Footprint Jordan Handbook

The travel guide

Ivan Mannheim

The crags were capped in nests of domes, less hotly red than the body of the hill; rather grey and shallow. They gave the finishing semblance of Byzantine architecture to this irresistible place...

TE Lawrence, *Seven Pillars of Wisdom*

Jordan Handbook
First edition
© Footprint Handbooks Ltd 2000

Published by Footprint Handbooks
6 Riverside Court
Lower Bristol Road
Bath BA2 3DZ. England
T +44 (0)1225 469141
F +44 (0)1225 469461
Email discover@footprintbooks.com
Web www.footprintbooks.com

ISBN 1 900949 69 5
CIP DATA: A catalogue record for this
book is available from the British Library

In USA, published by
NTC/Contemporary Publishing Group
4255 West Touhy Avenue, Lincolnwood
(Chicago), Illinois 60712-1975, USA
T 847 679 5500 F 847 679 2494
Email NTCPUB2@AOL.COM

ISBN 0-658-01086-7
Library of Congress Catalog Card
Number 00-132908

Credits

Series editors
Patrick Dawson and Rachel Fielding

Editorial
Editor: Alan Murphy
Maps: Sarah Sorensen

Production
Typesetting: Richard Ponsford, Emma
Bryers and Angus Dawson
Maps: Robert Lunn, Claire Benison and
Alasdair Dawson
Colour maps: Kevin Feeney
Cover: Camilla Ford

Design
Mytton Williams

Photography
Front cover: Impact Photos
Back cover: Impact Photos
Inside colour section: Pictures Colour
Library, Impact Photos, Travel Ink, Art
Directors & Trip, Getty One Stone and
Robert Harding.

Print
Manufactured in Italy by LEGOPRINT

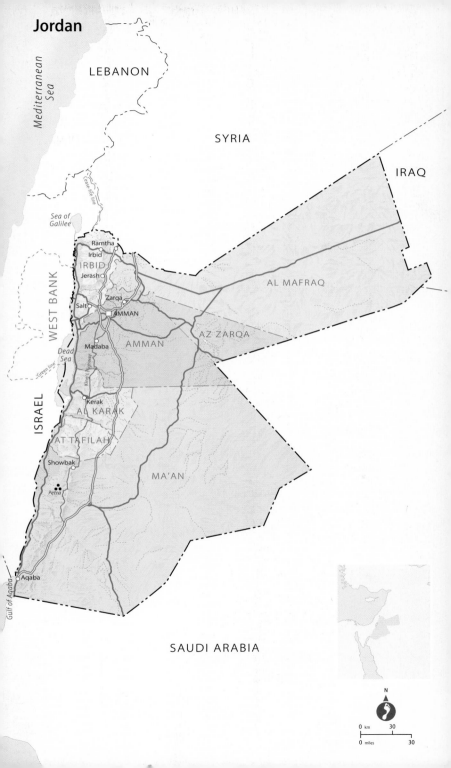

Contents

Left: The imposing entrance to The Treasury at Petra dwarfs the Bedouin guard

4

Right: Washing before prayer at a mosque in the capital, Amman.

A foot in the door

Highlights

Jordan, once one of the Middle East's best kept secrets, looks set to become the region's hot tourist ticket. This should come as no surprise to anyone familiar with this unassuming country, for it has an enormous amount to offer the visitor. There are more historic monuments and sites then you could shake a crook at, varied and stunningly beautiful landscapes, and a whole host of different activities, from diving in the Red Sea to rock climbing or gliding. Jordan combines all this with the desert romance of Lawrence of Arabia and a rich religious heritage more commonly associated with its neighbours. Add to this enticing mixture the most hospitable people this side of the Old Testament, and the result is a pretty appetising holiday prospect.

Rock legend Nothing can prepare you for your first glimpse of Petra. It simply has to be seen to be believed. The towering rock-cut temple façades of this Nabatean stronghold are truly awesome. That anyone should even have conceived of such an ambitious enterprise, let alone brought it into being, seems improbable, yet the evidence is there before your eyes. This was one of the ancient world's most opulent and unique cities, a hugely successful trading centre surrounded by imposing rock mountains and approached through a deep, narrow cleft, known as the *Siq*. No visit to Jordan would be complete without including Petra. In fact, you'd be *Siq* if you missed out.

When in Rome Jerash is one of the best-preserved Roman cities outside Italy, equal in grandeur to Palmyra in Syria or Baalbek in Lebanon. Under the Romans, Jerash flourished as an imperial centre, forming part of a loose regional federation known as the Decapolis or 'Ten Cities'. Today, you can roam through its colonnaded streets, theatres and temples, and imagine yourself in the city during its heyday, with the coming and going of chariots, the bustle of the marketplace, the political intrigue and perhaps even the occasional orgy or two, depending on just how vivid your imagination is!

Better Red Jordan's border with Israel is marked by the Great Rift Valley, one of the largest natural
or Dead? features in the world; a vast chasm in the earth's surface, with the Dead Sea, its lowest point, more than 400 m *below* sea level. The Dead Sea's high salt content means that you bob around like a cork on the water's surface. If that idea floats your boat, then why not go for the once-in-a-lifetime experience of reading a newspaper or book while afloat, with a drink balanced on a tray at your side. The unique combination of minerals and salts to be found here are also said to have great therapeutic properties, a fact that has spawned various luxury resorts on the shores of the Dead Sea specialising in health and beauty treatments.

With less than 30 km of coastline, the Red Sea is one of Jordan's attractions which is often overlooked. Yet Aqaba offers a variety of comfortable beach resorts with year-round sunshine, as well as the opportunity to dive or snorkel amongst some of the most impressive coral reefs in the world. Indeed, with the majority of divers heading for the large resorts in Sinai, Jordan's Red Sea coastline has the distinct advantage of being far less developed, and its coral reefs better preserved, than in Egypt or Israel.

Desert delight Alongside the Dead Sea, Wadi Rum is undoubtedly Jordan's most spectacular natural feature, much loved by TE Lawrence and made famous to the outside world by David Lean's *Lawrence of Arabia*, which was filmed here. Rising abruptly from the flat and featureless desert are massive pillars of sheer sandstone rock, weathered and eroded into fantastic shapes and towering majestically above the desert floor. Whether you come here for the rock climbing, to go on a jeep or camel safari, or simply to walk amidst such awesome grandeur, Wadi Rum is sure to leave a lasting impression.

Left: A hazy sunset lends a beautiful hue to Wadi Rum's already spectacular palette of colours. ***Below***: The hot springs spa resort at Ma'in provides the source water for the Dead Sea.

Above: The Times, it is a floatin'. Enjoying some R'n'R on the Dead Sea. ***Left***: The Monastery at Petra. ***Next page***: That's 'andy! One of Jordan's essential souvenirs is a famous sand bottle.

Right: King Abdullah Mosque in Amman is one of the country's main mosques, named after King Hussein's grandfather. *Below*: Qasr al-Abd (Fortress of the Servant), a third century Hellenistic palace, in Wadi as-Sir, west of Amman.

Right: The Royal Tomb, yet another of Petra's unmissable sights.
Above: A familiar sight. A group of friends enjoying a game of Mangala, an ancient Jordanian board game.
Next page: The Roman ruins at Jerash are one of the country's greatest archaeological treasures.

At the crossroads of history

As a nation state, Jordan is a young country, born out of the post-First World War carve-up of Europe's colonial empires (Winston Churchill famously and arrogantly claimed to have created it "with the stroke of a pen one Sunday afternoon"). Yet the land it occupies is an ancient one, lying at one of the great cultural and historical crossroads of the world. This region has witnessed the evolution of the three great monotheistic religions – Judaism, Christianity and Islam – as well as playing a central role in the development of civilization as we know it.

Unearthing the past

Jordan's ancient monuments may seem timeless and unchanging in their grandeur, but most have been conjured from the earth by the painstaking work of archaeologists over decades. It is a process which continues today, with new discoveries being made all the time. Only recently, a Byzantine church with beautiful mosaics decorating its floors has been added to the long list of Petra's attractions, while excavations at the Great Temple in Petra have revealed intriguing and previously unguessed-at features. Ongoing excavations at the Decapolis city of Gadara (modern Umm Qais), overlooking the Golan Heights and Lake Tiberias (Sea of Galilee), have uncovered whole stretches of the Roman colonnaded street where before there was nothing more than a dirt track. Undoubtedly there are many more treasures still to be found. Almost every year new wonders are revealed, while existing monuments are being lovingly restored and preserved for future generations.

Pilgrims' progress

The millenium visit of the Pope to Jordan raised hopes of a flood of pilgrims in his wake. The government's expectations may have been a little optimistic, but Jordan is increasingly being recognised for its claims to a stake in the 'Holy Land' mantle so jealously guarded by Israel. There is strong evidence supporting the theory that the recently excavated archaeological remains at Wadi Kharrar represent the elusive 'Bethany beyond the Jordan', a site of fundamental importance to Christians, being the place where John the Baptist pursued his vocation, and where Jesus himself was baptized.

A land of promise

Just 20 km or so to the southwest is Mount Nebo, identified in the Old Testament as the place where Moses looked out over the Promised Land. Today, housed in the remains of the 4th-6th century Memorial Church of Moses on the summit of Mount Nebo, are numerous beautiful mosaics. Together with the wealth of mosaic art to be found in the nearby town of Madaba (home to the famous Madaba Map), and at sites such as Umm ar-Rasas to the south, these reflect the extent to which Christianity flourished in Jordan during the Byzantine era.

Religious profit

Numerous other ancient sites in Jordan relate to biblical events. Lot's Cave Monastery, by the Dead Sea near Safi, stands on the site of an ancient cave which the Byzantines clearly believed was the place where Lot settled with his daughters, having fled the destruction of Sodom and Gomorrah and the 'cities of the plain'. Mukawir (ancient Machaerus) was the mountain stonghold of Herod Antipas, the son of Herod the Great, who was tricked into having John the Baptist beheaded by the guiles of the beautiful Salome and her mother. According to legend, Mohammad, too, travelled through Jordan as a young boy, and was identified as a future Prophet by a Greek Orthodox monk on the summit of Jebel Haroun, near Petra (also the resting place of the Old Testament Prophet Aaron).

Jordan today

Jordan sits right at the heart of the Middle East, a small, unassuming country with all the region's larger or more powerful players – Egypt, Israel, Syria, Saudi Arabia and Iraq – ranged around it. When it first emerged as an independent nation in 1946, many questioned whether it could ever survive, and its image has always been that of the underdog, the "stubborn survivor" in the face of adversity. Yet today it stands as something of a beacon of hope, commanding respect internationally as an island of stability and moderation in an often turbulent region.

A bright future Extremism may be foreign to the national psyche, but Jordan is far from staid either. In terms of its people, it is a young country; nearly half the population are under 15 years of age. With a young new King, Abdullah II, now installed on the throne and implementing modernising reforms, there is an almost tangible buzz of expectation in the air. Jordanians seem to sense that the future is theirs, and the majority are full of optimism as to what it will bring for them and their country.

Something old; something new Most people's first impressions are formed in Amman, Jordan's thoroughly modern capital city. With its wealthy uptown districts boasting numerous fancy restaurants and western-style cafés, bars and clubs, including the likes of *Planet Hollywood* and *Hard Rock Café*, it is easy to forget you are in the Middle East at all. On the other hand, a short excursion to the town of Salt, just outside of Amman, provides a glimpse of a bygone era; of graceful Ottoman architecture and tiny traditional coffee houses where people while away the hours chatting and playing cards. Drinking tea in a Bedouin tent in Jordan's eastern desert, meanwhile, you could be in just about any century.

Tradition and change The popular image of Jordan is closely associated with the Bedouin. Their nomadic lifestyle, wandering across vast expanses of desert with their sheep and camels, is a much loved and much romanticized theme in the West. Although undergoing rapid change, Bedouin society is still very much alive in Jordan today, while their history and traditions are held in high esteem. The Bedouin, however, are actually a minority. More than half of Jordanians are in fact of Palestinian origin. Many still hold on to the dream of returning one day to an independent state of Palestine, although the majority have now adopted Jordanian nationality. Indeed, one of the greatest challenges, and successes, for Jordan since independence has been in forging a national identity which incorporates these refugees from decades of Arab-Israeli conflict.

A welcome from the heart Although the majority of Jordanians are Muslim, there is also a significant Christian community in the country, belonging primarily to the Greek Orthodox church. Certain districts of Amman and towns such as Madaba are dotted with churches and have a very different atmosphere to Muslim-majority areas. Other minorities to be found in Jordan include the Circassians (non-Arab Muslims who came to Jordan in the 19th and 20th centuries from the Russian Caucasus), and the Druze (an obscure, some would say heretical, sect of Islam found mostly in Lebanon and Syria). Whatever their ethnic or religious background, Jordanians are united in the tradition of hospitality. It may sound like a cliché, but it is hard to imagine a more welcoming country. Hospitality lies at the heart of Arab society and codes of conduct, yet the welcome you will receive is not just a duty Jordanians feel obliged to fulfil, it comes from the heart. Don't be surprised if you are offered endless cups of tea on your travels, or invited to go for dinner at a complete stranger's house. That's the Jordanian way.

Left: Bedouins at their camp in Wadi Rum.
Below: Bedouin policemen at Petra.

Above: A moment of peaceful study in the King Hussein Mosque.
Left: Wadi Rum can be explored by four-wheel-drive or by camel. These visitors have chosen the less painful option. *Next page*: View of Amman from the Citadel.

Essentials

2

Essentials

Planning your trip

Where to go

The vast majority of visitors to Jordan come primarily to see its world-famous historical monuments, most notably Petra and Jerash, although there are plenty more which are also very impressive in their own right. The country's second major attraction is its natural beauty, embodied in the spectacular landscapes of Wadi Rum, the Dead Sea and the deep wadis which drain into it, the rolling hills in the north of the country, and the stunningly beautiful coral reefs of the Red Sea. These unique environments are also home to an impressive array of birds, animals and plants, many of them extremely rare and in some cases found nowhere else in the world. In the case of Wadi Rum, this awesome landscape of sheer rock amidst the desert has been adopted as a vast playground for rock climbers, gaining international recognition and inspiring many enthusiasts of the sport to visit Jordan for this reason alone. Likewise, the coral reefs of the Red Sea are enough in themselves to attract scuba divers and snorkellers to the country.

For most people, the real beauty of Jordan is that you can combine all these things in one visit. The majority of visitors, whether flying to Jordan or arriving overland, find themselves first in the capital Amman, although if you are coming from Eilat in Israel, or from Egypt's Sinai region, you will be starting off at Aqaba in the far south of the country. In either case, Jordan lends itself ideally to a north-south journey between these two cities. The scenic King's Highway takes you past Madaba, Kerak, Petra and a host of other fascinating sites along the way. Returning north, there is the option of the Desert Highway (fast but boring), or the more interesting Dead Sea/Wadi Arabah Highway, which runs along the shores of the Dead Sea for some of the way. From Amman, you can make day-trips or longer excursions to the sites to the north and east. Public transport is on the whole reasonably good in Jordan, although having your own transport gives you much greater flexibility in terms of visiting more out-of-the-way places. Hiring a car is easy in Amman or Aqaba. If your time is limited or you cannot afford a hire car, it is also worth considering joining an organized tour to get to those more remote sites. Organized tours to Wadi Rum and Petra are readily available in both Amman and Aqaba, while in Amman many of the hotels organize trips out to the Desert Castles to the east of the capital. There are of course also plenty of foreign tour operators offering package tours to Jordan.

Outlined below are suggested itineraries for visits to Jordan lasting from 1-4 weeks. They are designed to take in as varied a selection as possible of Jordan's most popular sights and attractions, both in terms of its historic monuments and natural scenic beauty. If you are visiting Jordan specifically for its nature and wildlife you will be spending much of your time in nature reserves administered by the Royal Society for the Conservation of Nature (RSCN) and you should contact them in advance. If you are visiting Jordan specifically for activities such as hiking, rock climbing or scuba diving, there are a number of specialist publications which will help you get the most from your trip. In either case, see under Sports and Special Interest Travel.

Day 1: Fly to Amman; visit Citadel & Museum, Downtown souks.   1 week
Day 2: Jerash (full day trip from Amman), plus Ajlun Castle if sufficient time.
Day 3: Visit Madaba and Kerak en route to Petra.
Day 4: Full day exploration of Petra.
Day 5: Visit Wadi Rum en route to Aqaba.
Day 6: Full day sun-bathing/swimming/diving in Aqaba.
Day 7: Return Amman and fly home.

Essentials

2 weeks **Days 1-3**: Amman, Salt, Wadi Seer, Dead Sea (using Amman as a base).
Day 4: Jerash/Ajlun (day trip, using Amman as base).
Day 5: Jordan Valley and Umm Qais (day trip, using Amman as base).
Day 6: Desert Castles (day trip, using Amman as base).
Day 7: Madaba, Mt Nebo, Hammamat Ma'in, (overnight in Madaba).
Day 8: Umm ar-Rasas, Kerak and Dana (overnight in Dana).
Days 9-11: Petra.
Day 12: Wadi Rum.
Day 13: Aqaba.
Day 14: Amman.

3 weeks **Days 1-3**: Amman, Salt, Wadi Seer, Dead Sea (using Amman as a base).
Day 4: Jerash/Ajlun (day trip, using Amman as base).
Days 5-6: Jordan Valley, Umm Qais, Abila (overnight at Pella or Umm Qais).
Days 7-8: Desert Castles and RSCN Azraq/Shaumari reserves (overnight in Azraq).
Days 9-10: Madaba, Mt Nebo, Hammamat Ma'in, Umm ar-Rasas (overnight in Madaba).
Days 11-12: Kerak, Hammamat Afra, Dana (overnight in Dana).
Days 13-16: Petra.
Days 17-18: Wadi Rum.
Days 19-20: Aqaba.
Day 21: Amman/fly home.

4 weeks **Days 1-3**: Amman, Salt, Wadi Seer, Dead Sea (using Amman as a base).
Days 4-5: Jerash and Ajlun (overnight in Ajlun or at Olive Branch resort).
Days 6-7: Irbid and Abila (overnight in Irbid).
Days 8-9: Umm Qais and Jordan Valley (overnight at Pella or Umm Qais).
Days 10-11: Desert Castles and RSCN Azraq/Shaumari reserves (overnight in Azraq).
Days 12-14: Madaba, Mt Nebo, Hammamat Ma'in, Mukawir/Machaerus, Umm ar-Rasas (using Madaba as base).
Day 15: Kerak and Lot's Cave (overnight in Kerak).
Days 16-18: Hammamat Afra, Dana, Showbak (using Dana as a base).
Days 19-22: Petra.
Days 23-24: Wadi Rum.
Days 25-27: Aqaba.
Day 28: Amman/fly home.

When to go

Roughly speaking, the best times to visit Jordan are during the spring (March-May) or autumn (September-November), when the climate is at its most pleasant. Even during these seasons, daytime temperatures at Petra and Jerash can reach as high as 25-30°C in the sun, although it does at least cool off from late afternoon through to early/mid-morning.

During the summer (June-August) it is scorchingly hot throughout most of the country, with temperatures often going well over the 40°C mark, and also extremely humid down on the Red Sea coast. Visiting sites such as Petra and Jerash in such conditions is very hard work. The Dead Sea and Jordan Valley meanwhile, where the humidity in summer is extremely high, are really unbearable. In the desert, although it gets extremely hot during the day, at night temperatures fall significantly, even in the height of summer. The higher altitudes and good forest cover of the northern highlands make the hills to the north of Amman somewhat cooler during summer.

Winters (December-February) can be quite severe in the hills of northern Jordan, with the majority of this region's rainfall coming during this period and temperatures often dropping to as low as freezing. Even as far south as Petra snow is not uncommon during December and January. On the other hand, if the weather is good, Petra at Christmas can't be beaten. Aqaba and Wadi Rum are likewise very pleasant during the winter, with average temperatures in Aqaba of 15-20°C (the sea temperature also remains very pleasant). In Wadi Rum, although the daytime temperatures are ideal for walking and climbing, it gets very cold at night. The Dead Sea and Jordan Valley are also at their best in winter, with temperatures of around 20°C, although it is in fact even more humid than during the summer.

Tour operators

Abercrombie & Kent Travel, Sloane Square House, Holbein Place, London SW1 8NS, T0207-7309600, F0207-7309376. **Ancient World Tours,** PO Box 12950, London W6 8GY, T07071-222950, F01328-823293, www.ancient.co.uk **Aquatours,** Charter House, 26 Claremont Rd, Surbiton, Surrey, KT6 4QU, T0208-2558050, www.aquatours.com **British Museum Tours,** 46 Bloomsbury St, London WC1B 3QQ, T0207-3238895, F0207-5808677. **Cricketer Holidays,** 4 The White House, Beacon Road, Crowborough, East Sussex, TN6 1AB, T01892-667459, F01892-662355. **Cox & Kings,** 4th floor, Gordon House, 10 Greencoat Place, London SW1P 1PH, T0207-8735000, F0207-6306038, www.coxandkings.co.uk **Eastern Approaches,** 33 Earlston Road, Stow, Selkirkshire, TD1 2RL, Scotland, T01578-730361, F01578-730714, w.ball@easynet.co.uk **Egyptian Encounter,** 36 High Street, Lymington, Hants SO41 9AF, T01590-677665, F01590-677373. **Exodus,** 9 Weir Road, London, SW12 0LT, T0208-6755550, F0208-6730779, www.exodus.co.uk **Explore Worldwide,** 1 Fredrick St, Aldershot, Hants, GU11 1LQ, T01252-319448, F01252-343170. **Fellowship Tours,** PO Box 29, Chard, Somerset, TA20 2YY, T01460-221406. **Freelance Travel,** Mere House, Dedmere Rd, Marlow, Bucks, SL7 1PB, T01628-483550, F01628-486954, JasSmith@compuserve.com **Inter Church Travel,** Saga Building, Middelburg Square, Folkestone, Kent CT20 1BL, T0800-300400, F01303-711100. **Jasmin Tours,** High Street, Cookham, Berks, SL6 9SQ, T01628-531121, F01628-529444. **Kuoni Travel Ltd,** 33 Maddox St, London, W1R 9LD, T0207-4998636, F0207-6386330. **Martin Randall Travel,** 10 Barley Mow Passage, Chiswick, London W4 4HP, T0208-7423355, F0208-7421066. **McCabe Travel,** 53-55 Balham Hill, London SW12 9DR, T0208-6756828, F0208-6731204. **Orientours Pilgrimages,** Sovereign House, 11 Ballards Lane, Finchley, London, T0208-3469114. **Page & Moy,** 136-40 London Road, Leicester LE2 1EN, T0116-250774, F0116-2549949. **Prospect Music & Art Tours,** 454-458 Chiswick High Road, London W4 5GT, T0208-9952151, F0208-7421969. **Sunvil Holidays** Sunvil House, Upper Square, Old Isleworth, Middx TW7 7BJ, T0208-5684499, F0208-5688330. **Swan Hellenic Tours,** 77 New Oxford St, London WC1A 1DS, T0207-8002300, F0207-8311280. **The Imaginative Traveller,** 14 Barley Mow Passage, Chiswick, London W4, T0208-7423113, F0208-7493045. **Voyages Jules Verne,** 21 Dorset Square, London NW1 6QG, T0207-7235066, F0207-7238629.

UK & Ireland

Finding out more

The Jordan Tourism Board has its own website (www.tourism.com.jo), and offices in the following countries. **France:** 32 Rue de Ponthieu, 75008 Paris, T01-45619258, F01-42256640. **Germany:** Postfach 160 120, 60064 Frankfurt T69-92318870, F69-92318879. **UK:** Representation House, 11 Blades Court, Deodar Rd, London SW15 2NV, T0208-8774524, F0208-8744219. **USA:** 3504 International Drive NW, Washington DC, 20008, T202-2441451, F202-2440534.

Tourist offices abroad
For a full list of useful websites, see page 63

Essentials

Jordanian embassies abroad

Australia: 20 Roebuck St, Redhill, Canberra, ACT 2603, T02-62959951, F02-62396236.

Belgium: 104 Ave DD Roosevelt, 1050 Brussels T02-6407755, F02-6402796.

Canada: 110, Bronson Ave, Ottawa, Ontario, K1N 6R4, T613-2388091, F613-2323341.

Egypt: 6 Sharia Al-Juhaini, Doqqi, Cairo, T02-3499912, F02-3601027.

France: 80 Blvd Maurice Barres, 92200 Neuilly Seine, Paris, T01-46242378, F01-46270206.

Germany: Beethovenallee 21, 53173 Bonn, T0228-357046, F0228-353951.

Israel: 14 Abba Hillel St, Ramat Gan suburb, Tel Aviv, T03-7517722, F03-7517712.

Italy: Via G d'Arezzo 5, 00198 Rome, T06-86205303, F06-86206122.

Lebanon: Elias Helou Ave, Baabda, Beirut, T01-922500, F01-922502.

Spain: Paseo de General Martinez Campos 41, 28010 Madrid, T091-4191100, F091-3082536.

Switzerland: Belpstrasse 11, 3007 Berne T031-3814148, F031-3822119.

Syria: I Jalaa (Abu Roumaneh) St, Damascus, T011-3334642, F011-3336741.

Turkey: Mesnevi, Dedekorkut Sokak No 18, Cankaya, Ankara, T312-4402054, F312-4404327.

UK: 6 Upper Phillimore Gardens, London, W8 7HB, T0207-9373685, F0207-9378795 (visa info T09001-171261, 'fax on demand' visa application form T09001-669917).

USA: 3504 International Drive NW, Washington, Washington DC 20008 , T202-9662664, F202-9663110.

In addition, *Royal Jordanian* airline offices abroad double as tourist information offices. **Australia**: Marland House, 570 Bourke St, Melbourne, T036424066. **Canada**: 1801 McGill College, Montreal, T2881655. **Egypt**: Zamalek Sporting Club, Sh 26 July, Mohaneseen, T3443114. **France**: 12 rue de la Paix, 75002 Paris, T42618060. **Germany**: 14a Budapest St, 10787, Berlin, T0302617057. **UK**: 32 Brook St (entrance on South Molton St), London W1K 5DL, T0207-8786300, F0207-6294068. **USA:** 535 Fifth Ave, New York 10017, T212-9490060.

Language   Arabic is the national language, although **English** is also widely spoken. The Arabic spoken in Jordan is known as Levantine Arabic, as opposed to Egyptian Arabic, although with Egypt being so close by, there is some blending of the two. Learning a few basic phrases of Arabic before you go really isn't that difficult and goes down very well once you are there. Learning to recognise and pronounce the numerals is also easy and of considerable practical use. See the Arabic Glossary in the Rounding up section at the end of this book.

Before you travel

Make photocopies of all your documents and keep them separate from the originals. Ideally, you should leave a set of photocopies with someone at home whom you can contact easily   A full passport valid for at least 6 months beyond your intended period of stay is required to visit Jordan. Make sure also that there is sufficient space in your passport for entry/exit stamps and any other visas you intend to buy while travelling. You should always carry your passport with you while in Jordan. Although the permanent checkposts along the Jordan valley and the Dead Sea/Wadi Arava highway have now been abolished, there is always the chance of random checkposts, or spot checks on buses. You will need to show your passport whenever you check into a hotel, or to change travellers' cheques. Some hotel managers may want to keep your passport until you check out; insist politely but firmly that you need to have it with you. A supply of passport photos is very useful for any visas or visa extensions might want to apply for while travelling.

Visa fees (2000)

Country	Fee (JD)
Australia	16
Austria	25
Canada	39
Denmark	12
France	11
Germany	15
Italy	11
New Zealand	16
Spain	17
UK	23
USA	33

Visas & immigration

All foreign nationals (except those from Egypt, Syria and the Gulf States) require a visa to enter Jordan. Visas can be obtained easily at any of Jordan's land, sea and air points of entry, **except the King Hussein (Allenby) Bridge crossing from Israel into Jordan** (other Jordanian/Israeli border crossings will issue visas). Fees vary according to nationality. For the fees being charged in 2000 for visas issued at point of entry, see box below.

Only single entry visas are issued at point of entry. Alternatively, you can apply at the Jordanian Embassy in your own country. For UK nationals this is slightly more expensive (£27/48 for a single/double entry visa issued in London), although for most other nationalities it is slightly cheaper (and in the case of Australians, free). Note that all visa fees, both abroad and at the point of entry, are subject to frequent changes. In London you must submit a completed application form (you can get this faxed to you by dialling T09001-669917), one passport photo and the appropriate fee. If you are going to Jordan on business, you must also submit a letter from your employer. The visa will then be issued within two working days (visa applications should be submitted between 0930-1300, and collected between 1330-1430). You can also apply by post (payments by postal order only; send a stamped self-addressed envelope), which takes around 10 days to two weeks. The Jordanian embassies in Damascus and Cairo will both issue visas without any problems (single or multiple entry). Visas obtained abroad must be used within three months of the date of issue. **All visas are initially valid for a period of only two weeks**, but they can be easily extended for up to three months in Amman free of charge.

Visa extensions All tourists must register with the police if staying for more than 15 days in Jordan. Registering with the police effectively extends your visa for three months. There is no fee and you are not required to submit any passport photos or other documentation. The best place to register is Amman (see page 115), where the whole process generally only takes half an hour or so. In theory, you can also register at the police headquarters of any governorate (administrative district) in Jordan, namely Irbid, Kerak, Ma'an and Aqaba, but in practice this can prove complicated and time consuming, so you are advised to do it in Amman.

If you intend to travel beyond Jordan, careful planning before setting off is very important. Obtaining a visa on arrival is no problem in Jordan or Lebanon, but it is impossible to get a Syrian visa at the Syrian border (or airport), and likewise all but impossible to obtain one in Amman. Basically, if you are planning to visit Syria as well, get your Syrian visa before leaving home. The same applies for Saudi Arabia; they do not issue transit visas on the border, and these can be very difficult to obtain in Jordan (or seemingly impossible around the time of the annual *Hajj*).

See page 115 for further details about getting visas in Amman for countries bordering Jordan

Currently both Syria and Lebanon (and Saudi Arabia) will not issue you with a visa, or allow you entry into the country even with a visa, if there is any evidence of a visit to Israel in your passport. If you do have any Israeli stamps in your passport, it is usually possible, at least for British passport holders, to obtain a new passport before leaving home if you explain the situation. Israeli officials will stamp your Israeli entry/exit stamps on a separate sheet of paper if you insist, but Syrian and Lebanese officials have become wise to this in recent years and will look to see if any of the entry/exit

The Entry/Exit Stamp Game

Even though the Israeli authorities are willing to stamp a separate piece of paper rather than your passport, the Syrian and Lebanese authorities have cottoned on to this fact. In their quest to prohibit people who have visited Israel coming to their countries they will scrutinise your passport for any evidence of an entry/exit stamp to/from a country neighbouring Israel. Thus if you enter or leave Israel via the Rafah or Taba border crossings with Egypt, the Egyptian entry/exit stamp (complete with the name of the border in Arabic) will alert the Syrian/Lebanese authorities to the fact that you have been in Israel. Likewise for the Wadi Arabah/Arava and Jisr Sheikh Hussein/Jordan River border crossings between Israel and Jordan. If you wish to visit Israel as well as Syria and/or Lebanon, the safest option is obviously to leave Israel till last. There are however two other options. If you fly between Amman and Tel Aviv, your Jordanian entry/exit

stamp will simply be for Queen Alia International Airport and therefore will not provide any conclusive evidence that you have been in Israel, allowing you to continue on to Syria and Lebanon (make sure your flight is into Queen Alia International Airport, and not Marka). The second option is to visit Israel from Jordan via the King Hussein (Allenby) Bridge border crossing, and return the same way. At this border crossing (and only this one), the Jordanian authorities are willing to put your exit/entry stamps on a separate sheet of paper, so leaving no evidence of a visit to Israel in your passport. Note that this will only work if you do a round-trip from Jordan to Israel and back again. If you fly to Israel and then enter Jordan and ask to have your entry stamp on a separate piece of paper, when you try to enter Syria, the absence of a Jordanian entry stamp will be enough to alert the authorities.

stamps from neighbouring countries indicate that you have crossed a land border to or from Israel (see box). Jordan does not apply any such restrictions with regard to visiting Israel. If you are planning to visit Israel and Syria/Lebanon during the course of your trip, the safest option is to leave Israel till last.

Travel insurance You are strongly advised to take out travel insurance before setting off. The medical component of such insurance is the most important. Check exactly what the level of cover is for specific eventualities, in particular whether a flight home is covered in case of an emergency, whether the insurance company will pay any medical expenses directly or whether you must pay in advance and claim back afterwards, and whether specific activities such as diving are covered (if not you can often get the policy extended to cover such activities). Most policies have very low ceilings on the value of individual items covered in the event of theft; if you have something of great value, the cheapest way of covering it is often through household insurance.

Vaccination certificates In theory, anyone arriving from a country where yellow fever or cholera occurs frequently must present the immigration authorities with up-to-date certificates of vaccination. In practice this is rarely enforced, but if you arriving by the overland route through Africa for example it is worth having these certificates just in case.

What to take
Always take more money and fewer clothes than you think you'll need
Most travellers take far too much. The only essentials are passport, money and ticket (and this book, of course). Everything else is a matter of personal choice, and it's all readily available once you get there anyway. We have not included a comprehensive list of what to take (if you can't pack your own bag, perhaps you should stay at home), but here are a few points worth bearing in mind.

Appropriate **clothing** is perhaps the most important consideration (see also page 35 for important guidelines on what is culturally acceptable). In the summer months, and for much of the spring and autumn, the daytime heat makes lightweight, loose-fitting cotton clothes a must. A hat, high factor sun-block and sunglasses are also essential. Bear in mind, however, that even in the height of summer night-time temperatures can drop dramatically in desert settings such as Wadi Rum. During winter, it can get extremely cold throughout the country (with the exception of the Jordan valley, Dead Sea and Gulf of Aqaba); biting winds, driving rain and even snow are not uncommon, so warm clothing and protection against the wind and rain is essential. Spring and autumn can also be surprisingly cold in the Northern Highlands, and at higher altitudes along the eastern plateau of the Great Rift Valley (ie along much of the King's Highway). Strong walking boots with firm ankle support are a good idea for exploring sites such as Petra, and essential if you plan to do any hiking. On the other hand, comfortable, open sandals are best for less strenuous town and city walking in summer.

Toiletries, including tampons, sanitary towels, condoms and contact lens cleaning equipment, are readily available in Amman and Aqaba, but outside these centres the range and availability of such goods is less reliable. If you are on medication, you are advised to bring adequate supplies. Locally available insect repellents are generally less effective than the stronger western varieties. Photographic products are widely available, but tend to be more expensive than at home, and film stock is not always as fresh as it could be.

If you're going to be staying in cheaper hotels and dormitories, a sheet sleeping bag is useful, as are earplugs and an airline-type eye mask. The campsites at Dana and Wadi Rum supply tents and bedding, but if you plan to do a lot of camping you should really bring your own equipment (a good sleeping bag is recommended in any case for late autumn through to early spring). Other useful items include a torch/flashlight for exploring dark nooks and crannies of Crusader castles and other historic sites, a Swiss Army knife and a universal sink plug (with a wide flange to fit any waste-pipe).

Customs The standard duty free allowance is 200 cigarettes/200g tobacco/25 cigars and two litres of wine/one litre of spirits. Details of video equipment, lap-top computers or other valuable items may be written into your passport (and checked on departure to ensure they have not been sold), but in practice the customs authorities are pretty easygoing about this. There are no restrictions on the import or export of foreign or Jordanian currency.

Money

Currency The Jordanian Dinar (JD; generally referred to as the "*jaydee*") is made up of 1,000 fils. However, this is made somewhat more complicated by the fact that there is a further subdivision of the JD into piastres (or qirsh), with 1 piastre/qirsh being equivalent to 10 fils. Coins are in denominations of 5, 10, 25, 50, 100, 250 and 500 fils. There are also now 1, 2.5, 5 and 10 piastre/qirsh coins. Notes are in denominations of JD0.500, 1, 5, 10, 20 and 50.

Changing money
Always take a credit card, even if you think you've got enough cash and TCs

All major currencies, whether in the form of cash or travellers' cheques (TCs), are easily exchanged at banks or money changers in the major towns and cities of Jordan. Money changers stay open later than the banks; in Amman you can generally even find at least one that is open on a Friday or Saturday morning. Most luxury hotels will also change cash and TCs, although their rates are well below those of the banks and money changers, so use them only as a last resort. **Credit cards** are the easiest way to keep in funds while travelling. As well as using them to pay bills in the upper range hotels, restaurants, shops etc, you can use them to get cash advances and to draw money from ATMs (cash-point machines). Practically every town of any note in Jordan now has at least one bank with an ATM. Perhaps the safest approach is to take the your money in a mixture of TCs and cash, and also a credit card as an extra emergency backup or for those little luxuries you hadn't budgeted for.

Cash All major foreign currencies can be changed without problem in Jordan and there should be no fees or commission for cash. On the whole, banks offer marginally better rates than money changers, although if you change large amounts of cash in high denomination bills, the money changers will usually match the bank rates. It is always useful to have some hard currency with you, particularly when crossing borders. US dollars (US$) are the most widely recognised foreign currency (useful if you find yourself in a remote area without any local currency). **NB** US$ bills dating from 1981 and 1988 are often more difficult to change, since there are apparently large numbers of forged US$ bills with these dates in circulation. Particularly in the case of $100 bills you are strongly advised to ask for the most recent series, which will be recognised as being the least prone to forgery.

There is no black market for foreign currency in Jordan. If you find yourself needing to change money outside of banking hours, see first if any money changers are open. If not, you will have to resort to one of the luxury hotels (although these give considerably lower rates), or you might be able to persuade a shop-keeper to change some US$ cash. The banks at Queen Alia International airport are open 24 hours.

Reconverting currency You can change JD back into hard currencies (US$, UK£ etc) without any problem, although you must show exchange receipts for the value you wish to reconvert. The rates for reconverting currency are, predictably enough, well below those for changing hard currency into JD. You can also buy currencies for neighbouring countries (Syria, Israel, Egypt) easily from money-changers; in the case of Syria, this is well worth doing as you will get considerably more than the official bank rate.

Travellers' Cheques (TCs) The great advantage with TCs is that if they are lost or stolen you can get them replaced. The main disadvantage in Jordan is that the commission charged for cashing them is sometimes very high. Commissions vary significantly between different banks, so it is well worth shopping around. In Amman there are a couple of banks which charge no commission. Elsewhere you can expect to pay around 3%, with a minimum charge of anywhere between JD3-7 per transaction. It therefore makes sense to change fairly large amounts less often, rather than small amounts frequently, although obviously you must balance this against the fact that you do not want to be carrying too much cash around at any given time. See the Directory sections of each town/city for details on which banks have the lowest commissions. Note that you will generally be asked to produce the original purchase receipt in addition to your passport, despite the fact that you are supposed to keep them separate. Moneychangers generally do not charge a commission on TCs, but instead offer a considerably lower rate than the banks. Both **Thomas Cook** and **American Express** have offices in Amman, while the latter also have an office in Aqaba. Note that while these offices will deal with lost/stolen TCs, they do not offer exchange services.

Credit Cards Many of the banks in Jordan will give cash advances against major credit cards, making them a convenient alternative to TCs. An increasing number also now have ATMs (cash-point machines) which can be used in the same way. Payment by credit card is accepted at most luxury hotels, more expensive restaurants and up-market shops. Credit cards which are recognised in Jordan include **Visa**, **Mastercard**, **Global Access**, **Visa Electron** and **+Plus**, with *Visa* being the most widely recognised. *Eurocard* is not accepted in Jordan. The *Visa* head office in Jordan is at Jordan Payment Services Co, 3rd floor, Housing Bank Centre, Amman, T06-5680554,

- -

Discount flight agents in the UK & Ireland

Usit Campus, 52 Grosvener Gardens, London SW1W 0AG, T08702-401010, www.usitworld.com; 53 Forest Rd, Edinburgh EH1 2QP, T0131-225 6111; Fountain Centre, College St, Belfast BT1 6ET, T01232-324073; 19 Aston Quay, Dublin 2, T01-602 1777. Student/youth travel specialists with branches also in Birmingham, Brighton, Bristol, Cambridge, Glasgow and Manchester.
Council Travel, 28a Poland St, London W1V 3DB, T020-7437 7767, www.destinations-group.com
The London Flight Centre, 131 Earl's

Court Rd, London SW5 9RH, T020-7244 6411; 47 Notting Hill Gate, London W11 3JS, T020-7727 4290.
STA Travel, 86 Old Brompton Rd, London SW7 3LH, T020-7437 6262, www.statravel.co.uk Also have other branches in London, as well as in Brighton, Bristol, Cambridge, Leeds, Manchester, Newcastle and Oxford and on many University campuses. Specialists in cheap student/youth flights and tours, and also good for student Ids and insurance.
Trailfinders, 194 Kensington High St, London W8 7RG, T020-7983 3939.

- -

Essentials

F06-5680570. The *Mastercard* head office in Jordan is at Jordan National Bank, 3rd Circle, Jebel Amman, T06-4655863/4654891.

Western Union Money Transfer is represented in Jordan by the *Cairo-Amman Bank*, which has a number of branches in Amman, and also a branch in Aqaba. In an emergency this is probably your best bet, although the fees charged are very high.

Transferring money

The cost of living in Jordan is significantly cheaper as compared with European and North American countries. It is considerably cheaper than Israel also, though generally a little more expensive than Syria and Egypt. Obviously, how much you spend will depend on the degree of comfort you want to travel in, but also how much you want to do into a given amount of time. Transport costs, while low, soon add up if you are moving around a lot, and entry fees to the major sites are relatively high. For budget travellers, the JD20-30 entrance fee to Petra is a major expense.

Cost of living/travelling

The tightest of budget travel (dormitory accommodation, a diet of cheap staples, only the occasional drink and travel by the cheapest local transport) will allow you to survive off the equivalent of around US$10-15 per day, but this involves keeping a very strict rein on what you spend. A more realistic figure for budget travellers, allowing a little leeway to treat yourself every now and again, would be $15-20 per day.

A mid-range budget (more comfortable hotel accommodation, generally with a/c rooms, restaurant meals, a/c buses) will mean spending in the region of $50-60 per day.

Luxury travel (international class hotels, gourmet restaurant food, private vehicle, perhaps with driver and guide) means moving into the equivalent price ranges as for luxury travel in Europe and North America – basically from $150-200 per day upwards.

Getting there

Air

The majority of international flights arrive at the **Queen Alia International Airport**, 35 km to the south of Amman, although there are also some charter flights into **Aqaba Airport**. There is also an airport around 4 km to the northeast of Downtown Amman, the **Marka Airport**, which is used mainly for the *Royal Wings* flights between Amman and Aqaba, as well as some of the *Royal Wings* and *El Al* flights between Amman and Tel Aviv.

Essentials

 Discount flight agents in North America

Air Brokers International, *323 Geary St, Suite 411, San Francisco, CA94102, T01-800-883 3273, www.airbrokers.com Consolidator and specialist on RTW and Circle Pacific tickets.*
Council Travel, *205 E 42nd St, New York, NY 10017, T1-888-COUNCIL, www. counciltravel.com Student/budget agency with branches in many other US cities.*
Discount Airfares Worldwide On-Line, *www.etn.nl/discount.htm A hub of consolidator and discount agent links.*
International Travel Network/Airlines
of the Web, www.itn.net/airlines Online air travel information and reservations.
STA Travel, *5900 Wilshire Blvd, Suite 2110, Los Angeles, CA 90036, T1-800-777 0112, www.sta-travel.com Also branches in New York, San Francisco, Boston, Miami, Chicago, Seattle and Washington DC.*
Travel CUTS, *187 College St, Toronto, ON, M5T 1P7, T1-800-667 2887, www.travelcuts.com Specialist in student discount fares, Ids and other travel services. Branches in other Canadian cities.*

Europe London is the cheapest place from which to buy flights to Jordan, although very good deals can nowadays also be found in other European cities such as Paris, Amsterdam, Berlin and Frankfurt. For discounted fares from London's so-called 'bucket shops', look through the travel advertisements of magazines such as *Time Out* and *TNT*, the latter being available free outside most Tube stations every Tuesday. The broadsheet newspapers all feature weekly travel supplements on Saturdays and Sundays which also contain many adverts for cheap flights. Shop around.

Bear in mind that the cheapest flights generally involve a lengthy stop-over along the way, and often arrive in the early hours of the morning. Prices vary according to the season and the period for which flights are valid. Be sure to check other details, such as penalties for changing the date of the return flight, and the frequency of flights. If you plan to set your return date while you are in Jordan and are flying with an airline which has a limited number of flights each week, you may run into problems with availability of seats during busy times.

Royal Jordanian offer daily direct flights from London from around £550 return (valid for 2 months). *Olympic Airways* and *Turkish Airlines* offer amongst the cheapest low season deals, at around £250 return. Other airlines offering good deals include *KLM, Air France, Lufthansa, Alitalia, Cyprus, British Mediterranean* (a subsidiary of *British Airways*) and *Czech*. An even cheaper option is to fly first to Israel (return flights to Tel Aviv can be found for as little as £175) and then travel overland into Jordan, though this is not advisable if you are planning to continue on to Syria and Lebanon. Both *Olympic Airways* and *British Mediterranean* offer the option of an 'open jaws' ticket which allows you to fly into Amman and out of Damascus or Beirut (or vica-versa), which is very useful if you are planning to visit Syria and Lebanon as well as Jordan. Note that buying tickets in Jordan for the UK or Europe will always be more expensive.

North America All flights to/from North America go via Europe. *Royal Jordanian* fly from New York via Amsterdam, and from Toronto and Montreal. There are several other airlines which also fly from New York via Europe. None of these are very cheap; the cheapest way to go is to buy a return flight to London and then to shop around for cheap deals there.

Australia & New Zealand Again, there are no direct flights to/from Australia and New Zealand, although both *Qantas* and *Royal Jordanian* operate flights via Singapore, Bangkok and Jakarta for between A$1500-2000 depending on the season and where you stop-over.

Discount flight agents in Australia and New Zealand

Flight Centres, 82 Elizabeth St, Sydney, T13-1600; 205 Queen St, Auckland, T09-309 6171. Also branches in other towns and cities.
STA Travel, T1300-360960, www.statravelaus.com.au; 702 Harris St,

Ultimo, Sydney, and 256 Flinders St, Melbourne. In NZ: 10 High St, Auckland, T09-366 6673. Also in major towns and university campuses.
Travel.com.au, 80 Clarence St, Sydney, T02-929 01500, www.travel.com.au

Royal Jordanian, Syrian Air, British Mediterranean and a number of other airlines operate daily flights between **Damascus** and Amman, though these are expensive (around JD54/93 single/return with *Royal Jordanian*) compared with the cost of a coach ticket (JD5). Given that the journey by road only takes around 4-5 hours depending on border formalities, by the time you take into account getting to and from the airports and checking-in etc, flying is certainly no quicker.

Middle East

Royal Jordanian, MEA (the Lebanese national carrier), *Olympic Airways* and *British Mediterranean* between them offer a number of flights daily between Amman and **Beirut.** It is much cheaper and more interesting (though not quicker) to travel overland.

Royal Jordanian and *Egypt Air* both offer daily flights between Amman and **Cairo.** The single/return fare with *Royal Jordanian* is around JD100/186.

There are now direct flights operating between Amman and **Tel Aviv** on the *Royal Jordanian* subsidiary *Royal Wings,* and with the Israeli national carrier *El Al.* Both cost in the region of JD55/90 single/return.

Boat

Passenger/vehicle ferries and faster 'sea cats' (passenger only) operate daily between Aqaba and Nuweiba in the Sinai. The ferry terminal is located 9 km to the south of Aqaba. Ferries are generally busy, carrying large numbers of migrant workers back to Egypt, en-route from Saudi Arabia. The period around the time of the annual *Hajj* is the busiest, with thousands of pilgrims going to or returning from Mecca. Whatever the level of chaos in Aqaba or Nuweiba ports, foreign tourists are generally helped through fairly rapidly. For details of timings, prices etc, see under Aqaba. Leaving Jordan by sea, there is a JD6 departure tax. Note that if you intend to visit the Sinai only, you can obtain a **Sinai Permit** which is valid for 14 days and is free. A Sinai Permit is only valid for visits to places along the Gulf of Aqaba coast between Taba and Sharm el-Sheikh. It does **not** permit you to visit Ras Mohammed National Park (either by boat or by land), or St Catherine's Monastery (although some travellers report being allowed through to here on just a Sinai Permit). If you wish to visit the rest of Egypt, get a full tourist visa in Aqaba. Coming from Egypt, Jordanian visas are available on arrival.

To/From Egypt

Road

Jordan has land borders with Syria and Israel, and of course Saudi Arabia and Iraq, although the latter is not very relevant for most travellers. For information on bringing a **private vehicle** into Jordan, see the Overland section below.

There are two land borders between Syria and Jordan. The one most commonly used by coaches and service taxis running between Damascus and Amman is the Jabir/Nasib border, for the simple reason that the whole route via this border is on a fast motorway. If you are travelling by your own transport, the Ramtha/Deraa border is probably a better bet, if only because it is not so busy. Both borders are open 24 hours, and each has currency exchange facilities on both sides. Jordanian visas can

To/From Syria

be obtained at either border without any problem, but it impossible to get Syrian visas at these border crossings (or indeed any other point of entry to Syria). Leaving Jordan there is a JD4 departure tax. Leaving Syria there is no departure tax. There are regular *JETT* and *Karnak* (the Syrian state-owned company) **a/c coaches** operating between Damascus and Amman for JD5/US$7 one way. The journey takes around 4-5 hours including border formalities. In addition there are regular **service taxis** which are slightly more expensive, but also slightly quicker (in theory) as there are fewer people to get through the border formalities. There is also a weekly **train** which runs between Damascus and Amman (via the Jabir/Nasib border) on the old narrow-gauge Hejaz railway which TE Lawrence spent so much time trying to blow up during the First World War. However this really is a trip for enthusiasts only, being just about the slowest way of going short of crawling on your hands and knees; the journey takes in the region of 11 hours, if you are lucky, but can take much longer.

To/From Israel & the Palestinian Authority areas

There are now three land borders which are open to tourists. Going from south to north they are; Wadi Arabah/Arava between Aqaba and Eilat; King Hussein (Allenby) Bridge between Amman and Jerusalem; and Jisr Sheikh Hussein/Jordan River between Irbid and Bet Shean. Note that the King Hussein (Allenby) Bridge crossing is not open to private vehicles. Most nationalities do not require a visa to visit Israel. The security checks and bureaucratic formalities entering/leaving Israel can be very lengthy.

Wadi Arabah/Arava Known as Wadi Arabah to the Jordanians and Arava to the Israelis, this border is located approximately 10 km northwest of Aqaba. A taxi from Aqaba to the border will cost in the region of JD4. The border is open Sunday-Thursday 0630-2200, Friday and Saturday 0800-2000, closed on Yom Kippur, Jewish New Year and Islamic New Year. Leaving Jordan, there is a JD4 departure tax. Private vehicles are allowed to cross at this border. On the Israeli side, bus number 016 runs to Eilat (4 km to the south) for 7 NIS, or a taxi will cost 20 NIS. Leaving Israel, there is an extortionate 60 NIS departure tax. Jordanian visas are issued at the border. Note that you will receive a Jordanian entry/exit stamp at this border whether you like it or not. There are currency exchange facilities on both sides.

King Hussein (Allenby) Bridge Known to the Jordanians as King Hussein Bridge (or Jisr Malek Hussein) and to the Israelis as Allenby Bridge, this border is located 45 km to the west of Amman and 55 km to the east of Jerusalem (or 16 km east of Jericho). The border is open Sunday-Thursday 0800-2400, Friday and Saturday 0800-1500, closed on Yom Kippur, Jewish New Year and Islamic New Year. There are currency exchange facilities on both sides. Leaving Israel, there is an astronomical 120 NIS departure tax (since both Israel and the Palestinian Authority collect a share). **Note that Jordanian visas are not available at this border.** For details of transport between Amman and the border, see Amman transport. Leaving Jordan there is a JD4 departure tax. The main advantage of this border crossing is that your Jordanian entry/exit stamps will not be entered in your passport, but on a separate sheet of paper. Likewise for your Israeli entry/exit stamps *provided you ask*. Therefore, if you wish to visit Israel from Jordan, as long as you enter *and leave* by this border, it is possible to continue on to Syria and Lebanon without any evidence of your having been in Israel. Private vehicles are **not** allowed to cross at this border. You are not even allowed to walk across here; instead an overpriced shuttle bus operates between the border posts (if you came by JETT bus from Amman, this is included in the price of the ticket). On the Israeli side, the easiest option is to take a shared taxi direct to Jerusalem's Damascus Gate (26 NIS, 45 minutes). Going via Jericho is no cheaper and takes considerably longer.

Jisr Sheikh Hussein/Jordan River Known to the Jordanians as Jisr Sheikh Hussein (or Prince Hussein Bridge) and to the Israelis as the Jordan River crossing, this is the northernmost border between the two countries, located around 35 km to the west of Irbid and 6 km to the east of the Lower Galilee town of Bet Shean. The border is officially open Sunday-Thursday 0630-2200, Friday and Saturday 0800-2000 (though it's best to cross before 1700 on Friday/Saturday), closed on Yom Kippur, Jewish New Year and Islamic New Year. There are currency exchange facilities on both sides. Leaving Israel there is a 60 NIS departure tax. Jordanian visas are issued at the border. Leaving Jordan there is a JD4 departure tax. There is a shuttle bus between the Jordanian and Israeli border posts (NIS3) or you can drive across in a private vehicle, but you cannot walk. On the Israeli side, buses and service taxis run regularly between the border and Bet Shean (NIS11/15). For details of transport between Irbid and the border, see page Irbid transport. Note that you will receive a Jordanian entry/exit stamp at this border whether you like it or not.

Overland from Europe

The overland route from Europe though the Middle East is alive and well. Travelling overland to this region is an enormously rewarding option. It's certainly not the cheapest or quickest way to get there, but if you have the time and resources, the advantages far outweigh the extra cost and effort involved.

Taking your own vehicle overland is very expensive. Although you can claim it back at the end, the deposit for your Carnet will be the single largest outlay (see page 39). Sparing any expense on preparing your vehicle is a false economy which could land you in serious trouble during your trip. As well as paying for local insurance, you will also be liable for administrative fees for processing your Carnet at each border ($30 in Egypt; $10 in Jordan; $2 in Syria; free in Lebanon). The ferry crossings from Italy to Greece and Israel to Greece are also comparatively expensive with a vehicle.

The difficulty of getting visas for Libya (impossible for US citizens; unpredictable for UK citizens; very time-consuming for others) and the current unrest in Algeria means that a complete circuit of the Mediterranean remains for the time-being impractical. However, by combining the overland route from Europe through Turkey and Syria to Jordan with sea routes across the Mediterranean, you can still make a very interesting circuit without having to double back the way you came. There is also the option of continuing down into Africa.

The most straightforward way of reaching Turkey is to travel down through Italy, take a ferry across to Greece and then cross from there into Turkey. This is more expensive, but saves you having to travel through eastern Europe (either through former Yugoslavia, or through Hungary, Rumania and Bulgaria), where many travellers report problems with corrupt border officials demanding large bribes. Ferries operate between **Ancona**, **Bari** or **Brindisi** in Italy and **Igoumenitsa** or **Patra** in Greece. From Igoumenitsa, the drive across Greece involves crossing the Pindus mountains to reach Thessalonika, from where you follow the Aegean coast before crossing the border at **Kipi** and carrying on to **Istanbul**. From Patras you must go via Athens to Thessalonika. Driving across Turkey, you have the choice of traversing the central **Anatolian plateau** or following the **Mediterranean coast**.

Through Italy, Greece & Turkey

Alternatively, you can take a ferry directly from Italy (**Bari**) to Turkey (**Çesme**, near Izmir on Turkey's west Mediterranean coast), and there are also ferry services operating from Greece (**Piraeus**) to **Rhodes**, from where you can get a ferry to **Marmaris** on Turkey's southwest Mediterranean coast. In addition, there are services operating along Turkey's Mediterranean coast, saving you the long drive across Turkey (including occasional ferries from **Izmir** direct to **Lattakia** in Syria).

The main land border crossing between Turkey and Syria is **Bab al-Hawa**, halfway between Antakya and Aleppo, although there are several more along the northern stretch of the Syrian/Turkish border. Once in Syria, as well as touring the country, you can make a detour into Lebanon (the only land route in and out of Lebanon is from

Through Syria & Lebanon

Essentials

Syria and at present the only sea route is on irregular passenger-only hydrofoils from Beirut/Jounieh to Cyprus). From Syria you can cross into Jordan via the **Deraa/Ramtha** or **Nasib/Jabir** border crossings.

From Jordan you can cross into **Sinai** (Egypt) by ferry from **Aqaba** to **Nuweiba**. If you are able to obtain a Libyan visa (this can take up to three months in Cairo unless you are able to organise it in advance), you can traverse **Egypt** and **Libya**, following the Mediterranean coast, and cross into Tunisia. From the capital, **Tunis**, there are ferry services back to **Marseille** (France).

Alternatively, from Jordan you can cross into **Israel** by land from **Aqaba** to **Eilat** via the **Wadi Arabah/Arava** crossing, or via the **Jordan River** crossing to the north (the King Hussein (Allenby) bridge between Amman and Jerusalem is not open to private vehicles). Weekly ferries operate from **Haifa** (Israel) to **Piraeus** (Greece) via Cyprus and Rhodes.

NB There are currently no public passenger/vehicle ferry services operating from Egypt (Alexandria) to Greece, Italy or France.

All the routes described above can be done by public transport. The distances are vast and the journey long, and at times boring and uncomfortable, but if this form of travelling appeals, it certainly beats sitting in an aeroplane. Coaches leave from London's Victoria station to Istanbul, from where you can take another coach on to Antakya and then another one on to Aleppo (NB it is more expensive to buy a ticket direct from Istanbul to Aleppo than to get tickets for each leg separately). You can also travel across Europe by rail, and indeed right across Turkey and into Syria. Once in the region, there are good public transport networks in all three countries, and in Israel and Egypt, while the Mediterranean ferry networks outlined above provide a means of getting back to Europe.

Touching down

Airport
information

Queen Alia International Airport, situated around 35 km to the south of Amman, handles the vast majority of international flights into Jordan. For those arriving without a **visa**, the proceedure for getting one is fairly straightforward and efficient. Unless you have your own supply of Jordanian Dinars, you will have to change the relevant amount to pay for your visa (see page 23) at one of the nearby **exchange booths**. These stay open for as long as there are international flights arriving at the airport. The rates given are slightly lower than in Amman itself, and commission charges for TCs are high, so only change the amount you need.

Note that the **landing card** which you have to fill in on the plane or in the airport is an important piece of documentation which you will have to submit when you leave; be sure not to lose it.

Once through immigration, there are further exchange booths, a friendly **tourist information** counter (also open as long as there are international flights arriving), a 24-hour **café** and several **car hire** booths. Whatever time you arrive, there will be no shortage of taxis touting for business. A **taxi** into the centre of Amman should cost no more than JD10-15, though you may have to bargain them down, especially late at night or in the early hours of the morning. Much cheaper (JD1.500) is the **Airport Express**, a comfortable a/c coach which goes to Abdali bus station via the *Meridien* hotel and 7th Circle. It leaves from directly outside the arrivals hall, with departures every 30 minutes between 0600-2200, and every 2 hours between 2200-0600 (after 2400, however, the service is not always 100% reliable, so check with the tourist information; taxi drivers will deny the existence of the service at any time of day).

Touching down

Official time
Jordan is 3 hours ahead of Greenwich Mean Time (GMT+3) all year round. This replaces the old system whereby Jordan was GMT+2, with Daylight Saving Time (effectively GMT+3) operating from April to October. Under this new system, Jordan is 8 hours ahead of American Eastern Standard Time, and 8 hours behind Australian Eastern Standard Time.

International Direct Dialling (IDD)
The IDD code to telephone Jordan from abroad is 00962, followed by the area code minus the initial 0, followed by the telephone number (eg to phone Amman from abroad you should dial 00962-6-XXXXXXX).

Emergency services
Police T191; **Traffic police** T190; **Ambulance/Fire brigade** T199. Directory enquiries National T1221/195; **International** T0132

Electricity
220 volts, 50 AC. European two-pin sockets are the norm. Electricity supply is reliable.

Weights and measures
The metric system is used in Jordan (kilogrammes, litres, kilometres etc).

Business hours
NB All government offices and Muslim shops/businesses close in the afternoon during Ramadan, though many shops re-open after sunset.
Banks are generally open Sunday-Thursday 0800-1530, closed Friday and Saturday.
Post offices are generally open Saturday-Thursday 0800-1900, Friday 0800-1300, though in smaller towns they tend to close earlier (usually by 1500) and may not open on Fridays.
Government offices are generally open Sunday-Thursday 0800-1400, closed Friday and Saturday. However, to stand a chance of getting anything done you should get there as early as possible.
Airlines/travel agents are generally open Saturday-Thursday 0900-1300 and 1600-1800, closed Friday.
Shops are normally open Saturday-Thursday 0800-1300 and 1530-1930 in summer (May-October) and 0830-1330 and 1500-1830 in winter, closed Friday. Note that you will always find some shops open on a Friday, particularly in Amman, Aqaba and Wadi Musa. The shops in the souks of Downtown Amman stay open on Fridays, which is generally their busiest day.

Essentials

Marka Airport (officially known as Amman Civil Airport), situated around 4 km northeast of Downtown Amman, handles some of the *Royal Wings* and *El Al* flights arriving from Gaza and Tel Aviv. Visas can be obtained on arrival here, and there are foreign exchange facilities. A taxi into Downtown Amman will cost around JD1-2, or you can catch a minibus from outside the airport to Raghadan bus station.

   Royal Jordanian City Terminal If you are flying by *Royal Jordanian,* when you leave Amman you have the option of checking in your luggage one day before your flight at their City Terminal (T585-6855), situated close to 7th Circle in western Amman. A shuttle bus operates between the City Terminal and Queen Alia International Airport, departing every 30 minutes between 0800-2030 (JD1). There is a **post office** and a branch of the *Arab Bank* with a 24-hour ATM in the City Terminal building.

Note that you will be charged a departure tax on leaving Jordan. It's a good idea to put this money aside as soon as you arrive, or you may find yourself having to change more money than you need right at the last moment (or worse still, without enough money to pay at all). Leaving Jordan by land the departure tax is JD4. By sea it is JD6 and by air JD10.

Airport tax
There is talk of departure tax going up to JD8 for land/sea and JD15 for air, so check when you arrive

Tourist Information There are tourist information offices or visitors' centres in Amman, Aqaba, Petra, Wadi Rum, Jerash, Madaba and Kerak. Their main purpose is to supply you with a selection of free pamphlets and maps of major sites. Other than this, depending on the staff, they range from the extremely helpful and resourceful to the largely useless. The head office of the Ministry of Tourism and Antiquities is in Amman. Though they have a public relations department, they do their best to deter humble tourists. The Jordan Tourism Board, also in Amman, is likewise geared up primarily to dealing with tour operators etc. See page 115 for the addresses of both.

Disabled travellers Provisions for disabled travellers are largely non-existent in Jordan. A few of the luxury hotels have provisions for wheelchair access (recent legislation is supposed to make this obligatory for all new public buildings), but this is still very much the exception rather than the rule. Urban areas generally feature uneven pavements which are often cracked or pot-holed, and ridiculously high kerbs. Visiting historic sites in Jordan almost invariably requires traversing rough, uneven ground unsuitable for wheelchairs. With some advanced planning, however, it is possible to see at least part of Petra (see Petra chapters for more details). If you can cope with a fairly rough ride in a 4WD, you can see a good deal of Wadi Rum also. Despite the considerable obstacles to disabled travel in Jordan, if you do decide to go, you can be sure that people everywhere will be extremely accommodating and helpful.

The following organisations can provide you with further advice and put you in touch with travel agents and tour operators specialising in travel for the disabled. **RADAR (Royal Association for Disability and Rehabilitation)**, 12 City Forum, 250 City Road, London EC1V 8AF, UK, T0207-2503222, minicom T0207-2504119. **Irish Wheelchair Association**, Blackheath Drive, Clontarf, Dublin 3, Republic of Ireland, T01-8338241, F01-8333873, iwa@iol.ie **Mobility International**, 25 Rue de Manchester, Bruxelles B-1070, Belgium, T02-4106297. **Mobility International USA**, PO Box 10767, Eugene, OR 97440, T541-3431284. **Society for the Advancement of Travel for the Handicapped** (*SATH*), 347 5th Ave, Suite 610, New York, NY 10016, USA, T212-4477284. **ACROD (Austalian Council for the Rehabilitation of the Disabled)**, PO Box 60, Curtin, Canberrra, ACT 2605, Australia, T02-62824333. **Disabled Persons Assembly**, 173-175 Victoria St, Wellington, New Zealand, T04-8119100.

Gay & Lesbian travellers Homosexuality is officially illegal in Jordan, and very much frowned on. A gay scene does exist in Amman, but it is extremely well-hidden. Pre-marriage homosexuality amongst men is probably far more widespread than most Jordanians would admit, but it remains a taboo subject. The idea of women engaging in lesbian relationships is something which Jordanian men seem totally unable to come to terms with, and most would deny that it occurs at all. Gay and lesbian travellers are therefore advised to be discreet about their sexuality. Paradoxically, the strictly segregated nature of Jordanian society means that public behaviour which would be seen as inappropriate between members of the opposite sex (eg holding hands, kissing on the cheek etc) is acceptable between members of the same sex.

Student travellers Anyone in full-time education is entitled to an **International Student Identity Card (ISIC)**. These are issued by student travel offices and travel agencies across the world. In Jordan they are essentially useless (although there is talk of introducing a 50% discount for students on entry fees to historic sites etc). They are useful, however, if you are travelling on to Syria, where entry to museums and historical sites is a fraction of the standard fee for students. If you do not have an ISIC, they are very easily obtainable in Cairo, even if you are not a student.

Jordanians love children. "Do you have children?", or more commonly "How many children do you have?", comes high up on the list of standard questions asked of foreigners after "what is your name/where are you from/are you married?". Unlike in Europe or North America, children are positively welcomed in restaurants, and most hotels will go out of their way to accommodate children. Indeed, travelling with children, you will constantly find yourself receiving offers of help and hospitality. There are of course important health considerations specific to children (see page 54), but facilities are reasonably good in all but the most out-of-the-way places, and it is easy to travel safely and comfortably with children in Jordan.

Travel with children

Generally, women travelling alone in Jordan experience no more harassment than is the norm in most European countries. The majority report Jordan to be amongst the most relaxed in the Middle East in this respect. While it can be more demanding, there are also distinct advantages. In the vast majority of situations women are treated with great respect. Seasoned female travellers in Jordan argue that they get the best of both worlds. As a foreigner they are generally accorded the status of 'honorary males' in public, while in private they have access to female society, from which men are excluded. When invited to a Jordanian household, male guests are usually confined to the guest room while women are whisked away behind the scenes into the 'real' household, where they can meet wives, mothers, sisters and other members of the extended family.

Women travellers

Women travellers should, however, make an effort to dress modestly. The main reason for this is to show respect for Islamic values and not cause offence. Wearing a wedding ring may help to classify you as 'respectably married', while photos of a husband and children (whether real or imaginary) will further raise your status.

Remember that most Jordanian women do not travel alone, and in remoter areas are rarely seen in public. The widely held perception of western women is based on the images in western magazines, films and satellite TV, which portray them as having 'loose' sexual morals. This, along with the fact that in their rigidly segregated society many young Jordanian males openly admit to feeling sexually frustrated, can lead to problems of sexual harassment. Cases of violent sexual assault are however extremely rare and a firm, unambiguous response will deal with most situations. In public, the best approach is to make a scene. Any form of impropriety towards women is a gross violation of the tenets of Islam and someone is bound to come to your aid; the perpetrator meanwhile will quickly vanish in a cloud of shame. It is worth remembering that a good Muslim would consider it improper to be alone with a female in private, so any attempt to contrive such a situation should set alarm bells ringing.

Rules, customs & etiquette

Just about everything, including the price of hotel rooms etc, can be bargained over. For some things such as souvenirs and handicrafts it is almost expected (although some souvenir/handicraft shops are fixed-price). Where bargaining is the norm, shop-owners will quote you a starting price well above what they actually expect to receive. Successful bargaining is something of an art. Trying to hurry things along never helps. Give yourself plenty of time and be prepared to sit around drinking cups of tea and exchanging small talk; it is all part of the process. It is always worth shopping around to compare prices and quality. Try also to establish in your own mind what you think the item you are after is worth, and use this as a basis for your negotiations. At the end of the day, if you think the final price is too high, be prepared to walk away empty handed (as often as not you will be called back to hear one 'final, last, lowest possible' price, at which point you can begin bargaining all over again).

Bargaining

Essentials

Clothing   You will be judged to a large extent by your appearance. Jordanians place a lot of importance on smartness and cleanliness and making the effort to be presentable in public will earn you greater respect. Skimpy, tight-fitting or revealing clothes cause great offence to Muslims. Much more acceptable are loose-fitting clothes that do not highlight the lines of your body, and not to expose anything more than head, hands and feet. For their own safety and well-being, women need to take particular care over this, although it applies just as much to men. For women, a scarf is useful for covering up further if you begin to feel exposed or uncomfortable in a given situation; it is also very good protection against the sun. Note that while very liberal dress-codes can be found in the affluent areas of Amman, as soon as you get out of the capital, far more conservative attitudes prevail.

Conduct   Jordanians are generally very open and welcoming and will often go out of their way to help foreigners. Return the gesture by being equally polite and friendly. It is not usually acceptable for foreign men (or indeed any unrelated male) to talk to Jordanian women on their own. Nor is it usual for men and women to shake hands. Do not take pictures of women without their consent, or more importantly that of their male escort. Female tourists are more likely to be given permission, but you should never take this for granted. Open displays of affection between couples can also cause offence and are not acceptable in public.

Drugs   Possession of narcotics is illegal in Jordan. Those caught in possession risk a long prison sentence and/or deportation. Although cannabis is said to be smuggled through the country in considerable quantities, it is not readily available and you are very unlikely to be offered it on the street. If you are after a smoke, you would do much better to head for places such as Dahab in Sinai, where it is not in short supply.

Photography   Avoid taking pictures of military installations, or anything which might be construed as 'sensitive', particularly if you are close to the Israeli border.

Tipping   The standard 10% is acceptable in more expensive restaurants; otherwise it is really down to your own discretion. Bear in mind that a 10% service charge is automatically added to your bill in most mid-range to luxury hotels.

Visiting   Non-Muslims are often not allowed to enter mosques in Jordan, or else are only
mosques   allowed into the outer courtyard but not the prayer hall itself. Always seek permission before entering a mosque, and be prepared to give way if you are refused entry. If you are allowed in, remember that shoes must be removed before entering the prayer hall, although socks can be left on. Both men and women should make sure their arms and legs are entirely covered. Women should also wear a headscarf. At some larger mosques, for example the King Abdullah Mosque in Amman, women are required to hire a full-length black hooded robe at the entrance (and men also if they attempt to enter in shorts).

Safety

Theft and violent crime are extremely rare in Jordan and even in the big cities it is possible to wander around freely at any time of the day and night (notwithstanding the inevitable offers of help if you are looking lost). Incidents of civil unrest are also extremely rare, with moderation rather than extremism being the norm in Jordan. If you are staying in cheap dormitory accommodation, there is always the danger of being robbed by a fellow-traveller, though this too is a rare occurrence. Never leave valuables in your hotel room (whether it is a dormitory or not); either take them with you, or hand them over to the management for safe-keeping.

Where to stay

Jordanian hotels are inspected annually by the government, and graded according to star-ratings (1-5, plus unclassified). Prices are set according to the star-rating, though invariably they are set too high and as a result few hotels stick to the the official government rates. Note that room charges in the medium and upper range hotels (**L+** to **B** category in this book) are liable to 10% 'service charge' plus another 13% 'government tax'. Clarify whether these charges are included in the price you are quoted, or you could be faced with an unexpectedly high bill when you come to pay. Below **B** category only the 13% government tax is usually applied, while the cheapest hotels generally do not bother with either the service charge or government tax. Many hotels include breakfast in the room price. Note that there are huge variations in hotel prices at Wadi Musa (Petra) according to the season and level of demand, with the high season generally running from January-May and October-November.

Hotels

There is a huge selection of hotels from all categories in Amman. In Aqaba and Wadi Musa (Petra) there is a more limited, though reasonable, selection of top-end hotels (**L+** to **A** category) and plenty of medium range (**B-D** category) and budget (**E/F** category) hotels. Elsewhere you will only find a limited selection of medium range and budget hotels.

In both Amman and Aqaba there are a number of hotels specialising in **family suites**. These are generally **AL-B** category, with separate sitting room/kitchen areas, and can make for comfortable, good value family accommodation, with good discounts for longer stays.

Wadi Rum is the obvious place to go for 'wilderness' camping. The Royal Society for the Conservation of Nature (RSCN) also has supervised campsites in a number of their nature reserves and protected areas. With the exception of Dana, where you can just turn up, you must make arrangements in advance to stay at these. Contact the RSCN in Amman (see page 115 for more details). Elsewhere, camping is not really advisable. This is not so much from a safety point of view, but because you are likely to attract a lot of attention from local people and possibly from the authorities. Some of the hotels in Aqaba and Petra will allow you to camp within their grounds.

Camping

Getting around

Air

The only internal air connection is between Amman and Aqaba, with *Royal Wings*, a subsidiary of *Royal Jordanian*, operating twice daily flights between the two cities.

Road

The state-run **JETT** company operates a/c coaches and minibuses between Amman and Petra, Aqaba, Hammamat Ma'in and King Hussein (Allenby) Bridge for Israel. They also run international a/c coaches between Amman and Damascus, Cairo and various other destinations in Saudi Arabia and Iraq. The privately-run *Trust International* company operates a/c coaches between Amman and Aqaba, and also between Amman and various destinations in Israel. There are a couple of other private coach companies offering a/c coaches and minibuses from Amman to Jerash, Irbid, Petra and Aqaba, and between Petra and Wadi Rum, and Aqaba and Wadi Rum. In addition there are numerous other local bus and minibus services connecting all the major and minor towns. These do not run to set timetables, simply departing when full.

Bus

Essentials

☞ Hotel Categories

The price categories used in this book are based on the cost of a double room, including all service and taxes, during the high season. They are **not** star ratings.

LL JD150+ Really prestigious international-class luxury hotels and resorts. There are very few of these in Jordan (only in Amman, Aqaba and down by the Dead Sea). All belong to multinational chains. They offer all the facilities for the business and leisure traveller to the highest international standard. Major credit cards accepted.

L JD100-149 International class luxury hotels and resorts, often part of a multinational chain. They offer all the usual facilities, including 24 hour room service, a/c, TV/dish, IDD, minibar, attached bath, choice of restaurants/bars, swimming pool and other sports such as tennis, health centre, conference/banquet hall, shopping, bank, car hire etc. Major credit cards accepted.

AL JD75-99 Luxury hotels, generally offering very comfortable, fully equipped rooms, but without the same range of other facilities to be found in L/L+ category hotels, and without that feeling of international luxury. Generally with only one restaurant and bar, although a choice of cuisines.

A JD50-74 Rooms are generally comfortable, with a/c, TV/dish, IDD, minibar and attached bath. You will find a restaurant, usually a coffee shop and/or bar, perhaps a swimming pool, and sometimes an impressive range of other facilities.

B JD30-49 Rooms with a/c, TV, phone, and attached bath. You will find a restaurant and usually a bar. Hotels in this category are usually modest but comfortable. Some have very grandiose reception areas which are somewhat out of keeping with the rest of the hotel.

C JD20-29 Rooms generally have a/c, TV, phone and attached bath. There is usually a restaurant. Reasonably comfortable. Can be very good value, and it is often possible to get good off-season bargains in this category.

D JD15-19 Rooms may have a/c (at the top of the category) or more usually just a fan; usually with attached bath. Good value when clean, but can be rather shabby. Sometimes with restaurant.

E JD10-14 Rooms with fan only and attached bath. Check to see if there is hot water. Rarely with restaurant. This is the cheapest accommodation you will find without resorting to dormitories or very basic F category rooms. Good value if clean, but otherwise you are better off moving up or down a category.

F under JD10 The very simplest of hotels. Very basic rooms or, more usually, dormitories, perhaps with a fan. Share toilet/shower facilities. Cleanliness and hygiene varies greatly. There are some real bargains, clean, friendly and well-run, but also some really squalid places. Women travelling alone should exercise caution.

Abbreviations The following abbreviations are used in the Accommodation sections; a/c = air conditioning; TV = television; dish = satellite television; IDD = international direct dialling; T = telephone; F = fax; bath = bathroom (which may include a bathtub in the more expensive hotels, but otherwise simply indicates a shower, sink and toilet.

Car With your own vehicle you have far greater freedom to explore more out-of-the-way places and to stop wherever you choose. The type of vehicle you select, whether it be a van/camper-van, car or motorcycle, depends very much on your own personal preferences and needs. Overlanding through the Middle East does not require a vehicle which has been specially modified in any way (unless of course you are planning to head down into Africa), although the vehicle should obviously be in excellent mechanical condition before you set off. For comfort, a car or van is the best option, or a camper-van if you want to be able to stop overnight wherever you choose. A motorcycle considerably cuts down on the cost of ferry crossings, petrol, local insurance etc, and is much more fun.

The road system in Jordan is generally very good. In the northern part of the country, an excellent motorway runs between Amman and the town of Ramtha on the Syrian border (via Jerash), while another excellent motorway runs between Amman and the Syrian border crossing at Jabir (via Zarqa and Mafraq). The minor roads in this part of the country, including the road along the Jordan Valley, are also fairly good, although you need to watch out for pot-holes, and well-concealed speed bumps in villages. In the southern part of the country, the Desert Highway carries practically all the heavy lorry traffic and is best avoided unless you want to get between Aqaba and Amman in a hurry. The King's Highway on the other hand is blissfully quiet as well as being stunningly beautiful. The Dead Sea/Wadi Arabah highway is a fast, good quality road, and usually very quiet. Amman is a hectic place to drive; as well as getting to grips with the impossibly complicated interchanges at major junctions, you have to cope with the legions of taxi drivers who merrily cut-up anything in sight. Except in well-lit urban areas, driving at night should be avoided altogether if at all possible; it is not uncommon to come across vehicles with faulty lights, or no lights at all, while others leave their main beams on permanently. In the majority of cases, routes are clearly signposted in English as well as Arabic; tourist sites are generally indicated by brown signs with white writing.

Vehicles drive on the right. The speed limit in built-up areas is 50 kph, outside of urban areas 90 kph, and on the Desert Highway 120 kph

Road users in Jordan tend to obey road rules. Traffic police are very much in evidence in and around Amman. On the whole, they are fairly lenient towards foreign tourists, providing you don't drive totally outrageously.

Documents

A Carnet de Passage is needed for private vehicles travelling through the Middle East. This must be obtained through a recognised motoring organisation (in the UK either the AA or RAC). A Carnet is in effect a guarantee to the various Customs authorities that the appropriate import duties will be paid if for whatever reason the vehicle is not taken out of the country again (eg if you sell it; or indeed if it is stolen or scrapped). Note that a Carnet is only valid for a maximum period of six months (180 days) in any one country. The maximum validity of a Carnet is one year from the date of issue, although it is possible to get it extended once it is nearing the expiry date. When applying for a Carnet you must specify which countries you will visit. The import fees for your vehicle for each of these countries will then be calculated and you will be required to provide a financial guarantee in the form of a **Bank Indemnity**. The figure will vary according to which counties you intend to visit and what vehicle you have, but the sum can amount to as much as *three times* the estimated value of the vehicle! One alternative is to obtain an **Insurance Indemnity**; in the UK this can only be done through **Irvine Campbell Ltd**, 48 Earls Court Road, London W8 6EJ, T0207-9376981. This in effect insures the organisation issuing the Carnet against the costs it is liable for if the vehicle is not taken out of a given country. **NB** Insurance Indemnity does not insure you personally against these costs; if any import duties are incurred, the insurance underwriters will still hold you liable for the amount they have paid out. It is however possible to take out further insurance (known as a **Double Indemnity**) with Irvine Campbell, which protects you from any liability. Note that at present Irvine Campbell will not provide Insurance Indemnity or Double Indemnity for Lebanon.

It is very important that the Carnet is correctly filled out and stamped at each border crossing. There is a page for each country, divided into three sections; on entering, the bottom section is retained by customs and the entry counterfoil filled in; on leaving, the middle section is retained and the exit counterfoil filled in. Always make sure that both the entry and exit counterfoils (which together form the third section and which you keep) have been correctly completed, as this is your proof that you exported the vehicle from each country, and when you return home it will ensure that you can reclaim your financial guarantee. In addition, when you return home, make sure that the customs officials fill in the Certificate of Location at the back of the Carnet. This confirms that the vehicle did return to the country of its origin, providing you with further documentary evidence should there be any problems in reclaiming your financial guarantee. Note however that in the UK at least customs officials are very reluctant to complete this section of the Carnet. If your vehicle is stolen or you are forced to abandon it while abroad, you must have the Certificate of Location completed, signed, stamped and dated by the local police or customs authorities and obtain a receipted Invoice/Bill of Entry showing the amount of Customs duties/taxes paid or exemption from duties/taxes granted.

Insurance A **Green Card** (providing third party insurance) is required for all EU countries. In the UK this can be easily obtained through your own insurance broker. If you request it when applying, a Green Card can be made valid for Israel also; this will save a considerable amount on the Israeli insurance you would otherwise have to pay for at the border. It is not possible to buy insurance in Europe for non-EU countries. Instead you must pay for it at the border of each country. Insurance is third-party only and valid for a period of one month.

Your own national **Driving Licence** is all that is required for Jordan. However, they are cheap and easy to get (in the UK from the AA) and have the advantage of containing a page in Arabic which you can always show to difficult officials.

International Certificate of Motor Vehicles This is an international vehicle registration document (or log book), and is likewise not compulsory, but again has the advantage of containing all the headings for your personal and vehicle details in Arabic.

NB Details of your vehicle will be written into your passport next to your visa/entry stamp for each country you visit. If for any reason you wish to break your journey and return home briefly without your vehicle, it is necessary to place your vehicle in a bonded customs warehouse and obtain the relevant authorisation from customs before leaving the country, otherwise you will not be allowed out. The bureaucracy involved can be labyrinthine; you are advised to enlist the help of your embassy in this eventuality.

Fuel   **Petrol** is very cheap, as compared with European prices. Where possible, always buy 'Super' (sometimes referred to as '*mumtaz*'), which is 98 octane petrol, roughly equivalent to '4 Star'; this is the best quality and generally cleaner than regular petrol ('*benzin*'). In Jordan 'Super' costs 300 fils (approx 50 cents/35 pence) per litre. Unleaded (same price) is available in Jordan. **Diesel** is even cheaper, costing just 110 fils per litre.

Except in very remote areas, petrol stations are found at fairly regular intervals. Basically, unless you plan to do an off-road trip, as long as you set off with a full tank, you will never have a problem with running out of petrol.

Spares/repairs   The range of vehicle spares is limited. The most common makes today tend to be Japanese (Nissan, Toyota, etc) or French (Renault, Peugeot). Make arrangements with a dealer at home to fly you out spare parts if necessary (make sure they know exactly what model and year of vehicle you have, and that they have stocks of the relevant spares).

Spare parts for motorcycles above 125cc are practically nonexistent in Jordan, reflecting the fact that only the police and certain other civil servants are allowed to drive motorcycles above this size. It is therefore essential that you bring all the spares you might reasonably need (and make arrangements to have them flown out if necessary); inner tubes, cables, spark plugs, oil filters, fork seals, brake/clutch levers, points/electronic ignition, etc. Likewise, a good tool kit (and the know-how to carry out basic repairs) is essential. In Amman there is one shop which stocks tyres, inner tubes, chains and batteries for the Suzuki motorcycles used by the police; **Suzuki Motorcycle Store** (proprietor Hani M Darwish Ahmad), Amphitheatre St (near the Roman Theatre), PO Box 6377, Amman 11118, T06-4651656.

AA Overseas Assistance, Copenhagen Court, New Street, Basingstoke, Hants, RG21 7DT, T01256-493819, F01256-460750, for information on applying for a Carnet.

Viamare Travel Ltd, Graphic House, 2 Sumatra Road, London, NW6 1PU, T0207-4314560, F0207-4315456, for details of Mediterranean passenger/vehicle ferries (Italy, Greece, Albania, Turkey, Cyprus, Israel).

Thomas Cook, PO Box 227, Thorpe Wood, Peterborough, PE3 6PU, T01733-503571, F01733-503596, publishing@thomascook.tmailuk.sprint.com (or any local branch of Thomas Cook), for its European and overseas timetables for rail and bus services, and for its *Greek Island Hopping* guidebook/timetable (published annually February/March) which covers the entire Greek ferry system, including the lines used by Inter-railers and Eurailers to cross the Adriatic from Italy to Greece, all international scheduled shipping across the eastern Mediterranean, and many Turkish ferries.

Royal Automobile Club of Jordan, Al Ameerah Sarvath al-Ibrahimi Shuhada St, near 8th Circle, Amman, T5850640.

Hiring a car is easy and relatively cheap in Jordan. It can save you a lot of time and **Car hire** makes life much easier for certain trips (notably the Desert Castles, Kings Highway, Jordan Valley and Dead Sea highway). Amman is the main place for car hire, with a range of international firms and literally hundreds of local companies scattered all over the city. There are also a few car hire places in Aqaba, while some companies have desks at the King Hussein (Allenby) Bridge border crossing with Israel and at Queen Alia International Airport. Hertz also has desks in the *Movenpick* hotels at the Dead Sea and Petra. The international firms are more expensive, but their insurance arrangements and other terms and conditions are likely to be more reliable. Local companies face huge competition, with the result that it is usually possible to secure some excellent deals if you are willing to shop around (prices have actually come down over the last three years). However, you should pay very careful attention to the insurance arrangements and general terms and conditions. An a/c car is more or less a must for the summer months. Even then, bear in mind that your car will behave like an oven when parked out in the sun; get some cardboard windscreen shades and carry a small towel for those occasions when the steering wheel is too hot to touch.

All companies require that you leave a deposit (generally JD200-500, either in cash or in the form of a credit card imprint), which you lose if you crash the car. Note that some of the small local companies may also try to charge you rental for the period that a damaged car is being repaired, or else a sum for depreciation. The better firms offer you the option of taking out additional Crash Damage Waiver (CDW) insurance (usually in the region of JD5-8 per day), which protects you from these charges (though even then, some still charge for an initial 'excess', so check carefully). Most companies have a minimum rental period of two or three days, and a choice of limited or open mileage. Limited mileage is usually 100-150 km per day, with a charge of 70-100 fils per extra km (if you are likely to go much above the set limit, open mileage usually works out cheaper). Most companies offer significant discounts for longer period rentals.

Prices tend to rise during the summer months, though ultimately this is very much a buyers' market and there are usually still good deals to be found. As a rough guide, the minimum rates (limited mileage, no CDW) for a small hatchback from a local company are generally JD12-15 per day. A medium size car with a/c will cost in the region of JD15-25 per day. Prices with the international firms start from around JD25 per day, though they also offer discounts, particularly for longer periods. Remember to check whether the 13% government sales tax is included or charged as extra. One-way rentals (eg hiring in Amman and dropping off in Aqaba or King Hussein Bridge) generally cost extra (JD10-35 for Aqaba, JD5-15 for King Hussein bridge), with the companies which also have offices at these locations charging the least. Most companies will deliver/collect to your hotel, or to Queen Alia International Airport, for no extra charge.

Taxis **Service Taxis,** or shared taxis – which are white – operate on all the major transport routes in Jordan. They are more expensive than coaches, buses and minibuses, but still very good value. They depart when full, but as they only take between five and seven passengers you don't usually have to wait around too long. They are also quicker than local buses and minibuses, since they do not stop as frequently to drop off or pick up passengers. In Amman they are also the main form of local transport around the city.

Private Taxis are yellow and readily available in all the major towns and cities. As well as providing local transport within towns and cities, you can also negotiate with private taxis for trips further afield. Nearly all the private taxis in Amman have working meters; if they do not (which is often the case outside the capital), you should always agree a price before getting in.

Train

The only passenger trains still operating are those which run between Amman and Damascus a couple of times each week. See page 107 for details.

Other

Bicycle Cycling is becoming increasingly popular in Jordan, although the hilly terrain and heat make this a particularly strenuous and demanding way of getting around. Head-winds and cross-winds can also be a real problem (though tail-winds always seem to be remarkably elusive). You can find spares for most imported hi-tech mountain or touring bikes in Amman. You will find workshops where you can get most repairs carried out in almost every town, but you should still carry your own basic tool kit and a supply of spares. The King's Highway is perhaps the most appealing route for cyclists in terms of the limited traffic and spectacular scenery, although it involves a number of very long and steep descents/ascents as you cross the wadis which drain into the Dead Sea. The rolling, forest-clad hill country to the north of Amman is also very beautiful. The Desert Highway is about as appealing to cyclists as London's M25 orbital motorway, while the Dead Sea/Wadi Arabah and Jordan Valley are simply too hot and humid for most of the year.

Hitching Hitching is not a widely accepted concept in Jordan, except in more remote areas where there is no regular public transport. Some sort of payment is often expected. Women are strongly advised not to hitch unless accompanied by a male companion.

Keeping in touch

Points of All European and North American countries (and the vast majority of other countries
contact from around the world) have **embassies** in Amman. If you passport is lost or stolen, your embassy should be able to help you obtain a replacement. However, except in the case of extreme emergencies (in the unlikely event of serious civil unrest, or a regional war breaking out, for example), foreign embassies are very reluctant to do anything else for their nationals. Several European countries, and the USA, also have **cultural centres** in Amman. These are generally geared primarily towards providing Jordanians with details of educational opportunities in their respective countries, and organising/hosting cultural events in Amman, but can also be a useful source of information and contacts, particularly for long-term residents in Jordan. For listings of all foreign embassies and cultural centres in Amman, see page 112.

Jordan has been quick to grasp the significance of the communications revolution. Computers and information technology are seen as being central to the country's future development. With computer hardware being beyond the means of most ordinary Jordanians, there has been a phenomenal growth in the number of internet cafés in recent years. There are now dozens of internet cafés scattered around **Amman** and **Aqaba**, and even a few in smaller centres such as **Madaba** and **Wadi Musa (Petra)**. The internet 'capital' of Jordan, however, is **Irbid**. Along the main street outside the large Yarmouk University in the southern part of Irbid there are now more than 70 internet cafés, with new ones opening up all the time. Indeed, Irbid's University Street, as it is known, reputedly has the highest concentration of internet cafés per block in the world!

Prices for internet access are falling steadily. In Irbid you can now hook up to the internet for as little as 500 fils per hour. In Amman the standard price is JD1 per hour. Elsewhere, internet access tends to be a little more expensive (from JD1.500 per hour upwards). This is because the nearest Internet Service Providers (ISPs) are in Amman, meaning that cafés have to keep a telephone line to Amman open while they are on-line. However, the introduction of low-cost 'lease lines' will result in these prices falling also.

With a few notable exceptions, the term 'internet café' is something of a misnomer in Jordan, as what most places offer is simply a room crammed full of computer terminals. They tend also to be very smoky, and male-dominated, though foreign women are usually welcome. In Amman, many of the foreign cultural centres offer internet access in a more appealing environment, though these are more expensive. Around the country, an increasing number of hotels also now offer internet access (and not just the luxury hotels), although again these tend to be more expensive.

Internet

For details of specific internet cafés, refer to the Directory in the Essentials section of each town/city.
For a list of Internet sites relating to Jordan and the Middle East, see page 63.

Essentials

There is at least one post office in every town and city in Jordan. **Airmail letters** and **postcards** to Europe cost 300 fils and 200 fils respectively, while to USA and Australia they cost 400 fils and 300 fils respectively. Postal services to Europe are fairly quick, taking 4-5 days on average. To North America and Australia takes up to two weeks. There are now postal services between Jordan and Israel, although they take longer than to Europe.

Sending **parcels** through the postal system is very expensive. By surface mail to Europe, the first kg costs JD9.500, with each additional kg costing a further JD3.400. By 'Express Mail' (air mail), a 3 kg package will cost JD72 (the Express Mail Service - EMS - office in Amman is located in Shmeisani, T563-0555).

Poste restante is available at the general post office in Downtown Amman. It consists simply of a box left on the counter which you look through yourself. Mail sent here should have your surname in capital letters and underlined. It should be addressed to; c/o Poste Restante, Central Post Office, Prince Mohammad St, Downtown Amman, Jordan. Alternatively, American Express offer a clients' mail service at both their Amman and Aqaba offices (see respective Essentials sections for their addresses).

Post

Courier services Branches of the major international courier companies can be found in Amman and Aqaba (see the relevant Essentials section), although they are very expensive.

Thankfully, crowded and chaotic government-run central telephone offices are a thing of the past in Jordan. The easiest and cheapest way to make local, national and international calls is now via the extensive network of public cardphones to be found in all towns and cities, and a surprising number of really out-of-the-way places. Cardphones are operated by two companies, *Alo* and *JPP*, with the former being the more ubiquitous. *Alo* phone cards come in values of JD3.300, JD8.800 and JD16.500 for national and international calls (including the 10% tax that is added), as well as a JD1.100

Telephone

card for local/national calls only. *JPP* cards come in JD2.200, JD5.500 and JD9.900 values. A JD3.300 card on an international call gives you around 5 minutes (you will be cut off before all your credit is gone, but can use the remainder for local/national calls). Local and national calls are very cheap; just 100 fils for a local call, or 300 fils for a national call. After 2200, and all day on Fridays and public holidays, you get 30% longer on all calls. Some *Alo* cardphones also accept *Visa* credit cards (these are marked with the *Visa* logo). The major downside of public cardphones is that so many of them are located on busy streets and junctions where traffic noise can easily drown out any chance of a conversation. Hotels and private telephone offices are better in this respect, though they too are often far from private, as well as being considerably more expensive than cardphones. **Faxes** can be sent from most hotels, and some main post offices.

Media

Newspapers and magazines
The *Jordan Times* is the national English language daily newspaper. It offers good coverage of events in Jordan and the Middle East, as well as world-wide. In addition it contains useful listings of emergency telephone numbers, flight information, films and exhibitions. There is also an English language weekly tabloid, *The Star*, which provides more detailed listings of events, as well as features and a section in French.

Most major foreign newspapers and magazines are readily available in Amman and Aqaba, in the luxury hotels or major bookshops. The foreign daily newspapers are generally only one or two days old, but are very expensive (eg *The Observer*, JD3.500).

Radio
Radio Jordan broadcasts in English from 1200-1300 and 1500-1730 on 11910 kHz and 11940 kHz (AM). It can also be picked up on 96.3 MHz (FM) in Amman, and 98.7 MHz (FM) in Aqaba. It is also often possible to pick up the numerous Israeli radio stations transmitting from across the border.

The best frequency for receiving the *BBC World Service* is 1323 kHz (MW), although it is also available in SW bands. *Voice of America* is on 1260 kHz (AM).

Television
Channel 2 of **Jordan TV** broadcasts in English, French and Arabic. The English news is at 2200, and the French news at 1900. Channel 1 is in Arabic only. Most hotels now also have satellite TV (if not in the rooms then at least in the lobby area), giving access to a broad range of international channels. Depending where you are in the country, it is also possible to pick up Syrian, Israeli and Egyptian terrestrial channels. The Israeli channels are popular, with far less in the way of censorship.

Food and drink

Amman has a vast range of eating options, including lots of up-market **gourmet restaurants** serving excellent Arabic cuisine, or else specialising in the cuisine of just about every other region/country of the world. In the past, the best restaurants were to be found only in the luxury hotels, but Amman now has a burgeoning scene in independent gourmet restaurants. There are some excellent restaurants in Aqaba, particularly for seafood, and in Madaba. In Petra, except at the luxury hotels, the selection is very limited and the quality not very good.

Though the **restaurants in luxury hotels** are invariably expensive, they often offer excellent value eat-as-much-as-you-want buffet meals, which are a great way to indulge yourself without breaking the bank. Western-style **fast-food places** (for burgers, pizzas etc) are numerous in Amman, and increasingly found in smaller towns throughout the country. In Jordan, Western-style fast-food is still something of a novelty and popular amongst the middle classes. **Cheap diners** can be found just about everywhere in the country and are generally excellent value, although the level of hygiene at these varies greatly. In terms of cheap snacks, *hummus*, *fuul*, *fatteh*, *falafel* or *shawarma* sandwiches, kebabs and roast chicken (whole or half portions) are the staples. *Mensaf* is considered something of a national dish in Jordan. Although vegetarians are not specifically catered for, the varied options provided by a *mezze* spread, the non-meat snacks such as *falafel* sandwiches, *fuul* and *hummus*, as well as a range of salads, mean that you can eat well without having to indulge in meat.

There are numerous traditional-style **cafés** in Downtown Amman where you can go for a cup of Arabic tea or coffee or a *nargileh*, as well as fancy Western-style cafés in the wealthier uptown districts. Freshly-squeezed fruit juices can be bought from **juice bars** in Amman and most larger towns. Fizzy soft drinks (Pepsi, Coca Cola, Seven Up and various local varieties) are widely available throughout the country, as is bottled mineral water.

Alcohol is also easy to obtain. In Downtown Amman there are some wonderfully atmospheric (if rather grotty/seedy) bars. Nearly all the luxury and mid-range hotels also have their own bars, and there are increasing numbers of up-market Western-style 'pubs' and bars. Outside of Amman, only the more expensive restaurants and hotels generally serve alcohol, or else you can buy it directly (and more cheaply) from liqueur stores in the Christian areas of most towns. Note that while alcohol is easy to obtain, it is forbidden to drink it in public (except of course in a licensed bar/restaurant); if you buy alcohol from a liqueur store, you should drink it in the privacy of your hotel room (with the permission of the manager).

A glossary of Arabic cuisine

Bread

Bread, known Arabic as *khubz* or *eish* (literally 'life'), is the mainstay of the Jordanian diet. It is baked unleavened (without yeast) in flat round discs and accompanies just about every meal or snack. Often it serves as an eating implement, or is rolled up with a filling inside to make a 'sandwich' snack. When it is fresh it is delicious although surprisingly for a country where so much of it is consumed, it has often been standing about for the best part of a day by the time it reaches your plate.

Mezze dishes

Perhaps the most attractive feature of Arabic cuisine is the *mezze*. When done properly, this consists of a spread of numerous small dips, salads and nibbles of fresh raw vegetables, olive etc, which are served as an extended starter course and, if the company is not tee-total, usually washed down with plenty of beer or *arak*. To fully appreciate a proper *mezze* spread you really need to be in a group of several people or you'll never get round the array of dishes; it also works out very reasonably when divided amongst several people. For smaller numbers you can just ask for a selection. If you do not want a full meal, you can always do away with the main courses and just concentrate on the *mezze*. Many of the items listed below are also served individually as a side dish in snack places and simple restaurants, or indeed as snacks in themselves. A selection of the more popular *mezze* dishes is given here.

Baba Ganoush (Moutabbal) Chargrilled eggplant (aubergine), tahini, olive oil, lemon juice and garlic blended into a smooth paste and served as a dip.
Falafel Small deep-fried balls of ground, spiced chick-peas. Very popular, both as part of a *mezze*, and as the basis of one of Jordan's most ubiquitous snacks (see below).
Fattoush Salad of toasted croutons, cucumbers, tomatoes, onion and mint.
Hummus Purée of chick-peas, tahini, lemon and garlic, served as a dip with bread. Probably the most common *mezze* dish, often also eaten along with salad as a side dish to a plate of meat in simpler restaurants, or as a light snack in its own right.
Kibbeh Ground lamb and burghul (bulghur/bulgar/cracked) wheat meatballs stuffed with olives and pine nuts and fried or baked. Something of a national dish in Lebanon.

Kibbeh Nayeh Raw kibbeh, eaten like steak tartare.
Loubieh (fasulya) Cooked French beans with tomatoes onion and garlic, served hot as a stew or cold as a kind of salad.
Mouhammara Mixture of ground nuts, olive oil, cumin and chillis, eaten with bread.
Rocca Rocket salad.
Tabouleh Finely chopped salad of burghul wheat, tomatoes, onions, mint and parsley.
Taratour Thick mayonnaise of puréed pine nuts, garlic and lemon, used as a dip.
Warak Enab (warak dawali) Vine leaves stuffed with rice and vegetables.

Main meat dishes So-called 'main' courses are more limited and consist primarily of meat dishes (usually lamb or chicken), or else fish (see below). Note that many listed below are also often served as snacks.

Bamia Baby okra and lamb in a tomato stew.
Bukhari rice Lamb and rice stir-fried with onion, lemon, carrot and tomato.
Kebab If you ask for 'kebab', you will most likely be offered *kofte kebab*, though strictly speaking *kebab* is just chunks of meat chargrilled on a skewer.
Kofte kebab Minced meat and finely chopped onions, herbs and spices pressed onto a skewer and chargrilled. You order by weight.
Kouzi Whole lamb baked over rice so that it soaks up the juice of the meat.
Mensaf A traditional Bedouin dish, consisting of lamb cooked with herbs in a yoghurt sauce and served on a bed of rice with pine nuts. Regarded as Jordan's national dish.
Saleek Lamb and rice dish cooked in milk.
Shish taouk Fillets of chicken breast chargrilled on a skewer.

Fish Fish is always expensive in Jordan; predictably enough it is the speciality in Aqaba, on the Red Sea coast. It is most commonly either grilled or fried and served with lemon, salad and chips.

Gambari Prawns.
Hamour Red Sea fish of the grouper family.
Najil Saddle-back grouper.
Samak nahri Trout.
Sayyadiya Delicately spiced fish (usually red mullet or bass) served with rice.
Shaour Red Sea fish of the emperor family.
Sultan Ibrahim (literally 'King Abraham', ie the king of fishes) Red mullet.

Snacks Traditional Arabic snack bars (and indeed many restaurants) serve a wide range of snacks. If you are on a tight budget, or vegetarian, many of these will become staples.

Ejje Omelette, usually with chopped onion and herbs. Makes a good breakfast dish.
Falafel The falafel sandwich must be the most ubiquitous snack throughout Jordan. You will find snack bars serving this (and often only this) everywhere you go. Several *falafel* balls (see under Mezze dishes) are crushed on an open piece of Arabic bread, garnished with salad and pickled vegetables (usually tomatoes, beetroot, onion and lettuce), topped by a yoghurt and *tahini* sauce and then rolled up into a 'sandwich'. They are very cheap and filling, though if you are on a tight budget and relying on them as a staple, they can get pretty monotonous. The freshness of the bread, as well as the filling, is what makes or breaks them.
Farouj Roast chicken. Although this should really appear under 'main' meat dishes, roast chicken is such a common form of light meal or snack that it is included here. Everywhere you go throughout Jordan you will find simple restaurants, snack places and shops with roasting ovens outside containing several spits of roasting chickens.

The standard portion is a half chicken ('*nuss farouj*'), sometimes served with a small portion of garlic dip and a few pickled vegetables and chips. As often as not, roast chickens are bought as take-aways to be eaten at home.

Fatayer Triangular pastry pockets filled with spinnach (*sbanikh*), meat or cheese. These make great snacks. Usually sold from bakeries specialising in these and other items, including *mannoushi*, see below.

Fatteh An excellent, very filling snack consisting of *fuul* and *laban* mixed together with small pieces of bread and topped with pine nuts and melted butter. Also sometimes served with fried minced meat mixed in.

Fuul Slow-cooked mash of fava beans and red lentils, dressed with lemon, olive oil and cumin, and sometimes a little yoghurt and *tahini* sauce. An excellent, filling and nutritious snack, traditionally a breakfast dish, though available any time of day.

Kushary Staple of pasta, rice and lentils mixed with onions, chilli and tomato paste. More common in Egypt, but found also in Jordan, Syria and Lebanon.

Mannoushi Thin, crusty '*pizzas*' topped with a thin layer of meat (*Lahmeh*), cheese (*Jebneh*), or *Zaatar*, a seasoning with thyme and *sumak*. A good breakfast snack.

'Sandweech' Both falafels and shawarmas are commonly referred to simply as 'sandwiches' (or *sandweech*). In addition, there are numerous other fillings available in many snack bars. *Shish taouk* and *kofte* can be ordered in sandwich form, or it's a case of looking to see what's on offer.

Shawarma This is essentially a meat version of a falafel sandwich, and an equally ubiquitous snack bar favourite. Layers of lamb or chicken roasted on a vertical spit are sliced off into small flat breads and rolled up with salad, pickled vegetables and a garlic sauce into a sandwich which is then steeped in extra fat as a special favour. Again they are cheap and filling, and if you are on a tight budget and not a vegetarian you will no doubt be eating plenty of them.

Dairy products

Some of these make an appearance in other dishes listed here, or else are popular as drinks in their own right.

Ayran Salty yoghurt drink, good refreshing rehydration material.
Haleeb Milk.
Jebneh (Jibni) Fairly hard and stringy white cheese.
Laban Slightly sour yoghurt drink, also widely used in cooking as a milk substitute
Labneh Thick creamy cheese, often spiced and used as a dip, for example *Labneh Maa Toum*, with garlic and olive oil.

Sweets

The Arab tooth is certainly very sweet. The range of sweets, pastries, biscuits and puddings on offer is enormous, although they all share one thing in common; copious amounts of sugar in one form or another. Most are served at restaurants, but to see the full range of what's on offer you should go to a patisserie, where you will be confronted by a bewildering selection. Many patisseries also have an area where you can sit and eat, and some also serve tea, coffee, soft drinks etc.

Asabeeh Rolled filo pastry filled with pistachios, pine nuts and cashews and honey. Often referred to as 'lady's finger'.
Atait Small pancakes stuffed with nuts or cheese and doused with syrup.
Baklawa Layered pastry filled with nuts and steeped in honey and lemon syrup. Probably the most common and best known Arabic sweet.
Barazak Crisp, light biscuits sprinkled with sesame seeds.
Basboosa Semolina tart soaked in syrup.
Booza Ice cream.
Borma Crushed pine nuts or pistachios wrapped in shredded pastry and sliced into segments.

Essentials

Halawat al-Jebneh Soft thick pastry stuffed with *labneh* cheese and steeped in syrup and ice cream.

Halwa A sweet made from sesame paste, usually studded with fruit and nuts and made in a slab.

Kamar ed-Dine Apricot nectar, often served as a break of fast during Ramadan.

Kunafi Pastry stuffed with sweet white cheese, nuts and syrup.

Ma'amul Biscuits stuffed with date, pistachio or walnut paste.

Muhalabiyyeh Fine, smooth textured semolina and milk pudding, sometimes with pistachios, pine nuts and almonds, served cold.

Sanioura Dry, crumbly macaroon-like biscuit. A speciality of Sidon in Lebanon.

Um Ali Literally 'Ali's mother', a pastry pudding with raisin and coconut, steeped in milk.

Tea & coffee Tea and coffee are widely drunk throughout the Middle East, though they are made very differently to in the West. Arabic coffee (or Turkish or Greek, depending on where you are) is known in the Middle East as *Kahweh (*or *Ah'weh)*. The Arab attitude to coffee is basically the stronger the better. The coffee is boiled up in tiny pots and served very strong in equally tiny cups, complete with a thick sludge of coffee grounds at the bottom. It is served without sugar (*balasekir* or *sadah*), with medium sugar (*wassad*), or with lots of sugar (*helweh*). Cardamom is sometimes added to give a delicate aromatic flavour. You can also often get excellent expresso coffee, just as strong but without the thick sludge at the bottom. Instant coffee is referred to everywhere as 'Nescafe' and is available on request in more expensive restaurants and hotels. The Arabic word for tea is *Shai (*or *chai)*, which is generally drunk strong and black, and with copious amounts of sugar. Mint tea and green tea are also available, though not so widely drunk.

Soft drinks You can get excellent freshly-squeezed **fruit juices** in Jordan, with dedicated fruit bars being a common feature of all larger towns and cities. What's on offer depends very much on the season; oranges, apples, pears, bananas, pomegranates, melons. Lemonade made from fresh lemon and fizzy mineral water is another one to look out for. *Laban* and *Ayran* (see above) are common **dairy**-based drinks, although straightforward milk (*haleeb*) is something of a rarity. Usually if you ask for milk, you will be given powdered or UHT milk. **Fizzy drinks** of all kinds are widely available, both international brands such as Coca Cola, Seven Up etc, and local lookalikes. **Mineral water** is widely available.

Alcoholic drinks **Arak** is an Arabic equivalent of the Greek *oozo* or Turkish *raki*, a potent liqueur made from grapes (in fact the left-overs of wine pressing) and flavoured with aniseed. It is very popular and is usually drunk with ice and/or cold water, which makes the otherwise clear alcohol go a cloudy white. The cheapest brands cost as little as US$2 for a litre, while the best ones cost as much as US$20. Only the most experienced drinkers however can actually detect any difference, except perhaps in the quality of their hangover the next day. Amman's trendy pubs and bars also stock a wide range of other spirits.

Almost all the **wine** to be found in Jordan comes from the West Bank, with that of the Latroun and Crémisan vineyards being the most popular. Amstel is the most widely available **beer** and is both imported and brewed in Jordan under licence. Canned Guinness, Kilkenny, Fosters etc is also available in the trendier bars.

Smoking **Nargileh** Not exactly an item of 'cuisine', the *nargileh* is nevertheless goes hand in hand with eating and drinking. it consists of a large waterpipe, known also as a *shish* or 'hubbly bubbly', through which tobacco, often flavoured with apple or strawberry, is smoked. *Nargilehs* are enjoyed at great length in cafés throughout Jordan alongside tea and coffee and endless games of cards and backgammon, or else after a meal.

Shopping

The best items to shop for in Jordan tend to be Bedouin handicrafts, since these are generally produced in Jordan itself; eg hand-woven woollen rugs and carpets, embroidery, fabrics, pottery, silverware, jewellery, finely decorated daggers and swords and items of traditional Bedouin dress such as the ubiquitous and distinctive head cloth or *keffiyeh* and the black cord or *aqal* used to tie it. Hand-blown glassware and hand-made ceramics (both of which were crafts traditionally practiced in Hebron but since the 1967 war moved from the West Bank to Amman) are also generally of a very high quality. There are several excellent outlets for all these goods in Amman (see page 102) and other major tourists centres in the country. Also worth checking out are the dried herbs, jams, olive oil and various 'natural' products sold through the RSCN's Dana shops (outlets in Amman, Madaba and those RSCN Reserves with Visitors' Centres). Popular as souvenirs are the bottles of different coloured sand from Petra, arranged in layers to make patterns, pictures and even writing. You will also find lots of Nabatean-style pottery souvenirs at the stalls in Petra. Another Jordanian speciality is the range of Dead Sea health products; salts, mud packs, soaps etc (available from the resorts on the Dead Sea, and various outlets in Amman, Madaba, Aqaba and elsewhere).

> **Handicrafts & souvenirs**

There is also a wide range of wood and inlaid wood products (chess-boards, boxes, carved camels etc), nargilehs, copper and brassware (particularly coffee pots), gold and silver jewellery, embroidered garments etc available from souvenir shops throughout the country. However, if you are heading for Syria, it is worth bearing in mind that items such as wood/inlaid wood products, copper and brassware are usually cheaper there, with much of it having been imported from Damascus in the first place.

The best place for English-language books is Amman, although even there the selection is rather limited. There are several bookshops with a range of publications on Jordan and the Middle East in Amman, while the top-end hotels generally have bookshops with a reasonable selection of fiction. Look out for the series of small booklets on tourist sites and areas of interest in Jordan by the local *Al Kutba* publishing company.

> **Books**

Colour negative and transparency (slide) film is widely available, and is usually fairly fresh. Black and white film is rarer. In terms of toiletries, 'luxury' foods and other provisions, these are all readily available in Amman and Aqaba, and to a lesser extent in most other smaller towns also. Away from Amman and Aqaba, the luxury hotels are usually a good place to look if you can't find what you want.

> **Miscellaneous**

Entertainment

Amman is developing into fairly happening place for nightlife, with a growing number of bars, pubs and nightclubs. On the whole, the best nightclubs are still to be found in the luxury hotels. The pub and bar scene, however, has gained its own momentum, with big names such as *Planet Hollywood* and the *Hard Rock Café* complementing a variety of local ventures. Aside from Downtown Amman's somewhat seedy/atmospheric bars, they are all very swish, trendy places catering for the wealthiest echelons of Jordan's international jet-set elite, with prices to match. Jordanians like to mix eating with dancing and drinking, so most places also serve food, and can be excellent restaurants in their own right, with DJs and bands appearing later in the evening.

> **Bars, pubs & nightclubs**

Away from the capital, there is much less in the way of nightlife. Popular tourist centres such as Petra and Aqaba have a certain amount going on in the luxury hotels, but the atmosphere (or lack of it) depends very much on the tour groups passing through. If Aqaba's nightlife gets you down, you can always hop across the border to Eilat, where there is a whole lot more going on.

Cinemas
There are numerous cinemas in Amman; those in Shmeisani and Jabal Amman show a fairly varied range of Hollywood films, while those in Downtown tend to focus on cheap kung-fu/action movies. The various cultural centres in Amman also show a variety of movies/videos.

Theatre & performing arts
Theatres in Jordan are fairly limited. There are a couple in Amman, although their performances are generally in Arabic. Some of the luxury hotels occasionally host theatre performances, as well as organising other evening entertainment for their guests, usually consisting of traditional music and dancing.

Sport and special interest travel

Diving & snorkelling
The coral reefs of the Red Sea's Gulf of Aqaba offer some of the most spectacular diving and snorkelling in the world. Jordan, however, tends to be overlooked as a diving destination in favour of the large resorts in Sinai. Certainly, diving in Sinai is much better promoted, but the five dive centres to be found in and around Aqaba are all professionally-run places with good reputations. The fact that far fewer divers come to Jordan also means that the reefs here are in an excellent state of preservation. If diving does not appeal, you can still see a great deal by simply snorkelling around on the surface. Indeed, Jordan's Gulf of Aqaba coastline is ideally suited to snorkelling since most of the coral reefs are in relatively shallow waters and easily accessible from the shore. All the dive centres hire out snorkelling equipment and will take snorkellers with them for a fairly small charge.

Diving courses All the diving centres run PADI (Professional Association of Diving Instructors) courses. The **Royal Diving Centre**, situated 17 km to the south of Aqaba, also offers BSAC and CMAS courses. Absolute beginners with no previous can go for an 'introductory dive' with a qualified instructor. The maximum depth you are allowed to go to is 6 m, but this is quite sufficient to see plenty of marine life and get a taste of what diving is about. If you like it, you can embark on a beginners (Open Water) course. These usually last around 5 days and include 10 dives. At the end you receive an 'Open Water' certification. After that there are Advanced courses, usually only 2-3 days, and a whole host of other speciality courses, including wreck diving, deep diving, night diving, navigation etc. Finally there is the Divemaster course, which is the minimum qualification needed to work as a diving instructor. This takes from 2-4 weeks.

A couple of the diving centres offer inclusive accommodation and diving 'packages' which can be good value. If you are interested, it may be worth booking before you leave home. The **Sea Star** diving centre in Aqaba is represented in the UK by *Aquatours* (see under page 21). For more details of diving centres, costs etc, see under Aqaba.

Nature reserves
All of Jordan's Nature Reserves and Protected Areas are managed by the **Royal Society for the Conservation of Nature (RSCN)**, an independent organisation established in 1966 under the patronage of King Hussein.

Dana Nature Reserve, situated to the west of the King's Highway between Tafila and Showbak, is the most attractive Reserve in terms of what it has to offer for tourists. There is a comfortable guest house with fantastic views, a field centre, two campsites, and the carefully restored 15th century village of Dana, not forgetting of course the various short hiking trails and longer hiking options through this stunningly beautiful area with its remarkable variety of flora and fauna. The **Wadi Mujib Nature Reserve**, situated to the west of the King's Highway between Madaba and Kerak, is equally dramatic and rich in flora and fauna, as well as being the focus of a captive breeding programme for the rare Nubian Ibex.

At the **Shaumari Nature Reserve**, situated to the southwest of the desert oasis of Azraq, you can see the endangered Arabian Oryx, two species of ostriches, and the onager, or wild ass, all of which have been successfully bred in captivity in this small Reserve and gradually re-introduced into the wild. There are also various species of gazelle. Nearby, the **Azraq Wetland Reserve** immediately to the east of Azraq is the focus for concerted efforts to restore this once extensive wetland habitat. Though still only a shadow of its former self, some migratory birds have once again begun stopping here en route between Africa and Europe and there are good opportunities for bird watching during the period of winter rains from February to April. The large lake at **Burqu** (yet to be officially established as a Protected Area), to the north of the Baghdad Highway in the far northeast of the country, is also a birdwatchers paradise.

Wadi Rum is now officially a National Park, although in practice measures to regulate activity here have yet to be implemented. With so many people visiting Wadi Rum, it is not the best place to look for wildlife, although Ibex, jackals and the Arabian sand cat can be found in the remoter areas, and there is of course the dramatic scenery and a surprising variety of plants and trees for a 'desert' region. Most of Jordan's coastline on the Red Sea is now incorporated into the **Red Sea Marine Peace Park**, providing the fantastic coral reefs here with some measure of protection. The **Dibeen** and **Zai** 'National Parks' to the north of Amman are essentially just picnic places with little or no active conservation work going on in them, although there are plans to rectify this at Dibeen. Currently, the only up and running Nature Reserve in this part of the country is **Zubia**, which covers an area of some 12 km of Mediterranean hill country between Ajlun and Irbid. There are plans to eventually establish a total of twelve Nature Reserves covering some 4% of Jordan's total land area.

Essentials

Essentials

The RSCN, based in Amman (see page 115), has its own 'eco-tourism' unit and can organise visits to all its reserves, as well as expeditions to other important wildlife areas. They can also put you in touch with other tour operators specializing in eco-tourism. In the case of Dana, you can also make all the necessary arrangements for a visit through the field centre there (see page 239), while at Shaumari you can just turn up to see the various animals in their breeding enclosures.

Rock climbing The spectacular landscape of **Wadi Rum** has been attracting increasing numbers of rock climbers to Jordan ever since the Ministry of Tourism commissioned a British climber, Tony Howard, to explore the area and map the possibilities. The result of his research is a book entitled **Treks and Climbs in Wadi Rum**, which gives detailed information on nearly 300 climbing routes in the region. There are a few local Bedouins who are now qualified to lead western-style ascents, but you will need to bring all your own equipment. For more details, see the section on Wadi Rum.

Trekking **Wadi Rum** offers plenty of opportunities for walkers and there is a book entitled *Walks and Scrambles in Wadi Rum* by Tony Howard and Diana Taylor which gives details of these. The **Dana** and **Wadi Mujib** Nature Reserves also offer excellent hiking; Dana has short, marked trails of 1-2 hours, while both provide the opportunity for expeditions of 1-3 days or more with RSCN park rangers to act as guides. The rolling hill country to the north of Amman also offers some great walking. The recently published *Jordan; Walks, Treks, Caves, Climbs & Canyons* by Tony Howard and Diana Taylor (Cicerone Press, 1999) provides an excellent overview of hiking option thoughout Jordan, as well as more strenuous and/or technical adventure activities.

Camel/4WD safaris Once again, **Wadi Rum** is the place to come for these. The **Resthouse** has official rates posted for both camel and 4WD trips lasting from half an hour to a couple of days. If you want to go for longer, you will have to negotiate a price. Be sure to establish exactly what is included in terms of food and camping arrangements. A number of tour operators based in Aqaba also offer camel/4WD safaris to Wadi Rum. It is also possible to travel by desert tracks between Wadi Rum and Aqaba. This takes a full day by 4WD, or 2-3 days by camel. Other off-road possibilities include a trip to Qasr Tuba, due south of Qasr Kharana (or due east of Qatrana on the Desert Highway).

Gliding & ballooning The **Gliding Club**, based at Amman's Marka Airport (T06-4874587), charges JD15 per hour to take you gliding over Amman and the surrounding area. Between March and November balloon flights over Petra and Wadi Rum are organised by *Balloons Over Jordan*, a company based in Amman (06-4825224). These should be booked well in advance. They are expensive, costing around US$200 for a 1-1$\frac{1}{2}$ hour flight.

Archaeology There is a wealth of archaeological sites in Jordan. Some of them (eg Petra) have been undergoing excavation for decades and still have far more work left to be done on them. Others have yet to be explored. Many Western countries have permanent archaeological missions in Jordan which work in partnership with the Jordanian Department of Antiquities. Each season, armies of archaeologists descend on new and ongoing sites to carry out excavations. Some of the digs have taken to recruiting amateur help by organising 'working holidays' where you actually pay to join the dig. Much of the work is very tedious and even if you are not particularly skilled, it is often possible to get involved. Note however that it is **not** possible to simply turn up at a dig and join in; official permits and authorizations have to be applied for well in advance and invariably take a long time to process. If you are interested in joining a dig, you need to plan ahead. For a list of archaeological missions and related bodies in Jordan, see page 114. Alternatively, get in contact with the archaeology department of a major university in your home country for possible leads. In the UK, London,

The Islamic Calendar

The Islamic calendar begins on 16 July 622 AD, the date of the Hijra ('flight' or 'migration') of the Prophet Mohammad from Mecca to Medina in modern Saudi Arabia, which is denoted as 1 AH (Anno Hegirae or year of the Hegira). The Islamic or Hijri calendar is lunar rather than solar, each year having 354 or 355 days, meaning that annual festivals do not occur on the same day each year, according to the Gregorian calendar. The 12 lunar months of the Islamic calendar, alternating between 29 and 30 days, are; Muharram, Safar, Rabi-ul-Awwal, Rabi-ul-Sani, Jumada-ul-Awwal, Jumada-ul-Sani, Rajab, Shaban, Ramadan, Shawwal, Ziquad and Zilhaj.

Cambridge and Edinburgh universities all send teams to the Middle East. In the USA, the Archaeological Institute of America (AIA, 135 William St, New York NY 10038), the parent body of ACOR (American Centre for Oriental Research) in Jordan, compiles an extensive annual listing of field work opportunities in the Middle East. You can also contact ACOR direct; 656 Beacon St, Fifth floor, Boston, MA 02215-2010, USA, T617-3536571, F617-3536575, acor@bu.edu In Australia, the University of Sydney's Near Eastern Archaeology Foundation (NEAF, SACAH, A14, University of Sydney, Sydney 2006) organises volunteer programmes to Jordan.

If you are simply interested in a more in-depth insight into Jordan's historical and archaeological sites, both the *Friends of Archaeology* and *ACOR* in Amman organise tours led by specialists.

Holidays and festivals

Note that the following are fixed public holidays – many of the major Muslim and Christian holidays are also public holidays, although their precise dates vary from year to year: **15 January** Arbour Day; **22 March** Arab League Day; **1 May** Labour Day; **25 May** Independence Day; **10 June** Army Day and Anniversary of the Arab Revolt; **11 August** King Hussein's Accession; **14 November** King Hussein's Birthday.

Public holidays

Islamic holidays are calculated according to the lunar calendar and therefore fall on different dates each year (see box for projected dates from 2000-2003).

Islamic holidays

Ras as-Sana Islamic New Year: 1st Muharram. The first 10 days of the year are regarded as holy, especially the 10th.

Ashoura: 9th and 10th Muharram. Anniversary of the killing of Hussein, commemorated by Shi'ite Muslims (Shi'ites are a small minority in Jordan, so this event is not widely commemorated). Ashoura also celebrates the meeting of Adam and Eve after leaving Paradise, and the end of the Flood.

Moulid an-Nabi The Prophet Mohammad's birthday:12th Rabi al-Awwal.

Leilat al-Meiraj Ascension of Mohammad from Haram al-Sharif (Temple Mount) in Jerusalem: 27th Rajab.

Ramadan The Islamic month of fasting. The most important event in the Islamic calender. 21st Ramadan is the *Shab-e-Qadr* or 'Night of Prayer'.

Eid al-Fitr Literally 'the small feast': three days of celebration, beginning 1st Shawwal, to mark the end of Ramadan.

Eid al-Adha Literally 'the great feast': begins on 10th Zilhaj and lasts for 4 days. Commemorates Ibrahim's (Abraham's) near sacrifice of his son Ismail (though in Christian and Judaic tradition it is Isaac who is nearly sacrificed), and coincides with the *Hajj*, or pilgrimage to Mecca. Marked by the sacrifice of a sheep, feasting and donations to the poor.

Essentials

 ### *Islamic Holidays*

The precise dates of Islamic holidays are determined by the appearance of the moon and are not known until shortly beforehand. As a general rule, however, they occur around 11 days earlier each year.

	2000	*2001*	*2002*	*2003*
Eid al-Fitr *(end of Ramadan)*	27 Dec	16 Dec	5 Dec	24 Nov
Eid al-Adha	-	6 Mar	23 Feb	12 Feb
Ras as-Sana *(New Year)*	-	26 Mar	15 Mar	4 Mar
Moulid an-Nabi *(Prophet's Birthday)*	-	3 Jun	23 May	12 May
Leilat al-Meiraj	23 Oct	12 Oct	1 Oct	20 Sep
Ramadan *(start of)*	27 Nov	16 Nov	5 Nov	25 October

Christian holidays The majority of Jordan's Christian population is Orthodox, meaning that Christian holidays are celebrated according to the Julian (as opposed to our own Gregorian) calender. **Christmas** is still generally celebrated on 25 December (Orthodox Christmas falls on 7 January). **Easter** is celebrated according to the Julian calender, and the date varies between two weeks before and after the Western Easter. For the Orthodox Church it is also the most important Christian festival, far outweighing Christmas in significance.

Health

On the whole, standards of hygiene are good in Jordan, and the health risks generally much lower than in Africa or Asia for example. Vaccinations are not absolutely necessary, but all the same you are advised to make sure that you are up to date with your polio, tetanus and typhoid shots. A hepatitis jab is also worth considering. Malaria is not a problem. As a rule, the worst you can expect is an upset stomach, though more serious food poisoning or gastric infections are not unknown. Tap water is generally safe to drink but if you prefer to be ultra-safe, bottled mineral water is widely available. Raw fruit and vegetables are a potential hazard unless you have washed or peeled them yourself. On the other hand, salads are an integral part of Middle Eastern cuisine and avoiding eating them in some form or other is not entirely practical. Perhaps the greatest health hazard is from heatstroke and/or dehydration. Proper protection against the sun and an adequate intake of water and salt are essential.

The standards of private medical facilities are high in Jordan. There plenty of international-standard hospitals in Amman and good medical facilities in Aqaba and Petra. Note that good medical insurance is absolutely vital as private healthcare is extremely expensive.

Before travelling

Take out good medical insurance. Check exactly what the level of cover is for specific eventualities, in particular whether a flight home is covered in case of an emergency, whether the insurance company will pay any medical expenses directly or whether you must pay and then claim it back, and whether specific activities such as diving are covered. You should have a dental check up. If you suffer from a chronic illness (such as diabetes, high blood pressure, ear or sinus troubles, cardio-pulmonary disease or nervous disorder) arrange for a check-up with your doctor, who can at the same time provide you with a letter explaining the details of your disability. If you are on regular medication, make sure you have enough to cover the period of your travel.

Children

More preparation is necessary for children than for adults and perhaps a little more care should be taken. Children can become more rapidly ill than adults (on the other hand they are quick to recover). Diarrhoea and vomiting are the most common problems, so take the usual precautions. Breastfeeding is best and most convenient for babies, but powdered milk and baby foods are widely available. The treatment of diarrhoea is the same for adults, except that it should start earlier and be continued with more persistence. Children get dehydrated very quickly in hot countries and can become drowsy and uncooperative unless cajoled to drink water or juice plus salts. Upper respiratory infections, such as colds, catarrh and middle ear infections are also common and if your child suffers from these normally take some antibiotics against the possibility. Outer ear infections after swimming are also common and antibiotic eardrops will help.

Vaccination and immunization

Vaccination for **smallpox** is no longer required anywhere in the world. Neither is **cholera** vaccination recognized as necessary for international travel by the World Health Organisation - it is not very effective either. You may be asked for a **Yellow Fever** certificate if you have been travelling in a country affected by the disease immediately before travelling to Jordan. The vaccination is practically without side effects and almost totally protective.

Vaccination against the following diseases are recommended:

Typhoid This is a disease spread by the insanitary preparation of food. A number of new vaccines against this condition are now available; the older TAB and monovalent typhoid vaccines are being phased out. The newer, eg Typhim Vi, cause less side effects, but are more expensive. For those who do not like injections, there are now oral vaccines.

Poliomyelitis Despite its decline in the world this remains a serious disease if caught and is easy to protect against. There are live oral vaccines and in some countries injected vaccines. Whichever one you choose it is a good idea to have booster every 3-5 years if visiting developing countries regularly.

Tetanus One dose of the vaccine should be given with a booster at 6 weeks and another at 6 months and 10 yearly boosters thereafter are recommended. Children should already be properly protected against diphtheria, poliomyelitis and pertussis (whooping cough). Measles, mumps and rubella vaccine is also given to children throughout the world, but those teenage girls who have not had rubella (German measles) should be tested and vaccinated. Hepatitis B vaccination for babies is now routine in some countries.

Infectious Hepatitis This disease is less of a problem for travellers than it used to be because of the development of two extremely effective vaccines against the A and B form of the disease. It remains common however and protection is strongly recommended. A combined hepatitis A & B vaccine is now licensed and available; one jab covers both diseases. Use condoms against Hepatitis B.

Other vaccinations These might be considered in the case of epidemics eg meningitis. There is an effective vaccination against rabies which should be considered by all travellers, especially those going through remote areas or if there is a particular occupational risk, eg for zoologists or veterinarians.

Staying healthy

Travellers' diarrhoea and vomiting is due, most of the time, to food poisoning, usually passed on by the insanitary habits of food handlers. As a general rule the cleaner your

Intestinal upsets

Essentials

surroundings and the smarter the restaurant, the less likely you are to suffer.

Foods to avoid: uncooked, undercooked, partially cooked or reheated meat, fish, eggs, raw vegetables and salads, especially when they have been left out exposed to flies. Stick to fresh food that has been cooked from raw just before eating and make sure you peel fruit yourself. Wash and dry your hands before eating; disposable wet-wipe tissues are useful for this.

Tap water is generally safe to drink in larger towns and cities. If you want to be on the safe side however, bottled mineral water is readily available throughout Jordan. Ice generally gets delivered in a pretty unhygenic fashion, so is best avoided.

Travellers' diarrhoea
Infection with various organisms can give rise to travellers' diarrhoea. They may be viruses, bacteria, eg Escherichia coli (probably the most common cause worldwide), protozoal (such as amoebas and giardia), salmonella and cholera. The diarrhoea may come on suddenly or rather slowly. It may or may not be accompanied by vomiting or by severe abdominal pain and the passage of blood or mucus - when it is called dysentery.

Types of diarrhoea and how to treat it
If you can time the onset of the diarrhoea to the minute (`acute') then it is probably due to a virus or a bacterium and/or the onset of dysentery. The treatment in addition to rehydration is Ciprofloxacin 500 mg every 12 hrs; the drug is now widely available and there are many similar ones.

If the diarrhoea comes on slowly or intermittently ('sub-acute') then it is more likely to be protozoal, ie caused by an amoeba or giardia. Antibiotics such a Ciprofloxacin will have little effect. These cases are best treated by a doctor as is any outbreak of diarrhoea continuing for more than 3 days. Sometimes blood is passed in ameobic dysentery and for this you should certainly seek medical help. If this is not available then the best treatment is probably Tinidazole (Fasigyn) – one tablet four times a day for three days. If there are severe stomach cramps, the following drugs may help but are not very useful in the management of acute diarrhoea: Loperamide (Imodium) and Diphenoxylate with Atropine (Lomotil) They should not be given to children.

Any kind of diarrhoea, whether or not accompanied by vomiting, responds well to the replacement of water and salts, taken as frequent small sips, of some kind of rehydration solution. There are proprietary preparations consisting of sachets of powder which you dissolve in boiled water or you can make your own by adding half a teaspoonful of salt (3.5 gms) and four tablespoonsful of sugar (40 gms) to a litre of boiled water.

Thus the linchpins of treatment for diarrhoea are rest, fluid and salt replacement, antibiotics such as Ciprofloxacin for the bacterial types and special diagnostic tests and medical treatment for the amoeba and giardia infections. Salmonella infections and cholera, although rare, can be devastating diseases and it would be wise to get to a hospital as soon as possible if these were suspected.

Fasting, peculiar diets and the consumption of large quantities of yoghurt have not been found useful in calming travellers' diarrhoea or in rehabilitating inflamed bowels. Oral rehydration has on the other hand, especially in children, been a life saving technique and should always be practised, whatever other treatment you use. As there is some evidence that alcohol and milk might prolong diarrhoea they should be avoided during and immediately after an attack.

Diarrhoea occurring day after day for long periods of time (chronic diarrhoea) is notoriously resistent to amateur attempts at treatment and again warrants proper diagnostic tests (most towns with reasonable sized hospitals have laboratories for stool samples). There are ways of preventing travellers' diarrhoea for short periods of time by taking antibiotics, but this is not a foolproof technique and should not be used other than in exceptional circumstances. Doxycycline is possibly the best drug. Some preventatives such as Enterovioform can have serious side effects if taken for long periods.

Paradoxically **constipation** is also common, probably induced by dietary change, inadequate fluid intake in hot places and long bus journeys. Simple laxatives are useful in the short-term and bulky foods and plenty of fruit are also useful.

Heat & cold

Full acclimatization to high temperatures takes about 2 weeks. During this period it is normal to feel a bit apathetic, especially if the relative humidity is high. Drink plenty of water, use salt on your food and avoid extreme exertion. Tepid showers are more cooling than hot or cold ones. Large hats do not cool you down, but do prevent sunburn. Remember that, especially in the desert, there can be a large and sudden drop in temperature between night and day, so dress accordingly. Loose cotton is still the best material when the weather is hot.

Insects

These are mostly more of a nuisance than a serious hazard. Mosquitos are the most troublesome. Malaria however is very rare in the region, although there have been cases reported in Syria. It is sensible to avoid being bitten as much as possible; cover bare skin and use an insect repellent. The most common and effective repellent is diethyl metatoluamide (DEET). DEET liquid is best for arms and face (care around eyes and with spectacles; DEET dissolves plastic). Aerosol spray is good for clothes and ankles and liquid DEET can be dissolved in water and used to impregnate cotton clothes and mosquito nets. Impregnated wrist and ankle bands can also be useful.

If you are bitten or stung, itching may be relieved by cool baths, antihistamine tablets (care with alcohol or driving) or mild corticosteroid creams, eg. hydrocortisone (great care: never use if any hint of infection). Careful scratching of all your bites once a day can be surprisingly effective. Calamine lotion and cream have limited effectiveness and antihistamine creams are not recommended – they can cause allergies themselves. Bites which become infected should be treated with a local antiseptic or antibiotic cream such as Cetrimide, as should any infected sores or scratches. When living rough, skin infestations with body lice (crabs) and scabies are easy to pick up. Use whatever local commercial preparation is recommended for lice and scabies. Crotamiton cream (Eurax) alleviates itching and also kills a number of skin parasites. Malathion lotion 5% (Prioderm) kills lice effectively, but avoid the use of the toxic agricultural preparation of Malathion.

Ticks

Ticks attach themselves usually to the lower parts of the body often after walking in areas where cattle have grazed. They take a while to attach themselves strongly, but swell up as they start to suck blood. The important thing is to remove them gently, so that they do not leave their head parts in your skin because this can cause a nasty allergic reaction some days later. Do not use petrol, vaseline, lighted cigarettes etc to remove the tick, but, with a pair of tweezers remove the beast gently by gripping it at the attached (head) end and rock it out in very much the same way that a tooth is extracted.

Sunburn

Most people fail to appreciate the burning power of the sun until it is too late. Always wear a wide brimmed hat and use some form of suncream lotion on untanned skin. Normal temperate zone suntan lotions (protection factor up to 7) are not much good; you need to use the types designed specifically for the tropics or for mountaineers or skiers with protection factors up to 15 or above. These are often not available in Jordan. Glare from the sun can cause conjunctivitis, so wear sunglasses especially on beaches, where high protection factor sunscreen should also be used.

Prickly heat

A very common intensely itchy rash. Best avoided by frequent washing and by wearing loose clothing. Cured by allowing skin to dry off through use of powder and spending two nights in an airconditioned hotel!

Athletes foot

This and other fungal skin infections are best treated with Tolnaftate or Clotrimazole.

Essentials

Other afflictions

Rabies If you are bitten by a domestic or wild animal, do not leave things to chance: scrub the wound with soap and water and/or disinfectant, try to have the animal captured (within limits) or at least determine its ownership, where possible, and seek medical assistance at once. The course of treatment depends on whether you have already been satisfactorily vaccinated against rabies. If you have (this is worthwile if you are spending lengths of time in developing countries or travelling far from the five-star circuit) then some further doses of vaccine are all that is required. Human diploid vaccine is the best, but expensive: other, older kinds of vaccine, such as that derived from duck embryos may be the only types available. These are effective, much cheaper and interchangeable generally with the human derived types. If not already vaccinated then anti rabies serum (immunoglobulin) may be required in addition. It is important to finish the course of treatment whether the animal survives or not.

AIDS AIDS is not a major problem in Jordan, but care is obviously neccessary. Heterosexual transmission is now the dominant mode and so the main risk to travellers is from casual sex. The same precautions should be taken as with any sexually transmitted disease. The Aids virus (HIV) can be passed by unsterilized needles which have been previously used to inject an HIV positive patient. Check that needles have been properly sterilized or disposable needles have been used. The risk of receiving a blood transfusion with blood infected with the HIV virus is greater than from dirty needles because of the amount of fluid exchanged. Supplies of blood for transfusion should be screened for HIV in all reputable hospitals. Catching the AIDS virus does not always produce an illness in itself (although it may do). The only way to be sure if you feel you have been put at risk is to have a blood test for HIV antibodies on your return to a place where there are reliable laboratory facilities. The test does not become positive for some weeks.

Infectious hepatitis (Jaundice) The main symptoms are pains in the stomach, lack of appetite, lassitude and yellowness of the eyes and skin. Medically speaking there are two main types. The less serious, but more common is Hepatitis A for which the best protection is the careful preparation of food, the avoidance of contaminated drinking water and scrupulous attention to toilet hygiene. The other, more serious, version is Hepatitis B which is acquired usually as a sexually transmitted disease or by blood transfusions. It can less commonly be transmitted by injections with unclean needles and possibly by insect bites. The symptoms are the same as for Hepatitis A. The incubation period is much longer (up to 6 months compared with 6 weeks) and there are more likely to be complications.

Hepatitis A can be protected against with gamma globulin. It should be obtained from a reputable source and is certainly useful for travellers who intend to live rough. You should have a shot before leaving and have it repeated every 6 months. The dose of gamma globulin depends on the concentration of the particular preparation used, so the manufacturer's advice should be taken. The injection should be given as close as possible to your departure and as the dose depends on the likely time you are to spend in potentially affected areas, the manufacturer's instructions should be followed. Gamma globulin has really been superceded now by a proper vaccination against Hepatitis A (Havrix) which gives immunity lasting up to 10 years. After that boosters are required. Havrix monodose is now widely available as is Junior Havrix. The vaccination has negligible side effects and is extremely effective. Gamma globulin injections can be a bit painful, but it is much cheaper than Havrix and may be more available in some places.

Hepatitis B can be effectively prevented by a specific vaccine (Engerix) - 3 shots over 6 months before travelling. If you have had jaundice in the past it would be worthwhile having a blood test to see if you are immune to either of these two types, because this might avoid the necessity and costs of vaccination or gamma globulin.

There are other kinds of viral hepatitis (C, E etc) which are fairly similar to A and B, but vaccines are not available as yet.

Typhus is carried by ticks. There is usually a reaction at the site of the bite and a fever. Seek medical advice.

Typhus

These are not very common in Jordan. The more serious ones such as hookworm can be contracted from walking barefoot on infested earth or beaches.

Intestinal worms

This is a very rare event indeed for travellers. If you are unlucky (or careless) enough to be bitten by a venomous snake, spider, scorpion or sea creature, try to identify the creature, but do not put yourself in further danger. Snake bites in particular are very frightening, but in fact rarely poisonous – even venomous snakes bite without injecting venom. What you might expect if bitten are: fright, swelling, pain and bruising around the bite and soreness of the regional lymph glands, perhaps nausea, vomiting and a fever. Signs of serious poisoning would be the following symptoms: numbness and tingling of the face, muscular spasms, convulsions, shortness of breath and bleeding. Victims should be got to a hospital or a doctor without delay. Commercial snake bite and scorpion kits are available, but usually only useful for the specific type of snake or scorpion for which they are designed. Most serum has to be given intravenously so it is not much good equipping yourself with it unless you are used to making injections into veins. It is best to rely on local practice in these cases, because the particular creatures will be known about locally and appropriate treatment can be given.

Snake bite

Reassure and comfort the victim frequently. Immobilize the limb by a bandage or a splint or by getting the person to lie still. Do not slash the bite area and try to suck out the poison because this sort of heroism does more harm than good. If you know how to use a tourniquet in these circumstances, you will not need this advice. If you are not experienced do not apply a tourniquet.

When you return home

If you have had attacks of diarrhoea it is worth having a stool specimen tested in case you have picked up amoebas. If you have been living rough, blood tests may be worthwhile to detect worms and other parasites. Report any untowards symptoms to your doctor and tell the doctor exactly where you have been and, if you know, what the likelihood of disease is to which you were exposed.

The above information has been compiled from information supplied and received from Dr David Snashall, who is presently Senior Lecturer in Occupational Health at the United Medical Schools of Guy's and St Thomas' Hospitals in London and Chief Medical Adviser to the British Foreign and Commonwealth Office. He has travelled extensively and keeps in close touch with developments in preventative and tropical medicine.

Further Information

Further information on health risks abroad, vaccinations etc may be available from a local travel clinic. If you wish to take specific drugs with you such as antibiotics these are best prescribed by your own doctor. Beware, however, that not all doctors can be experts on the health problems of remote countries. More detailed or more up-to-date information than local doctors can provide are available from various sources. In the UK there are hospital departments specializing in tropical diseases in London, Liverpool, Birmingham and Glasgow and the Malaria Reference Laboratory at the London School of Hygiene and Tropical Medicine provides free advice about malaria, T0891-600350. In the USA the local Public Health Services can give such information and information is available centrally from the Centre for Disease Control (CDC) in Atlanta, T404-3324559.

Essentials

There are other computerized databases which can be accessed for up-to-the-minute, destination-specific information. In the UK there is the MASTA (Medical Advisory Service to Travellers Abroad) Health Line, T0906-8 224 100 (calls charged at 60p per minute) and website, www.masta.org, and Travax (Glasgow, T0141-9467120, ext 247). Other information on medical problems overseas can be obtained from the book by Dawood, Richard (Editor) (1992) *Travellers' Health: How to stay healthy abroad*, Oxford University Press 1992, £7.99. We strongly recommend this revised and updated edition, especially to the intrepid traveller heading for the more out of the way places. General advice is also available in the UK in *Health Information for Overseas Travel* published by the Department of Health and available from HMSO, and *International Travel and Health* published by WHO, Geneva.

Further reading

There is a wealth of books on all aspects of Jordan and the Middle East, in fact probably enough to fill a few libraries and keep you going for a lifetime. The following is just a small selection. Many contain more detailed bibliographies for those who wish to explore further.

History & politics
Aburish, Saïd K *A Brutal Friendship* (1997) Victor Gollancz. A very readable and often highly controversial book which identifies the collusion between the Arab elite and the West as being at the heart of the Middle East's current problems.

Dent, Martin Gilbert *Atlas of the Arab-Israeli Conflict.* The history of the Arab-Israeli conflict told through the medium of maps.

Glubb, John Bagot *Syria, Jordan, Lebanon* (1967) Thames and Hudson. An account of the history of the region up until immediately before the Six Day War, written by 'Glubb Pasha' who helped found the modern Jordanian army in his role as Commander in Chief of the Arab Legion from 1938-56.

Hart, Alan *Arafat; A Political Biography* (1994) Sidgwick & Jackson. Hart swallows Arafat's line every time, though the book provides some very interesting insights into the Palestinian perspectives on Jordan and Lebanon.

Hourani, Albert *A History of the Arab Peoples*, (1991) Faber and Faber. A comprehensive and highly regarded work which focuses as much on the social as the political history of the Arabs.

Hourani, A, Khoury, P, Wilson, M (editors) *The Modern Middle East.* An authoritative survey of the Middle East.

Joffe, Lawrence *Keesing's Guide to the Middle East Peace Process*, (1996) Cartermill. An excellent reference book on the Peace Process, including detailed analysis of its relevance for Jordan, Syria and Lebanon, and brief overviews of all the countries concerned.

Lawrence, TE *Seven Pillars of Wisdom*, various editions. Lawrence's own account of the Arab Revolt and his part in it. Despite his somewhat impenetrable style of writing, the book is a compelling one. Perhaps the most awe-inspiring fact about this man is that he lost the original manuscript while changing trains in Reading and then started all over again!

Maalouf, Amin *The Crusades Though Arab Eyes*, (1984) Al Saqi. An excellent, highly readable account of the Crusades, original and refreshing in its Arab perspective on this period of history which is otherwise all too often approached from a European viewpoint. Strongly recommended.

Mansfield, Peter *The Arabs*, (1992) Penguin. A good, readable overview of the history of the region, including short analyses of each of the Arab countries since independence and an excellent discussion of the Western versus Arab perspectives, recommended.

Ovendale, Ritchie *The Longman Companion to The Middle East Since 1914*, (1992) Longman. A good reference book consisting of chronologies of the key strands in Middle Eastern history, as well as a comprehensive topic bibliography and other useful information.

Mack, JE *The Secret Lives of Lawrence of Arabia*, (1976). Reasseses many of the myths associated with Lawrence's life.

Runciman, Steven *A History of the Crusades*, (1978). A detailed and definitive account in three volumes.

Kamal Salibi *The Modern History of Jordan*, (1993) IB Tauris. A lucid and highly readable account of Jordan's modern history. Recommended.

King Hussein bin-Talal *Uneasy Lies the Head; An Autobiography of HM King Hussein of Jordan*, (1962). King Hussein's own account of his life.

Wilson Lawrence of Arabia, the Authorised Biography, (1989). Includes a discussion of Lawrence's disputed significance.

Yapp, ME *The Making of the Modern Near East 1792-1923* and *The Near East since the First World War*, (1987 and 1991). Together these provide a lucid and scholarly overview of the region's history.

Brenton Betts, Robert *The Druze*. Gives some fascinating insights into this secretive sect. <!-- Religion -->

Dawood, NJ (translator) **The Koran**, (1993) Penguin. A well-regarded translation of the Qur'an.

Esposito, John L *Islam; The Straight Path*, Oxford UP. Excellent analysis of the origins and significance of Islam.

Fernea, Elizabeth Warnock (editor) *Middle Eastern Muslim Women Speak*, University of Texas Press (USA). Anthology of writings giving excellent insights into contemporary Middle Eastern culture and society from women's perspectives.

Halliday, Fred *Islam and the Myth of Confrontation*, IB Tauris. Challenges the idea that a show-down between Islam and the rest of the world is imminent.

Lewis, Bernard *The Assassins*, (1985) Al Saqi. A detailed and scholarly work, though still readable, examining the origins and history of the Assassins.

Netton, Ian R *A Popular Dictionary of Islam*, (1992) Curzon Press. Useful reference book for those interested in learning more about Islam.

Said, Edward *Covering Islam*, (1997) Vintage. Examines the basis of western steroetypes of Islam

El Hassan Bin Talal *Christianity in the Arab World*, (1995) Arabesque (Amman). A detailed and interesting study of the intricacies of the Christian church in the Middle East. Available in Jordan.

Religion

Wijdan Ali *Modern Art in Jordan*, Royal Society for the Fine Arts. Excellent and extensively illustrated overview of Jordanian and Palestinian art. Available in Jordan.

Bienkowski, Piotr (editor) *Treasures from an Ancient Land; The Art of Jordan*, (1996) Alan Sutton Publishing. An excellent overview of Jordan's heritage, with a brief history of the country, lots of beautiful photos, and sections on sculpture, pottery, art and technology, mosaics, writing, traditional costumes and folk jewellery.

Ammar Khammash *Notes on Village Architecture in Jordan*, Arabesque (Amman). Interesting and readable, despite being a university thesis.

Ghazi bin Mohammad *The Tribes of Jordan at the Beginning of the Twenty-first Century*. An interesting study of contemporary tribal society in Jordan, including a look at the issue of 'honour crimes'.

Piccirillo, Michele *The Mosaics of Jordan*, ACOR. Huge volume with colour photos and accompanying interpretations/explanations of practically every mosaic discovered in Jordan. Available in Jordan (from ACOR in Amman).

Art, architecture & culture

Essentials

Vine, Peter *Jewels of the Kingdom; The Heritage of Jordan,* (1987) Immel. Excellent overview of Jordanian heritage covering history, flora and fauna, cultural traditions and art.

Specialist guides to historic/archaeo logical sites Browning, Iain *Petra* and *Jerash and the Decapolis,* (1989 and 1982) Chatto & Windus. Detailed and comprehensive historical and architectural guides to these sites. Well written and interesting, but becoming dated in places. Available in Jordan. **Rami Khouri** Jerash *A Frontier City of the Roman East,* (1986) Longman. A compact and well-written guide to Jerash, complete with numerous site plans. Available in Jordan and worth buying if you see it in Amman bookshops. **Harding Lankester G** *The Antiquities of Jordan,* (1959) Jordan Distribution Agency. With various reprints; gazeteer of most archaeological sites by the former British director of the Department of Antiquities. Comprehensive, though now rather outdated in places.

Available in Jordan are **Rosalyn Maqsood's** *Petra; A Travellers' Guide,* (1996) Garnet, 1996, a detailed practical guide to Petra with a good history section and carefully researched walking tours. Available in Jordan; and **Michele Piccirillo's** *Mount Nebo, Custodia Terra Sancta* (Jerusalem), a detailed historical guide to Mount Nebo and its surroundings. Available in Madaba and Mount Nebo.

Specialist guides to activities Buckles, Guy *The Dive Sites of the Red Sea,* New Holland. Comprehensive guide to the whole of the Red Sea area. **Howard, Tony** *Treks and Climbs in Wadi Rum,* (1994) Cicerone Press. Indispensible for anyone intending to go rock climbing in Wadi Rum. **Howard, Tony and Taylor, Diana** *Walks and Scrambles in Wadi Rum,* (1993) Al Kutba. An offshoot of the *Treks and Climbs* book, ideal for non-climbers interested in exploring Wadi Rum. Also by Diana Taylor and Tony Howard is *Jordan; Walks, Treks, Caves, Climbs & Canyons,* (1999) Cicerone Press. Covers a wide range of walking and trekking opportunities throughout the country, as well as some more technical climbing and caving options. Currently the only book with a detailed overview of the possibilities for such activities in Jordan.

Nature & wildlife Andrews, Ian J *The Birds of the Hashemite Kingdom of Jordan,* IJ Mathews. Compact guide, available in Jordan. **Dawad MH al-Eisawi** *Field Guide to Wild Flowers of Jordan,* Jordan Press Foundation. Compact guide, available in Jordan. **Kingdon, Jonathan** *Arabian Mammals; a Natural History,* Harecourt Brace Jovanovich. **Porter RF, Christensen S, Schiermacker-Hansen P** *Field Guide to the Birds of the Middle East,* T&AD Poyser. Very detailed and comprehensive guide, available in Jordan.

Travelogues Asler, Michael *The Last of the Bedu; in search of the myth,* (1996) Viking. Michael's travels bring him into contact with Bedouin tribes from all over the Middle East. Gives a good insight into Bedouin culture and its myths.

Bell, Gertrude *The Desert and the Sown,* Virago, Beacon, various reprints. The story of Bell's travels from Jerusalem to Antioch in the early 1900s. Something of a classic, though focused more on Syria. **Burckhardt, Johan Ludwig** *Travels in Syria and the Holy Land,* Darf, various reprints. First published in 1822, Burckhardt's account of his travels is still very readable. **O'Rourke, PJ** *Holidays in Hell* and *Give War A Chance,* (1988 and 1992) Picador. Ascerbic wit and no concessions to political correctness by a man said to be able to "irritate both Salman Rushdie and Ayatollah Khomeini"! **Raban, Jonathan** *Arabia,* Picador. Excellent insight into the region, covering the Gulf States, Yemen, Egypt and Jordan, during the late 1970s.

Fiction Inea Bushnaq (editor) *Arab Folktales,* Pantheon; includes a selection of Bedouin folktales under the heading 'Tales Told in Houses made of Hair'.

Nur and Abdelwahab Elmessiri (editors) *A Land of Stone and Thyme,* Quartet; excellent anthology of Palestinian short stories.

Fadia Faqir *Pillars of Salt*, Quartet, Interlink; beautifully written novel set in Mandate-period Transjordan recounting the experiences of two women in a mental hospital (one from a Bedouin village, the other from Amman), and how they came to be there. **Fadia Faqir** *Nisanit,* Penguin; moving and often harrowing story of the impact of the Arab-Israeli conflict on three central characters.

Salma Khadra Jayyusi (editor) *Anthology of Modern Palestinian Literature* and *Modern Arabic Poetry; An Anthology,* Columbia UP (USA).

Ghassan Kanafani *Men in the Sun,* Three Continents (USA); a series of touching, sensitive short stories by the former spokesman for the Popular Front for the Liberation of Palestine. The title story recounts a journey from Amman to Kuwait.

Abd al-Rahman Munif *Story of a City; a Childhood in Amman,* Quartet; diverse tales of life in Amman during the 1940s, charting many of the dramatic changes that the city has undergone. **Abd al-Rahman Munif** *Cities of Salt, The Trench* and *Variations on Night and Day,* Vintage; engaging and insightful trilogy set in a fictional Middle Eastern state thrown into turmoil by the discovery of oil.

Maps

Two makes of maps stand out for their coverage of Jordan; GEO Projects and Freytag & Berndt. In the UK the best place for maps is **Stanfords**, 12-14 Long Acre, London WC2E 9LP, T0207-8362121. The address for *GEO Projects* in the UK is 9-10 Southern Court, South Street, Reading, Berkshire, RG1 4QS, T01734-393567, F598283.

Regional Probably the best map covering the whole of the region is the **Hildebrand's** *Travel Map* of Jordan Syria and Lebanon (1:1,250,000), 1996.

Jordan *GEO Projects* (1:730,000), 3rd edition (1996) and **Freytag & Berndt** (1:800,000), 1997, are the two best available maps of Jordan (buy them before you go, as they are not on sale within Jordan). Both include good maps of Amman on the reverse side, as well as site plans of Jerash and Petra. Note that they do not give details of minor roads in the northern half of the country.

The free handout maps of Jordan and Amman (published by the Jordan Tourism Board) available from tourist information offices within the country are of little use, although their town/site maps of Jerash, Madaba, Petra and Aqaba are better. Note that the English-language editions of all these maps are in short supply, so pick up any you need wherever you see them; they may not be available at the town/site itself. *Luma Khalaf/Nahhas* (T06-5813353/5815814, F06-5863607, jrdn.map@nets.com.jo) publish two excellent free maps of Jordan and Amman. The front cover of the Jordan map comes in various guises, though the information inside is identical. Finding copies of either map is something of a hit-and-miss affair; your best bet is to try the luxury hotels or larger car hire firms. The *Royal Jordanian Geographic Centre* produces a series of maps (available in Amman bookshops), including a road map of Jordan and maps of all the major towns and cities, which are reasonably good, if a little out of date at times and, in the case of the road map of Jordan, rather difficult to read.

Websites

The following is a small selection of what the web currently has to offer on Jordan and the Middle East. There is a vast amount more, with new sites opening all the time.

www.oranim.macam98.ac.il/geo/meast.htm ORANIM school of education (Dr Arnon Medzinin); geography of the Middle East. Vast number of excellent links listed under Middle East General Information, Magazines and Newspapers on the Web, Economy, Development and Environment, Regional Geography, Middle East from Space, Maps of the Middle East, Geology, Political Geography, Water Issues, etc.

www.columbia.edu/cu/libraries/indiv/area/MiddleEast/index.html Columbia University; Middle East Studies page. Excellent site, includes listings of internet resources on the Middle East by subject; the links to be found under 'Water in the Middle East' are particularly good for those interested in water issues.

www.arab.net/ Arab Net; a comprehensive site with country by country listings and lots of links to other relevant and interesting sites.

http://almashriq.hiof.no/ Al Mashriq; a wide-ranging site focusing principally on Lebanon, but with useful links to sites related to all the other countries in the region.

www.birzeit.edu/links/ Complete guide to Palestine's websites; listings of all websites relating to things Palestinian, with short reviews of each one.

www.accessme.com/jordantimes Homepage of Jordan's only English language daily newspaper, the Jordan Times. With links also (via www.accessme.com/) to various other sites.

www.arabia.com/ Arabia On line; includes news, (www.akhbar.com) business, culture, and lots more data and links to other sites.

www.menewsline.com Middle East Newsline; the new regional internet service, now has a site updated daily with the latest Middle East news, a diary of events, and special reports.

www.nic.gov.jo/ National Information Centre for the Hashemite Kingdom of Jordan. Lots of official statistics on Jordan.

www.odci.gov/cia/publications/factbook/jo.html CIA Factbook; outline of Jordan's geography, people, government, economy etc.

www.rscn.org.jo Royal Society for the Conservation of Nature (RSCN) homepage.

www.elmaghtas.com Dedicated to the Wadi Kharrar Baptism Site (Al Maghtas), with background on the excavations and historical sources.

www.hrw.org/ Human Rights Watch; with an extensive Middle East section.

www.kinghussein.gov.jo/hash_intro.html Hashemite family homepage.

www.johotels.com Jordan Hotels Association; provides an information and booking service for luxury hotels in Jordan.

www.mideasttravelnet.com.jte Jordan Travel Exchange; travel information and airline booking service.

www.tourism.com.jo Jordan Tourism Board.

www.jordanembassyuk.gov.jo/ Jordanian Embassy in London

Archaeological Institutes in Jordan: see page 114.

Amman

3

Amman

Most visitors to Jordan pass through Amman at some stage, though the city doesn't have the same exotic appeal as other regional capitals such as Damascus, Cairo or Jerusalem. Amman is generally seen as something of a transport hub, or a place to get your visas as part of an onward journey. But this is a pity, since Amman does deserve a little time. In fact, Jordan's capital falls neatly into the image that the Ministry of Tourism strives so hard to present, of "a young country dense with history". On the surface Amman is a new city, built almost entirely during the latter half of the 20th century. Yet significant archaeological remains attest to the ancient city's importance and splendour. In recent years there have been concerted (and largely successful) efforts to restore some of these remains to something of their former glory, providing visitors with an interesting day's sightseeing. Amman also provides a good base from which to visit neighbouring attractions such as Jerash, Madaba, Mount Nebo, the Dead Sea and the eastern 'Desert Castles'. With a lively and increasingly sophisticated dining and nightlife scene, lots of cultural activity and some excellent shopping opportunities, it also has plenty to offer in its own right. Indeed, Amman is a city which grows on most people who give it any time, perhaps because despite all the modern development, Ammanis still remain so disarmingly friendly, generous and hospitable.

Ins and outs

Getting there

See page 30 for detailed information on all international and long-distance transport to and from Amman, and also local transport within the city

Air   Queen Alia International Airport, situated 35 km to the south of Amman, is the main arrivals and departure point for international flights to and from Jordan. There is also the smaller Marka airport 4 km to the northeast of Amman, which primarily deals with *Royal Wings* flights to and from Aqaba, as well as some of the flights between Amman and Tel Aviv.

Road   Luxury coaches, buses, minibuses and long-distance service taxis link Amman with just about every town or site of any importance within Jordan. There are also plenty of international buses and service taxis linking it with Damascus (and indeed Cairo, Riyad and Baghdad). The relatively central **Abdali** bus station, along with the **Jett** bus station a little to the north of it, are the main terminals, although if you are arriving from the south you might find youself at the inconveniently located **Wahadat** bus station, way out to the south of the city. **Trust International**, by 7th Circle, offer services to Aqaba, and also to Tel Aviv, Haifa and Nazareth in Israel. The **Muhajireen** bus station, near Jabal Amman and a short bus or service taxi ride from

Amman overview

Related maps
A Shmeisani, page 90
B Western Amman, page 86
C Jabal Amman &
Al-Weibdch, page 84
D Abdoun, page 92
E Swafiyeh & Umm
Uthayna, page 82

the Downtown district, serves Suweimah (for the Dead Sea), Madaba, Wadi Seer and South Shunah, all of which are within a 50 km radius of Amman. Finally, the **Raghadan** bus station, within walking distance of Downtown, is primarily for local buses, although it also serves the nearby towns of Salt, Zarqa and Madaba.

Getting around

For ordinary Ammanis, service taxis and buses are the primary means of getting around the city. The **local bus** system is very confusing and, with a couple of exceptions, best left to the locals. White **service taxis** (shared taxis, known as 'serveece') run along fixed routes for a fixed fare (the majority are 100 fils), carrying up to 5 or 6 passengers at a time. Almost all of them begin from various points around Downtown, shuttling out to surrounding districts and back. Once you get the hang of them, they are a cheap and convenient means of getting around, but first you must familiarize yourself with the routes and learn to read the Arabic numerals which identify the route a particular service taxi operates along. Far easier, and also relatively cheap (usually 300-500 fils, rarely more than JD1), are the yellow **private taxis**, which are both plentiful and ubiquitous. **Walking** is an option for getting around within specific districts of Amman. The Downtown area in particular is relatively compact, flat and best explored on foot. However, walking to any other district from Downtown involves a steep – and in summer, swelteringly hot – climb. Similarly, walking between any of the uptown districts almost invariably involves crossing a deep wadi (valley) between tall jabals (hills). Even within some of the uptown districts, distances are considerable, while the busy main roads and complicated intersections are anything but pedestrian-friendly. Wherever you are, you will also have to contend with a steady stream of taxis hooting enthusiastically at the prospect of a fare.

Amman

To Wahadat Bus Station, Queen Alia
Airport, Desert Highway & King's Highway

Tourist information

The tourist information centre (Downtown Visitors Centre) is based in an office adjacent to the Roman theatre in Downtown Amman; T4646264, T.I.C@N2.com (open summer 0900-1900, winter 0900-1800, Fri and holidays 1000-1600). The staff here are generally very helpful and well-informed. As well as supplying you with copies of the various free magazines, pamphlets and maps of Amman (and all the other important sites in Jordan), they can book hotels for you anywhere in Jordan, arrange car hire, guides, organized tours etc. In fact, if you need assistance with any aspect of your visit, this is the best place to come; they are more than willing to get on the phone and do whatever they can to help. The **Jordan Tourism Board** is located in the

Orientation

The modern city of Amman is actually spread over a series of hills (jabals or jebels) and in the narrow valleys (or wadis) between. As a consequence of this undulating terrain, Amman is not an easy city to explore on foot. Nor is it the easiest place in which to orientate yourself. **Downtown** is the main focus of the city. In addition to its budget hotels and bustling markets, it features some of the main historical places of interest; namely the Roman theatre, Odeon and Nymphaeum, all just to the east of the central Downtown area. Rising steeply above Downtown to the north is **Jabal al-Qal'a**, or Citadel Hill (featuring the Roman Temple of Hercules, Byzantine church, Umayyad palace and Jordan Archaeological Museum). Rising to the west of Downtown is **Jabal Amman**, initially a quiet, leafy residential area with a number of nice restaurants and some embassies, but giving way further west towards Third Circle to a busier, more congested area with a number of luxury hotels. From Third Circle a major transport axis runs west along Zahran St, with the major intersections along it numbered Fourth Circle, Fifth Circle, Sixth Circle etc (though not all are actually roundabouts). Each Circle also has a name (eg First Circle is also King Abdullah Circle), though they are generally more easily identified by their number. The stretch of Zahran St between Third and Fifth Circle is dominated by the royal Zahran Palace, government institutions, ambassadors' residences and embassies. To the north and south of Zahran St between Sixth and Seventh Circle are the affluent districts of **Swafiyeh** and **Umm Utheina**, with their upmarket shops and restaurants. Due south of Fourth Circle is Amman's newest and most affluent suburb of **Abdoun**, with its pristine streets, luxurious mansions, trendy restuauants, cafés and bars, and of course the obligatory latest-model Mercedes or BMWs cruising around.

Another major transport axis runs northwest from Downtown along King Hussein St, passing the district of **Jabal al-Weibdeh** (or Luweibdeh), a largely residential area with some shops, hotels and embassies, through **Abdali** (bus stations, government institutions) to **Shmeisani** (a relatively upmarket commercial area with lots of hotels and restaurants, and some embassies). Further northwest from Shmeisani is the large University of Jordan complex.

Most hotels, restaurants, offices etc just give their address in terms of the 'Circle' or prominent landmark to which they are closest, or the district that they are in. For example, the Inter-Continental hotel would give its address as just 'Jabal Amman' or 'near Third Circle', rather than 'Al Kulliyah al-Islamiyah (Zahran) St, between Second and Third Circle, Jabal Amman'. In this Handbook full addresses are given in order to aid orientation. Many streets have two names; an official one which appears on the ubiquitous blue street signs around the city but is rarely known to anyone other than the city planners who dreampt it up, and a popular one which everybody uses. Thus Al Kulliyah al-Islamiyah St is almost universally referred to as Zahran St. Other notable official/popular street names include Quraysh/Saqf al-Seel; Abu Bakr as-Siddiq/Rainbow; Omar Bin Khattab/Mango; Wasfi al-Tall/Gardens and Arar/Wadi Saqra. Where there are two options for street names in an address in this Handbook, the official one is written first, with the popular name in brackets. To add to the confusion, many of the English language street signs are transliterations of the Arabic, so that Prince Mohammad St may be written Shariah Al Amir al-Mohammad, or King Hussein St as Shariah al-Malek al-Hussein (shariah being street, Amir prince and Malek king).

Ammon hotel, 10 Tunis St (off Zahran St), between 4th and 5th Circle, T5678294, F5678295, www.jordan-tourism.com.jo It produces the monthly *Visitor* magazine and a variety of other glossy brochures on Jordan, as well as a CD-rom.

History

Excavations on and around the citadel area have provided evidence of settlement in the Neolithic period (5500-4500 BC), though it is in the biblical accounts of the city that the first real interest lies. There can be little doubt that modern Amman occupies the site of the Old Testament Rabbath-Ammon, first mentioned in the context of the 12th century BC war between the Ammonites and Og, king of Basham (Deuteronomy 3: 11). As the 'royal city' of the Ammonites, Rabbath-Ammon was fought over many times, and despite being captured by the Israelite king David (II Samuel 12: 26-31, I Chronicles 20: 1-3), it flourished as the capital of an independent Ammonite Kingdom until the sixth century BC. The city even managed to recover from its sacking (and probable destruction) at the hands of Nebuchadnezzar II in 581 BC, regaining something of its former prosperity.

Around 259 BC, the city fell under the influence of the **Ptolemids**, subsequently being renamed **Philadelphia** by Ptolemy II Philadelphus (285-246 BC). Several ancient texts refer to the city during this period, usually in the context of the battle for hegemony between the Ptolemids and the Seleucids; in fact the latter dynasty captured and ruled over the city for a short period in the early second century BC. Nabatean influence over Philadelphia grew in the second half of the second century BC until 63 BC, when Pompey subdued the city and attached it to the Roman *Provincia Syria*.

Under Roman influence Philadelphia thrived, taking its place with pride as one of the cities of the Decapolis (see History section in Background). The administrative reforms that followed the Roman annexation of the Nabatean Empire in 106 AD saw Philadelphia become part of the newly created *Provincia Arabia*; a move that enhanced the city's status through the increase in trade between Damascus and the Hejaz. It was this trading wealth that paid for the construction of a number of important monuments that can still be seen today.

Philadelphia remained an important centre during the **Byzantine** period (324-635 AD), being the seat of a bishopric. Currently two of the churches from this period (on the citadel mound) has been excavated. Though the city was referred to by the name of Amman during the Byzantine period, it was only after the Arab conquest of 635 AD that this name gained general usage. Amman's prosperity during the Early Arab period is attested to by the remains of the magnificent Umayyad palace built on the citadel mound sometime between 720-750 AD and currently the focus of an imaginative restoration programme.

Amman appears to have undergone a gradual decline under subsequent Arab dynasties and was probably abandoned completely by the 16th century. The process of rejuvenation began in 1876 when a group of Circassians resettled the site, though by the turn of the century Amman's population was still little over 2,000.

The new set of political realities that accompanied the conclusion of World War I saw Amman established as the headquarters of King Abdullah, effectively as the capital of the internally autonomous Emirate of Transjordan. Following independence from Britain in 1946, it officially became the capital of the Hashemite Kingdom of Jordan. The city's rapid population growth was given further impetus in 1947-49 by the need to resettle Palestinian refugees displaced by the creation of the State of Israel. This process was repeated again following the Six Day War of 1967. Around one third of Amman's population are Palestinians, and the city was the scene of major fighting between Palestinian groups and the Jordanian army in 1970/71. Amman's population now stands at around 1.8 million, or around 30% of the country's population.

Amman

Sights

The Citadel (Jabal al-Qal'a)

Standing at the centre of the modern city, just to the north of the Downtown area, is an L-shaped hill known as Jabal al-Qal'a (literally 'Citadel Hill'), which contains some of Amman's most important, and indeed most impressive, ancient remains. At 837 m above sea-level the citadel is one of the highest points in Amman. There are excellent views from here out across the city and down onto the Roman theatre below. The citadel served as a stronghold from the Middle Bronze Age onwards, and is surrounded by a massive **defensive wall**. In its present form, this dates primarily from the Roman period, with evidence of repairs and additional fortifications dating from the Islamic era. Extensive restoration of these defensive walls is currently being carried out by the Jordanian Department of Antiquities, the results of which can be seen most clearly at the northern tip of the citadel mound and along the northeastern side. As well as the three main structures on the citadel mound – the Roman Temple of Hercules, the Byzantine Church and the Ummayad palace complex – which each date from three key periods in the city's history, there is an excellent museum here.

Roman Temple of Hercules On the south side of the citadel mound (to the left of the access road leading to the museum), are the remains of what is popularly referred to as the Roman Temple of Hercules (or Heracles). Although it has never been conclusively indentified as such, the discovery here of an elbow and hand from a larger-than-life statue of Hercules makes this identification seem very likely. A dedicatory inscription firmly dates the temple to 161-166 AD, during the term of the Roman governor Geminius Marcianus (the period of joint reign of the emperors Marcus Aurelius and Lucius Versus). When first discovered, the remains comprised a large part of the temple podium (44 m by 28 m), the bases of three columns, plus a large fallen column. The columns have subsequently been rebuilt, and a section of the decorative architrave restored to its original position. The re-erected columns, together with the various fragments scattered around on the ground, give a good idea of the huge scale of this temple (each column section, or 'drum', weighs up to 11 tonnes). Excavations have also revealed the remains of what appears to be a 6th-7th century BC Iron Age temple, and it seems likely that the Temple of Hercules was built over the ruins of the Ammonite Temple of Milkon which was destroyed by King David (11 Samuel 12; 26-31). The Roman temple originally stood within a large rectangular *temenos* surrounded by a colonnade, though nothing of this remains. A stairway would have led from the civic area of the city below up to the temple, passing through a monumental gateway in the southwestern corner of the temple's *temenos*. Nothing survives of this either, but the views from this point out over Downtown are excellent.

Byzantine churches To the north of the Roman temple (on the opposite side of the approach road to the museum) stand the remains of a Byzantine church dating from the sixth century AD. Trapezoidal in shape, the church features a central nave divided from the side-aisles by two rows of seven columns. Some of the columns have been re-erected, with decorative capitals placed on the top. The nave originally featured a geometric mosaic floor whilst the two aisles were paved with plain stone slabs. Nearby, traces of a smaller and older church have been uncovered. The discovery here of a coin from the reign of the Byzantine Emperor

The Citadel

The citadel is open daily until sunset. Entry is free (except for the museum). The easiest way to get there is to take a taxi (around 300 fils from Downtown). Though it looks enticingly near to Downtown, to get there on foot you actually have to walk all the way round to the northeast side, where an access road leads onto the mound. From the southern side (nearest Downtown), it is possible – but not easy – to scramble up onto a retaining wall above the road and then walk up to the Roman temple.

Constantius, dated to 348 AD, has led to the tentative dating of this church to the fourth century AD. If this is confirmed, it would make it one of the earliest known churches in Jordan.

The contrast between the two churches provides an interesting insight into the development of Christianity in the region. The earlier church was rather poorly built of rubble masonry and earth-based mortar, without making use of any materials from the Roman temple. It was also tucked away in an inconspicuous position, away from the main street and public areas. The later church on the other hand was a larger and altogether more prominent affair, standing right beside one of the main streets of the citadel, and built almost entirely with materials taken from the Roman temple. The implication is that the earlier church existed alongside a still functioning temple, at a time when Christianity was only just beginning to be tolerated; by the time the later church was built, Christianity was firmly established as the official religion of the empire, and the Roman gods had been abandoned.

The **excavated street** which runs northwards from the sixth century church leads directly into the 'great square' of the Umayyad period settlement. Of Roman origin, this street is on the same axis as the stairway which led up from the lower city to the temple of Hercules and thus was a major approach to the upper area of the citidel. Paved with large stones, it continued to be used during the Byzantine period, before being surfaced with hard lime and earth during the Umayyad period. The different levels of the street, corresponding to different periods of use, are clearly visible at various points along it.

To the north of the Byzantine church and museum building is the highest area and main focus of the citadel. Almost certainly the site of another Ammonite and later Roman temple and other important buildings, what survives today is the extensive eighth century Ummayad settlement, consisting of a 'great square', a large congregational mosque and a lavish palace complex. Standing as a testimony to the new Umayyad ascendancy, both the architecture and the overall layout of these buildings are in part the result of Sassanid and Byzantine influences; they also bear a close resemblance to Ummayad projects in Andalucía such as the Alhambra Palace of Granada. Unfortunately, the Umayyads had barely finished their building work before the earthquake of 749 razed much of it to the ground. The palace complex has for some years been the subject of an ambitious restoration project by a joint Spanish-Jordanian team, the most visually striking aspect of this being the reconstruction of the dome over the audience hall. It is only recently that the team has excavated and restored the great square and the congregational mosque, adding greatly to our overall understanding of the settlement.

Umayyad palace complex, 'Great Square' & cogregational mosque

The **'Great Square'** lies at the heart of the Umayyad settlement, providing a link between the palace complex and congregational mosque to the north and south. As well as serving as an important meeting place, the square was also a focus for commerce, with rows of small shops running along its east and west sides. In addition to the street leading into it from the Byzantine church to the southeast, two further streets appear to have converged here.

Wide steps lead up from the south side of the square into the **congregational mosque**, which occupied a raised platform measuring just over 33 sq m. The cobblestone floor of the mosque has been restored, along with the numerous column bases which would have supported the roof, and the *mihrab* in the southern wall, oriented towards Mecca. In the centre of the mosque was a small open courtyard.

Amman Citadel

Source: Ignacio Arce, Spanish Archaeological Mission

1 Roman Temple of Hercules	10 Plaza
2 Byzantine Church (6th century)	11 Gateway
3 Early Byzantine Church	12 Colonnaded Street
4 Excavated Street	13 Court
5 Great Square	14 Iwan
6 Congregational Mosque	15 Throne Room
7 Audience Hall	16 Court
8 Baths Complex	17 Jordan Archaeological Museum
9 Cistern	

0 metres 50
0 yards 50

The large **palace complex** to the north of the great square was almost certainly built as the residence and administrative base of the governor or emir. It comprises three main parts. At the south end is the domed audience hall, a baths complex and open square. The central section is the main residential block, comprising nine residential buildings (of which four have been extensively excavated). The northern section was the palace proper, housing a throne room and the residence of the governor/emir.

The domed **audience hall** provides a suitably grand introduction to the palace complex. It was built over the remains of an earlier Byzantine building and follows the same cruciform plan as its predecessor, the lowest course of stonework actually being of Byzantine origin. The recently installed lead-covered domed roof has drawn mixed responses in terms of aesthetics, but on a practical level is at least providing some protection against the elements and is removeable if necessary. The whole of the front façade has also been extensively restored, complete with the decorative minature pilasters and arches running in a band along the top. Inside, the wooden ribs and lattice of the new dome complement the further decorative bands of stonework in the walls, also extensively restored.

To the east of the audience hall stands the partially restored royal **baths complex**, modelled on the Greco-Roman style. The present remains include what may have been an audience chamber and the *frigidarium* (cold room), though the *tepidarium* (warm room) and *caldarium* (hot room) have not survived. An interesting feature of these baths is that they could be entered from both inside and outside the palace complex, suggesting that they were used by the general public as well as the palace elite. The baths would have been fed by water from the deep circular **cistern** just to the east. You can see some of the original plaster lining inside the cistern, which could hold some 1,368 cubic metres of water, along with part of a column in the centre which acted as a depth gauge. Both the cistern and the system of clay pipes and stone drains which channelled water from the area around the audience hall into it have been restored. Rain provided the sole source of water on the citadel, and the Umayyads made careful use of the extensive water collection system which had been developed over the centuries, modifying it to suit their needs.

From the audience hall you pass into an open **plaza** (probably formerly a Roman courtyard) immediately to the north. A **gateway** in the north wall of the plaza leads via a **colonnaded street** to the governor's residence. You can see an exposed section of the sewage system which ran under part of the street. On either side of the open plaza and colonnaded street are a series of residential buildings, labelled by the excavators as buildings **A-I**. Four of the nine buildings have been fully excavated, though all follow roughly the same plan of an inner courtyard surrounded by porticoes with a series of rooms leading off it. The site's excavators draw particular attention to '**building F**', suggesting that its superior architectural features and proximity to the audience hall indicate its use for some form of official functions.

The northern section of the complex, or palace proper, is entered via the colonnaded street (as it would have been in the eighth century), which leads into a small porticoed **court**. The room that opens onto the court's north side probably served as an audience chamber, or **iwan**, whilst the cruciform room to its north may well have been the **throne room**. Beyond is a further small court. At the northernmost tip of the palace complex there is another large cistern, this one bell-shaped and hewn into the bedrock.

Amman

Jordan Archaeological Museum

This small, well-presented museum is packed with impressive exhibits which reflect the complete history of the region. The exhibits are presented more or less in chronological order, from prehistoric times through the Chalcolithic, Bronze and Iron Age periods, to Hellenistic, Roman and Early Arab times. There are some very beautiful artefacts here, along with good, clear explanations of the major developments and themes of each period. Well worth a visit. ■ *Open 0800-1700, Fri 1000-1600. Entry JD2.*

Head of Tyche (goddess of fortune), 2nd century AD.

Roman theatre

Whilst parts of the upper city of Roman Philadelphia are preserved on the citadel mound, most of the lower city has been submerged beneath modern Amman. A few relics remain, however, most notably in the form of the impressive Roman theatre (just to the east of the main Downtown area, and south of the citadel mound). The theatre partially fills a natural depression in the ground, with three tiers of seating cut out of the hillside. It was built during the reign of Emperor Marcus Aurelius, between 169-177 AD. At its peak the theatre would have had a capacity of around 6,000, though it should be noted that unlike other contemporary Roman theatres (eg Petra), the seats themselves were not actually cut out of the rock but were stone built. In recent years the *scaena* and *scaenae frons* (stage and backdrop) have been partially rebuilt. The acoustics of the theatre are remarkably good; even from the very highest row of seats you can hear conversations on the stage below with startling clarity. The views from up here are also good. Cut into the rock face above the tiered seating of the *cavea* is a small shrine with decorative niches on either side. A broken statue of the goddess Athena was found during restoration work on the *cavea*, suggesting that the shrine may have been dedicated to her.

Museums

Two small museums flank the Roman theatre, housed within the vaulted rooms either side of the stage area. On the east side (to your left as you enter the theatre) is the **Museum of Popular Tradition**, which features various pieces of mosaic work from the churches of Madaba and Jerash, as well as traditional Bedouin costumes, embroidered fabrics, woven carpets and various pieces of jewellery and ornamental headdresses. On the west side (to your right as you enter the theatre) is the **Folklore Museum**, featuring displays of weaponry, musical instruments, jewellery, glassware, looms, woven rugs, embroidered fabrics etc, as well as recontructions of traditional Bedouin households and an example of a traditional camel-mounted *howdah*. Together, the two museums are reasonably interesting, though they don't really warrant the separate entrance fees. ■*Both musuems open daily 0800-1700. Entry JD1 to each.*

Agora & Odeon

Just to the north (in front) of the theatre is a small colonnaded plaza, now identified as Roman Philadelphia's **agora** (forum, marketplace, or place of assembly). The east side of the agora is occupied by a smaller theatre, or **Odeon**. Probably built a little before the main theatre, this had a capacity of just 500 or so, and was perhaps primarily used for council meetings and other official gatherings. Now fully restored, the odeon provides an additional venue to the theatre for occasional performances of live music etc.

Nymphaeum

Another reminder of Amman's previous incarnation as Roman Philadelphia is provided by the Nymphaeum, currently being restored, though at a pain-fully slow rate. Most public areas in Roman cities were marked by some sort of monumental structure – usually a fountain – though given the way that Amman's modern buildings have crowded and dwarfed this nymphaeum, it is hard to envisage this fine example dominating a large open area. It is located to the southwest of the Roman theatre, on Quraysh (Saqfa al-Seel) Street. This street almost exactly follows the course of the Roman **decumanus maximus**, or main street. This was also the course of the lower city's main stream and water source, which the Romans paved over with their decumanus maximus ('Saqfa al-Seel' translates roughly as 'roof of the stream', though the stream itself has long since dried up, its sources tapped to provide drinking water to the city). It seems likely that the nymphaeum also stood close to the junction of the decumanus maximus with the **cardo maximus**, which is thought to have run northwest from here, following the approximate alignment of mod-ern-day King Hussein Street.

King Hussein Mosque

Though not generally open to non-Muslims, it is still possible to appreciate the attractive façade of the King Hussein Mosque in the Downtown area. Built in 1924 by the present king's grandfather (reputedly on the site of the seventh century mosque built by the caliph Umar), it was substantially refurbished in 1987 by the late King Hussein. On Fridays the praying crowds extend to the large plaza outside, whilst during the rest of the week this area acts as an infor-mal employment market for construction labourers and craftsmen.

King Abdullah Mosque

While the King Hussein Mosque was built by the grandfather but named after the grandson, the King Abdullah Mosque reverses the compliment. Located in the Abdali area (just behind the Parliament House), the mosque's huge dome, decorated with pale blue and black geometric designs, serves as one of Amman's principal landmarks. Built in 1990, the brightness of the exterior is matched only by the simplicity of the interior. Tourists can go inside the huge octagonal dome-topped prayer hall of the mosque (take your shoes off). There is a small **Islamic museum** in the grounds of the mosque, with various Qur'ans, photographs and bits of Islamic pottery (open 0800-1400, closed Fri-day). Below it is a small 'bazaar' of souvenir/handicraft shops, the proceeds of which go to various charitable causes (full length black gowns for women wishing to enter the prayer hall are available down here).

Abu Darwish Mosque

Situated high up on Jabal Ashrafiyeh, to the south of Downtown, is the Abu Darwish mosque, built in 1961 by the Circassian community which came to set-tle in Amman during the late 19th century, and was responsible for much of its early development. The most striking feature of this mosque is the alternating black and white bands of stonework, and the rather bizaarre chess-piece

Amman

decorations topping the walls. Non-Muslims are not encouraged to go inside, and the interior is very simple anyway. The mosque can be reached by taking service taxi No 25 or 26 from Italian Street, by the Church of St Saviour (see Downtown map).

Darat al-Funan

Situated in an elegant turn-of-the-century residence on the slopes of Jabal al-Weibdeh (a short, steep walk from Downtown), the Darat al-Funan houses an attractive art gallery, as well as the ruins of an interesting Byzantine church in the grounds. First built by the wealthy Hmoud family, it became the home of Lieutenant Colonel FG Peake ('Pasha Peake'), the founder and first leader of the Arab Legion, from 1920-39. TE Lawrence was one of the many guests to stay here during this period. In its present form, the Darat al-Funan (literally 'House of the Arts') was established by the Abdul Hameed Shoman Foundation, a charitable foundation dedicated to "promoting the fine arts and fostering knowledge and cultural dialogue" in the Arab world.

Entering by the gates at the bottom of the grounds, you come first to the excavated remains of **St Georges Church**. Dated to the late sixth century or early seventh century, an inscription mentioning a "humble priest of St George" found near the altar forms the basis of its presumed dedication. The outline of the church is clearly visible, with the foundations of the apse to the east, and a number of re-erected columns, a couple topped by ornate Corinthian capitals, separating the central nave from the side-aisles. Traces of mosaic floors and some marble tilework can also be seen. Cut into the rock of the steep hillside on the north side of the church is a small **cave**, with four niches in the walls, one of which appears to have contained a sarcophagus. The cave was clearly incorporated into the plan of the church and, along with a rectangular room opposite it (on the south side of the church), would have given it cruciform shape. Another inscription found here mentioning the god Hercules, as well as the fact that the columns and capitals are clearly of Roman origin, suggest that the church was built over the remains of an earlier Roman temple, possibly dedicated to Hercules. The church was probably abandoned sometime during the eighth century, although it appears to have continued to be used as a place of worship during the Islamic period, in the form of a shrine dedicated to *el-Khadr*, a semi-mystical Islamic saint.

Dotted around the gardens are various pieces of contemporary artwork, while just above the church is the carefully restored former residence of 'Pasha Peake', containing the main **art gallery**, with its impressive exhibitions of Jordanian and Arab art, as well as an excellent art library. Further up the hill, at the top of the grounds, is another smaller art gallery housing occasional exhibitions, while the small tranquil terrace outside acts as a small *café*. ■ *Open 1000-1900, Thu 1000-2000, closed Fri. Entry free. T4643252. To get there on foot from Downtown (a 5-10 min walk), head up Omar Khayyam St, turn right at the first hairpin and where the road forks there is an gateway with a sign in Arabic to the left in the wall facing you. This leads you into the lower part of the grounds. There is also an entrance (with a sign in English) at the top of the grounds, on Mohammad Ali al-Sa'di St. Service taxi No 4 passes here.*

Swafiyeh Mosaic

Preserved somewhat incongruously in the heart of the affluent Swafiyeh district of western Amman there is a small fragment of beautifully preserved mosaic floor, all that is left of a sixth century Byzantine church which once stood here. The mosaic fragment originally lay within the grounds of a private garden, but now it has been opened to the public and a protective shelter built over it. The detail of the mosaic is wonderfully clear, particularly the faces of the men. ■ *Open 0800-1400, closed Fri. Entry free. A taxi is the easiest way to reach Swafiyeh district, or else there are some buses which come this far out along Zahran St (see Local Transport). Heading west along Zahran St, turn left at Sixth Circle, take the 1st right, 2nd left and then 4th right into Hamra St; the mosaic is around 700 m further on, inside a small hangar.*

University of Jordan Museums

For those who enjoy museums or with a specialist interest, the small, well-presented **Archaeological Museum** run by the archaeology department of the University of Jordan is worth a visit, with exhibits spanning the Paleolithic through to Islamic periods. Next door is the **National Folklore Museum**, housing various 'ethnographic' displays of traditional costumes, jewellery and everyday household scenes. ■ *Both museums open 0800-1700, closed Fri and Sat. Entry free. T5343555. Minibuses and service taxis from either Raghadan or Abdali bus station bound for Salt, Jerash or Irbid all pass by the entrance to the university (get off at the green domed mosque by the main entrance and ask directions from there), or take a taxi.*

Essentials

Sleeping

Amman has a huge selection of hotels in all categories. They have been grouped below according to areas. Given the ever-increasing abundance of accommodation options, many hoteliers are open to bargaining, particularly out of season. There are some particularly good deals in the **LL**, **A** and **B** categories. Note that all hotels must add a 13% 'government sales tax' to their room prices, while those in **C** category and above must add a further 10% 'service tax'. This means that the cost of a room can jump by nearly a quarter once tax and service is added, so it is important to clarify whether these taxes are included in the price you are quoted (waiving tax and service is often the starting point for discounts). Many hotels offer breakfast; again, check whether this is included in the room price. Note that most Amman hotels use a PO Box, and rarely use the street name in their address. Street names are used below in order to help you find them.

Downtown, Abdali & Jabal al-Weibdeh

Downtown is the main focus for **cheap** (**E-F** category) accommodation. By Amman's standards it is congested, noisy and chaotic, but it is also the most 'atmospheric' part of Amman, contrasting sharply with the generally rather bland and sterile environment of the city's more affluent districts. As a result, this is where the majority of independent travellers choose to base themselves (much to the bemusement of Ammanis). **Abdali** has more budget hotels concentrated around the large bus station, though these tend to be rather noisy and unappealing. There are however a couple of reasonable **B** and **D** category hotels in the vicinity. **Jabal al-Weibdeh** (or Luweibdeh) is a quiet, largely residential area with some good **B**, **C** and **D** category hotels which have the added advantage of being within easy walking distance of either Abdali or Downtown.

B *Amman Mirage*, King Hussein St, Abdali (opposite the top end of Abdali bus station), PO Box 82, T5682000, F5688890, mirageh@go.com.jo A/c, TV/dish, minibar,

Downtown

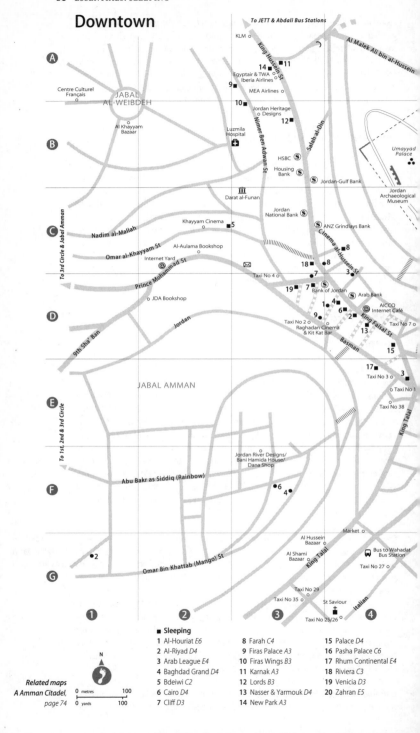

Sleeping

1 Al-Houriat E6	8 Farah C4	15 Palace D4
2 Al-Riyad D4	9 Firas Palace A3	16 Pasha Palace C6
3 Arab League E4	10 Firas Wings B3	17 Rhum Continental E4
4 Baghdad Grand D4	11 Karnak A3	18 Riviera C3
5 Bdeiwi C2	12 Lords B3	19 Venicia D3
6 Cairo D4	13 Nasser & Yarmouk D4	20 Zahran E5
7 Cliff D3	14 New Park A3	

Related maps
A Amman Citadel,
page 74

	0	metres	100
	0	yards	100

JABAL
AL-QAL'A

Byzantine
Church

Roman Temple of
Hercules

To Raghadan Bus Station & Roman Theatre

■16

Yaqut al
Hamawi

Shabsaouh

Yaqut al Hamawi

Ibn Al-Adeen

Hashemi

o Taxi No 6

Ⓢ Union Bank

Al-Ridha

Quraysh (Safa al-Seel) St

Rashin al-

Ibn al-Altheer

1■

Quraysh (Safa al-Seel) St

King
Hussein Mosque

Nymphaeum

20

Madfa

●5

Quraysh (Safa al-Seel) St

Ⓢ

Ⓢ

● Eating
1 Abu Khania &
   Abu Saleh *D4*
2 American Bakehouse *G1*
3 Biffa Billa *D4*
4 Books@Café *F3*
5 Cairo *E5*
6 China *F3*

7 Hashem *D3*
8 Jerusalem
   (Al Quds) *C3*
9 Jordan Bar *D3*

Amman

attached bath, restaurant, bar, roof terrace, parking. Comfortable, nicely furnished, good double glazing so not too noisy, excellent value for money. Recommended. **B** *Firas Palace*, Nimer Ben Adwan St (off King Hussein St), Jabal al-Weibdeh, POBox9119, T4650404, F4650122. A/c, TV/dish, phone, attached bath, restaurant, bar. Rooms arranged around large internal 'courtyard' covered by a rather ambitious skylight. Vertigo sufferers may be put off by the lift arrangement! Quiet location, within easy reach of Downtown. **B** *Toledo*, Umayah St, Abdali (or Ar Razi St, Jabal Hussein), PO Box 927335, T4657777, F4656688, www.toledohotel.com A/c, TV/dish, IDD, attached bath, overlooks Abdali bus station (entering from this side the hotel is up on the 7th floor, but the main entrance is in fact from Ar Razi St, which being high up on Jabal Hussein, is at 'ground' level). Contained within a large shopping complex which includes a health club, 4 restaurants, coffee shop, travel agents etc, this fancy new hotel is aimed very much at the Arab market. Rooms are very plush at first glance, though some show signs of damp problems.

C *Canary*, 17 Al-Karmaly St, Jabal al-Weibdeh, PO Box 9062, T4638353, F4654353, canary_h@hotmail.com Fan, TV, phone, attached bath, clean, comfortable rooms, very friendly staff. Quiet residential location, but within easy walking distance of Abdali bus station. Good value (only just outside **D** category). Recommended. **C** *Caravan*, corner of Al-Ma'moun/Khalil Toutah St, Jabal al-Weibdeh, PO Box 9062, T5661195, F5661196, caravan@go.com.jo Fan, phone, TV, attached bath, located in quiet residential street opposite King Abdullah Mosque and within walking distance of Abdali bus station. Friendly, helpful staff, popular with overland groups. **C** *Pasha Palace*, Shabsoah St, Downtown, PO Box 1, T4639181, F4645313. A/c, TV, phone, fridge, attached bath, quieter rooms at rear, simple but popular Arabic restaurant downstairs, central location close to

Raghadan bus station and Downtown shopping, great rooftop terrace with BBQ in summer and excellent views of the Amphitheatre. Clean, well run, friendly staff, good value (only just outside **D** category). Recommended. **C** *Rhum Continental*, Basman St, Downtown, PO Box 109, T4623162, F4611961. A/c, TV, phone, fridge, attached bath, restaurant. Small rooms, but clean and good value, quieter at rear.

D *Firas Wings*, Nimer Ben Adwan St (off King Hussein St), Jabal al-Weibdeh, PO Box 9119, T4622103, F4621999. A/c, TV, attached bath, restaurant, rooms are clean but rather small, though the a/c makes them good value, quiet location, within easy reach of Downtown. **D** *Merryland*, off King Hussein St, Abdali, T/F4630370. Fan, phone, TV, fridge, some rooms with a/c (JD2 extra), restaurant, reasonably good value, though the rooms don't quite live up to the grandiose lobby. Some travellers have complained about noise from the nightclub below. **D** *New Park*, King Hussein St, opposite law courts, Downtown, PO Box 1790, T/F4648145. Fan, phone, TV, attached bath, quieter rooms at rear, big old building, a bit rundown but reasonable value. **D** *Remal*, 4 Sa'id bin al-Harith, Abdali, PO Box 910477, T/F4630670. Fan, phone, TV, attached bath, some rooms with balcony, clean, good value (discounts available), convenient for Abdali bus station, some rooms surprising quiet given location.

Cheap Downtown is awash with really cheap (and sometimes very unappealing) 'hotels' which cater primarily for Syrian and Jordanian labourers. Many of these are unused to dealing with foreigners, and may turn you away (places listed here all accept foreigners). On the other hand, there are some well-run, excellent value places to be found. In many of the cheapest hotels you pay per bed, though there may be only 2-3 beds per room. For a private room you generally have to pay for all the beds in the room. Accommodation in Amman can be had for as little as JD1.500 per night, though you will generally have to pay around JD3-4 for a 'dormitory' bed, and from JD5 or JD8 for a single or double room. You will also pay a couple of JD more for an

Swafiyeh & Umm Uthayna

■ Sleeping	7 San Rock International	4 Dar al-Anda Teashop
1 Amra Forum	8 Sheraton	& Gallery
2 Comfort Suites &	(under construction)	5 McDonalds
Rovers Return Pub		6 Mays al-Reem
3 Córdoba	● Eating	7 Mosaic
4 Dana Plaza	1 Bayerischer Hof	8 Seven Seas
5 Four Seasons	2 Chili House	9 Szechwan Gardens
(under construction)	& Dunkin Donuts	10 Tannoureen
6 Red Rose	3 China Inn	

attached (as opposed to shared) bathroom. Note that some places charge extra (500 fils) for a hot shower. Ascertain whether the 13% 'government sales tax' is included in the price you are quoted. **NB** Some of the cheap hotels can be slightly seedy, and women travelling alone should exercise caution (those which can be considered safe for women travelling alone are indicated).

E *Al-Houriat*, Saqfa al-Seel/Amanah St, Downtown, T4646903, F4646908. Doubles with fan and attached bath JD12 (or JD8 with shared bath). Fairly good value, a step up from the **G** category hotels around here. **E** *Al Monzer*, King Hussein St, opposite Abdali Bus Station, PO Box 926595, T4639469, F4657328. Fan, phone, attached bath, rooms reasonably clean, but bathrooms rather grotty, overlooks bus station so noisy (but convenient; quieter rooms at rear), a little expensive at JD14 for a double. Note that this hotel shares its street entrance with the cheaper but really very unattractive and best avoided *Cleopatra* next door, whose staff will do their best to drag you up to their hotel. **E** *Happyland*, King Hussein St, opposite Ministry of Finance, T4639832, F4628550. Fan, phone, attached bath, doubles JD10, singles better value at JD5.500, a bit tacky and somwhat isolated (midway between Abdali Bus Station and Downtown). **E** *Karnak*, 58 King Hussein St, Downtown, PO Box 6095, T4638125. Fan, phone, attached bath, old building with large rooms (quieter at rear), bathrooms a bit grotty, otherwise reasonable value at JD10 for a double. **E** *Lords*, 41 King Hussein St, Downtown, PO Box 6293, T4622167. Fan, phone, attached bath, big old building with a slightly rundown, shabby air to it, but reasonable value at JD10 for a double. **E** *Palace*, King Faisal St, Downtown, PO Box 6916, T4624326, F4650603. Fan, phone, TV, attached bath, large, rather old-fashioned hotel, but with clean rooms and good clean bathrooms (nicest rooms have balconies away from the main street), good value (double room JD11.300), the best in this category, and a dramatic improvement on the **F** category cheapies in King Faisal St. Recommended.

F *Al Riyad*, King Faisal St, Downtown, PO Box 1612, T4624260, F4625457. Double room with fan and shared shower/toilet JD6, or bed in shared room (fan, sink) JD3, fairly clean showers (free) and passable toilets, use of kitchen, TV/dish in reception, basic but friendly and well run. Good budget choice. **F** *Arab League*, Al Sa'adi St, Downtown (near King Hussein mosque), PO Box 1518, T4623143. Fan, sink, share shower/toilet, clean rooms with firm beds, rather noisy location, but very good value at JD2 per bed (doubles JD4, 3-bed JD6), hot shower 500 fils extra, no heating in rooms, so cold in winter, friendly staff, safe for women. Recommended. **F** *Baghdad Grand*, King Faisal St, Downtown, T4625433. Double room with fan and shared toilet/shower JD5, or bed in shared room JD3, free showers and use of kitchen, all rather basic and slightly seedy. **F** *Bdeiwi*, Omar Khayyam St, Downtown, PO Box 182426, T4643395, F4643394. Fan, share shower (hot/free) and toilet, simple but spotlessly clean rooms, quiet location, JD8 for a double (JD10 with attached bath), or JD4 per bed, friendly staff, safe for women. Recommended. **F** *Cairo*, King Faisal St, Downtown, PO Box 20199, T4638230. Double room with fan and attached bath JD8, or bed in shared room with shared bath JD3, fairly clean, friendly staff, plans to get rid of dorms and upgrade rooms in future. **F** *Cliff*, Prince Mohammad St, Downtown, PO Box 184381. T4624273, F4638078. Fan, sink, share shower/toilet, TV lounge, can arrange car-hire, tours, airport taxi etc, doubles JD9, bed in shared room JD4, more basic rooms upstairs (JD3 per bed/double JD6), or sleep on the roof in summer for JD2, the No1 choice with backpackers for years because of guidebook recommendations, and used to catering for foreigners, though the hotel itself is hugely over-rated, mattresses are lumpy with knackered bed-springs, there's no heating in the rooms (an important consideration in winter), it's not the cheapest around, and a hot shower is 500 fils extra (and with only 2 showers you will certainly have to queue when it's busy), on the other hand, it's a good place to meet fellow travellers, the staff are friendly and the

Amman

manager is a mine of useful practical information, and it's safe for women. **F** *Farah*, Cinema al-Hussein St, Downtown, T4651443, F4651437. Fan, phone, TV, locker, share shower/toilet, can arrange car-hire, tours, etc, and offers free airport pickup/drop, doubles JD9, bed in shared room JD4, or sleep on the attractive roof area in summer for JD2. 2 clean (single-sex) showers (free, hot) and toilets on each floor, fridge on each floor, lift to all floors, a/c reception/TV/lounge area. Safe for women. Recommended. For those with their own vehicle, this is the only budget place in Downtown with its own parking lot. **F** *Nasser*, King Faisal St, Downtown, T4623342. Rather basic and unremarkable doubles with shared shower/toilet JD6. **F** *Riviera*, King Hussein St,

Abdali, Jabal Amman & Al-Weibdeh

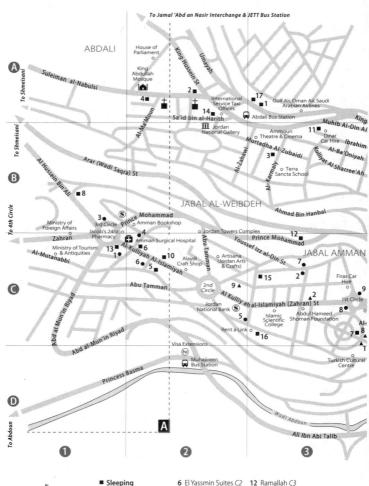

Related maps
A Western Amman,
page 86
B Downtown, page 80

■ **Sleeping**	6 El Yassmin Suites *C2*	12 Ramallah *C3*
1 Al-Monzer *A3*	7 Granada *C3*	13 Razan *C1*
2 Amman Mirage *A2*	8 Grand Hyatt *B1*	14 Remal *A2*
3 Canary *B3*	9 Happyland *B4*	15 Sabeel Suites *C3*
4 Caravan *A2*	10 Inter-Continental *C2*	16 Shepherd *C3*
5 Carlton *C2*	11 Merryland *B3*	17 Toledo *A3*

Downtown, PO Box 20455, T/F4622629. Fan, sink, share shower/toilet, double room JD8, bed in shared room JD3, or sleep on roof for JD2.500, fairly clean, friendly staff. **F** *Venicia*, Prince Mohammad St, Downtown PO Box 182350, T4638895. Shared showers/toilets, free use of kitchen area, double rooms JD8, bed in shared room JD3, or sleep in roof dorm for JD2 (discounts out of season), scruffy, somewhat rundown place, but friendly staff. **F** *Yarmouk*, King Faisal St, Downtown, T4624241. Rather basic rooms with shared shower/toilet, some with balconies over busy/noisy road. **F** *Zahran*, Betra St, Downtown, T46254473. One of the cheapest in town (JD1.500 per bed), not much English spoken, close to mosque, very basic, slightly seedy.

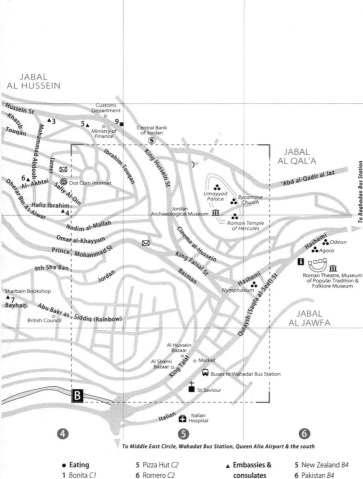

• Eating	5 Pizza Hut *C2*	▲ Embassies &	5 New Zealand *B4*
1 Bonita *C1*	6 Romero *C2*	consulates	6 Pakistan *B4*
2 Fakhr el-Din *C3*	7 Saluté/Grappa *C3*	1 India *C3*	7 Saudi Arabia *C4*
3 FRIENDS *B1*	8 Terrasse Cafeteria	2 Iraq *C3*	8 Sri Lanka *C3*
4 New Orient (Abu	Petros *C3*	3 Ireland *B4*	9 Turkey *C2*
Ahmad) *C2*	9 The Diplomat *C3*	4 Italy *B4*	

Jabal Amman The slopes of Jabal Amman rise steeply to the southwest of Downtown, with this affluent district extending westwards in a long ridge as far as 3rd Circle. There are some excellent **B** category hotels in the quieter, more residential areas to the east of 2nd Circle. In the vicinity of 3rd circle there are 2 **luxury** and some **A** and **B** category hotels, though 3rd Circle itself is a large, busy and unattractive intersection designed with a view to instilling fear in any sane pedestrian. The main advantage of this district is its relatively central location.

LL *Inter-Continental*, Al Kulliyah al-Islamiyah (Zahran) St, between 2nd and 3rd Circle, Jabal Amman, PO Box 35014, T4641361, F4645217, amman@interconti.com. Centrally located, 5-star luxury (recent extensive refurbishment), full business, conference and banqueting facilities, swimming pool, health club, extensive shopping plaza including excellent bookshop, Royal Jordanian reservations office, Arab bank (Visa/Mastercard ATM) and post office. Restaurants include *Bukhara* (Indian), *Atrium* (International) and *Mama Juanita* (Mexican), as well as the mouth-watering *Deli Café* and in summer the rooftop *Terrace*. Very swish, but equally pricey.

L *Grand Hyatt*, Al Hussein Bin Ali St, near 3rd Circle, Jabal Amman, PO Box 831159, T4651234, F4651634, www.amman.hyatt.com. Recently opened, 5-star luxury, full business, conference and banqueting facilities, shopping, car hire, tours etc, outdoor

Western Amman

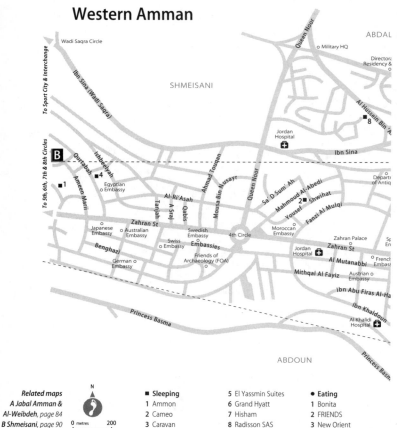

Related maps	Sleeping	5 El Yassmin Suites	● Eating
A Jabal Amman &	1 Ammon	6 Grand Hyatt	1 Bonita
Al-Weibdeh, page 84	2 Cameo	7 Hisham	2 FRIENDS
B Shmeisani, page 90	3 Caravan	8 Radisson SAS	3 New Orient
C Abdoun, page 92	4 Dove	9 Razan	(Abu Ahmad)

0 metres 200
0 yards 200

Amman

and indoor swimming pools, health club. Restaurants include *L'Incontro* (Italian), *Indochine* (French-Vietnamese) and soon-to-open *Arabian* (Middle Eastern), as well as *Grand Café*, *Grand Deli* and *Orynx* lounge and bar. Also featuring the exclusive *JJ's* nightclub. Standard rooms very reasonably priced (and sometimes substantially discounted), with more expensive options ranging from 'Regency' rooms right the way through to the astronomically priced 'Royal Suite' (JD1,500!).

A *Carlton*, Al Kulliyah al-Islamiyah (Zahran) St, between 2nd-3rd Circle, Jabal Amman (opposite *Inter-Continental*), PO Box 84049, T4654200, F4655833. Reasonable rooms with a/c, TV/dish, IDD, minibar and attached bath. Restaurant and coffee shop. Quick to offer substantial discounts, which make it good value. **A** *El Yassmin Suites*, Al Kulliyah al-Islamiyah (Zahran) St, near 3rd Circle, Jabal Amman, PO Box 3335, T4643216, F4643219. Rooms feature attached bath, separate bedroom and lounge areas with a/c, phone, TV/dish and sink/cooker/fridge units. Rather pricy for the quality of facilities, though discounts are available.

B *Granada*, near 1st Circle, Jabal Amman, PO Box 2321, T4638031, F4622617. A/c, TV/dish, IDD, fridge, attached bath, quiet area, close to the British Council, clean, pleasant rooms, though some are a bit small. Discounts of up to 20% available, making it good value. **B** *Razan*, 3rd Circle, Jabal Amman, PO Box 2674, T4649391, F4649397. A/c, TV/dish, phone, attached bath, sink/cooker/fridge unit, restaurant, bar, newly-built hotel located right on 3rd Circle (good double glazing, so reasonably quiet), friendly, well-run establishment. **B** *Sabeel Suites*, Ibrahim al-Muwaylehi St, near 2nd Circle, Jabal Amman, PO Box 2206, T4630571, F4630572, hsabeel@nets.com.jo Choice of small, medium or large suites, all with a/c, TV/dish, phone, attached bath, sitting room and kitchenette area, pleasant restaurant, friendly, family-run, small hotel (just 9 suites), nicely furnished, quiet residential location, homely atmosphere, good value. Recommended. **B** *Shepherd*, Zaid Bin Harethah St (near 2nd Circle), Jabal Amman, PO Box 2020, T/F4639197. A/c, TV/dish, IDD, fridge, attached bath, restaurant, bar, coffee shop, spacious rooms at front, smaller but quieter ones at rear. A little overpriced.

'Western Amman' Running west from 3rd Circle all the way to 8th Circle, the busy thoroughfare of Zahran St represents the main transport artery through 'Western Amman', where several of the luxury hotels and many of the mid-upper range (**A-B** category) hotels are located. This broadly defined area includes the districts of **Al Radhwan** and **Zahran** (respectively to the north and south of Zahran St between 3rd and 5th Circle), **Umm**

Uthayna (the commercial heart of which lies to the north of Zahran St between 5th and 6th Circle) and **Swafiyeh** (centred around a compact grid of streets immediately to the south of Zahran St between 6th and 7th Circles). Zahran St (along which most of the luxury hotels in this area are locate has no great appeal in itself. Al Radhwan and Zahran districts are quiet, affluent and nondescript, with many of the foreign embassies and consulates located here. Umm Uthayna and Swafiyeh are both very affluent; the former is home to a couple of Amman's most expensive restaurants, while the latter has a mix of restaurants, bars, western-style fast food places and lots of trendy designer-label shops.

L *Amra Forum*, King Faisal Bin Abdul Aziz St, 6th Circle, PO Box 950555, T5510001, F5510003, amrafh@nets.com.jo. Owned by the Inter-Continental group. The rather ugly tower block exterior conceals an extensively refurbished and upgraded 5-star interior, full business, conference and banqueting facilities, large outdoor (and smaller indoor) swimming pool, tennis, excellent health club (see under Sport), rooftop *Shehrazad* restaurant (Moroccan chéf), *Wadi Rum* bar, *Zee* nightclub, large shopping complex attached to hotel. **L** *Dana Plaza*, Zahran St, 6th Circle, PO Box 850577, danaplaza@net.com.jo. Modern, compact, recently opened hotel, rooms comfortable and pleasantly furnished, though a bit small, business, conference and banqueting facilities, small rooftop and indoor pools, restaurant, bar, health club.

A *Ammon*, off Zahran St, between 4th and 5th Circle, PO Box 950271, T5680090, F5605688, achte@go.com.jo Modern, newly-opened hotel with comfortable, well-appointed rooms (a/c, TV/dish, IDD, minibar, attached bath), business, conference and banqueting facilities, swimming pool, tennis, restaurants, bar, coffee shop. Jordan Tourism Board offices located here, as well as a 'Duty-free' shopping centre. **A** *Comfort Suites*, Ali Nasouh al-Taher St, Swafiyeh, PO Box 850049, T5856184, F5865997, www.comforts.com Choice of 'deluxe' or 'elegant' suites (separate bedroom/sitting room or studio layout), all with a/c, TV/dish, IDD, attached bath and kitchenette, comfortable and nicely furnished, though a little on the small side (some with connecting doors), free use of all facilities (pool, sauna, gym etc) at the nearby *Plaza Fitness Centre*. Popular *Rover's Return* pub at rear, helpful, friendly staff. **A** *Hisham*, junction of Hazza' al-Majali/Ibn Abu Firas al-Hamdani St, between 3rd-4th Circle, T4642720, F4647540, hishamhotel@nets.com.jo A/c, TV/dish, phone, attached bath, restaurant, 'English pub'. Small, pleasant, well-run residential hotel, popular with nearby embassies. **A** *San Rock International*, Dijlah St, 6th Circle, T5513800, F5513600. Decent size rooms with a/c, phone, TV/dish and attached bath, lively place, featuring café, games room, coffee shop, bar and *Scandal* disco. Friendly staff, though the hotel is much in need of a promised renovation, after which prices will go up.

B *Córdoba*, Shat al-Arab St, Umm Uthayna, PO Box 3278, T5536166, F5510255. A/c, TV/dish, IDD, minibar, attached bath, restaurant, coffee shop, bar, modern new hotel with marble extavaganza of a lobby. Rooms are more modest, but comfortable and very good value. **B** *Dove*, 16 Qurtabah St (off Zahran St, next door to Egyptian Embassy), between 4th and 5th Circle, PO Box 950701, T5697601, F5697683, dove@go.com.jo A/c, TV, phone, fridge, room safe, attached bath, restaurant, popular Irish Pub (*Céad Míle Fáilte*) downstairs, reasonable rooms, though nothing special, discounts available. **B** *Gondola*, Sa'id ibn Abi Waqqas St, 5th Circle, T5515656, F5528847. Apartments and suites for long-stay guests, complete with a/c, TV/dish, phone, attached bath, kitchen, sitting room, balcony, restaurant, bar, weekly/monthly rates very competitive. Recommended. **B** *Red Rose*, Shat al-Arab St, Umm Uthayna, PO Box 950504, T5512301, F5512305, redrose@go.com.jo Spacious, nicely furnished suites with large sitting room, small kitchenette area, a/c, TV/dish, IDD, attached bath, *Extreme* nightclub downstairs, restaurant. Luxurious new hotel, very competitively priced (for the moment at least).

C *Cameo*, 25 Mahmoud al-Abedi St, near 4th Circle, T4644515, F4644579. A/c, TV/dish, phone, attahed bath, favoured by overland companies, pretty good value, quiet area. Discounts available.

Shmeisani is the upmarket version of Downtown, a busy commercial area with lots of **Shmeisani** luxury and mid-upper range hotels, restaurants, shops and offices. Note that several of the hotels listed here are in the vicinity of Shmeisani, but not strictly speaking within the district. The *Holiday Inn*, also included here, is in Al Salheen district, which is miles from anywhere.

LL *Meridien*, Queen Noor St (next door to Housing Bank Centre), Shmeisani, PO Box 950629, T5696511, F5674261, meridien@go.com.jo A huge hotel with spacious rooms boasting all the mod cons, full business, conference and banqueting facilities, new extension under construction to include indoor and outdoor pools, health club and new conference centre (scheduled for 2001), large shopping arcade with car hire, travel agents etc, restaurants include the *China Town* (Chinese and Japanese) and *Casa Mia* (Italian), various bars and coffee shops, popular *Boiler Room* nightclub, rather pricey, though low season discounts make it a better value **L** category hotel. **LL** *Regency Palace*, Queen Alia St, near Jamal 'Abd an-Nasir Interchange, Shmeisani, PO Box 927000, T5607000, F5660013, regency@nets.com.jo Full business, conference and banqueting facilities, small indoor pool on top (20th!) floor with health club 1 floor down, *Al Madafa* restaurant, *Al Alali* nightclub, bar, library, car hire, good book-shop, rooms comfortable (great views from upper floors), but a bit dated and not 'luxurious' enough to warrant the price tag. In fact, this hotel really belongs in the **L** or **AL** brackets; low season discounts put it in the latter, making it much better value.

L *Holiday Inn*, off Al Madeenah al-Munawarah St, Al Salheen, PO Box 941825, T5528822, F5529944, holidayn@nol.com.jo. Huge, modern, recently opened hotel, suitably luxurious but unremarkable rooms, extensive business, conference and ban-queting facilities (main hall seats up to 1000 people), nice outdoor pool, good health club, shopping, car hire, travel agent etc, resturants include *Beyond Rangoon*(Chi-nese/Thai cuisine) and *Senate* (international cuisine), also *Cappuccino Café* for coffee, pastries and ice cream, and the popular *French Quarter* bar/nightclub. All very fancy and shiny-new, but pricey (almost **LL** category), and remote location. **L** *Jerusalem International*, University (Al Jami'a) Rd, near Sports City Interchange, PO Box 926265, T5151121, F5159328. A luxury hotel in the old style, all very elegantly furnished (vel-vet wallpaper, period furniture etc), full business, conference and banqueting facili-ties, shopping, car hire etc, health club (gym, sauna, massage, but no pool), *Al Yarmouk* restaurant, *Al Andalus* nightclub. Rather a long way from the centre of town. **L** *Marriott*, Isam al-Ajlouni St, near Jamal 'Abd an-Nasir Interchange, Shmeisani, PO Box 926333, T5607607, F5670100, www.cns.com.jo/marriott. Rooms pleasantly fur-nished to a high standard. Full business, conference and banqueting facilities, shop-ping, car hire etc, indoor and outdoor pools, tennis, *Oasis* health club, choice of restaurants, popular *Champions* bar/nightclub, very reasonably priced for quality of facilities, with low season deals bringing room prices into **AL** category, attentive ser-vice. Recommended. **L** *Radisson SAS*, Al Hussein Bin Ali St, Shmeisani, T5607100, F5665160, www.radisson.com Pleasantly furnished and suitably luxurious rooms, business centre, huge conference and banqueting hall (one of the largest in Amman, seating up to 2000 people; also 7 smaller rooms), outdoor pool, health club, restau-rants include *Al Liwan* in lobby (international cuisine) and *Royal Club* on top floor with great views and pleasant garden terrace (Continental cuisine), also *Wings Club* bar. Extensive refurbishment nearing completion at the time of writing.

Amman

Amman

AL *Arwad*, Queen Alia St, near Jamal 'Abd an-Nasir Interchange, Shmeisani, PO Box 921091, T5673849, F5677024, arwad@firstnet.com.jo Modern, recently opened hotel, comfortable rooms, small outdoor pool, fitness centre, restaurant, bar, discounts in low season make this a more reasonably priced **A** category hotel. **AL** *Paradise Suites*, Sharif Abdul Hameed Sharaf St, Shmeisani, PO Box 17222, T5677072, F5676980. Modern, recently opened hotel with well appointed single and double suites (separate sitting room/kitchenette areas with sofabeds, 1/2 double bedrooms, 1/2 attached baths). Good value for families, particularly during the low season when single/double suites can be had for as little as JD40/50.

A *Amman Orchid*, Ash Sharif Nasir Bin Jamil St, Shmeisani, PO Box 940537, T5522111, F5522113, orchid@firstnet.com.jo. Modern, recently opened hotel, comfortable rooms with a/c, TV/dish, IDD, minibar and attached bath, business, conference and banqueting facilities, restaurant, popular with UN agencies. Good value during low season when discounts put it in **B** category. **A** *Commodore*, Sharif Abdul Hameed

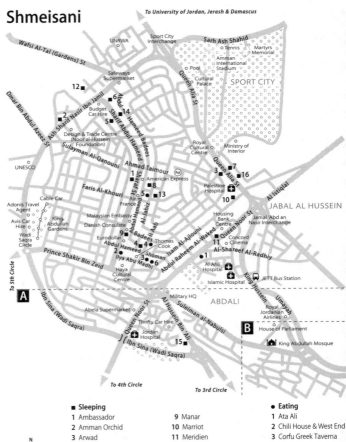

Shmeisani

To University of Jordan, Jerash & Damascus

To 5th Circle

To 4th Circle

To 3rd Circle

N

| 0 metres | 400 |
| 0 yards | 400 |

■ **Sleeping**		● **Eating**
1 Ambassador	9 Manar	1 Ata Ali
2 Amman Orchid	10 Marriot	2 Chili House & West End
3 Arwad	11 Meridien	3 Corfu Greek Taverna
4 Blue Marine	12 Middle East	4 Leonardo da Vinci
5 Commodore	13 Nefertiti	5 Peking
6 Gardenia	14 Paradise Suites	6 Pizza Hut
7 Grand Palace	15 Radisson SAS	
8 Howard Johnson (Al Qasr) Plaza	16 Regency Palace	

Sharaf St, Shmeisani, PO Box 927292, T5607185, F5668187, comedest@go.com.jo. Comfortable (recently renovated) rooms with a/c, TV/dish, phone, minibar and attached bath, restaurant, coffee shop, bar, nightclub, use of pool at Middle East hotel. Unremarkable, but good value during low season when discounts put it in **B** category. **A** *Grand Palace*, Queen Alia St, near Jamal 'Abd an-Nasir Interchange, Shmeisani, PO Box 9224444, T5691131, F5695143. Comfortable spacious rooms with a/c, TV/dish, phone, minibar and attached bath, restaurant, bar, use of facilities (including pool and health club) at *Regency Palace* next door. Good value. **A** *Middle East*, off Ash Sharif Nasir Bin Jamil St, Shmeisani, PO Box 927292, T5517160, F5517422, comedest@go.com.jo A/c, phone, TV/dish, minibar and attached bath, outdoor pool, *Churchill's* English-style pub, *Talk of the Town* disco, restaurant, coffee shop, *Hertz* car hire, despite all the facilities, an ageing hotel whose rooms are rather in need of refurbishment, quick to offer substantial discounts, but overall its sister hotel, the *Commodore*, nearby on Sharif Abdul Hameed St, is better value for money.

B *Ambassador*, 55 Sharif Abdul Hameed Sharaf St, Shmeisani, PO Box 925390, T5605161, F5681101, ambashtl@go.com.jo A/c, TV/dish, phone, minibar, attached bath, rather old-fashioned despite recent renovations, small but still comfortable rooms, *Marco Polo* restaurant (Arabic/international), *Aladin Bar*, business and conference facilities. **B** *Gardenia*, Sharif Abdul Hameed Sharaf St, Shmeisani, PO Box 940490, T5667790, F5604744, gardeniahotel@index.com.jo Modern, recently opened hotel featuring spacious rooms complete with kitchenette area, as well as the usual a/c, TV/dish, IDD, minibar and attached bath, restaurant, small outdoor pool, fitness centre. Good value, particularly with low season discounts. **B** *Howard Johnson (Al Qasr) Plaza*, 4 Al Arroub St, off Al Jahiz St, Shmeisani, PO Box 926192, T5689671, F5689673. Comfortable rooms with a/c, TV/dish, IDD, minibar and attached bath, coffee shop, *Vinaigrette* restaurant on top floor with good views, *Absolute* nightclub, recently taken over by the Howard Johnson group and undergoing extensive refurbishment at the time of writing. Quiet residential location. **B** *Manar*, 20 Sharif Abdul Hameed Sharaf St, Shmeisani, PO Box 20730, T5662186, F5684329. A/c, TV/dish, phone, minibar, attached bath, OK rooms (some with balcony), small outdoor pool. Rather overpriced and in need of refurbishment.

C *Blue Marine*, off Abdul Hameed Shoman St, Shmeisani, PO Box 926038, T5667165, F5664312. A/c, TV/dish, phone, attached bath, clean, pleasant rooms, though a little small. Good location for Shmeisani nightlife.

D *Nefertiti*, 26 Al-Jahiz St, Shmeisani, T5603865. Simple rooms with fan and attached bath, the only budget hotel (doubles JD15) to be found in Shmeisani district. Quiet residential location.

Eating

Amman has a wide range of restaurants to suit all tastes and budgets. **Expensive** and **mid-range** restaurants are scattered all over the city's more prosperous districts, with major concentrations to be found around **Jabal Amman**, **Shmeisani**, **Abdoun**, **Umm Uthayna** and **Swafiyeh**. The majority of the Western-style fast food places (Pizza Hut, Baskin Robbins, Dunkin Donuts and the like, as well as local derivatives) are also to be found in these areas (such outlets, though they fall just inside the budget range in terms of prices, are very much a middle class preserve in Jordan). Note that although the number of independent restaurants at the upper end of the market is growing rapidly, many of the best restaurants are still to be found in the luxury hotels. Bear in mind also that many of the places listed under 'Cafés', and under 'Bars and nightclubs', also serve food.

Amman

Amman

The majority of Amman's **budget** eating options are focused around **Downtown** and **Abdali**, although there are cheap places all over the city for *shawarma* and *falafel sandwiches, hummus, fuul* etc. Note that with the exception of *Hashem*, most the cheap eateries in Downtown close by around 2100 or 2200, and even earlier in winter. In all but the cheapest budget diners you need to bear in mind the 13% government tax that is always added to the bill, and sometimes the further 10% service charge. The expensive restaurants in the luxury hotels generally add both tax and service, though some of the upmarket independent restaurants just add the government tax, leaving service to your discretion. Where given, prices per head are obviously only very approximate guides. Unless otherwise stated, they have been calculated to include the relevant service/tax, but not alcohol. If you stick to vegetarian dishes you can usually reduce the overall bill significantly.

Expensive (more than JD10) **Jabal Amman and Al-Weibedh** *Bonita,* off Kulliyah al-Islamiyah (Zahran) St, near 3rd Circle, Jabal Amman, T4615061. Open 1200-late. Continental/Spanish cuisine with lots of fish and seafood on the menu. Pleasant outdoor terrace. JD10-15 per head upwards. The Tapas bar next door is open from 2100. *Bukhara, Inter-Continental* hotel, Al Kulliyah al-Islamiyah (Zahran) St, between 2nd and 3rd Circle, Jabal Amman, T4641361. Open 1200-1500, 1900-2330. Very elegant and classy, with prices to match, but equally with a reputation for excellence. Indian restaurants are something of a rarity in Amman; this one could compete with the best anywhere in the world.

Abdoun

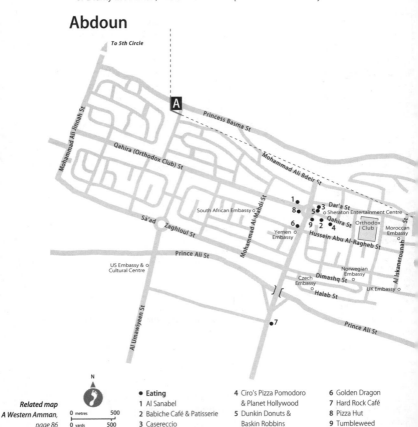

To 5th Circle

Princess Basma St

Mohammad Ali Jinnah St

Qahira (Orthodox Club) St

Mohammad Ali Bdeir St

South African Embassy

Mohammad Al-Mahdi St

Dar'a St

Sheraton Entertainment Centre

Sa'ad   Zaghloul St

Qahira St

Orthodox Club

Moroccan Embassy

Al Iskanerounah St

Yemen Embassy

Hussein Abu Al-Ragheb St

Prince Ali St

US Embassy & Cultural Centre

Norwegian Embassy

Czech Embassy   Dimashq St

UK Embassy

Halab St

Al Umawiyeen St

Prince Ali St

N

Related map
A Western Amman,
page 86

0 metres   500
0 yards   500

● Eating
1 Al Sanabel
2 Babiche Café & Patisserie
3 Casereccio

4 Ciro's Pizza Pomodoro & Planet Hollywood
5 Dunkin Donuts & Baskin Robbins

6 Golden Dragon
7 Hard Rock Café
8 Pizza Hut
9 Tumbleweed

JD15-20 per head upwards. **Fakhr el-Din**, 40 Taha Hussein St, between 1st and 2nd Circle, Jabal Amman, T4652399. Open 1300-1530, 1930-late. Booking essential, one of Amman's best Lebanese restaurants, with a reputation for excellence (the brass plaque in the entrance lobby listing eminent diners, including practically all the royal family, gives an idea of its pedigree). The menu offers a choice of more than 70 different hot and cold *mezze* dishes, as well as the usual grilled meat and fish main courses. The interior is spacious, airy and elegantly furnished in keeping with the Ottoman-style architecture of the building (a former residence of Jordan's first Prime Minister, and later of the Spanish ambassador). There is also a pleasant outdoor terrace for summer dining. JD15 per head upwards. If you are in a group of 4 or more, their special set menu is a great way to sample a typical Lebanese spread, and excellent value at JD10 per head (+13% tax). **Indochine**, *Grand Hyatt* hotel, Al Hussein Bin Ali St, Jabal Amman, T4651234. Vietnamese and French cuisine served in elegant 'French-colonial' surroundings. JD10-15 per head upwards. **L'Incontro**, *Grand Hyatt* hotel, Al Hussein Bin Ali St, Jabal Amman, T4651234. Very elegant Italian restaurant with a generally excellent reputation, though some complain of erratic standards. JD10-15 per head upwards. **Mama Juanita**, *Inter-Continental* hotel, Kulliyah al-Islamiyah (Zahran) St, between 2nd and 3rd Circle, Jabal Amman, T4641361. Open 1230-1530, 1930-late. Popular as much as a drinks and snacks place as a restaurant, though the standard of the food is generally high. Around JD10 per head (good value set-price lunch menu for just under JD7). **Romero**, off Kulliyah al-Islamiyah (Zahran) St, between 2nd-3rd Circle (opposite *Inter-Continental* hotel), T4644227. Open 1300-1500, 2000-1130. Part of an upmarket chain with restaurants at Umm Qais, Pella, Madaba and Aqaba. Elegantly furnished, with a pleasant outdoor patio for summer dining. Generally excellent reputation, though some aficionados claim that it has gone downhill a bit in recent years. JD10-15 per head. **Tower**, off Prince Mohammad St, on top floor of Jordan Towers complex, near 3rd Circle, Jabal Amman. Open 1100-2330. The food here is unspectacular, but, being up on the 23rd floor, the view certainly is. JD8-12 per head (there is also a café here, so you can get the views without splashing out on a full-scale meal).

Swafiyeh and Umm Uthayna *Bayerischer Hof,* Al Hamra St, Swafiyeh, T5819730. Open 1100-late. Smart, upmarket German restaurant and bar. Mainly European cuisine, with occasional Oriental flourishes. German specialities include Wienerschnitzel (Bavarian sausages), various pork and beef dishes, and home-made apple Strudel (from the tempting deli counter which greets you when you walk in). Extensive wine list. JD10-15 per head. Downstairs is a cosy bar area, complete with open fire in winter, featuring occasional quiz nights and

To Downtown

Princess Basma St

Wadi Abdoun St

Lebanese Embassy

Amman

Amman

☞ *Getting up-to-date information on restaurants*

The restaurant scene in Amman, particularly at the upper end of the market, is expanding very rapidly. This is good news for foodies, with new establishments opening practically every month (Lebanese and Italian cuisine are very much in vogue at the moment). At the same time, however, there is a great deal of fluctuation in the fortunes of these new restaurants. Some fail to make their mark in what is a highly competitive market, and fall by the wayside rather abruptly. Others open to great critical acclaim, only to slide rapidly into mediocrity or worse. Others still appear to be highly inconsistent, with the quality of the food and/or service varying dramatically from one week to the next.

The restaurant information given in this Handbook inevitably represents something of a 'snapshot' of what was on offer at the time of writing. For those interested in getting a more in-depth and up-to-date insight into Amman's gourmet restaurant scene, the Grumpy Gourmet *magazine provides impartial reviews of both newly-opened and long-established restaurants (though only at the upper end of the market). Published on a quarterly basis, this free magazine is available by subscription (grumpy@gourmet.com). Copies can also be found at the receptions of many of the luxury hotels, and also at some of the more expensive restaurants. The magazine is complemented by a small booklet, the Jordan Restaurant Guide, which provides fairly comprehensive listings of restaurants, cafés and pubs, categorized under headings such as 'Elegant Affairs', 'Hip and Happening' and 'Late Night Dining'.*

live music (check the *Jordan Times*). *La Casa Rosa*, Princess Sarvath al-Hassan St, near 8th Circle (heading east along Zahran St from 8th Circle, take the first left turn and it is on the left after a few hundred metres), T5816521. Open 1230-1530, 1900-late. Recently opened. Very classy and elegant. Live piano music nightly except Fri. JD10-12 upwards per head. *Mays al-Reem,* Shat al-Arab St, Umm Uthayna, T5536990. Open 1200-late. Booking advisable. Elegant Lebanese restaurant, not as classy as the nearby *Tannoureen*, but still of a high standard, with a wide selection of hot and cold *mezze* dishes. JD12 per head upwards. *Mosaic*, King Faisal Bin Abdul Aziz St, Umm Uthayna, T5532510. Open 1300-1500, 2000-1130. Simply but elegantly furnished with a large patio garden for summer dining. Menu combines European and Arabic (Lebanese) aspects of 'Mediterranean' cuisine (hot and cold *mezze* dishes, mixed grill etc, as well as paella, lasagna, grilled pigeon and the like). JD10-15 per head upwards. *Seven Seas,* Shat al-Arab St, Umm Uthayna, T5510051. Open 1200-1600, 1900-late. Booking advisable. Modern, elegant fish/seafood restaurant. JD15-20 per head. *Shehrazad,* Amra Forum hotel, King Faisal Bin Abdul Aziz Rd, 6th Circle, T5510001. Situated on the top floor of the hotel, with stunning views out over Amman. Arabic cuisine with a Moroccan focus. Occasional live entertainment in the evenings. JD10-15 per head upwards. *Tannoureen,* Shat al-Arab St, Umm Uthayna, T5515987. Open 1130-1630, 1930-late. Booking essential. Excellent Lebanese restaurant, in the same league as the *Fakhr el-Din* and attacting similar clientelle (this place served as the art studio of Princess Fakhr el-Nissa Zeid, the mother of Prince Ra'ed). Short menu of classic Lebanese salads, *mezze* dishes, grills, fish etc, with an emphasis on simplicity and quality. Light, airy decor, with an understated elegance. Conservatory area for *nargileh* sessions, and outdoor summer terrace. JD15 per head upwards.

Abdoun *Al Afandi*, Sheraton Entertainment Centre, Qahira (Orthodox Club) St, Abdoun, T5934794. Open 1300-1530, 2000-late. Upmarket, glass-roofed affair on the top floor of the Sheraton centre (good views), live music nightly except Thu and Sun. Good food, varied menu. JD12 per head upwards. *Tumbleweed,* Abdoun Circle,

Abdoun, T5932050. Open 1100-late. Smart, upmarket American franchise Tex-Mex restaurant and bar. Wide range of snacks (nachos, burritos, enchiladas, fajitas etc), as well as high quality ('Grade A' US beef) steaks. Light, airy interior with glass-roofed section. Though it's really best known as a lively nightspot (see under Bars and night-clubs, below), a lot of effort goes into the food side. Perhaps the only place to give prices including taxes. JD10-15 per head.

Shmeisani *Beyond Rangoon*, *Holiday Inn* hotel, off Al Madeenah al-Munawarah St, Al Salheen, T5528822. Open 1145-1500, 1845-2300. Chinese and Thai cuisine. 'Japa-nese Garden' style setting complete with waterfall, plants and wooden pagodas above each table. JD10-15 per head upwards. *China Town*, *Meridien* hotel, Queen Noor St, Shmeisani, T5696511. Choice of Chinese or Japanese cuisine. Set menus JD15/20 per head (+23%), or à la carte. *La Maison Verte,* off Abdul Hameed Shoman St (next door to *Blue Marine* hotel), Shmeisani, T5685746. Open 1300-1500, 1900-late. Booking advisable. Elegant, cosy interior with candle-lit tables. One of the few genuinely French restaurants in Amman, with a reputation for excellent food. JD10-15 per head. *Leonardo da Vinci*, 11 Arab St (off Abdul Hameed Shoman St), Shmeisani, T5662441. Open 1230-1530, 1930-2300. Long-established Italian restau-rant with a good reputation. Live music every evening. Extensive menu. JD10-15 per head. *Peking*, Al Arroub St, off Al Jahiz St (opposite *Howard Johnson Al Qasr Plaza* hotel, Shmeisani, T5660250. Open 1300-1530, 1900-2330. Large, elegant Chinese res-taurant with a good reputation. JD8-12 per head upwards. *West End,* Abdul Hameed Shoman St (above *Chili* House), Shmeisani, T5693053. Open 1230-late. Huge T-bone steaks (JD13) are the house speciality here, or there are various cheaper chargrill options (eg chicken breast JD5), as well as a range of light snacks (chicken wings, potato skins, soups, sandwiches etc) for JD2-3.

Jabal Amman *American Bakehouse*, Motran St (off Rainbow St), Jabal Amman, T4643470. Great breakfast menu (pancakes, waffles, French toast, omlettes etc; set breakfasts JD3/4). Lunch/dinner menu of sandwiches, burgers, chips etc. Small, easy-going diner-style place. *China*, off Rainbow St, Jabal Amman, T4638968. Open 1200-1530, 1900-late. Pleasant, unpretentious Chinese restaurant within walking dis-tance of Downtown. JD7-10 upwards. *The Diplomat,* 1st Circle, Jabal Amman, T4625592. Open 0800-2200. Mixed Arabic and European cuisine. Unpretentious diner-style place with a good breakfast menu, as well as *mezze* dishes, sandwiches, pizzas and main meals (the daily specials are filling and good value). JD5-7 per head (less for snacks). Serves alcohol. *FRIENDS*, 3rd Circle, Jabal Amman, T4642830. Located right on 3rd Circle (formerly the *Nouroz*). Bills itself as a 'restaurant/pub'. The menu is a mixed bag of *mezze* snacks, sandwiches, pasta, pizza, steaks etc. Relaxed, 'smart/casual' atmosphere, with a small bar room and a separate couples area. More a drinking place in evenings, with occasional live music. Bit pricey for what you get. *New Orient (Abu Ahmad)*, Basman St, 3rd Circle, Jabal Amman. T4641879. Open 1100-late. Long-established and popular place with a good reputation for Arabic food. Extensive, reasonably priced menu. Pleasant outdoor garden terrace for sum-mer dining. JD5-8 per head.

Mid-range (JD5-10)

Swafiyeh and Umm Uthayna *Szechwan Gardens,* Shat al-Arab St, Umm Uthayna, T5531174. Open 1130-1530, 1800-2330. Booking advisable for evenings. Looks a little shabby from the outside (at least in comparison to its swish neighbours), and inside the seating is in 2 slightly cramped rooms, but the food is good. JD8-10 per head.

Abdoun *Café de Paris*, Sheraton Entertainment Centre, Qahira (Orthodox Club) St, Abdoun, T5934765. Open 0800-late. On the ground floor of the Sheraton Entertain-ment Centre, with a pleasant outdoor patio terrace and indoor seating. As well as

Amman

being a café, complete with enticing patisserie, and a bar, this outlet also has an extensive food menu, ranging from soups, salads, sandwiches, burgers, grills etc, through to excellent wood-oven pizzas. JD5-10 per head upwards. *Casereccio,* Abdoun Circle, Abdoun, T5934772. Open 1300-1600, 1900-2400. Tucked away in small side street off to the right immediately north of Abdoun Circle. Small, pleasant restaurant serving excellent wood oven pizzas, pastas, etc. Good value (JD5-8 per head), but no alcohol served. Also incorporates *La Creppina* for crépes featuring super-indulgent fillings such as nutella, banana and hazelnuts. *Ciro's Pizza Pomodoro,* Qahira (Orthodox Club) St, Abdoun, T5928515. Better known as a lively bar/nightclub (see under Bars and nightclubs, below), though the food also has a good reputation, and it now also opens for lunch (1230-1700). There are also plans for a weekly 'dinner' night (as opposed to the usual DJs, live music and drinking). JD7-10 per head. *Golden Dragon,* just south of Abdoun Circle, Abdoun, T5929362. Open 1230-1600, 1900-2400. Upstairs on 2nd floor above *Jordan Supermarket* (entrance round the corner). Recently opened, good quality, upmarket Chinese restaurant featuring an unusually large bar. JD7-10 per head upwards.

Shmeisani *Corfu Greek Taverna*, off Queen Noor St, Shmeisani, T5680185. Open 1230-1600, 1930-late, closed Fri. Family-run restaurant with a varied menu encompassing Arabic and International as well as Greek cuisine. Pleasant outdoor terrace during summer. Often with live entertainment in the evening. JD7-10 per head. *Houston's*, off Abdul Hameed Shoman St (in same side street as *Blue Marine* hotel), Shmeisani. Open 1200-late. Lively, popular Tex-Mex restaurant and bar. Gets very busy on Thu evenings, when it is more of a nightspot than a restaurant. JD8-10 per head upwards.

Cheap (less than JD5) **Downtown** *Abu Khania & Abu Saleh*, off King Hussein St, Downtown. Situated in the same alley as the entrance to the *Baghdad Grand* hotel, simple, relatively clean(ish) diner with the usual range of Arabic dishes on offer. Popular with backpackers and so used to dealing with foreigners. There is a reasonable vegetarian selection here, though overall the food is distinctly mediocre. Around JD3-4 per head (less for vegetarian). *Cairo*, off King Talal St, near King Hussein Mosque, Downtown. This cheap, friendly Egyptian-run diner is always busy, and the food generally fresh. A half chicken, salad and tea here is a very reasonable JD1.750. The meat or vegetable stews with rice are another cheap and filling option. There is also seating upstairs. *Hashem*, Downtown. Whether you are on a budget or not, this small unassuming eatery in the alley opposite the *Cliff* hotel is a must for all *hummus* and *fuul* lovers. Open 24 hrs a day, and always busy, it has been serving excellent *hummus, fuul* and very sweet tea (that is all they do) for over 40 years. A bowl of *hummus* or *fuul* with bread and tea costs just 450 fils, and you can buy fresh falafels (50 fils for 4) from the shop opposite to eat with your meal. When the bread arrives fresh and steaming hot from the local bakery, the combination is unbeatable. Recommended. *Jabri*, King Hussein St, Downtown. The downstairs section is entirely given over to Arabic sweets; upstairs is a simple, brightly lit and spotlessly clean diner-style restaurant and coffee shop serving the usual range of Arabic dishes. A good, stress-free budget option. Popular with Jordanian families, so women will feel comfortable here. Open for breakfast (including omlettes etc) and lunch, but closed in the evening. Eat well for JD3-5 per head. *Jerusalem (Al Quds)*, King Hussein St, Downtown. Situated a couple of doors along from the *Jabri* and very similar in setup (Arabic sweets at the front, restaurant behind), though not as good. Prices are a bit inflated here; eg JD2.600 for an unremarkable half chicken, salad and tea, or JD2.400 for an equally unremarkable *mansaf*. Menus are in Arabic only. Service can be pretty slack but the waiters are greedy for tips. *Pasha Palace*, on ground floor of *Pasha Palace* hotel, Shabsoah St (opposite Roman Theatre), Downtown. Simple Arabic fare. Clean, friendly and very good value (eg rice, bean stew and quarter chicken JD1.250). Reassuringly popular with locals.

Abdali and Jabal Al-Weibedh *Granada, Toledo* hotel, by Abdali Bus Station. Situated on the ground floor of the Toledo complex on the Abdali side. Spotlessly clean and pleasantly decorated throughout with traditional blue and white patterned tilework. Prices here are a little higher than your average budget diner (JD2.500 for a half chicken or 250 g of grilled meat, 500 fils for hummus etc), but the quality is also that much better. They also do good shwarmas and falafel sandwiches. A great haven if you've just arrived by bus and need to recover a little before moving on. Recommended.

Shmeisani *Tarweea*, Haya Cultural Centre, Ilya Abu Madhi St, Shmeisani. Unpretentious restaurant serving a good selection of Arabic/Lebanese food. Good value at around JD2 per head. One of the few genuinely budget places in Shmeisani.

Fast food, takeaway & snacks *A La Saj*, Qahira (Orthodox Club) St, Abdoun. Tucked away beside the entrance to *Planet Hollywood*. This small, unassuming-looking take-away with a couple of tables outside serves excellent 'sandwiches' consisting of huge crêpes made on the spot and stuffed to the brim with the filling of your choice. Very tasty, very generous portions and very reasonable prices (around JD1.200 depending on the filling). Recommended. *Bifa Billa*, off King Faisal St, Downtown. Located in the alley beside the Arab Bank. Mainly a takeaway, but with some seats inside. Good shawarmas, as well as burgers, pizzas, chips and milkshakes. Ask prices before you order, or you may find yourself being charged somewhat randomly. *Chili House*, various branches, including Shmeisani (Abdul Hameed Shoman St) and Swafiyeh (Salah al-Shaimat St). Chilli/spaghetti meals for JD2-2.500, also burgers, sandwiches and other snacks. *China Inn*, Al Hamra St, Swafiyeh, T5861303. Open 1200-2300. Fast food-style Chinese eat-in or takeaway. Combination meals good value at around JD3-3.500, though the portions are on the small side. *Pizza Hut*, various branches, including Shmeisani (Abdul Hameed Shoman St); Abdoun (on Abdoun Circle); Jabal Amman (Zaid Bin Harethah St, near 2nd Circle); T5856700 for all Amman branches. Pizzas from around JD2 upwards. *Snack Box*, Suleiman al-Nabulsi St (directly opposite King Abdullah Mosque), T5662402. Open 1200-2200, closed Fri. Takeaway only place offering good value sandwiches, burgers, chips, pasta dishes, stir-fries, etc. JD1.500-3.000.

Cafés

Downtown cafés are generally very traditional, wood-and-sawdust type places where men with time on their hands come to while away the hours drinking tea or coffee, smoking a *nargileh*, chatting, playing cards or backgammon, reading the papers, or just watching the world go by. In sharp contrast, the cafés to be found in Amman's more affluent districts (notably Jabal Amman, Jabal al-Weibdeh, Abdoun and Shmeisani) tend to be very sophisticated (and equally pricey), Continental-style places. All the luxury hotels also have their own coffee shops, of which only a couple of the more notable ones are listed below.

Downtown There are numerous traditional Arabic coffee houses dotted around Downtown. In a Jordanian context they are exclusively male environments, though foreign women are generally tolerated (modest dress and a male escort will help reduce the amount of attention you receive). Of those listed below, the *Eco-Tourism* café is the least intimidating for women. Alternatively, both the *Jabri* and *Jerusalem (Al Quds)* restaurants (see under Budget Eating), and the *Habibah* in between these 2, are also coffee shops where women will feel comfortable, though they lack the atmosphere of the more traditional places. There are also plenty of cafés around Hashemite Square (between the Roman Theatre and Raghadan Bus Station), though these are more expensive, being geared towards local and foreign tourists.

Arab League, King Faisal St. Situated up on the first floor (below the budget hotel of the same name), this cavernous place is the epitome of a traditional Arabic coffee house. A seat by the window gives you a bird's-eye view over King Hussein mosque and the busy pavement area in front. *Auberge*, Prince Mohammad St. Situated on the 1st floor (in the same building as the *Cliff* hotel). Much the same as the *Arab League*. Small balcony overlooking Prince Mohammad St. Also serves some food, and alcohol, in a separate room. *Eco-Tourism*, King Faisal St. Situated on the first floor (next door to the *Cairo* hotel). Slightly more expensive than the more traditional places in Downtown, and attracting a younger, fashionable crowd. Great balcony (distinctively decorated with painted flags from around the world) overlooking King Faisal St. The name derives from strong interest that the owner, Ibrahim el-Wahsh, has in regional environmental issues.

Jabal Amman & Jabal al-Weibdeh
Books@Café, Omar Bin al-Khattab (Mango) St, Jabal Amman, T4650457, www.books-cafe.com Open 0900-2300. (See also pages101 and 110). Wide selection of real coffees and speciality teas (both rather expensive, but discounted if you are accessing the internet here). Also serves a range of snacks, sandwiches, salads, soups, cakes etc, and more substantial dishes (JD3-5 per head). Casual, relaxed atmosphere (popular with Amman's young and trendy set). Pleasant patio terrace overlooking Jebel al-Ashrafiyya. *Darat al-Funan*, Jabal al-Weibdeh. As well as the art gallery (see under Sights), this complex also includes a café (right at the top) with a delightfully tranquil garden terrace. *Deli Café*, *Inter-Continental* hotel, Zahran St, between 2nd and 3rd Circle, Jabal Amman. A very swish and modern café and patisserie serving Bodum teas, Green Mountain coffees, fresh fruit juice cocktails, a delicious range of cakes, sweet and savoury pastries; a great place to come for a little bit of indulgence. The drinks are predictably expensive, but some of the food is surprisingly reasonable. *Terrasse Cafeteria Petra*, 1st Circle, Jabal Amman. Pleasantly situated right on 1st Circle, with seating inside on 2 floors, or out on the street. A simple, Arabic-style place, also serves *hummus, fuul,* grills etc, as well as tea and coffee.

Abdoun
Abdoun's cafés are all to be found clustered around a very small area, either on Abdoun Circle itself, or just along Qahira (Orthodox Club) St immediately to the east of it. In keeping with this district, they are very elegant and trendy affairs. On Abdoun Circle itself there is the *Lambada* and *TCHE*. On Qahira (Orthodox Club) St, in the Sheraton Entertainment Centre, there is the *Café de Paris*, which also does food (see under Eating, above). Next door (just by the entrance to the *Big Fellow* Irish pub) is the basement *Ya Lail Ya Ain*, as upmarket as the others around it, but with more of an Arabic rather than European feel. More or less opposite the Sheraton Entertainment Centre is the *Café Moka*, and the *Babiche*, which is also a very enticing patisserie.

Shmeisani
Most of Shmeisani's cafés are to be found in the area of Ilya Abu Madhi St and Abdul Hameed Shoman St, in the southern part of the district (where many of Shmeisani's fast food places are also located). Though not as trendy as Abdoun's cafés, they are still very upmarket places. Most have outdoor seating on terraces overlooking the street.

Bars, pubs and nightclubs

Downtown
There are various tiny, exclusively male and somewhat seedy bars to be found clustered around a small area of Downtown (mostly around the *Cliff* hotel). The beer is relatively cheap in these places (between JD1.500-1.700 for a large bottle of Amstel), and they are convenient if you are staying in Downtown and want a drink without making an expedition out to the more expensive nightspots. Women, however, will attract a considerable amount of attention and should steer well clear unless they have a male escort with them and don't mind dealing with occasional drunken advances (not to mention the problem of going to the toilet, as most only have a very basic urinal.)

Hilton, situated up on the first floor, next door to the stairway leading up to the *Riviera* hotel. Fairly spacious, but very unappealing. *Jordan*, entrance in the alleyway parallel to *Cliff* hotel. Arguably the friendliest of the Downtown bars, with some attempt to create a bit of atmosphere (if you don't agree, a couple more beers may bring you round). *Kit Kat*, entrance on Cinema al-Hussein St, opposite the cinema. Even seedier than the others (if that's possible). *Orient*, entrance in same alleyway as entrance to *Cliff* hotel. Situated up on the first floor. Not quite as cramped as the others, and with the added attraction (?) of a real toilet. Also serves food (*mezze* dishes, chicken, kebabs etc). *Saloman*, entrance in same alleyway as entrance to *Venicia* hotel. Cleaner and neater than the others, and with Amstel on draught, but hopelessly small and cramped.

There is a burgeoning scene in fancy, upmarket 'pubs', bars and nightclubs to be found **'Uptown'** scattered all over 'uptown' Amman. Frequented by the affluent, trendy 'Euro-Arab' (or more often 'US-Arab') set, the contrast between these places and Downtown's bars couldn't be greater. If you are after a bit of 'real' nightlife, they can certainly deliver, though they are also pretty expensive. A large Amstel (draught, not bottled) generally costs around JD3, with standard cocktails costing between JD4.500-6.500 upwards. Some places charge an entrance fee if there are DJs or live music. Almost all of the more expensive hotels also have their own bar or nightclub, although only a few of these have any real atmosphere or popular appeal. Ask around to find out which are the 'in' places of the moment. Traditionally, Mon and Thu nights are the 'big' nights, when things really get going, though Fri nights are increasingly popular.

The Big Fellow, Sheraton Entertainment Centre, Qahira (Orthodox Club) St, Abdoun, T5934766. Open 1200-0200. Large, slightly glitzy (this is the Sheraton Entertainment Centre after all), but authentic Irish pub (it's even Irish-run!). At the time of writing this was the only place in Amman offering Guinness and Killkenny on draught, though at JD4 per pint it doesn't come cheap. Friendly, easygoing atmosphere, popular with expats. Shows most major football, rugby and boxing fixtures on its large satellite screens. Happy hour 1700-1900. Come before 2100 if you want a seat. Also does food (exclusively Irish cuisine, of course, without a hint of foreign influence). *Boiler Room*, *Meridien* hotel, Queen Noor St, Shmeisani. One of Amman's 'in' nightclubs at the time of writing (apparently). *Champions*, *Marriot* hotel, near Jamal 'Abd an-Nasir Interchange, Shmeisani. Open 1200-late. Popular, trendy 'sports bar' with a steady stream of live international sports events beamed at you from large screens dotted around the place. Live DJs on Thu nights (when it becomes more of a nightclub). Also serves food (Tex-Mex snacks, burgers, chips, steaks etc). *Ciro's Pizza Pomodoro* ("*of Knightsbridge*", to give it its full name), Qahira (Orthodox Club) St, Abdoun, T5928515. Open 1900-late (also as a restaurant from 1230-1700, see above). Part of the international chain. Here in Amman, it's best known as a bar/nightclub venue, with DJs and live music every night, though it also serves food in the evening (see under Eating, above). Cosy, going on cramped, basement setting. Very popular, particularly on Mon and Thu nights, and increasingly on Fri nights. Wed is Salsa night. 'Happy hour' 1900-2200. DJs start around 2100, live bands around 2300. Entry JD3.

French Quarter, *Holiday Inn* hotel, off Al Madeenah al-Munawarah St, Al Salheen. Spacious 'New Orleans' style bar/restaurant, with a large hexagonal bar in the centre, dance floor and outdoor terrace in summer. DJ and live music on Mon and Thu nights (JD3-5 entrance). The menu is mainly burgers, steaks and Tex-Mex offerings. *Hard Rock Café*, Prince Hashem Bin Al Hussein St, Abdoun, T5934901. Open 1230-late. Part of the international Rock'n'Roll-theme chain. Stylish, cavernous interior with a grand stairway leading down to the spacious dining area and bar. Live band on Thu nights from around 2100/2200. The menu is mostly US/Mexican food, with a few Arabic offerings. Impressive venue, but rather a remote location, away from the main focus

Amman

Amman

of activity around Abdoun Circle. *Irish Pub (Céad Míle Fáilte)*, *Dove* hotel, off Zahran St, between 4th and 5th Circle. Open 1900-late. Not entirely convincing as an 'Irish pub', but a good atmospere and very popular with a younger crowd, perhaps reflecting the fact that the beer is that bit cheaper than average (though not the Guinness). Starts to get busy from around 2200, with full-on dance music after midnight. *JJ's*, *Grand Hyatt* hotel, Al Hussein Bin Ali St, near 3rd Circle, Jabal Amman. Very trendy, exclusive nightclub (officially members only, though hotel guests and well-dressed foreigners will have no problems getting in) with British DJs playing all the latest sounds. *Planet Hollywood*, Qahira (Orthodox Club) St, Abdoun, T5930972. Open 1200-late. Part of the international chain, with the usual movie screens and Hollywood memorabilia dotted all over the place. Very trendy and popular. Actually quite small, but friendly and suitably American in feel. Outdoor 'tropical' theme terrace bar in summer. Restaurant section serves a variety of US, Italian and Tex-Mex food (booking advised Thu and Fri nights). *Rover's Return*, Ali Nasouh al-Taher St (behind *Comfort Suites* hotel), Swafiyeh, T5814844. Open 1200-late. Popular English-style pub inspired by the Coronation Street (popular UK TV soap opera) watering hole of the same name. Relaxed, friendly atmosphere, but, despite the careful attention to detail, it somehow manages to feel a like an airport pub, or perhaps a film set? Famous for its fish and chips (just under JD4.500), though it also does a range of other traditional English pub meals. No bookings taken. *Saluté/Grappa*, opposite *Fakhr el-Din* restaurant, Ibrahim al-Muwaylehi St, between 1st and 2nd Circle, Jabal Amman, T4651458. Open 1900-late. Easy-going, trendy bar with loud music. Also serves food (pizzas, pasta etc). *Tumbleweed*, Abdoun Circle, Abdoun, T5932050. Open 1100-late. Tex-Mex restaurant/bar (See also Eating, above). Trendy nightspot with DJs every night. Live Spanish music Mon, Wed and Fri nights from around 2030. Booking advised Thu and Fri nights. *Zee*, *Amra Forum* hotel, 6th Circle. Not yet fully opened at the time of writing, but looking promising. Large dance floor, good sound system and enthusiastic British DJ. Entry JD3 (smart casual dress). Open from 2100 (closed Sat).

Entertainment

Art galleries   *Dar al-Anda*, 38 Dijlah St, Umm Uthayna, T5519122. Elegant, privately run 'tea salon' and art gallery displaying works of contemporary local artists. *Darat al-Funan*, Nadim al-Mallah St, Jabal al-Weibdeh. T4643252. Open 1000-1900, Thu 1000-2000, closed Fri. Features a small but impressive art gallery with permanent exhibitions of Jordanian artists, as well as a regular exhibitions of artists from all over the Arab world, and beyond. Well worth a visit (see also under Sights, above). *Jordan National Gallery*, 6 Husni Fareez St, Jabal al-Weibdeh (near Abdali Bus Station), T4630128. Open 0900-1700, closed Tue. Entry JD1. As the name suggests, this is Jordan's main government-sponsored art gallery, with an extensive collection of works. Well worth visiting for those interested in art.

Children   *Haya Cultural Centre*, Ilya Abu Madhi St, Shmeisani, T5665194. Open winter 0830-1630, summer 0830-1730, closed Fri. Entry 500 fils. This is a dedicated children's complex for 6-12 year olds. As well as a pleasant supervised playground there is a wide range of facilities, including a library, science museum, planetarium, theatre and various courses and activities. *Amusement World*, Abu Bakr as-Siddiq (Rainbow) St (next door to the British Council), Jabal Amman. Offers a range of activities, including video games, roller-skating, dodgem cars, tenpin bowling and snooker.

Cinemas   Amman's newest cinema is the 2 screen *Galleria*, Sheraton Entertainment Centre, Qahira (Orthodox Club) St, Abdoun, T5934793. It is the most expensive (JD6), but it is usually the first to show new releases and is also the best, with comfortable seating and good projection and acoustics. Other good cinemas include the *Philadelphia*,

Jordan Towers Complex, Prince Mohammad St, near 3rd Circle, Jabal Amman, T4634144 (2 screens, JD4); *Plaza*, Housing Bank Centre, Queen Noor St, Shmeisani, T5699238 (1 screen, JD4); and *Concorde*, off Queen Noor St, Shmeisani, T5677420, (1 screen, JD4). Programmes for all of these cinemas are advertised in the *Jordan Times*.

Books@Café, Omar Bin al-Khattab (Mango) St, Jabal Amman, T4650457 (see also under Cafés above, and Shopping and Communications below), shows films on Sun and Tue nights at 2030 (JD2). They are listed – somewhat erratically – in the 'What's On' section of the *Jordan Times* (inside back page). Most of the foreign cultural centres show movies on video (see page 111 for addresses and phone numbers); *American Center*, Thu at 1700; *British Council*, Wed at 1800 (adults), Tue at 1700 (children); *Centre Culturel Français*, Mon at 2000. The *Abdul Hameed Shoman Foundation* (see below for address/ phone number), has a film club every Tue night at 1900 (free), showing the works of Arab film makers (usually with English subtitles). They are also involved in organising various film festivals, including the annual Franco-Arab Film Festival (usually in Jun/Jul each year, with films being screened at the Royal Cultural Centre, Shmeisani). There are several cinemas to found around Downtown, including the *Hussein*, Cinema al-Hussein St; *Khayyam*, Omar al-Khayyam St; and *Raghadan*, Basman St. These places specialise in Hong Kong made shoot-'em-up action movies, enticing punters in with lurid billboards featuring the obligatory leggy blonde bombshell and billings such as "spies, thighs, bikinis and bullets" (though the censors are quick to cut the fleshy bits). Tickets cost just JD1.500.

General

Royal Cultural Centre, Queen Alia St, Sports City, Shmeisani, T5661026. Combining a theatre, cinema, conference and exhibition halls, this complex is the primary venue for major cultural events in Amman. These are generally advertised in the *Jordan Times*. Getting information over the phone from the centre is something of a hit and miss affair. *Abdul Hameed Shoman Foundation*, Zahran St, between 2nd and 3rd Circle (directly opposite the Iraqi embassy), T4659154. As well as a film club, this cultural foundation hosts weekly lectures (Mon) and occasional symposiums on contemporary issues (usually in Arabic). It also houses a large public and children's library (around 50/50 English/Arabic books).

Theatre

Both the *Ammoun*, 17 Murtadha al-Zubaidi St, Jabal al-Weibdeh (just up from Abdali Bus Station), T4618274, and the *Hisham Yanes*, Abu Bakr as-Siddiq (Rainbow) St, near 1st Circle, T4625155, feature regular plays (usually in Arabic, though with an increasing number in English). The *Ammoun* is also a cinema. See the *Jordan Times* for programmes.

Festivals

The *Jerash Festival Committee* has its offices in Shmeisani, behind the Arab bank, T5675199.

Shopping

Books

The selection of books in English is not exactly brilliant, and prices are comparatively high.

Of the bookshops in the luxury hotels, the one in the *Inter-Continental* hotel is probably the best, while those in the *Regency Palace* and *Marriot* hotels are also good. *Al Aulama Bookshop*, Prince Mohammad St (near Post Office), T4636192. Small selection of books on Jordan and the Middle East, and also some of the Royal Jordanian Geographic Centre maps of Jordan. *Amman Bookshop*, 207 Prince Mohammad St, near 3rd Circle, T4644013. One of the better bookshops, with a wide range of books on Jordan and the Middle East, as well as some fiction, but not cheap. **Books@Café**, Omar Bin al-Khattab (Mango) St, Jabal Amman, T4650457. Good but relatively pricey selection of new and second-hand fiction. Usually also stocks a range of newspapers. **Jordan Distribution Agency (JDA)**, 9th Sha'ban St, off Prince Mohammad St, Downtown, T4630191. This shop actually supplies many of the bookshops in the luxury hotels and has an excellent selection on the history and politics of the Middle East, as well as a good selection of general fiction and a wide range of international magazines and newspapers (including all the British newspapers). However, it is rather expensive. **Sharbain**, Abu Bakr as Siddiq (Rainbow) St, just off 1st Circle, T4638709. Small but good selection of books on the history and politics of the Middle East, as well as a reasonable range of Penguin Classics and some contemporary fiction. Prices here are significantly lower than most other bookshops.

Handicrafts & souvenirs There are plenty of souvenir shops to be found dotted around Downtown, particularly along Hashemi St and King Talal St. **Jordan Handworks**, on Hashemi St, is one of the larger places, with a sometimes rather garish collection of *nargilehs*, copperwares, decorated pottery goods, wood and inlaid wood items etc. It is worth shopping around as there are lots of smaller places nearby offering a similar range of goods, but perhaps without the same tourist mark-up and hard-sell. Despite attempts to 'talk-up' Downtown Amman's souks (notably the gold souk), they do not measure up to regional rivals in Damascus, Aleppo, Cairo or Jerusalem. However, they are still interesting – as much for the general atmosphere and people-watching experience as for the goods on offer.

Away from Downtown, nearly all the luxury hotels have souvenir shops, though they tend to be expensive. Of more interest are the various independent shops specialising in high quality locally made (often Bedouin) handicrafts. Many of these are in fact outlets for income-generating projects from around the country. All those listed below accept major credit cards and can arrange to have larger purchases air-freighted home for you.

Alaydi (*Jordan Craft Development Centre*), off Zahran St, near 2nd Circle, Jabal Amman, T4644555. Wide selection of traditional handicrafts (jewellery, embroidery, woven rugs, baskets, pottery, glassware etc). Good quality but expensive. **Artisana** (*Jordan Arts and Crafts Centre*), M Krishan St, near 2nd Circle, Jabal Amman, T4647858. Open 0915-1830, closed Fri. Wide selection of handicrafts in a similar vein to the nearby *Alaydi*. **Jordan Design and Trade Centre** (*Noor al-Hussein Foundation*), off Ash Sharif Nasir Bin Jamil St (opposite the *Amman Orchid* hotel), Shmeisani, T5699141, www.nhf.org.jo Open 0800-1900, closed Fri. Outlet for the Noor al-Hussein Foundation's various income-generating projects. Large showroom with a wide selection of beautiful hand-woven rugs and pottery, as well as embroidered items, fabrics, jewellery, ceramics, furniture etc. See also under Salt and Wadi Seer in the 'Around Amman' section. **Jordan Heritage Designs**, Nimer Ben Adwan St (off King Hussein St), Jabal al-Weibdeh, T4611454. Open 0900-1800, closed Fri. Workshop and showroom/shop specialising in beautiful, high quality traditional pottery designs. The larger articles are expensive (eg JD25-50 for decorative plates), but there are also lots of smaller items (candle holders, cups, ashtrays etc) for JD3-12. **Jordan River Designs/Dana Shop/Bani Hamida House**, off Abu Baker as-Siddiq (Rainbow) St, Jabal Amman, T5933211, jrd@nets.com.jo Open 7 days, 0900-1900. This complex houses outlets for projects of the *Jordan River Foundation*, as well as the RSCN's project at Dana. There is a wide selection of goods on offer here, including jewellery, pottery, woven rugs, home furnishings, baskets, embroidered items, jams, dried herbs, olive oil, soaps etc, as well as some books on Jordan's flora and fauna. Prices are high but the quality of the merchandise is also excellent.

Safeways, Ash Sharif Nasir Bin Jamil St, near Sport City Interchange, Shmeisani. Open **General**
24 hrs, features food hall, clothing, plus just about anything else that you could need
(includes internet café). There is another branch, also 24 hr, near 7th Circle. Also near
7th Circle is the trendy *C-Town* supermarket. *Ahlia Abela*, Queen Noor St, near
Shmeisani Circle, Shmeisani. Similar to *Safeways*, but rather more upmarket.

Sport

Orthodox Club, Qahira (Orthodox Club) St, Abdoun, T5920491. Members-only club, **General**
but if you can get entry as a guest they have good facilities, including Olympic-size
indoor and outdoor pools, gym, tennis, squash and basketball, as well as a restaurant
and bar. *Sport City*, Queen Alia St, Shmeisani, T5667181. This extensive complex
includes the Amman International Stadium, where football matches and other sporting events are staged, as well as tennis courts and an Olympic-sized outdoor pool.

Royal Jordanian Gliding Club, Marka Airport, T4874587. JD15 per hour. Bookings **Gliding**
should be made well in advance.

Amman Golf Club, Airport Highway, T5736955. JD15 per day, plus JD10 for club hire. **Golf**

Amra Forum Fitness and Recreation Centre, *Amra Forum* hotel, 6th Circle T5510001, **Health/fitness**
ext1611. This is the best of the various health clubs contained in Amman's luxury hotels. **centres**
As well as the large outdoor pool and smaller indoor pool (both extensively refurbished
and kitted out with jacuzzis), there is a spacious fully-equipped fitness centre, sauna,
steam room, massage, Turkish bath and 2 floodlit tennis courts. Open 0700-2200, Fri
0900-1800. Use of all facilities JD15 per day (hotel guests JD12; massage, Turkish bath,
tennis courts extra), or you can become a member for a minimum of 1 month. *Dana
Plaza Health Club*, *Dana Plaza* hotel, 6th Circle. Considerably smaller and a little less luxurious than the Amra Forum, but the equipment is all very new. Pool, gym, jacuzzi,
steam room, sauna, massage, Turkish bath. Use of all facilities JD10 per day (massage,
Turkish bath extra). *Holiday Inn Health Club*, *Holiday Inn* hotel. Large outdoor dou-
ble-hexagonal pool. Fitness centre, aerobics room, steam bath, sauna, massage, jacuzzi,
jet shower. Use of the pool or health club is JD10 each (hotel guests free; massage extra).
Oasis Health Club, *Marriott* hotel, near Jamal 'Abd an-Nasir Interchange. Indoor and
outdoor pools, fitness centre, jacuzzi, sauna, Turkish bath, massage. Use of all facilities
JD11 per day (hotel guests free; Turkish bath, massage extra). *Sanctuary Zara Spa*,
Mövenpick Resort and Spa, Dead Sea. For the ultimate in health centres, head down to
Mövenpick's luxurious hotel on the Dead Sea (less than a 1 hr drive from Amman).

Arabian Horse Club, Airport Highway, T591678. Riding lessons etc. *Royal Racing* **Horse-riding**
Club, T5850630. Horse and camel racing during spring and summer.

Hash House Harriers undertake a brief jog/walk through an Amman neighbourhood, **Jogging**
followed by some serious drinking and a BBQ, every Mon night. Enquire discreetly at
the British Embassy (or British Council). More serious runners may want to join up with
the *Amman Road Runners*, who meet every Sat evening at 1830 at Abdoun Circle.

Nearly all the luxury hotels have their own swimming pools, and will allow non-guests **Swimming**
to use them for a daily fee. The outdoor pool at the *Amra Forum* hotel is one of the largest and nicest in Amman. The *Marriott*, *Radisson SAS* and *Holiday Inn* hotels also have
good pools. The *Meridien* hotel was in the process of building a whole new health/fit-
ness complex, complete with swimming pools, at the time of writing. The open-air public pool at the Sport City complex is open 0630-1800 daily, and costs JD6). Bathing is
mixed and women may prefer to use a private pool at one of the luxury hotels.

Tennis The public courts at the Sport City complex (T5682796 to book) cost JD1 per hour. Bring your own equipment and clothing. The tennis courts at the *Amra Forum* hotel cost JD2 per person per hour, or JD3 at night when they are floodlit.

Tour Operators

The tourist information centre by the Roman theatre in Downtown can arrange guided tours of Amman, or put you in touch with various tour operators offering organized tours of the country. A number of the budget hotels in Downtown (notably the *Cliff* and *Farah*) organize 1 day tours to various sites around Jordan (most popularly to the Desert Castles); these require a minimum number of people before they will run, so you may need to ask around and get others interested. The *Friends of Archaeology* (see page 114) organize regular tours to archaeological sites around the country. The *RSCN* (see same page) has an eco-tourism unit responsible for organising visits to its various wildlife reserves and protected areas, and can also put you in touch with other tour operators specialising in 'ecological' tours.

There are literally hundreds of tour operators in Amman. The free tourist booklet *Your Guide to Amman* has extensive listings. *Adonis Travel & Tourism*, 8 Ash Sharif Nasir Bin Jamil St (near King Abdullah Gardens), Shmeisani, PO Box 142930, T5697434, F5697437, www.adonistravel.com Good, professional service, aimed very much at the luxury end of the market. Organizes tailor-made tours for individuals/couples or groups. Also with offices in Damascus and Beirut, so well placed to provide tours taking in Syria and Lebanon as well as Jordan. *Alia Tours*, Wasfi al-Tal (Gardens) St, T5620501, F5620503, aliatours@nets.com.jo Specialises in 'pilgrim tours'. *Jordan Eco-Tours*, T5533526, F5536964, www.jordanecotours.com *Middle East Tours*, Shamieh Trading Centre, Wafsi al-Tal (Gardens) St, T5533494, F5531903. Long established, with a good reputation. *NET (Near East Tourist Agency)*, *Grand Palace* hotel, Queen Alia St, Shmeisani, T5662518, F5685490. Helpful, reliable service. *Petra Travel and Tourism*, Sharif Abdul Hameed St, Shmeisani, T5667028, F5681402, www.petratours.com Efficient and reliable, also with office in Aqaba.

Transport

Local **To/From Airport** The **Airport Express** runs between Queen Alia International Airport and Abdali Bus Station (going via the *Meridien* hotel and 7th Circle), departing every 30 mins between 0600-2200 and every 2 hrs between 2200-0600 (though after 2400 the service is not 100% reliable). Tickets cost JD1.500, with an additional 250 fils sometimes charged for baggage. The trip takes 40 mins to 1 hr. A similar service from Raghadan Bus Station was not operating at the time of writing. A taxi to/from the airport will cost in the region of JD10-15.

Bus Few people get to grips with the bus system during a short stay in Amman. The numbering system is complicated, and buses from one route are sometimes transferred to another route without the numbers being changed. Generally, it is easier to use the service taxis or a private taxi. However, there are a couple of routes which can be used without too much difficulty. Regular buses (yellow) shuttle between the Raghadan and Mujahareen bus stations; ask around at either for the correct bus. Of the buses which head up Prince Mohammad St from Downtown, most go up to 3rd Circle and continue along Zahran St as far as 7th Circle (the remainder branch off along Arar St). Similarly, if you are in western Amman, the majority of the buses heading east along Zahran St are bound for Downtown. All bus fares within Amman are 100 fils (or 150 fils for longer journeys to outlying districts); you need to have the right change and deposit your coins in the box by the driver when you board.

Car hire For important general information about car hire in Jordan, see page 41. The following represents just a small selection of what is on offer. The free tourist brochures such as *Your Guide to Amman* have more extensive listings. The staff at the Downtown tourist information centre can also help you arrange car hire.

International firms Avis, King Abdullah Gardens, Shmeisani, T5699420, F5694883, avis@go.com.jo Also with offices at Queen Alia International Airport, King Hussein Bridge and Aqaba, though they still charge a hefty JD35 for a one-way rental to Aqaba. **Budget**, Sharif Abdul Hameed Sharaf St (near Commodore hotel), Shmeisani, T5698131, F5673312. Service not up to the standard one might expect from an international franchise. **Euro Dollar**, Sharif Abdul Hameed Sharaf St (near Manar hotel), Shmeisani, T5693399, F5687233, eurodollar@nets.com.jo Reasonable service and rates. **Hertz**, Middle East hotel, off Sharif Nasir Bin Jamil St, Shmeisani, T5538985, F5538406, hertz@go.com.jo Probably the best of the international companies, but also the most expensive. No small cars. Also with offices in Mövenpick hotels at Aqaba, Petra and Dead Sea, and at Queen Alia International Airport. **Thrifty**, off Al Hussein Bin Ali St, near Radisson SAS hotel, T5622384, F5624654, thrifty@nets.com.jo Helpful, professional service. Good rates on longer rentals with inclusive CDW. Also with desks in Radisson SAS, Meridien and Amra Forum hotels in Amman.

Local companies Al Amin, Jaber Centre, Mecca St, T/F5827201. Good rates on small cars. Also with an office at King Hussein Bridge. **Assaraya**, King Abdullah Gardens, Shmeisani, T5684771, F5684973. **Dallah**, Amra Forum hotel, near 6th Circle, T5511112, F5511116 (airport office T4451345) dallah@index.com.jo **Dinar**, off King Hussein St (next to Merryland hotel), Abdali, T4654238. Small company, conveniently located, excellent deals on small cars, especially for longer periods. **Firas**, on 1st Circle, Jabal Amman, T4612927 (Shmeisani office T5676856). Good service and reasonable rates. **Rally**, King Abdullah Gardens, Shmeisani, T5699983, F5620878. **Twins**, Jaber Centre, Mecca St, T5822481. Small company with good deals on small cars.

Private taxi Amman's numerous legions of private taxis are generally yellow (as oppose to the service taxis, which are white). The vast majority have working meters, which reduces the possibility of being taken for the wrong sort of ride. Most drivers do it as a matter of course, but check that the meter is switched on; if a taxi driver claims his meter isn't working, either agree the fare in advance or find another taxi. As a rough guide it's generally 150 fils plus 100 fils per km on the meter. Short journeys generally come to around 300-500 fils, while longer journeys within Amman are rarely more than JD1. At late hours of the night most drivers expect at least double the standard fare. Some of the taxis working the 5-star hotels like to try for 5-star prices at any time of day.

Service taxi Service taxis (shared-taxis) are the best cheap way of getting around, with numbered cabs (usually white Mercedes) running along fixed routes (see box) for set fares. Most fares are 100 fils, or 150 fils for some longer routes; it always helps to have the right change handy. All start from various point around Downtown, shuttling back and forth to the surrounding districts of the city, and dropping off or picking up anywhere along the way. Obviously it's much easier to get a seat at the start point rather than half way along a route. The Downtown queues can get very long during the morning rush hour, but they are very orderly affairs, and generally fast moving. Service taxis generally keep running until around 1 or 2 hrs after sunset, though much less frequently, and late at night any that you see are likely to be operating on a private hire basis.

Air Amman has 2 airports. The main international gateway is **Queen Alia International Airport** (T5678321 for airport info, or T64453200 for Royal Jordanian), located approximately 35 km south of Amman along the Desert Highway (see Local transport,

Long distance

Amman

Amman

 Service Taxi Routes

Some of the main shared-taxi routes are given below. Destinations and route numbers are written on the front doors, though the majority are in Arabic script only (the route number is the top one of the two, or the first one if they are side by side). The starting points for most are marked on the Downtown map.

1 starts from a small side street off Basman St, near King Hussein Mosque, and travels past First and Second Circles to Third Circle.

2 begins on Basman St (more or less opposite Raghadan cinema), and travels via Omar Bin al-Khattab (Mango) St up to Second and Third Circles.

3 starts from a small side street off Basman St, near King Hussein Mosque, and heads up to Third and Fourth Circles.

4/5 leaves from the bottom of Omar al-Khayyam, behind the post office, and heads via Jabal al-Weibdeh to Al-Amaneh Circle.

6 leaves from the southern end of Cinema al-Hussein St, Downtown, and passes via Abdali and JETT bus stations on its way to Jamal 'Abd an Nasir Interchange (Interior Circle).

7 leaves from the southern end of Cinema al-Hussein St, passing via Abdali bus station and King Abdullah Mosque, as far as the Ambassador Hotel in Shmeisani.

19 runs from Raghadan bus station to Wahadat bus station.

25/26 leaves from Italian St (off Quraysh St, to the south of King Hussein Mosque), and runs to Jabal al-Ashrafiyeh (for Abu Darwish Mosque).

27 runs from Italian St to Wahadat bus station.

29 leaves from Quraysh St, near the Church of St Saviour, and heads out along Al Quds (Jerusalem) St, to the southern district of Ras al-Ain.

35 leaves from Quraysh St, near the Church of St Saviour, and passes within walking distance of the Muhajireen Bus Station and Police Station (for visa extensions), before heading up to Third Circle.

38 starts from a small side street off Basman St, near King Hussein Mosque, going via Prince Mohammad St, Arar (Wadi Saqra) St to Wadi Saqra Circle, then along Mecca St and down Abdullah Ghosheh St.

above, for getting to/from the airport; for detailed airport information see page 32). Between them, Royal Jordanian and the 2 dozen or so other international airlines which serve Amman offer connections world-wide, many of them direct (see Directory, below, for addresses of airline offices in Amman). As well as long-haul flights, there are 1-3 flights daily with *Royal Wings* (a subsidiary of *Royal Jordanian*) to and from **Aqaba**. Both *Royal Wings* and *El Al* have daily flights between here and **Tel Aviv**. *Royal Jordanian* has regular services to **Beirut**, **Cairo**, **Damascus** and **Istanbul**. Remember the JD10 departure tax on international flights.

Amman's much smaller second airport is **Marka Airport** (officially known as Amman Civil Airport), T4875201, situated in the district of North Marka ('Marka al-Shamaliyeh'), about 4 km northeast of the Downtown Raghadan bus station. There is a daily *Royal Wings* flight to **Aqaba** from here, and currently 3 flights weekly to **Tel Aviv** (Mon, Wed, Fri) and **Gaza** (Tue, Wed, Sun), though timetables change frequently. **NB** If you fly into Marka Airport from Israel, the Jordanian entry stamp that you get here will betray the fact that you have been to Israel (and thus may prevent you from continuing on to Syria/Lebanon). If flying into Jordan from Israel (and intending travelling on to Syria/Lebanon), take 1 of the flights that arrive at Queen Alia Airport and not Marka. Marka Airport can be reached by minibus from Raghadan bus station in Downtown, or take a taxi.

Train The railway station ('Al Mahatta') is situated about 2 km to the northeast of Downtown (the buses which run between Raghadan bus station and Marka airport pass close by). Oil-fired steam trains still run from here along a section of the old Hejaz narrow-gauge railway line to **Damascus**. At the time of writing there were 2 trains weekly (Mon and Thu, departing at 0800, JD2.500), with talk of a 3rd train on Fri at 1300. The journey takes an absolute minimum of 9 hrs, with frequent lengthy delays. Cancellations are also common, and the timetable is liable to change. Indeed, for many years the line teetered on the verge of permanent closure, although there have been concerted efforts to revive it in recent years. Ask at the Downtown tourist information for up-to-date information, or you can try phoning the station directly (T4895414), though you are unlikely to get anyone who speaks English on the other end.

Road There are no less than 6 bus stations in Amman which are of use to tourists. **Abdali Bus Station**, King Hussein St, Abdali, is the major transport hub for buses, minibuses and service taxis serving destinations to the north of Amman. The Airport Express service also leaves from here (see Local transport, above). International service taxis to Damascus (amongst other places) also operate from around here. **JETT Coach Station**, situated around 1 km further up the hill from Abdali Bus Station, also on King Hussein St (look out for the Mercedes car showroom), operates a/c coaches (comfortable but ageing) to a number of important destinations (Petra, Aqaba, Hammamat Ma'in, King Hussein Bridge). Just around the corner, is the international JETT office, for a/c coaches to Syria (amongst other places). **Trust International Coach Station**, near 7th Circle has regular a/c coaches (brand new and very comfortable) to Aqaba and various destinations in Israel. **Wahadat Bus Station**, inconveniently located on the southern outskirts of Amman, just to the west of Middle East Circle, serves destinations to the south of Amman (coming from the south you may well find yourself deposited here; if you are heading south, for most destinations it is possible to depart from one of the more central bus stations). **Raghadan Bus Station**, just to the east of the Roman theatre in Downtown, is the main transport hub for Amman's chaotic and confusing local bus network, but is useful for a number of destinations in the vicinity of Amman (Madaba, Salt and Zarqa). **Muhajareen Bus Station**, situated to the south of Jabal Amman, is also useful for destinations close to Amman (South Shunah, Suweimah, Madaba and Wadi Seer).

Abdali Bus Station (Service taxi Nos 6 or 7 from Downtown, or a steep 30 min walk). **Buses/Minibuses** to the following destinations all leave from the top half of the bus station, departing when full; **Jerash**, 350 fils, 1 hr; **Ajlun**, 450 fils, 1½ hrs; **Irbid**, 500 fils, 1½ hrs; **Ramtha**, 500 fils, 1½ hrs; **Mafraq**, 450 fils, 1½ hrs; **Salt**, 200 fils, 45 mins; **King Hussein (Allenby) Bridge**, JD1.500, 1 hr; **Deir Alla**, 500 fils, 1 hr; **Zarqa**, 180 fils, 30 mins; **Suweileh**, 100 fils, 25 mins. In addition, Hijazi, situated in the middle part of the bus station, run a/c coaches to **Irbid**, departing every 15-30 mins, 820 fils. **Service Taxis** run from the middle and lower parts of the bus station, departing when full to the following destinations; **Jerash**, 550 fils; **Irbid**, JD1; **King Hussein (Allenby) Bridge**, JD1.500-2.000. There are several **International Service Taxi** companies on King Hussein St, opposite the top end of the bus station. These depart when full to **Damascus**, JD5.500, 2½-3 hrs (they also operate to a number of other destinations in Syria, as well as to Lebanon, Egypt, Turkey, Saudi Arabia and Iraq; see also *Afana Tourist Transport*, below).

JETT Coach Station(Service taxi No 6 from Downtown). The small ticket office is towards the top end of King Hussein St, next door to a Mercedes car showroom. Coaches leave from outside the ticket office. Open 0600-2000, T5664146. Bookings may be made up to 1 month in advance; you are advised to book at least 1 day ahead (JETT have a habit of altering their schedules according to demand, so it is worth checking them first anyway). **Aqaba**, 5 departures daily, 0700, 0900, 1100, 1400, 1600,

☞ *Amman to Israel on a Budget*

Many visitors use Amman as a jumping off point to/from Israel. For a cheaper option than the JETT coach which costs JD6 to get you to the the Israeli side of the border or the Trust International coaches which cost JD14/10.500 to get you to Tel Aviv/Haifa, take either a service taxi (JD2) or a bus (JD1.500) from Abdali bus station to King Hussein (Allenby) Bridge (one hour). Neither run to a timetable, both departing when full, though if taking the bus an early start is recommended. You will be dropped at the customs/immigration post on the Jordanian side where you complete exit formalities (including paying a JD4 departure tax). You are not allowed to walk across the no-man's land that divides the two countries (including the

unimpressive bridge over the Jordan River), and thus there is little choice but to take the bus for an extortionate JD1.5. Once on the Israeli side there is no entry tax, though entry and security formalities can be lengthy. The crossing is open Sunday-Thursday 0800-2200, Friday-Saturday 0800-1300, closed on the Jewish holiday of Yom Kippur. Having cleared entry formalities on the Israeli side, service taxis await to take you to Jerusalem's Damascus Gate (26 shekels). There may be cheaper buses/service taxis to take you to Jericho, though you save little money (and waste a lot of time) if you intend continuing on to Jerusalem. For details on entering Jordan from Israel via the King Hussein (Allenby) Bridge see page 30 .

JD4, 4 hrs approx; **Petra**, 3 departures weekly, Sun, Tue, Fri at 0630 (may increase to every other day), JD5.500/JD11 one way/return, 3½ hrs approx; **Hammamat Ma'in**, daily at 0730 if there are 2 or more passengers, JD4 return including entrance (no one-way tickets), 1½ hrs; **King Hussein (Allenby) Bridge** (takes you across to the Israeli side), daily at 0630, JD6, 1 hr. Just up the hill and around the corner is the *International JETT office*, T5664146. **Damascus**, 2 departures daily 0700, 1500, JD4.500, 3½ hrs approx; **Aleppo** (via Homs and Hama), 1 departure daily at 1430, JD7, 8½ hrs approx; **Beirut**, 2 departures weekly, Sun and Thu at 0900, JD15; **Cairo**, 2 departures weekly, Tue and Sat at 0630, US$52; **Riyadh**, 1 departure daily at 1030, JD31; **Baghdad**, 3 departures weekly, Sun, Tue, Thu at 0800, JD12. Next door to the International JETT office is *Afana Tourist Transport,* T5681560, which sells tickets for international buses and service taxis, although departures are from Abdali or Wahadat bus stations (they also have a ticket office at Wahadat). **Damascus**, 1 bus daily at 2100, JD5 (from Wahadat), service taxis hourly, JD6 (from Abdali); **Beirut**, 2 service taxis daily at 0600 and 2400 (from Abdali, though the morning service will pick-up from your hotel); **Cairo**, 1 bus daily at 0800, JD25 (from Wahadat).

Trust International Coach Station Most of the local buses heading up Prince Mohammad St run past 7th Circle, but ask as some branch off along Arar St; a private taxi will cost under JD1. The ticket office for Trust International is immediately to the south-west of 7th Circle, tucked away between the Royal Jordanian City Terminal office (look out for the *Royal Jordanian* and *Pizza Hut* bill-boards on the roof) and the 24 hr *Safeways*. Coaches depart from outside the ticket office. Open 0600-2200, T5813427. Bookings can (and should) be made up to 1 day in advance. **Aqaba**, 4 departures daily, 0730, 1130, 1430, 1700, JD4, 4 hrs approx; **Tel Aviv** (via Irbid and Jordan River border crossing), daily except Sat at 0730, J14, 6 hrs approx; **Nazareth/Haifa** (via Irbid and Jordan River border crossing), daily except Sat at 0800, JD10.500, 4½-5½ hrs approx.

Wahadat Bus Station This is the most arkwardly-situated of Amman's bus stations, being a good 5 km from Downtown (note that it has moved 1 block to the west of its old location on Middle East Circle. Service taxis (No 19) shuttle between here and

Raghadan Bus Station, or there are buses and service taxis (No 27) which run from Quraysh St and Italian St respectively (see Downtown map). A private taxi from Downtown will cost around JD1-1.500. **Buses/Minibuses** depart when full with varying frequency (there are more departures in the morning) to the following destinations (amongst others); **Madaba**, frequent, 350 fils, 45 mins; **Ma'in**, erratic, JD1.500, 1½ hrs; **Kerak** (via Desert Highway), frequent, 750 fils, 1½ hrs; **Tafila** (via Desert Highway), frequent, JD1, 2 hrs; **Ma'an**, frequent, JD1.500, 3 hrs; **Petra** (via Desert Highway and Showbak), not so frequent, JD1.650, 4 hrs; **Aqaba**, frequent (also some a/c coaches), JD3, 4½-5 hrs; **Service-taxis** depart when full to most of the above destinations, charging around 50-100% more than the buses/minibuses. You will have to bargain hard for fares to Petra and Aqaba. There are also some international buses from here, see *Afana Tourist Transport,* above.

Raghadan Bus Station (Within walking distance of Downtown hotels). This bus station is convenient for its regular minibus services to **Madaba**, **Salt** and **Zarqa**. Also useful are the local bus services to North Marka ('Marka al-Shamaliyeh'; for Marka airport and the train station) and Muhajireen bus station.

Muhajireen Bus Station To get there, either take one of the new yellow local buses from Raghandan Bus Station, or service taxi No 35 from Quraysh St (in front of the Jordan National Bank), passes close to the bus station before heading up to 3rd Circle. Minibuses from here run to **Suweimah** (for the *Dead Sea Resthouse*) (600 fils); **South Shunah**, 400 fils; **Madaba**, 250 fils; and **Wadi Seer**, 100 fils.

Directory

Airline offices

Aeroflot, Inter-Continental hotel, Zahran St, between 2nd and 3rd Circle, T5521642. *Air Canada, Nahas Travel and Tourism,* King Hussein St, Downtown, T4630879, F4629333. *Air India, Al Karmel Travel & Tourism,* King Hussein St, Downtown, T4653691, F4653693. *Air France,* 50 Sharif Abdul Hameed Sharaf St, Shmeisani, T5666055, F5692314. *Alitalia, Testco,* Yacoub Iwais St, Shmeisani, T4625203, F4657341. *American Airlines, Space Tourism & Travel* (also agents for *Thomas Cook*), Ilya Abu Madhi St, Shmeisani, T5668069, F5688919. *Austrian Airlines,* Sharif Abdul Hameed Sharaf St (opposite *Commodore* hotel), Shmeisani, T5677503, F5677509. *British Airways* (including British Mediterranean), *Hashweh Corporation,* Swafiyeh, T5828801, F5862277. *Cyprus, Petra Travel & Tourism,* Sharif Abdul Hameed Sharaf St (near *Commodore* hotel), Shmeisani, T5667028. *Egypt Air, Za'atarah & Co,* King Hussein St, Downtown, T4630011, F4655011. *El Al, 5 Continents Travel Services,* Ibn Sina (Wadi Saqra) St, near Wadi Saqra Circle, Shmeisani, T5622526, F5622574. *Emirates,* Al Seyagh Centre, Abdali, T4643341. *Gulf Air,* King Hussein St, Abdali (just down hill from Bus Station), T4653613, F4646190. *Iran Air, Nahas Travel and Tourism,* King Hussein St, Downtown, T4630879, F4629333. *KLM,* King Hussein St, Downtown, T4655267, F4622167. *Kuwait,* Strand Centre, Sharif Abdul Hameed Sharaf St (next door to *Ambassador* hotel), Shmeisani, T5690144, F5697144. *Lufthansa,* Ilya Abu Madhi St, Shmeisani, T5601744. MEA, King Hussein St, Downtown, T4636104. *Olympic, Grand Travel,* Wasfi al-Tal (Gardens) St, northwest of Shmeisani, T5682140. *Palestinian Airlines, Al Karmel Travel & Tourism,* King Hussein St, Downtown, T4653691, F4653693. *PIA, Jordan International for Travel & Tours,* King Hussein St, Downtown, T4625981, F4615721. *Quantas, Hashweh Corporation,* Swafiyeh, T5828801, F5862277. *Royal Jordanian,* Head Office, Housing Bank Complex, Queen Noor St, Shmeisani, T5607300, F5672527. Sales offices around Amman include *Inter-Continental* hotel, Zahran St, between 2nd and 3rd Circle, Jabal Amman, T4644266, F4642152; King Hussein St, Abdali (up hill from Bus Station), T5663525; Amman City Terminal, 7th Circle, T5856835, F5851875; Jordan University, T5346868; Queen Alia International Airport (information), T644532000. *Royal Wings,* Marka Airport, T4875201, F4875656 (or book/reconfirm through any *Royal Jordanian* office). *Saudi,* King Hussein St, Abdali (just down hill from Bus Station), T4639333. *Sudan, Alpha International,* Strand Centre, Sharif Abdul Hameed Sharaf St (next door to *Ambassador* hotel), Shmeisani, T5667100, F5669555. *Swissair, Near East Tourist Centre, Inter-Continental* hotel, Zahran St, between 2nd and 3rd Circle, Jabal Amman, T4641906, F4659792. *Syrian Arab, Seikly Travel & Tourism,* Prince Mohammad St (near *Jordan Towers* complex), T4622147, F4622148. *Tarom*

(Romanian), *Petra Travel & Tourism*, Sharif Abdul Hameed St (near *Commodore* hotel), Shmeisani, T5667028. *Thai*, 24 Sherif Abdul Hameed Sharaf St (same building as Danish consulate), Shmeisani, T5699701. *Turkish*, Riyadh Centre, Al Hussein Bin Ali St, near 3rd Circle, T4659102. *TWA*, *Khoury Travel Agency*, 61 King Hussein St, T4623430, F4622684.

Banks   There are numerous banks, both Jordanian and international, all across Amman which will change cash and TCs. Bank hrs are generally Sun-Thu 0830-1530, closed Fri and Sat. Although exchange rates are fairly similar, commissions vary enormously and are ridiculously high in some cases. Current exchange rates for most major currencies are listed daily (except Fri/Sat) in the *Jordan Times*. The majority of banks now have ATMs (cash-point machines) which between them accept most major international credit/debit cards, making this a good way to carry your money in Jordan. Many places that cash TCs will ask to see the original purchase receipts in addition to your passport – so much for the idea of keeping them separate. Note that although there are representatives for both *American Express* and *Thomas Cook* in Amman, they are travel agents and cannot cash TCs, not even their own. For changing TCs, the Downtown branch of *Arab Bank*, on King Faisal St, offers the best deal. Service is fairly efficient (go straight up to the 1st floor), although they do not receive the daily rate until around 1030. For TCs up to a value of US$500 they do not charge any commission at all (likewise for cash to any value). For TCs from US$500-1,000 in value there is a US$3 postage charge. The ATM here accepts *Visa* and *Mastercard*. Their head office is in Shmeisani, with other branches and ATMs across the city, including Jabal al-Weibdeh (Luweibdeh Circle, near the *Centre Culturel Français*); Abdali (at the top end of the Bus Station); Jabal Amman (*Inter-Continental* hotel, Zahran St, between 2nd and 3rd Circle); and Abdoun (Qahira St, opposite the *Sheraton Entertainment Centre*). The *Union Bank*, with a branch on Al Ridha St, Downtown, also changes TCs without charging a commission.

For ATM withdrawals, the *HSBC* (formerly *British Bank of the Middle East*) is the most convenient, as its ATMs accept *Visa*, *Cirrus*, *Mastercard*, *+Plus* and *Global Access*. They have a branch on King Hussein St, Downtown (around 200 m up the hill from the junction with Prince Mohammad St), with others across the city, including Shmeisani (Al Istiqlal St, just northeast of Jamal 'Abd an-Nasir Interchange) and Abdoun (right on Abdoun Circle). Other banks with branches and ATMs around the city include *Jordan National Bank* (*Mastercard*), Housing Bank (*Visa*, *+Plus*), *ANZ Grindlays* (*Visa*) and *Citibank*. *Western Union Money Transfer* is through the Cairo-Amman Bank, though this is an expensive way to have money wired to you. This bank also has perhaps the most outrageous commission charges; US$10 for cash or TCs! *Thomas Cook* are represented by *Space Tourism & Travel*, Ilya Abu Madhi St, Shmeisani, T5668069, F5688919, space@go.com.jo. In case of lost or stolen TCs, you must first contact Thomas Cook directly using the number they provide. They will then fax through authorisation for Space Tourism and Travel to issue new ones. *American Express* are represented by *International Traders*, 58 Sherif Abdul Hameed Sharaf St, Shmeisani, PO Box 408, T5607014, F5687183, guest@traders.com.jo In case of lost or stolen TCs, they will call the relevant Amex office themselves for authorisation to issue replacements. They also offer a clients' mail service. For changing cash the easiest option is to go to one of the numerous licensed **money changers** to be found around the Downtown area, particularly along King Faisal St. Their rates are generally only fractionally lower than the banks (although you should shop around as they do vary) and they offer a lightening quick service. They also stay open well into the evening (usually until around 2100 in summer), and there are always at least 1 or 2 which open on Fri and Sat mornings. Most will also change TCs, offering lower rates than the banks, but without charging commission. As a last resort, most larger **hotels** will change cash and TCs, though their rates are generally well below the bank rate and the commission charged on TCs amounts to licensed banditry.

Communications   **Internet** The number of internet cafés in Amman is growing rapidly, and prices for internet access falling steadily. In addition to the independent outfits listed below, many hotels now offer internet access, though their rates are generally more expensive. Many of the foreign Cultural Centres also offer internet access. Again, their rates are more expensive, although the working environment is generally more pleasant and if you are going to be in Amman for a long time they have good membership-based deals (eg *British Council*, 1 year membership – JD25 – gives you 12 hrs free access, then JD6 per 12 hrs after that; *American Center*, 1 year membership – JD10 – gives you free access for up to 1 hour per session). There are also various internet cafés to be found along the main road opposite the university although, unless you are already in this area, they are too far from the centre to be of practical use. AICCO, King Faisal St (next door to Arab bank), Downtown,

T4648649. Open 1000-2400. Situated up on the first floor, above *Sahloul* money changers. The most conveniently located of the Downtown internet cafés, with 9 terminals (more planned), though rather cramped and smoky. JD1 per hour (minimum 30 mins), or buy time in advance; JD4 for 5 hrs, JD7 for 10 hrs, JD10 for 15 hrs, JD14 for 20 hrs. Also acts as an agent for *TNT*.

Al Saha, Hashemi St, opposite Roman Theatre, Downtown. Open 24 hrs. One of a number of similar functional and smoky places to be found along this stretch of Hashemi St. JD1 per hr (minimum 30 mins), or buy time in advance; JD7.500 for 10 hrs, JD10 for 15 hrs, JD12.500 for 20 hrs. ***Books@Café,*** Omar Bin al-Khattab (Mango) St, Jabal Amman, T4650457. Open 1000-2300. (See also under Cafés). One of the first internet cafés to open in Amman, and far and away the most pleasant (indeed, the only one to pay any attention whatsoever to the café side of the equation), but also the most expensive (JD2 per hr, minimum 30 mins, or buy time in advance; JD25 for 20 hrs). *Dot Com*, Kulliyat al-Sharee'ah St, Jabal al-Weibdeh (near *Centre Culturel Français*), T4659593. Open 1100-2400. Clean, pleasant place, 11 terminals (new machines), not too cramped and with a no smoking policy which will come as a welcome relief to choking non-smokers. JD1 per hr (minimum 30 mins), or JD10 for 12 hrs per month, or monthly membership of JD5 plus 500 fils per hr. *Internet Yard,* Prince Mohammad St (just down from junction with 9th Sha'ban St), Downtown (sign out on street just says 'Internet'; café is inside the small arcade of shops below). Small outfit with 6 terminals. JD1 per hr (minimum 30 mins), or buy time in advance; JD4 for 5 hrs, JD7 for 10 hrs, JD10 for 13 hrs etc.JAI, 3rd Circle, Jabal Amman, T4617764. Open 24 hrs. Located up on the 4th floor, in building next door to *Razan* hotel, right on 3rd Circle. Spartan and smoky place, but friendly, with 8 terminals. JD1 per hr (minimum 30 mins), or buy time in advance; JD6 for 10hrs, JD10 for 20 hrs, JD20 for 50 hrs etc.

Post   The Central Post Office is towards the bottom of Prince Mohammad St, near its junction with King Faisal St, Downtown (a short walk up from the *Cliff* hotel, on the right). Open Sat-Thu 0800-1900, Fri 0800-1300. The poste restante service is a box placed on the counter, available to all. If you wish to send a parcel, first take it unwrapped to the Parcel Post Office on Omar al-Khayyam St, behind the Central Post Office for weighing. You will then be directed to the customs department across the road for a cursory search, and to sign a customs declaration form, before returning to the Parcel Post Office for packaging and payment. There are a number of .branch post offices dotted around other districts of Amman, including Jabal Amman (at the *Inter-Continental* hotel on Zahran St between 2nd and 3rd Circle, and on Rainbow St opposite the Saudi embassy near 1st Circle); Jabal al-Weibdeh (on Kulliyat al-Sharee'ah St, a short walk west from Luweibdeh Circle and the *Centre Culturel Français*); and Shmeisani (in the basement of the Housing Bank Centre).

Courier service   There are a number of international courier companies based in Amman, providing a much safer (though very expensive) way to send valuable items compared with the parcel post service. If you are heading for Syria, bear in mind that courier services there are significantly cheaper. *DHL*, 7th Circle, T5818351. *FedEx*, Abu Saud Centre, Ash Sharif Abdul Hameed St, Shmeisani, F5695415, F5695720. *TNT Worldwide*, Zahran St, between 4th-5th Circle, T5703966 (also with an agent at the *AICCO* internet café in Downtown).

Telephone   Alo and JPP card phones (see page 43 for more details) are distributed liberally all over Amman, though finding a kiosk which is in a reasonably quiet location can be difficult. If you are staying in Downtown, there is a good Alo card phone at the top of the stairway leading up past the entrance to the *Riviera* hotel; during the evenings at least, when there are fewer service taxis struggling up the steep slopes of Jabal al-Weibdeh, this is probably the quietest one in the area. Nearby, along Omar al-Khayyam St (in the vicinity of the old government-run central telephone office), there are a few private telephone offices, though these cost around twice as much the card phones for international calls. International (and national/local) calls can also be made from almost all hotels, though the rates charged by the luxury hotels (and some mid-range hotels) can be exhorbitant, so be sure to check first. The budget hotels are generally more reasonable (comparable with the private telephone offices). Most private telephone offices and nearly all hotels can also send/receive faxes for you, as can the Central Post Office in Downtown (see below). For **mobile phone hire**, try Rent-a-Link, Zaid Bin Harethah St, near 2nd Circle, Jabal Amman, T4656593. The require a deposit of JD50 on the phone, plus around JD100 against call charges.

The foreign cultural centres listed below are primarily geared towards providing language courses and information on their respective countries for Jordanians, but are also of interest to tourists for their newspapers and magazines, internet facilities (see also under Communications, above), film nights (see also under Entertainment above), cultural programmes and spoken Arabic courses.

Cultural centres

Amman

American Center, 79 Al Umawiyeen St, Abdoun, PO Box 359, T5920101, F5920121, www.usembassy-amman.org.jo. Part of the enormous US embassy complex. Library open Sun-Wed 1300-1700, Thur 0900-1700, closed Fri and Sat. Includes an extensive collection of periodicals, from *Time* and *Newsweek* to more scholarly regional journals such as *Middle East International, ME Journal, ME Report* etc. Annual membership costs JD10, allowing you to borrow books and get internet access for free. Check the embassy website or get hold of their monthly magazine *Dimensions* for details of current films and cultural events. **British Council,** Abu Bakr as-Siddiq (Rainbow) St, near 1st Circle, Jabal Amman, T4636147, F4656413, www.britishcouncil.org/jordan. Library open Sat 1100-1900, Sun-Wed 1000-1900, Thu 1000-1500, closed Fri. Includes a selection of British newspapers and periodicals. Annual membership costs JD25, allowing you to borrow books and access the internet. Check their website or get hold of their monthly newsletter for details of current films and cultural events. Copies of the *Friends of Archaeology* newsletter are also usually available here. *Centre Culturel Français*, 4 Kulliyat al-Sharee'ah (College) St, Jabal al-Weibdeh, T4612658, F4630061, cccljor.citeweb.net Open Sat 1330-1945, Sun-Wed 1100-1945, Thu 1030-1300, 1500-1945, closed Fri. More active than most on the cultural front, with a continuous programme of exhibitions, films, music, conferences and social gatherings. Check their website or get hold of their bi-monthly *agenda culturel* pamphlet for current details.

Goethe Institute (German Cultural Centre), 5 Abdul Mune'm al-Rifa'i St (off Al Hussein Bin Ali St), near 3rd Circle, T4641993, F4612383, giammvw@go.com.jo Open Sun-Wed 0900-1300, 1600-2000, Thur 0830-1400, closed Fri and Sat. *Instituto Cervantes* (Spanish Cultural Centre), behind *Inter-Continental Hotel*, near 3rd Circle, Jabal Amman, T4610858, F4624049, www.cervantes.es Open Sun-Thur 0900-1300, 1600-1900, closed Fri and Sat.

Embassies & Unless otherwise stated, all the below are embassies. Embassy hours are generally Sun to Thu from
consulates 0800 or 0900 to 1200 or 15000, closed Fri and Sat, though some close Fri and Sun, and others Fri only. All seem to subscribe to an unspoken international convention of inscrutable unhelpfulness. *Australia*, 13 Ameen Mar'i St, just off Zahran St (next door to the Ministry of Social Development, with its distinctive blue sign), between 4th and 5th Circle, PO Box 35201, T5930246, F5931260, ausemb@nets.com.jo *Austria*, 36 Mithqal al-Fayez St, between 3rd and 4th Circle, T4644635. *Canada,* Abdul Hameed Shoman St, Shmeisani, T5666124, F5689227. *Denmark* (consulate), 24 Sharif Abdul Hameed Sharaf St, Shmeisani, PO Box, 222, T5603703, F5672170 (nearest full embassy in Damascus). *Egypt*, 22 Qurtabah St, off Zahran St between 4th and 5th Circle (close to the *Dove* hotel), T5605200, F5604082 (see box). *France,* entrance at 36 Al Mutanabbi St (behind ambassador's residence on Zahran St), between 3rd and 4th Circle, T4641273, F4659606, www.ambafrance.org.jo *Germany*, 25 Banghazi St, between 4th and 5th Circle, T5930351, F5932887 (emergency number 079-534261). *India*, Al Imam Maalek St, near 1st Circle, Jabal Amman, T4622098, F4659540. *Iraq*, 16 Al Kulliyah al-Ilmiyah al-Islamiyah (Zahran) St, between 1st and 2nd Circle, T4623175, F4619172 (see box). *Ireland* (consulate), 109 King Hussein St, Downtown, T4614268, T/F4630878. *Israel*, *Meridien* hotel, Queen Noor St, Shmeisani, T5524686, F5524689. *Italy*, 5 Hafiz Ibrahim St, Jabal al-Weibdeh, T4638185, F4659730. *Japan*, 26 Tarablus al-Gharb St, between 4th and 5th Circle, T5932005, F5931006. *Lebanon,* 17 Mohammad Ali Bdeir St, Abdoun, T5929111, F5929112 (see box). *Morocco,* 17 Al Iskanderounah St, Abdoun, T5921771, F5925185. *New Zealand* (consulate), 4th floor, Khalaf Building, 101 King Hussein St, Downtown, PO Box 586, T4636720, F4634349 (nearest full embassy Ankara, Turkey). *Norway*, 25 Dimashq St, Abdoun, T5931646, F5931650.*Pakistan*, Al Akhtal St, Jabal al-Weibdeh, T4624680, F4611633. *Palestine*, 27 Qurtabah St, off Zahran St between 4th and 5th Circle, T5677517, F5661727. *Saudi Arabia*, Abu Bakr as-Siddiq (Rainbow) St, near 1st Circle, Jabal Amman, T4630338. *South Africa,* 15 Mohammad al-Mahdi St, Abdoun, T5922288, F5920080. *Spain,* 17 Zahran St, between 3rd and 4th Circle, T4614166, F4614173. *Sudan,* Ibrahim al-Qattan St, northwest of 7th Circle, T5854500, F4644187. *Sweden,* 12 Al Sarafat (Embassies) St, near 4th Circle, T5931177, F5930179. *Switzerland,* 19 Al Sarafat (Embassies) St, near 4th Circle, T5931416, F5930689. *Syria*, Tawfiq Abu al-Huda St, between 3rd and 4th Circle, T4641935, F4641945 (see box). *Turkey*, 31 Abbas Mahmoud al-Aqqad St, near 2nd Circle, Jabal Amman, T4641251, F4612353. *UK*, 45 Dimashq St, Abdoun, T5923100, F5923759. USA, 20 Al Umawiyeen St, Abdoun, T5920101, F5920121, www.usembassy-amman.org.jo *Yemen,* Salamah B Hisha St, Abdoun, T4642381.

Getting visas for neighbouring countries in Amman

Egypt *Egyptian visas can take up to two days to be issued at the busy and chaotic Egyptian embassy in Amman (applications 0900-1200, closed Friday, collection 1200-1400). It is quicker and a lot less hassle to make the application at the consulate in Aqaba, where they can be processed the same day if you go early. At the Aqaba consulate (see page 320), one month single entry tourist visas cost JD12 for all nationalities, while multiple entry tourist visas are JD15 (bring one passport photo, as well as a photocopy of your passport details). The Amman embassy sometimes quotes different fees. If you are planning to visit Sinai only, you can obtain a free Sinai Permit on the ferry to Nuweiba, or at the Taba border if you are going via Israel. This is valid for 15 days, but cannot be extended and restricts you to the Sinai's Gulf of Aqaba between Taba and Sharm el-Sheikh. It does not allow you to visit the Ras Mohammad National Park at the southern tip of Sinai, or St Catherine's Monastery (there is confusion amongst officials regarding the latter site and some tourists report being allowed to visit with just a Sinai Permit). Note that, contrary to what embassy or consulate officials may say, it is not possible (or at least difficult) to obtain a full tourist visa on arrival; if you wish to travel beyond the limits of a Sinai Permit, get a full tourist visa in advance.*

Israel *Almost all nationalities are issued with a free tourist visa (consisting effectively of your filled-in 'landing' card) on arrival in Israel (arriving by land you usually get one month, by air three months). Exceptions include nationals of most African and Central American countries, Arab/Muslim nations, India, Singapore and many of the former Soviet republics. Nationals of these countries should apply first to the embassy in Amman (open 0800-1100, closed Friday and Saturday).*

Syria *It is almost impossible for foreign tourists to get a Syrian visa in Amman. The only people officially being issued with Syrian visas here are Jordanians, or those with permanent Jordanian residency. The only possible exception to this rule is if there is no Syrian embassy in your home country (as is the case with Australia and New Zealand*

for example). However, the Syrian embassy is far from consistent on this point and, even assuming that they do concede, you will have to do battle with their Kafka-esque bureaucracy in order to get the visa. Be safe and get your visa before coming to Jordan (Syrian visas are available in Cairo and Ankara, although they are much easier to obtain in your home country). Contrary to some rumours, it is impossible to get a Syrian visa on the Jordanian-Syrian border (or any other entry point to Syria for that matter). Note also that even if you have already obtained a Syrian visa, if there is any evidence in your passport of a visit to Israel, you will be refused entry (see Essentials for more details).

Lebanon *The Lebanese embassy in Amman issues tourist visas with a minimum of fuss. A one month single entry tourist visa costs JD14 for all nationalities, or JD28 for a three month multiple entry (bring one passport photo, as well as a photocopy of your passport details). The consular section is open for applications 0800-1100, closed Friday and Saturday. Visas can be collected the following working day between 1330-1400. Tourist visas are also issued at all points of entry into the country. There is no Lebanese embassy in Syria. As with Syria, the Lebanese will not issue you with a visa, or allow you entry into the country, if there is evidence in your passport of a visit to Israel.*

Saudi Arabia *The Saudi authorities do not issue tourist visas as such, but those wishing to travel overland through into Africa can apply for a transit visa (it is currently impossible to cross from Egypt into Sudan). Travellers' experiences in dealing with the Saudi embassy in Amman vary greatly, and you are strongly advised to apply in your home country. During the period between Ramadan and the annual Hajj, it appears to be almost impossible to obtain a Saudi transit visa in Amman.*

Iraq *Obtaining tourist visas to visit Iraq is extremely difficult (surprise, surprise). Determined efforts in February 2000 by a couple with British/Dutch passports eventually produced an offer of tourist visas, on condition that they joined a US$500 per day luxury tour.*

Amman

Medical services   **Chemists**: The *Jordan Times* publishes a daily list of doctors and chemists (pharmacies) on night duty. Night duty lists are also published outside main chemists (though in Arabic only). In emergency consult your hotel reception or embassy. 2 good 24 hr chemists are Jacob's, on 3rd Circle, T4644945 and Rawhi, near Al-Khalidi Hospital, T4644454. **Hospitals:** There are at least 30 hospitals in Amman, offering a high standard of care and expertise. Phone numbers are listed daily in the *Jordan Times*. The following ones are recommended by major hotels and by foreign embassies in Amman. Amman Surgical, Zahran St, near 3rd Circle, Jabal Amman, T4641261. Al-Khalidi, Ibn Khaldoun St, south of Zahran St between 3rd and 4th Circle, T4644281. Palestine Queen Alia St, near *Marriot* hotel, T5607071. Hussein Medical Centre, Wadi Seer, T5856856. Luzmila, Jabal al-Weibdeh (near *Darat al-Funan*), T4624345.

Language   All of the foreign cultural centres (see above) offer language courses, primarily in their respective
schools   tongues, but most also offer spoken Arabic courses. They also have information on other language schools in Amman.

Laundry   Nearly all hotels can arrange laundry services for their guests if they do not provide it themselves. There are several small independent laundries and dry cleaners to be found around Downtown. An average load at one of these should not cost more than around JD4.

Libraries   The Amman Central Library is situated beside the Roman Theatre in Downtown (occupying the main part of the building that the tourist information is housed in). As well as its extensive Arabic collection it has a reasonable selection of books in English. Open 0900-1700, closed Fri. The foreign cultural centres (see above) all house libraries, as does the Abdul Hameed Shoman Foundation on Jabal Amman, while the Haya Arts Centre in Shmeisani has a good children's library (see under Entertainment). **Specialist**: The Department of Antiquities Museum, near 3rd Circle (see the Western Amman map), T4644320, F4615848, has an excellent library upstairs with an extensive selection of books on the archaeology and history of Jordan. Open 0800-1400, closed Fri. ACOR and CBRL, both out near the University (see under Useful addresses: Archaeology, below), have specialist archaeology/history libraries open to the public. The Darat al-Funan on Jabal al-Weibdeh has an excellent art library.

Travel agents   Almost every business address in Amman that is not a car-hire firm is a travel agent. Many of the airline offices listed above are in fact travel agents; a good number of these are to be found towards the lower end of King Hussein St, in Downtown. They generally deal only with international ticketing. For tour operators, see page 21.

Useful   **Archaeology**: Those interested in archaeology, perhaps wanting to take part in a 'dig', should
addresses &   contact one of the following. American Center for Oriental Research (ACOR), PO Box 2470,
phone numbers   T5346117, F5344181, www.bu.edu/acor. Open 0830-1700, Sat 0830-1200, closed Fri. Their office
Police: T192 (Emergency   is inconveniently situated near the University of Jordan on the northeast outskirts of Amman. To
T191; Traffic accidents   get there head northeast from Jamal 'Abd an-Nasir Interchange along Queen Alia St, going
T4896390). Ambulance: straight at the Sports City Interchange and at the next major junction. When you reach the traffic
T193. Fire: T4622090/93   lights by the university mosque (a distinctive green-domed affair), continue straight on (U-turns
(Emergency T199).   not allowed here), then do a U-turn at the next set of lights. Continue back through the lights by
Tourist Police HQ: the university mosque and then take the first right turn after passing under a pedestrian
T5861271   footbridge. Head straight up the hill and take the second right, towards the top; ACOR is the first building on the right. They have an excellent library and give lectures on current projects and digs in Jordan (see their website for details). Friends of Archaeology, PO Box 2440, near 4th Circle, T/F5930682, http://corp.arabia.com/foa. Open 0900-1500, closed Fri. To get there, head west along Zahran St from 3rd Circle, turn left at 4th Circle and sharp right immediately after (into Embassies St), then turn left by the mosque and then first left after that; the office is opposite the building with a Jordanian flag flying from it. They organize lectures and visits to historical/archaeological sites in Jordan with specialist guides/lecturers (see their website for details, or the British Council usually has copies of their monthly newsletter). Petra National Trust (in same building as *FOA*), T5930338, F5932115, www.petranationaltrust.com. NGO dedicated to the preservation of the cultural heritage and environment of the Petra region. Council for British Research in the Levant (CBRL) (formerly BIAAH), PO Box 519, near University of Jordan, T5341317, F5337197, www.britac.ac/institutes/cbrl/index To get there, follow directions as for *ACOR*, but turn right at the traffic lights by the university mosque, then first left and first right. Follow the road

until it bends round to the left, then take the second right and the office is on the right, on the corner at the bottom of the hill. They have a good library (though for members only) and also offer accommodation for visiting archaeologists and researchers (£17 per night including meals; for more than 1 night you must become a member – £22/11 normal/student; long-term accommodation – more than 1 month – £14 per night). Other bodies include Department of Antiquities, T4644336, F4615848 (see under Libraries). German Protestant Institute for Archaeology (acronym in German; DEIAHL), PO Box 183 (c/o German Embassy), T5342924, F5336924, gpia@go.com.jo. Institute Francais d'Archéologie du Proche-Orient (IFAPO), T4611872, F4643840, ifapo@nets.com.jo. University of Jordan Archaeology Department, T5343555, ext 3739.

Ministry of Tourism & Antiquities Al Moutanabi St, near 3rd Circle, Jabal Amman, T4642311, F4648465. Not the most penetrable of bureaucracies; unless you have a contact name or introduction, they will do their best to fob you off. The public relations department on the ground floor (to your right as you enter the building) is the best place to start.

Conservation RSCN, PO Box 6354 (near University of Jordan), T5337931, F5347411, tourism@rscn.org.jo To get there, follow directions as for *ACOR*, continuing past the traffic lights by the university mosque and turn right at the next set of traffic lights. Turn right again at the first roundabout you come to, and then right again immediately after; the building is on the left. The RSCN can organize guided visits to Jordan's Wildlife Reserves and Protected Areas, as well as accommodation or camping where appropriate.

Motorcycle spares The Suzuki Motorcycle Store (proprietor Hani M Darwish Ahmad), Amphitheatre St (near the Roman theatre), PO Box 6377, Amman 11118, T4651656, stocks spares for the police Suzuki GSXs and other government motorcycles. This is perhaps the only place in Jordan where you can get tyres, inner tubes, chains, batteries etc for anything larger than a 125cc motorcycle.

Visa extensions All foreigners travelling on tourist visas must register with the police within 2 weeks of arrival (unless of course you are staying in Jordan for less than 2 weeks), a simple process usually only taking half an hour or so which effectively extends your visa for 3 months. There is no fee. You should register at the main police station of the district of Amman in which you are staying. If you are staying in Downtown, you should register at the *Muhajireen Police Station*, in a converted mosque near Muhajireen Bus Station, Princess Basma St (take service taxi No 35 from near Church of St Saviour, Downtown, or a local bus from Raghadan Bus Station). Jabal Amman is served by *Zahran Police Station*, near 3rd Circle (on side street more or less opposite *Inter-Continental* hotel); Shmeisani by *Shmeisani Police Station* (see Shmeisani map); Abdali and Jabal al-Weibdeh by the Foreigners' Affairs Department of the *Directorate of Residency and Borders* on Suleiman al-Nabulsi St (just up from King Abdullah Mosque). If you have entered Jordan from Israel without receiving an entry stamp in your passport, you should also go to the Directorate of Residency and Borders; likewise if you wish to apply for a second extension. Since most long-term travellers stay in Downtown, the Muhajireen Police Station deals with more tourists than the others and is therefore the most efficient. Even if you are staying elsewhere, it does no harm to come here and give a Downtown hotel address.

Amman

Around Amman

4

118

Around Amman

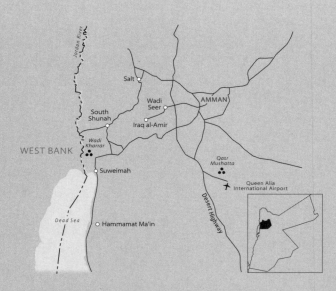

Amman makes for a convenient base from which to explore the surrounding countryside. As well as the sights dealt with here, there are plenty of other places which can be visited as day-trips from the capital. Most spectacular are the Roman ruins at Jerash (see page 150). With your own transport, the Desert Castles to the east of Amman can also be covered in one day (see following chapter), although staying overnight in Azraq allows for a more leisurely circuit. Madaba and Mount Nebo are both within easy reach of the capital (see page 205). As well as Wadi Kharrar (covered here), the other main sites in the Jordan valley (see page 181) are manageable in one long day with your own transport.

Dead Sea

The Dead Sea and the barren, arid hills around it form one of Jordan's most aus-
tere and dramatic natural features. Extending north-south for around 80 km and
up to 18 km wide, the Dead Sea (actually a large lake) comprises part of the Great
Rift Valley which extends from Turkey all the way through into East Africa. Here
can be found the lowest point on earth (more than 400 m below sea level), and a
body of water with the highest salt content in the world (see also page 374). To the
Romans it was known as the lacus asphalitis (sea of asphalt), while Muslim writ-
ers referred to it as Al Bahr Lut ('Sea of Lot') or Al Bahr Sodom ('Sea of Sodom'),
in reference to the biblical stories associated with it. It was the Crusaders who
named it the Dead Sea, an obvious enough label given the almost complete
absence of life in it. For most visitors to the Dead Sea, the main attraction is taking
that obligatory dip in its waters to experience the bizarre sensation of floating on
the surface. The various resorts near the northern end of the Dead Sea are the best
place to do this and, being less than one hour's drive from Amman, make for a
convenient day-trip from the capital. Each offers accommodation and a range of
health treatments associated with the waters and mud of the Dead Sea, or you can
just use their beaches (and more importantly their showers).

Ins and outs

Getting there **By public transport** Given the importance of the Dead Sea as a tourist attraction, public transport facilities are pretty appalling. Providing there is sufficient demand, there are usually 2 buses a day departing in the morning (between around 0700-0800, 600 fils, 1 hr) from Amman's Muhajireen bus station for the *Dead Sea Resthouse* near Suweimah. If these are not running, you have to take a bus from here to South Shunah, and then another one from there to Suweimah. Returning to Amman, ask the tourist police at the *Dead Sea Resthouse* to make sure you get the last bus (usually around 1600). If you miss this, or it is not running, they will help arrange a lift for you as far as South Shunah, from where there are fairly regular services to Amman. There is no public transport to the other resorts to the south of the *Dead Sea Resthouse.*

By private car Head west out of Amman along Zahran St and turn left at 7th Circle (signposted for the airport). Around 6 km after 7th Circle, take the exit clearly signposted for the Dead Sea (going straight takes you onto the Desert Highway, for Queen Alia International Airport and ultimately Aqaba). Keep following this road, past an exit signposted for Madaba, Ma'in spring and Tell Hisban, and then through an almost lunar landscape of barren hills as you begin the descent to the Dead Sea. Look out for a marker to the right of the road indicating sea level. Soon after there is an exit signposted for South Shunah ('Ash Shuna al-Janubiyeh' or 'Shunat Nimrin' on most maps) and King Hussein Bridge. About 5 km further on is the small village of **Al Rameh**, with a petrol station, cafés and simple restaurants clustered around the junction here (turning right at this junction will also take you to South Shunah). Around 500 m beyond the junction there is a left turn clearly signposted for Mount Nebo and Madaba, the start of a newly resurfaced road which snakes its way up through the mountains (see page 213). Continuing straight on, a further 5 km or so brings you to a T-junction. Turn left here (the right turn takes you to Wadi Kharrar/the Baptism Site, see below; the track straight ahead leads to the King Abdullah Bridge crossing into Israel, closed since 1967, and still strictly off-limits in a military zone). After a further 5 km you pass a left turn leading to the village of Suweimah, followed soon after by a right turn for the *Dead Sea Resthouse.* The *Mövenpick Resort and Spa* and the *Dead Sea Spa* hotel are around 5 km further on, while the hot springs at Ain Zarqa and the archaeological site of Callirhoë are another 13 km or so further south.

The Dead Sea has a desert microclimate all its own, combining the extreme heat of the Rift Valley with local features of humidity. Temperatures in summer (Jun-Sep) are very high, averaging 27°-34°C. This may not sound too bad, but these are for conditions in the shade; out in the open it is scorchingly hotter, at times over 56°C! The best months are Oct-late May, when it is very pleasant at around 20°C. At night however temperatures drop significantly. Summer relative humidity in the Rift Valley as a whole is low at 45% but along the sea edge humidity is much higher and the atmosphere can best be described as 'muggy' or 'close' to the point of unbearability. Winter relative humidity rises to over 60%.

Best time to visit

The resorts

For years the only tourist facility on the Jordanian side of the Dead Sea was the rather shabby government-owned *Dead Sea Resthouse*. This was then supplemented by the more upmarket *Dead Sea Spa* hotel, and more recently by the ultra-luxurious *Mövenpick Resort and Spa*. Next to this, the *Marriott* chain are building another luxurious establishment. Compared with the generally overpriced resorts on the Israeli side, all of these are fairly good value for money.

LL *Mövenpick Resort and Spa*, T05-3252030, F05-3252020, www.movenpick-deadsea.com A sprawling, super-luxurious, though on the whole tasteful and creatively designed resort. The lavish main buildings, just off the Dead Sea Highway, house the reception, a bar and restaurant. Spread over the sloping land leading down to the Dead Sea are the accommodation blocks, swimming pools, health spa and numerous other facilities (they even lay on a golf buggy to transport you and your luggage from reception down to your room). Accommodation is in a 'village' of 2-storey chalet-type buildings made from local stone and plaster, following traditional architectural designs. Inside, they are very elegantly and tastefully furnished to the highest standard, as well as sporting all the mod cons you would expect from a luxury hotel. Each has its own balcony or terrace. Restaurant options include the *Al Saraya* (mixed menu; buffet or à la carte), *Chopsticks* (Chinese/oriental), *Luigi's* (Italian) and *The Grill*, and there are various bars and cafés. There are conference, banqueting and business facilities, shopping arcades, a Roman-style amphitheatre (for occasional live entertainment), outdoor swimming pools and tennis courts. The star feature, however, is the *Sanctuary Zara Spa*, managed by the UK-based Sanctuary Spa group and billed as the 'largest and most advanced Spa in the Middle East', with a choice of more than 60 different treatments. Entry to the Spa (open Sun-Wed 0900-1800, Thu-Sat 0900-2100) is JD25 for non-guests (hotel guests JD10), which includes use of the changing/shower facilities outdoor pools, thermariums, hydropool, Dead Sea pools (salt water) and of course the Dead Sea itself. Treatments are extra; as a guide, the one day packages cost JD89-100! After all this, the resort's access to the Dead Sea is somewhat disappointing, consisting of just a tiny patch of pebble beach. It's a long walk down to it, with lots of steps, making disabled access tricky to say the least.

AL *Dead Sea Spa*, T05-546101, F05-546108 (Amman T06-5601554, F06-5688100). Choice of rooms with sea or 'mountain' views, all with a/c, TV/dish, IDD, minibar, attached bath and balcony. There are 2 restaurants, a bar, 2 swimming pools and a reasonably-sized beach. The main emphasis however is on the 'medical centre' offering a variety of skin and health treatments. A JD10 entry fee (or JD15 including lunch; children JD5/9) allows visitors use of the swimming pool, showers and changing facilities. A comfortable, modern, though unremarkable hotel, somewhat overshadowed by the new *Mövenpick* resort. Some refurbishment work to the beach-side facilities in progress at the time of writing. Popular with German package tours.

B *Dead Sea Resthouse*, T05-546110, F05-546112. Accommodation is in reasonably comfortable though somewhat small bungalows with a/c, TV, phone, attached bath and separate sitting room. Room prices (currently JD35 for a double) are

Around Amman

inclusive of breakfast and taxes. **Camping** Is also allowed, either in the car park (suitable for campervans only) or in the grounds (fine for tents), for JD5 per person. Visitors to the resthouse pay a JD2.500 entry fee which allows them use of the swimming pool (under repair at the time of writing), showers and changing facilities. The large restaurant and bar serves mediocre food; bear in mind the 23% tax and service charge which is added to your bill. On Fri and holidays there is usually a set buffet (JD6 per person). Various mud packs and other skin treatments are available. The resort is at its busiest on weekends from Oct-end of May (the rest of the year it is just too hot), and particularly so during Ramadan. Although much in need of refurbishment, the resthouse actually has the best 'beach' and easiest access to the Dead Sea. Just to the north of the resthouse there is another area of **public beach**, with free access and simple shower/changing facilities.

Ain Zarqa If you have your own transport the hot sulphur springs at Ain Zarqa (or 'Zara'), 13 km further south from the *Mövenpick Resort and Spa*, are worth a visit. Look out for the distinctive blue fencing by the road on the left; there are usually also several cars parked here, and people offering camel rides. Here the hot springs of Hammamat Ma'in (see page 216) finally drain into the Dead Sea. At the point where one spring emerges from the rocks, the stream below has been landscaped into three shallow pools with mini-waterfalls between them. On weekends it can get very busy, although this is unfortunately a male-dominated activity. Jordanian women are rarely seen bathing, and if so it is always fully-clothed. This is a good alternative place to go for a float in the Dead Sea, since afterwards you can wash off the salt in the hot springs.

Callirhoë Around 300 m to the south of Ain Zarqa, more blue fencing and a sign mark the archaeological site of Callirhoë, where Herod the Great would venture out from his stronghold of Machaerus (see page 219) to treat his skin diseases. More hot springs emerge from the mountainsides here, used today to irrigate vegetable plots. Above the road you can see a section of wall built of huge blocks of vocanic stone. Excavations have identified this as the remains of a large villa and baths complex. However, other than the foundations and lower courses of walls and several excavation trenches, there is not much for the untrained eye to see here.

Dead Sea/Wadi The road leading south past the Dead Sea resorts and Ain Zarqa springs con-
Arabah tinues on all the way to Aqaba, following first the shores of the Dead Sea and
Highway later the broad Wadi Arabah valley. This highway provides a fast alternative route between Amman and Aqaba, with link roads connecting it with the King's Highway at Kerak and Tafila. There is no public transport (other than a few local services) and, apart from the huge potash lorries which crawl along it, very little traffic. For more details on this route, see page 321.

Wadi Kharrar (the Baptism Site/'Al Maghtas')

Wadi Kharrar is a small spring-fed wadi which flows into the Jordan river around 10 km north of the Dead Sea. Extensive archaeological excavations and research here have identified this in all probability as the elusive 'Bethany beyond the Jordan' mentioned in the Bible, where John the Baptist came to live in the wilderness, where Jesus himself was baptised, and where in an earlier age the Old Testament recounts how Elijah was carried up to heaven in a chariot. The area is still being excavated, but already there are substantial archaeological remains to be seen and the site is receiving lavish attention from the government in the hope that it will become a major pilgrimage centre and tourist attraction.

Ins and outs

At the time of writing there was no public transport to the site itself, but once it is fully open a minibus service from Amman will hopefully be initiated; ask at the tourist visitors centre in Downtown Amman. In the meantime, there are regular buses from Amman's Muhajireen bus station to South Shunah (400 fils, 1 hr), from where you will have to get a private taxi (approximately JD1 return, plus waiting time). A taxi all the way from Amman will cost in the region of JD10-15 for the return trip, depending on how long you spend there. With your own vehicle, the best way to get there from Amman is to drive down as if to the Dead Sea (see page120), but instead of turning left towards Suweimah turn right onto a brand new road clearly signposted for the 'Baptism Site'. The site itself is off to the left of this road after 2 km or so, while the visitors' centre currently under construction (and future site entrance) is 3 km further on.

Getting there

Due to be completed sometime in 2001, the visitors centre is part of a US$8 million development plan for the site. Located a considerable distance away to avoid any unecessary disruption of the site itself, the centre will include a restaurant, café, bar etc, as well as shops and a small museum and interpretation centre. A pathway will wind its way from the visitors centre to Tell Kharrar, and then follow the course of Wadi Kharrar down past the various other archaeological remains and points of interest to the Jordan river. A shuttle bus (perhaps in the form of an electric tram car) will also run from the visitors' centre to Tell Kharrar (and possibly on to the Jordan river) for those who do not want to walk the 2½ km each way. As to the entry fees for the site, these had not been agreed at the time of writing, but if the authorities follow the example of Petra, they are likely to be considerable. At the time of writing there was a temporary visitors' centre close to Tell Kharrar. All visits had to be arranged in advance through the Public Relations department of the Ministry of Tourism and Antiquities in Amman (but check first at the Downtown visitors' centre for current arrangements).

Visitors' centre/entrance

Around Amman

History

Being so close to the Israeli border, Wadi Kharrar lay within a sensitive military area until the 1994 peace treaty, when the army cleared the area of landmines and allowed the Department of Antiquities to carry out a survey. Since then, a Jordanian team of archaeologists led by Dr Mohammad Wahib have uncovered extensive remains, including churches, water cisterns, caves and other buildings. The site shows clear evidence of occupation from the Roman period (1st century AD), though most the surviving structures appear to date from the Byzantine period, with a further period of occupation from the 12th century.

The website www.elmaghtas.com has more detailed information on the excavations and research at Wadi Kharrar

For years scholars and archaeologists have searched for archaeological evidence of the biblical 'Bethany beyond the Jordan' (not to be confused with the Bethany near Jerusalem which was the hometown of Lazarus), a site depicted on the famous Madaba Map of the Holy Land (and known then as *Saphsaphas*), but never identified. The New Testament accounts are clear that John the Baptist settled on the east bank of the river when he went out into the wilderness and began his mission of baptism; *"This all happened at Bethany beyond the Jordan, where John was baptising."* (John 1; 28); *"Then Jesus went back across the Jordan to the place where John had been baptising in the early days. Here he stayed and many people came to him."* (John 10; 40-41). Though not explicitly stated in the New Testament, it was presumably also on the east side that Jesus himself was baptised by John. Certainly, the accounts of travellers from the 4th century onwards indicate that a number of places on the east bank of the Jordan developed into important pilgrimage sites associated with the life of St John and the baptism of Jesus, and also with the Old Testament story of the prophet Elijah (Mar Elias in the Qur'an), who was swept up to heaven in a chariot (2 Kings 2; 11).

In 570 AD, Piacenza writes; *"We arrived in the place where the lord was baptized. This is the place where Elijah was taken up. In that place is the little hill of Hermon. In that part of the Jordan is the spring where John used to baptize, and which is two miles from the Jordan... the whole valley is full of hermits"*. Forty years earlier, Theodosius relates that; *"In the place where the Lord was baptized there is a single marble pillar and on the pillar an iron cross has been fastened. There too the church of St John which the emperor Anastasius built; this church is very lofty, being built above layer chambers, on account of Jordan when it overflows."* The description of the church of St John fits very closely with one of the churches found close to the present course of the Jordan river. That the Jordan river should have changed its course is both highly likely in terms of the topography of the region, and backed up later accounts, such as that of Willibalad in the 8th century; *"Here is now a church raised up on stone columns and under the church it is now dry land where our lord was baptized."*

It seems likely that a pilgrimage route developed between Jericho and Mount Nebo, with the various sites of Wadi Kharrar representing important stops along it. Between the 12th and 18th centuries, Tell Kharrar was occupied by Greek Orthodox monks, before being abandoned (when the area was first de-militarized, it was found that the land in fact still belonged to the Greek Orthodox church). Though there is still a huge amount of work to be done, the excavations so far, together with the historical accounts, certainly indicate that from the Byzantine period onwards at least Wadi Kharrar was recognized as 'Bethany beyond the Jordan'.

Around the site

The Wadi Kharrar site spreads over several square kilometres, and is part of a much wider area of related archaeological research (in all, some 20 sites have been identified between Wadi Kharrar and Mount Nebo). In terms of visible remains, there are three main areas of interest; the complex of churches, baptism pools and related structures on and around Tell Kharrar at the head of the wadi; the large pool and pilgrims' resthouse around halfway down to the Jordan river and the caves in the cliffs just below; and the three churches close to the Jordan river itself.

Tell Kharrar Approaching the site, the land stretching away towards the Jordan river appears largely desolate; a semi-arid plain of stunted bushes and trees crushed beneath oppressive heat in summer. However, by the low mound of Tell Kharrar a spring emerges, feeding a small stream, its bed thick with reeds, tamarisk bushes and even a palm tree, as it flows down the small narrow valley of Wadi Kharrar to the Jordan river.

Close to the tell, on the south side, are a number of structures. To the southwest of the tell are the foundations of a rectangular building with sections of plain mosaic floor remaining, thought to have served as a **prayer hall**. Nearby are the foundations of another rectangular building which has been indentified as a **church** dating from the 4th or 5th century. One of its arches has been reconstructed to give a better idea of its form, and a small fragment of its mosaic floor has also been preserved. Beside the church are restored sections of **water channels** and **settling pools** (for sediment) feeding a large, deep rectangular **cistern** built of well-cut sandstone blocks covered by lime and rendered with plaster. The cistern was originally covered by a barrel vault, a small section of which has been reconstructed, and a small fragment of the mosaic floor which covered the vault has been preserved. Next to the cistern is a deeper **circular cistern** which reaches down to the water table. Further away to the southeast, traces of ceramic pipes and aquaducts have been discovered, and it would appear that water was brought to these cisterns from the nearby Wadi Kafrayn and Wadi al-Ramah. An aquaduct supported on stone pillars is then thought to have carried the water to the pools on Tell Kharrar.

A wooden walkway has been constructed around the tell itself to allow visitors to view the excavations here without damaging them. In all, three pools and two churches have been identified. Stone stairs lead up onto the tell, bringing you first to the **southern pool**, which dates from the Byzantine period (probably 5th or 6th century). Rectangular in shape, with four steps leading down into it, traces of the lime and plaster which lined it can still be seen. The fact that the steps occupy the whole length of one of the short sides of the pool suggests that it was designed for people to immerse themselves in it, rather than simply for water storage.

Higher up on the tell, on the northeast and northwest sides, are two further **pools** of very similar construction and probably also dating from the same period. In the centre of the northeast pool there is a deep well (excavated to 12 m) which was clearly dug in order to tap into the water table, possibly during the Roman period, although this is difficult to confirm. Lower down, on a terrace on the far (north) side of the tell overlooking the wadi, are the remains of the **northern church**. Dated to the late Byzantine period, much of the nave and apse of the church are still covered by mosaic floors with geometric designs, though these have been damaged, probably when the roof of the church collapsed. In the apse is a Greek inscription which reads; "By the help of the grace of Christ our Lord. The whole monastery was constructed in the time of Rhetorius, the most God-beloved presbyter and Abbott. May God the Saviour give him mercy." The **western church** occupies a similar terrace on the western slope of the tell, and probably dates from the same period. Its apse is formed by a perhaps earlier cave cut into the natural rock of the tell under the northwestern pool. Inside there is a lamp niche in the wall. The nave of the church was also originally covered with mosaics, though these have been largely destroyed.

Around 1 km to the west of Tell Kharrar there is a large irregular shaped **pool**. The foundations and lower courses are built rough stone, while the upper courses are of well-cut sandstone. The inside was lined with lime and plaster. A channel from a nearby **spring** led into the north side of the pool, with an outlet on the south side, where there are also steps leading down into it. On the higher ground just to the east of the pool are the foundations of what was perhaps a **pilgrims' resthouse**, consisting of a series of rooms built around a central courtyard. Both the building and the pool date from the Byzantine period. A little further on, low cliffs mark the boundary between the *Ghor* area (the broader plain of the Jordan river) and the *Zor* (the deeper, narrower plain bordering the river on either side). Cut into the chalky lissan marl of these cliffs are two **caves,** each with rooms and niches inside. Clearly, these served as hermits' retreats, though when they were originally built is harder to determine. Stone steps and a wooden stairway and walkway have been built against the cliffs giving access to the caves.

The pool, spring, pilgrims' resthouse and caves

Just 300 m from the present course of the Jordan river, amidst dense tamarisk trees, are the ruins of three churches. At the time of writing, excavations were still

The three churches

Around Amman

An explosive discovery?

For decades pilgrims have flocked to one of two sites in Israel and the Palestinian territories which lay claim to be the place where Jesus was baptised, though neither has a shred of evidence to support their claims. Though there is still much work to be done, the Jordanian site appears to have a firm archaeological basis for its claim, strongly supported both by biblical sources and the contemporary accounts of writers over the centuries. The Jordanian government has set great store by this new discovery and invested vast amounts of money in excavating and preserving the remains and developing

Wadi Kharrar as a pilgrimage site, hoping for a share of the huge revenues Israel earns through 'pilgrimage tourism'. Perhaps with a touch of paranoia, the Jordanian Department of Antiquities has undertaken sole responsibility for the excavations at Wadi Kharrar, fearing that if foreign archaeological missions were brought in they could come under pressure from Israel to deny the authenticity of the site. At the same time, foreign teams have been somewhat reluctant (more understandably perhaps) to get involved with excavating a site once riddled with landmines.

ongoing here and the site consisted of a rather confusing jumble of ruins and excavation trenches. The first church (largely ruined) is thought to be **John the Baptist Church**, which Theodosius states was built during the reign of the emperor Anastasius (491-518 AD). The church was raised up on pillars and arches in order to allow the Jordan river to flow underneath in times of flood, though ultimately the foundations appear to have been undermined (either by flood or earthquake), causing the church to collapse. Adjacent to this are the two remaining **churches**, one built on top of the other. A square reservoir was built over the ruins of these churches during the Islamic era. An excavation trench in this reservoir has reached down to the floor of the lower (earlier) church, which was paved with marble tiles, traces of which can be seen. A broken marble column can also be seen in the trench, reused from the earlier church in foundations of the later one. Near the square reservoir is a small fragment of well-preserved mosaic floor from the later church. Adjacent to the two churches is another area of mosaic floor which has been badly damaged by falling stone blocks, perhaps due to an earthquake. Just to the east of the two churches is a terrace, originally paved with marble, with steps leading down on the east side. It seems likely that the terrace and steps were for baptisms, either in the Jordan river itself (assuming that it did indeed once flow directly past the churches), or else in the waters of a nearby spring which is still active today.

Jordan river A tour of a site such as this would hardly be complete without a visit to the Jordan river itself (which hopefully will be allowed when the site fully opens). But for all its vast historic and symbolic importance, the Jordan here is in reality just a small, muddy and altogether unassuming stream where you find yourself all of a sudden nose to nose with an Isreali military post on the other side, and next to it a small Greek Orthodox chapel marking the Israeli/Palestinian version of the baptism site. That chapel, however, is a 20th century construction (built when the West Bank still belonged to Jordan) and, despite protracted efforts, no ancient ruins have been discovered here. Ruins of a church on the Jordanian side are reported to have existed up until 1900, but were subsequently completely swept away. Bits of twisted metal and concrete rubble by the river are all that remains of a bridge destroyed during the 1967 war.

Wadi Seer: Iraq al-Amir and Qasr al-Abd

This is an easy excursion which only takes a few hours if you have your own transport. The green and fertile valley of Wadi Seer makes for a pleasant contrast to all the congestion and concrete of Amman, while the restored ruins of the impressive Tobiad palace of Qasr al-Abd and the picturesque village of Iraq al-Amir with its various handicrafts projects are both well worth a visit.

Getting there by public transport   Fairly regular minibuses run from Muhajireen bus station in Amman as far as Wadi Seer village. From the village there is a somewhat erratic service on to Iraq al-Amir and Qasr al-Abd. Fris are the best day since there are usually plenty of people heading out there for picnics and so services are more frequent.

By private car   Head west out of Amman along Zahran St and keep going straight through 4th, 5th, 6th, 7th and 8th Circle (the latter junction is signposted straight ahead for Wadi Seer), after which the road descends steeply to Wadi Seer (12 km), a small town which still has a predominantly Circassian population. Entering Wadi Seer, follow the road sharply round to the right, and then turn left immediately after (part of the one-way system through the town). A little further on, the road again works its way round a one-way block. Immediately after this, bear right at a small roundabout. The road descends steeply to cross the Wadi Seer River (16 km); on the right by the bridge is a section of arched **aqueduct**. Having crossed the river, up on the hillside to your left can be seen the rock-cut façade known as **Ed Deir** (literally 'The Monastery'), with a newly built stone stairway snaking steeply up to it. Despite the name, its origins and purpose are not known, although it is generally agreed that it probably served as a dovecote in ancient times. To reach it, double back and take the sharp right immediately after the river, and then walk from the small village nearby. The main road continues west, winding its way along the right bank of the picturesque Wadi Seer, to arrive at the village of **Iraq al-Amir**, off to the left of the road (21 km). Just over 1 km further on are the ruins of **Qasr al-Abd**.

Arriving at Iraq al-Amir, a signpost points left from the road to "Iraq al-Amir Handicrafts Village". To the right of the road here there are some **caves** which have been carved into the cliff-face. It is from these caves that the village takes its name, Iraq al-Amir translating as the 'Caves of the Prince'. The large, carefully carved rectangular doorway which stands out from the rest leads into a network of rooms. Inscriptions in Aramaic suggest that the caves were carved by members of the Tobiad Dynasty (see below). They probably served as a defensive refuge against attack, and perhaps also as tombs. A newly built stone stairway leads up to the various caves, although, aside from their importance from an epigraphic point of view, there is not that much to see. More interesting is the **'Handicrafts Village'**, part of the Wadi Seer Community Development Project established by the Noor al-Hussein Foundation to help regenerate the village and provide local women with additional sources of income. Heading into the village, to the left of the small mosque is a carefully restored complex of Ottoman-period buildings housing workshops for **handmade paper** and **ceramics**. The paper workshop is the first of its kind in Jordan and produces beautiful cards and other paper products. The ceramics workshop produces a variety of pottery and ceramic wares, some very nice, although there are perhaps rather too many kitschy souvenirs. Going straight ahead at the mosque takes you past a **weaving** centre on the right, where you can see beautiful shawls etc being woven on small wooden looms. A little further on is a **food processing** centre, where locally available items such as *zarta*, figs, olives etc are prepared. There are delicious miniature pizzas on sale here, as well as cold drinks. Further on, at the end of the village, there are fantastic

Ins & outs

Iraq al-Amir

Around Amman

views out over Wadi Seer and Qasr al-Abd. Much of this end of the village is in ruins, the beautiful Ottoman buildings crying out for restoration. One contains a standing column section, believed to be part of an earlier Byzantine church, and has been earmarked for excavation. There are plans to further develop the handicrafts enterprises here by establishing workshops for woodworking, ironworking and perhaps also glass making. All the handicrafts here can be bought directly from the workshops, and are also available at the Noor al-Hussein Foundation's **Jordan Design and Trade Centre** showroom/shop in Amman (see also page 102).

Qasr al-Abd   Standing in the centre of a broad, level terrace of land is a large reconstructed palace known locally as the Qasr al-Abd (literally 'Palace of the Servant'). Although visited by various European travellers in the 19th century, the first detailed description of the site was given by Butler's Princeton archaeological expedition in 1904, and it was not until 1976 that work started on its restoration. French archaeologists spent three years cataloguing all the stone blocks which lay scattered on the ground, and then a further seven years were spent on the reconstruction itself. As to the origins and purpose of the building, most scholars agree that it was built by Hyrcanus, a member of the locally powerful Tobiad Dynasty, in the 2nd century BC. Writing in 93AD, Josephus (*Antiquities XII, 230*) describes how Hyrcanus *"built a strong fortress which was constructed entirely of white marble up to the very roof, and had beasts of gigantic size carved on it..."*. Hyrcanus is known to have been driven from Jerusalem early in the 2nd century BC and this is where he is believed to have established himself. According to Josephus the building was called *Tyros*, literally 'mountain' or 'rock' in Greek; in Arabic this becomes *seir*, hence the name of the valley. Opinions are divided as to whether the building was in fact a palace or a temple, or perhaps a combination of the two, though most now agree that it served as a palace. The tiny rooms which occupied the ground floor were almost certainly used as storage, with the upper floor used for accommodation or religious functions. The building probably formed part of a substantial estate and is thought to have been surrounded by a lake, with a network of aqueducts supplying water to orchards and fields. Having been defeated by the Seleucid forces of Aniochus IV in 175 BC, Hyrcanus committed suicide, leaving the Qasr al-Abd still uncompleted and soon after the Tobiad Dynasty appears to have died out. During the Byzantine period the building was again occupied, perhaps as a monastic settlement, and substantial modifications were carried out. It was however completely destroyed by an earthquake in 362 AD.

The site is today enclosed within a fence and there is a small shop selling cold drinks, biscuits etc by the entrance. There is no entrance fee as such, but the palace is kept locked and the caretaker who will no doubt appear to open it up for you will expect around JD1 for his troubles. The most intriguing features are the carved reliefs of lions on the huge blocks of the outside walls. Two of these (in fact more resembling panthers), one in either side wall at ground level, are well preserved and now protected by an iron railing, while on top of the far side wall from the entrance is an excellently preserved relief of a lion suckling a cub. What also stands out about the building is the shape of the stone blocks from which it is constructed; although these measure as much as 6 m by 3 m, they are all less than 1 m thick, suggesting that it was never meant to serve as a defensive structure. The unusual proportions of these blocks made it particularly susceptible to the earthquake which destroyed it in the 4th century. Beside the palace there is a small museum which the caretaker will also open up for you. Inside there are various photographs of the site before it was reconstructed (giving a sobering insight into the enormity of the task which the French archaeologists faced), as well as a translation of the extract from Josephus' Antiquities in which he tells the story of the Tobiads. The centre-piece, however, is the video presentation, which gives details (in English, French and Arabic) of the history, architecture and reconstruction of the ruins, complete with funky computer-generated images showing the original layout of the two floors.

Salt

The small town of Salt, situated 29 km to the northwest of Amman, provides intriguing glimpses of a bygone age. It is richly endowed with beautiful Otto-man-period buildings and retains a quieter, more easygoing pace of life that is altogether absent in the capital (and most other Jordanian towns and cities for that matter). The museum and handicrafts training centre are both well worth a visit, but otherwise Salt's real charm is best appreciated simply by admiring the fine Ottoman architecture, exploring the narrow souks in the centre, and the stairways which climb the steep hillsides, or joining the locals whiling away the day in one of the many traditional cafés to be found here.

Ins & outs
There are regular minibus services between Amman's Abdali or Raghadan bus sta-tions and Salt (200 fils, 45 mins). You can also get minibuses from Salt to Deir Alla in the Jordan Valley, and to South Shunah, from where there is regular transport to the King Hussein (Allenby) Bridge crossing into Israel, and south to the Dead Sea. For details of the route from Amman, see page 184. The town itself is small enough to be easily explored on foot.

Like Amman, Salt is built on several hills, each of which originally represented a separate village. Inhabited at least from the Byzantine era onwards, a large fortress was built on one of the hills during the early 13th century. The fortress was destroyed by the Mongols in 1260 but rebuilt a year later by the Mameluke Sultan Baibars. Under Ottoman rule Salt was an important administrative cen-tre and a large barracks was built on the site of the fortress. This was also where King Abdullah I had his residence in the early years of his reign. The town was originally earmarked to become the capital of Jordan, but due in part to the resistance of the local people, Amman was chosen instead. King Abdullah moved to Amman and his palace became the town's first school.

Salt Archaeological Museum
The beautiful Ottoman-period building in which the Salt Archaeological Museum is housed belonged originally to Ibrahim Tokham, the grandfather of Queen Alia. Inside is a small but interesting collection of pottery, glassware, jewellery, coins and other items spanning the Iron Age through to the Islamic period, including the head from a Roman Statue and reproductions of busts found at Amman, Jerash and Umm Qais. Upstairs is a courtyard with various fragments of decorated mosaic floors arranged around it, and two rooms with rather contrived 'ethnographic' displays depicting scenes of traditional every-day life (weaving, grinding wheat, making coffee etc), along with pieces of fur-niture, rugs and traditional costumes. ■*Open 0800-1200, 1300-1800, Fri 0800-1200. Entry free. If coming from the bus station, head uphill along the main road; keep going straight and the museum is on the right after around 500 m.*

Salt Handicrafts Training Centre
Adjacent to the mosque in the centre of town is the Salt Handicrafts Training Centre, funded by the Noor al-Hussein Foundation and Salt Development Corporation. The centre trains students in traditional pottery, ceramics, silk

screen and weaving techniques. Visitors are welcome to wander round the extensive ceramics and pottery workshop, which processes its own clay from raw materials gathered from the Jordan Valley and Madaba areas, and produces some very beautiful decorated ceramic and pottery wares (tiles, vases, plates etc). The silk screen and weaving workshops are on a smaller scale, but also impressive. The best students are employed by the centre to produce wares for the Noor al-Hussein Foundation. There is also a small shop here selling pottery, ceramics and silk screen and woven fabrics. The goods on sale here are discounted, being items which have been made by the students undergoing training; the top-quality stuff goes to the Noor al-Hussein Foundation's *Jordan Design and Trade Centre* showroom/shop in Amman (see page 102). ■*Open 0800-1500, closed Fri and Sat. Entry free. T05-3551781. Coming from the bus station, head uphill along the main road and take the second left (shortly before the museum) and it is on the left.*

Qasr Mushatta

You must have your passport with you as you will be required to leave it at one of the checkposts along the perimeter road

Although this is really one of the so-called 'Desert Castles' which are covered separately under the East of Amman chapter, Qasr Mushatta is not directly on the circuit which covers the other main ones. Located on the north perimeter of the Queen Alia International Airport, it can be conveniently visited as a short excursion from Amman if you have your own transport. Without your own transport, you would need to hire a private taxi, which is expensive and not really worth it for this site.

Arriving at the entrance to the airport (see page 322 for details of the route along the Desert Highway to the airport turn-off), you must make an anti-clockwise circuit of the entire perimeter to reach the site, a distance of 10 km. This was originally the largest of the palaces built by the Umayyads, probably by Walid II in the 8th century. However like Qasr Tuba, it was never finished. More importantly, the decoration on the façade of the palace was donated to Kaiser Wilhelm by the Ottoman Sultan Abd al-Hamid shortly before WW1 and shipped off to Germany where it can still be seen in the Pergamum Museum in Berlin. Little remains of the 145 m square surrounding walls. Fragments of the richly decorated façade can still be seen dotted around the palace itself. Unlike the other Desert Castles, much of this palace was built of burnt brick. Although what survives of it is visually quite impressive, it is only a shadow of its former self.

East of Amman

5

East of Amman

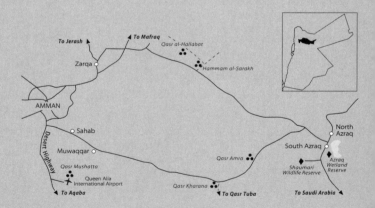

To the East of Amman are the vast expanses of the Arabian desert, extending far into Iraq and Saudi Arabia. Although seemingly fiercely inhospitable and totally bereft of life, these expanses have been traversed for centuries by nomadic tribes, for whom this wilderness is home. Indeed, the Umayyads, who assumed the Caliphate in the second half of the 7th century following the Arab Muslim rise to power in the Middle East, were first and foremost nomads. Despite adopting Damascus as their capital, they retained a strong attachment to their desert roots, maintaining numerous desert complexes, many of which still survive today in varying states of ruin in the deserts of Jordan and Syria. The exact purpose of these complexes, often adapted from pre-existing Roman fortresses, is not entirely clear and appears to have varied from place to place. Some served as agricultural settlements, trading stations, or perhaps frontier outposts designed to exert control over the newly conquered tribes of the deserts. Others appear to have been lavish miniature palaces where the Umayyad rulers could escape from the pressures of city life and indulge themselves. Several of these so-called 'Desert Castles' can be visited in a convenient loop by heading east into the desert from Zarqa (just to the northeast of Amman) as far as the oasis settlement of Azraq, and then returning by a more southerly road. An added attraction are the two impressive conservation projects at Azraq; the Shaumari Wildlife Reserve and the Azraq Wetland Reserve, both managed by the Royal Society for the Conservation of Nature (RSCN).

By far the easiest way of visiting the Desert Castles is with your own transport, and it is well worth considering hiring a car, or else enquiring in the budget hotels in Amman to see whether a group tour by minibus is being organized (these can be very good value; try at the *Cliff* or *Farah* hotels). With your own transport it is possible to cover all the Desert Castles on or near the main road in one long day, although a more leisurely option is to stop overnight in Azraq. If your time is limited, you are advised to concentrate on Azraq, Qasr Amra (definitely not to be missed) and Qasr Kharana. Only Qasr Hallabat/Hammam al-Sarakh and Azraq are accessible by public transport (from Amman's Raghadan or Abdali bus stations you must get a bus first to Zarqa and then change there). To reach Qasr Amra and Qasr Kharana involves hitching or hiring a taxi from Azraq.

Hammam al-Sarakh and Qasr al-Hallabat

Hammam al-Sarakh

The Umayyad baths complex of Hammam al-Sarakh was built to serve the nearby Qasr Hallabat. Originally the baths would have been lavishly decorated with mosaics and frescoes, but although they have been extensively restored in recent years, there is not that much to see. An arched entrance leads through into a small domed chamber with recesses to the left and right containing windows. Note the quality of the stonework in the semi-domes of the recesses. Straight ahead, an arch leads through into a second vaulted chamber. Arranged in rows on the floors of each room are squat columns of small circular discs which once supported the raised floor under which hot water would have been channelled. Outside, to the left of the main building is a deep well covered by a metal grill, while between the well and the main baths complex is a raised platform, all that remains of an audience hall.

Qasr al-Hallabat

The traces of a small fort found in one corner of the larger fortress/palace have been identified by some as being of Nabatean origin (early 2nd century AD). During the Roman period a more substantial fortress was built, probably by Marcus Aurelius (emperor 161-180 AD), in order to defend the *Via Nova Traiana*, the road built by Trajan linking Bosra (in Syria) with Aila (present-day Aqaba). An inscription discovered in the ruins reveals that the fortress was enlarged and the corner towers added between 212-215 AD, during the reign of Caracalla. Another inscription suggests that the fortress served as a monastery during the Byzantine era (late 5th-early 6th century). Early in the 7th century it appears to have been abandoned, probably following the Sassanid Persian invasions of 611-14. Under the Umayyads, probably during the rule of the Caliph Walid II (743-44), it was extensively restored, and a mosque added. The same basic layout of the earlier Roman fortress was retained, but internally it was lavishly rebuilt to serve as a palace or royal residence, with elaborate mosaic floors, wall frescoes and other decorations.

The ruins stand within a large fenced-off enclosure; if you have your own transport the Bedouins on duty will allow you to drive in and right up to the ruins. There is no entrance fee as such, but if one of the Bedouins shows you around he will expect a tip. You reach first the **mosque**, of which only the west wall, along with parts of the north and south walls, is still standing. The west wall has a fine doorway with a decorated relieving arch above the lintel and pilasters on either side. In the south wall the base of the *mihrab* has been reconstructed.

The **fortress/palace** itself lies to the northwest of the mosque and follows the traditional square plan with towers in each corner typical of a fortified Roman *castrum*. Today it is largely in ruins, with piles of rubble strewn all around, although the basic layout of many of the rooms can still be seen, along with some of the walls and doorways, and the odd fragments of arches and sections of staircases leading up to sheer drops. As you enter, you pass under a particularly precarious-looking free-standing stone arch. Of the Umayyad-period decorations nothing remains to be seen; the frescoes have now all been weathered away, although in places you can still see traces of the plaster, while the mosaics, where they survive, have been covered over to protect them from the elements. In the northwest corner (far right as you enter), are the remains of the older, smaller fort identified by some as Nabatean, although this corner is the most heavily ruined and little can be made out. Perhaps the most striking feature of the ruins is the mixture of black basalt and lighter limestone used in the construction. The black basalt stones, many of them bearing Greek inscriptions, are believed to have been transported here from Umm al-Jimal to the north by the Umayyads when they rebuilt the fortress and converted it into a palace.

Ins & outs

Getting there by public transport Regular minibuses run from Amman's Raghadan and Abdali bus stations to Zarqa, where you must transfer to another bus station (there is a shuttle bus) to catch the much less frequent minibuses running to the village of Hallabat. The minibus passes both Qasr al-Hallabat and Hammam al-Sarakh as it runs between the western and eastern parts of Hallabat village.

By private car From Downtown Amman, head east along Hashimi St past Raghadan bus station and follow signs for Zarqa/Mafraq to join the motorway heading northeast out of Amman. After 19 km, take the exit signposted `Iraq/Syria'. Keep going straight, past a sign and turning for Hashimiyya and past the Zarqa Private University, and then take the exit signposted for the Iraqi border and Azraq (30 km). 5 km further on, take the right turn signposted to Azraq (and Qasr Hallabat). After 3 km you come to a left turn signposted for 'Hilbat' and a towering cement factory close to the road; ignore this turning, as it is a very long-winded and confusing route on an appalling road. Instead, continue straight on for a further 10 km and then take the left turn (clearly signposted) to Qasr al-Hallabat. After 3 km, turn left at a T-junction and the ruins of Hammam al-Sarakh are on your left after about 200 m. The signposted left turn for Qasr al-Hallabat is 3 km further along this road (the ruins are in fact visible from Hammam al-Sarakh, perched on top of a small hill).

Distances in brackets are the cumulative distance from the starting point

Azraq

Situated in the midst of the desert, yet blessed with abundant water, the oasis town of Azraq is best known for its well-preserved fortress, where TE Lawrence stayed for a winter during the Arab Revolt. It is also increasingly gaining recognition for the two excellent RSCN nature reserves here. Being the only place in the eastern desert with any accommodation, it makes for a convenient overnight stop if you do not want to rush back to Amman the same day.

Ins and outs

Azraq is a further 53 km east of Hallabat (101 km from Amman). Returning to the main road at the turning for Hallabat and continuing east, after 44 km you come to a right turn signposted for Qasr Amra and Qasr Kharana. Continue straight on here for Azraq, to arrive after a further 9 km at a T-junction. Azraq is in two parts; turning left here takes you past the *Azraq Tourist Resort* and *Al Sayad* hotels to North Azraq, 5 km further on, where the fortress is located; turning right takes you into South Azraq where numerous brightly-lit restaurants catering for the traffic running between Amman, Saudi Arabia and Iraq line the road.

There is no local public transport as such between North and South Azraq, but there is a steady trickle of traffic between the two and it is generally easy to hitch a lift. There are usually several taxis hanging around by the T-junction for the road to Amman which are always eager to take tourists out to Qasr Amra, and on to Qasr Kharana and Amman if necessary. The minibuses which run between Zarqa and Azraq go right into North Azraq, taking you past the fortress. On the return trip they ply up and down between North and South Azraq touting for passengers until they are full. If you want to get back to Amman the same day, check what time the last one is leaving.

History

Azraq owes its existence to the large natural oasis here, which represents the only significant water supply to be found in the vast expanses of the desert to the east of the Jordan River. As such, it has since ancient times been an important stopping place for caravans traversing the desert en route between the Hejaz region of Saudi Arabia and Syria. Flint tools and other artefacts discovered here indicate that Stone Age man lived and hunted in this area during the Paleolithic era (around 200,000 years ago), when the climate would have been more temperate and fauna even more abundant than in the recent past. Until a few decades ago the large area of wetland immediately to the east of Azraq provided an important watering place for a wide variety of migratory birds and indigenous wildlife (see below).

Today, however, apart from the occasional stands of palm trees, it is hard to imagine Azraq as a fertile and verdant oasis. The dusty, rapidly growing town has retained its importance as a transport hub, with a steady stream of traffic passing through, ranging from improbably overloaded long-distance service taxis to huge lorries. It is also an important salt producing centre. North Azraq ('Azraq al-Janubi'), where the salt production takes place, is also known as Druze Azraq, the population consisting largely of Druze who settled here following the 1920 uprising against the French in the Jebel Arab region of the Hauran in Syria. South Azraq ('Azraq ash-Shamali') is also known as Shishan after one of the springs here, and consists of a mixture of Circassians who settled here in the 19th century and local Arab Bedouins.

Azraq Fort (Qasr al-Azraq)

Azraq's chief claim to fame is the imposing fortress built of black basalt rock which TE Lawrence used as his headquarters during the winter of 1917. In its present form this is an Ayyubid construction undertaken by the Ayyubid-appointed Mameluke governor Aybak in 1236-7, as indicated by an Arabic inscription above the main entrance. Other inscriptions in Greek and Latin dedicated to Diocletian (284-305) indicate that the Romans first built a fortress here around 300 AD, and it is known that the Umayyad Caliph Walid II used it as a hunting lodge in the 8th century. During the early Ottoman period it served as a barracks.

The main entrance tower is in the southern wall. The doors consist of two solid slabs of basalt weighing around one tonne each, which still swing on their hinges. In the entrance hall, with its corbelled roof of basalt slabs (as at Umm al-Jimal, the shortage of wood necessitated using this building technique, see page 188), are various architectural fragments with inscriptions, patterned designs and depictions of hunting scenes. Directly above this hall is the room used by TE Lawrence (see next page). There is a central arch supporting the corbeling, and decorative arches framing the arrow slits in the outward facing walls and the window overlooking the central courtyard of the fortress.

The largest surviving tower is in the western wall. From the courtyard of the fortress, if you go through the doorway to the right of the tower, you come to another, even larger single-slab basalt door which was the postern gate. Though extremely stiff, this one also still swings on its hinges. When Lawrence occupied the fortress the main entrance was sealed shut so that the entrance hall could be used as accommodation, and it was through this gate that people came and went. Each night it was closed and Lawrence describes how: *"It took a great effort to start swinging, and at the end went shut with a clang and crash which made tremble the west wall of the old castle."*

Along the north wall, on either side of the central tower, were the kitchens, store rooms and stables, with arches supporting the corbel ceiling. In the stables (to the right of the tower as you face it) mangers and tethering rings for the horses can still be seen. In the northeast corner is a deep pit with steps leading down into it, originally a water cistern. Standing in the courtyard, offset towards the northeast corner and aligned towards the cardinal points of the compass, is the mosque. This was originally a church dating from the Byzantine era. Two rows of supporting arches resting on oddly slender column segments formed the central nave and side-aisles of the church, with the *mihrab* being built into the south wall when it was converted into a mosque by the Umayyads. ■*Open daily 0800-sunset. At the time of writing there was no entrance fee, but you should make clear beforehand whether you want the guided tour that the caretaker will attempt to give you, for which he expects a tip. The fort is situated by the road on the left as you drive into North Azraq.*

Azraq Fort

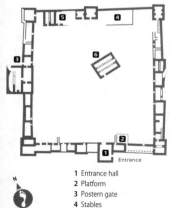

1 Entrance hall
2 Platform
3 Postern gate
4 Stables
5 Kitchens & store rooms
6 Mosque

0 metres 20
0 yards 20

Azraq Wetland Reserve

Just to the east of South Azraq is the Azraq Wetland Reserve, a small area of wetland (currently around 12 sq km) which has been the focus of intensive conservation efforts in recent years. A new visitors' centre has been opened on the edge of the wetland, while walkways running through the reserve, along with a bird-hide overlooking one area of water, provide an excellent opportunity to see this remarkable natural habitat, and the birds which flock to it, at close quarters. The best time for bird watching is from February to April. There are plans to extend the walkways and develop longer nature-trails with more wildlife and birdwatching opportunies in the future.

East of Amman

The Azraq wetland (and indeed the whole oasis of Azraq) lies at the heart of the vast Azraq Basin, a shallow depression in the Eastern Desert extending over nearly 13,000 sq km. Declared an internationally important wetland under the RAMSAR convention in 1977, the wetland once covered more than 50 sq km and consisted of large areas of permanent marshland, spring-fed pools and mudflats. This environment provided an important watering point for numerous species of migratory birds en route between Africa and Europe. Less than 35 years ago, during the height of the migratory season in February, as many as 350,000 teal, pintail, coot, wigeon, tufted duck and mallard were recorded in one count. The wetland also supported indigenous wildlife including water buffalos, ducks, carp and catfish.

However, during the 1980s the water from the springs which fed the wetlands began to be pumped first to Zarqa and then to Amman, to supply them with drinking water. These springs are fed by water percolating down into underground aquifers in the Jebel Druze (or Jebel Arab) in Syria before emerging eventually at Azraq. The rate of water extraction far exceeded the inflow and the wetlands steadily started to dry up. By the late 1980s they had been reduced to just a few small pools and the majority of the migratory birds were stopping instead on the shores of Lake Tiberias (Sea of Galilee) in Israel. The intensive hunting of the water buffalo, meanwhile, along with the destruction of their natural habitat, rapidly reduced their numbers until they had disappeared altogether. By 1993 the water table had fallen to 12 m below ground level.

Since 1993 concerted efforts have been made to restore the wetlands, most importantly by pumping 1.5 mn cubic metres of water back in each year. However, Azraq is still the source of around 25% of Amman's water supply, and the amount of water being pumped back in is estimated to be only sufficient to restore around 10% of the original wetland habitat. Nevertheless, some migratory birds are stopping here now, with the marshes reviving to a certain extent after winter rains. During April 1999 as many as 150 different species of birds were recorded, with many more stopping here over the rest of the year. Water buffalo have also been re-introduced, and to date the herd has grown to seven in number. These animals play an important role in eating and trampling down areas of reed, preventing this extremely hardy plant (*Phragmites australis*) from completely dominating the wetland, and so helping to maintain a wider variety of habitats for other wildlife.

Around the reserve The centrepiece of the newly-opened **visitors' centre** at the edge of the reserve is a room with excellent displays and explanations of the ecology and natural history of the wetlands. There are also education facilities for visiting school groups, and a shop selling various handicrafts made at Azraq and Dana as part of RSCN sponsored income-generating projects. If you are interested in a guided tour of the wetland with one of the reserve's staff, contact the centre in advance. The roof of the visitors' centre provides a good vantage point from which to get an overview of the reserve.

Going round the reserve anti-clockwise, a combination of paths and wooden walkways lead you through tall reedbeds rustling in the wind to the so-called **'Roman wall'**. The small section of wall you see is part of a much larger structure running to nearly 5 km which enclosed an important spring and its related pool. At first the wall was thought to be of Roman origin and later raised in height during the Ummayad era, but recent research suggests that it is an entirely Umayyad structure, built during the short reign of Caliph Walid II (743-744 AD). As to its purpose, it was clearly intended to provide a means of regulating and utilising the waters of the spring, with two sluice gates allowing water to be channelled to fields and gardens. An interesting feature of

A Bitter Winter in the Desert

Most visitors' experience of Azraq is of the relentless heat of the desert, when even to imagine the sensation of coldness is all but impossible. However, when TE Lawrence stayed here in the winter of 1917, his experience was a very different one.

"We hurried up the stoney ridge in high excitement, talking of the wars and songs and passions of the early shepherd kings, with names like music, who had loved this place; and of the Roman legionaries who languished here as a garrison in yet earlier times. Then the blue fort on its rock above the rustling palms, with fresh meadows and shining springs of water, broke on our sight. Azrak lay favourably for us, and the old fort would be convenient headquarters if we made it habitable, no matter how severe the winter. So I established myself in the southern gate-tower, and set my six Haurani boys (to whom manual labour was not disgraceful) to cover with brushwood, palm-branches, and clay the ancient split stone rafters, which stood open to the sky. At last the sky turned solidly to rain, and no man could approach us. In loneliness we learned the full disadvantages of imprisonment within such gloomy ancient unmortared places. The rain guttered down within the walls' thickness and spouted into the rooms from their ancient chinks. We set rafts of palm-branches to bear us clear of the streaming floor, covered them with felt mats, and huddled down on them under sheepskins, with another mat over us like a shield to throw off the water. It was icy cold, as we hid there, motionless, from the murky daylight until dark, our minds suspended within these massive walls, through whose every shot-window the piercing mist streamed like a white pennant." (TE Lawrence, Seven Pillars of Wisdom)

the wall is the triangular and circular buttresses to be found at irregular intervals along its length on both the inside and outside. Given that the wall is quite low and was never actually built to be watertight (there is no evidence of a plastering lining on the inside of the wall), these appear to have been a purely decorative feature. There are striking parallels with similar structures built at the Umayyad palaces of Qasr al-Heir al-Gharbi and Qasr al-Heir al-Sharki in the Syrian desert, and it is thought that the Azraq wall was modelled on these. Whatever the exact purpose of the enterprise, it was never completed, with the murder of Walid II bringing it to an abrupt halt. In recent years, the spring enclosed by the walls has dried up and the surrounding land is dry and cracked, giving a stark insight into the state of these wetlands before they began to be restored.

Continuing on through the tall reeds, past inviting pools of water teeming with the small Azraq Killifish (a fish found nowhere else in the world), you come next to the **bird-hide**, which overlooks a larger water pool. Here you can see coots feeding in the water and harriers wheeling in the skies above at any time of the year, and a host of other birds during the peak migratory period from February to April. From the bird-hide, a path leads on to a large **circular stone wall**. The exact function of this wall is still not known, though, like the other wall, it also dates from the Umayyad period and was in all likelihood related to it in some manner. From here it is a short walk back to the visitors' centre. ■*Open daily 0800-sunset. Entry JD3 (with a 25% discount if you have already paid for a Shaumari Reserve ticket). T/F3835225, azraq@rscn.org.jo To get there, take the signposted left turn around 200m south of the T-junction and the visitors' centre is 500m further on. Allow 30 mins-1 hr for a tour of the wetland, more if you want to stop and watch for wildlife.*

Shaumari Reserve

Half an hour's drive to the southwest of Azraq is the Shaumari Wildlife Reserve, where you can see oryx, ostriches, onagers, gazelle and a host of other birds and animals. There is also an excellent nature centre here, a picnic and play area for children, an observation tower from which to view the wildlife, and 'oryx safaris' for those who wish to head further out into the reserve.

Covering an area of 22 sq km, the Shaumari Reserve was established in 1975 in an attempt to re-introduce some of the species of wildlife previously found in this area before they were destroyed by excessive hunting. One of the reserve's greatest success stories has been in the breeding of oryx. Having become extinct in Jordan, eight of these were imported from Santiago (Chile) in 1978. Five years later just over 30 of them were released into the reserve and left to breed on their own. There are now over 200 of them and it is hoped that in the future they will re-establish themselves in the wild. At the time of writing, 25 were shortly due to be released into the wild in Wadi Rum. Indeed, Shaumari has gained an entry in the Guinness Book of Records for the most successful oryx breeding programme in the world, with oryx from here being sent to other breeding programmes in Syria, Saudi Arabia, UAE, Qatar and Iraq. The blue necked ostrich has also established itself here, having been imported from the Montpellier zoo in France, with these remarkable birds now numbering 32. The onager, or wild ass, is the third re-introduced species to be found here. Imported from Switzerland and Germany, it is a very close relative of the now extinct local species of wild ass. There are also various species of gazelle. A survey in 1999 also recorded over 140 different species of birds, making the reserve increasingly attractive for bird-watchers too. The stands of Eucalyptus trees in the reserve are not in fact native to this area. They were planted in the 1970s when Shaumari was a government-run agricultural research centre. Though they do provide welcome shade in summer, their deep roots take almost all the available water from the ground, preventing other plants from flourishing, and there are attempts to re-establish native trees and bushes instead.

Around the reserve Approaching the entrance to the reserve, keep an eye out for Oryx, which can often be seen close to the perimeter fence to your left. On the track itself, the footprints of wild animals (notably wolves and jackals) can also often be seen, and perhaps even the odd snake slithering across. Inside the entrance, to the right, is the newly opened **nature centre**, a truly inspiring place aimed very much at children, with lots of well-presented interactive displays which are both highly informative and great fun. The centre hosts visits from around 7000 students each year, with groups coming from throughout Jordan and the Middle East. Ahmad al-Zouby, the Education Officer posted here, is bursting with enthusiasm and ideas to get children interested in the conservation work of the reserve. Nearby there is a **rehabilitation centre** for injured birds and animals. Further on is the picnic and children's play area, and then a tunnel which leads though to the 4-storey **observation tower** overlooking the breeding enclosures. You can get a bird's-eye view from here of ostriches and gazelle in nearby pens, as well as oryx and onagers further afield. A small pool has been dug around 500 m from the tower, to encourage the oryx, as well as other animals and birds, to come and drink, and there are plans to establish a bird-hide and nature trail nearby. **'Oryx safaris'** (JD20; maximum 15 people) are on offer to take you out into the rest of the reserve. In summer, when the oryx tend to remain close to the observation tower, these last around 30 minutes, though in winter and spring, when the oryx tend to venture further afield, they can take much longer. ■*Open daily 0800-sunset. Entry JD3 for tourists (with a 25% discount if you have already paid for an Azraq Reserve ticket), JD1 for Jordanians, 50% discount for students. To get there head south through South Azraq and after 7 km take the right turn signposted to the reserve. It is a further 6 km to the entrance. Only soft drinks are available at the reserve, so bring your own food; binoculars, strong boots or shoes and a hat are also recommended.*

Essentials

B *Azraq Resthouse*, set back 1½ km from the main road, on the left, 2 km north of the T-junction as you head towards North Azraq, T3834006, F3835215. Accommodation in bungalows arranged around swimming pool, a/c, TV, phone, fridge, attached bath. Clean and reasonably comfortable (rooms about to undergo full refurbishment at time of writing; prices currently **C** category, but will edge over into **B** category afterwards). Large restaurant (set buffet lunch/dinner JD4.500 per head, or a la carte and snacks) and bar. Non-guests can use the swimming pool for JD1. Room prices include breakfast and taxes, but watch out for the 23% tax and service added to everything else. Pleasant but unremarkable government-run establishment. **B** *Al Sayad (Hunter)*, situated to the left of the road, past the *Azraq Resthouse*, shortly before you arrive in North Azraq, T/F06-4644988 (in Amman). Rooms with fan, heater and balcony, share shower/toilet. Restaurant, bar, swimming pool (though often empty – with water in short supply only the government-owned hotel gets the luxury of a full pool). Unusual hotel set in pleasant gardens. Lots of character, with paintings by the owner, Lydia, dotted around the place, and some nice architectural touches, but the rooms are rather basic and some of them are very small.

C *Azraq Lodge (RSCN)*, coming from Amman, signposted off to the right of the road shortly before you reach the T-junction, T3835017. Formerly a British hospital and later a hunting lodge, the accommodation here consists of 5 carefully refurbished cabins, each with 2 double rooms with attached bath (but currently no fan or a/c, so hot in summer). There are plans to convert the old hospital wing into more luxurious accommodation and open a restaurant as well.

D-E *Al Zoubi*, set back from the road on the left as you drive south through South Azraq, no phone. Clean, pleasantly furnished rooms with fan and attached bath (water solar heated). Good value for money (JD15 for double/triple room, will come down to JD10 for single occupancy with a little firm persuasion).

F *Al Waha* (sign in Arabic only), situated on the main road in South Azraq, no phone. Very grotty shared rooms, with even worse shared shower/toilet and vicious bed-bugs. Best avoided if at all possible. Chicken and kebab restaurant out front.

Being way out in the middle of nowhere, food is more expensive here, and pretty limited. The restaurant at the *Azraq Resthouse* offers lunch and dinner buffets for JD4.500, as well as cheaper snacks. Just beyond the fortress a right turn is signposted to the *Al Montazah Restaurant*, which has a pleasant, palm-shaded garden area as well as an indoor section and a bar. A reasonable meal of roast chicken, salad, hummus and *moutabbal* will cost around JD5 per head. On the main road just south of the fortress the *Azraq Palace Tourist Restaurant* will try to charge you whatever they think they can get for chicken, kebabs, hummus etc; ask prices first and bargain. There are several simple and cheap falafel, hummus and fuul restaurants to the north of the fortress, in North Azraq. The Lebanese-run *Al Arez*, on the right around 500 m past the fortress, and the *Al Sufara* next door are among the better of these. The numerous transport restaurants/cafés lining the road in South Azraq offer the

Sleeping

Eating

East of Amman

standard selection of roast chicken, kebabs, hummus etc. Most will try to charge tourists premium prices so negotiate before you order.

Directory There is a branch of the *Bank of Jordan* on the main street in North Azraq which offers foreign exchange facilities. The **post office** is nearby. There are a couple of **Alo** cardphones in the garden of the *Al Montazah* restaurant, making this the best place to phone from.

Around Azraq

There are a number of other places further afield which can be visited as short excursions from Azraq. Around 20 km to the northeast of Azraq are the ruins of **Qasr Aseikhim**, a hilltop fortress dating from the late Roman era (3rd century AD), built over an earlier Nabatean structure. The ruins themselves are not particularly impressive, but the setting is dramatic in a desolate sort of way, and there are numerous ancient rock carvings to be found on the basalt boulders scattered around the hill. A 4WD is essential to visit these ruins, as is a local guide. Both can be arranged through the RSCN (contact the staff at Azraq Wetland Reserve or Shaumari, or try at the RSCN Azraq Lodge). Around 10 km to the southwest of Azraq are the even scantier ruins of **Qasr Uweinid**, also only accessible by 4WD and again only really of interest for their isolated setting.

Qasr Amra

The low, squat buildings of Qasr Amra seem somewhat small and unassuming from the outside, though its delicate dome and series of three barrel vaults hint at something special, and indeed this is perhaps the most rewarding of the desert complexes to visit. Designated a World Heritage Site, Qasr Amra is unique in that preserved here are beautiful and unusual frescoes dating from Umayyad times, the only ones to have survived from this period.

Ins & outs Heading back out of Azraq the way you came, take the left turn after 9 km, signposted for Qasr Amra etc. The ruins of Qasr Amra are signposted and clearly visible off to the right of the road 17 km further on. There is no public transport along this branch of the highway between Azraq and Amman, so, unless you arrange your own transport, to visit Qasr Amra (or Qasr Kharana further west) the only option is to catch a Zarqa-bound bus as far as the turn-off and then hitch. Make sure you have plenty of water and adequate protection against the sun. A private taxi from Azraq to Qasr Amra and back should not cost more than around JD5.

History The site is thought to have served as a caravanserai before the arrival of the Umayyads, but under them, probably during the rule of the sixth Umayyad caliph, Walid I (705-15), it was made into a luxurious hunting lodge and baths complex. The frescoes provide a fascinating insight into the life of the Umayyads, who under Walid I experienced a remarkable cultural and artistic flourishing. While other Umayyad desert complexes appear to have been more functional, Qasr Amra betrays the recreational, pleasure-seeking side of the Umayyads. Most striking is the depiction of human forms, including naked female figures, and scenes of singing and dancing. Under the later Umayyad caliph, Yazid II (720-24), any representation of the human form in art (let alone a naked one) was forbidden as blasphemous and un-Islamic. Nevertheless, the Abbasids, who overthrew the Umayyads in the mid-8th century to assume the Caliphate, still viewed the latter as licentious and degenerate and set about imposing an altogether stricter interpretation of Islam.

There is a brand new parking area and **visitors' centre** adjacent to the site. The latter includes a room with displays offering interpretations of the the frescoes, including a diagram of the constellations depicted on the inside of the domed *caldarium*, as well as an explanation of the hydraulic system which supplied the baths. A pathway lined with newly-planted shrubs winds from the visitors' centre across to the baths complex itself.

The simple entrance leads into the **main audience chamber**, divided by two supporting arches into three barrel-vaulted aisles. At the end of the longer central aisle is an alcove with two side-rooms leading off it, while a door in the left-hand side-aisle leads through into the baths complex. It takes your eyes a while to adjust, and only gradually do you fully appreciate the rich detail of the frescoes for which Qasr Amra is so famous. With the passage of time they have been badly damaged and only partly saved by the painstaking restoration work carried out by a team from the Madrid Archaeological Museum in 1972, but they are still clearly discernible and very impressive. All around you are scenes of hunting, feasting and scantily clad women. In the centre of the right-hand wall as you enter is the figure of a nude woman bathing. To the left of her, indistinctly, can be made out six figures, four of which have been identified by the writing below in Greek and Kufic Arabic; `Ceasar', a Byzantine emperor; `Roderick', the king of the Spanish Visigoths; `Chosroes', the Sassanid Persian ruler; and `Negus', an Abyssinian king. The other two figures are thought to be Chinese and Central Asian. To the right of the bathing woman are athletes in various action poses. Higher up the wall is a long panel depicting a hunting scene of onagers being trapped in a net by horsemen, helped by figures (partly obscured by flags) holding burning torches. In the alcove at the end of the central aisle, the Caliph is depicted seated on his throne, surrounded by courtiers. The panels on the barrel-vaulting of the left-hand aisle have well-preserved pictures of craftsmen at work, while the supporting arch on this side also has well-preserved frescoes of two women, their features very much in the Graeco-Roman tradition. The wall on this side includes another particularly vivid hunting scene. The floors of the side alcoves still have traces of mosaic flooring surviving.

Going through into the baths, the first room was the **changing room**. The human figures depicted here, to the left of the small window and above the doorway, are wonderfully expressive, while on the ceiling are panels depicting men and animals, including a bear playing a lute! Next is the *tepidarium*, with small circular discs to support the raised floor which would have been heated by water from underneath. Lastly you come to the *caldarium*, with a beautiful small domed ceiling pierced by four windows and frescoes of the heavens painted on the inside of the dome. These are thought to be the earliest surviving representations of the Zodiac on a spherical surface. The small holes in the walls were for marble cladding.

Outside the main building is a **well** which was dug to a depth of 40 m to reach the water table. The animal-driven water drawing mechanism (known as a *saqiyah*) beside the well has been reconstructed to demonstrate how it worked. The large

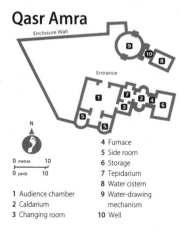

Qasr Amra

Enclosure Wall

Entrance

N

0 metres 10

0 yards 10

1 Audience chamber
2 Caldarium
3 Changing room
4 Furnace
5 Side room
6 Storage
7 Tepidarium
8 Water cistern
9 Water-drawing mechanism
10 Well

stone structure attached to the well itself was a **water cistern**. The section of **enclosure wall** built in a V-shape between the well and the baths served to prevent the complex being flooded by the nearby Wadi al-Batum. Though dry for most of the year, this wadi is subject to flash floods in winter and is believed to have been more active during the Umayyad era. Today there are still tamarisk and pistachio trees to be found beside it. ■*Open daily until sunset. Entry JD1. The baths complex itself is kept locked, so go first to the visitors' centre, where the caretaker can usually be found. There are good, clean toilet facilities at the visitors' centre but, apart from the Bedouin tent outside offering tea, postcards and souvenirs, there is nothing in the way of refreshments, so bring your own supplies.*

Qasr Kharana

Qasr Kharana is a further 16 km west from Qasr Amra, situated just to the left of the main road. The impressive and excellently preserved building stands within a fenced-off enclosure with the obligatory Bedouin tent outside selling postcards, tea etc.

The style of the building is strongly reminiscent of Qasr al-Heir al-Sharki in Syria, particularly in the herringbone lines of decorative brickwork running around the outer walls. Built to a square plan, with rounded buttresses in each corner and in the centre of each wall, it has all the appearance of a castle, although experts are divided as to exactly what purpose it served.

It may have been a defensive fortress, though what appear at first sight to be arrow slits in the walls were more probably intended for ventilation, being too narrow on the inside and high off the floor to be of any use to archers. It may have served as a khan to accommodate passing trading caravans, but although the internal plan of a central courtyard surrounded by rooms conforms to that of a traditional khan, the number of rooms and the elaborate architectural decoration found in some of them seems a little too grand for a khan, while the lack of a substantial water supply nearby also makes this function unlikely. According to the American archaeologist Urice, who carried out a detailed survey in 1979, it may have acted as a kind of conference centre where the Umayyads could meet with local tribal chiefs to forge alliances and negotiate agreements. As to the date of its construction, an inscription in ink above one of the doorways to an upper floor hall includes the date November 710 AD, during the rule of Walid I. However certain architectural and decorative features have led some archaeologists to suggest that it may have originally been built by the Sassanid Persians. Stones bearing Greek inscriptions strongly suggest that the building stands on the site of an earlier Roman or Byzantine site.

The ground floor rooms around the central courtyard almost certainly served as stables and storage. The upper floor rooms are the most interesting, many of them retaining (with a little restoration) substantial and elaborate decorative and architectural features, including triple engaged colonnettes

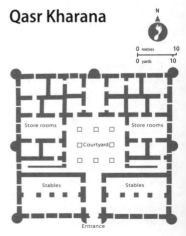

Qasr Kharana

supporting the cross arching, rosette friezes and semi-domes engaged into the right-angle corners of the walls with that wonderfully named architectural device, the squinch. Stairs lead from the upper floor up onto the roof. ■ *Open daily 0800-sunset. Entry free. The building is usually kept locked. The caretaker, who is always on hand to open it up, will offer you a guided tour and expects a small tip even if you go round on your own.*

Qasr Tuba

Situated approximately 50 km due south of Qasr Kharana (or around 35 km east from Qatrana on the Desert Highway) are the ruins of Qasr Tuba, striking mostly for their isolated setting far from any modern roads. If you want to head out here, 4WD is essential, as is a good local guide who is familiar with the desert tracks. Qasr Tuba was started by Walid II, but left uncompleted after his death in 744. If completed, it would have been the largest of the desert complexes.

Continuing west along the main road from Qasr Kharana, around 22 km further on the road suddenly widens out rather dramatically, this stretch of the highway having been earmarked as an emergency alternative landing strip for the nearby Queen Alia International Airport. Just over 35 km from Qasr Kharana, you arrive at the small town of **Muwaqqar** just off to the left of the road. If you take the turning immediately after the sign for the town, you will see on your left a large water cistern, built by the Umayyad Caliph Yazid II (719-724 AD). Relined in the 1960s with funding from the US, the cistern is still in use today. There was once also an Umayyad palace/fortress up on the hill above the village, but today the scant remains of this have all but disappeared. Returning to the main road, after 20 km turn right to join the main highway into Amman (or left for Madaba or the Desert Highway heading south towards Aqaba). For details of Qasr Mushatta, on the north perimeter of the Queen Ali International Airport, see page 130.

Qasr Kharana to Amman

East of Amman

Jerash & the North

Jerash & the North

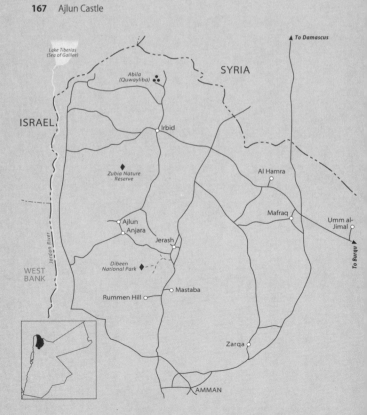

To Damascus

Lake Tiberias
(Sea of Galilee)

Abila
(Quwayliba)

SYRIA

ISRAEL

Irbid

Zubia Nature
Reserve

Al Hamra

Mafraq

Umm al-
Jimal

Jordan River

Ajlun
Anjara

Jerash

Dibeen
National Park

To Burqu

WEST
BANK

Rummen Hill

Mastaba

Zarqa

AMMAN

The northern part of Jordan consists of rolling hills and uplands (the northern, or Ajlun, highlands). This region is well-watered and fertile, supporting rich agricultural land, orchards and olive groves, as well as remnants of the thick pine forests which once would have covered the whole area. With such a favourable environment, however, it is today unsurprisingly the most densely populated part of the country. Due north from Amman is the most spectacular site to be found in this part of the country, the ruins of the Roman city of Jerash – Jordan's answer to Syria's Palmyra and Lebanon's Baalbek. Nearby is the beautiful Dibeen National Park and the picturesque Arab castle of Ajlun. Further north, the town of Irbid boasts an excellent archaeological museum and makes a convenient base from which to visit surrounding sites such as Umm Qais (ancient Gadara) and Abila. Many people combine a visit to the northern highlands with a journey along the Jordan Valley (covered separately in the following chapter). To the northeast of Amman, close to the border with Syria, is an altogether different environment of black basalt desert, geographically part of Syria's Hauran and Jebel al-Arab region, where the intriguing ruins of Umm al-Jimal can be found.

Public transport services are relatively good in northern Jordan, though a car is useful for some of the more out-of-the-way sites, and allows you to stop wherever you want, to enjoy the scenery or have a picnic perhaps. Services between Amman and Jerash are frequent. On the route between Jerash and Irbid via Ajlun they are more erratic but adequate. Irbid is the major transport hub in the far north, with services to most places in this part of the country. Other transport hubs include Zarqa, around 22 km to the northeast of Amman (for services to Azraq in the eastern desert), and Mafraq (for services to Umm al-Jimal).

Amman to Jerash

Jerash is just 65 km to the north of Amman, a 45-minute drive on a fast new section of motorway. Note that most maps of Jordan do not show this new motorway, which bypasses Jerash en route from Amman to the border town of Ramtha.

From Downtown, follow King Hussein St up past Abdali bus station and turn left at the Jamal Abd an-Nasir Interchange. Keep going straight at the Sports City Interchange, following signs for Suweilah, and then turn right at a large roundabout (14 km from the centre, signposted for Jerash) to join the motorway leading north towards Jerash. After a further 18 km there is an exit signposted for `Rummen Hill'. Taking this exit, the road goes under the motorway to head west. Arriving at a T-junction, turn right to reach a picnic spot on the wooded hillside overlooking a large lake created by the King Talal dam across the Zarqa River. The views from up here are lovely, although the road down to the lake itself is closed. The more popular picnic spots amongst the trees on the hillside are unfortunately strewn with litter.

Returning to the motorway and continuing north, you pass after 3 km an exit signposted for Mastaba, and then after another 8 km an exit signposted for South Jerash. Taking this exit, you follow a road lined with eucalyptus trees running along a green valley with plentiful water, past a number of restaurants, to arrive at a roundabout. Going straight (left for Ajlun), you come first to Hadrian's Triumphal Arch, marking the southern end of the ruins, to the left of the road. Adjacent to this is the south parking area and ticket office.

Jerash

Phone code: 02 *The extensive and superbly preserved ruins of Roman Jerash, one of the great cities of the Decapolis, represent Jordan's most significant historical site after Petra. Jerash does not have the awesome scale and lavish decoration of Baalbek in Lebanon, or the dramatic setting of Palmyra in Syria, but rather a sense of grace and proportion which makes these ruins a pleasure to explore. Bear in mind, however, that during the summer, if you visit at any time other than early morning or evening, your lasting impressions are likely to be of the searing heat, and the air conditioned restaurant will be the main attraction. You really need at least half a day or more to do the site justice, preferably with breaks in-between if it is hot, although if you are in a hurry it is possible to get round in a couple of hours. There are no hotels in Jerash itself, although if you have your own transport, there are a couple of places nearby.*

Ins and outs

Getting there There are regular a/c coaches from Amman's Abdali bus station direct to Jerash (350 fils, maximum 1 hr). The bus station in Jerash is in the modern part of town, on the east side of the small river that runs through the centre. Coming from Amman, ask to be dropped off by Hadrian's Arch (an unmissable edifice immediately to the left of the main road, south of the town centre). This will save you having to walk back down to buy a ticket. Even from the bus station, however, it is only a short walk to the ruins, and everything is relatively easily accessible on foot (with the exception of the Birkentein Reservoir and Theatre, 2 km to the north of the main ruins, for which you will need to negotiate a private taxi if you do not have your own transport).

The site is open daily 0730-sunset. Entry JD5. At the time of writing, tickets were only available from the newly-built complex at the **south parking area** adjacent to Hadrian's Arch. The complex consists of a 'souk' with a selection of souvenir, handicraft and antique shops, including an outlet for the *Noor al-Hussein Foundation* (see under Shopping in the Amman section). There are toilet facilities here, and a café/restaurant which is due to open shortly. **Site information**

This arrangement is a little confusing in that there is also a **visitors' centre** around 500 m to the north, adjacent to the Southern Gate (which gives access to the main body of the ruins). In the past, tickets could be bought from a small booth by the Southern Gate. However, at the time of writing this booth had been closed down, and the visitors' centre was empty except for a small tourist information office (T6351272) with copies of the Jordan Tourism Board's free map/pamphlet about the site, and an office for the tourist police (T6350670). There are plans to install a scale model of the site here (currently this is in the museum), and perhaps open a post office and other facilities, though progress so far has been painfully slow. Presumably tickets will also be available here in the future, though no one seems very sure about this, so you are advised to buy your ticket from the complex at the south parking area by Hadrian's Arch and save yourself the possible inconvenience of having to walk all the way back down here. Opposite the visitors' centre there is a large a/c restaurant, the *Jerash Resthouse* (see page 165), with a couple of **Alo** and **JPP cardphones** outside.

Multi-lingual **guides** are on hand to provide guided tours of the site (ask at the visitors' centre). The Jordan Tourism Board's map/pamphlet on Jerash gives a reasonable outline of the site. If you want a more detailed guide, *Jerash, A Frontier City of the Roman East*, by Rami Khoury is a small, well-written booklet which is worth looking for, though it may only be available in Amman. The most detailed book on the site is *Jerash and the Decapolis* by Iain Browning, which is usually stocked by the shops at the south parking area. The ubiquitous glossy coffee-table book on Jerash has nice photos but is otherwise useless. There are a couple of banks in the modern part of Jerash offering **foreign exchange**, and a branch is likely to open either at the south parking area or visitors' centre in the future.

History

Despite evidence of settlement dating from the Stone Age onwards, the history of the city really begins during the **Hellenistic** period. Exactly when it was founded is not known. One tradition relates that Alexander the Great himself founded it, sometime after his conquest of Syria in 332 BC, while another holds that it was founded during the reign of Ptolemy II Philadelphus (283-246 BC), the man responsible for Hellenizing Amman and naming it Philadelphia. An inscription found on the site suggests that it was in fact founded by Perdiccas, one of Alexander the Great's generals. As with most of the Hellenistic cities `founded' in the Middle East, it appears to have been built on the site of a pre-existing settlement, known by the ancient Semitic name of *Garshu*, which was Hellenized to *Gerasa*.

For more than a century after Alexander's death in 323 BC, the region of Jerash was contested by his two main successors, Ptolemy and Seleucus. In 200

Jerash

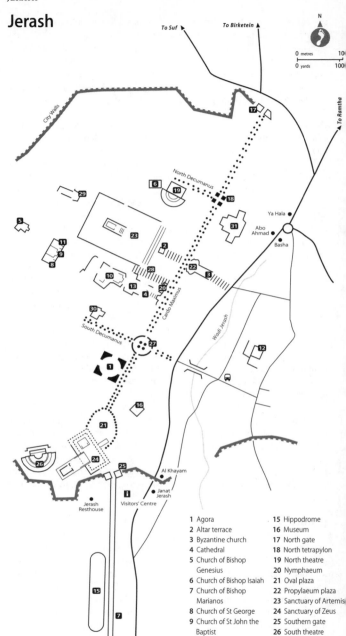

To Suf
To Birketein
To Ramtha

N

0 metres 10(
0 yards 100|

City Walls

North Decumanus

Ya Hala

Abo Ahmad

Basha

Cardo Maximus

South Decumanus

Wadi Jerash

Al Khayam

Janat Jerash

Visitors' Centre

Jerash Resthouse

South Car Park & Ticket Office

To Ajlun & Amman

Jerash & the North

1 Agora
2 Altar terrace
3 Byzantine church
4 Cathedral
5 Church of Bishop Genesius
6 Church of Bishop Isaiah
7 Church of Bishop Marianos
8 Church of St George
9 Church of St John the Baptist
10 Church of St Theodore
11 Church of SS Cosmas & Damien
12 East baths
13 Fountain Court
14 Hadrian's Arch
15 Hippodrome
16 Museum
17 North gate
18 North tetrapylon
19 North theatre
20 Nymphaeum
21 Oval plaza
22 Propylaeum plaza
23 Sanctuary of Artemis
24 Sanctuary of Zeus
25 Southern gate
26 South theatre
27 South tetrapylon
28 Stepped street
29 Synagogue church
30 Umayyad house
31 West baths

The Decapolis

Meaning literally 'Ten Cities', the term Decapolis appears to have emerged in the early Roman period. According to Pliny, writing in the 77 AD, the ten cities of the Decapolis were Damascus, Philadelphia (Amman), Scythopolis (Bet Shean, in present-day Israel), Gadara (Umm Qais), Pella (Tabaqat Fahl), Gerasa (Jerash), Canatha (Qanawat, southern Syria), Hippos (Qalat al-Hosn, in Israel), Dium and Raphana (neither of the last two have been identified). Pliny notes that the Decapolis is "so-called from the number of its towns, though not all writers keep to the same list" (Pliny, Natural History, 5; 74). Writing in the 2nd century AD, the geographer Ptolemy lists a total of 18 cities, although this appears to combine cities of Ceole Syria with those of the Decapolis.

Although there are plenty of other literary references to the Decapolis, including in the Bible (Matthew 4; 25, Mark 5; 20, 7; 31) and Josephus (Antiquities), nowhere is its exact nature explained. It appears to have represented a federation or league of some sort, but what level this operated on -

political/military, commercial or purely cultural - is not known. Early theories of a close political alliance have given way to ones suggesting a loose commercial relationship. The term may simply have been descriptive of a geographical area encompassing the cities or an administrative label, as perhaps suggested by one inscription found in Turkey detailing the posting of a Roman soldier to the 'Decapolis of Syria'.

Whatever its exact nature, it clearly expanded and contracted during its existence, and most probably its significance changed over time in any case. With the administrative reorganization of 106 AD, which led to the creation of the new province of Arabia next to that of Syria, the cities of the Decapolis became divided between the two. Thriving on trade and agriculture, they were prosperous but essentially provincial towns that never played a major role in the affairs of the empire. The delight of Jerash is that it preserves such a complete record the layout and architecture of a typical Roman city of this period.

BC the **Seleucid** emperor Antiochus III defeated the Ptolemids in the battle of Panium and Jerash fell firmly under Seleucid control. What had until then been just a small settlement of Macedonian soldiers from Alexander's armies soon began to develop into a substantial city, named *Antiochia ad Chrysorhoam* (`Antioch on the Chrysorhoas River'). Its prime function during the Hellenistic period would have been defensive, forming part of a chain of fortified cities protecting Seleucid territory from the nomadic desert tribes to the east. Almost nothing of the city during this period has survived, although it appears to have been centred around the hill on which the temple of Zeus stands.

In the late 2nd century BC it appears to have fallen under the control of Zeno and Theodorus, the tyrant rulers of Philadelphia, as the historian Josephus records that they hid their treasure in the temple of Zeus in Jerash (Josephus, *War*, I, 104; *Antiquities*, XIII, 398). It remained in their hands following the Maccabean revolt against Seleucid rule in 173 BC, which saw the **Hasmonean** Dynasty founded by Judas Maccabeus in Judea capture many of the Seleucid cities to the east of the Jordan River. However under Alexander Jannaeus (103-76 BC), the Hasmoneans were eventually successful in capturing the city in 84 BC. With the Seleucid Empire crumbling, control of the region wavered between the Nabateans to the south, the Hasmoneans of Judea and the Itureans, a local tribal dynasty from the Bekaa valley. To complicate matters, following the death of Alexander Jannaeus, control of the Hasmonean kingdom was contested by three rival Judean tribes.

The Graeco-Roman Tradition

Although what remains to be seen of Jerash today dates entirely from the Roman rebuilding of the city and later Byzantine modifications, the architecture displays strong Hellenistic influences. Indeed, long after becoming part of the Roman empire, socially and culturally Jerash continued to be shaped by Hellenistic traditions. Greek remained the official language and the Romans relied heavily on pre-existing Hellenistic administrative structures to provide cohesion and stability. Thus, as with so many cities in the region which evolved during the early centuries before and after Christ, the transition from Hellenistic to Roman was very much a process of development rather than abrupt change, and the product essentially Graeco-Roman. At the same time Jerash was also subject to the influences of Nabatean culture emanating from Petra to the south, with which it had strong commercial ties, as well as its own Semitic population.

In 64 BC the **Romans**, anxious to prevent the Parthians expanding westwards through the disintegrating Seleucid Empire, succeeded in bringing order to this disarray, the general Pompey establishing the Roman province of Syria. Although militarily they asserted themselves firmly, the Romans exercised only loose political control, declaring the former city-states of the Seleucid Empire `free cities' and allowing them a large degree of internal autonomy. It was probably during this early Roman period that the Decapolis emerged as an entity (see box).

Roman rule brought peace and stability to the region – the famous *Pax Romana* – and Jerash began to flourish. Its success was founded primarily on commerce, standing as it did close to the important north-south trade route between Damascus and the Red Sea, and being linked also with the Mediterranean via Pella and the Jordan valley. The rich agricultural land surrounding the city likewise brought it prosperity.

From around the middle of the 1st century AD the Romans began to completely rebuild the city and by 76 AD the walls and basic city plan with its main colonnaded street, the north-south Cardo Maximus, and two intersecting east-west streets, the southern and northern Decumanus, had been completed. In 106 AD Trajan annexed the Nabatean kingdom to the south and Jerash became part of the new province of Arabia, with Bosra (in present-day Syria) as its capital.

An ambitious programme of building works continued under both Trajan (98-117 AD) and Hadrian (117-138 AD), the latter visiting the city in 129-30 AD. By the early 3rd century AD Jerash boasted lavish temples, theatres, public baths, colonnaded streets, its unique oval plaza and all the other trappings of a thriving provincial Roman city. The Roman Empire however was starting to experience its own difficulties, with internal political instability and economic decline being matched externally by the rising Sassanid Persian threat from the east. Under Caracalla (211-217 AD), Jerash was made a colony and renamed Colonia Aurelia Antoniniana, but its most prosperous years were coming to an end.

Under Diocletian (284-304 AD), the city's fortunes were somewhat revived. By the time of Constantine's Edict of Milan in 313 AD, which officially allowed Christians to practice their religion, there was already a sizeable **Christian** community at Jerash. By the middle of the 4th century the city had its own cathedral and was the seat of a bishopric. It was represented at the Council of Seleucia in 359 AD and at the Council of Chaldecon in 451 AD. During the **Byzantine** era, particularly during the reign of Justinian (531-565), many of

Hadrian's Triumphal Arch

Jerash's former temples were converted into churches. So far a total of 15 churches have been uncovered, although it is likely that there are more still to be found. In 614 the **Sassanids** led by Chosroes II sacked the city and occupied it until 630, when the Byzantines briefly regained control. With the decisive defeat of the forces of Byzantium at the Battle of Yarmouk in 636, Jerash became part of the newly emergent **Muslim** Arab Empire. In 747 it was rocked by a serious earthquake and although it continued to be inhabited until the 12th century, the once glorious Roman city remained in ruins. By the 13th century it had been completely abandoned.

The ruins of the Roman city were made known to the outside world in 1806 by a German traveller named Ulrich Seetzen. In 1878 Jerash was resettled by a community of Circassian refugees from Russia, who borrowed stones from the ruins to build a new town. Serious excavations at the site began soon after and are still continuing, with current work focusing on the reconstruction and restoration of the existing monuments.

Around the site

Approaching from the south, Hadrian's Triumphal Arch looms up impressively as the first of Jerash's monuments to come into view. Built to commemorate Hadrian's visit in 129-30 AD, it consists of a huge central gateway flanked by two side portals. At a later date two side pavilions were added, the right-hand one being a reconstruction. Note the intricate carved decoration on the four semi-engaged columns flanking the gateway and side portals. Unusually this is at the base of the columns, which stand on high pedestals. Above each side portal is a recessed niche which would have held statues. Just inside the arch are numerous richly decorated architectural fragments laid out on the ground. The triumphal arch stands around half a kilometre to the south of the Southern Gate of the walled city and is linked to it by a long street. Clearly, the plan was to extend the city limits southwards, but this was never completed. **Hadrian's Triumphal Arch**

Having passed through the gate, on the left, running along most of the length of the street, is the Hippodrome. In the context of Jerash it seems huge, and indeed it was capable of holding up to 15,000 spectators, but it is in fact the smallest so far found in the Roman Empire. Exactly when it was built is not known for sure, though recent excavations by a Polish team point to the mid-2nd century AD. The south end of the hippodrome has been the focus of a reconstruction project, with the large central arch flanked on either side by five smaller arches now **Hippodrome** having been completely restored. A short section of the tiered seating along the eastern side (by the street) has also been rebuilt. The partially reconstructed rooms you see built against the hippodrome, extending partly beneath the tiered seating, probably served as shops. Inside the hippodrome, about two-thirds of the way up, traces of a retaining wall can be seen, thought to date from the Sassanid Persian occupation of 614-30 AD, and perhaps representing an attempt to consolidate a smaller area after the western side subsided.

Church of Bishop Marianos A short distance up from Hadrian's arch, to the right of the street, the foundations of the Church of Bishop Marianos can be seen, discovered in 1982. Only the outline of its plan is visible, although its floors were originally decorated with mosaics. It has been dated to 570 AD and pottery finds indicate that it continued to be used up until the earthquake of 747. A little way beyond the church, also on the right, is a series of shafts with steps leading down to **rock-cut tombs**. These date originally from the Roman period, although they appear to have been reused during the Byzantine era. Further on, steps take the street down to a lower level and at this point a brand new section of street has been built which takes you to the *Jerash Resthouse* and Visitors' Centre. Just beyond these is the entrance to the main site, through the Southern Gate.

Southern Gate Though considerably smaller, the much restored Southern Gate mirrors exactly the style of Hadrian's arch. As a result, it is thought to date from around the same time, although it may be earlier, and Hadrian's arch a copy of it. Before passing through it, note on the right the well-preserved section of the city walls, with the different stones of the lower and upper courses representing the different stages of construction.

Once through the gate, immediately on your left, excavations have revealed a small area of shops and an underground room containing a huge olive press. These date from the 3rd century AD. The press was made from reused columns and capitals. Deeper soundings uncovered pottery dating from the Middle Bronze Age (c 1500 BC) as well as evidence of construction dating from the 2nd century BC Hellenistic and 1st century AD Roman periods.

Sanctuary of Zeus, south theatre & oval plaza

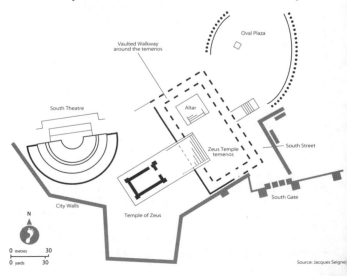

Source: Jacques Seigne

From the Southern Gate the path splits, the left-hand branch running alongside the partly reconstructed supporting wall of the *temenos* of the Temple of Zeus and under the steps leading up to it. Under the *temenos* is a long barrel-vaulted hall, inside which are various stone slabs bearing Greek inscriptions. The right-hand branch of the path slopes gently up to the Oval Plaza, with the stairs on the left leading up into the *temenos* of the Sanctuary of Zeus, which spreads up the hillside. To your right is a sign and path leading up to the museum (see page 164), which is also accessible from the southern stretch of the Cardo Maximus).

Climbing the stairs leading up into the Sanctuary of Zeus, you pass through the remains of an outer and inner wall. This formed a vaulted *peristyle* running around the edge of the large rectangular paved area of the *temenos* or sacred enclosure which preceded the temple. In front of you, on the slopes of the steep hillside, is a confusion of huge tumbled column sections, stone blocks and other architectural fragments, with the remains of the *cella* or temple itself at the top. The sight of such enormous and seemingly immovable chunks of fashioned stone scattered so haphazardly across the hillside is somehow highly evocative – the story of the glory and decline of the Roman Empire captured in stone.

Sanctuary of Zeus

The existing sanctuary and temple dates from 162-166 AD. In the lower *temenos* (to your right as you enter) is a rather confused area of excavations. These have revealed an altar and parts of what is believed to have been an earlier Sanctuary of Zeus dating from the mid-1st century AD. Traces of an earlier Hellenistic temple have also been found here, as well as a cave and altar which appear to have served as a pre-Hellenistic temple of some sort. A monumental staircase (its outline still just discernible) led up the hillside to the *cella*, with an upper terrace half way up which, like the *temenos*, was supported by a long barrel-vaulted chamber. The *cella* occupies a platform at the top of the hill. It was surrounded on all sides by tall columns forming a *peristyle* around it. Three of these columns have been re-erected on the northwest side and one towards the rear of the southeast side.

The partially collapsed walls either side of the entrance reveal the thickness of their construction and on the left-hand side contain a staircase which led up to the roof. Also on the left side of the front façade is a semi-circular niche with a shell-patterned half-dome. This feature is repeated all the way round the side and rear walls. At either corner of the front façade are sections of the decorative *architrave* which once ran around the top of the walls; chunks of it can be seen close-up, laid out on the ground to the right of the temple. The interior is plain, with shallow pilasters along the walls and no trace of the altar and inner shrine or *adyton*. The platform on which the *cella* stood was surrounded by its own mini *temenos* marked by a pilastered wall which was built against the hillside on the northwest side facing the South Theatre, and at the rear, where it has now been fully excavated.

From the Temple of Zeus you can conveniently walk across to the huge South Theatre. This is the larger of the two theatres found at Jerash and has been extensively restored to provide a remarkably complete picture of its former glory. During the Jerash Festival it forms the main focus for events. It was built in the late 1st century AD, during the reign of the emperor Domitian (81-96 AD) and was able to seat up to 3,000 spectators. The lower half of the tiered semi-circular seating area or *cavea* was built into the hillside while the upper half rises above it. Greek letters can still be seen carved below some of the seats of the lower tiers, apparently part of a numbering system for the most desirable seats.

South Theatre

Jerash & the North

Two arched entrances lead via vaulted passageways into the semi-circular *orchestra* area between the stage and seating. The front of the stage is elaborately decorated with niches. The backdrop or *scaenae frons* behind was originally two storeys high, and is also elaborately decorated. There are three doorways in it, topped by triangular pediments, and between them four semi-circular niches with shell half-domes, each flanked by small columns supporting richly decorated triangular pediments.

Oval Plaza Both the Temple of Zeus and the South Theatre make for good vantage points from which to look down on the Oval Plaza. In architectural terms this is the most distinctive feature of Jerash, being unique to this site. Surrounded by a full complement of re-erected Ionic columns and connecting architrave, and still with its original paving, it's very striking. To begin with it was assumed that this was the city's *agora*, but the uncovering of what appears to be an *agora* along the Cardo Maximus has put paid to that theory.

What has most interested scholars and archaeologists is its unusual oval shape, which was perhaps intended to provide a visual link reconciling the differing axes of the Cardo Maximus and Sanctuary of Zeus (this is best appreciated when approaching the plaza from the north along the Cardo). In the centre is a pedestal, now topped by a column, which would originally have

Cardo Maximus

sported a statue. There are also traces of a building which surrounded it, later converted into a water cistern when the plaza area was built over during the late 7th century. The two lines cut into the plaza's paving slabs coming from the north and west conceal buried ceramic water pipes. At two points in the surrounding colonnade on the western side the columns are slightly wider apart and the connecting architrave slightly raised; streets led off from these points into the residential and commercial districts of the town.

The Cardo Maximus leads off from the Oval Plaza in a north-easterly direction. Lined with colonnades, this was Jerash's principal thoroughfare, and was laid out as part of the original Roman city plan of the early 1st century AD. Along the first stretch, on the left, note how the original Ionic columns are topped by Corinthian capitals. This dates from the late 2nd century AD when the Cardo as far as the North Tetrapylon was widened. Also along this first stretch, on the right, you can see the small shops which lined the street behind the colonnade. The street is still paved with its original stone slabs.

Cardo Maximus

A little way along on the left, four much taller columns mark the entrance to what is believed to have been the agora. This was first excavated in the 1970s and so identified because of the word `agora' found inscribed on one of the taller columns. Behind the four taller columns was a central portico and triple gateway, of which only the right-hand portal survives along with parts of two columns in front. Flanking the central portico and gateway on each side are four small cells, believed to have been shops. In front of the two northernmost shops is an area of mosaic floor. This has been fenced off behind barbed wire. Traces of it are visible. Inside the northernmost shop there is another mosaic, though this has been reburied to protect it.

Agora

Passing through what remains of the triple gateway, the interior layout consists of a large central octagonal area surrounded by a colonnaded *peristyle*. In the centre there is an elaborate pond/fountain structure in what appears to be the shape of a Byzantine cross. Outside the octagonal *persityle*, the four corners of the large square compound are marked by semi-circular *exedras*, with square pilasters at either end of each semi-circle and two free-standing columns in between. It is only in recent years that a Spanish team have completed excavation and reconstruction work here, and their efforts have revealed an impressive and intriguing monument.

Returning to the Cardo and continuing north, along the next section you can see traces of the ruts left by chariot wheels in the smooth and weathered paving slabs. You come next to the intersection of the Cardo with the South Decumanus, marked by a huge tetrapylon. The four large pedestals can still be seen, but the four granite columns and crowning entablature which would have stood on each of these are now all gone. During the Byzantine period this junction appears to have been widened out into a circular plaza, the outline of which can still be seen, and surrounded by shops and houses. Turning left (west) at the junction, towards the end of the re-erected line of columns on the right there are the excavated remains of an **Umayyad house**. Turning right (east), the street slopes down before being interrupted abruptly by a fence and beyond it the modern road. On the far side of the road however you can see a now completely restored **bridge** which carried the decumanus over the small river running through Jerash, known today as the Wadi Jerash and in ancient times as the Chrysorhoas River (literally `Golden River').

South Tetrapylon

Nymphaeum Continuing north along the Cardo, you reach on the left the main group of ruins. Just beyond the monumental gateway and stairs leading up to the Cathedral complex (see below) is a huge Nymphaeum or public fountain dating from the late 2nd century AD. You will come across the remains of many nymphaeums if you spend any time exploring Graeco-Roman ruins in Jordan, but all consist of just the basic foundations with the rest being left to your imagination (the nymphaeum at Petra is a good example). Here at Jerash, however, you can appreciate what is a superbly decorated and remarkably well-preserved nymphaeum. It consists of a towering recessed semi-circle flanked by side walls. Within the recessed semi-circular area are a series of niches, alternately rectangular and semi-circular, on two levels. The carved decoration on the triangular pediments above the niches of the upper level is particularly beautiful. In front of the nymphaeum is a huge shallow stone basin. Note also the drainage channel immediately below the front wall of the nymphaeum; the drainage holes in it are decorated with carved fish. The recessed area of the nymphaeum would originally have been covered by a semi-dome.

The Cathedral complex & churches The monumental gateway and stairs immediately to the south of the nymphaeum lead up to what became a **Cathedral** during the Byzantine era. The gateway and stairs are believed to have originally formed the *propylaeum* of the 2nd century AD Temple of Dionysus. Four flights of stairs ascend to a small semi-circular niche with a shell-patterned semi-dome. This was a shrine dedicated to the Virgin Mary, probably dating from the 5th century when the cult of the Virgin Mary was gaining in popularity. The shrine is built against what is the eastern retaining wall of the Cathedral. Worshippers had to walk around the sides to enter the Cathedral via the opposite, western end. Built sometime during the second half of the 4th century AD, it is today completely in ruins, though its basic basilica shape can be made out and three of the columns separating the nave from the side-aisles have been re-erected.

Immediately to the west of the Cathedral is the **Fountain Court**. This was in fact the atrium of the Cathedral, but a fountain/pool was built here at a later date, hence the name. The fountain appears to have been the venue for an annual feast celebrating the miracle of Cana, when Jesus turned water into wine at a marriage. The foundations of the polygon-shaped apse of the Church of St Theodore, which occupies the higher ground to the west, intrudes into the original plan of the atrium/fountain court.

The Cathedral complex

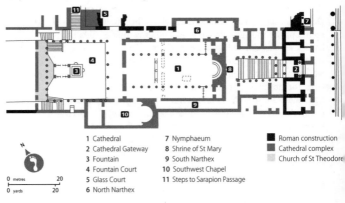

1 Cathedral	7 Nymphaeum	■ Roman construction
2 Cathedral Gateway	8 Shrine of St Mary	■ Cathedral complex
3 Fountain	9 South Narthex	☐ Church of St Theodore
4 Fountain Court	10 Southwest Chapel	
5 Glass Court	11 Steps to Sarapion Passage	
6 North Narthex		

0 metres 20
0 yards 20

On either side of the Fountain Court stairs lead up to the **Church of St Theodore**. Built between 494-6 AD, this is in better condition, with the base of the apse still intact, and two rows of seven re-erected columns marking the central nave and side-aisles. Like the Cathedral, the entrance was via the western end, through a triple doorway which is still intact. Preceding the entrance was a large rectangular atrium. This would have been surrounded by a colonnade, parts of which have been re-erected.

Further to the west, reached via a path, is a group of three parallel churches sharing a common atrium. The most northerly (the one nearest you on the right as you approach from St Theodore's) is the **Church of SS Cosmas and Damien**, the middle one the **Church of St John the Baptist** and the southerly one the **Church of St George**. All three were built between 529-33 AD. You get a good view down onto them from the path as you approach.

The Church of SS Cosmas and Damien contains Jerash's best-preserved mosaic floor. Covering the central nave, it consists of alternating rows of squares and diamonds containing geometric patterns, inscriptions, animals, birds and portraits of benefactors. Immediately in front of the raised altar area is a large rectangular mosaic inscription in Greek which mentions Bishop Paul as the patron of the church and gives the date 533 AD. On either side of it are panels portraying the two saints Cosmas and Damien, each of them flanked by trees. Cosmas and Damien were twin brothers who gained fame as accomplished doctors who charged nothing for their services. They are thought to have been martyred by Diocletian and subsequently achieved cult status in the Byzantine era. The walls of the church have been reconstructed to a considerable height and the gate is kept locked to prevent people walking on the mosaics.

The other two churches are open and contain small but impressive fragments of mosaics. The Church of St John the Baptist is interesting in that its layout is cruciform in shape, with semi-circular recesses extending out from the side-aisles to the north and south, and four columns forming a square in the centre.

From the churches you can walk across to the Temple of Artemis, but to fully appreciate this awesome temple, and approach it as worshippers would have done, you should climb up to it from the Cardo Maximus. Returning to the Fountain Court, near the foot of the stairs joining it with the Church of St Theodore, a set of stairs on the left lead north to what is known as the **Sarapion passage**, after an inscription dating from 67 AD found here which records its construction by Sarapion, son of Apollonius. At the top of the stairs, the path passes through what were once three gateways in succession, though the middle one is now missing.

The passage brings you out on what is known as the **Stepped Street**, which runs east-west between the Cathedral/Fountain Court complex and the Sanctuary of Artemis. Turning left into it, it climbs to the west, its long-interval steps subsided and leaning this way and that. On the right as you ascend is a long barrel-vaulted chamber built under *temenos* of the Sanctuary of Artemis. The chamber has been restored and once housed a museum, though it is currently used as a store room by the Department of Antiquities.

Returning to the Cardo, note the sections of massive, richly decorated architrave lined up on the floor; these would once have crowned the colonnade on either side. A little further to the north, past the Nymphaeum, you come to four columns on the left which tower above those of the colonnade, marking the entrance to the Sanctuary of Artemis, the largest and most important

Sanctuary of Artemis

temple sanctuary at Jerash. Built during the 2nd century AD, probably between 150-180 AD at a time when the city was flourishing and expanding, the temple was dedicated to Artemis, the daughter of Zeus, sister of Apollo and patron goddess of the city. The glory of this sanctuary is not in its individual components, but rather in the way they combine to form a unified complex which would have unfolded before worshippers as they approached via a sacred way, monumental entrance and monumental staircase to arrive finally at the holy of holies, the temple itself.

In fact, the approach to the sanctuary began to the east of the Cardo, by the river. Turn right therefore and go as far as you can (the way is blocked by the apse of a Byzantine **church** built here in the 6th century) to get a view of the `sacred way' as it would have looked. Beyond the church you can see the vague remains of a stairway which ascended from the river. By climbing up onto the apse of the Byzantine church you can get a particularly good view of the whole approach to the inner temple.

From the apse of the church a colonnaded square extended to a `**Propy-laeum Plaza**' (today a rather jumbled confusion of ruins), which in turn led out onto the Cardo. After crossing the street and passing through the four taller columns of the colonnade, steps lead up through the **Propylaeum Gate-way** of the complex. The gateway is of massive proportions, with four free-standing columns preceding a huge central portal flanked by smaller side-portals. Above each side-portal is an elaborate niche with a shell-patterned half-dome topped by a richly decorated triangular pediment. Only a fragment of the massive triangular pediment which once crowned the whole gateway remains in place.

Passing through the gateway a monumental stairway ascends in a series of seven flights, each of seven steps interspaced by a terrace, until you reach the **Altar Terrace**, with the foundations of a large altar in the centre. From here the monumental staircase, thought to have originally been over 100 m across, con-tinues in three further flights up to the *temenos* of the temple itself. A total of 22 Corinthian columns originally formed a colonnade along the top of the stairs, several of which have been re-erected, to your left as you ascend. Beyond this colonnade was a wall pierced by a doorway (of which almost nothing remains) which led through into the *temenos* proper, a large rectangular enclosure mea-suring 161m by 121m and originally surrounded on all sides by colonnades (some of the columns along the south side have been re-erected).

Sanctuary of Artemis

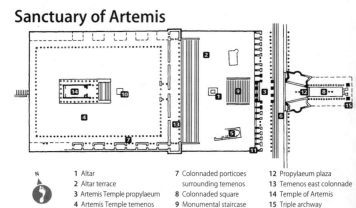

N

0 metres 100
0 yards 100

1 Altar
2 Altar terrace
3 Artemis Temple propylaeum
4 Artemis Temple temenos
5 Byzantine church
6 Cardo
7 Colonnaded porticoes surrounding temenos
8 Colonnaded square
9 Monumental staircase
10 Open-air altar
11 Propylaeum gateway
12 Propylaeum plaza
13 Temenos east colonnade
14 Temple of Artemis
15 Triple archway

The *temenos* is dominated by the **Temple of Artemis** itself, described by CS Fisher, who excavated it in the 1930s, as "in all probability the finest single structure ever erected at ancient Gerasa". A modern set of steps lead up onto the platform on which the *cella* of the temple stood. In front of the *cella* itself was a massive *portico* supported by three rows of towering Corinthian columns, still standing after more than two millennia; six at the front (one of which is missing), followed by four, followed by two.

One of the columns (the middle one of the three along the south side) sways slightly in the wind. On a windy day you can actually see the movement with the naked eye, but even when the wind is very light, if you wedge some coins and a long flat object into the small gap at the base of the column, you can see the movement.

Inside the *cella* itself, in the wall opposite the entrance, you can see the shrine which would have contained the sacred idol of the goddess Artemis. In front of the Temple of Artemis there are the remains of an **altar**. Excavations have revealed that this was partly covered over by a ceramics workshop dating from the late Byzantine to early Umayyad period. From the *temenos* it is possible to walk across to the Church of the Bishop Isaiah and North Theatre to the north (see below).

Returning once again to the Cardo and continuing north, you cross a dirt road leading up to the North Theatre before arriving at the North Tetrapylon, marking the junction of the Cardo Maximus with the North Decumanus. It consists of four solid piers in each corner, with arches spanning the line of each road. At the time of writing, it was undergoing extensive restoration, with its domed roof now fully reconstucted. This tetrapylon was added after the basic city plan had been laid out, probably during the late 2nd century AD.

North Tetrapylon

Immediately before the North Tetrapylon, to the east of the Cardo, are the West Baths. Dating from the 2nd century AD, the complex is huge (originally 75 m by 50 m) though now in an advanced state of ruin. Only the north pavilion with its domed roof is standing, along with one of the supporting arches of the central *fridgidarium/caldarium* complex.

West Baths

From the North Tetrapylon the Cardo continues north for 200 m or so to the North Gate of the city. Built in 115 AD during Trajan's reign, this gate is today largely in ruins; if you are hot and tired it can be skipped. More interesting is the last stretch of the Cardo itself, which here retains the original colonnade with its Ionic columns and capitals, this part of the Cardo (along with the section immediately to the south of the North Tetrapylon) never having been widened.

North Gate

Following the North Decumanus westwards from the North Tetrapylon, you come to the North Theatre on your left. This was preceded by a plaza and portico, both of which, along with parts of the theatre, have been extensively restored. To the right (north side) of the street the plaza is marked by a series of six columns (two consisting of engaged columns and pilasters, and all but one re-erected) standing on huge pedestals and crowned by Corinthian capitals and plain interconnecting architrave. To the left, steps lead up to the portico, from where two doorways lead through to the stage of the theatre. The *scaenae frons* (a reconstruction) is much simpler than that of the South Theatre. The marble paving decorating the orchestra is a modern reconstruction of the original design. Climbing up from here via the steps between the tiered seating of the *cavea*, you can gain access to a vaulted tunnel which runs beneath the uppermost tiers of seating. Doorways lead out from the tunnel onto the higher

Theatre

ground between the theatre and the Temple of Artemis, while at the eastern end steps lead steeply down to an entrance beside the stage.

Excavation of the North Theatre only began in 1982-3, carried out by British, American and Australian teams. In its original form, the theatre appears to have been completed around 164/5 AD, at which time it was much smaller, really only counting as an *odeon* rather than a full-blown theatre, and probably also serving as a civic centre. During the early 3rd century AD it was enlarged, although it still remained much smaller than its southern counterpart, seating only around half as many spectators.

Church of Bishop Isaiah On the high ground just to the west of the North Theatre is the Church of Bishop Isaiah. Built in 559 AD, the church was first excavated in 1982 by an American team. They uncovered rich mosaics decorating all the floor area of the church except for the apse. At the time of writing these had been reburied to protect them from the elements and only the basic outline of the church could be seen, with its triple apse and some of the recycled Ionic columns and capitals which separated the nave from the side-aisles.

Museum Up on the hillside to the east of the southern section of the Cardo Maximus is a small museum which houses a collection of mosaics found at Jerash, along with various architectural fragments and items of pottery, glassware, metalware, coins, jewellery etc. At the time of writing there was also a scale model of ancient Jerash, although there are plans to install this in the new visitors' centre opposite the *Jerash Resthouse*. The museum, which can be reached by a path from the oval plaza or by steps leading up from the southern section of the Cardo, is well worth a visit. ■ *Open daily 0730-sunset, but sometimes closed on Fri. Entry free (included in the price of your ticket for the rest of Jerash).*

Birketein Reservoir & Theatre Just over 2 km to the north of the main ruins of Jerash is a large reservoir and the remains of a theatre. To get there, head north along the main road running alongside the ruins. Go straight across the first roundabout you come to and then take the left turn signposted to `Suf'. Very soon after, more or less opposite the North Gate of ancient Jerash, bear right where the road forks to arrive at the reservoir and theatre on the left. The name Birketein means literally `double pool' or `two pools' and the large rectangular reservoir has a dividing wall sectioning off one portion of it. The reservoir is still in use today, although in summer it gets rather stagnant and smelly.

Above it on the hillside are the remains of a small theatre, today rather worn and eroded, not having undergone restoration or reconstruction work of any sort. Both the reservoir and theatre date from the late 2nd or early 3rd century AD. The reservoir was the site of the Maiuma Festival, a Syrian festival celebrated every three years. According to literary sources dating from the 4th century onwards, this included various water sports involving naked women. It appears to have continued to be celebrated up until the 6th century, although its somewhat promiscuous nature led to it being banned and then reinstated on several occasions during the Byzantine era.

Eastern Baths By the bus station are the remains of the Eastern Baths. Originally even larger than the Western Baths, they are today in an advanced state of ruin. Their setting amidst the crowded press of the modern town provides a stark contrast with the ruins within the site. The baths have never been closely studied and the date of their construction is not known.

Jerash Festival

First organised in 1980 by Yarmouk University, the Jerash Festival has grown into a major annual cultural event in Jordan. Featuring theatre, music, dancing, singing, crafts etc, it starts at the end of July and lasts for 2-3 weeks, attracting large crowds throughout its duration. If your visit to Jordan coincides with the festival, it is certainly an event not to be missed. For more information on exact dates, programmes etc contact the Jerash Festival Office in Amman, T06-5675199.

Essentials

Unfortunately there is at present no accommodation at Jerash itself, although there are a couple of places nearby which are convenient if you have your own transport. By far the best option is the **B** *Olive Branch Resort*, to the west of Jerash, T079-523546 (mobile), F06-5826034. To get there, follow the road from Jerash towards Ajlun (see below), and after 6 km take the right turn signposted for the resort (and for the village of Souf). Keep following the signs for a further 2 km to arrive at the hotel. Located high up in the hills, with stunning views out over the surrounding countryside, the hotel offers comfortable rooms with fan, heater, TV/dish and attached bath (some rooms also with balconies). There is a restaurant, swimming pool (JD5 for non-guests) and children's play area.

Sleeping

Camping is also allowed here (JD5 per person including use of the pool and toilet/shower facilities), and you can also come for a do-it-yourself barbecue (you bring the food, they provide the barbecue, JD1 per person). The hotel is well-run and friendly. Recommended.

Rather less appealing is the **C** *Dibeen Rest House*, situated in the Dibeen National Park some 14 km southwest of Jerash (see below for directions), T6639710. There are 8 bungalows here (choice of doubles or 3/4-bed) with heater, phone, TV and attached bath. Somewhat rundown and in need of proper refurbishment, but passable. There is a large restaurant and **camping** is also allowed (JD3 per person).

Finally, if you are on a tight budget, it is worth asking at the *Jerash Resthouse* adjacent to the visitors' centre in Jerash. There are basic dormitory rooms below the resthouse which were originally intended for staff but are generally empty. Talk to the manager; with permission from the tourist police, he may be able to let you stay the night here.

The *Jerash Resthouse*, opposite the visitors' centre, is open daily from 0730 until sunset, T6351146, F6351437. It offers a full buffet of various mezze/salad dishes plus main course meat dishes for JD6 per person. Alternatively you can just have the mezze/salad dishes for JD4 per person, or there is an à la carte menu. There is also a bar and a cafeteria where you can get snacks, drinks etc. Prices all round are a little on the steep side, though the manager claims he is willing to offer discounts for 'students'/ budget travellers.

Eating

Next door to each other on the main road running alongside the site, more or less opposite the visitors' centre, are the *Janat Jerash* and *Al Khayam* restaurants. Both have pleasant shaded terrace areas and offer a fairly standard (and somewhat overpriced) selection of kebabs, chicken, mezze dishes, salads etc for around JD5 per head upwards. The latter is usually the busier (and perhaps better) of the two.

By the roundabout some 700 m further north there is the *Abo Ahmad*, T6352520, a simple, clean and unpretentious restaurant with a large upstairs dining hall and an outdoor terrace, offering a standard selection of Arabic fare from around JD4 per head. Nearby is the *Ya Hala* restaurant and bar, T6351289, a rather over-the-top place pitched very much at the Arab market and featuring some supremely tacky interior decor. Meals here cost in the region of JD7-10 per head upwards. Across the road, the *Basha* restaurant is a simple budget diner offering shawarma and falafel sandwiches, roast chicken, kebabs etc. There are several more cheap eateries to be found in the vicinity of the bus station.

Of the cluster of restaurants to be found around 2 km to the south of Jerash, the *Green Valley* is long established and has a good reputation, though all are rather expensive and geared primarily towards catering for wedding parties and the like. A meal of kebabs and salad etc will cost around JD7-10 per head upwards.

Transport As well as the regular a/c coaches and minibuses running between Jerash and **Amman's** Abdali bus station, minibuses also operate from Jerash to **Ajlun** (200 fils), **Irbid** (290 fils), **Zarqa** (300 fils) and **Mafraq** (300 fils). Service taxis also operate from here to all these destinations. All services depart when full. Note that there are very few (if any) services to anywhere after nightfall, so make sure you get to the bus station a little before sunset.

Around Jerash

Dibeen National Park Around 12 km to the southwest of Jerash is the Dibeen National Park, incorporating some of Jordan's richest forests, which spread across the Mediterranean hill country of this area. Consisting predominantly of Aleppo pine, they also contain oak, cypress, acacia and wild pistachio trees. Some of the Aleppo pines (*Pinus halepensis*; known locally as *Aihadaa*) are as much as 200 years old, and are now the focus of conservation efforts through a joint Jordanian-German forestry project. First established in 1972, Dibeen is unfortunately only really a 'national park' in name, although there are plans to designate it as a 'Protected Area' under the auspices of the RSCN. This is a beautiful place to come for a picnic and enjoy the cooler air of the hills, and with your own transport it takes less than half an hour to reach from Jerash.

To get there, head west at the roundabout at the southern end of Jerash, as if for Ajlun, but take the left turn signposted to `Ghazza Camp' and 'Dibeen National Park' after around 400 m. Keep following this road, going straight through Ghazza Camp 4 km further on (originally a Palestinian refugee camp of makeshift tents, but now a fully developed village). The road winds its way through beautiful wooded hills. Around 6 km beyond Ghazza Camp, you come to a right turn signposted to *Dibeen Resthouse*, which is located in the midst of the forest 2 km further on. Continuing past the resthouse, the road leads eventually back to the Jerash-Ajlun road, though the route is rather confusing in places.

The resthouse itself is a rather rundown, sprawling and unattractive place of concrete paths and terraces. As well as the accommodation here (see above), there is a restaurant with a cavernous dining hall and seating outside during summer. It can get very busy with visiting Jordanian families on weekends and holidays during the summer, but otherwise it is usually pretty deserted, and somewhat forlorn. The surrounding forests are altogether far more appealing, and you don't have to venture far to find a lovely secluded spot for yourself.

Jerash to Ajlun

It is a pleasant drive through rolling hills to Ajlun, some 22 km to the northwest of Jerash. Head west at the roundabout at the southern end of Jerash (signposted for Ajlun). After 6 km you pass the right turn for the *Olive Branch Resort* (see above). Just under 13 km further on, turn right in the town of Anjara (signposted for Ajlun; going straight takes you down into the Jordan

Valley). Just over 5 km further on you arrive in Ajlun. Go left at the round-about in the centre of town (signposted only to `Directorate of Ajloun Tourism') to head up to Ajlun Castle, 3 km further on, passing on the way the *Al Rabad Castle* and *Ajloun* hotels, and the *Bonita Ajloun* restaurant (see below).

Ajlun Castle (Qalat ar-Rabaad)

Perched on top of a hill with commanding views out over the surrounding countryside, Ajlun castle is unique in that it is the only entirely Arab castle in Jordan. It has been extensively restored and is well worth a visit, as much for its beautiful setting and views as for the castle itself.

The castle was first built in 1184 AD by Izz ud-Din Usama ibn Munqidh, a nephew of Salah ud-Din (Saladin) and a commander in his army. Its strategic position allowed it to control trade and communications between southern Jordan and Syria, as well as the important iron mines in the area. It was probably also intended to counter the Crusader castle of Belvoir near Lake Tiberias (Sea of Galilee). In 1214 AD, following the death of Izz ud-Din, it was enlarged by Aibak ibn Abdallah, who added the southeast tower and entrance gate. In 1260 the castle was largely destroyed by the Mongols, but subsequently rebuilt by the Mameluke Sultan Baibars. During the early Ottoman period a contingent of soldiers was based here and during the early 17th century Fakhr ud-Din II Maan, a powerful Emir from Mount Lebanon, used it as a base for his campaigns. Two major earthquakes, in 1837 and 1927, caused serious damage. Soon after the second earthquake, excavation and restoration work was carried out, with the Jordanian Department of Antiquities carrying out further restoration work to the walls in the 1980s.

From the outer entrance portal, stairs lead up past arrow slits set within recessed arches in the wall to the left, while on the right is the wall of one of the castle's original towers. On the way up, note the carved stone single-slab door lying on the shelf of one of the windows. Entering the inner castle, you pass through a double archway with a gap in-between, from where boiling oil could be poured on any would-be attackers. Once inside, you find yourself in a veritable maze of vaulted passageways and rooms which seem almost designed to disorientate and confuse, though this is more a reflection of the different stages of construction. The views from the upper towers are very impressive; you really get a sense of the strategic significance of the castle's location, overlooking a long stretch of the Jordan Valley to the west, as well as three small wadis leading down to the Jordan Valley; the Wadi Kufrajeh, Wadi Rajeb and Wadi al-Yabees.

■ *Open daily 0800-1900 in summer, 0800-1700 in winter. Entry JD1 (Jordanians 250 fils). There is a small souvenir shop and tourist police post by the castle. Official guided tours cost JD4. The Ajlun Directorate of Tourism (open 0800-1500, closed Fri and Sat, T6420115), located in the same building as the Bonita Ajloun restaurant, can provide you with a free brochure and pamphlet about the castle.*

Ajlun Castle (Qalat Ar-Rabaad)

Entrance

N

■ Construction dating from 1184
▨ Additions dating from 1214

0 metres — 20
0 yards — 20

Jerash & the North

Sleeping & eating Both the hotels on the road up to the castle offer very similar deals. They are a little rundown, though comfortable enough. The room rates they advertise are the official ones set by the Ministry of Tourism, and are somewhat inflated. If it is quiet (which it usually is) they are generally willing to drop their prices. **B-C** *Al Rabad Castle*, T6420202. Rooms with TV, heater, phone and attached bath. The rooms at the front all have balconies, the best one being the corner room on the 1st floor (room 101), which has a larger terrace balcony and excellent views of the castle. There is a restaurant and seating outside in summer on a pleasant shaded terrace with great views. **B-C** *Ajloun*, T/F6420524. Rooms with TV, heater, phone, fridge and attached bath. The rooms at the front have good views but no balconies. There is a large restaurant hall on the top floor, also with good views,

Entrance to Ajlun Castle

and plans for a swimming pool in the grounds. A rather ugly, modern building, not as nice as the *Al Rabad Castle*, but appears more willing to drop prices.

Around 400 m below the castle is the *Bonita Ajloun* restaurant and bar, T6420981. Open 0900-1800 in winter, 0900-2300 in summer. This rather smart establishment is linked to the *Bonita* restaurant in Amman and caters mainly for groups. The set-menu buffet here costs JD6 per person, or there is an à la carte menu (around JD4-6 per head, but watch out for the 23% tax and service). There are great views of the castle from the terrace. In the town of Ajlun itself, clustered around the roundabout in the centre, there are a few cheaper restaurants and snack places serving the usual selection of falafels, shawarmas, kebabs, roast chicken, hummus, salad etc.

Transport There are regular minibuses and service taxis between Ajlun town and **Jerash**, **Amman** (Abdali bus station) and **Irbid**. These leave when full and stop running around sunset. There is also a shuttle bus service which runs between Ajlun town and the castle (60 fils) on a 'depart when full' basis (in summer, and especially on Fri and Sat, there is usually sufficient demand to make services pretty frequent) or you can take a taxi (around 500 fils), or walk.

Ajlun to Irbid

The drive from Ajlun to Irbid, some 30 km to the north, is a beautiful one, taking you up into the rolling Ajlun highlands. From the roundabout in the centre of Ajlun town head north (signposted for Irbid). The road climbs steeply up, and after just under 5 km there is a sharp left turn signposted to Deir Abu Saed and Halawah, and, on a separate tourist signpost, to Ishtanafaina. This road takes you into the area of the RSCN-administered **Zubia Nature Reserve**, established in 1988 and comprising 12 sq km of oak and pistachio woodland where a captive breeding programme for the Roe Deer has been initiated.

There is a simple **campsite** here, but visits must be arranged in advance through the RSCN in Amman (see page 115). Continuing straight, just over 1 km further on there is a right turn signposted to Suf and Jerash. The main road continues north to arrive eventually in Irbid, running along the hilltops of the Ajlun highlands, where precariously leaning pine trees stand (just) as a testament to the powerful winds which sweep across from the west. Entering the town, continue straight past the right turn signposted to 'Al Himma' and 'Umm Qays' (this is the ring-road around Irbid), along the busy University St (with Yarmouk University on your right), and then do a left and a right to follow the one-way system into the centre of town, around 1½ km north of the university.

Irbid

Irbid is the largest town and administrative centre of northern Jordan, with a thriving local economy fuelling rapid growth. Perhaps the greatest influence on the town, however, is the **Yarmouk University***. Established in 1976, the university is the country's second largest, and gives Irbid an added vibrancy, not least in terms of the proliferation of internet cafés which now vie with all the fast food outlets and snack bars on University St (said by some to have the world's highest concentration of internet cafés!)*

Phone code: 02

Although Irbid presents itself very much as a modern town, evidence of settlement dating back to the Early Bronze Age has been uncovered on the ancient tell in the centre of the town. Irbid has also been identified with the settlement of Beth Arbel mentioned in the Bible, and with Byzantine Arbela (not to be confused with Abila), at one time part of the Decapolis. However, there is very little in the way of monuments recording the town's history, and for most travellers it is seen mainly as a convenient base from which to visit sites in the surrounding area, or as a transport hub when travelling between them. Nevertheless, the town's museums are certainly worth a visit (in particular the Museum of Jordanian Heritage on the university campus). There are also a couple of interesting things to see around the ancient tell, *a lively town centre and souks area to explore, as well as the altogether different ambience of the university area.*

Ins and outs

Being an important transport hub, there are regular bus and minibus services connecting Irbid with all the towns and sites in northern Jordan, although the various bus stations are all somewhat inconveniently located away from the centre.

Getting there

The old centre of town is relatively compact and easily explored on foot, though the unversity area to the south, and various bus stations dotted around town, are far away enough to warrant making use of the local buses, or the readily available private taxis.

Getting around

There will be a tourist information office in the newly restored Ottoman Dar es-Saraya when it opens. Until then, you are best off enlisting the help of your hotel.

Tourist information

Sights

Located in the university grounds and part of the university's archaeology department, this is an excellent, well laid-out and well presented museum. It is one of the best in Jordan, combining 'ethnographic' displays of Jordan's cultural heritage with archaeological displays covering Jordan's history from the earliest origins of agriculture and settlement up to the present. Well worth a visit. ■ *Open 0900-1600, closed Fri and Sat. Entry free. The nearest university entrance for the museum is the west gate on University St, just to the south of the Hijazi Palace hotel, or you can enter through the north gate.*

Museum of Jordanian Heritage

Jerash & the North

Irbid

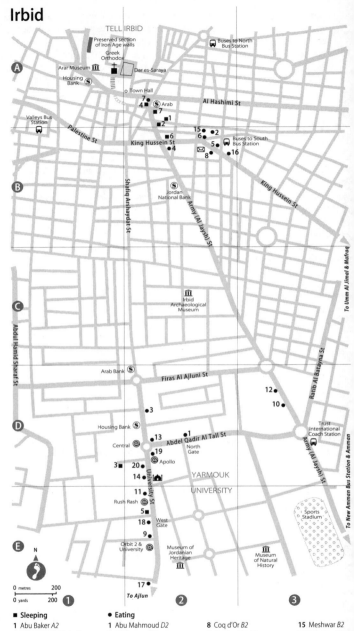

■ Sleeping
1 Abu Baker A2
2 Al Ameen al-Kabir A2
3 Al Joude D1
4 Al Wahadat al-Arabie A2
5 Hijazi Palace E2
6 Omayed B2
7 Tourism (Siyaha) A2

● Eating
1 Abu Mahmoud D2
2 Al Khayyam B2
3 Al Madi D2
4 Al Saadi B2
5 Andalucia B2
6 Auto Burger B2
7 Café A2

8 Coq d'Or B2
9 Cortina d'Or E2
10 Grill House D3
11 Habibah Patisserie E2
12 Kamer al Zaman D3
13 Les Champs Elysées D2
14 Mankal Chicken Tikka D2

15 Meshwar B2
16 Palestine B2
17 Pizza Hut E2
18 Popeye's E2
19 Tiger Brazil D2
20 Toronto Fried
   Chicken D2

Also part of the university, this museum comprises of a huge collection of stuffed birds and mammals, many of them chronicling Jordan's long list of vanished species. There are also corals and aquatic specimens, lizards, snakes, insects etc as well as dried plants/herbs and a geology section. ■ *Open 0900-1600, closed Fri and Sat. Entry free.*

Museum of Natural History

At the time of writing, this small museum was housed in the carefully hidden and little visited Department of Tourism and Antiquities building, between the university and town centre. The collection includes some very beautiful mosaics from sites around northern Jordan, as well as pottery, figurines, sculptures etc. The artefacts are only temporarily housed here and will be displayed in the newly restored Ottoman Dar es-Saraya, on the *tell* in the centre of town, when it opens. ■ *Open 0800-1400, closed Fri and Sat. Entry free.*

Irbid Archaeological Museum

A short section of the **Iron Age walls**, consisting huge, rough-hewn and worn stone blocks, can be seen on the west side of the ancient *tell*. The large **Dar es-Saraya** on the *tell* housed the Ottoman and then Hashemite governor of the town before being converted into a police station/jail. At the time of writing, the restoration of this attractive Ottoman building was nearing completion; when it opens it will house the Irbid Archaeological Museum, and also a tourist information office. Nearby, the **Araar Museum** is the former house of the Jordanian poet Mustapha Whab'il at-Tal (1899-1949). Also dating from the Ottoman period, this building has a pleasant open courtyard and a small museum chronicling his life and works. The sign outside is in Arabic only (white writing on a blue background). Just beside the Araar Museum there is a **Greek Orthodox church**, as well as the **King Abdullah mosque**, with its graceful minaret. Note that there is a military base on top of the *tell*; don't try wandering in, they will not be amused.

Tell Irbid

Jerash & the North

Essentials

Irbid has 2 mid-range hotels, both to the south of the town centre, beside the University. All the budget accommodation is in the centre of town. **B** *Hijazi Palace*, University St, T7279501, F7279520. Rooms with a/c, TV/dish, phone, fridge and attached bath (those at the front are a little noisy). Restaurant, coffee shop/bar, conference hall. Reasonably comfortable but expensive and a bit tacky. The lobby area is much nicer than the rooms themselves. **B** *Al Joude*, off University St, T7275515, F7275517. Large, comfortable rooms with a/c, TV/dish, fridge, phone and attached bath. Good café/restaurant downstairs (see below). Pleasantly located at the end of a quiet dead-end street, yet just a stone's throw from the university. Friendly, helpful management. Recommended.

Sleeping

D *Omayed*, King Hussein St (3rd floor, above *Irbed Supermarket*), T/F7245955. Fan, heater, TV, phone, attached bath. Rooms at the front are smaller and noiser, those at the rear larger and quieter. The only hotel in the town centre above rock-bottom budget. Friendly, helpful manager.

F *Al Wahadat al-Arabie*, Arar St, T7242083. Basic but reasonably clean rooms, some with fan, all share shower (clean, solar heated, free) and toilet. Doubles JD8, singles JD5 or dorm beds JD2. Friendly manager. **F** *Tourism (Siyaha)*, Al Uruba St, T7242633. Basic rooms, no fan, shared shower (abysmal) and toilet (more or less OK). Doubles JD8, singles JD5 or dorm beds JD2. **F** *Al Ameen al-Kabir* (or just *Amin*), Al Uruba St, T7242384. Basic but spotlessly clean rooms with ceiling or table fan, shared shower (750 fils, clean, hot) and toilet (also clean; one room with attached toilet), use of kitchen. Doubles JD8, singles JD5 or dorm beds JD2. Well-run hotel, very friendly and helpful. Recommended. **F** *Abu Baker*, Wafsi al-Tall St (above *Bank of Jordan*), T7242695. Reasonably clean rooms with fan, share shower (clean, free) and toilet (one room with attached shower/toilet). Doubles JD8, singles JD5 or dorm beds JD2. Good views from top floor rooms.

Eating   Eating options in Irbid are divided between those places in the town centre, all of which are fairly simple affairs, and the numerous fast-food outlets and smarter restaurants in the vicinity of the university, most of them along Arshaydet (University) St.

Town centre Easily the best budget diner, for vegetarian food at least, is the *Palestine*, on King Hussein St, a simple, spotlessly clean restaurant specialising in hummus, fuul, fateh and falafels (also serves tea and soft drinks). It's popular with locals and always busy, so everything is very fresh. Excellent value. Nearby, also on King Hussein St, is the *Coq d'Or*, which does good roast chicken. More or less opposite is the *Andalucia* (up on the 6th floor), which is a little more upmarket, though unremarkable, serving a fairly standard selection of Arabic fare for around JD4 per head upwards. The *Al Saadi*, opposite the *Omayed* hotel, offers a very similar deal. On Wasfi at-Tall St there is the *Al Khayyam*, which serves food for around JD2 per head, but is more a place to come for a drink (large Henniger beer JD1.400). Nearby is the *Meshwar*, serving a varied selection of sandwiches as well as fresh juice, and round the corner the *Auto Burger* serving shawarmas, burgers etc. There are dozens more simple budget diners offering roast chicken, kebabs etc, as well as numerous falafel, shawarma and sandwich bars dotted around the town centre.

University area Amongst the cluster of cafés and fast food/snack places on University St, opposite the west gate of the university, there is the popular *Cortina d'Or*, which has comfortable seating indoors or a pleasant covered terrace outside, and serves a varied selection of pizzas, pasta, spaghetti, omlettes, meat grills, fruit juices, milkshakes, ice cream, tea, coffee etc (around JD4-5 per head for a full meal, less for snacks). Around 300 m to the south of the west gate there is a branch of *Pizza Hut*. Fast food outlets and restaurants along this stretch of street to the north of the west gate include *Popeye's*, *Mankal Chicken Tikka* and *Toronto Fried Chicken*, as well as the *Habibah Patisserie* with a mouthwatering selection of cakes, Arabic sweets and biscuits (takeaway or seating upstairs), the *Tiger Brazil* restaurant and coffee shop (mostly sandwiches and burgers, but also roast chicken and meat grills), and the *Concorde*, a Canadian-theme restaurant/coffee shop and *Planet Donuts*, both in the same complex as the *Apollo* internet centre. On the roundabout just to the north of here is *Les Champs Elysées*, T7258999, situated up on the 1st floor. Despite the name, it serves mostly Arabic food (around JD4 per head). The decor here is on the tacky side of tasteful, but the staff are friendly and helpful and they also serve beer (large bottle JD1.500). They often have live music in the evenings. Further north along University St, where it narrows and becomes one-way southwards, there are several pleasant traditional falafel, hummus and fuul restaurants. Below the *Al Joude* hotel is the *News Café*, a nicely furnished, spacious place serving sandwiches, pizzas (from a wood oven) and various 'international cuisine' dishes, as well as real coffee (JD4-6 per head for a full meal, coffee JD1.250). They also have a pool table here and three terminals for internet access. On Abdel Qadir al-Tall St, opposite the north gate of the university is *Abu Mahmoud* (aka *Al Moqbel*), a popular student hang-out offering a mixture of Arabic and western-style fast food and snacks. On Army (Al Jaysh) St, to the northwest of this roundabout, is the *Kamer al-Zaman*, T7253683, a swish place with modern decor offering a choice of Chinese, 'international' and Arabic cuisine (around JD10 per head, or lots more for fish dishes). Serves alcohol, downstairs is a coffee shop. The *Grill House* (aka *Omayed 2*) nearby is essentially a somewhat upmarket fast food place serving burgers, pizzas, grills etc.

Cafés   There are several traditional Arabic cafés in the centre of town. Perhaps the nicest of these, with a pleasant balcony overlooking Al Hashemi St, is next door to the *Al*

Wahadat al-Arabie hotel (go up the stairway immediately to the right of the hotel as you face it). Many of the fast food places and restaurants on University St also serve as cafés. For something fancy, try the posh European-style *Pravista*, up on the 1st floor in the same shopping complex as the *Apollo* internet centre.

New Amman bus station (in Arabic; 'Mujama Amman al-Jadide). Inconveniently   **Transport** located around 3 km to the southeast of the town centre, near the university, although there are frequent minibuses (70 fils) and service taxis (100 fils) between the centre (see map) and the bus station. *Hijazi* operate a/c coaches between here and Amman's Abdali bus station, departing every 15 mins between 0600-1900 (820 fils, 1½ hr). There are also minibus services to Jerash, Ajlun, Ramtha, Zarqa and Mafraq from here, all of which depart when full and cost less than 500 fils. Service taxis operate from here to Damascus in Syria, going via the Ramtha-Deraa border, and also operating on a 'depart when full' basis (JD4, approx 3 hrs). The ticket office for both *Hijazi* coaches and service taxis to Damascus is in the large building in the centre of the bus station. Minibuses to other destinations leave from various points around the bus station.

North bus station (in Arabic; 'Mujama Shamali'). Located a couple of kilometres north of the town centre and also served by service taxis and minibuses shuttling to and from the centre (see map). Minibuses run from here to **Umm Qais** (220 fils), **Al Himma** (280 fils) and **Hartha** (for **Abila**, 150 fils)

Valleys bus station (in Arabic; 'Mujama al-Agwar'). Situated just off Palestine St, within walking distance of the centre of town. Minibuses and service taxis run from here to destinations in the Jordan valley. **North Shunah** (250 fils), **Al Mashari** (for **Pella**, 300 fils), **Jisr Sheikh Hussein** (Prince Hussein Bridge/Jordan River, the most northerly border crossing into **Israel**, service taxi, JD2; a bus takes you from the Jordanian customs/immigration post to the Israeli side for NIS3 (US$0.75), and from there buses run to Bet Shean for NIS9 (US$2.22), and **Deir Alla** (600 fils).

Trust International coach station Situated on Army (Al Jaysh) St, near the university, T7251876. The shuttle buses and service taxis between the centre and the New Amman bus station pass this way. A/c coach services to **Tel Aviv** (daily except Sat, 0830, JD14) and **Nazareth/Haifa** (daily except Sat, 0930, JD8.500) stop here en route from Amman. Note that timings are approximate and it is not possible to book tickets in advance; during May, Jun and Jul in particular the coaches may well already be full when they leave Amman.

Banks The *Bank of Jordan,* in the same building as the *Abu Baker* hotel, changes cash and TCs   **Directory** (3% commission). The *Arab Bank,* opposite *Al Wahadat al-Arabie* hotel, has an ATM which accepts *Visa, Mastercard* and *Cirrus*. On Al Hashemi St, to the west of the town hall, there is a branch of the *Housing Bank* with an ATM which accepts *Visa* cards. Both these latter two banks also have branches with ATMs near the university (see map). There are also several licensed money changers opposite the town hall on Al Hashemi St, and round the corner on Arar St.

Communications Internet Irbid is the internet capital of Jordan, boasting a plethora of internet cafés along University St (more than 70 at the last count), with new ones opening practically every week. At the time of writing, prices for internet access were also cheaper here than anywhere else in Jordan. The majority are better described as 'internet offices', since few have any sort of café facilities, consisting only of as many computer terminals as can be crammed into the available space. Almost all claim to be open 24 hrs. A small selection of the better ones are listed here (see map for exact locations). *Central*, 500 fils/hr, 27 terminals, separate area for women downstairs. *Apollo*, JD1/hr before 2000, 500 fils/hr after 2000, 45 terminals, also incorporates café and juice bar complete with large-screen TV. *Rush Rash*, 750 fils/hr, 30 terminals, reasonably spacious with good partitions. *University*, 500 fils/hr, 24 terminals, free tea and coffee, fairly cramped. *Orbit 2*, 24 terminals, free tea and coffee, fairly cramped. *News Café*, below Al Joude hotel. JD1.500/hr, 3 terminals, pricey but comfortable and pleasant setting. **Post** The Central Post Office is on King Hussein St. Open 0700-1700, Fri 0700-1330. **Telephone** There are numerous **Alo** and **JPP** cardphones to be found all over the town

Around Irbid

Sites in the area which can conveniently be visited from Irbid include Abila, due north of Irbid (see below), Umm Qais, in the extreme northwest corner of Jordan (see page 193), and Pella, to the south of Umm Qais, in the Jordan Valley (see page 188). Although it is quite a drive, you can also reach Umm al-Jimal in the northeast (see below), and the route from Irbid is more interesting than from Amman.

Abila (Quwayliba)

Situated 15 km to the north of Irbid, Abila is rarely visited by tourists, tending to be overlooked in favour of more important (or at least better known) sites in the area. However, if you have the time, it is well worth visiting, both for the substantial archaeological remains to be found here, and for its beautiful setting amidst rolling hills of olive groves and wheat fields. There are no facilities of any kind here, so bring your own food and plenty of water (it's an idyllic place for a picnic).

Getting there **By public transport** There are irregular minibuses from Irbid's North bus station to Hartha, which run past the spring of Ain Quwayliba. If you do come out here by public transport, be sure to leave plenty of time for the return journey, as minibuses back to Irbid are even less frequent towards the end of the day. Really, though, Abila is one of those places best visited with your own transport (if you do not have a hire car or your own vehicle, it is worth chartering a private taxi from Irbid).

By private car From the centre of Irbid, head east along Al Hashimi St and turn left at the first roundabout you come to (marked by a large white concrete sculpture in the centre). Turn left again at a T-junction 1 km further on, and then right after around 600 m (both turnings are signposted for 'Umm Qais'). After another 1½ km, bear off to the left at a large roundabout (again signposted for 'Umm Qais'). The road passes through the village of **Beit Ras**, which has been identified as the site of the Decapolis town of **Capitolias**, though today there is not much to see. Where the road to Umm Qais forks off to the left (4 km from the last roundabout; taking this turning, it is a further 20 km to Umm Qais), continue straight on (signposted for `Makaren', `Kreibah' and `Hreima'). Just under 7 km further on, by a mosque, take the fork off to the left signposted to `Hartha' and `Akraba'. Soon after taking this turning, the tops of the columns of a Byzantine basilica church can be seen straight ahead across the wadi, poking up from amidst an olive grove. The road then descends to a spring 1 km further on. This is the spring of **Ain Quwayliba**, the source of the stream by which Abila flourished, and which still contributes to making the surrounding land so fertile. You can either begin your visit here, or continue on to the Byzantine basilica church (on top of Khirbet Umm al-Amad, see below). To do this, continue past the spring and fork right around 700 m further on. Immediately after the fork, turn right down a rough track, following the edge of an olive grove. Keep following the track straight until it swings to the left, taking you right up to the ruins of the church.

History Excavations here have revealed evidence of settlement dating from around 3500 BC through to the 15th century. This site, known in Arabic as Quwayliba (or Quailibah), has been identified as the ancient Abila, one of the cities of the Decapolis. Abila was one of the places captured by the Seleucid ruler Antiochus III in 218 BC, after which time it began to develop into an important town, becoming part of the Decapolis during the Roman era. Archaeological evidence indicates that Abila reached its zenith during the late Roman and early Byzantine periods. Its classical name, Abila, appears to have been derived from the Semitic word *abel*, meaning literally `meadow' or `lush' or `green' in Hebrew and Arabic. Not much else is known about the history of the site; the excavations still being conducted here will no doubt reveal more in time.

The excavated remains at Abila are to be found on two mounds, Tell Abila to the north and Khirbet Umm al-Amad (literally the `Ruins of the Mother of Columns') to the south, and also down in a 'saddle depression' area just to the east. On either bank of the Wadi Quwayliba, meanwhile, between here and Ain Quwayliba, are numerous rock-cut tombs. If you visit the site between autumn and spring when the weather is not too hot, a pleasant walking circuit (minimum one hour plus resting time) is to begin at Ain Quwayliba, follow the left-hand side of the wadi (facing downstream), climb up to Khirbet Umm al-Amad, across to Tell Abila, down to the 'saddle depression' area and then return to Ain Quwayliba along the opposite (east) bank of the wadi. In the sweltering heat of summer, however, you may prefer to drive directly to Khirbet Umm al-Amad and restrict your visit to the ruins in the immediate vicinity.

Around the site

Arriving at Ain Quwayliba, the spring itself is to the right of the road, protected by a concrete structure. A little way up the hillside to the left of the road, just before the spring, there are a couple of easily accessible **rock-cut tombs**. One of these still has its original single-slab stone door and portal intact, the lintel featuring a wreath with rosettes on either side, while inside there are two tiers of loculi lining the walls on three sides. Adjacent to it is another tomb with a similar lintel, though the doorway is now largely blocked by earth. Right by the road is another cave with small separate cavities (loculi) inside, but no portal, and also a low narrow tunnel, thought to have been a Roman/Byzantine aquaduct, which emerges from the hillside in two places. From the spring, if you follow the left-hand bank of the wadi (facing downstream), the hillside is dotted with more rock-cut tombs, most with loculi cut into the walls, though the most impressive tombs, with traces of frescoes still surviving, are on the opposite bank. Keep working your way gradually up the hillside, then head for an olive grove to reach the basilica church on top of Khirbet Umm al-Amad.

The **Byzantine basilica church** was first excavated between 1984-1990 and has been dated to the 7th or 8th century. The two rows of 12 columns separating the side-aisles from the central nave have been partially re-erected. The basic outline of the church is clearly visible, including the central semi-circular apse and two side-apses at the eastern end (partially restored in 1998), and the porch at the western end, marked by four hefty limestone columns. Note the mixture of granite and black basalt used in the columns dividing the nave from the side-aisles, suggesting that they were taken from earlier buildings at the site. Note also the unusual capitals on some of the columns, with beak-like faces protruding from them. Excavations in 1996 revealed a small apse alongside the north wall of the church on the outside, probably belonging to a chapel attached to the church. Immediately to the west of the church, excavations have revealed the foundations and first course of the walls of another building consisting of large rough-hewn blocks. This is an earlier **basilica** dating from the 5th-6th century which appears to have been modified and occupied again during the Umayyad era.

On Tell Abila to the north traces of a large **acropolis** have been uncovered (looking across from Khirbet Umm al-Amad you can still see the foundations of the defensive walls which surrounded the tell). On top of Tell Abila

Double window, Umm al-Jimal

are the partially excavated remains of another **basilica church**, this one dating from the 6th century. The church was built of huge basalt and limestone blocks which have clearly been recycled from earlier structures. Excavations in 1994 along the north wall of the basilica uncovered an armless and headless life-size white marble statue of Artemis. Just outside the north wall at its eastern end, the corner of a large building dating from the Hellenistic or Roman period has also been uncovered. The deep trenches just to the north of this have revealed evidence of occupation from the Early Bronze Age all the way through to the Umayyad era.

Down in the 'saddle depression' area to the east of the two mounds traces of what appear to have been the civic centre during the Roman and Byzantine periods have been uncovered. A large semi-circle cut into the hillside is really all that remains today of the *cavea* of a **theatre**, but within this the remains of a later **Ummayad fortress/palace** are clearly visible. In front of the theatre, a section of **Byzantine street** paved with black basalt flagstones has been uncovered. To the north of the theatre are the jumbled ruins of a large structure which is thought to have been a **nymphaeum/baths** complex.

The most striking feature of the civic centre, however, is the large **Byzantine cruciform basilica** just to the northeast of the nymphaeum/baths complex, which has now been extensively excavated and partially restored. Five doorways led into the nave and side-aisles of the church from the western end, and excavations have revealed that the outside of the western wall was faced with marble. Inside, four rows of re-erected columns divide the church into a central nave flanked on each side by two side-aisles. The majority of the columns are of basalt and topped with Ionic capitals, though two are of marble and one is topped with a Corinthian capital. At the eastern end of the church is the raised altar area. The main semi-circular apse extends out from the east wall, while at the eastern end of the north and south walls, two smaller semi-circular apses also extend out beyond the rectangular plan of the building, giving it its cruciform shape. In the southwest corner of the church, traces of the original marble which paved the floor can be seen.

To the east of the cruciform basilica is a **bridge** (the foundations of which are of Roman origin) giving access to the east bank of Wadi Quwayliba, where a good track leads south back to Ain Quwayliba. Following this track south, you pass on your left a half-excavated rectangular structure with a half-dome 'conch shell' niche of basalt which is thought to have been a **Byzantine shrine**, modified from an earlier Hellenistic or Roman building. Up on the hillside above the track there are numerous **rock-cut tombs** and **shaft graves** (to date more than 90 have been discovered on both sides of the wadi), dating mostly from the Roman and Byzantine periods. Some of the rock-cut tombs are particularly interesting for the beautiful frescoes which survive within them. You really need a guide to locate the best tombs (if there are shepherds camped at Ain Quwayliba, they may be able to help, or else there is sometimes a tourist policeman on duty in the area), and a good torch is essential.

Umm al-Jimal

Situated to the northeast of Amman, close to the border with Syria, Umm al-Jimal lies within an area of black basalt desert which geographically forms part of Syria's Hauran and Jebel al-Arab region. After the splendours of Jerash, Umm al-Jimal may seem a little disappointing, consisting as it does of the tumbled remains of a very ordinary town, but exploring the ruins there are plenty of interesting surprises, and if you can visit on a sunny day (ideally towards

● ●

The architecture of Umm al-Jimal; Corbels and Cross-beams

The scarcity of wood in this region made the use of timber beams as a building material impractical. Instead, a system known as corbelling was adopted. This involved the use of cantilevered ceiling supports built into the walls of the buildings, on which long slabs of the ubiquitous basalt could be rested. The maximum length of these slabs was limited to around 3 m (any more and they would crack under their own weight). As a

result, many of the buildings tended to be rather narrow, although there was no limit to their length. To achieve wider rooms, supporting cross-arches were built, so that two or more parallel lines of roofing slabs could be laid. Staircases were also built of solid basalt slabs, which were likewise cantilevered into the walls of buildings, usually on the outside because of the narrowness of the rooms internally.

● ●

evening when in summer the heat is not so intense and the light is at its best), the overall effect is highly atmospheric.

Getting there Regular minibuses run between Amman's Abdali bus station and Mafraq's 'Bedouin bus station' (450 fils). From here you can pick up less frequent minibuses on to Umm al-Jimal (200 fils). There are also regular minibuses between Irbid's New Amman bus station and Mafraq (300 fils), although these arrive at what is known as the 'Irbid bus station' in Mafraq, around 1 km from the 'Bedouin bus station'. Taxis run between the two for 500 fils. Returning from Umm al-Jimal, check in advance what time the last bus back to Mafraq leaves, or else ask at the Department of Antiquities office at the site, where they will help you flag down transport to Mafraq.

If you're driving from Irbid to Umm al-Jimal head southeast out of the centre of Irbid along King Hussein St and keep going straight, crossing the ring road and over another crossroads. After 15 km you pass under a motorway (north for Ramtha and the border crossing into Syria; south for Jerash and Amman). Keep straight, past a right turn signposted to Zarqa, a left turn signposted to Hamra and a right turn signposted to Mafraq, the latter turning 43 km from Irbid. A few kilometres further on the road passes underneath the motorway running between Amman/Zarqa and the border crossing into Syria at Jaber, and then after a further 12 km take the left turn signposted to Umm al-Jimal, 4 km away. **From Amman** follow the route as if for the Desert Castles (see page 134), but keep on the motorway, following signs for Mafraq. After around 62 km take the exit signposted for Iraq and Umm al-Jimal (highway 10) and then after a further 12 km take the left turn signposted to Umm al-Jimal, 4 km away.

Site information At the time of writing there was no entrance fee, although there are plans to charge one in the future (probably JD1-2). By the surfaced road on the south side of the site is the Department of Antiquities building. Ask here for the caretaker who will be glad to show you around; a guided tour of the site certainly helps bring the ruins to life and makes it much easier to identify the different buildings. Only a small selection of the more interesting buildings are described here. There are no refreshments at the site (the nearest restaurants – very basic – are at Mafraq), and precious little in the way of shade; bring your own food, plenty of water and adequate protection against the sun.

History Probably first established as a caravan station by the Nabateans during the 1st century BC, Umm al-Jimal became part of the Roman province of Arabia following the annexation of the Nabatean kingdom in 106 AD. Partially destroyed during the 3rd century, it continued to be occupied during the Byzantine and early Islamic periods, only being abandoned in the 9th century. Throughout its existance, Umm al-Jimal was never a settlement of any great

Jerash & the North

significance, although its population is thought to have reached around 3,000. There are no traces here of the monumental public buildings (theatres, baths, etc) which adorned other cities in the region such as Jerash. Rather, it was a simple provincial town, and its interest to archaeologists today is that it gives an unique insight into the everyday life and vernacular architecture of a typical town from this period.

Around the site Entering the site from the south (leave the surfaced road opposite the Dept of Antiquities building and follow the track into the site), the first building you come to on the left of the track, the **barracks**, is easily identifiable by the well-preserved square tower in one corner. An inscription in Greek gives a construction date of 412 AD, at a time when Umm al-Jimal was being strengthened as a frontier town. It was however modified and enlarged during the late Byzantine period. A small doorway complete with its single-slab basalt door still on its hinges (and still swinging, though very stiffly) leads inside. Above it are openings for dropping stones etc on attackers. The well-preserved late Byzantine period corner tower has these openings in each face, and lower down on the outside walls, Greek inscriptions. The older, more ruined corner tower has sections of corbelling and stairways still protruding from its walls. The large room which extends beyond the rectangular plan of the barracks was a chapel, also added in the late Byzantine period.

Inside one house in the cluster of ruins to the west of the barracks is a room which has been dubbed the **Nabatean temple** due to what appears to be an altar standing in the centre of the room. The cross-arches and corbelling date from repair works carried out by the Druze at the start of this century. The courtyard itself is thought to have been used as a khan during the Roman period due to the carving of a wheel by the entrance. Note the well-preserved stables in the courtyard. Immediately to the east of this, **house III** has a circular window above the doorway in the south wall, and a Byzantine cross just above it.

Umm Al Jimal

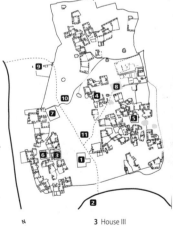

Continuing north along the track past the barracks, bear right where it forks to head northeast. The first building on the left was the **Numerianos church**, now in an advanced state of ruin though with its apse still discernible. In the large courtyard of the building to the north of the church (originally the church cloister?) is an underground water cistern.

Further along the track, if you work your way through the ruins to the right of the track, you will arrive at **house XVIII**, evidently one of the wealthier houses of Umm al-Jimal and easily distinguished by its distinctive second storey double-arched windows. Note the arched doorway to the courtyard of this house, and the well-preserved stairs built into the walls. Below the double-arched windows, outside the building, is an

0 metres 200
0 yards 200

1 Barracks
2 Department
  of Antiquities
3 House III
4 House XIII
5 House XVII
6 Nabatean Temple
7 Praetorium
8 Reservoir
9 West Church
10 Cathedral
11 Numerianos Church

underground chamber with cross-arching (a water cistern), and to the right a doorway with one of its single-slab basalt doors still in place. Returning to the track, a little further on you pass a low mound with a reservoir next to it, to arrive at another **water cistern** with four cross-arches. Just beyond it is a large square reservoir, now relined and still in use, but dating originally from the Roman period.

Doubling back the way you came, in the cluster of ruins to your right, roughly diametrically opposite house XVIII, is **house XIII**. You need to scramble over the collapsed walls of the adjacent house to get in, but once inside you have the pleasure of a nice shady room with excellently preserved corbelling (the supporting arch and roofing slabs are however a recent addition, having been added by Druze farmers at the start of this century). Note the latrine and washbasin in the northeast corner of the room, and the ventilation screen partitioning off the stables in the room beyond, with its row of mangers.

Taking the left-hand branch of the track to the north of the barracks to head northwest, you pass on your left what is known as the **praetorium**, although the true function of this building is not known. At the time of writing this was undergoing restoration and was partially supported by heavy wooden joists. There are three doorways in the south wall. The central doorway leads into an atrium, where four columns once supported a partial roof. The left-hand doorway leads into what appears to have been a basilica, though today this is all rubble. The right-hand doorway is the most interesting, leading into a courtyard with barrel-vaulted chambers in each wall. Originally there would have been a corbelled roof over the courtyard area. Two of the five rooms along the rear (north) side of the building retain their precisely engineered cross-arches, and one of them its associated corbelling.

Just beyond the praetorium, to the right of the track, is the **cathedral**, dating from 556 AD. A Latin inscription on the lintel of the right-hand doorway includes the date 371 and mentions the emperors Valens, Valentinian and Gratian, although this must have been recycled from an earlier building as such a date is far too early for a building of this kind. Inside, the cathedral is entirely in ruins.

Further on, to the left of the track, is the **west church**, striking for its surviving line of four arches which originally divided the central nave from the southern side-aisle. Note the Byzantine crosses carved on the arches. Its position outside the city walls suggests that it was built at a later date, when the town was already fully developed, or that it served as a funerary church (or both).

Around Umm al-Jimal

There are a number of other archaeological sites in the area, though you need to have your own transport and a guide to visit them. Note that all the sites described here are very close to the Syrian border and there are plenty of military checkpoints around where you may be required to show your passport.

Around 7 km to the northwest of Umm al-Jimal, near the village of **Al Ba'ij**, there is a well preserved section of **Roman road**. This is part of the *Via Nova Traiana*, an important trunk road which ran from Bosra (in Syria) to Aqaba (then known as *Aila*) on the Red Sea. It was built by the Emperor Trajan between 111-114 AD in order to help consolidate control over the newly-formed province of Arabia, created following the annexation of the Nabatean kingdom of Petra.

Around 55 km to the east of Umm al-Jimal is **Deir al-Kahf**, the site of a **Roman fort** dating from 306 AD. The fort stood on the *Strata Diocletiana*, another Roman military road, this one built by the Emperor Diocletian, who remodelled an earlier road which ran between the Euphrates and Palmyra, extending it south to Damascus and then on to Azraq. The walls of the fort are reasonably well preserved and inside you can still make out the various rooms and stables which surrounded the central courtyard.

Another 25 km to the east of Deir al-Kahf are the atmospheric black basalt ruins of **Jawa**, accessible only by 4WD. The ruins themselves may not be that substantial, but the setting amidst vast expanses of basalt desert is dramatic and beautiful in a bleak, rugged sort of way. The ruins here date back at least 5,000 years, to the Chalcolithic era. Very little is known about the settlement, other than the fact that it was only occupied for as little as 50 years before being abandoned. To the untrained eye the site presents itself primarily as a jumble of basalt rubble, though the massive walls are clearly discernible, along with some of the many gates which pierced them. An important feature of the settlement was the extensive system of canals, dams and reservoirs which served to collect precious rainwater. After suffering a major attack soon after it was completed, the fort and its water system fell into disrepair, leading soon after to its abandonment.

Burqu

Situated a little over 180 km to the east of Mafraq, to the north of the Baghdad Highway, the vast lake at Burqu is a birdwatchers' paradise, and also the site of a small fort. Around 75 km to the east of Mafraq, at the junction of the Baghdad Highway with Highway 5 which runs south to Azraq, is the town of **Sawafi**, a major truck stop with lots of garages and cheap eateries but little else. Another 90 km or so brings you to a checkpost at **Muqat** (10 km short of the village of Ruwayshid), where a turning left signposted for 'Burqu Islamic Palace' points north towards the lake and fort at Burqu, some 18 km away across open desert. A 4WD is essential for this last stretch, as is a guide. Your best bet is to organise a visit through the RSCN in Amman (see page 115).

The **lake** has been formed by a dam built at its northern end, probably dating from the same time as the fort, during the Roman era. Burqu, rather like Azraq, is at the centre of a depression, or *qa*, where underground aquifers emerge, allowing such a substantial lake to form in so unlikely a setting. As a magnet for wildlife, the lake is unsurpassed, attracting a wide variety of birds and animals, while in spring the shores blossom with wild flowers. The area has been earmarked to become a 'Protected Area' managed by the RSCN in the future.

The **fort** consists of a well-built tower standing in a courtyard surrounded by more ruinous walls and rooms. The tower is thought to date from the 3rd century AD, and is clearly Roman in style. Although a long way to the east of the Roman frontier, the presence of a water source is likely to have attracted caravans travelling between Syria and Arabia, giving Burqu a strategic significance. The site appears to have been continually inhabited throughout the Byzantine period, perhaps as a monastic community, with the outer walls and rooms being added during the Umayyad era, when it perhaps served as a fortified caravanserai.

Jordan Valley

Jordan Valley

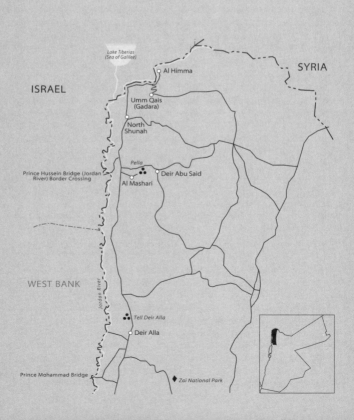

To the west and north of Amman is the deep Jordan
Valley, a dramatic cleft in the earth's surface which forms
part of the much larger Rift Valley system (see page
373). As a natural feature, the Jordan Valley is
awe-inspiring to behold. Like the Dead Sea, into which it
drains, it is below sea level, and its depth is accentuated
by the mountains which rise to over 900 m on either
side. Its physical scale is matched also by its
archaeological and historical significance. Dotted
around the valley floor are literally hundreds of
archaeological sites which are evidence of man's presence
here since earliest antiquity, while the Jordan river has a
deep historical and religious significance for Jews,
Christians and Muslims alike. Sites such as Tell Deir
Alla, Tell as-Sa'idiyeh and Pella, in the middle and
northern sections of the Jordan Valley, are not the most
impressive in Jordan, and certainly no match for the
glories of Jerash, but the drive along the valley is
interesting, and the ascent at its northern end along the
Yarmouk valley to Umm Qais is very striking. The ruins
of ancient Gadara at Umm Qais, though not strictly
speaking in the Jordan Valley, are highly atmospheric
and well worth a visit.

Ins and outs

Getting there & getting around
There are regular minibus services from Amman's Abdali bus station to Deir Alla, the first site dealt with in this chapter, or else from Amman's Muhajireen bus station to South Shunah, close to Wadi Kharrar and the King Hussein (Allenby) Bridge border crossing into Israel. Public transport between the various towns along the Jordan Valley is adequate, though somewhat erratic in places. If you have your own transport, you can easily visit all the sites in the Jordan Valley and return to Amman in one long day. A more leisurely and preferable option is to stay overnight at Pella or Umm Qais, giving you the benefit of the sunset and sunrise over these sites, or else to continue on to Irbid (in the northern highlands), which can then be used as a base to visit other sites in this area.

Best time to visit
The climate of the Jordan Valley is on average 8°C warmer than in adjoining areas. Summers are hot and sultry, with temperatures rarely dropping below 38°C, making this an exhausting time to visit. Spring and autumn temperatures are much more bearable, with spring offering the added attraction of blossoming wild flowers in the surrounding hills. Winters are also very mild (frosts are virtually unheard of), providing a pleasant contrast to the rest of the country, which can experience cold winds, rain and even snow.

Amman to Deir Alla

There are numerous routes down into the Jordan Valley. The one described here is the major access route from Amman, although another alternative is to go down to the Dead Sea (see page120) and then head north past Wadi Kharrar to join the main road along the Jordan Valley at South Shunah.

From Downtown, follow King Hussein St up past Abdali bus station and turn left at the Jamal Abd an-Nasir Interchange. Keep going straight at the Sports City Interchange, following signs for Suweilah, and at the next major roundabout (14 km from Downtown) go straight also (right for Jerash). After a further 11 km you pass an exit signposted for Salt, 4 km to the south (see page 129). Further on the road begins to descend, giving dramatic views down into the Jordan Valley. Around 7 km beyond the first Salt exit, having passed another exit for Salt (and for Zai), there is a right turn signposted for `Zay Park' and 'Zai National Park'.

Zai National Park
This turning takes you into the Zai National Park which, like the Dibeen National Park to the north, is a forested hill area clad predominantly in Aleppo pine. Being close to Amman it is a popular day-trip/picnic spot and tends to get very busy on weekends. Taking the turning, bear left where the road forks to arrive at the government-owned *Jalaad* restaurant, with its large terrace area and superb views. The restaurant is open 1000-2000 daily and serves a fairly standard range of Arabic food for around JD4 per head. There is also a cheaper self-service section. If you bear right instead of forking left to reach the restaurant, the road leads up to a military base at the top of the hill. On the way up however there are some lovely views and plenty of good picnic spots.

Returning to the main road and continuing northwest, it soon begins to descend steeply in a series of sweeping switchbacks. Just under 3 km further on, go straight past a large turning off to the right (signposted for 'Sumya', 'Sihan' and 'Subihi'). After another 9 km or so, look out for a stone marker by the road on the right indicating sea level. There is a good viewpoint and small picnic area here. Another 3 km brings you to a T-junction, (58 km from Amman). Turn right here to head north towards Deir Alla and Pella (left for South Shunah and the King Hussein (Allenby) Bridge crossing into Israel, and for Wadi Kharrar).

A Garden of Eden

Travelling along the Jordan Valley in 1852, the Dutch engineering captain, Charles WM van de Velde, wrote: "But just imagine, all the things which could be done with this wonderful water! Even without the Jordan the Ghor is susceptible to general irrigation due to its multiplicity of tributaries; what a garden of Eden could this valley become if the waters of the Jordan were to be tapped!... One day this will be realized. How people will gaze, when Israel's curse is changed to blessings!" The building of the East Ghor Canal (later re-named the King Abdullah Canal) bringing water into the valley from the Yarmouk River in the 1950s allowed vast areas of land to be brought under irrigation, and the results were indeed dramatic. Since the 1970s the Jordan Valley Authority has been responsible for further extending the area under irrigation and today the Jordan Valley has become the country's most important food-producing area. Another important (though somewhat unattractive) innovation has been the introduction of polytunnels. In places you are confronted by huge expanses of sheet plastic shimmering in the sun like water or a mirage. The main crops grown in these tunnels are vegetables such as tomatoes, cucumbers, onions, aubergines, peppers, watermelons etc, and citrus and other fruits, with as many as three harvests being achieved each year in these favourable conditions.

Heading north, you arrive after around 5 km in the centre of the village of **Deir Alla**. On the northern outskirts of the village, the tall mound or *tell* of Deir Alla appears unmistakably by the road on the left.

Tell Deir Alla

Although archaeologically very significant, other than the ubiquitous pottery sherds scattered all over the *tell*, and the outlines of the excavations on the north side (corresponding with the Late Bronze Age sanctuary complex), there is little for the non-specialist to actually see. That being said, the views from the top of the mound are quite impressive, and work is underway to preserve some of the excavations.

History Tell Deir Alla translates literally as `monastery situated high up'. Most biblical scholars identify Tell Deir Alla with the biblical Succoth, primarily due to the fact that the Talmud (a Jewish commentary on the Old Testament dating from around 400 AD) identifies Succoth with Tar'ala, from which the name Deir Alla is in all likelihood derived. However this has never been conclusively proven and some scholars point out that nowhere in the Old Testament is there any mention of a sanctuary at Succoth, or on the `plain of Succoth'. Another interpretation identifies Tell Deir Alla with the biblical site of Penuel, which is recorded as having a sanctuary. Excavations began here in 1960, conducted by a team from the Netherlands led by HJ Franken, and over the 30 or so years that they have continued, have revealed Tell Deir Alla to be an important archaeological site.

The most significant finds date from the Late Bronze Age, when a large sanctuary complex was built. The earliest stages of the sanctuary date from the 16th century BC and it appears to have been rebuilt at least five times until finally being destroyed by a severe earthquake in the 12th-13th century BC. Artefacts found in the sanctuary indicate that during this period trading relations existed with Egypt, Cyprus and northern Syria. During the Iron Age, a furnace appears to have been built on the site for smelting bronze and a

Jordan Valley

sizeable settlement grew up. Interestingly, the Old Testament records that the bronze furnishings for the Temple of Solomon were all made in this area (1 Kings 7: 46), and the furnace dates from the 10th century BC, corresponding with the date of the building of the Temple of Solomon.

Head of terracotta female figurine found in Tell Deir Alla

Around the site The *tell* is now entirely fenced-in, with a gate on the north side by the road and a small hut just inside; if the caretaker is not in the hut, he is usually close at hand to open the gate. There are plans to establish a small café and garden here, and to build a retaining wall to prevent further erosion of the lower slopes of the tell. On top of the *tell*, on the north side, some restoration work has been carried out on the **Late Bronze Age sanctuary** complex. All the same, this does not amount to much, consisting only of mud and straw render aimed at protecting the original mud-brick walls from the elements, though a detailed reconstruction of the complex is planned for the future. A small road loops round the tell from the main road; taking the turning at the southern end of the tell, where this road swings round to follow the west side of the *tell*, off to the left is the **Deir Alla Archaeological Station** (the building is not that obvious; ask for the `mat-haf'; unless there is an archaeological team in residence you may also have to get the caretaker to open it up for you). This includes a tiny room displaying some of the artefacts found on the *tell*, along with explanations of the significance of the settlement, particularly the Balaam text which was found on the site. Photographs of the excavations give an idea of what the santuary complex looked like when it was first excavated. ■*The site is open daily until sunset. Entry is free.*

Deir Alla to Pella (Tabaqat Fahl)

Continuing north from Deir Alla, after a little over 3 km you pass on the left a huge new mosque complex, built around the original mosque and tomb of **Abu 'Ubaydah Amir Bin al-Jarrah**, one of the Prophet Mohammad's generals and a veteran of the Battle of Yarmouk which saw the Muslim army inflict a decisive defeat on the Byzantines. Exactly 3 km further on there is a right turn clearly signposted for Ajlun castle, and also for Jerash and Irbid (this road leads directly to Jerash, passing the turning for Ajlun and Irbid in the centre of Anjara. After a further 2 km there is an unmarked left turn which weaves its way between various irrigation canals and past numerous polytunnels to Tell as-Sa'idiyeh.

Tell as-Sa'idiyeh The large mound of Tell as-Sa'idiyeh was first excavated by a team from the University of Pennsylvania between 1964-67. Since 1985 a team from the British Museum has been carrying out further excavations and restoration work each season. The earliest period of occupation, found at the foot of the *tell*, dates from the Early Bronze Age, though this was destroyed by fire around 2800 BC. During the Late Bronze Age (13th-12th century BC) the site was again occupied, with a large settlement being established this time on the summit of the *tell*. Identified by some as ancient *Zarethan*, in all probability this settlement was an outpost of the Egyptian empire, since the New Kingdom

The Balaam Text

One of the most exciting finds from the excavations at Tell Deir Alla was made in 1967, when fragments of plaster bearing lettering in black and red ink were discovered. Careful salvage work resulted in two coherent pieces of text being pieced together, written in a North-West Semitic dialect related to Aramaic and Canaanite. The first piece relates a prophecy made by Balaam, the son of Beor, who appears in the Bible (Numbers 22-24). The following is a translation of the text, with some of the gaps filled in on the basis of guesswork and interpretation, and with an accompanying explanation.

"`This is the history of Balaam the son of Beor, the visionary of the gods. As far as he is concerned; the gods appeared to him in the night'...*This is the start of the text, and what immediately follows is hard to translate. Some scholars have suggested moving the fragments closer together and also to add pieces in between based on the content, but much of this is speculation.* `Balaam got up the following morning' *and is asked what is the matter; then he replies;* 'Sit down and I shall tell you what has happened'. *He speaks of a council of gods in his vision;* 'The Shadday gods came together for a meeting and said to Sh....', *- here the name of the chief goddess will have been written, possibly Shagar, who appears further on, and she is requested not to take severe measures against mankind, with the following words;* 'Do not break the bolts of heaven, in your cloud is darkness and no light... Do not pour out the fear of you nor the fright... and never say that the swift has insulted the eagle. Then the voice of the vulture shall sound in...' *...The text continues;* 'The shepherd's crook shall lead hares to the place where nursing ewes graze' *...the nursing ewe stands for successful animal husbandry and hare indicates the wilderness. In the following fragment it is reported how the prophet tries to convert his listeners and calls to the enemies of the goddess;* 'Listen to the admonition'. *At the end of this piece mention is made of the terrible situation which will come about if the punishment of the gods is realised. For example;* 'Man will mock the wise', *something which is typical for that world where maintaining the social order was an obvious good." (*Picking Up The Threads...edited by G van der Kooij and MM Ibrahim).

The second piece is far more fragmentary, but includes a number of curses and proverbs. The Balaam text consists of a mixture of prose and poetry. The curses which Balaam gives reflect closely his role in the Bible, where he constantly chastises the Israelites. The Bible describes Balaam as a non-Isrealite prophet, a fact reflected also in the Semitic dialect in which the Balaam text is written, which differs markedly from the Hebrew of the Old Testament. The name of the chief goddess at Deir Alla remains uncertain, but is generally identified as Shagar, most probably a fertility goddess, who appears elsewhere in the text, together with Ashtar, the male equivalent of Astarte, and El, the chief god of this pantheon. The reference to the 'Shadday gods' is interesting, appearing also in the Bible, where it is translated as 'the Almighty'; in the Book of Job for example, God is often referred to as 'Shadday'.

pharaohs held sway in the region by this time. Certainly, the Late Bronze Age complex on the summit shows clear signs of Egyptian architectural influences, while the majority of the graves in the large burial ground which was established at the foot of the *tell* during this period are also Egyptian in style. Early in the 12th century BC, this settlement was in turn destroyed, perhaps as a result of the invasion of the so-called "Sea Peoples" (see page 187). However, it was soon re-occupied, and by the 9th-8th century BC had grown into a substantial Iron Age town. It continued to be occupied up until the Roman period before being permanently abandoned.

The team from the British Museum have restored an Iron Age stairway (probably originally a covered tunnel) which leads down from the summit of the *tell* to a stone-lined cistern containing a spring on the north side. Today this is visually the most impressive aspect of the archaeological remains here, though excavations of the complex at the top of the *tell* are ongoing, and hopefully will lead eventually to a more detailed restoration of the settlement. The views from the top of the *tell* of the intensively worked farmland surrounding it – a mosaic of lush green interspersed with hundreds of polytunnels – are excellent, though the nearby Jordan river is in fact hidden from view. ■ *The site is not as yet officially open to the public. If you are interested in visiting, contact the Department of Antiquities' Archaeological Inspector at Deir Alla, Mohammad al-Balawneh. His office is in the new building across the road more or less directly opposite the entrance gate to Tell Deir Alla, T05-570412, mobile T079-596328.*

Continuing north past the turning for Tell as-Sa'idiyeh, you pass soon after through the small town of **Kraymeh**, from where minibuses run to the various villages to the north and south along the Jordan valley, and also to Ajlun. Around 23 km from Deir Alla there is a right turn signposted to the "Wadi Rayan Project Handicrafts Showroom (Jordan River Foundation)". At the time of writing this was actually only a workshop; to see the woven wicker and reed handicrafts made here, you need to visit their shop in Amman (see page 188). After a further 5 km (28 km from Deir Alla), you arrive in the village of **Al Mashari**. At the north end of the village there is a right turn signposted to Pella, 3 km further on up the hill.

Pella (Tabaqat Fahl)

Nestled in the hills of the east bank of the Jordan, Pella enjoys panoramic views out over the Jordan Valley and across into Israel. A spring feeds a splash of lush green down in the wadi, while the surrounding hills, largely dry and rocky other than the occasional olive groves and patches of cultivation, blossom with wild flowers after rains. As well as preserving remains of the important Decapolis city of Pella, this site has proved to be of enormous archaeological significance, with evidence of human activity in the immediate vicinity reaching right back to the earliest pre-historic periods. The surviving monuments from the Hellenistic, Roman and Byzantine periods in no way match those of Jerash or Umm Qais (Gadara), but they do have their own charm, particularly when bathed in morning or evening sunlight.

Getting there If you have your own transport, drive up to the *Pella Resthouse*, which overlooks the ruins and is a good point from which to start your visit (after turning off the main road, ignore the first right turn you come to signposted for a 'Pella Resthouse', which leads to a rather tacky 'tourist park' below the site, and then bear right higher up where the road forks to reach the resthouse). If you are walking up from Al Mashari, you can enter the site after around 1½ km from a point opposite the Western Church (a good track leads from this entrance up to the dig-house), or else by the excavated remains of the Roman Gate further up. If you don't fancy walking, you should be able to negotiate a taxi from Al Mashari. At the time of writing, although the site was fenced-in, there was no entrance fee or fixed opening times. Deeb Hussein, the manager of the *Pella Resthouse* (a restaurant) offers simple but comfortable accommodation nearby in the modern village of Tabaqat Fahl. He is also an excellent source of information on the archaeology and local ecology of the area.

Until the 1970s, the small village of Tabaqat Fahl stood on the main mound, but **History** this was moved to the west and the land acquired by the Jordanian government, allowing a detailed archaeological survey, still ongoing today, to be carried out.

The combination of a plentiful water supply from springs in the area with a favourable climate of mild, frost-free winters made this site ideal for habitation since earliest times. Indeed, the earliest evidence of human activity dates back to the Lower and Middle **Paleolithic** periods (as much as 1 million years ago). During this period the climate would have been cooler and damper, the hills would have been forest-clad and deer, gazelle, sheep, pigs and other smaller animals would have been plentiful, making the area ideal for hunter-gatherers. Natufian artefacts dating from the **Mesolithic** period (20,000-8000 BC) and Pre-Pottery/Pottery **Neolithic** periods (8000-4500 BC) have also been found, with the first evidence of settled agriculture and the domestication of animals dating from these latter periods. By the **Chalcolithic** period (4500-3300 BC) houses of stone and mud-brick were being built, along with storage pits for grain, indicating that surpluses were being generated and that some sort of social organization existed.

During the **Early Bronze Age** (3300-2200 BC), the first evidence of a walled settlement begins to emerge and by the **Middle Bronze Age** (2200-1500 BC) Pella was clearly a prosperous Canaanite town with flourishing trade links. Excavated tombs from this period have yielded a rich variety of artefacts, including imported pottery, inlaid ivory boxes, alabaster bottles and various gold and silver trinkets and jewellery. The Arabic name Fahl appears to have been derived from the site's ancient Semitic name, *Pihil*, which is to be found in Egyptian texts dating to 1800 BC. The Tell Armana tablets (a series of letters written to the Egyptian Pharaohs in the 14th century BC, found at Tell Armana in Egypt) indicate that during this period Pella effectively paid tribute to the Egyptian Pharaohs. The upheavals brought about by the arrival of the so-called `Sea Peoples' during the **Iron Age** (from around 1200 BC onwards), followed by the arrival of the Israelite tribes on the west bank of the Jordan, had their impact at Pella also. Contact with Egypt faded, although Pella appears to have clung to its Canaanite pantheon of gods in the face of the new influences of the Israelites.

The **Neo-Babylonian** conquest of Pella in the early 6th century BC appears to have led to the almost complete abandonment of the site until the **Hellenistic** period. According to later Byzantine sources, Alexander the Great himself re-established the city after his conquest of the region in 332 BC. The Hellenistic name for the city, Pella, was the name of Alexander the Great's birthplace in Macedonia, although very little is known about the city during this early Hellenistic period and it may only have been re-established by the **Seleucid** emperor Antiochus III in 198 BC after he had conclusively defeated the Ptolemids at the Battle of Parnium in 200 BC. It subsequently flourished as an important trading city. In 83 BC it was destroyed by the **Hasmonean** king Alexander Jannaeus, appparently for refusing to adopt various Jewish customs.

Incorporated into the **Roman** Empire in 64 BC, Pella did not really begin to recover until the late 1st century BC and early 1st century AD, when a new Roman civic centre was built and Pella became firmly established as one of the cities of the Decapolis. In 82 AD it began minting its own coins and by the 2nd century AD Pella was once again a flourishing town, with colonnaded streets, an odeon, public baths, nymphaeum and large temple. Little however remains of the Roman period city, with much of it being built over or reused during the **Byzantine** period. Christians had already established themselves in the city as early as the 1st century AD, taking refuge there from the Roman siege of Jerusalem in 70 AD. During the early 4th century AD,

Jordan Valley

with Christianity now recognized as the official religion under the emperor Constantine, three churches were built and Pella became the seat of a bishopric. It continued to expand and flourish throughout the Byzantine era, reaching its zenith by around the 6th century.

On 23 January 635 AD, the Byzantines clashed with the invading forces of the Arab **Muslims** at the Battle of Fihl, close to Pella. The Byzantines were resoundingly defeated and Pella became part of the Muslim Empire, reverting back to its ancient Semitic name of *Pihil* (or *Fihl*), later becoming Fahl and then Tabaqat Fahl. A reduced Christian population remained in the city during most of the period of Umayyad rule (661-750), although by 700 both the east and west churches had fallen into disuse. The civic centre church appears to have continued to function as a place of worship until an earthquake in 717 caused severe damage to the city. Another earthquake in 747 finished off what was left of the major monuments and it was subsequently all but completely abandoned, surviving only as an insignificant village through the Abbasid, Mameluke and Ottoman periods.

Around the site   From verandah of the *Pella Resthouse* there are excellent views out over the site, with the Jordan River to the west, and beyond it Israel. On a clear day you can see Nazareth, Mount Tabor (scene of Christ's Transfiguration) and the Crusader castle of Belvoir. As you look out from the verandah, to your left, on a terrace half-way down the hillside, is the East Church, and beyond it the steep hill of Tell al-Husn. Straight ahead of you, at the bottom of the hill, by the spring, is the Civic Complex Church. To your right is the `main mound' (Khirbet Fahl), which has been the focus of much excavation work in recent years.

A rough path descends steeply from the verandah of the *Resthouse* to a convenient hole in the perimetre fence and then traverses across to the **East Church**.

Pella

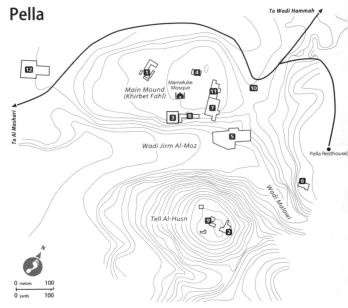

1 Archaeological dig house
2 Bronze Age platforms
3 Canaanite Temple
4 Central cut
5 Civic Centre complex
6 East Church
7 East cut
8 Iron Age residential area
9 Roman/Byzantine fortress
10 Roman gate
11 Ummayad residential area
12 West Church

Jordan Valley

The terrace on which it stands was originally a quarry. Built around 575 AD and largely destroyed by the earthquake of 747, the church was preceded by a colonnaded and marble-paved atrium at its western end. Some of the columns have been re-erected and you can still see traces of the marble paving, although it is in poor condition. The lower walls of the church still survive along with the triple apse at its eastern end, built into the hillside. The central aisle is strewn with rubble, but a raised altar area in front of the triple apse can still be seen.

From the East Church the rough path traverses and descends, steeply in places, down to the **Civic Centre complex** by Pella's main spring. The main feature here is what has been dubbed the **Civic Centre Church**, being built over the remains of the earlier Roman civic centre. Dating from around 400 AD, it was the largest church at Pella and probably served as a cathedral. A wide stairway (added in the early 7th century) led from the west up to a large colonnaded atrium. Many of the columns have been re-erected. Inside the church, the columns scattered on the ground which once divided the central nave from the side-aisles are all clearly taken from earlier Roman buildings. In the left-hand side-aisle the original paving still survives largely intact. The triple apse at the eastern end of the church was a later 6th century addition. Of the Roman-period Civic Centre, little remains.

Just to the south of the church are the ruins of an **Odeon** (small covered theatre), though it's in a poor state of repair, the best preserved part of it being the semi-circular passage running behind the tiers of seating. To the west of the church, at the foot of the stairway, are the half-sunken ruins of a **baths complex**. Both the odeon and bath complex date from the early Roman period and were clearly used as a source of building materials during the Byzantine era.

A wide track leads north from the Civic Centre up to the excavated foundations of a **Roman gate**, along with what are thought to have been guard rooms, kitchens and barracks. To the west of this, up on the `main mound' (Khirbet Fahl), is a long rectangular area of excavations aligned north-south. The southern half of this is generally referred to as the **east cut**. Excavations here by an Australian team over a period of 16 years or so have revealed evidence of more or less continuous settlement dating from the Mameluke period all the way back to the Early Bronze Age.

The northern half consists mainly of an **Umayyad residential area**. Running along the steep southern edge of the hillside, overlooking the spring and facing Tell al-Husn, is another long rectangular area of excavations consisting mostly of an **Iron Age residential area**. At the far western end of this, ongoing excavations have revealed what is now confirmed to be a massive **Canaanite temple**. Sections of the walls, built of huge rough-hewn stone blocks, along with floors on various different levels and column drums from later periods can be seen. More or less in the centre of the `main mound' is a **Mameluke mosque** (fenced-off); you can see clearly the neatly restored lower walls and rectangular plan of the mosque with its *mihrab* in the south wall. To the north of the mosque is a fenced-off rectangle of excavations, known as the **central cut**, including one very deep trench which reaches down to a depth of 15 m. Though nothing more than a very deep hole to the untrained eye, it has helped give some understanding of all the layers of settlement at Pella.

The **West Church**, off to the left of the road coming up from Al Mashari, is in a fairly advanced state of ruin. Three columns of the *atrium* have been re-erected, although the outline of the church itself is only vaguely discernible.

It is a steep climb up to the summit of **Tell al-Husn**. There are traces here of a large **fortress** dating from the late Roman-early Byzantine period, and to the east of it an area of stone **platforms** dating from the Early Bronze Age (around 3000 BC), probably part of a fortified structure of some sort.

Jordan Valley

Heading up towards Pella from Al Mashari, if instead of bearing right to go up to the *Resthouse* you bear left, after just under 3 km a rough track continues straight on where the road hairpins sharply round to the right. Taking this track, park up shortly after and then walk down into the gulley to arrive at a set of sulphurous springs known as **Wadi Hammah**. Some of the earliest traces of human activity were found in the vicinity of these springs, although today the main attraction is the prospect of a bath in the warm (32°C) sulphurous water. There is a somewhat murky bathing pool in an old building with a new concrete roof, or various natural open-air pools if this doesn't appeal. Nearby is a natural rock arch through which the spring water flows.

Sleeping *Pella Resthouse*, situated on hillside overlooking Pella, T079-574145 (mobile), or try the manager's home number T/F02-6560899. An attractive, tastefully designed restaurant with unbeatable views from its verandah. Its speciality is `St Peters fish' caught from the Jordan River and served with a selection of *mezze* dishes (JD6), or you can get freshly grilled chicken and *mezze* dishes for the same price. They also serve good red and white wine from the Cremisan cellars in Bethlehem (JD10.500 per bottle), as well as other refreshments and light snacks. For cheaper snacks (falafels etc), try down in Al Mashari, though the eateries here are very basic. *Tourist Park*, situated in the wadi below Pella (and somewhat confusingly signposted 'Pella Resthouse'). This small complex includes a restaurant, café and tiny swimming pool set within a walled compound. It was closed when I visited, so unable to comment on the facilities, but seen from the outside it's undeniably an ill-considered eyesore.

C *Pella Countryside Guesthouse*, set amidst olive groves on the edge of the modern village of Tabaqat Fahl and run by the manager of the *Pella Resthouse* (contact numbers as above). Simple but clean and pleasantly furnished accommodation in a converted house. 3 bedrooms (1 with attached bath, other 2 sharing), kitchen, sitting room. Lovely peaceful location with great views. Recommended.

Transport Fairly regular minibuses run between Al Mashari and Irbid's West Bus Station. There are also fairly regular minibuses running north and south from Al Mashari along the Jordan valley to North Shunah and South Shunah. Regular minibuses run between South Shunah and Amman's Abdali station, or else you can pick up minibuses to Amman from the junction 5 km to the south of Deir Alla.

Pella to Umm Qais

Continuing north from Al Mashari on the main road along the Jordan Valley, after a little over 5 km there is a left turn signposted for '**Jordan River Crossing** (cars and buses)'. This is the northernmost border crossing into Israel, also known as Jisr Sheikh Hussein or Prince Hussein Bridge. Just under 2 km further on there is a signposted right turn for Irbid via Deir Abu Said (also signposted for 'Ajlun Castle'), followed after another 2 km by a second left turn for the Jordan River Crossing (presumably for commercial freight). Just over 8 km further on you pass another right turn signposted for Irbid, before arriving soon after in the centre of **North Shunah** ('Shunah al-Shamaliyeh'), 19 km from Al Mashari.

Ash Shunah As you enter the town of North Shunah from the south, there is a right turn
baths signposted for 'Hot Springs'. Taking it, the extensive baths complex is on the left after around 700 m. Parking costs 250 fils and after that it costs 500 fils per person for entry to the swimming pools. There are separate male and female bathing areas (men get an outdoor and indoor pool, women an indoor pool only) as well as private family pools (JD5 for 2 hours, a little pokey) and a restaurant. The springs here are excellent, issuing a plentiful supply of really hot

sulphurous water (the swimming pools are hot also). The resort is popular with Jordanians, though somewhat ageing and seemingly right off the tourist track. There is also accommodation at the resort, consisting of reasonable though slightly damp units with 2 double rooms, a/c and fan, TV/dish, phone, kitchen, lounge and attached bath for JD25-35.

Arriving in the centre of North Shunah, turn right at the roundabout (clearly signposted for Umm Qais; straight on leads to an off-limits military/border area). After following the main feeder of the King Abdullah Canal for a while, the road begins to follow the Yarmouk River through a narrow, fairly deep gorge overlooked by the towering mass of the Golan Heights. The scenery here is strikingly beautiful, though with Israel just across the narrow gorge, taking photos is prohibited. Turn right at a crossroads just over 13 km from North Shunah (left for Al Himma baths, see below) to arrive in the centre of Umm Qais 5 km further on. Arriving from this direction, the ruins of the ancient city of Gadara are to the right of the road as you enter the modern town.

Umm Qais (Gadara)

Situated up on the northern slopes of a plateau with stunning views north across to Lake Tiberias (Sea of Galilee) and the Golan Heights, the setting for the Decapolis city of Gadara is beautiful and atmospheric. The ruins themselves are also highly impressive, with extensive ongoing excavations and restoration work continually uncovering new features of this substantial city. Gadara was in Graeco-Roman times a flourishing cultural and artistic centre strategically located at the junction of a number of important trade routes. It was also easily defended (important given its frontier position overlooking the natural border formed by the Yarmouk River), and blessed with a reliable water supply from nearby springs, a good climate and rich agricultural land. Today it is one of those out-of-the-way places (for the time-being at least) which is thoroughly enchanting; if you can, it is well worth timing your visit to catch the sunset or sunrise, or better still staying overnight.

Ins and outs

Getting there Regular minibuses run between Irbid (see page 173) and Umm Qais (220 fils, 45 mins). If you are coming from the Jordan Valley by public transport, you will have to go first to Irbid (there are minibuses to Irbid from Deir Alla, Al Mashari or North Shunah) and then catch a minibus from there to Umm Qais (if you do not have your own transport and want to follow the picturesque Yarmouk gorge up to Umm Qais, you will have to negotiate a private taxi from North Shunah). For details of the route from North Shunah, see above. For details of the route from Irbid, see page 193.

Site information Open daily 0700-1900 in summer, 0700-1700 in winter. Entry JD1. An optimistically vast new parking area and entrance to the site, with toilet facilities, has now been established along the south side of the acropolis/Ottoman village area. Entering the site from here, you can take the steps and path at the eastern end of the parking area (to your right as you face the acropolis/Ottoman village) which will take you up to a track leading round to the museum, or from the western end of the parking area you can work your way through the ruins of the Ottoman village to arrive at the west theatre. The description given below begins at the old site entrance, where you turn off the main road, as this allows for a more chronological tour of the remains. There is a good restaurant and bar, the *Umm Qais Resthouse*, inside the site on the edge of the acropolis/Ottoman village area, and a simple but reasonably comfortable hotel (as well as various other cheap

Jordan Valley

eateries) a short walk from the site in the modern village. Tourist police are on duty at the site (their office is in the Ottoman village). Ask here or at the museum if you want to hire a guide. Another good source of information is Abdullah Qassem, the owner of one of the small gift shops you pass on your way from the main road to the new parking area. He worked for a long time with the German Protestant Institute on the excavations at Umm Qais and was formerly curator of the museum. His shop stocks copies of the useful introductory booklet *'Umm Qais, Gadara of the Decapolis'*, published by Al Kubta (and indeed the rest of the series), as well as other more scholarly offerings.

History

In all probability the setting for human activity in pre-history, little is known about Gadara until it rose to prominence during the **Hellenistic** era. The town appears to have been `founded' following the death of Alexander the Great in 323 BC. Controlled at first by the Ptolemids, it was subsequently captured by the Seleucid emperor Antiochus III in 218 BC. During the early part of the 1st century BC it was, like Pella to the south, besieged and destroyed by the **Hasmonean** ruler Alexander Jannaeus and remained under Hasmonean control before being incorporated into the **Roman** Empire in 64 BC.

Under Pompey the city was rebuilt in recognition of the services of Demetrius the Gadarene, a freedman and important figure in Pompey's court who is said to have financed the building of the monumental theatre on Campus Martius in Rome. It soon began to flourish once again as one of the cities of the Decapolis, minting its own coins and adopting the new Pompeian calendar. In 30 BC however Octavian (the future emperor Augustus) gave Gadara and its territory as a gift to Herod the Great, the king of Judaea, in return for his help in defeating his rival Anthony at the battle of Actium the previous year. This change of rulers was bitterly opposed by the Gadarenes, who twice petitioned to be reincorporated into the Roman Empire and freed from the tyrannical rule of Herod, sending petitions first to the imperial legate Agrippa in 28 BC and later to Augustus himself when he visited Syria in 20 BC. According to Josephus, having failed in their attempts and fearing the retribution of Herod for their disloyalty, "... *they killed themselves for fear of torture, some with their own hand, some flung themselves into the valley or drowned themselves in the river*".

Following Herod's death in 4 BC, Gadara was reincorporated into the Roman province of Syria. During this period the city (or at least its territory) finds mention in the Bible as the place where Jesus drove the demons from two possessed men into a herd of swine (see next page). By the late 1st century AD the benefits of the *Pax Romana* began to make themselves felt and Gadara entered its golden age. Most of the important public buildings which survive date from the 2nd century AD. Gadara became famous as a cultural and artistic centre with its own university, two large theatres and the nearby hot spring baths complex of Hammath Gader (present-day Al Himma, see below) which attracted people from throughout the empire to its therapeutic waters. Already during the Hellenistic era the city had gained a reputation as the birthplace of Menippos, a freedman who rose to become a noted satirist and philosopher, and of the poet Meleager. Under the Romans this tradition continued. Philodemos, the mid-1st century BC Epicurean philosopher (a contemporary and friend of Virgil and Horace) came from here, as did the 2nd century AD philosopher Oinomaos, and the famous orators Theodoros (1st century AD), who founded a school of rhetoric in Rome and taught the emperor Tiberius, and Apsines (3rd century).

A Christian community developed from the 1st century AD onwards, with Gadara producing two martyrs, Zacharias and Alpheios, in 303 during the

The Gadarene Swine

The New Testament story of the miracle which Jesus performed at Gadara, driving the demons from two men into a herd of pigs is best told by Matthew:

"When he arrived at the other side in the region of the Gadarenes, two demon-possessed men coming from the tombs met him. They were so violent that no one could pass that way. `What do you want with us, Son of God?' they shouted. `Have you come here to torture us before the appointed time?' Some distance from them a large herd of pigs was feeding. The demons begged Jesus `If you drive us out, send us into the herd of pigs.' He said to them, `Go!' So they came out and went into the pigs, and the whole herd rushed down the steep bank and died in the water. Those tending the pigs ran off, went into the town and reported all this, including what had happened to the demon-possessed men. The whole town went out to meet Jesus. And when they saw him, they pleaded with him to leave their region.'"(Matthew 8: 28-34)

This miracle is one of many which Matthew relates, all illustrating the divine powers of Jesus, though in this case the Gadarenes seem more concerned with the fate of their pigs.

reign of Diocletian. With the recognition of Christianity and the start of the **Byzantine** era, Gadara continued to flourish, becoming the seat of a bishopric and sending its bishop, Sabinus, to the Council of Nicaea in 325. Becoming part of the Arab **Muslim** Empire in 635, it initially continued to fare reasonably well under the Umayyad caliphs, but when they were replaced by the Abbasids and the capital of the empire moved from Damascus to Baghdad, Gadara fell into decline, suffering also from the earthquakes of 717 and 747. It continued to exist as an insignificant settlement throughout the medieval period, with a more substantial Ottoman village (Umm Qais) growing up on the main acropolis mound during the 19th century. The site was first identified as the Decapolis city of Gadara by Ulrich Seetzen in 1806. Excavation and restoration work only began in the 1970s and is still continuing today, led by the Jordanian Department of Antiquities and the German Protestant Institute.

Around the site

Starting at the old entrance to the site, where you turn off the main road, there are various underground tombs by the turning, though all of them are rather dank and smelly inside. The first is the **tomb of Germani**, identified as such by the inscription in Greek on the lintel above the doorway. On the strip of stone between the lintel and the *pediment* above are various motifs. The two solid stone doors are still in place, jammed solid in an open position. To the right of the main portal is a small, plain side-entrance. To the right of this tomb there is another, the **tomb of LS Modestus**, which, appropriately enough, is rather more modest. In the centre of the lintel above the doorway is a carved wreath containing the dedicatory inscription, with rosettes on either side. The door consists of a single slab of solid stone. Taking the track leading off to the right, on level ground (if you head straight up the hill to the west you can work your way through the remains of the Ottoman village, past the museum, to the main area of ruins), on the left there is another **tomb**, also with a small simple entrance and single-slab stone door. Scattered outside are various sarcophagi. The tomb contains more sarcophagi and gives some idea of the original layout, with supporting columns around the sides and *loculi* cut into the walls.

Underground tombs

Jordan Valley

North theatre & decumanus maximus Continuing along this track you come to the indistinct remains of the **north theatre** on the left, once Gadara's largest but almost completely dismantled over the centuries as a source of building materials. Nevertheless, excavations in recent years have revealed parts of the stage area and *scenae frons*, built of cleanly-cut basalt blocks, while trenches cut into the *cavea* area have revealed sections of the vaulting which supported the different levels of seating. To your right, opposite the north theatre, excavations by a German team in 1995/6 have revealed traces of a **temple**. Although there is little for the casual visitor to see, the temple, probably dedicated to Zeus Nikephorus and dating from the 1st century BC, is of considerable importance in that it is the first to be discovered at Gadara, despite the fact that evidence from coins suggests there were at least two other temples here during the Graeco-Roman period, dedicated to Tyche and the Three Graces. The track at this point has already given way to the large flagstones of the Roman **decumanus maximus**, which swings round by the theatre to run east-west, extending for nearly one kilometre.

Just three years ago most of this street was hidden under centuries of accumulated earth, but excavation work by the Jordanian department of Antiquities has now largely uncovered it, along with parts of other important monuments still to be fully excavated and conclusively identified. An extensive canalisation system has been found below the street, as well as traces of cisterns and wells. Continuing west, you come to the main body of the ruins. A set of stairs on the left leads up to the *Resthouse*, its terrace offering excellent views along the length of the decumanus maximus, lined in places with re-erected columns.

Basilica terrace & west theatre Immediately below and to the west of the *Resthouse* is a large rectangular terrace, generally referred to as the **basilica terrace**, aligned north-south. At its northern end is a large **courtyard** surrounded by a colonnade of limestone columns. The courtyard dates originally from the Roman period when it is thought to have served as a plaza or forum, but during the Byzantine era it probably served as the atrium of the **church** which was built at the southern end of the terrace during the late 5th-early 6th century AD. The church follows a rectangular basilica plan, within which is a central octagon of basalt columns with the outline of an apse extending out from the east side of the octagon. At either end of the eastern wall of the church are two *exedra*; the northern one containing a black basalt basin which perhaps served as a baptismal, and the southern one a hexagonal pedestal. Outside the line of the western wall is a row of eight columns which originally formed the *narthex*. Outside the southern wall, up against the hillside, is what appears to be a further chapel, its apse still clearly visible.

Umm Qais (Gadara)

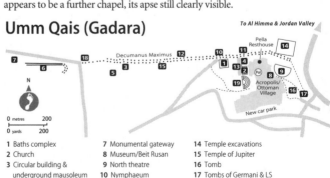

To Al Himma & Jordan Valley

1 Baths complex	**7** Monumental gateway	**14** Temple excavations
2 Church	**8** Museum/Beit Rusan	**15** Temple of Jupiter
3 Circular building & underground mausoleum	**9** North theatre	**16** Tomb
4 Courtyard/atrium	**10** Nymphaeum	**17** Tombs of Germani & LS Modestus
5 Five-aisled Basilica church	**11** Public building	**18** Western city gate
6 Hippodrome	**12** Semi-circular church	**19** West theatre
	13 Street with shops	

To the south of the church is the **west theatre**, which along with the terrace containing the courtyard and church forms one of the visually most impressive feature of Gadara. Built of volcanic black basalt stone, the theatre dates from the late 1st-early 2nd century AD. The stage area is largely in ruins, though the tiered seating of the *cavea* is better preserved, along with the vaulted passageway running underneath and the *vomitoria* by which people entered and exited. The views from the upper tiers of the *cavea* out over Lake Tiberias (Sea of Galilee) and the Golan Heights are truly spectacular, especially around sunset. At the time of writing the theatre was still undergoing extensive restoration, with a large crane standing in the orchestra.

Returning to the decumanus maximus, across the street directly opposite the basilica terrace, a large **public building** has been partially excavated. It is possible that this might be one of the other two temples thought to have existed at Gadara, though at the time of writing there was still considerably more work to be done before any coherent theories could be put forward. What is already clear is that the building underwent several stages of modification; note the water channel running in front of it at street level (added at a later stage), which appears to have supplied some sort of fountain arrangement. Adjacent to this is another smaller building, still to be excavated and identified. **Civic centre ruins**

Directly opposite, a street leads off to the left towards the west theatre, running parallel to the basilica terrace at a lower level. The whole western length of the basilica terrace is in fact supported by barrel vaulting, and the street on this side is lined with **shops** which occupied the vaults beneath the terrace. Dating from the Roman period, some of the classical square façades which fronted the barrel vaults have recently been restored. Continuing west, the decumanus maximus descends slightly, its flagstone paving giving way to limestone bedrock for a stretch. At the point where a modern track forks off to the left, to the right of the decumanus maximus are the remains of a late 2nd century AD **nymphaeum**, today rather forlorn and ruinous, although if you have already seen the nymphaeum at Jerash you will be able to imagine at least what it would have looked like.

For many years the true function of this structure was the subject of speculation amongst archaeologists, but in 1998 the plinth of a statue was discovered here, with an inscription which explicitly refers to it as a nymphaeum. More or less directly opposite, on the other side of the street, are the ruins of a **baths complex** dating from the Byzantine period (early 4th century AD). Seen from the decumanus maximus, the baths appear as little more than a confused jumble of stones and earth, but if you walk round to view them from the south, you can see a little more of their structure, including the remains of a domed room, and lots of the minature columns that supported the raised floors under which hot water was channelled.

Continuing west along the decumanus maximus, you come next to the partially excavated foundations of what appears to have been a **semi-circular church** on the right. The apse is clearly discernable on the east side, though, interestingly, the church is too close to the decumanus maximus for the semi-circle which extends from its northern side to be mirrored on the south side. **Western decumanus & its monuments**

Traces of an earlier building have been identified below the church, this quite possibly being a Roman temple given the Byzantines' habit of building over pagan structures. Again, however, further excavations are needed before either structure can be properly understood. Around 20 m to the north of here, a **mosaic floor** measuring 6 m by 4 m has been discovered, though for the moment it has been reburied until a protective structure can be built over it. On the decumanus, by the semi-circular church, there is a small step in the street, thought to mark the threshold of a gateway built during the Byzantine era to further control movement in and out of the city.

A little further along the decumanus, on the left, a series of taller re-erected columns decorated with ornate Corinthian columns marks another important monument. An inscription on the pedastal at the base of one of the columns reads IOVA, one of the names of Jupiter, suggesting that this was perhaps the Roman **temple of Jupiter**. During the Byzantine period the building appears to have been converted into living quarters, and then further modified and used again during the Umayyad period. In front of the building, a niche (taken from the nymphaeum) has been used to form the *mihrab* of an Umayyad mosque, with column drums laid horizontally on the floor to serve as foundations.

At various points along the decumanus, similar arrangements can be found, with column drums and other architectural fragments (presumably already toppled by the earthquakes of 717 and 747) having been used to build houses during the Islamic period. Further on, on the right, an opening can be seen into a large **water cistern** under the decumanus, which would have fed another bath house to the north of here, built according to an inscription by a nobleman named Herakleides, though there is little to see today. Just beyond the cistern is another step in the street, as well as the foundations of a wall and tower on the left, indicating another Byzantine gateway. Beside the wall and tower is what is believed to have been a market place, also Byzantine, though slightly earlier.

You come next to the foundations of a **circular building** on the left, and beyond it a well-preserved **underground mausoleum**. The circular building formed one tower of a 1st century AD Roman arched gateway with a barrel-vaulted passage which straddled the decumanus maximus at this point. During the late 2nd or early 3rd century AD it was dismantled and used instead as a water pool, with the stone from the tower being used to expand the entrance hall of the mausoleum into a Christian tomb in its own right, probably dedicated to the Gadarene martyr Zacharias. The mausoleum itself dates originally from the Roman period. Steps lead down to the entrance hall; the four columns and semi-circular structure would once have supported a roof. Behind it is the porch of the mausoleum itself, consisting of a broad arch flanked by two smaller ones. Under the main arch was a shaft tomb while to the left of the door of the mausoleum is another tomb which was once covered by a mosaic, now displayed in the museum. The mausoleum itself is kept locked, but the *loculi* in the walls are clearly visible.

Immediately to the west of the mausoleum, excavations in 1998 have uncovered the foundations of a **five-aisled basilica church** dating originally from the early 4th century, but modified and renovated in the 6th century. According to the archaeologist Thomas Weber, the large size of this church could indicate that it was built to commemorate Jesus' healing of the two demon-possessed men.

Continuing west (if you are tired or short of time this last section can be skipped), on the right, where you come to a surfaced road, are the excavated remains of the **western city gate**, consisting only of the foundations along with sections of the original street paving. From here, if you follow the surfaced road west, you reach after around 500 m the ruins of a **monumental gateway**, with only the base of it still standing. This gateway is thought to date to the early 3rd century AD, when the city was expanded. All along this stretch of road, off to the left, are large amounts of rubble, thought to be the remains of a **hippodrome** which may never have been completed completed.

The Pharaoh's Aquaduct

Running beneath the Graeco-Roman acropolis is a section of underground water channel carved into the soft chalk limestone, known locally as Qanawat al-Far'oun (literally 'the aquaduct of the pharaoh') after a legend which attributes its construction to an Egyptian pharaoh. Some archaeologists have suggested that the aquaduct began far away in the fertile Hauran plains around 60 km to the south of Damascus (according to legend, the volcanic mountains of Subbe and Garara in the Hauran region are mounds of wheat which were stolen from local farmers by the Pharaoh's workmen, but which turned to stone when they tried to transport them to Gadara). Others have disputed this, arguing that it would not have been possible to build such a long aquaduct, especially given that it would have had to traverse some very hilly terrain, and suggested instead that it began at Ain Turab, some 13 km to the east of Umm Qais. As to the date of its construction, the 10th century Persian historian Hamza al-Isfahani attributes it to the 3rd century AD Ghassanid ruler Gebele II, though most scholars now agree that it was built during the Hellenistic or Roman period, some time between the 2nd century BC and 1st century AD.

If you are interested in having a look, ask the museum curator, who has a key to a locked access stairway located nearby, 100m to the east of the museum. Electric lighting has been installed, though this may not be working so take a torch. Other than the small niches cut into the walls for oil lamps, there is not much to see down here. However, the existence of such an aquaduct is a testimony to the advanced levels of hydraulic technology achieved in antiquity, and also the importance of a reliable water supply to cities such as Gadara.

Jordan Valley

Returning to the *Resthouse*, the area of higher ground to the east of the west theatre marks the **Graeco-Roman acropolis**, now largely covered by the ruins of an **Ottoman village**. From the new parking area along the south side of the acropolis, you can clearly see the lower courses of the Graeco-Roman walls and towers which once surrounded the city, built of large limestone blocks, and above this the Ottoman-period ruins consisting primarily of smaller black basalt blocks.

Graeco-Roman acropolis/Ottoman village

From the *Resthouse*, signs point you through the Ottoman village ruins to the **museum**, housed in one of the more substantial buildings known as *Beit Rusan* and formerly used as an Ottoman official's residence. Entering the museum, on your right is a cross-vaulted reception hall dominated by the imposing white marble statue of a seated woman. More than twice life size, though now unfortunately headless, the statue is almost certainly that of the Goddess Tyche, the patron of the Hellenistic city. It was found atmospherically placed amongst the seating of the west theatre, but moved to the museum to better preserve it.

Also in this gallery is a large section of mosaic recovered from the underground mausoleum, and the marble lid of a sarcophagus. The picturesque main courtyard is dotted with trees and a variety architectural fragments. Along the covered portico at the far side of the courtyard, various other mosaics are displayed, though unfortunately none of them is labelled. A single-slab stone door to a mausoleum has also been reconstructed here. Off the main courtyard is another cross-vaulted gallery (formerly the stables) containing some impressive fragments of statuary, including a marble statuette of an enthroned Zeus, this being a copy of the gold and ivory statue of Zeus found at Olympia. Other interesting exhibits here include a large coiled serpent carved from limestone, reminiscent of the Snake Monument at Petra, and a statue of woman, found in the Nymphaeum, her head intact for once. ■*Open daily 0700-sunset. Entry free (included in the price of your ticket for entry to the ruins).*

Sleeping & eating On the main street of the modern village is the **D** *Umm Qais Hotel*, T7500080. Double rooms with fan and attached shower/toilet JD16, or **F** category dorm beds (JD6, share shower/toilet). Clean pleasant rooms, nice roof patio, well-run friendly hotel. Meals served, though these are uninspiring and overpriced (watch out also for the `government tax' charged on the overall bill).

Inside the site is the ***Umm Qais Resthouse***, T7500555. Managed by the *Romero* restaurant in Amman, the star feature has to be the views from its terrace. Meals cost around JD10 per head (watch out for the 23% tax and service on the bill). Alcohol served. On Thu and Fri nights it stays open late, with entertainment and a buffet dinner being laid on. There are a number of simple restaurants on the main road in the modern village which serve good hummus, fuul etc.

Al Himma

Around 9 km to the north of Umm Qais are the hot springs of Al Himma (also known as Al Mukhayba al-Fawqa), situated nearly 200 m below sea level amongst lush banana and palm trees, and surrounded by steep hills, with the looming mass of the Golan Heights dominating the skyline. Known in Roman times as *Hammath Gader* and famed then for their therapeutic waters, there are extensive remains of a Roman-period baths complex just across the border in Israeli-occupied territory. The baths complex to be found on the Jordanian side is however an entirely modern (though somewhat rundown) construction.

Entry to the complex costs 500 fils. Inside, there is a large central outdoor pool where the water is around 32°C. The only problem is that it fills up with leaves from the surrounding trees and gets to look rather murky, although the water is in fact being continually replenished. In theory this is a mixed pool, though in practice Jordanian women are never seen swimming (foreign women can give it a go if it is quiet, but are advised to steer clear when it is busy). Use of the outdoor pool costs an extra JD1.130. There are also several indoor pools ranging from very hot through to warm (entry JD1.130). The hottest pool is considered especially beneficial for the treatment of rheumatism etc. Use of this pool alternates between men and women for two hour periods throughout the day, starting at 0600 and closing at 2000. Another of the indoor pools is for families only, or you can reserve it exclusively for around JD10.

Sleeping & eating There is a **C** *Hotel* (T7500512, F273554) within the complex, consisting of 3-bed chalets with a/c, phone, kitchenette and attached shower/toilet for JD28, or simpler double rooms in an older wing with fan, fridge and attached shower/toilet for JD9 per person. There is also a *Restaurant* with a pleasant terrace area overlooking the main outdoor pool. Just past the baths complex, in the village itself, is the **F** *Sah al-Noum* hotel, with basic but clean double rooms with fan and attached shower/toilet for JD8, a restaurant and a pleasant garden area at the rear with a small pool area fed by hot spring water. At the time of writing, the *Mövenpick* hotel chain was conducting a detailed feasibility study into building a large spa resort at Al Himma.

Transport From Umm Qais, follow the main road north, past the ruins off to your left, after which it begins to descend steeply. Go straight on at the crossroads 5 km from Umm Qais (left for North Shunah and Pella). After another 3 km you must pay a car toll of 300 fils before arriving at the baths 1 km further on (entry 500 fils). The minibuses which run between Irbid and Umm Qais continue down to Al Himma (280 fils, 1 hr from Irbid). They can be picked up in Umm Qais along the main road through the village. Check what time the last one leaves Al Himma for the return journey.

King's Highway

King's Highway

The ancient King's Highway runs south from Amman to the world-famous site of Petra. Already a major caravan route at the time of Moses, today it is a small, quiet road, thankfully relieved of heavy traffic by the Desert Highway to the east. Unassuming it may be, but the King's Highway takes you through some of Jordan's most spectacular scenery, running along the eastern edges of the Great Rift Valley, and descending precipitously every so often to cross the deep wadis which drain into the Dead Sea from the east. Along the way, it passes an array of fascinating and impressive sites: Madaba and Mount Nebo, with their stunning mosaics and views out over the Dead Sea; the hot springs at Hammamat Ma'in; Herod's mountain-top stronghold at Mukawir (ancient Machaerus); the rambling ruins and beautiful mosaics of Umm ar-Rasas; the mighty Crusader castles of Kerak and Showbak; and the breathtaking Dana Nature Reserve, to name just a few. There are also several points at which you can descend to the Dead Sea, a unique experience in itself.

With such a wealth of sites, you could easily spend several days en route to Petra, using Madaba, Kerak and Dana (all of which have accommodation) as bases from which to explore. If you are in a hurry, two days is adequate to see the main sites, with Kerak (roughly half way) making for a convenient overnight stop. But a whirlwind one day marathon, which so many tour groups are unfortunately subjected to, is really best avoided if at all possible.

An Ancient Route

The King's Highway is a route as ancient as the land it passes through, first finding mention in the Old Testament as the road along which Moses led the Israelites, requesting free passage from the king of the Edomites and the king of the Amorites (Numbers 20; 14-17, 21; 22). As a caravan route, the King's Highway was of vital importance, linking the biblical sea-port of Ezion-Geber on the Red Sea (present-day Aqaba) with Amman and Syria to the north. It was by taxing (and plundering) the trade along this route that the Nabateans acquired the fantastic riches which enabled them to build the city of Petra. During the Roman era, it became part of Trajan's Via Nova Traiana linking Damascus with the Red Sea. The Muslim Arabs modified its ancient biblical name, referring to it as the Tariq as-Sultani ('Sultan's Road'), though its strategic significance remained unchanged, with the Crusaders attempting to exert control over it with their castles at Kerak and Showbak.

Ins and outs

Getting around by public transport Travelling along the King's Highway by public transport is a pain, with minibus services along sections of it being highly erratic or non-existent. Nevertheless, if you have time and are prepared to do a little hitching in places, it is possible, and certainly well worth the extra effort. From Amman to Madaba is no problem. From Madaba to Kerak there is only one direct bus which runs along the King's Highway, a student bus which leaves early in the morning, going to Mut'ah University near Kerak, though this is often full. The only other guaranteed option is to go back to Amman and catch a bus direct to Kerak from Wahadat bus station. Alternatively, there are fairly regular services as far as Dhiban; occasionally there are minibuses running south from Dhiban, but more often than not you have to hitch or negotiate a ride across the deep Wadi Mujib to Ariha on the south side. From Ariha you can usually find minibuses running to Kerak. There are irregular minibuses running from Kerak across the deep Wadi Hasa to the small town of Tafila. From there, however, picking up onward public transport or hitching can be tricky (see page 204). The easiest option by public transport is to go from Kerak to Ma'an, just off the Desert Highway, from where there are regular services to Petra. There are regular minibus services from Petra to Wadi Rum and Aqaba, and also to Amman (via the Desert Highway).

Amman to Madaba

The easiest way to join the King's Highway from Amman is to head west along Zahran St and, around 8 km from Downtown, turn left at 7th or 8th circle to head south (signposted for the Airport; both roads join up). Around 6 km further on, take the exit clearly signposted for the Dead Sea (going straight takes you onto the Desert Highway, for Queen Alia International Airport and ultimately Aqaba). After another 7 km, take the exit signposted for Madaba, Ma'in Spring and Tell Hisban (straight on for the Dead Sea), and then fork right 1 km further on. You are now on a small, relatively quiet road which leads directly to Madaba, 13 km further on, passing along the way (after around 4 km) two right turns both clearly signposted for Tell Hisban (see below, under Around Madaba).

Madaba

Madaba is a small but lively town boasting a wealth of mosaic art. During the Byzantine era it flourished to become one of the most important centres of Christianity to the east of the Jordan River, and today it still has a large Greek Orthodox community. Here, and at the nearby site of Mount Nebo, can be found some of the best-preserved and most beautiful Byzantine mosaics in the Middle East, amongst them the famous `Madaba Map' of Palestine which has provided fascinating insights into the region during the Christian era. Being so close to Amman, Madaba can easily be visited as a day-trip from the capital. It is also becoming increasingly attractive as a base in its own right. The range of hotels and restaurants here may be limited, but they are of a high standard and good value, and the town is altogether more manageable than Amman, with none of its sprawling congestion.

Phone code : 05

Ins and outs

The main bus station is a rather chaotic yard just off the King's Highway where it runs through the outskirts of town. There are buses and minibuses to most destinations from here, though minibuses for Mount Nebo and Hammamat Ma'in leave from different points in the town (see Transport, page 212). All the main sights are dotted around the centre of the town, within easy walking distance of each other, though taxis are readily available if needed.

Tourist information The tourist information office (open 0800-1500, closed Fri and Sat, T545527) is currently located by the 'Burnt Palace', directly behind the Madaba Society shop, though it may move to the new visitors' centre and parking area nearby, which at the time of writing was due to open shortly. The staff can supply you with free copies of the Jordan Tourism Board's pamphlet on Madaba, which includes a good map, but are otherwise of limited help. The *Madaba Society* shop has a number of excellent publications for those wanting more in-depth information about Madaba and Mount Nebo.

History

The earliest evidence of settlement at Madaba now goes back to the late Early Bronze Age period (around 3100 BC). The town finds mention in the Bible on several occasions, where it is referred to as *Medeba*. It is first recorded as being amongst the cities of Moab conquered by the Israelites: "But we have overthrown them; Heshbon is destroyed all the way to Dibbon. We have demolished them as far as Nophah, which extends as far as Medeba." (Numbers 21: 30). It was also in the vicinity of Madaba that the armies of King David defeated the coalition of Ammonites and Aramaeans (1 Chronicles 19).

By the 9th century BC, however, according to the Mesha Stela (see page 205), Madaba was recaptured by the Moabite king Mesha, and it appears in later biblical texts as being amongst the towns of Moab (Isaiah 15: 2). In the 2nd century BC it appears to have been under Nabatean control, with the "sons of Jambri" (thought to be members of a Nabatean tribe) ambushing a convoy led by John, the brother of Judas Maccabeus (I Maccabees 9: 35-42). Josephus records how the city was captured by John Hyrcanus following a lengthy siege and restored to Jewish rule (Antiquities XIII, 15, 4). Later, control of Madaba and other cities in the area was handed back to the Nabatean king Aretas III by Hyrcanus II in return for the help he had provided in his wars with his brother Aristobulus (Antiquities XIV, 1, 4).

Madaba's Mosaics

The wealth of mosaic art in Jordan is something which most people are quite unprepared for. The roots of this art go back to Hellenistic traditions which flourished throughout the region from the 4th century BC and continued through the Roman period, changing and evolving until they found renewed expression during the Byzantine era. The tradition of mosaic making which developed in and around Madaba did so in the context of a social and cultural flourishing under the emperor Justinian (527-65), often referred to as the Justinian renaissance. Working from pattern books emanating from Constantinople and other cultural centres, the craftsmen of Madaba created their masterpieces, mixing the figures and legends of classical mythology with the new messages of Christianity. Mosaics such as the Madaba Map meanwhile point to a renewed interest in achieving geographical accuracy in representing the world. Many of the mosaics are anonymous, but on others we find the mosaicist's name; Salamanios in the Church of the Apostles in Madaba; Soelos, Kaiomos and Elias in the Memorial of Moses on Mount Nebo; Staurachios son of Zada and his colleague Euremios in the Church of St Stephen at Umm ar-Rasas. The tesserae from which the mosaics were made are solid cubes of stone, their natural colours drawn from the rich variety of stone to be found in the region, and it is for this reason that they have survived so vividly over the centuries.

In 106 AD Madaba became part of the Roman province of Arabia and under Roman rule developed into a small but significant provincial town laid out along typical Roman lines with colonnaded streets, baths and temples. It soon became a focus of Christian activity. During the persecution of Christians carried out by Diocletian (284-305 AD), several of Madaba's inhabitants were martyred, including an army officer named Zenon and his servant Zena, and Theodore and his five companions, Julian, Eobolus, Malkamon, Mokimos and Salamon. During the Byzantine period Madaba continued to prosper, becoming the seat of a bishopric by the mid-5th century, as mentioned in the Acts of the Council of Chalcedon of 451 AD. The height of the town's prosperity came during the rule of Justinian (527-65) and it was from this period onwards that all the great mosaics were laid. Interestingly, Madaba continued to flourish even after the Archamenid Persian invasions of 611-14, when most other Christian centres fell into decline, and also during the early Islamic period. The later mosaics in the Church of the Saviour for example date from the early Umayyad period. Unfortunately, however, the iconoclastic movement of the 8th century led to many of the mosaics depicting animal and human forms being dug up and replaced.

Although it continued to be inhabited well into the Islamic period, at least until the 14th century, the town lost its significance and sometime during the late Mameluke or early Ottoman period it was abandoned altogether. The present town dates from the 1880, when Christians from the nearby town of Kerak were settled here following disturbances between the Christian and Muslim inhabitants. The discovery of the Mesha Stela in 1868 had already aroused interest in the *tell* at Madaba, and excavations carried out from 1872 onwards resulted in various of the Roman and Byzantine period remains being uncovered.

The Madaba Map was discovered in 1896 and a year later the mosaics in the crypt of St Elianos and in the Church of the Prophet Elias. Further excavations were carried out during the next century, on the Church of el-Khadir in 1966 and the Church of the Apostles in 1967. Since 1968 excavations have been carried out by the Jordanian Department of Antiquities and are continuing to this day.

Sights

Most tour groups stop here only to look at the Madaba Map before hurrying off to Petra. However, the other excavated mosaics at Madaba are in many respects even more impressive and certainly not to be missed. The nearby monastery at Mount Nebo (see below) should also really be included as part of a visit to Madaba.

St George's Church & Madaba Map

The Greek Orthodox St George's church was built in 1896 over the foundations of an earlier Byzantine church. The full extent of the famous Madaba Map, parts of which had been traced by a local priest in 1890, was only revealed when the floor tiles of the new church were being laid. The map originally depicted an area extending from the Egyptian delta in the south to the Levantine coast in the north, including the cities of Tyre and Sidon. Although only a quarter of the original has survived, this includes most of the all-important city of Jerusalem as well as the Jordan river flowing into the Dead Sea and sections of Sinai. As such, it still represents perhaps the most significant mosaic discovery in the whole of the Middle East, and the historical and geographical information it contains continues to fuel research and debate to this day.

The glory of the map is in the detail, and in the remarkable geographical accuracy it achieves. Essentially a document of biblical geography, it was most probably intended as a guide for religious pilgrims to the Holy Land. A total of 157 captions in Greek identify important religious sites as well as indicating the twelve tribes of Israel. The map is oriented to the east, with the Jordan river and Dead Sea forming the central axis. The highlight is the detailed bird's-eye view plan of the Holy City of Jerusalem. The walls and gates of the city, its cardo maximus running north-south (left to right on the map) through the centre, and its principal buildings are all clearly discernable, including the Constantinian complex of the Holy Sepulchre half way down the cardo and two large basilica churches towards its southern end. The detail elsewhere is just as meticulous; fish swimming in the Jordan river, two boats on the Dead Sea, palm trees at the oasis of Jericho, tributary rivers, mountains, sea etc.

As well as being an important source of information to contemporary scholars regarding as yet unidentified biblical sites, the map has also provided the only available clues as to the date of its execution. Thus the large basilica church in the plan of Jerusalem, on the east side of the cardo at its southern end, has been identified as the Nea Theokotos (New Church of the Mother of God), which was built by Justinian and dedicated in 542, leading most experts to agree that the map dates from the second half of the 6th century. To the left of the main area of the mosaic map, concealed beneath a small rug, is a further fragment. There are also a number of very beautiful painted icons in the church. ■ *Open 0800-1800, Fri 0900-1800, Sun 1000-1800. Entry JD1. There is usually someone on hand to give a detailed 'tour' of the Madaba Map, if required.*

King's Highway

Madaba Archaeological Park

Included in the Madaba Archaeological park are the Church of the Virgin and Hippolytus Hall, the Church of the Prophet Elias, and a section of the Roman *decumanus*. Entering the `park', an impressive selection of mosaics discovered in the Madaba region are displayed: from the 1st century BC Herodian fortress at Machaerus (the oldest in Jordan); the upper mosaic church of Massuh (3 km east of Hisban, 6th century); the Acropolis Church at Ma'in (early 8th century); and the hall of the Seasons in Madaba (6th century)

The highlight is the **Church of the Virgin** and the surviving parts of the **Hippolytus Hall**, housed within a large modern structure with walkways around the inside. The Church of the Virgin dates from the late 6th century AD. It was built over a late 2nd-early 3rd century AD Roman temple to which a further hall had been added in the early 6th century AD (the so-called Hippolytus Hall). Covering the floor of the circular central nave of the Church of the Virgin, which corresponds with the platform of the Roman temple, is a beautiful mosaic. The floral designs around the outer border of the mosaic date from the late 6th to early 7th century AD, while the central square enclosing a circular medallion was added later, during the early Umayyad period by the then bishop of Madaba, Theophane. The inscription in the centre reads: "If you want to look at Mary, virginal Mother of God, and to Christ whom she generated, Universal King, only Son of the only God, purify mind, flesh and works! May you purify with prayer the people of God." The date accompanying the inscription is incomplete, but is believed to correspond with 662 AD.

The Hippolytus Hall contains a beautifully preserved rectangular mosaic, one part of which formed the floor of a private house until it was fully excavated in 1982. The border consists of acanthus scrolls and hunting scenes, with personifications of the Four Seasons at each corner. Along the east wall, outside the border of the main mosaic, the cities of Rome, Gregoria and Madaba are personified as three Tyches, each seated on a throne and holding a cross on a staff. To one side of them is a small medallion with two sandals surrounded by four birds, while on the other side are monsters and birds. The central section of the mosaic consists of three panels. The bottom one contains flowers and birds. The central one contains characters from the Greek tragedy of Phaedra and Hippolytus (as recounted in Euripides' *Hippolytus*, hence the hall's name), although parts of it were destroyed when the hall was divided into two rooms at a later date. The top one contains various scenes from the legends of Adonis and Aphrodite, who are seated on a throne and surrounded by a number of Cupids and Graces.

The Church of the Virgin and the Hippolytus Hall borders the Roman period **decumanus**, a section of which has been excavated revealing the large flagstones with which it was paved. Running roughly east-west, this would have originally linked two of the city's gates and would have been lined by a colonnade.

On the other side of the decumanus is the **Church of the Prophet Elias**. The church was first discovered in 1897 and a fragment of mosaic flooring was uncovered near the steps leading to the presbytery which included a dedicatory inscription referring to the Prophet Elias and giving a date for the church of 607-8. Another mosaic inscription in a circular medallion in the centre of the nave reads: *"You who with your prayers set in motion, as is fitting, the clouds, bearers of rain, and who give mercy to the people, O Prophet, remember also the benefactors and this humble city"*. The church suffered damage during the early part of the 20th century and today only the apse of the church is clearly discernible along with traces of the mosaics which covered the floor of the nave and side-aisles. Beneath the apse is the **Crypt of St Elianus** with further traces of mosaics surviving, and an inscription which reads: "The Christ God has erected this house at the time of the most pious Bishop Sergius for the care of Sergius, the priest of Saint Elianus, the year 490 [595-6 AD]…"

Also within the grounds of the archaeological park, though not open to the public, is the recently established **Madaba Mosaic School**, a joint Italian-Jordanian project involved in training people in the art of making and conserving mosaics. ■ *Open daily 0800-1900 in summer, 0800-1700 in winter, Fri 1000-1600. Entry JD2, which covers the Archaeological Park, the Museum and the Church of the Apostles (3 separate sites).*

£4000 worth of holiday vouchers to be won!

... that can be claimed against any exodus, Peregrine or Gecko's holiday, a choice of around 570 holidays that set industry standards for responsible tourism in 90 countries across seven continents.

exodus

The UK's leading adventurous travel company, with over 25 years' experience in running the most exciting holidays in 80 different countries. We have an unrivalled choice of trips, from a week exploring the hidden corners of Tuscany to a high altitude trek to Everest Base Camp or 3 months travelling across South America. If you want to do something a little different, chances are you'll find it in one of our brochures.

Peregrine

Australia's leading quality adventure travel company, Peregrine aims to explore some of the world's most interesting and inaccessible places. Providing exciting and enjoyable holidays that focus in some depth on the lifestyle, culture, history, wildlife, wilderness and landscapes of areas that are usually quite different to our own. There is an emphasis on the outdoors, using a variety of transport and staying in a range of accommodation, from comfortable hotels to tribal huts.

Gecko's

Gecko's holidays will get you to the best places with the minimum of hassle. They are designed for younger people who like independent travel but don't have the time to organise everything themselves. Be prepared to take the rough with the smooth, these holidays are for active people with a flexible approach to travel.

To enter the competition, simply tear out the postcard and return it to Exodus Travels, 9 Weir Road, London SW12 0LT. Or go to the competition page on www.exodus.co.uk and register online. Two draws will be made, Easter 2001 and Easter 2002, and the winner of each draw will receive £2000 in travel vouchers. The closing date for entry will be 1st March 2002. If you do not wish to receive further information about these holidays, please tick here. ☐ No purchase necessary. Plain paper entries should be sent to the above address. The prize value is non-transferable and there is no cash alternative. Winners must be over 18 years of age and must sign and adhere to operators' standard booking conditions. A list of prizewinners will be available for a period of one month from the draw by writing to the above address. For a full list of terms and conditions please write to the above address or visit our website.

To receive a brochure, please tick the relevant boxes below (maximum number of brochures 2) or telephone (44) 20 8772 3822.

exodus	Peregrine	Gecko's
☐ Walking & Trekking	☐ Himalaya	☐ Egypt, Jordan & Israel
☐ Discovery & Adventure	☐ China	☐ South America
☐ European Destinations	☐ South East Asia	☐ Africa
☐ Overland Journeys	☐ Antarctica	☐ South East Asia
☐ Biking Adventures	☐ Africa	☐ India
☐ Multi Activity	☐ Arctic	

Please give us your details:

Name: ---

Address: ---

Postcode: ---

e-mail: ---

Which footprint guide did you take this from?

----

exodus
The Different Holiday

getaway tonight on **www.exodus.co.uk**

exodus
The Different Holiday

getaway tonight on

www.exodus.co.uk

exodus
The Different Holiday

exodus

9 Weir Road
LONDON
SW12 0BR

BUSINESS REPLY SERVICE
Licence No SW4909

Across the street immediately to the west of the Archaeological park, behind **Burnt Palace**
the Madaba Society shop, is the so-called Burnt Palace. When part of it was
first uncovered in 1905, it was thought to be a church. However, excavations
since 1985 have confirmed that it was a lavish complex, probably secular in
nature, dating from the late 6th-early 7th century. It was destroyed by fire
(hence the name), perhaps as a result of the earthquake of 747.

The palace consists of a central courtyard surrounded by rooms. Walkways
have been constructed overlooking the various fragments of mosaics preserved here. Part of the central courtyard is obscured by the tourist office; in
the basement of this building plans are displayed giving an overview of the layout of the Burnt Palace. On the north side, only small fragments of mosaic
floors in two rooms have been excavated, with the remainder lying beneath the
Madaba Society shop and other modern buildings.

Preserved in the first room is a mosaic of the bust of the goddess Tyche
(complete), along with a fragment of a personification of one of the seasons.
The second room contains a mosaic of scale patterns framed within a plaited
border. On the west side is a long room containing three square mosaic panels
with geometric designs. Between the northern-most and central panel is a strip
of mosaic depicting a lion attacking a bull. The southernmost panel actually
belongs to a separate room. To the west again of these mosaics is a futher complex of rooms, and also a deep water cistern. It is in the large hall on the east
side of the central courtyard that the most impressive mosaic has been uncovered. It consists of a broad border decorated with birds, fish, animals, plants
and trees. Within this is a large panel depicting pastoral and hunting scenes,
each encircled within an acanthus scroll. On the south side of the Burnt Palace,
another section of the Roman **decumanus** has been excavated (this would
have joined up with the section across the road in the Archaeological Park).

At the time of writing, the Burnt Palace had not been as yet officially opened to
the public, though visitors were allowed to enter the site (access via the tourist
office, or from a path off the road just to the west) and wander around the
walkways overlooking the various fragments of mosaics. Once officially open,
it will be incorporated into the Madaba Archaeological Park.

Immediately to the southeast of the Burnt Palace is the 6th century basilica **Church of El**
Church of El Khadir (literally Martyrs' Church). At present this is enclosed **Khadir (Martyr's**
within a high-walled compound and not open to the public. However, from **Church)**
inside the Burnt Palace site, where the corner of this compound obscures part
of the decumanus, there is a hole where you can peer inside. The semi-circular
apse and altar area are clearly discernable, while two rows of corinthian columns separate the nave from the side-aisles. The mosaic floors of the church
have been reburied under sand to protect them from the elements. Though
they suffered damage from iconoclasts in the 8th century, much of the intricate
mosaic decoration, depicting hunting and pastoral scenes, still survives, and
once properly protected and displayed will make an impressive addition to
Madaba's monuments.

The site of the Church of El Khadir actually belongs to the Greek Orthodox
church, and negotiations are in progress to decide whether it should be managed by the Department of Antiquities as part of the Archaeological Park, or by
the Greek Orthodox church.

One room of the Madaba museum is built around the mosaic floor of a 6th **Madaba**
century house, with panels depicting a Bacchic scene, with a lute-playing satyr **museum**

King's Highway

still discernible, and a scene containing Achilles and Patroclus. Two other rooms also contain mosaic floors; one large room given over to floral and geometric designs and a small one with a central medallion of a ram nibbling at a tree. The folklore section includes traditional jewellery, costumes and head-dresses while the archaeology section contains a range of artefacts including "ballistic missiles" (Byzantine slingshot stones) and a copy of the Mesha Stela. ■ *Open daily 0900-1700, Fri 1000-1600, closed Tue. Entry included in the price of the Madaba Archaeological Park ticket.*

Church of the Apostles Located on the southern edge of the town, by the junction of the King's Highway with Al Nuzha St, the Church of the Apostles is also enclosed by a modern protective building. First discovered in 1902, an inscription in a room at the eastern end of the church (now gone) identified the church as having been dedicated to the Apostles and built in 578 AD. The nave is covered by a large mosaic consisting of a border of ananthus leaves enclosing a geometric pattern of birds and plants. In the centre is a medallion with a personification of the sea represented as a woman, Thetis, emerging from the waves and surrounded by fish and sea monsters. The inscription around the edge of the medallion reads: "O Lord God who has made the heavens and earth, give life to Anastasius, to Thomas, to Theodore and to Salamanios, the mosaicist".

Both the side-aisles of this basilica church are decorated with geometric patterns. On the north side are two small chapels. The first contains a mosaic of stags, sheep and gazelles standing amidst fruit trees. The second is divided into two areas, one with a square mosaic consisting of four trees oriented towards the centre and dividing the square into four triangles, within each of which is a pair of animals and at the top a dedicatory inscription referring to the "temple of the Holy Apostles". The other area consists of a smaller rectangle of mosaic with a floral grid within which are depicted various trees, flowers etc and a bird in the centre. ■ *Open daily 0800-1900 in summer, 0800-1700 in winter, Fri 1000-1600. Entry included in the price of the Madaba Archaeological Park ticket.*

Madaba

To Amman via Tell Hisban

■2

Al Quds St

■1

Al Quds St

Yarmouk St

To Mount Nebo

Buses to Mount Nebo · Buses to Tell Hisban

Palestine St

Jordan-Gulf · @ Tour dot Net

1● (S) Housing · (S) Arab

Al Malik Hussein St

2●

† St George's

3■ · Madaba Society Shop/Office

Site for New Tourist Information Office

Al Malik Abdullah St

Haret Jdoudna o · Church of El Khadir & Burnt Palace

■4

🛈

4■ · Car Park o

o Madaba Archaeological Park

New Souk Complex

6●
5● · Buses to Hammamat Ma'in

To Hammamat Ma'in

▥

Al Nuzha St · ●3

King's Highway

N
△

Church of the Apostles †■

To Kerak

0 metres   100
0 yards   100

To Main Bus Station (150m) & Amman (direct)

To Desert Highway

● Eating
1 Abu Ghassan
2 Ayola
3 Dana
4 El Cardo
5 Mankal Chicken Tikka
6 Sam's Café & Lounge

■ Sleeping
1 Black Iris
2 Lulu's Pension
3 Madaba
4 Queen Ayola

King's Highway

Essentials

Though the range of hotels in Madaba is somewhat limited, the overall standard of **Sleeping** accommodation is excellent as compared with hotels of a similar price range in Amman. All hotels include breakfast in the price of the room.

C *Black Iris*, T541959. Clean, pleasant rooms with fan, heater and attached bath. Friendly management. Restaurant hall and more rooms under construction, also planning to install a/c in some rooms. **C** *Lulu's Pension*, T543678, F547617. Large private house offering choice of rooms with attached or shared bath, all with heater. Sleep on roof terrace in summer or in upstairs common area in winter for JD6 (access to cooking facilities and bathroom, very good value). Camping in garden JD5. Homely, very comfortable and spotlessly clean. **C** *Queen Ayola*, T/F544087. Choice of rooms with attached or shared bath, all rooms with fan and heater. Small, recently opened hotel with just 8 rooms, all spotlessly clean and pleasantly furnished, some with balcony.

D *Madaba*, T/F540643. Reasonably clean rooms with fan, heater and shared bath (also two rooms with attached bath), somewhat erratic plumbing and elusive hot water. During summer you can sleep under a tent structure on the roof for JD3.

'Pilgrim' hostel St George's Church, T544982, F541842. Next door to St George's church is a newly built hostel with 13 rooms, a lounge and dining area, and a kitchen. The accommodation here is meant primarily for bona fide 'pilgrims', but if the other hotels in Madaba are full, they will let tourists stay providing they have space. The rooms are simple but spotlessly clean with heater, attached bath and hot water. There are no charges for staying here as such, but guests are invited to make a donation which will go towards the upkeep of both hostel and the school which the church also runs.

Mid-range Easily the nicest place is the *Haret Jdoudna*, Talal St, T548650, F548609. **Eating** This delightful complex of restored Ottoman buildings (see also under Shopping) includes an excellent restaurant upstairs (managed by the *Romero* chain), complete with a lovely outdoor terrace, serving high quality Arabic food for around JD7-10 per head. Downstairs there is the *Pizza Giordania*, serving excellent wood-oven pizzas (around JD2.500-4.500) as well as burgers, chips, alcohol, soft drinks, tea etc. Both recommended. There are two other mid-range restaurants in Madaba. Both are comfortable, well-run establishments geared primarily towards large groups, though they will happily cater for individuals and couples. *Dana*, Al Nuzha St (near Church of the Apostles), T545749, F545452. Mostly Arabic cuisine, but also Indian, Chinese and Mexican (the chef is Indian, and his speciality *Saaj* - leg of lamb cooked in a spicy sauce with onions and yoghurt). Buffet meals (when there is a group) JD6 per head, or à la carte JD6-8 upwards per head. Serves alcohol. Occasional live entertainment in the evenings. *El Cardo*, Abu Bakr as-Sideeq St, opposite the entrance to the Madaba Archaeological Park, T3251006. Seating for up to 200 and outdoor terrace in summer, serving Arabic and 'international' cuisine, with a daily buffet for around JD6 or an à la carte menu (JD6-8 per head). Serves alcohol. Occasional live entertainment in the evenings.

Budget Note that all these places close relatively early; by around 2100-2200 in summer, and even earlier in winter. Near St George's Church, the *Ayola* is nicely decorated in Bedouin style to attract the tourists and serves snacks of shawarmas, falafels and sandwiches etc, and drinks including filter coffee. Prices, however, are a little above the budget mark. More reasonable is *Abu Ghassan*, on Al Malik Abdullah St, a typical Arabic diner which does good falafels, hummus, fuul, roast chicken etc. In the small side-street opposite the post office there is an even simpler place (sign in Arabic only) which does excellent hummus, fuul and falafel. The branch of *Mankal Chicken Tikka* on Al Malik Abdullah St is reasonable value at around JD2-3 for a chicken tikka meal. There are a couple of other cheap Arabic-style diners nearby on the same street. On the King's Highway, in the vicinity of the bus station, there are plenty more cheap eateries offering the standard hummus, roast chicken etc. There are a number of

King's Highway

shops along Yarmouk St, to the north of St George's Church, selling an array of traditional Arabic sweets and biscuits.

Bars With such a large Christian community, you might expect more in the way of bars in Madaba. However, the only places to go for a drink are those restaurants listed above which serve alcohol. There are also several liquor stores around town (two of them are on Al Malik Abdullah St; the one next door to *Mankal Chicken Tikka* is known as *Sam's Café and Lounge* and features a small backroom bar, though the introduction of satellite TV here, permanently tuned into European soft porn, makes it a singularly seedy men-only experience).

Shopping On Talal St, opposite the entrance to St George's Church, the **St George Bazaar** has a wide range of souvenirs and postcards etc, as well as some books on Madaba and Jordan. Just nearby, also on Talal St, there are a number of shops selling the rugs for which Madaba is famous, and various other handicrafts and souvenirs. Next door to the *Madaba* hotel, and also by the *Madaba Society Shop* (see below) there are small workshops where you can see these rugs being woven. The **Haret Jdoudna**, further south on Talal St, is an extensive complex of craft shops housed in beautifully restored Ottoman-period premises. There are outlets for the *Noor al-Hussein Foundation*, *Dana Nature Shop* and *Alburgan*, amongst others, while in the basement there are various workshops where you can see crafts such as mosaic making, rug weaving, silverwork, sand art and carpentry in progress. The **Madaba Society Shop** is run by the snappily-named National Society for the Preservation of the Heritage of Madaba and its Suburbs. The shop includes a selection of handicrafts and books on Madaba and Jordan. Funds raised from the shop are used towards the work of the society, which helps fund some of the excavation and conservation work and has also sponsored local people to study tourism at university.

Transport Regular minibuses run between the main bus station and **Amman's** Raghadan,
See also the Ins Muhajireen and Wahadat bus stations for 350 fils. For **Kerak** there is one bus daily, a
and Outs section student bus which leaves at 0630-0700 and goes to Mutah University near Kerak,
at the beginning though this is often full (approaching Kerak, get off at the T-junction and catch a local
of this chapter bus from there into the centre of Kerak). Fairly regular minibuses operate to **Dhiban**, just to the north of the deep Wadi Mujib (350 fils). For **Mukawir** (Machaerus) there are around 5 minibuses daily (250 fils). For **Umm ar-Rasas** there are a couple of minibuses daily (150 fils, get there early). Regular minibuses and service taxis to **Faissaliyeh** (4 km short of Mount Nebo) leave from here, or, more conveniently, can be caught from the roundabout just to the north of St George's Church (150 fils). Minibuses for **Hammamat Ma'in** leave from Al Malik Abdullah St, see map (2-3 daily, 500 fils). See also the `Ins and outs' sections for each of these sites for more detailed information on reaching them.

Directory **Banks** There are three banks clustered together in the centre of town. The *Arab Bank* and *Housing Bank* both have cash machines outside which accept *Visa* and *+Plus* cards, and will also change cash and TCs, as will the **Jordan-Gulf Bank**. **Communications** Internet There are a couple of internet cafés in Madaba. The most central is *Tour dot Net,* just to the north of St George's Church, T325523. Open 7 days, 1000-2400. Six terminals, JD2/hr (minimum 30 mins). Further away (though convenient if you are staying at *Lulu's Pension*) is *Let's Go!*; from the roundabout at the north end of Yarmouk St, go north and take the first right, then turn left at a T-junction and it is on the next crossroads you come to. Open 7 days, 0900-2400, 9 terminals, J1.500 per hr (minimum 30 mins). **Post** The main post office is next door to the *Jordan-Gulf Bank*. **Telephone** There are *Alo* and *JPP* cardphones dotted around the town.

The Promised Land

"Then Moses climbed Mount Nebo from the plains of Moab to the top of Pisgah, across from Jericho. There the Lord showed him the whole land from Gilead to Dan, and all of Naphtali, the territory of Ephraim and Manasseh, all the land of Judah as far as the western sea, the Negev and the whole region from the Valley of Jericho, the City of Palms, as far as Zoar. Then the Lord said to him, "This is the land I promised on oath to Abraham, Isaac and Jacob when I said, `I will give it to your descendants.' I have let you see it with your eyes, but you will not cross over into it." And Moses the servant of the Lord died there in Moab, as the Lord had said. He was buried in Moab, but to this day no one knows where his grave is. Moses was a 120 years old when he died, yet his eyes were not weak nor his strength gone." (Deuteronomy 34: 1-7)*

Around Madaba

Mount Nebo (Siyagha)

On Mount Nebo, 8 km to the west of Madaba, is the Memorial Church of Moses, in which are preserved more beautiful mosaics, now cared for by the Franciscan monks there. The mosaics are in themselves reason enough to visit, while the hilltop on which they are situated offers truly stunning views across the Jordan River and Dead Sea towards the West Bank (biblical Judaea and Samaria).

Mount Nebo consists of several peaks, the highest reaching 800 m, although this is above sea level; if you take into account the altitude of the Dead Sea you are looking at nearly 1,200 m. The Memorial of Moses is on a peak known as Siyagha, while at Khirbet Mukhayyat (identified as the ancient town of Nebo) are the Church of St George and the Church of SS Lot and Procopius.

Ins & outs To get there, head northwest out of Madaba along Palestine St, following the signs for Mount Nebo. The road passes through the small village of Faissaliyeh (4 km), past a left turn signposted to Khirbet Mukhayyat (6 km) and then a right turn signposted to `Mosa Spring', before arriving at the monastery and Memorial of Moses on the right.
   The minibuses and service taxis from Madaba go only as far as the village of Faissaliyeh. From there it is a pleasant walk (providing it is not too hot), or you can pay the driver an extra JD1 or so to take you right up to the entrance to the Memorial Church of Moses. A private taxi from Madaba will cost in the region of JD5 for the return trip, including waiting time (or more if you include also a visit to Khirbet Mukhayyat and Moses Spring).

History The ridges of Mount Nebo are littered traces of settlement dating back as far as the Stone Age. Historically famous as the scene of the final vision and death of Moses, the mountain also finds mention in the Bible in relation to the passage and camp of the Israelites (Numbers 21: 20) and the story of Balak and Balaam (Numbers 23: 13-26), and in Maccabees (the four books of Jewish history and theology, two of which form part of the Aporcrypha) in relation to the conceal-ment of the tabernacle, the ark and the altar of incense in a cave (2 Maccabees 2: 4-8). Several references in the Bible include Nebo amongst the cities of the land of Moab, in the territory of Madaba. The Mesha Stela meanwhile relates how King Mesha captured it (lines 14-18), "*Next Chemosh said to me, Go take Nebo from Israel. So I went by night, and fought against it from break of dawn till noon; and I took it and slew all in it, seven thousand men and women, both*

Mosaic of gazelle (7th century AD), Mount Nebo

natives and aliens, and female slaves; for I had devoted it to Ashtar-Chemosh. I took from thence the vessels of Yahweh and dragged them before Chemosh."

By the 4th century AD Mount Nebo was an important pilgrimage site marked by the Memorial Church of Moses and several accounts of pilgrims visiting it can be found in the writings of the late Roman and Byzantine periods. Exactly when the monastery and town were abandoned is not known, but it was only in 1864 that the ruins of Siyagha were brought to the attention of the outside world. Various explorations and surveys of Siyagha, Mukhayyat and the surrounding area were carried out and in 1933 the land was bought by the Franciscan Custody of the Holy Land order. By 1937 excavations had uncovered the Memorial Church of Moses with its mosaic floors, and the surrounding monastery complex. Work on the preservation and further excavation of this site continues to this day.

Memorial Church of Moses The Memorial Church of Moses was originally built in the second half of the 4th century as a small triapsidal church with a vestibule in front and two funeral chapels on either side, although little of this remains to be seen today. Various additions over the years culminated in the construction of the full three-aisled basilica incorporating the earlier church (in the second half of the 6th century, in the time of the Bishop Sergius of Madaba). In the meantime the monastery surrounding it steadily grew in size, giving rise to a substantial complex which would have been able to accommodate several hundred monks and pilgrims at its height.

A rather bizarre sculpture greets you as you walk up towards the church, built to mark the millenium and bearing the legend "Unus Deus, Pater Omnium, Super Omnes" ("One God, Father of all, above all others"). Further on is a terrace with another modernistic sculpture, this time in the shape of a cross, and stunning views out over the Dead Sea and Jordan river, and Israel beyond. Today the excavated remains of the 6th century basilica are covered by a modern protective building. Entering the main church, to the left (north) of the central nave, is a walkway overlooking an earlier baptistry (the `Old Diaconicon'), dominated by a large panel of mosaic which is beautifully preserved and perhaps the most impressive in the church. Depicted on it are scenes which appear to chart the progression of man's relationship with animals from primitive hunting to domestication: lions, a bear and a boar being hunted; sheep and goats grazing from trees; and finally an ostrich, a zebra and a camel being led by two men. An inscription in Greek gives the date of the mosaic as 530 and the mosaicists' names: Soelos, Kaiomos and Elias. Dotted around the church are various other mosaics, either in situ or mounted on the walls, the detail on some of them being equally impressive. The restored monastery buildings of the Franciscan monks are not open to the public. At the time of writing a small museum and a cafetería were under construction.
■ *Open daily 0500-1900 in summer, 0700-1700 in winter. Entry 500 fils. Included in the price of the ticket is a rectangular card with a detailed plan of the site; ask for the 'naksha' (map) if it is not offered. There is a 250 fils fee for the car park by the entrance to the site, and for the toilet facilities nearby. Various postcards of the mosaics are on sale inside the Memorial Church.*

There are several handicraft shops, a glass-blowing factory and the huge *Siyagha* restaurant by the turning down to Moses Spring. The road winds its way steeply down into the beautiful though desolate hills to the spring, just over 2 km away. This is unfortunately now marked by a modern pumping station, although below it where the water re-emerges is a miniature waterfall. It is possible to scramble down beside it to a pleasant area of green ideal for a picnic. Although there is not much to see, dolmens, rock cut tombs and hermitages, traces of fortresses and Byzantine buildings have been recorded, along with milestones of the Roman road which linked Nebo with Heshbon (Tell Hisban).

Moses Spring (Wadi Ayoun Musa)

Excavations in 1984 revealed two small churches near the spring, both dating from the first half of the 6th century. The **Church of Deacon Thomas**, located on the path between spring and the Roman road, contains beautiful and largely intact mosaics covering the central nave, side-aisles and presbytery. At the time of writing it was not however open to the public. The **Church of Kaianos**, consisting of an upper and a lower church, has poorly preserved mosaics which have been removed for restoration.

The small *tell* at Khirbet Mukhayyat has been identified fairly conclusively as the site of the ancient town of Nebo. Excavations have revealed three churches, a chapel and a monastery in the vicinity of the *tell*. Tombs dating from the Early Bronze Age through to the Hellenistic period as well as an Iron Age tower have also been discovered here. This was probably the settlement attacked by king Mesha, although his claims as to the number of people it contained at that time are certainly exaggerated.

Khirbet Mukhayyat

From the turning off the main Madaba-Mount Nebo road, it is a further 2 km down to Khirbet Mukhayyat. The **Church of SS Lot and Procopius** is at the road-head, housed within a nondescript modern building. If it is locked someone should soon turn up to open it for you. The mosaics preserved inside are very beautiful. The raised presbytery directly in front of where the altar stood depicts two sheep grazing from a tree. The central nave consists of two panels enclosed within a border; that nearest the presbytery depicting hunting and pastoral scenes woven through by vine scrolls, while the other depicts four trees and pairs of animals in-between. The dedicatory inscription gives the date of the mosaic as 560. Just by the door is a small panel depicting a church (perhaps the original church of Lot and Procopius) with a boatman on one side and a fisherman on the other.

The dilapidated ruins of the **Church of St George** are visible up on a hillock beyond the Church of SS Lot and Procopius. The mosaics from this church, which depict various hunting scenes and personifications of the Four Seasons and of Earth, are now all housed within the Memorial Church of Moses on Mount Nebo. The **Church of Amos and Casiseos**, built on the western slopes of Wadi Afrit and including also the **Chapel of Priest John**, is equally ruinous. On the eastern slopes of Wadi Afrit are the remains of a small monastery known as **El Keneiseh**.

King's Highway

From Mount Nebo you can descend through dramatic barren hills to the Dead Sea via a narrow and winding road (continue straight past the entrance to the Memorial Church of Moses; the road is signposted 'Dead Sea; Baptism Place'). At the time of writing, resurfacing and widening work on this road was nearing completion, making an excursion down to the **Dead Sea** and/or **Wadi Kharrar** (Al Maghtas, or the Baptism Site) by this route an attractive proposition. Note, however, that while the new road may be excellent, the numerous hairpin bends and precipitous drops are just as treacherous – so take care!

The road down to the Dead Sea

Mosaic of wine pressing (6th century AD), Church of SS Lot and Procopius

From the Memorial Church of Moses it is just under 16 km down to a T-junction on the main road between Amman and the Dead Sea, just to the west of the village of Al Rameh and the turning for South Shounah and the Jordan Valley. The return trip from Madaba to Wadi Kharrar by taxi costs around JD10-15. For details of both the Dead Sea and Wadi Kharrar, see the 'Around Amman' chapter, page 216.

Hammamat Ma'in

Nestled in a sheer ravine as it plunges down from the Eastern Plateau towards the Dead Sea are the hot sulphur springs of Hammamat Ma'in. Both the setting and the springs themselves are dramatic, with hot water cascading down from the cliffs and feeding pools below. Unfortunately, the large resort which has been developed here is a rather ugly affair, although at the time of writing it was undergoing extensive renovation which hopefully will make it more appealing in the future. On weekends and holidays it can get very busy, though at other times it is usually fairly deserted. When the new roads being built in the area are completed, it will be possible to combine a visit to Hammamat Ma'in with visits to the Dead Sea and Mukawir (Machaerus).

■*Open daily (NB at the time of writing the resort was closed between 1600-0800 each day while renovations were in progress). Basic entry is JD2 (children 550 fils), which allows you to enjoy the pools below the main waterfall; there are separate fees for the various other facilities at the resort.*

Ins & outs　**Getting there** Hammamat Ma'in is situated 30 km to the southwest of Madaba. To get there, head southwest out of Madaba on Ibn Kuthayr St. After 8 km, go straight on at the roundabout in the village of Ma'in (right for the village centre). Around 4 km further on, the Dead Sea and the barren moonscape of hills leading down to it come dramatically into view. The road runs along the side of a ridge before arriving at 2 viewpoints close together (18 km from the roundabout in Ma'in). The first looks west out over the Dead Sea, while the second looks south across the deep Wadi Zarqa Ma'in towards Mukawir. Nearby, a road is under construction which will eventually lead right down to the Dead Sea near Ain Zarqa (see page 216). Immediately after the viewpoints, the main road descends precipitously to arrive at the resort entrance. On the way down you can see another road (still under construction at the time of writing, but nearing completion) which climbs equally precipitously from the resort up towards Mukawir (see page 216).

　　The minibuses from Madaba only go all the way to Hammamat Ma'in if there is sufficient demand; otherwise they stop in Ma'in village, and you will either have to negotiate with the driver to take you the rest of the way, or else hire a taxi. There is also a daily JETT bus which leaves Amman at 0730 (though only if there are sufficient passengers), charging JD4 for the return trip including entry (no one-way tickets).

The resort　On the left, as you head down into the resort from the entrance gate, there is the so-called **"Roman bath"** (signposted 'The Baths', entry JD1.650), a somewhat rundown complex consisting of separate pools for men and women, a sauna (artificial) and treatment rooms. Further on down, there is a **'Family Spring'** consisting of a small waterfall feeding a bathing pool, complete with its own cave (entry JD1.100), as well as an outdoor **swimming pool** (cold water, entry JD2.200). However, the primary attraction at Hammamat Ma'in is the **main waterfall** just to the right of the *Mercure* hotel. With steam rising off it, the waterfall cascades down over rocks rounded smooth and caked with the accumulated deposits of millenia, like a thick sludge dripping slowly down. At the bottom there are several pools in the stream where you can immerse yourself in the hot water and treat yourself to a high-powered, pummelling sort of 'massage' from the waterfall above.

Being free, this is where most Jordanians come to bathe, though you will notice that Jordanian women, if they are bathing at all, do so fully clothed. Women may find some privacy if they continue downstream, round the corner and out of sight of the more popular spots, though on weekends and holidays these stretches are likely to be just as busy. The road which passes underneath the *Mercure* hotel brings you to a mosque and a stairway which leads up to the **Al Amir Spring**, with alternating 2 hour sessions for men and women (entry 250 fils; at the time of writing these were closed, but due to open again in the near future).

For hiking enthusiasts there is a wealth of possibilities, including following the stream down from Hammamat Ma'in to the Dead Sea, a distance of around 8 km. Around halfway down, you enter a particularly narrow section of gorge (rather like the *Siq* at Petra) which involves some demanding scrambling over rocks. Unless you are experienced, a guide is advisable for this section of the route. There are plans (still very much at the 'ideas' stage at the time of writing) to create a network of trails around Hammamat Ma'in, both for hiking and mountain biking, and also to explore the rock climbing potential of the area.

Sleeping & eating The centerpiece of the resort is the luxury **AL** *Mercure* hotel (formerly the *Ashtar*, now taken over by the French company *ACCOR*, which is responsible for renovating the whole resort), T545500, F545550. Comfortable, pleasantly furnished rooms with a/c, TV/dish, IDD, attached bath and balcony. Those at the front overlook the resort, while those at the rear overlook the hotel's swimming pool and the Al Amir spring. Guests here get free use of all the various facilities of the resort, and also the hotel's own health centre (separate fees) and pools. For non-guests, use of the swimming pool (cold water) costs JD6.250, and JD5 for the 2 hot spring water 'treatment' pools. At the time of writing, the cheaper *Chalets* (consisting of self-catering units) and *Caravans* (unappealing portakabin-type units) were both closed for renovations.

Currently, the only proper restaurant at the resort is inside the *Mercure* hotel, where buffet meals are overpriced at around JD10-12 per head, or you can opt for a cheaper snack at their coffee shop. The *Drop and Shop Supermarket*, in front of the *Caravans* complex, has a very limited and overpriced range of biscuits, chocolate bars, crisps and cold drinks. Though you are officially not meant to bring food and drinks into the resort, in practice this is not enforced and bringing your own picnic is a very good idea.

Tell Hisban

Tell Hisban is a little visited site within easy reach of Madaba. There are some interesting excavated remains to be seen on top of the *tell*, including a recently discovered complex of caves, and excellent views out over the surrounding countryside.

Ins & outs It is a short drive out to Tell Hisban, situated 9 km to the north of Madaba (head due north from the roundabout at the north end of Yarmouk St). There are 2 left turnings off the main road for Tell Hisban itself (both signposted), with a road doing a loop

King's Highway

through Hisban village and past the site entrance, around 500 m from the main road. There are reasonably frequent minibuses running along this stetch of road, which you can catch from the bus station (make sure you specify Hisban as your destination as Amman-bound services mostly go via the Desert Highway, not the Hisban road). Alternatively, you can catch minibuses for Hisban from the roundabout a little to the north of St Georges Church.

The site is fenced off. If the gate is locked the caretaker is usually close at hand to open it up. There are no fixed opening times or entrance fee. The role of caretaker is unofficially fulfilled by Abu Noor, who lives close by and has helped the archaeologists working here in recent years. His colourful interpretations of the ancient history of the site, should you be treated to them, will add a whole new dimension to your visit.

History First excavated in the late '60s and early '70s by a team from St Andrew's University in Michigan, the large *tell* or mound here has revealed evidence of human activity dating from the Paleolithic era all the way through to Islamic times. In 1997 a team from St Andrew's University returned to carry out further excavations as part of the Madaba Plains Project, with the aim of shedding more light on the history of this fascinating site.

Hisban is generally identified with **Heshbon**, which first finds mention in the Bible as "… *the city of Sihon king of the Amorites*" (Numbers 21: 26) which Moses captured; "*Israel captured all the cities of the Amorites and occupied them, including Heshbon and all its surrounding settlements.*" (Numbers 21: 25). The archaeological record indicates that there was a permanent settlement here at least from the Early Iron Age onwards, with distinct periods of building activity during the 10th century BC and 7th-6th century BC (during the latter period Heshbon appears to have been part of the Ammonite kingdom). Sometime during the 5th century BC this settlement came to an abrupt and violent end, and it was not until the late Hellenistic period (2nd century BC) that it really began to flourish again. Later, Josephus includes Heshbon (or Hesebon) amongst the fortresses and fortified cities built by Herod the Great (37-4 BC) to strengthen his kingdom (Antiquities XV, 294). During the Roman period the town, then known as Esbus, benefited from its position at the junction of the road from Jerusalem with the *Via Nova Traiana*. Under the rule of Elagabalus (218-222 AD), it was raised to municipal status and began to mint its own bronze coins.

During the 4th century it became a Christian centre of some importance, appearing in the Acts of the Council of Nicaea (325 AD) as an episcopal see. It remained an important bishopric until at least the 7th century, appearing in correspondence with Pope Martin I. After disappearing for a while from historical records, it reappears in the 9th century (Abbasid period) when the Arab geographer Yaqut relates the existence of a strong fortress here. In the 14th century, under the Mamelukes, it became the capital of the Belqa district but thereafter appears to have lost its significance.

Around the site With the help of the Jordanian Department of Antiquities, Friends of Archaeology and local schools, considerable effort has gone into making the site more accessible to the general public and developing it as an "open air classroom" to provide Jordanian children with a first-hand insight into the field of archaeology and its significance for Jordan.

Following the path up from the entrance gate, on your right, near the top of the mound, is the entrance to a recently discovered system of **caves** (kept locked; the caretaker has the key). Inside, an arch of limestone blocks supports the roof, while in the floor a deep hole opens out into what appears to be a cistern, with two tunnels leading from it (presumably added at a later date). Moving into the second part of the cave, there is another supporting arch and a shaft in the roof leading up to the surface. A passage leads through into another chamber with three tall square columns supporting the roof, which is pierced by two further shafts. The discovery of stone hammer tools, scrapers and arrowheads in these caves confirms that they were occupied during the Epipaleolithic and Neolithic eras (from around the 10th-4th millenium BC). The deep cistern appears to have been dug during the Iron Age I period (1200-918 BC) and perhaps reused as a tomb during the Iron Age II period (918-539 BC). The supporting arches and columns, meanwhile, are thought to date from the Hellenistic era. These caves are part of a larger complex and, while further work is needed in order to develop a more complete picture, it is clear that they were of integral importance to the settlement from prehistoric times through to the Hellenistic era, perhaps even amounting to a whole 'city' underground where the inhabitants could retreat in times of danger.

Further up the path, you can look out over an area of excavations, the deepest level of which has revealed a massive bedrock trench dating from the Iron Age I period (during the mid-13th century BC). This is thought to have served as a **dry moat** protecting the settlement on the summit. Just to the south of this can be seen the eastern wall of a huge plastered **reservoir** with a capacity of some 2.2 million cubic litres dating from the Iron Age II period (during the 10th century BC). At a higher level, the remains of a late Roman period **plaza** are visible, along with the first few steps of a **stairway** which led up to a **Roman temple**, possibly erected by the emperor Elagabalus, and later destroyed by an earthquake. Part of the *portico* of the temple survives and there are plans to partially reconstruct it. Standing within the compound of this temple (and almost certainly built using materials taken from it) can be seen the clear outline of a 5th-6th century **Byzantine basilica church**, with its semi-circular apse and the bases of columns marking the central nave. Beside the church is a rectangular **stone basin** and a circular stone with a hole in the centre leading down into a deep **water cistern**. The highest point of the *tell* (on the west side) is occupied by the indistinct remains of a **Mameluke palace complex**, which included a bathhouse, reception hall, mosque and store rooms.

Across the valley, on the hillside to the west of the tell, the entrances to numerous **caves** can be seen. These were no doubt also occupied during prehistoric times, and perhaps later used as tombs. Until recently, they were lived in by local people, though today the serve only as animal shelters. A recent survey, funded by the Swedish government, has identified an elaborate agricultural and **water management system** down in the wadi, consisting of terraced fields, various agricultural cisterns, a reservoir and numerous check dams in the bottom of the wadi to prevent gulley formation. On the edges of the modern village of Hisban are the remains of various Mameluke and Ottoman period buildings, many of them clearly built with stones taken from earlier structures on the *tell*.

The route south along the King's Highway from Madaba takes you across the spectacular **Wadi Mujib**, which cuts a deep gorge through the eastern plateau as it descends from the desert to the east down into the Dead Sea. En route there are two worthwhile diversions, east to **Mukawir**, the site of the Herodian stronghold of Machaerus, and west to the Byzantine ruins and mosaics at **Umm ar-Rasas**. Both can also be conveniently visited as an excursion from Madaba.

Madaba to Kerak

Mukawir (Machaerus)

As the place where John the Baptist was beheaded, the mountain stronghold of Machaerus is today perhaps most impressive for its stunning views and dramatic setting. The detour off the King's Highway takes you through rugged,

Bani Hamida House

The large and well-appointed shop, Bani Hamida House, which you see on the way out of Mukawir village, is part of the Bani Hamida Women's Weaving Project initiated by Save the Children Fund and now incorporated into the Jordan River Foundation. Aimed at providing 'self-sustaining income generation for rural women in Jordan', the project works with Bedouin women who have recently been settled in villages in the area, which is known locally as Jebel Bani Hamida (after the name of the Bedouin tribe). Drawing on the women's skills and knowledge of traditional weaving techniques, including the spinning and dying of wool, the project allows mothers to work from home, producing handwoven rugs, cushions etc from locally derived wool. More than 1,600 women in 13 villages are now employed in this way. The products are then sold directly to the public through this shop and another one in Amman, and also marketed abroad. As well as generating additional income for the Bedouin women while allowing them to continue their pastoral lifestyle and raise their children, the project, which is self-run, has encouraged the women to take up education and training opportunities.

The handwoven woollen rugs etc are very beautiful, combining vivid colours and pastel hues, as well as traditional and contemporary Bedouin designs. The prices are not cheap (most of the rugs are more than JD200, and the smallest ones around the JD50 mark), but they reflect the quality and real value of the goods. Even if you are not interested in buying, a visit to this shop or the one in Amman (see page 220) is worthwhile just to see the designs.

Open 0800-1500 (or later if there are tour groups around), closed Fri and Sat (but again, may open for tour groups). For more information contact the Jordan River Foundation in Amman; T06-5933211, F06-5933210, jrd@nets.com.jo

striking countryside, and also offers the opportunity to visit Bani Hamida House, a showroom and shop for the beautiful handwoven rugs made by local Bedouin women from the Bani Hamida tribe.

Ins & outs The turning right for Mukawir (signposted both for 'Mukawir' and 'Memorial of John the Baptist') is 14 km south of Madaba, in the small village of Lib. Fork right immediately after taking the turning and follow the winding road through desolate landscape with occasional spectacular views down into Wadi Zarqa Ma'in and the Dead Sea. Around 19 km after turning off the King's Highway, just before the village of Mukawir, there is a right turn signposted for 'Mukawir Rest Area', situated 300 m further on (see under Eating below). This road joins up with the new road leading down to Hammamat Ma'in, which was nearing completion at the time of writing, but not as yet open. Continuing past this turning, follow the road through the modern village of Mukawir, to arrive at **Bani Hamida House**, less than 1 km further on, on the right (see next page). Just over 1 km past Bani Hamida House, the road ends in a parking area a short walk from the ruins of Machaerus, which are perched on top of a distinctive conical-shaped hill visible from some distance away.

The minibuses which run from Madaba come only as far as Mukawir village. It's an easy walk from there to the ruins, or you can negotiate with the driver to take you the rest of the way for a small fee. Check what time the last minibus back to Madaba leaves; they are much less frequent in the afternoon, and stop operating altogether well before nightfall.

History The earliest defensive stronghold at Machaerus dates from the rule of the Hasmonean (Jewish) king Alexander Jannaeus (103-76 BC), when it formed an important frontier post on the border with the Nabatean kingdom to the

King's Highway

south. Following the arrival of the Romans, it was destroyed in 67 BC by Pompey but later rebuilt by Herod the Great (37-4 BC). It was under Herod the Great's son, Herod Antipas (4 BC-39 AD) that John the Baptist's execution took place. Herod Antipas had married Herodias, the former wife of his brother Philip. Both Herodias' divorce and her subsequent remarriage were forbidden in Jewish law, and John the Baptist had denounced her. Herodias, keen to silence John, achieved her wishes through Salome, her beautiful daughter from her first marriage:

"*Now Herod had arrested John and bound him and put him in prison because of Herodias, his brother Philip's wife, for John had been saying to him, `It is not lawful for you to have her.' Herod wanted to kill John, but he was afraid of the people, because they considered him a prophet. On Herod's birthday the daughter of Herodias danced for them and pleased Herod so much that he promised with an oath to give her whatever she asked. Prompted by her mother, she said, `Give me here on a platter the head of John the Baptist.' The king was distressed, but because of his oaths and his dinner guests, he ordered that her request be granted and had John beheaded in the prison. His head was brought in on a platter and given to the girl, who carried it to her mother.*" (Matthew 14: 3-11)

Following the First Jewish Revolt of 66 AD and the subsequent capture of Jerusalem by the Romans in 70 AD, many Jews fled the Holy City and took refuge at Machaerus. Along with the more famous stronghold of Masada in Israel, it became a centre of Jewish resistance, holding out until 72 AD when it was finally destroyed by the Roman governor Bassus.

It is a 15-20 minute walk from the road-head/car park, down and then up to the summit along a good path. Nearing the top, there is a restored section of the original defensive walls and glacis. The views from the summit are really stunning (you can see Jerusalem on a clear day, if you know where to look, while at night its lights are clearly visible). Of the original buildings there is very little to see; just the outlines of their foundations and a few low walls. In the centre of the hilltop, however, work is in progress to restore the main palace complex. The newly-paved courtyard and brand new columns surrounding it, all smooth and immaculate, look rather incongruous, and what the site will be like when finished is questionable. In the centre of the courtyard is a rectangular opening to an enormous water cistern cut into the bedrock.

Around the site

The surrounding hills are strikingly patterned with the swirling shapes of folded rock formations and dotted with numerous caves, many of which can easily be visited. As you descend the stairway from the car park to the low saddle which joins with the conical hill of Mukawir, at the bottom on your right is a doorway of cut stone blocks leading into a cave with a side room. Further on, if you branch off to the right on a rough path (instead of following the main track around to the left), you come to a series of caves cut into the side of Mukawir hill itself. Some of these have been carefully hewn out into square rooms, others have doorways of cut stone blocks and traces of mud plaster on the walls, and in one case, a square supporting pillar in the centre. According to local legend, it was in one of these caves that John the Baptist was beheaded.

At the time of writing, the ***Mukawir Rest Area*** was still under construction; according to the billboard outside, it will feature a restaurant and coffee shop, as well as horse riding and camping facilities. In the village of Mukawir, right by the road just 200 m or so before you reach Bani Hamida House, there is a restored Ottoman complex which is due to open soon as a ***Café*** and shop. Also located here are the partially restored remains of a Byzantine Church. Next to it is a deep water cistern, and various other remains awaiting excavation.

Eating

King's Highway

Dhiban

Returning to the King's Highway and continuing south, the road passes through the village of **Mulagh** and then descends into the green and wooded **Wadi Wala,** climbing up the other side to arrive shortly after in the town of **Dhiban**, 20 km from the Mukawir turning and 34 km from Madaba. Although today a small, dusty place without any real attractions, Dhiban was the site of the ancient city of Dibon, the capital of King Mesha of Moab, who ruled in the 9th century BC. It was here that the famous Mesha Stela was discovered (see pag 223). Excavations on the *tell* at Dhiban have revealed evidence of more or less continuous settlement from the Early Bronze Age through to the Byzantine period, with a peak of settlement activity during the Iron Age II period (late 10th-9th century BC). However there is almost nothing to see on the *tell* other than a small section of the ancient city wall.

Umm ar-Rasas

A detour east from Dhiban takes you to the sprawling Roman/Byzantine ruins at Umm ar-Rasas. The highlight of this site are the spectacular and beautifully preserved mosaics of the churches of St Stephen and Bishop Sergius, easily comparable with anything on display at Madaba or Mount Nebo and well worth the extra effort involved in coming out here. ■ *There are no fixed opening times or entrance fee to the site. The hangar containing the mosaics of the churches of St Stephen and Bishop Sergius is kept locked. The caretaker is on hand during daylight hours to open it up.*

Ins & outs **Getting there by private vehicle** Heading south along the King's Highway, take the left turn immediately after the roundabout in the centre of Dhiban (clearly signposted for Umm ar-Rasas). After 9 km you pass a right turn signposted to Al Lahun (or Lehun, 4 km, see below), the road taking you through rolling countryside cultivated with wheat. Soon after, bear left to continue along the 'main' road, and after a further 2 km take the left turn signposted for Umm ar-Rasas and the Desert Highway. Around 4 km further on the low, sprawling ruins are clearly visible beyond a left turn signposted, amongst others, for 'Nitel' (going straight on here takes you to the Desert Highway). Take this left turning and 500 m further on, immediately after a post office on the right, turn right onto a rough track, to arrive after another 500 m at the green metal hangar housing the mosaics of the churches of St Stephen and Bishop Sergius. (An alternative route from Madaba is to take the road southwest to Nitil, and then south from there to Umm ar-Rasas.)

Getting there by public transport There are only a couple of minibuses daily which run from Madaba via Nitil to Umm ar-Rasas; check what time the last one leaves for the return journey. Alternatively, there are more regular minibuses to Dhiban, from where you will have to negotiate for a private taxi to take you out to Umm ar-Rasas and back.

Umm Ar Rasas

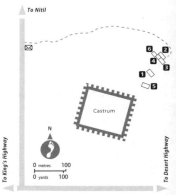

1 Church
2 Church of Bishop Sergius
3 Church of St Stephen
4 Church of the Courtyard
5 Church of the Lions
6 Church of the Niche

The Mesha Stela

The Mesha Stela was discovered at Dhiban in 1968 by a Prussian missionary, FA Klein. The solid block of basalt measures 115 cm in height and is 70 cm wide and 35 cm thick. The lengthy inscription on it (34 lines) records the exploits of the Moabite King Mesha, particularly in his wars against the Israelites. Mesha ruled from around 853-830 BC and the inscription is believed to date from the end of his reign. It is written in an early form of Hebrew derived from the Phoenician script which developed in centres such as Tyre, Sidon and Byblos, though the language itself is essentially Moabite. To biblical scholars and historians the great significance of the stela was that it provided for the first time an alternative literary source which described events previously related only in the Bible. A total of seventeen site names appear on the Stela, twelve of which correspond to places mentioned in the Old Testament.

According to some accounts of the discovery, Klein promised to pay the villagers the princely sum of £60 for the stone and headed back to Jerusalem to fetch the money. In the meantime the villagers argued as to how the money should be divided amongst them until one of them, jealous of the majority view, lit a fire on the stone and then poured cold water on it, causing it to shatter. Another version suggests that after Klein had expressed such interest in the stone, the villagers became convinced that it contained evil spirits and lit a fire around it to drive them out. Whatever the truth of the matter, Klein had fortunately made a imprint of the stone, allowing the fragments, which were sent back to France, to be pieced back together. The original is now on display in the Louvre; those that you see in various museums around Jordan are copies.

History

Umm ar-Rasas has been identified with the site of *Kastron Mefaa*, an important Roman/Byzantine settlement. According to Eusebius, a unit of the Roman army was stationed here, and he goes on to identify the site with the Old Testament city of Mephaath. The identification with biblical Mephaath remains to be confirmed, although it seems likely and excavations have revealed evidence of settlement during the Iron Age II (7th-6th century BC). The site appears to have been abandoned until the Roman period, when it developed as a military outpost and went on to flourish during the Byzantine era. At first the identification of Umm ar-Rasas with Kastron Mefaa had been rejected by scholars in favour of Khirbet Nefa, 10 km to the south of Amman and it was only recently that attention was really focused on the site. To date a total of at least 15 churches have been discovered (four within the walled *castrum*, and the remainder dotted around the open area of ruins to the north), though only a few of these have been properly excavated.

Around the site

Inside the large green corrugated-iron hangar a raised walkway around the sides allows you to view the beautiful mosaic floors of the **Church of St Stephen**. The main mosaic covering the central nave of the single-apsed church depicts men, animals and birds in various hunting and rural scenes, although it suffered damage at the hands of iconoclasts. The borders are the most interesting. The inner border depicts a river with boats and people fishing, along with 10 cities of the Nile Delta: Alexandria, Kasin, Thenesos, Tamiathis, Panau, Pilousin, Antinau, Haraklion, Kynopolis and Pseudostomon.

Along the north side, between the spaces where the columns separating the nave from the side-aisles would have stood, eight Palestinian cities are depicted: Jerusalem, Neapolis (Shechem), Sebastis, Caesarea, Diospolis (Lydda), Eleutheropolis (Beth Guvrin), Ascalon and Gaza. Along the south side seven Transjordian cities are shown: Kastron Mefaa, Philadelphia

King's Highway

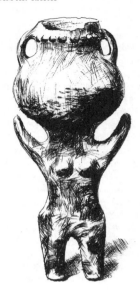

Female figurine with amphora on her head, Early Bronze Age (3200-2900 BC), Bab adh-Dhraa

(Amman), Madaba, Esbounta (Heshbon/Tell Hisban), Belemounta (Ma'in), Aeropolis (Rabba) and Charach Mouba (Kerak).

The great detail with which all these cities are depicted, amounting to a plan in the case of Kastron Mefaa, represents a source of information of equal importance to scholars and historians as that of the more famous Madaba Map. The two dedicatory inscriptions confirm the identification of Umm ar-Rasas with Kastron Mefaa and date the church to the 8th century. One indicates that the mosaic around the presbytery was completed in 756 by two mosaicists from Heshbon, Staurachios and Euremios, while the other indicates that the full mosaic decoration was not completed until 785.

Also preserved within the hangar is part of the mosaic floor of the adjacent **Church of Bishop Sergius**. Only a rectangular panel of mosaic in front of the altar has survived. In the centre of the panel is a circular medallion containing a dedicatory inscription dating the church to 586, flanked on either side by rams and pomegranate trees. The mosaics of the central nave were largely destroyed by iconoclasts, although a particularly striking personification of one of the seasons has survived, having been hidden under the foundations of a pulpit which was added at a later date.

Outside the protective hangar, on its northwest side, is a courtyard which was later converted into a church (the so-called **Church of the Courtyard**), and adjoining it, another church, dubbed the **Church of the Niche**. Together, these four churches formed an integrated liturgical complex surrounded by a wall.

Heading southwest from the hangar, towards the ruins of the castrum, you come to the remains of another **church** (as yet unnamed). Its basic structure is well-preserved, with the the semi-circular apse clearly discernable, along with doorways, pilasters, niches and various architectural elements bearing carved decorations. Adjacent to it is a complex of rooms, some with mosaic floors (covered for protection against the elements), as well as stone basins and deep cisterns.

Further on, close to the northeast corner of the castrum, are the remains of a larger, triple-apsed church with impressive mosaic floors. At the time of writing these mosaics were hidden under a layer of sand and plastic to protect them from the elements, although a proper protective structure is planned for the future. An interesting feature of this church's mosaics is the depiction of two lions facing each other (hence its name; the **Church of the Lions**), along with a pair of gazelle, both these motifs being usually associated with synagogues. Like the Church of St Stephen, it also contains a plan of Kastron Mefaa, although this one is far more detailed, providing archaeologists with important clues as to the layout of the town during the 6th century (the mosaic was laid during the time of Bishop Sergius, possibly in 587).

From here it is a short walk to the large rectangular walled **castrum**, which represented the main Roman/Byzantine settlement. It is possible to scramble through the ruinous walls, though inside is a scene of almost total dereliction,

Wadi Mujib Nature Reserve

Established in 1987, the Wadi Mujib Nature Reserve is amongst the largest in Jordan, covering an area of some 212 sq km. The reserve begins around 18 km downstream from where the King's Highway crosses Wadi Mujib and extends westwards all the way down to where it finally emerges from a narrow canyon to drain into the Dead Sea. North-south it extends for more than 20 km to incorporate a number of other perennial wadis. Like Dana to the south, Wadi Mujib incorporates a huge diversity of habitats, with five different vegetation zones and more than 400 species of plants. Rare mammals found here include the Golden Jackal, Grey Wolf, Egyptian Mongoose, Blandford's Fox, Honey Badger, Striped Hyena, Caracal, Nubian Ibex and Rock Hyrax. Others such as the leopard and mountain gazelle once existed here but are now believed to be extinct. For a time the Nubian Ibex seemed condemned to the same fate due to excessive hunting, but a captive breeding programme here has so far proved highly successful, and some are now being released into the wild.

Wadi Mujib is also home to nearly 200 species of birds, including the extremely rare Griffin vulture, lesser kestrel and Egyptian vulture.

Visits to the reserve must be organised in advance through the RSCN in Amman (see page 115). There are two designated campsites. The first is located close to where the Wadi Mujib enters the reserve. The second is close to the captive breeding centre for Ibex (known as Radas Station), around 4 km to the southeast of where the Wadi Mujib emerges from its canyon to drain into the Dead Sea. The potential for hiking in the reserve is almost limitless, ranging from easy walks of 2-3 hours to extremely strenuous treks of 3-4 days or more involving some abseiling and swimming. A number of the hikes are described in some detail in the excellent book Jordan; Walks, Treks, Caves, Climbs & Canyons, by Di Taylor & Tony Howard (Cicerone Press, 1999). Note that summer temperatures in Wadi Mujib can be pretty unbearable, while in winter (and occasionally during spring and autumn) there is the possibility of flash floods.

with numerous arches and the occasional outline of a building rising out of the rubble of what must have been a densely-packed town.

Just over 1 km to the north of the hangar housing the churches of St Stephen and Bishop Sergius there is a 14 m high **tower** standing in a courtyard along with the remains of a small church. The tower, which had a small room on top and no stairs, is believed to have been a stylite tower in the tradition of St Simeon in Syria.

Lehun Excavations at the tiny village of Lehun, currently being carried out by a joint Belgian-Jordanian team, have revealed evidence of a substantial settlement dating from the Late Bronze Age and an Iron Age fortress with a large central courtyard. The excavations are just beyond the village school. There is not that much to see other than the foundations of buildings, and visitors should avoid walking over the area of excavations. Just beyond the excavations the land drops sharply down into the Wadi Mujib. The views from here are absolutely stunning.

Wadi Mujib and the road south to Kerak

Continuing south along the King's Highway from Dhiban, you soon come to the deep and spectacular **Wadi Mujib**, now a Nature Reserve administered by the RSCN (see above). This is the biblical *Arnon*, which formed the border between Moabite and Amorite territories at the time of the Exodus. In Deuteronomy Moses relates to his people the instructions God has given them: "*Set* *out now and cross the Arnon Gorge. See, I have given into your hands Sihon the Amorite, king of Heshbon, and his country."* (Deuteronomy 2: 24). The views from the top are truly awesome, this massive gorge measuring some 4 km across at the top and more than 400 m deep. Where the road begins its descent, there is a parking area and viewpoint, with basic toilet facilities and a souvenir shop hidden away below. The road hairpins its way down to the bottom, where lush green vegetation grows all the year round, in sharp contrast to the surrounding bare earth and rock. At the time of writing a large dam was under construction in the bed of the wadi, to the west of the road.

Climbing back up the other side, you pass the *Trajan* restaurant near the top on the right (T03-390295). This large, pleasantly furnished establishment has great views from its terrace, and also a Bedouin tent for outdoor dining in summer. A meal of standard Arabic food here costs around JD5 per head. The owner, a former guide for German tour groups, has plans to establish a hotel here in the future; until then, he is happy to allow people to **camp** on the grounds. A little further on, the road passes the tiny settlement of **Ariha** and continues through arid hills to arrive at the small town of **Qasr**, 35 km from Dhiban. To the left (east) of the road in the centre of the town, just before the traffic lights, are the ruins of a small Nabatean **temple**, known locally as the `Beit Karam'. The lower walls remain, along with four massive column bases. Inside it is largely in ruins, with various architectural fragments scattered around.

Five kilometres further south is the small town of **Rabba**, where the remains of a Roman **temple** can be seen next to the road on the right as you drive through. Rabba has been identified with the biblical city of *Rabbath Moab*, known to the Greeks as *Rabathmoba* and to the Romans as *Aeropolis*.

After a further 12 km you come to a T-junction, with the *Al Mujeb* hotel shortly before on the right (see Kerak Essentials). Turn right here for Kerak (left takes you east to the Desert Highway) and then after just over 3 km turn right again at the next T-junction (left for Mutah and the King's Highway south towards Petra). Just over 1 km further on, turn left for the centre of Kerak, (126 km from Amman; signposted clearly for Kerak Castle) or carry straight on for the Dead Sea (see Around Kerak, page 234).

Kerak

Phone code: 03   *Kerak's greatest attraction is the imposing Crusader castle which dominates this hilltop town, offering stunning views west across a deep wadi and out towards the Dead Sea. The town itself is of less interest, although it provides a convenient overnight stopping place en route between Amman and Petra. It also makes a good base from which to visit a couple of archaeological sites down by the Dead Sea.*

Ins and outs

Getting there &   Public transport links between Amman and Kerak (via the Desert Highway) are reason-
getting around   ably frequent, though to and from other regional centres they are more erratic. Public
transport north or south along the King's Highway is, as always, problematic (see under
Transport, below, and also page 108). Kerak itself is small enough to be easily explored
on foot. The commercial centre of the town is focused around the Statue of Salah
ud-Din on Madyan/Italian Hospital St. The castle is at the higher southwest corner of the
town, with a cluster of tourist-oriented restaurants and hotels close by.

The tourist information is currently on Al Mujama St, in an upstairs office between the **Tourist** *Sewar* and *Peace Ram* restaurants, near the castle, though it will probably move to the **information** restored Ottoman complex beside the castle when this opens. Open 0800-1500, closed Fri and Sat. T351150, F354263. Mahmoud Saoup, the assistant director of tourism here, is extremely helpful and when he is on duty here you should have no problems; at other times the staff are of limited help. Tourist police are on duty here and at the castle; they can be contacted on T352909.

History

Kerak's strategic position guarding the all-important King's Highway and obvious advantages as a natural defensive stronghold have attracted settlement here since ancient times. During the Iron Age it belonged to the kingdom of Moab, and was known then as Kir or Kir Haraseth, finding mention in the Bible in the context of the Moabite revolt against Israelite domination (2 Kings 3: 25). Even then, it must have been a formidable stronghold, being the only place to successfully hold out against the Israelites, though not before the Moabite king had offered his firstborn son "as a sacrifice on the city wall". Later, during the Roman period, it was known as Charach Mouba, while the Byzantine era saw it flourish as a bishopric, and it is depicted as a substantial walled city on the Madaba Map.

The present castle dates from the Crusader period, built in around 1140 by Payen de Bouteiller (see Showbak, below). It was one of the largest and best defended of the string of castles which stretched from the Gulf of Aqaba all the way to Turkey, protecting the Crusader states from attack from the east, and controlling movement along the King's Highway. Standing halfway between Jerusalem and Showbak, Kerak served as the capital of the Crusader administrative district of Oultre Jourdain (part of the Seigneury of Montreal). Perhaps the most colourful (or at least, most notorious) period of its history was under the governorship of Reynald of Châtillon (see next page), who made a habit of tossing prisoners over the walls. Despite its strong fortifications, it was eventually taken in 1188 by Salah ud-Din's forces, more than a year after the battle of Hattin. From 1264, having wrested control of it from the Ayyubids, the Mameluke Sultan Baibars, and later his successor Sultan Qalaun, carried out extensive modifications and rebuilding work on both the castle and the city's outer walls. Subsequently, however, it fell into relative obscurity.

The later Ottoman period was eventful for Kerak. Ibrahim Pasha based himself here for a time when he rose up against Ottoman rule, but went on to demolish parts of the city's outer walls when he withdrew in 1840 (these were further dismantled following subsequent periods of unrest, but you can still see a short section along with one of its towers from the bus station). In the 1880s, as a result of a rebellion against Ottoman rule and associated unrest between Muslims and Christians, most of the town's Christian population were forced to flee south to Ma'an and north to Madaba. Another rebellion in 1908 resulted in the Ottoman garrison taking refuge in the castle while they awaited reinforcements from Damascus. In 1920, during the period of British Mandate rule over Palestine, Kerak even became the capital of the short-lived Arab Government of Moab (see page 227).

More recent events also belie the town's present sleepy appearance. In August 1996, Kerak hit the headlines when the townspeople rioted against the government's decision to follow IMF advice and raise bread prices. Kerak now serves as a provincial market town and administrative centre, and is home to the regional court and government offices.

King's Highway

Reynald of Châtillon

The period of the Crusades threw up many disreputable characters, but few were as repugnant as Reynald of Châtillon, who ruled the district of Oultre Jourdain from the castle here at Kerak. Born into a family of low-level nobles with no title and no land, Reynald arrived in the Holy Land in the entourage of King Louis VIII's Second Crusade (1147-49). A fortuitous marriage to Princess Constance, cousin of the King of Jerusalem, Baldwin III, elevated Reynald into a position of considerable wealth and power; a position he continued to abuse until his dying day. Reynald accumulated further wealth by raiding Arab caravans, though eventually this was to lead to his first downfall. On one particular raid he attempted to carry off so much booty that his own party became too slow to escape, and Reynald himself was captured; he was to spend the next sixteen years in prison in Aleppo.

On his release in 1176 Reynald headed straight for Kerak, where he set about wooing Lady Etiennette, who was descended from Payen de Bouteiller, the former lord of Kerak. As charming and dashing as ever, Reynald succeeded in his quest and was quickly installed as the new lord. Kerak provided him with the ideal base from which to continue his caravan raiding activities, prompting Salah ud-Din (Saladin) to lay siege to the castle in 1183, though his chivalrous

nature was perhaps the reason for his failure on this occasion. According to legend, a wedding was in progress inside the castle at the time; on learning this, Salah ud-Din ordered his siege engines to direct their fire away from the tower where the wedding was taking place. Reynald by contrast had no such scruples and soon returned to his favourite pastime of raiding caravans, despite the fact that a truce signed between the Christian king Baldwin IV and Salah ud-Din outlawed such practices. In 1186 he even went so far as to raid a pilgrim caravan en route to Mecca. Ignoring the petitions of Baldwin IV, and subsequently King Guy, Reynald was unrepentant, refusing to pay the compensation that had been agreed. Eventually Salah ud-Din caught up with Reynald at the battle of Hattin in 1187 and personally saw to it that his head and body parted company very quickly.

Reynald's widow continued to hold out in Kerak castle for more than a year, with the inhabitants becoming so desperate that they apparently took to eating horses and dogs, and even bartering their women and children for food. Eventually, however, they had no choice but to surrender. In another display of chivalry Salah ud-Din is said to have been so impressed by their courage and tenacity that he spared them their lives.

Sights

Kerak Castle　The entrance to the castle is currently at the south end of Castle St, via a wooden footbridge over the dry moat. However, when the nearby Ottoman complex (see below) is completed, the entrance will be via another footbridge leading to the castle's original Crusader gate. Just inside the current entrance is the ticket office and beside it a detailed plan of the castle. There are now a number of excellent interpretation boards dotted around the castle, giving clear explanations of the various phases of construction and strategic thinking behind the design and architecture.

Heading up the ramp from the ticket office, you find yourself in the **Upper Court** of the castle. Along with the northern and eastern walls and towers, this dates mostly from the Crusader period, with some later additions. Running along the northern wall of the Upper Court are two **barrel-vaulted galleries**, one above the other. Towards the end of the lower gallery, steps on the left lead down to the **Crusader gate**. Further along there is a re-used stone block in the wall featuring a carved torso (now headless) of Nabatean origin. The complex of rooms in the northeast corner served as **barracks**, **kitchens** (complete with an olive press and a huge brick oven) and **storerooms**.

Working your way south from here, you come next to a complex of buildings which includes a **Crusader church** and **sacristy**. The towers, walls and glacis running along the east side of the castle here were undergoing extensive restoration at the time of writing. Further on is a **Mameluke Palace** and **mosque** complex (this can also be reached from the north via a long

Kerak Castle

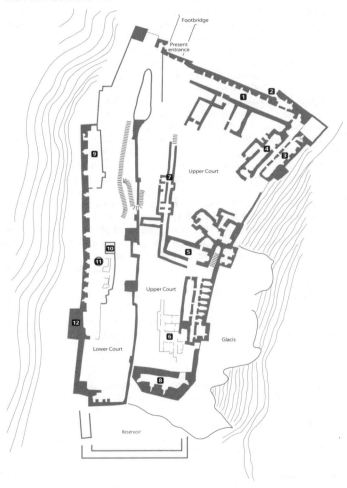

1 Barrel-vaulted galleries
2 Crusader gate
3 Barracks
4 Kitchens & storerooms
5 Crusader church & sacristy
6 Mameluke palace
   & mosque complex
7 Underground passage
8 Mameluke keep
9 Kerak archaeological museum
10 Entrance to underground
   vaulted galleries
11 Domed skylight
12 Monumental west gate
   & bastion

N

0 metres   30
0 yards   30

g **underground passage** which brings you to the entance court of the palace). The south end of the Upper Court is dominated by the **Mameluke keep**, its massive fortifications providing improved defences against attack from the south - the castle's most vunerable point.

The **Lower Court** can be reached either by doubling back the way you came and following the ramp/steps down from the ticket office, or via a set of stairs leading down through the castle's inner wall. This part of the castle dates almost entirely from the Mameluke period, with traces of Crusader foundations in places.

At the northern end of the Lower Court is a long, narrow vaulted hall which probably served as soldiers' barracks and now houses the **Kerak Archaeological Museum**. The museum has a small but interesting collection of artefacts from the Neolithic period through to the late Islamic era arranged around the walls (work your way round anti-clockwise for a roughly chronological tour, with a few anomalies). Along the centre of the hall are displays of various coins, as well a series of display boards, unfortunately somewhat jumbled up, but with some interesting photos and extracts from Gertrude Bell's accounts of her travels through Jordan in the early part of the 20th century.

Running beneath almost the entire length of the Lower Court are two long **underground vaulted galleries**, and between them a cross-shaped chamber with a domed skylight. The entrance to these (via a modern square structure) is kept locked, but the caretaker of the museum has the key and is usually happy to open it up. Both galleries have been extensively restored and are worth a look. The longer north gallery (running to some 80 m), is occasionally used by the *Kerak Resthouse* to host 'banquets' for tour groups. Originally these galleries probably served as barracks and store rooms, though the arrow slits in the western wall indicate that they also served a defensive purpose.

Back on ground level, towards the southern end of the Lower Court, is the **monumental west gate** and **bastion**. The full dimensions of this structure are difficult to appreciate from up the castle itself, but if you drive down to the Dead Sea from Kerak, you get an excellent view of the whole western wall and its fortifications.

■ *Open daily 0800-1800 in summer, 0800-1700 in winter, opens 1 hr later on Fri. Entry JD1 (including the museum). A torch/flashlight is essential if you want to explore the underground passageways and chambers of the Upper Court in any detail. Guides are available (JD4 for a 30 minute tour; ask at the ticket office).*

Ottoman complex Opposite the northern walls of the castle is a complex of buildings which served as the administrative centre of the Ottoman governor of the town, with a prison, mosque, offices and accommodation. At the time of writing, restoration work on this complex was nearing completion. When finished, it will serve as a sort of visitors' centre, featuring a museum, theatre hall, shops, restaurant and coffee shop, as well as a post office and currency exchange facilities. Entry to the castle will also be via this complex, across a footbridge and in through the original Crusader gate.

St George's Church In the lower, northern part of town is Greek Orthodox St George's Church (or 'St Jawerjius' as per the Jordan Tourism Board's transliteration of the Arabic). Inaugurated in 1849, the church stands on the site of a much older Christian settlement, possibly dating right back to the Byzantine era, as indicated by the discovery a complex of underground grain storage silos and water cisterns. Various architectural fragments in and around the church also clearly predate its present form. Entering the church, on the right is a massive stone **baptismal font** consisting of a huge cylindrical stone block hollowed out in the shape of a cross, deep enough to stand in and submerge oneself, with steps leading down into it in two of the arms. A series of beautifully painted **icons** decorate the *iconostasis* (the screen which separates the altar area from the main body of the church). The second one from the left is considered to be of special importance. It depicts Jesus flanked by Mary on his left and John the Baptist on his right, and an assembled host of more than 500 saints and holy figures. Below it is a smaller identical copy, apparently by the same artist. ■ *If the church is locked the caretaker is usually close at hand to open it up. Alternatively, if you want to arrange to be shown around, contact Father Michael, who lives opposite, in advance (T352176).*

The unassuming low, square building on Al Khadr St is in fact a 12th century **Al Khadr shrine** church dedicated to St George, though it was subsequently converted into a Muslim shrine dedicated to the mystical Islamic saint Al Khadr. Today it is kept locked and remains in a somewhat sorry state of delapidation pending the outcome of a court case between the Greek Orthodox church and the Islamic authorities to decide its ownership.

Essentials

Most visitors to Kerak only stay long enough to look around the castle, before continu- **Sleeping** ing on their journey. Given that the supply of hotels exceeds demand, this puts visitors in a fairly good bargaining position. Most include breakfast in the price of the room, but check first.

B *Al Mujeb*, King's Highway (coming from Wadi Mujib, situated on the right just before you reach the T-junction), T386090, F386091. Modern, recently opened hotel, the best in Kerak, though only really convenient if you have your own transport, being a good 5 km from the castle. Comfortable rooms with a/c, heater, TV/dish, fridge, phone and attached bath. Restaurant (buffet lunch JD6, popular with groups), bar and coffee shop. Well run. Recommended.

B-C *Kerak Resthouse*, Castle St, T351148, F353148. Reasonably comfortable rooms with fan, heater, TV, phone and attached bath. Somewhat in need of refurbishment, though the views from the rooms out over the deep wadi to the west make up for this. Great views also from the restaurant and bar (buffet meals for JD5-6 per head when there are groups around, or à la carte; small beer JD2.500). Rooms can be bargained down to **C** category when it is quiet.

C *Kerak Guest House*, Castle St, T355564. Newly-opened hotel owned by the manager of the *Kerak Resthouse*. Comfortable, pleasantly furnished rooms with TV, fridge, heater and attached bath. The best rooms are those at the rear with the views. Small restaurant (for breakfasts, snacks, tea and coffee).

D-E *Ram* (aka *Rum Cottage*), Mujama St, T351351, F354293. Choice of rooms with attached bath (JD15) or shared bath (JD10). Reasonably clean and comfortable, though a bit on the expensive side, rooms with shared facilities pretty basic for the price. Small restaurant. *Al Shuhba* supermarket below.

E *Towers-Castle*, Castle St, T352489, F354293. Under the same ownership as *Ram* hotel. Top floor rooms clean and pleasant with heater, phone and attached bath. Cheaper, more basic rooms on floor below with shared bath. Restaurant. Simple but friendly place.

F *New*, Maydan/Italian Hospital St, T351942. Cheapest hotel in Kerak at JD3 per bed (share shower/toilet), but rather basic and not exactly clean.

The best restaurants are in the **Kerak Resthouse** and *Al Mujeb* hotels (both around JD6 **Eating** per head upwards). With advance warning, the manager of the former can arrange 'banquets' in the vaulted underground gallery of the castle's lower court for large groups. When the Ottoman complex is completed it will also house an upmarket restaurant.

King's Highway

The *Sewar*, *Peace Ram* and *Al Fid'a* restaurants, all on Mujama St near the castle, serve overpriced Arabic and European dishes, shamelessly hassling passing tourists to come inside. Usually around JD5 per head, but check prices before ordering.

For budget eating, the *Al-Habiba* and *Akkash*, just around the corner on King Hussein St, are more down-to-earth, traditional Arabic diners offering fuul, hummus, falafels etc. Towards the bottom of Al Khadr St there is a place which does excellent shawarmas and falafels, and is often quite busy in the evenings. Around the corner on Madyan/Italian Hospital St is the *Delicious Meal*, which is also popular for shawarmas and falafels, as well as more substantial meals of roast chicken etc. Further along this street, near the statue of Salah ud-Din, there is a branch of *Mankal Chicken Tikka*, and next door the rather dingy *Turkey* restaurant. For great cheap snacks, the small bakery off Al Khadr St (see map) does great *mannoushi* – Arabic style mini-pizzas topped with meat (*lahmeh*), cheese (*jebneh*) or *zaatar* – and various savoury pastries.

Transport The main bus station, an open parking lot on Al Birka St, on the lower eastern slopes of the town (it's a steep walk from here up to the castle). **Buses** and **minibuses**, and the occasional **service taxi** (always a little more expensive), operate on a `depart when

Kerak

To Dead Sea
Arch over road
Italian
Chemist
Carpet Shop
Chemist
Maydan/Italian Hospital St
Chemist
St George's
Statue of Salah al-Din
3
6
5
Tower
4
Minibuses to Ar-Rabba & Ariha
Buses to Mazraa
Buses to Safi
King Hussein St/Salah ad-Din St/Main St
Al Qala St/Castle St
Al-Khadr St
Women's College
Al Khadr Shrine
Main Bus & Minibus Station
Al-Birka St
1
5
8 7
2 1
3
Car Park
Pol
2
4
Ottoman Complex
Tower
Castle
Tower
Arch over road
To Amman
To Petra

N
0 metres   200
0 yards   200

■ Sleeping	● Eating	
1 Kerak Guest House	1 Akkash	6 Mankal Chicken
2 Kerak Resthouse	2 Al Fid'a	Tikka & Turkey
3 New	3 Al-Habiba	7 Peace Ram
4 Ram	4 Bakery (Arabic style pizzas)	8 Sewar
5 Towers-Castle	5 Delicious Meal	

King's Highway

The Destruction of Sodom and Gomorrah

"Abram lived in the land of Canaan, while Lot lived among the cities of the plain and pitched his tents near Sodom. Now the men of Sodom were wicked and were sinning greatly against the Lord…. Two angels arrived at Sodom in the evening, and Lot was sitting at the gateway of the city. When he saw them, he got up to meet them and bowed down with his face to the ground. `My Lords,'he said, `please turn aside to your servant's house. You can wash your feet and spend the night and then go on your way early in the morning.'…. Before they had gone to bed, all the men from every part of the city of Sodom – both young and old – surrounded the house. They called to Lot, `Where are the men who came to you tonight? Bring them out to us so that we can have sex with them.' Lot went outside to meet them and shut the door behind him and said, `No, my friends. Don't do this wicked thing. Look, I have two daughters who have never slept with a man. Let me bring them out to you, and you can do what you like with them. But don't do anything to these men, for they have come under the protection of my roof.' `Get out of our way' they replied. But the men inside reached out and pulled Lot back into the house and shut the door. Then they struck the men who were at the door of the house, young and old, with blindness so that they could not find the door…. With the coming of dawn, the angels urged Lot, saying, `Hurry! Take your wife and your two daughters who are here, or you will be swept away when the city is punished.' When he hesitated, the men grasped his hand and the hands of his wife and of his two daughters and led them safely out of the city, for the Lord was merciful to them. As soon as they had brought them out, one of them said, `Flee for you lives! Don't look back, and don't stop anywhere in the plain! Flee to the mountains or you will be swept away!' But Lot said to them, `No my lords, please! Your servant has found favour in your eyes, and you have shown great kindness to me in sparing my life. But I can't flee to the mountains; this disaster will overtake me and I'll die. Look, there is a small town near enough to run to, and it is very small, isn't it? Then my life will be spared.' He said to him, `Very well, I will grant this request too; I will not overrun this town you speak of. But flee there quickly, because I cannot do anything until you reach it….' By the time Lot reached Zoar, the sun had risen over the land. Then the Lord rained down burning sulphur on Sodom and Gomorrah – from the Lord out of the heavens. Thus he overthrew those cities and the entire plain, including all those living in the cities – and also the vegetation in the land. But Lot's wife looked back, and she became a pillar of salt. "(Genesis 13; 12-13, 19; 1-26)

full' basis. There are regular buses and minibuses to **Amman** (Wahadat bus station) via the Desert Highway (750-850 fils). If you wish to travel by public transport along the King's Highway to **Petra/Wadi Musa**, your best bet is to take a minibus south to **Tafila** (regular departures, 500 fils). From Tafila there are irregular minibuses (or you can try hitching) to Qadisiyyeh (for **Dana**) and Showbak, from where there are onward minibuses to Wadi Musa (but see warning under Tafila). An easier alternative, though it avoids the King's Highway altogether, is to go first to **Ma'an** on the Desert Highway (only 1 or 2 departures in the morning, JD1), from where there are regular services on to Wadi Musa. There are usually at least 2 departures each morning for **Aqaba** via the Dead Sea/Wadi Arabah Highway (JD1.750).

Minibuses heading north along the King's Highway to **Qasr**, **Rabba** and **Ariha** (500 fils) leave from a side-street off Al Khadr St (see map). From Ariha you have to hitch or negotiate a ride across the Wadi Mujib to Dhiban, from where you can pick up onward transport to Madaba. There is also one student bus daily which leaves from Mutah university (around 9 km to the south of Kerak) and goes directly to Madaba along the King's Highway; it leaves the university in the afternoon, around 1600, though this is not fixed and the bus is often full. Minibuses to **Safi**, down by the Dead Sea (for Lot's Cave/Deir Ain Abata, 500 fils), leave from a side street off King Hussein St (see map). A little further along the same side street there are minibuses for **Mazraa** (also on the Dead Sea, heading north, 500 fils).

There are a couple of **private taxi** companies based on Mujama St, near the castle, including **Al Riad** (or *Al Raed*), T352297, which are always happy to hire out their taxis for longer trips, though they try to charge tourists extortionate rates (eg Wadi Musa JD35-40, or Safi JD20 return, including 1 hr waiting time). Bargain hard.

Directory   **Banks** On the street immediately to the south of Madyan/Italian Hospital St there is a cluster of banks, including the *Housing Bank* and *Arab Bank*, both of which can change cash and TCs, and have cash machines outside (*Visa, +Plus*).

Communications Post The small, easily missed main post office is in the lower part of town, towards the northern end of Al Khadr St. More convenient is the branch inside the police station on Mujama St, near the castle. **Telephone** There are **Alo** and **JPP** cardphones dotted around the town. There are no internet cafés here as yet.

Medical services The **Italian Hospital** is at the western end of Madyan/Italian Hospital St. There are several pharmacies close by.

Around Kerak

Bab adh-Dhraa (Sodom and Gomorrah)

The road from Kerak down to the Dead Sea is a good one, and takes you past what is believed to be the site of Sodom and Gomorrah, the infamous "Cities of the Plain". There is very little to see as such, but the views of the Dead Sea and the scenery on the way down are dramatic, and you must pass this way to visit the impressive Lot's Cave Monastery to the south.

Ins & outs   **Getting there** Turning left onto the main road below Kerak to head west, after 17 km you come to a checkpost where you may be asked to show your passport. (Officially the passport checks along the Dead Sea Highway and on the routes leading down to the Dead Sea have been abolished, but, perhaps out of boredom or plain curiosity, the soldiers on duty here still sometimes ask to see your passport.) Around 2 km further on there is a marker to the left of the road indicating sea level. After a further 6 km, having passed through the tiny, almost non-existent settlement of 'El Thrae', you come to a large fenced-off enclosure to the right of the road, which is the site of the excavations here.

The minibuses from Kerak bound for Safi or Mazraa pass right outside the site. Those bound for Aqaba via the Dead Sea/Wadi Arabah road also pass this way, although they are likely to charge you the full Aqaba fare.

First identified in the early 1920s by a team led by Melvin Grove Kyle, a Doctor of Divinity at Jerusalem, excavations here have uncovered evidence of a huge Bronze Age settlement dominated by a fortress and surrounded by ramparts up to 4 m thick in places. Occupied from approximately 3200-1900 BC, the settlement subsequently appears to have been abruptly abandoned, with no evidence of further occupation until the Byzantine period, a sequence which certainly makes it a viable contender for the site of Sodom and Gomorrah. The Israelis of course have their own contender for the site, on their side of the Dead Sea, a little further south. However the conclusive identification in recent years of the Byzantine Lot's Cave Monastery gives added weight to the Jordanian site.

King's Highway

The gate in the site's perimeter fence is kept locked, but it's fairly easy to scramble underneath. Inside, the basic outline of the ramparts can be seen, but otherwise there are only mounds of earth and stone, the excavations long since having been all but erased by the elements. Across the road is the site of a large graveyard dating from the same period, which yielded thousands of flint artefacts and pottery shards. Today absolutely nothing can be seen of this.

Lot's Cave Monastery (Deir Ain Abata)

Perched on a steep hillside a little to the north of Safi is the site of Lot's Cave Monastery. Unlike Bab adh-Dhraa, this atmospheric site is well worth visiting in its own right, with the Byzantine church here boasting some impressive mosaics. Considerable effort has gone into making the site accessible to visitors. The views from here, out over the Dead Sea and the fertile agricultural lands around Safi, are also very impressive.

Ins & outs
Follow directions as for Bab adh-Dhraa, above. From Bab adh-Dhraa it is just over 1 km down to the T-junction with the Dead Sea/Wadi Arabah Highway. Turn left here to head south. After 18 km, having passed the huge 'Arab Potash Company' factory, there is a petrol station on the right. Just under 4 km further on, take the left turn signposted 'Cave and Monastery of the prophet Lut (Lot)', and then 1 km further on, branch off to the left along a rough track (signposted 'Lot's Cave'), to arrive after around 700 m at a parking area below the site.

The minibuses which run between Kerak and Safi pass the turning off the Dead Sea/Wadi Arabah Highway for Lot's Cave. From the turning, you will have to walk or hitch the remaining 2 km to the site. Leave plenty of time for the return trip, as minibuses back to Kerak can be rather thin on the ground in the afternoon.

Around the site
Although local people had long known of the existence of this site, it was only officially reported in 1986. The church is depicted on the Madaba Map, but until then the attempts of scholars to locate it had proved fruitless. Excavations began in 1988, sponsored by the British Museum, and are still continuing. More work needs to be done on the site to build up a detailed picture of its history, but the Byzantine basilica church (only uncovered in 1991) and monastery complex was clearly built around what pilgrims believed was the cave where Lot retreated after the destruction of Sodom and Gomorrah.

The parking area below Lot's Cave features a reconstruction of a 'pillar of salt' as recounted in the biblical story. From here a stairway climbs steeply up to the site, the focus of which is a triple-apsed **basilica church**. The outline of the church is clearly visible, with two rows of four re-erected columns separating the central nave from the side-aisles. The northern (left-hand) side-aisle, the nave and the raised chancel area in front of the altar are all decorated with mosaic floors (at the time of writing these were covered by a layer of sand to protect them from the elements, but a protective structure is planned for the church, after which the mosaics will be exposed to view).

The apse at the end of the northern side-aisle contains a doorway which leads through into a **cave**. Immediately before it, there is a four-line inscription in the mosaic floor which gives the names of church and monastery officials and the date 606 for the construction of the church. Another inscription in the mosaic floor of the central nave giving the date 691 is thought to refer to later building work carried out on the church. The discovery nearby of a stone inscribed with the name St Lot confirms the dedication of the church. The lintel of the doorway to the cave is carved with a cross and two rosettes. Inside, the cave is paved with a plain mosaic floor. Interestingly, excavations in the cave have revealed evidence of occupation and burials dating not just from Byzantine and later times, but right back through the Hellenistic, Middle Bronze Age, Early Bronze Age and Neolithic periods.

To the south (right) of the church is a large 7 m deep **water cistern** in two sections, with steps leading down into it and a feeder channel coming from the west. Originally the whole cistern was covered by a roof supported on cross arches. To the north (left) of the church is a **Byzantine tomb**, a **bread oven** and perhaps a later **Abbasid children's tomb**. Beyond these, the foundations of a series of rooms can be seen, thought to be part of the **monastery** complex.

Kerak to Petra

To rejoin the King's Highway heading south from Kerak, turn right onto the main road below the town and then continue straight on at the junction and traffic lights after just over 1 km (left takes you past the turning for the King's Highway heading north, and eventually to the Desert Highway). The road climbs steadily up onto the rolling plains of the Trans-Jordan Plateau, to arrive after a further 9 km at a crossroads in the cente of the town of **Mutah**.

Continuing straight on here, after 3 km you come to a junction in the town of **Mazar** with a large modern mosque complex beside it. Although only notable today for its large university, Mutah was the site of the first great battle between the Byzantines and Muslim Arabs in 629 AD. Three of the leaders of the Muslim army who were killed here, Zaid ibn Harith, Jaafar ibn Abu Talib and Abdullah ibn Ruaha, were buried at Mazar, and this modern mosque, complete with a small museum, is built around the site of their original mausoleum. Bear left at this junction (signposted for Petra), and after 5 km there is a left turn variously signposted for 'That Ras' and 'Zat Ras' (Dhat Ras).

Dhat Ras Taking this left turn, bear right at the roundabout soon after to reach the village of Dhat Ras, 5 km away. Entering the village a left turn takes you up to the Roman ruins here, clearly visible from the road. There is really not a lot to see here other than a small section of wall still standing, although judging from the precarious angle at which it leans, it won't be long before even this has gone. The wall is all that remains of the *cella* of a temple, originally Nabatean but modified during the Roman era. The foundations of the large compound or *temenos* in which it stood are still discernible, along with a few scant remains dotted around, but much of the site has all the appearance of having been recently bulldozed. During the Byzantine era Dhat Ras was known as *Kyriacoupolis* and boasted a large church.

Wadi Hasa Continuing south along the King's Highway from the turning for Dhat Ras, the road soon descends into the deep Wadi Hasa, not as spectacular as Wadi Mujib to the north, but impressive nevertheless. This was the biblical *Zared* which formed the border between Moab and Edom. As the road climbs out the southern side there is a right turn signposted to Hammamat Afra and Borbita (20 km from the Dhat Ras turning).

Hammamat Afra & Hammamat Borbita These hot sulphur springs are just two of more than 350 hot springs to be found dotted around this area. Taking the turning, the road follows the Wadi La'ban, a tributary of Wadi Hasa, winding its way through barren hills eroded and twisted into fantastic rock formations. After 7 km the road forks; right leads down to Hammamat Borbita a few hundred metres away, left continues on to Hammamat Afra, 5 km further on.

Hammamat Borbita has the nicer setting, the valley being wider at this point, with thick stands of reeds growing on the banks of the river (an ideal spot for camping; there are also cold springs nearby for drinking water). It is also free, although the hot spring here is very small, consisting of just one pool enclosed within a small concrete structure.

Hammamat Afra by contrast has now been developed into a resort along the lines of Hammamat Ma'in (though much smaller), with an entrance gate (and entrance fee) shortly before you arrive at the springs themselves. Down by the springs there is a small shop selling cold drinks and snacks, a pleasant cafeteria which is due to open shortly, and landscaped terraces on different levels where you can relax. There are plans to establish a camping area, and also possibly a hotel in the future. The wadi here narrows to a gorge with sheer rock cliffs on either side. There are several artificial pools alongside the stream. The pool furthest upstream is the hottest, with the water here being around 47°C. The next pool down is walled-in and reserved for women, and the one after that is inside a cave, creating a 'steam room' effect (when it is busy, use of the cave pool alternates between men and women at hourly intervals). If you work your way upstream from the hottest pool, there are several cooler natural pools in the stream.

■ *Open daily 0800-sunset. Entry JD3 (children JD1). Note that on Fri and Sat, and public holidays, it can get extremely busy here.*

On the south side of Wadi Hasa, on top of the steep-sided, conical mountain of **Khirbet Tannur** Jebel Tannur, is Khirbet Tannur, the site of an important Nabatean temple. The finds from here have provided archaeologists with an unique insight into the richness of Nabatean religious art. Today all these finds have been removed from the site, most of them to the Jordan Archaeological Museum in Amman, and there is little to see here beyond the basic foundations. It is also difficult to reach, involving a strenuous climb, although the views are as usual spectacular.

An inscription found here indicates that the main temple was built in 7 BC, during the reign of the Nabatean king Aretas IV, although it appears to have been built over an earlier temple, thought to date from the early 1st century BC. Most of the religious art found here dates from the early 2nd century AD, around the time that the Nabatean kingdom was incorporated into the Roman province of Arabia by Trajan in 106 AD. Soon after, the temple was destroyed by an earthquake and subsequently abandoned. The religious art included carvings of the complete pantheon of Nabatean deities, with the goddess Atargatis and her consort Hadad at their head. One particularly beautiful piece depicts a Tyche framed within a circle, with the signs of the zodiac around the edge.

Getting there   Take the rough track leading off to the west, 1 km north of the turning for Hammamat Borbita and Afra. This follows the north bank of Wadi La'ban. After around 1 km, branch off to the right and then soon after, depending on the state of the tracks you must continue on foot. It is a stiff 20-30 min climb up to the top.

Continuing south from the Hammamat Borbita and Afra turn-off, after 18 km **Tafila** you come to a junction. Bear right for Petra (left for the Desert Highway and Ma'an; signposted clearly). A further 5 km or so brings you to the centre of the town of Tafila. Once there was a Crusader castle here, forming part of the chain of castles along the King's Highway. Today, all that remains of it is a square tower to the west of the main road. Go straight across the traffic lights in the centre of town and bear right after a few hundred metres. There is not much to see, but just beyond the tower there are spectacular views down into the

The restored mosque in Dana village

precipitous wadi which flows into the Dead Sea here.

There are several simple eateries on the main road in the centre of town. A couple of kilometres to the south, on the outskirts of town, are two more upmarket restaurants, the *Adom Resthouse* and the *Petra*. There is no hotel here. Though there are regular minibuses between Kerak and Tafila, services south from Tafila are more erratic. Occasionally you get mini-buses running through to Showbak, though generally they go only as far as Qadisiyyeh. The locals meanwhile have cottoned-on to the potential for ripping-off stranded tourists, so beware of being taken for a different sort of ride here. A number of people who have attempted to hitch also report rather jittery reactions from local police and army.

Buseira Around 4 km south of Tafila, you pass a right turn signposted for Aqaba and Ghore Fida, this being a new road not marked on most maps which connects with the Wadi Arabah/Dead Sea Highway between Aqaba and Amman. A lit-tle under 14 km further on there is a sharp right turn signposted to the village of **Buseira** (or Busayra), 3 km away.

Excavations carried out here in the '30s and '70s revealed evidence of an extensive Edomite settlement dating from the 8th-7th century BC and the site is generally identified with the biblical city of *Bozrah* (not to be confused with the Roman city of Bosra in southern Syria), which is thought to have been the capital of Edom. The Edomite settlement is situated on a promontory at the westernmost edge of the village; keep straight along the road through the vil-lage, and the site is just past the modern school buildings at the end of this road. There is not much for the untrained eye to see, other than the excavated outlines of various buildings and traces of the settlement's defensive walls and one of its gates. However, on a clear day the views westwards are dramatic and spectacular. On either side of the road shortly before you reach the site are the ruins of Ottoman-period buildings.

Dana Nature Reserve

In terms of natural beauty, the Dana Nature Reserve, just to the south of Buseira, offers one of the most breathtaking experiences in Jordan and is certainly not to be missed. There is a choice of mid-range or budget accommodation here and an infi-nite range of hiking options from short walks to full-scale treks. Or you can simply to take in the awesome views and wander round the picturesque Dana village.

Ins and outs

Getting there There are two turnings off the King's Highway giving access to the Dana Nature Reserve. The 1st (to the north) takes you down to the 'Tower Centre' viewpoint and *Rummana Campsite*, while the 2nd (to the south) takes you down to the Dana Field Centre/*Dana Guest House* and Dana village. A 3rd entry point is at Wadi Feinan (where there is another *campsite*), reached via a turning off the Wadi Arabah/Dead Sea High-way, and accessible only by 4WD.

Dana; a Model for Small-Scale Sustainable Development?

The Dana Nature Reserve certainly seems to have gone a long way towards achieving its aim of integrating conservation and development. The $3.3 million project was funded by the Jordanian government, RSCN, World Bank and UNDP. The reserve is now run entirely by local staff, and has created more than 50 full and part-time jobs. The income generating activities associated with the reserve (handicrafts, local produce, guiding etc) have had a dramatic effect on the local economy, encouraging many people to come and settle here once again. With visitor numbers increasing steadily, the revenues from the entry fee alone now cover most of the reserve's running costs.

It is not all sweetness and light in Dana however; inevitably there are conflicts of interest. The most pressing problem is overgrazing. When it was first set up, around 9,000 sheep, goats and camels were recorded within the reserve's area. For the 550 or so semi-nomadic pastoralists of the Azazmeh tribe who have traditionally grazed their flocks on Wadi Dana's lower elevations, this represents their sole livelihood and getting them to change their habits is going to be difficult. More worrying perhaps is the potential threat from mining interests; already the Jordanian Natural Resources Agency had made attempts to sample the copper deposits around Wadi Feinan, and were these ever to be mined on a large scale, the environmental impact would be disastrous.

Continuing south along the King's Highway from the turning for Buseira, the road climbs up onto a high plateau. After nearly 4 km you come to a small right turn signposted to 'Rummen Camp'. This turning leads down to the 'Tower Centre' viewpoint overlooking Wadi Dana, and below it the *Rummana Campsite*. For a short while the track joins the wide access track linking the nearby Rashadiya Cement Factory to its large quarry works on the edge of the reserve. After 3 km take the signposted left turn (straight on takes you back to Buseira), to arrive at the Tower Centre, just over 2 km further on.

If you continue straight past the 'Rummen Camp' turning off the King's Highway, a little further on there is a left turn for the towering hulk of the Rashadiya Cement Factory, followed soon after (4 km from the first turn-off) by a right turn signposted to Dana Village, 3 km away. The Dana Field Centre and *Dana Guesthouse* are just outside the village, while in the village itself there are two budget hotels.

There are erratic minibuses which shuttle between Tafila and Qadisiyyeh (a small village 1 km or so south of the Dana Village turning). Either ask to be dropped off at the Dana Village turning and walk down from there, or else it is usually possible to negotiate a ride from Qadisiyyeh. Coming from the south, you will either have to charter a private taxi from Wadi Musa or Showbak, or else try hitching. There is a shuttle bus which operates between the visitors' centre adjacent to Dana village and the Rummana campsite (included in the entrance/camping fee).

Entry to the reserve itself costs JD5 per person, although you can visit the Dana Field Centre, Dana village and Tower centre for free. If you are planning to stay overnight at the *Dana Guest House* or at either of the campsites, or if you wish to undertake any of the longer hiking trails with a guide, the RSCN strongly recommends that you book in advance. All arrangements can be made directly through Dana Field Centre, T368497, F368499, dhana@rscn.org.jo, www.rscn.org.jo **Reserve information**

The Wadi Dana drops from 1,500 m above sea level to 100 m below sea level as it plunges from the eastern plateau of the Great Rift Valley down to the lowlands of the Wadi Arabah. As such, it contains a remarkable variety of habitats ranging from Mediterranean semi-arid forests through to sub-tropical wadis **Background**

King's Highway

and sand dune desert. With this comes an equally remarkable variety of flora and fauna, bringing together in one area species from Europe, Asia and Arabia. There are a total of nearly 700 species of plants, more than 100 of which are rare, and 8 of them endemic (not found anywhere else in the world). The last stand of cypress trees in Jordan can also be found here. Amongst the 565 species of animals are the Nubian ibex, sand cat, Blandford's fox, honey badger, Syrian wolf, Asiatic Jackal, Rock Hyrax and desert gazelle. With more than 200 species of birds, Dana is also one of the most important non-wetland sites for birdlife in the Middle East; here you can see the Spotted and Imperial Eagles, Lesser Kestrel, Tristam's Serin and Cyprus Warbler, to name just a few.

First established in 1993 and encompassing an area of 320 sq km, the Dana Nature Reserve has become something of a model for integrated conservation and development projects. A strong emphasis has been placed on making the nature reserve of tangible economic benefit to local people, on the basis that this is the only way of giving conservation efforts any long-term prospects of success. Developing the "eco-tourism" potential of the reserve has been of primary importance in this respect and a centre-piece of this strategy has been the restoration of **Dana village**. Dating back originally to the 15th century, many of the buildings in the village had been abandoned in recent decades. These have been restored and local Bedouin families have been encouraged to settle here once again. Fruit from previously neglected orchards is now harvested, dried and sold commercially, and likewise for locally-occurring medicinal herbs. Small jewellery workshops have also been established, producing beautifully delicate silverware.

The reserve covers what was the heartland of the ancient Edomite kingdom and contains hundreds of sites of archaeological interest, including **Wadi Feinan** (down in the lower Wadi Arabah part of the reserve), where evidence of occupation dates back as far as the 7th millennium BC. The ancient copper mines in the area were of vital economic importance and supported a sizeable settlement. According to Eusebius, Christians were sent here to work in the copper mines as a punishment for their beliefs, and the remains of numerous churches and other public buildings dating from the late Roman period have been recorded. Indeed, Wadi Feinan is considered by archaeologists to be the most important site in southern Jordan after Petra (though, it has to be said, only from a specialist's point of view at present). A British team is currently carrying out work here and a camp with accommodation facilities has been established, which is shared between archaeologists and visitors to the reserve.

Around the reserve The **Dana field centre** adjacent to Dana village is a good place to start, and offers some of the best views out over Wadi Dana. The staff can provide you with further information about the reserve, and help you plan and organize hiking trips into the reserve. There is a nature shop here selling a range of local produce and handicrafts, and you can also visit a number of craft workshops. A short walk away, the small, picturesque **Dana village** is a lovely place to wander around. The mosque here and many of the old houses have now been fully restored. There are also more craft workshops located here which can be visited. A couple of kilometres to the northwest, the **Tower centre** provides another spectacular viewpoint out over the reserve, and also features a small shop and toilet facilities. If you visit **Wadi Feinan** when there are archaeologists working there, they may be able to show you around the excavations in the area.

Hiking in the reserve Though you can get a taste of the unique beauty of Dana from the viewpoints, to really appreciate the richness of this natural environment you have head into the reserve itself. Various clearly signposted short hiking trails have been established (1-2 hours), most of which start from the *Rummana campsite*. The short marked trails can be undertaken without a guide. Longer expeditions lasting anywhere from 1-3 days (or more) can also be arranged, for which an official guide in the form of a trained park ranger is compulsory. To hire a guide costs JD6 for up to 2 hours, JD10 for up to 3 hours, or JD30 for a full day (maximum 10 people per group). One of the more spectacular short hikes runs from Dana village around the upper reaches of Wadi Dana to the Rummana campsite. As well as being relatively flat and therefore not too demanding, if you do this walk you can take the shuttle bus back to Dana village rather than retracing your steps. A guide is required for this walk, which takes around 2½-3 hours. More demanding is the hike from Dana village or Rummana campsite down to Feinan camp, which takes at least 5 hours but takes you through a wide range of the reserve's different habitats.

If you can afford it, the RSCN-run *Dana Guest House* is well worth splashing out on. If not, there are two locally-run budget hotels in Dana village itself. **Sleeping & eating**

    B *Dana Guest House*, T368497, F368499. Elegantly designed Ottoman-style building. Simple but tastefully furnished and immaculately clean rooms with shared toilets/showers and balconies opening onto what Queen Noor described as "ten star" views (hyperbole fully justified). Also cheaper (**C** category) rooms without balcony. Breakfast is included in room price. Lunches and dinners (JD6 per head) can also be provided, though they should be booked in advance. Recommended.

    F *Dana*, situated near the mosque in Dana village. Basic but clean rooms with shared shower/toilet for JD5 per person. Also serves simple meals. Good, friendly budget option. **F** *Dana Tower*, situated further down in village. Similar deal to *Dana* hotel. Upper floor rooms (in the 'tower') with great views.

    Camping Note that camping is only allowed in the 2 designated campsites. The prices are expensive, but the money does at least go back into the project and into the pockets of local people. The *Rummana Campsite* is open from Mar to Oct only (exact dates depend on the weather each season, so check). The *Feinan Campsite* is open all year round. At both campsites you must use the tents provided. Hire of tents (each sleeping up to 4 people) costs JD5, on top of which there is an additional charge of JD12 per person (JD6 for Jordanians or those resident in Jordan). This includes the JD5 entrance fee to the reserve. Mattresses, blankets and pillows are provided (also included in the price). There are simple toilet and shower facilities. If there are 6 people or more, meals can be provided (breakfast/lunch box JD3; lunch/dinner JD6).

Dana to Petra

As it passes Dana, the King's Highway is running along the top of the Great Rift Valley and from here on down to Wadi Musa and Petra the landscape is particularly austere and dramatic. About 1 km beyond the turning for Dana village, you pass through the small village of **Qadisiyyeh**. After a further 16 km you arrive at a T-junction; turn right here (clearly signposted for Showbak and Petra; left takes you to Ma'an and the Desert Highway). Around 4 km further on there is a right turn signposted for **Showbak castle**, followed by a second right turn signposted for the castle (2½ km further on), and then the village of **Showbak** itself on the main road just over 1 km past the second turning. Continuing south from Showbak village, after 23 km bear right at a fork for Wadi Musa and Petra (signposted), to arrive after a further 2 km at a junction by Musa Spring, marking the start of Wadi Musa. Go straight on to descend to Wadi Musa village and Petra.

King's Highway

Showbak castle

Showbak castle is strikingly situated on a conical hilltop. Though smaller and more delapidated than Kerak, the ruins are nevertheless fascinating to explore. Extensive restoration work was in progress at the time of writing. For most of the year the surrounding hills are barren and austere, but in spring they are clothed in grass and wild flowers.

Ins & outs   **Getting there**   From either turning off the King's Highway it is around 3 km to the castle of Showbak. Unless you have your own transport, probably the best option is to hitch or catch a bus out here as an excursion from Petra. The minibuses which run from Wadi Musa to Ma'an pass through Showbak village, from where, if you do a little cross-country walking, you can cut the distance down to around 2 km to the castle. Alternatively, it is usually possible to negotiate a ride from the village.

Site information   At the time of writing there was no entrance fee to the castle. Outside there are a few souvenir stalls (also offering tea) and the caretaker is usually on hand to show you around. He expects a tip, but speaks reasonable English and, given the sometimes confusing jumble of ruins inside the castle, a guided tour will certainly make it easier to identify the various surviving features. In Showbak village itself, on the main road, is the *Family Restaurant,* which serves standard Arabic fare in clean surroundings for around JD4-6 per head.

History   Like Kerak, Showbak formed part of the chain of Crusader castles along the King's Highway. Known as *Mont Realis* (or *Montreal*) to the Crusaders, it was originally built by Baldwin I in 1115 AD when he founded the Seigneury of Montreal. Baldwin appointed Peyen de Bouteiller as lord of this Seigneury, and Payen resided here until moving to Kerak around 1140 and building the larger castle there. In 1187 the castle was besieged by Salah ud-Din (Saladin) after the battle of Hattin, but it only fell to him two years later in 1189. Under subsequent Ayyubid control repairs were made to the fortifications. During the 13th and 14th centuries the Mamelukes used Showbak as their main base in southern Jordan, carrying out further repairs and significant alterations. In 1840 it was used for a time as a barracks for Ibrahim Pasha's troops.

Around the site   The Arabic inscription on the large rectangular tower to the right of the entrance gate dates from the Mameluke-period modifications; during the Ottoman period, this tower served as a prison. Going through the entrance gate, turn left to follow the path running between the inner and outer walls of the castle. On your left, steps lead down into a chamber with two holes in the floor giving access to a large water cistern below. This chamber leads in turn to a small **church** with a vaulted ceiling. At the eastern end is the apse, flanked by two niches, while at the opposite end is a broad flight of steps marking the original entrance. The room to the west of this is lined with a series of square basins which are thought to have served as wine presses. A passageway runs under the stairs before descending steeply to a deep chamber (a torch/flashlight is essential if you wish to explore this).

Returning to the path, note the water channels which fed the wine presses. You come next to a cross-vaulted **entrance hall** which gives access to the inner castle. Once through it, on your left is the partially restored **south tower**, with a series of rooms each containing arrow slits built into arched recesses. Follow the path from the entrance hall, around past the entrance to a large hall on the right, to arrive at a long flight of slippery stone-cut stairs leading down to the castle's **main water cistern**. No-one seems to count the same number of stairs (anywhere between 350 and 375) but it is certainly a long way down. A good torch and sure footing are required if you want to go to the bottom. This water cistern was perhaps Showbak's most important feature, providing it with an almost limitless water supply, and the reason behind its ability to hold out for so long against Salah ud-Din following the battle of Hattin.

Doubling back from here and going through the entrance to the large hall, you pass the remains of a large olive press before joining a street lined on either side by what are thought to have been shops. Going through any of the entrances to the left, you can get a good view of the walls and bastions of the castle on this side. At the end of the street is a building on the left, believed to have been a **madrassa** (religious school) with three arched entrances. Above the third entrance arch is a large Arabic inscription attributing the building to Hosam ud-Din (Salah ud-Din's brother).

If you go through the remains of the madrassa (only two barrel-vaulted rooms survive) and turn right, you come to a long rectangular bastion containing barracks and stables. A long passageway leads from here past rooms with arrow slits to the castle's **north tower**, consisting of a single room with four arched recesses containing arrow slits (seen from the outside, as you approach the castle, this tower is the rounded one with a long band of Arabic inscription commemorating the Ayyubid rebuilding work carried out on it).

From here, loop round to follow the eastern wall of the castle, then climb up to what is generally referred to as the **palace complex**. This dates originally from the Crusader period, though it was largely rebuilt by the Ayyubids. In recent years it has been the focus of extensive restoration work. The main reception hall of the complex is in three sections, separated by two sets of tall arches, each flanked by smaller ones on either side. At the far end there is a false wall with three arches in it, supposedly used for hangings. Next door are the heavily ruined remains of a **baths complex**.

Working your way back towards the entrance gate by which you first entered the castle, you come next to the **main church** (undergoing extensive restoration at the time of writing). Dating (obviously) from the Crusader period, this was converted into a mosque by Salah ud-Din. Below the church is a small vaulted chamber which acts as a kind of ad-hoc **museum** (this may be moved to one of the restored towers in the future). Inside there is an interesting collection of artefacts; a stone block bearing an Arabic inscription, a carved lintel from the church above decorated with geometric and floral designs, olive presses, a hand corn mill, a pestle and mortar, and stone cannonballs of various different sizes (for catapult siege engines).

Petra

Petra

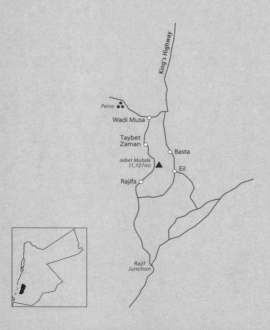

Petra is undoubtedly Jordan's most famous attraction, and justifiably so, being amongst the most impressive historical sites in the whole of the Middle East. The huge temple façades, carved into the sandstone rock, are truly awe-inspiring, and all the more so for their impregnable location, surrounded by imposing rock mountains and approached through a deep narrow cleft, the famous Siq. If at all possible, you should really devote at least one full day (preferably two or three) to exploring this fascinating site.

The Petra that Burckhardt finally managed to penetrate in 1812 is very different to that which greets today's visitor. A glut of ill-planned and generally unappealing hotels now line the road leading down to the entrance from Musa Spring, with more appearing along the road to Taybet. The Bedouins who used to live amongst the ruins now only come in from the new village of Bdoul to set up souvenir stalls for the tourists, while young children sidle up to you on their donkeys offering `Taxi?' At times it can feel more like a bazaar, rather than an ancient historical site, but then again Petra was once a great centre of commerce.

Ins and outs

Getting there

Public transport connections to Petra are surprisingly poor, given that this is Jordan's premiere attraction. The *JETT* coach services between Amman and Petra currently only run on Tue, Fri and Sun, though this may change to a daily service in the future. In addition, there are more regular minibus services between Amman's Wahadat bus station and Petra. Minibus services between Aqaba and Petra are reasonably frequent, though the majority of the departures are early in the morning. Between Wadi Rum and Petra there is only one minibus daily. The most frequent connections with Petra are from Ma'an, an important transport hub just off the Desert Highway. Ma'an is easily accessible from both Amman and Aqaba, as well as most other regional centres inbetween, though other than its importance as a transport hub, it has little to recommend it.

Many people coming from Aqaba opt to share a private taxi. This is expensive, costing anywhere between JD20-30, depending on how desperate the Aqaba taxi drivers are for business. There are frequent reports (particularly at the Wadi Arabah border crossing with Israel) of taxi drivers quoting fares of JD14, 15 or 16 to Petra and then once you arrive, claiming they said 40, 50 or 60. Beware also of taxi drivers who try to take you to a specific hotel; invariably they are working on a commission basis, so you will be charged more for your room. The same goes for taxis from Wadi Rum to Petra.

Getting around

There is no shortage of private taxis shuttling between Musa Spring and the visitors' centre/entrance to Petra. This 4 km trip costs an inflated JD2. A taxi between Wadi Musa town and the entrance to Petra, or between Wadi Musa town and Musa Spring will cost a minimum of JD1 (again, this is a 'tourist' price, but you will have to be a consummate bargainer to get them down to the 'locals' fare of 500 fils). Nearly all the hotels in Wadi Musa town and along the road up as far as Musa Spring offer free transport to and from the visitors' centre/entrance to Petra. This arrangement generally works smoothly for getting down to the entrance in the morning, but be sure to agree clearly in advance a time in the afternoon/evening for them to pick you up when you emerge exhausted from the ruins.

It is a good 20 minute walk from the entrance gate through the *Siq* to the Treasury. There are horses for hire at the entrance gate which will take you as far as the dam at the start of the *Siq* proper (just under 1 km). The price for this trip is officially fixed at JD7. Organized groups visiting Petra pay this whether they take a horse or not, as a way of giving a guaranteed income to the 350 or so Bedouin families who provide the horses, donkeys and camels. Part of that guaranteed income goes towards funding a veterinary clinic and animal welfare centre at the entrance to the site. Individuals can choose whether to pay for a horse and in practice can usually negotiate one for much less. Only horse-drawn carriages are now allowed to make the journey from the entrance gate all the way to the Treasury (ie the whole length of the *Siq*) and are reserved for elderly and disabled people. They cost JD20 for two people. Once inside, there are camels available for hire which can take you to most of the sites (though not up to the High Places or the Monastery) or else unofficial donkeys, usually ridden by children of no more than 9 or 10 years of age. You are officially encouraged to arrange all such rides through the Visitors' Centre, but in practice you can negotiate a deal directly with those in charge of the animals, probably for much less than the official rates. In any case it is much more pleasant to skip the whole tourist-trap and simply walk.

Killing the goose?

In 1994 the Ministry of Tourism and Antiquities raised the entrance fee to Petra from JD1 to JD20 for one day. With such vast numbers of people visiting the site, this turned Petra into Jordan's most profitable tourist attraction by far, generating huge amounts of revenue for a tourist industry which already plays a central role in the country's economy. The effects of the new entrance fee have been various. The flood of complaints from indignant tourists was predictable, while Jordanians working there have become adept at pointing out that it is worth every penny. From the point of view of the local hotel industry it has not been popular. Many complain that it has reduced Petra to a day-trip or at most two-nights stop for many visitors, whereas before there was always a sizeable contingent of dedicated people who would stay for weeks at a time exploring the site. Certainly the rise has been very bluntly applied, with no concessions for students or children over twelve years old.

The phenomenal growth in the number of hotels, all hoping to cash in on the popularity of Petra, has brought with it serious pressures. There are now well over 3,000 beds near the site. When you add to this all those who visit as a day-trip from Amman, Aqaba or even Israel and Egypt, the potential number of visitors in one day during peak times exceeds 4,000, as compared with a limit suggested by UNESCO of 1,500 per day. During 1999 there were nearly half a million visitors to Petra, generating more than JD7 million in entrance fees. In the month of April alone there were more than 64,000 visitors. The sheer weight of numbers in itself threatens to speed the rate of erosion, with tourists clambering over the monuments and something as seemingly harmless as the accumulated sweat of people's hands deposited on the rock contributing significantly to the process.

To date the authorities have made no attempts to limit the numbers of visitors to the site. However, on a more positive note, the Petra Regional Planning Council (PRPC) was established in 1997. This new body is charged with the "management, development and protection of Petra and its archaeological sites". An area of some 264 sq km, encompassing all the main ruins in Petra, has been declared an 'Archaeological Park'. Within the Archaeological Park considerable efforts are being made to further excavate, restore and preserve the ruins, with the PRPC overseeing the work of a number of bodies, including the Petra National Trust (PNT), the Conservation and Restoration Centre in Petra (CARPIC) and foreign archaeological missions such as the American Centre for Oriental Research (ACOR). Outside of the Archaeological Park, the PRPC is responsible for regulating further hotel construction. Thus all new hotels must submit a feasibility study before planning permission is granted, and the maximum height for new hotels is now limited to two storeys. Of lesser benefit perhaps was the decision that all the buildings in the area had to be painted pink! In addition, the PRPC is responsible for developing the infrastructure of the region; building new roads, developing sewage, drainage and irrigation systems, planting trees and restoring parts of Wadi Musa town – notably the Elgee Souk – as tourist amenities.

Disabled access

You can reach the `basin' at the centre of the ruins by taking a horse-drawn carriage as far as the treasury and then a camel or donkey the rest of the way. From there, many of the other sites can be reached in a similar way. However, the carriage ride is quite a bumpy one and if you are not able to ride on a donkey or camel once you reach the Treasury, there is the possibility of being driven into the site. A good track, surfaced for part of the way, leads directly to the central city ruins from the new Bedouin village of Bdoul (also known as Umm Sayhoun). Although vehicles are officially banned from the site, it is possible to get special permission. You are advised to arrange this well in advance, either through the Ministry of Tourism in Amman, or else through the Visitors' Centre in Petra. Once you reach the central basin, many of the sites can be seen from there and it is possible to be driven up close to those which surround the immediate valley-floor.

Site layout There are 3 distinct centres along the main road leading down to the site, although pretty soon they will have merged into one long linear development. First you reach **Musa Spring** (Ain Musa) on the right, now with a couple of hotels and shops around it. Heading down the hill you pass isolated hotels and the Health Centre before arriving in **Wadi Musa** (2½ km), a sizeable village-going-on-town, its current growth fuelled almost entirely by new hotel construction. Continuing down the hill, just before you reach the Visitors' Centre and entrance to the historical site of **Petra**, there is another rapidly growing focus of new hotel construction (4 km from Musa Spring). **NB** If you take the the old route to Petra along the King's Highway from Aqaba, via Taybet (also written Taybeh or Tayyibeh), you join the main road between Musa Spring and Wadi Musa, just above the town of Wadi Musa.

Best time to visit The high season is usually from mid-Jan to the end of May when the weather is at its best (Apr is invariably the busiest month), then from the begining of Oct to the end of Nov. From Jun to Sep it is generally extremely hot during the day, while in Dec it gets extremely cold at night and snow is not uncommon. Christmas and New Year can get quite busy. If you are lucky with the weather in Dec you can have glorious sunny days without the crowds, and likewise at either end of the Jan-May season. At peak times the site can get very busy, although it is big enough to get away from the crowds. However, it may be neccessary to book hotel rooms in advance.

Site information

Entrance fees & opening hours
If a Jordanian is caught helping you to enter the site without a ticket, they face the prospect of 6 months in prison

Entrance fees are JD20 for 1 day, JD25 for 2 days or JD30 for 3 days. The JD30/3 day ticket also entitles you to a 4th day's visit for free. Children under 12 are charged half price. Jordanians pay JD1. There are no concession for students at present, though this may change in the future. Note that students of archaeology or other specialists are no longer able to get a letter from the Ministry of Tourism in Amman allowing them free entry to the site (or at least not unless you can get a personal recommendation from the Minister of Tourism himself). The site is open 7 days; the ticket office opens at 0600, although this is somewhat flexible, and closes shortly before sunset. You can leave the site much later, but cannot enter after these times. It is forbidden to spend the night in the site without prior permission. **NB** The temptation to try to find a way into the site for free may be strong if you are travelling on a tight budget. However, there are frequent spot-checks by tourist police inside the site and anyone found there without a ticket risks a fine and will certainly be made to pay the full fee.

Tourist information There is a large Visitors' Centre (T2156020, F2156060) close to the entrance of Petra which acts as the tourist information centre. The centre is open 0700-2200 for general information. To arrange for guides, horses etc for the following day you must go there before 1800. There is a bank, post office and toilet facilities inside the building, as well as various souvenir shops. The tourist police (T2156441) are also based here.

Guides Official guides are probably best arranged through the Visitors' Centre. There is a regular city tour (around 2½ hrs) which takes in the most easily reached sights; the Siq, Treasury, Theatre, Obelisk Tomb, Qasr al Bint and museum (guide fee JD8). After that there are *additional* charges for guided tours of the remaining sights, eg to the High Places (JD7); Monstery (JD9); Umm al Biyara (JD15); Nabi Haroun (JD25). Thus if you wish to include the High Places and the Monastery in your guided tour, you will pay

The Significance of Petra

To gain an understanding of the history of Petra and of the way in which it developed, one needs to understand also its strategic significance. That it should have played such a crucial role in the early history of the region is a testament to its unique attributes. Initially, during the pre-historic and Edomite periods, its main attraction lay in its excellent natural defences coupled with a reliable water supply.

As the civilizations of the wider region began to develop, Petra came into its own for other reasons. Most importantly, it commanded a bottleneck in the trade route connecting the two great cradles of civilization, Egypt and Mesopotamia. Moreover, the immediate region proved to be rich in natural resources, particularly copper, which was extensively mined throughout the Wadi Arabah region and was obviously of central importance during the emerging Bronze Age. Indeed, the perpetual state of antagonism which existed between the Edomites and the Israelites was largely the product of competition for the control of trade and copper resources. Control over trade routes brought with it prosperity, while control over copper resources ensured a technological advantage (many argue that it was the Edomite's comparatively advanced metal-working skills that allowed them to hold their own against the Israelite tribes).

Over time, it was in the role of a trading capital that Petra excelled. Trade coming up the Red Sea and across the Arabian Peninsula by necessity flowed through Petra en route to the Mediterranean sea ports of Gaza and Alexandria. Trade coming from Syria to the north meanwhile tended to favour the eastern side of the Rift Valley due to its more frequent fresh-water springs, giving rise to the ancient King's Highway which passed right by the gates of Petra.

By the 1st century AD there is evidence that trade was being conducted as far afield as China. It is believed that caravans arrived at the Indian Ocean and followed its coast as far as the Straits of Hormouz, discharging their goods onto ships which then skirted the Arabian Peninsula to connect with the land or sea routes up the Red Sea. Alternatively they may have proceeded up to Bahrain and Kuwait from where they would have made the arduous journey directly across the Arabian desert to Petra.

The other great trade route passed through the sea port of Spasinu-Charax at the head of the Persian Gulf and headed up the Tigris river to Ctesiphon, from there either crossing the desert to Palmyra and thence to the Levantine ports or else continuing up the Euphrates as far as Dura Europos before crossing the Syrian highlands to Aleppo and on to Antioch. However, it was not until the Roman Empire was able to consolidate its control over what was a highly turbulent region that this important ancient trade route once more provided a viable alternative to the southerly routes, all of which passed through Petra.

Petra

JD24 (JD8 regular tour, plus JD7 and JD9). A guide for the whole day will cost JD35. All prices are displayed inside the Visitors' Centre; they are for the guide only and if you wish to hire horses, camels or donkeys, these are extra. You can also arrange for guides to any of the places around Petra, including to Showbak Castle and Wadi Rum.

Eating

Once inside Petra, the *Basin*, near the Qasr al-Bint Pharon at the centre of the site, is the only formal restaurant (open 0800-1700; sometimes closes earlier off-season depending on demand). The buffet lunch here is reasonably good, but expensive at JD8.700 per head. In addition there are a couple of large `Bedouin tents' nearby serving slightly cheaper (though far inferior) buffet lunches for JD6 per head. A cup of tea at these costs JD1, while their 'lunch box' (consisting of nothing more than a couple of sandwiches, a tomato, cucumber, biscuit and yoghurt pot) is a monumental rip-off at

JD4. There are several similar places along the route from the Treasury to the Central City Ruins. Further afield there are tea/cold drinks stalls strategically located near most the major sites, although these only really get going during the high season. Bottled water can be bought inside the site, although it is more expensive than in Wadi Musa. Bring your own supplies of food and water if you want to be free to take lunch wherever you want.

Toilets   There are good clean toilet facilities in the Visitors' Centre at the entrance to the site; in a cave near the Theatre; in the *Basin* restaurant; and behind the Qasr al-Bint (in what was formerly the *Nazzal* hotel).

Anthropomorphic idol (possibly the Egyptian/Nabatean goddess Isis/Al Uzza), Temple of the Winged Lions, Petra

Safety   The greatest risk is from dehydration, so make sure you bring plenty of water. Adequate protection against the sun is also vital; take sun-block cream and wear a hat and loose-fitting clothes which cover the skin, including the back of the neck. Practically all of the sites can be easily reached in normal shoes or trainers. However proper boots with good ankle support considerably reduce the risk of a sprained ankle, and given that much of the terrain is rough and uneven, will also make walking that much less tiring.

A sign by the Pharaoh's Column near the Qasr al-Bint warns "Venturing from the regular routes on your own is not advisable ... should you wish to do so beyond this point we strongly advise either a local guide or at least one companion." Exploring the site on your own is perfectly safe providing you are sensible (and actually finding the various monuments is also far easier than lurking guides would have you believe), but if you intend to do any climbing or to venture very far from the central ruins, the advice to go with at least one other person is very sound. If you were to be injured on your own, you would probably face a night out in what can be bitterly cold conditions before you were found. A guide is recommended for the climb up to Jebel Umm al-Biyara and Jebel Haroun since the route is not clear and tricky in places. Emergency medical facilities, including oxygen and if neccessary helicopter evacuation, are available from the *Basin* restaurant and museum complex.

History

Pre-history to the Edomite period

Petra has been a focus of settlement since pre-historic times, as confirmed by the excavation of Neolithic settlements at Beidha and Basta which date back to the 7th millennium BC. Evidence has also been found at these sites of semi-nomadic hunter-gatherers occupying the region during the Mesolithic period (10,000-7,500 BC). During the Bronze Age much of the region fell under the orbit of Egypt, with the Hyskos kings being keen to maintain control over this vital trade route connecting the Nile valley with the civilizations along the Euphrates and Tigris rivers to the north.

Other than what can be gleaned from archaeological evidence, nothing more is known about the region until references to the land of Edom begin to appear in the Bible. Various tribes occupied Edom over time, the most

A Note on Biblical References and Place-Names

As a historical record, the Bible is both valuable and misleading. Many of the events it relates occur at the very beginings of recorded history and remain shrouded in myths and legends. The events and places mentioned in Exodus are notoriously difficult to date and locate, yet from them have emerged the Arabic place-names Musa (Moses), Haroun (Aaron) and Pharon (Pharaoh) along with their associated biblical stories, all firmly fixed around Petra in popular local tradition. Most scholars reject such geographical certainties as being unfounded. But the very uncertainty which clouds all of these events also leaves the debate wide open; that they are closely linked with the region as a whole is undeniable. Perhaps it is fitting that their exact location should be left to imagination.

With regards to Petra, part of the problem lies in the fact that it did not yet exist as a city during biblical times (later, Petra was referred to as Reqem, its Semitic name, which again causes problems since there are many Reqems in the region). Instead we find references in the Bible to

Seir and Sela (both meaning 'rock') as the abode of the Edomites. This is popularly identified with the high rocky mountain of Umm al-Biyara, although archaeological evidence suggests that it was not occupied by the Edomites until at least a century after the famous biblical massacre of Edomites by the Judean king Azamiah. Numerous sites in the region have been identified as possible alternative locations, with one near present-day Tafila currently favoured as the true Sela.

Similarly, the numbers of people quoted as being massacred in the numerous clashes between the Edomites and Israelites need to be treated with caution. At this point in history the population of the region would have been very small and it seems unlikely that the various massacres were in the order of thousands. Either the numbers were deliberately exaggerated or else, as seems much more likely, it has been pointed out that the Hebrew word for 'thousands', 'alaf', also translates as 'families, clans or tents', thus rendering the numbers much more realistic.

important of these being the Edomites, described as the sons of Esau in the Bible. Esau was the twin brother of Jacob (the sons of Isaac) who left Canaan after Jacob tricked him out of his birthright and came to the region with his family. Most of what we know about the Edomites (see also page 333) is derived from biblical references, which focus almost exclusively on the continual state of antagonism between the Edomites (sons of Esau) and Israelites (sons of Jacob). Thus, during the time of the Exodus:

"*Moses sent messengers from Kadesh to the king of Edom, saying: `This is what your brother Israel says: You know about all the hardships that have come upon us. Our forefathers went down into Egypt, and we lived there many years. The Egyptians ill-treated us and our fathers, but when we cried out to the Lord, he heard our cry and sent an angel and brought us out of Egypt. Now we are here at Kadesh, a town on the edge of your territory. Please let us pass through your country. We will not go through any field or vineyard, or drink water from any well. We will travel along the King's Highway and not turn to the right or to the left until we have passed through your territory'. But Edom answered: `You may not pass through here; if you try, we will march out and attack you with the sword'. The Israelites replied: `We will go along the main road, and if we or our livestock drink any of your water, we will pay for it. We only want to pass through on foot – nothing else.' Again they answered: `You may not pass through.' Then Edom came out against them with a large and powerful army. Since Edom refused to let them go through their territory, Israel turned away from them.*" (Numbers 20: 14-21)

Petra

Burckhardt the Explorer

The Anglo-Swiss geographer and explorer Johann Ludwig Burckhardt was born in Lausanne, Switzerland, on 24 November, 1784. He studied at London and Cambridge between 1806-9 and lived in Syria where he learned Arabic and converted to Islam, taking the Muslim name Ibrahim Ibn Abd Allah. He left Syria in 1812, en route for Cairo and the Fezzan (Libya) from where he intended to attempt to cross the Sahara. Along the way he overheard his local guides talking about the ruins of a lost city hidden in the mountains of Wadi Musa. Suspecting that they were referring unknowingly to the legendary city of Petra, he devised a plan to trick his guides into revealing its location. "I pretended to have made a vow to have slaughtered a goat in honour of Haroun (Aaron), whose tomb I knew was situated at the extremity of the valley, and by this strategem I thought that I should have the means of seeing the valley on the way up to the tomb."

The plan worked worked exactly as he expected and he was led through the Siq, past the Khazneh and the main monuments of the central basin en route to Jebel Haroun. Barely able to conceal his excitement, he managed to make a couple of sketches, arousing the suspicions of his Bedouin guides with his excessive interest in what were after all pagan monuments of no significance to a Muslim pilgrim wishing to make a sacrifice at the tomb of Nabi Haroun. In any case he had seen enough to be convinced that this was indeed the lost city of Petra. When he arrived in Cairo he could find no immediate transport to Fezzan. Instead he journeyed up the Nile, discovering the Temple of Ramses II at Abu Simbal. He next travelled to Saudi Arabia, visiting Mecca. He returned to Cairo where he died on 15 October, 1817, the rigours of his travels evidently proving too much for him. Five years later his journal was finally published as a book entitled Travels in Syria and the location of the lost city of Petra was once again revealed to the outside world.

Having established themselves in the Promised Land, the Israelites, led by King Saul, "*fought against their enemies on every side; Moab, the Ammonites, Edom, the kings of Zobah and the Phillistines*" (1 Samuel 14: 47-8). The Edomites were not however fully subdued and continued to make raids into Judah. When King David (circa 1000-960 BC) came to the throne he launched a ferocious attack on the Edomites, defeating them once again and this time, according to the Bible, massacring 18,000 of them in the valley of Salt (2 Samuel 8: 13-14 and 1 Chronicles 18: 12).

King Solomon (circa 960-922) consolidated his control over Edom, replacing the small port of Eloth with a much larger one able to accommodate a merchant fleet which plied the Red Sea, trading along the coast of Africa and with the Queen of Sheba in southern Arabia. In doing so he effectively diverted trade away from the Petra region, to the detriment of the Edomites. Biblical references to Solomon's splendour suggest that he profited handsomely from the control he exercised: "*The weight of gold that Solomon received yearly was 666 talents [nearly 23 metric tons], not including the revenues from merchants and traders and from all the Arabian kings and the governors of the land.*" (1 Kings 10: 14-15).

With the death of Solomon, the Israelite kingdom became divided between Judah in the south and Israel in the north, while the fate of Edom became closely tied to the former. Edom remained nominally under the control of Judah, but in practice exercised a large degree of autonomy and continued with the frequent raids into Judah. It was during the reign of the Judean king Amaziah (796-781 BC) that the famous massacre of Edomites, hurled from the summit of their rock stronghold (the Sela) took place.

Uncovering Petra's past

The majority of the great Nabatean monuments at Petra consist of façades carved into the sides of cliff-faces and therefore they did not actually have to be excavated in the first place. However, there was also a sizeable city consisting of free-standing buildings in the central basin of Petra. The colonnaded street which ran through the centre of this city along with a number of buildings nearby have been, or are in the process of being, excavated. Ongoing excavations include the Great Temple just to the south of the Colonnaded Street, being carried out by an American team from Brown University, and the

nearby Zantur site consisting of Nabatean/Roman housing, being excavated by a Swiss team from Basle Unversity. The excavations by the American Centre for Oriental Research (ACOR) of the Petra Church to the north of the Colonnaded Steet, and the Ridge Church beyond it, have recently been completed. Most experts agree that what is visible today represents only a tiny fraction of the original city and that there is still a wealth of ruins buried under the accumulated debris of centuries, with funding being the only obstacle to uncovering more details about the history and life of Petra.

By the end of the 8th century BC, the Edomite kingdom was entering its `classical' period, the height of its social and economic development, which was to last until the early 6th century BC. The Edomites had become accomplished metal-workers, as attested by the numerous copper smelting slag heaps dating from this period found dotted around Wadi Arabah. Spinning and weaving were practised for the manufacture of cloth, high quality pottery was being produced and some form of writing is thought to have been in use. All of this was complemented, and fed to a certain extent, by the trade which was passing through the land of Edom, providing both a source of revenue and new ideas.

By the 7th century BC the Assyrians were rising as the great new power to the north and east, and extending their control over the region. However in 612 BC they were in turn overthrown by the Babylonians, who destroyed their capital at Nineveh and by 605 BC had consolidated their control over Judah, Edom and Moab. Judah responded by revolting against them, forming allegiances with Moab and Edom against this new common enemy. In the event, the Babylonians defeated Judah resoundingly in 587 BC, successfully laying siege to Jerusalem and razing it to the ground. The Bible records how the Edomites, allies of convenience only, rejoiced at this turn of events, much to the disgust of the Judeans. With the kingdom of Judah crushed, the Edomites began to settle in large numbers in the lands they had previously only been able to carry out raids upon.

The Nabateans

This migration of Edomites into Judah had begun long before the fall of Jerusalem as a gradual expansion westwards across the Wadi Arabah. At the same time, a new influx of peoples into the land of Edom was underway. This tribe, referred to as the *Nabaitu* in Assyrian texts, are believed to have originated from the Arabian Peninsula and were effectively the forefathers of Nabateans. They gradually replaced the Edomites and by the time the Persian Archaemenid Empire, led by Cyrus, overthrew Babylon in 539 BC, the Nabateans are known to have been in possession of the biblical Sela. By the late 4th century BC they had firmly established themselves and were beginning to benefit significantly from the trade they controlled through Petra. In 312 BC they were able to repulse attacks by Antigonos, the Greek Seleucid ruler of

Syria, who was battling with the Greek Ptolemid ruler of Egypt for control of the now divided Empire of Alexander the Great. The Nabateans eventually established a status quo with him, presenting gifts as a form of appeasement.

This last act was very much at the heart of the Nabateans' policy towards the outside world. They were a nomadic Bedouin people who were gradually settling down in their new stronghold of Petra and relying increasingly on the peaceful passage of trade to support themselves. Thus they practised a delicate balancing act, buying off the rulers of Egypt and Syria in order to maintain a certain degree of autonomy. This was to the mutual benefit of both Egypt and Syria, which each profited from the trade which passed between them via Petra. From around the 3rd century BC, the Nabateans began to abandon the tents of their nomadic roots and build a city at Petra. The trade passing through brought with it great wealth and a synthesis of Hellenistic and Egyptian architectural influences, along with the indigenous styles (which themselves stemmed largely from former Assyrian and Babylonian influences) of these increasingly sophisticated Arabs.

The collapse of the Seleucid Empire in 64 BC left the two great regional powers, Rome in the west and Parthia in the east, struggling for control of the Middle East. Like Palmyra, the other great caravan city to the northeast, Petra took advantage of this state of affairs to increase its autonomy. Under King Aretas II

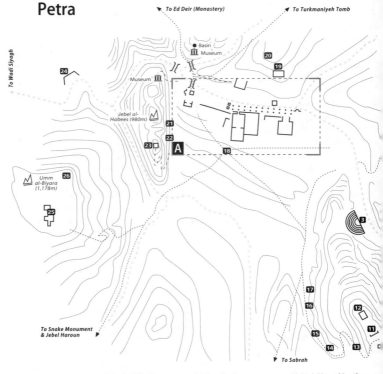

Petra

To Ed Deir (Monastery)

To Turkmaniyeh Tomb

To Wadi Siyagh

Basin
Museum

Museum

Jebel al-Habees (980m)

Umm al-Biyara (1,178m)

To Snake Monument & Jebel Haroun

To Sabrah

Petra

Related map
A Petra Siq, page 259

0 metres	200
0 yards	200

1 Tomb of Uneisha
2 Streets of the Façades
3 Theatre
4 Urn Tomb
5 Silk Tomb
6 Corinthian Tomb

7 Palace Tomb
8 Sextius Florentinus Tomb
9 Jebel Umm al-Amr
   High Place of Sacrifice
10 Obelisks
11 Fortress Ruins

12 High Place of Sacrifice
13 Lion Fountain
14 Garden Tomb
15 Roman Soldier
   Tomb & Triclinium
16 Renaissance Tomb

(110-96 BC) the Nabateans, by now relatively powerful in their own right, were able to carve out an independent kingdom for themselves, which under Aretas III (84-56 BC) was briefly extended as far as Damascus. Pompey responded by sending Scaurus to lay siege to the city in 63 BC. The Nabateans were able to hold out and, true to style, subsequently bought him off.

Roman period

At the same time, Rome was exerting an increasingly strong influence on Petra, both culturally and politically. Thus Strabo records how the succession of Aretas IV to the throne after the death of King Obodas in 9 BC was officially confirmed by the Roman Emperor, despite the supposed status of Petra as an independent kingdom. King Aretas IV was highly successful in pursuing a diplomatic policy of close allegiance with Rome, even obtaining possession of Damascus from Caligula. Nevertheless, the power of Rome continued to increase until finally in 106 AD Trajan was able to incorporate Petra into the newly-established Roman Province of Arabia.

Petra continued to flourish under the Romans, the new political arrangement representing more a natural development than a watershed. Certainly the Roman influence became more pronounced in architectural terms, with the Romans building the Colonnaded Street and a number of other typically Roman features, but on the whole a process of synthesis continued, with the architectural tradition of the Nabateans being too strong to be wholly obliterated. Indeed, immediately after being annexed, Petra appears to have undergone something of a renaissance.

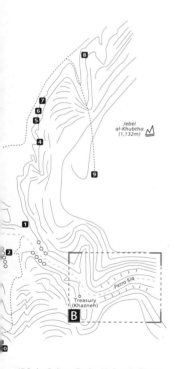

Jebel al-Khubtha (1,132m)

Petra Siq

Treasury (Khazneh)

Subsequently however it began to fall into decline, with Palmyra taking over as the great caravan city and trading crossroads of the Roman Empire.

Byzantine period to the present

Petra continued to be inhabited well into the Byzantine period, as attested by the conversion of some of its monuments into churches or monastic retreats, as well as the recently discovered Petra Church and Ridge Church to the north of the Colonnaded Street. By the 4th century AD, Petra had its own bishop, although its life-blood in the form of trade had ceased to exist. The Byzantine occupation probably continued well into the 6th century, but Petra appears to have fallen steadily into obscurity, certainly disappearing from the historical records. It next reappears during the

Petra

Itineraries and timescales

How long you devote to exploring the monuments of Petra obviously depends on how long you have. If you are really pushed for time, it is possible in half a day to see most of the main monuments situated close to the central basin. In a strenuous full day you can see nearly all the most important monuments. Over two or three days you have time to explore in considerable detail without ever running out of new things to discover. If you are really dedicated, you could easily spend weeks here.

Half Day; main sights *To devote just a half-day to Petra limits you considerably, but it is nevertheless possible to see a substantial amount. Walk or ride through the Siq to arrive at the Khazneh. Continue along valley floor past the Theatre and then divert up to the Urn, Corinthian and Palace Tombs. Return down and walk on to Colonnaded Street and Qasr el-Bint, exploring surrounding excavations and tombs of the central city ruins as time permits. Visit the museums and return.*

Full Day; main sights *This is a strenuous day involving long climbs and descents, and a lot of walking. Walk or ride through the Siq to the Khazneh. Continue on and climb up to the High Places on Zibb Attuf, either descending the same way or continuing down past the Lion*

Monument, Garden, Roman Soldier and Renaissance Tombs. Then, in whichever order, explore the Cardo Maximus, Qasr al-Bint, museums and surrounding excavations and tombs of the central city ruins as time permits; visit the Monastery (Ed Deir) high up to the northwest (best in evening light); and, on returning, visit the Urn, Corinthian and Palace Tombs at the foot of Jebel el-Khubtha.

2 Days *Day 1; cover the sights listed above. If you want a less strenuous day, either the Monastery or the High Places can be incorporated into the next day (the Monastery is a must if you can make it up there, the High Places are great if you like, well... high places). Day 2; choose between a full day outing to Sabrah or Nebi Haroun (both of which can include the Snake Tomb), a full day to the summit of Umm el-Biyarah, a half-day to Beida and Siq el-Bared, or shorter visits to Wadi Siyagh, Wadi Turkmaniyeh, Al Madras and Al Woaira Castle.*

3 Days *This gives you the chance to see all the sights covered here in detail, provided you are willing to undertake a fairly strenuous programme. Visit them all in whatever order you choose, or be selective and give yourself more time to appreciate certain sights.*

Crusader period, when Baldwin I built two fortresses here (Wu'eira and Al Habees) between 1108-1116 as part of the strategic chain of castles extending from the Sinai Coast up through Jordan. The aim was to control the land route between Cairo and Damascus, both held by Salah ud-Din (Saladin) at this time, and to tax the caravan trade along it. However following the victory of Salah ud-Din over the Crusaders, these fortresses were abandoned and this time Petra fell into total obscurity for nearly 800 years, its existence known only to the local Bedouins who guarded their secret jealously from outsiders. Finally, in 1812, the Anglo-Swiss explorer Johann Ludwig Burckhardt `redis-covered' it.

Around the site

The Siq

Having passed through the ticket gate, you follow the course of a wide, dry wadi-bed (part of Wadi Musa), down towards the Siq. First you pass on the right three large free-standing rock cubes known as **Djinn Blocks**. There are more than 20 of these carved rock cubes dotted around Petra, some of them up to 9 m tall and hollowed out inside. Their exact purpose is not clear, although they are believed to have been created as the dwelling places of Nabatean spirits. All of them are found near water (or at least seasonal water courses), leading some to believe that the spirits they housed were meant to stand guard over flows and sources of water.

A little further on, on the left, there is a double monument, the Obelisk Tomb (above) and the Bab as-Siq Triclinium (below). The **Obelisk Tomb**, so called because of the four obelisks each originally over 7 m high carved above the entrance, dates from the 1st century AD and shows an interesting mix of Egyptian and classical influences in the use of obelisks alongside the standard pilasters, niches and pediments. Immediately below it is the **Bab as-Siq Triclinium** (`Gate of the Siq Triclinium'), a façade with two heavily weathered tiers of pediments and a large cave chiselled out of the rock in the lower tier. A Triclinium is a banquet hall in which feasts were held, usually in honour of the dead. Immediately opposite the Obelisk Tomb, about 5 m up in the cliff-side, there is an **inscription** in both Nabatean Aramaic and Greek announcing the burial place of a Petran. The monuments described so far are not the most impressive and are easily missed.

Beyond the Obelisk Tomb, the path swings round to the right, passing on the left the route up to Al Madras (see page 259), before entering the Siq proper. A **dam** blocks the wadi at this point, its purpose to divert the flow of water through a tunnel off to the right in the event of flash-floods. The dam was built following one such flash-flood in 1963 when a group of 23 tourists was drowned. The tunnel is of Nabatean construction and in the course of building the modern dam, the foundations of an earlier dam dating from the Nabatean period were discovered, along with the fragments of various water channels. The problems of flooding were just as real in Nabatean times, and in addition they had to supply their city with water, hence they built an elaborate system of water channels, some fed originally by the spring at Ain Musa, which wound their way into Petra. One of these started at a large rock-cut reservoir opposite

Petra

Petra Siq

the *Petra Forum Resthouse* and ran north then west through carved channels to reach the Nabatean city centre. Another ran through the Siq and sections of it can still be seen carved into the left-hand wall of the Siq at about head height, along with sections of ceramic piping on the right.

Crossing over the dam and entering the narrow Siq, if you look up you notice the remains of a **triumphal arch**, now collapsed, but still intact 100 years ago, as shown by the watercolours of David Roberts. Much of the floor of the Siq has now been consolidated with concrete to prevent further erosion. Originally, the full length of the Siq would have been paved, and sections of this paving, dating from the Nabatean and Roman periods, can be seen at various points, along with traces of heavily weathered niches carved into the cliff-sides. The Siq itself is an entirely natural feature, a narrow cleft produced by earth movements which literally split a solid section of limestone mountain in two. In places you can clearly match the cross-section patterns in one cliff-side with those opposite. The effects of weathering and erosion meanwhile have carved fantastic shapes in the rock higher up. The Siq runs for a length of 1.2 km and in places is just 3 m wide, while the walls tower up to a height of 200 m. The overall effect of walking through this remarkable natural feature is truly awe-inspiring and is half the magic of approaching the great monuments of Petra.

The Treasury (Al Khazneh Pharon)

The numerous twists and turns bring you suddenly to your first glimpse of the Treasury, one of Petra's best preserved and most impressive temple façades, framed between the narrow walls of the end of the Siq. The contrast of bright light after the gloom, and the sheer improbability of the scale of this monument, combine almost to challenge your sense of reality. The morning is the best time to see the Treasury (between around 1000-1100 in summer and 0900-1000 in winter), when the sun falls directly on its façade, illuminating the warm hues of the rock.

The Treasury towers to a height of over 40 m and is comprised of two tiers. The lower tier consists of six huge Corinthian columns topped by ornate capitals, with a frieze running in a band above them, decorated with pairs of grifffins each flanking a vase with plant tendrils. A pediment sits over the four central columns and is decorated with plant designs. The upper tier consists of two side pavilions and a central *tholos*, or small circular shrine. Each pavilion is supported by Corinthian columns and contains barely discernible carved figures. On top of each are the end-wedges of a broken pediment. The *tholos* rises up in the centre, topped by a dome and then a Corinthian capital surmounted by a 4 m tall urn. The interior consists of a large central chamber flanked by two smaller side chambers. These are reached by steps that lead into the portico formed by the four central columns and pediment. Each is disappointingly bare and simple in contrast to the grandeur of the exterior, though this is a feature common to all the Nabatean monuments of Petra.

Surprisingly little is known about the Treasury. Locally it is referred to as *Al Jerrah*, meaning `the urn', a reference to the huge solid-stone urn which sits on top of the central *tholos* of the upper storey. Local legends told that this urn was filled with gold, hence its rather reduced state, chiselled and shot at countless times over the centuries by hopeful treasure hunters. Hence also its name *Al Khazneh*, `the Treasury', or *Al Khazneh Pharon*, `the Pharaoh's Treasury'; according to one variation of the legends it was the very same Pharaoh that pursued the Israelites from Egypt in the Old Testament Book of Exodus who stored his treasures here.

Restoration and preservation

For all their seeming timeless endurance, the ruins at Petra are fading fast. The carved sandstone façades are steadily being eroded away, some surveys suggest by as much as 1 cm each year. That earthquakes and the elements should have taken their toll over more than a thousand years seems inevitable, but the actual rate of loss is striking when today's façades are compared against the early 19th century watercolours of Petra by David Roberts. Detailed studies of the site by the Conservation and Restoration Centre in Petra (CARCIP) suggest that out of around 3,000 monuments found in Petra, only 100 remain whose original features are still discernable.

A major problem is from groundwater penetrating the stones and, on evaporating in the heat, leaving behind salt crystals which cause the rock to crumble. To a lesser extent rain and sand storms mechanically erode the rock, while freeze-thaw splits and cracks it. Chemical and mechanical weathering are not easily combated in a site as large as Petra, but the Petra Stone Preservation Project, a bi-lateral project between the German Agency for Technical Cooperation (GTZ) and the Jordanian Ministry of Tourism and Antiquities was set up in 1994 with the aim of doing this. Having completed a survey of the site, work has begun on the actual restoration of a number of temple façades. The project has a budget of around JD3 million (US$4.3 million) and aims to hand over management and running to a Jordanian team after a training programme.

Various theories exist as to its true origins and purpose. Perhaps it was the tomb of King Harith IV or King Aretas III, thus dating to somewhere between 86-62 BC, or else the tomb of King Aretas IV, which would put it as late as 25 AD. Others suggest that it was not a tomb at all, but a temple dedicated to the goddess Al Uzza, equated with the Egyptian goddess Isis. The statue contained within the central *tholos* is recognized by some as being of Isis, although it has been badly damaged and is today only just discernible as female. Another theory suggests that it was dedicated to the Nabatean god of caravans and caravaneers, She'a-alqum.

As well as being an architecturally stunning monument, the Treasury is intriguing for the wide range of different styles and influences it displays – a fascinating blend of local, Hellenistic and Egyptian. This reflects both the far-flung extent of trade (and therefore exchange of ideas) carried out from the Nabatean capital, and in all probability the extensive use of craftsmen from far afield, along with their own distinctive styles.

Continuing past the Treasury, after a couple of hundred metres you pass on your left three large, heavily weathered tombs (the central one incomplete) and a fourth smaller one, while on your right is a series of tombs ascending in size. At the time of writing the last of these was being restored under the auspices of CARPIC, with work on the upper parts of the façade now largely completed. The wadi here begins to open out. Ahead of you on the left is the theatre. To your right, up on a higher level around the corner from the façade undergoing restoration, is the Tomb of Uneisha and, further away, the Royal Tombs, ascending in a series along the base of Jebel al-Khubtha. To your left, just past a tent for souvenirs and refreshments, steps mark the start of the route up to the Jebel Madhbah High Place of Sacrifice (see page 261). Just beyond the steps, also to the left before the Theatre, are the Streets of the Façades, cut into the cliffs on four levels.

Tomb of Uneisha The Tomb of Uneisha is strictly speaking one of the Royal Tombs. Reaching it involves a bit of a scramble. An inscription suggests that Uneisha was either the brother or a minister of Queen Shaqilat, wife of King Aretas IV. The internal chamber is of interest in that it demonstrates the complete layout of a royal tomb. There are a total of 11 recesses, four in the side walls and three in the rear, each of which would have held a sarcophogus. Once up here you can explore a number of other un-named tombs and caves, as well as getting some good views down onto the theatre.

To the left of the Tomb of Uneisha (as you face it), rock-cut steps lead up into a ravine. Following this ravine you can pick up another flight of steps which continue up the rock face; however the route is tricky and only for those who feel comfortable clambering around on exposed rock.

Streets of the Façades The Streets of the Façades consists of more than 40 `tombs' (in fact the majority were probably dwellings rather than tombs), their façades carved into the cliffs on four levels (or `streets', hence the name). They are thought to be early examples of Nabatean workmanship, classified as Assyrian I and II in style after the strong Assyrian influence shown in the crow-step decoration of the façades.

Theatre The Theatre dates originally from around 25 AD and was constructed by the Nabateans. After 106 AD, however, it was greatly extended by the Romans to seat a capacity of between 7,000 and 8,000 spectators in 40 rows of concentric semi-circles. The construction cut into an earlier street of tombs which can be seen above. The devastating earthquake of 363 AD, and the subsequent removal of materials for other building works have severely damaged the theatre, leaving it a poor reflection of its former state. Parts of the stage were restored in the 1960s by an American team, although the crisp, new stonework used still stands out rather incongruously. It has been suggested that the theatre was originally conceived by the Nabateans in order to perform funeral rites and other religious rituals, rather than for entertainment purposes, although under the Romans it would certainly have fulfilled the latter function. From the upper tiers of seating you get good views of the rock face opposite, which is riddled with heavily weathered caves.

Royal Tombs

The Royal Tombs, as with so many of Petra's monuments, are so called with little firm basis. Only one, the Tomb of Sextus Florentinus, is definitely a tomb; the others may have been tombs, temples or royal houses. To reach them, continue along the valley floor past the theatre until you reach a good stairway on the right, just past a large restaurant and souvenir stall. This leads directly up to the Urn Tomb.

The **Urn Tomb** is distinctive for the two tiers of arched vaults below the main façade. Locally it is referred to as *Al Mahkama* (`the Court'), and the arched vaults as *As Sijn* (`the Prison'); whether or not it ever served this purpose is uncertain, although the name is at least a little more imaginative than `Urn Tomb'. The vaulting serves to extend the courtyard in front of the tomb further than the natural rock allowed. The stairways on either side leading up to the courtyard are however later additions, most probably built in the 5th century AD by the Byzantine Bishop of Petra, when the tomb was used as a church. On either side of the courtyard is a recessed portico cut into the rock, the one on the left supported by five columns.

The main façade consists of four huge pilasters topped by an enormous lintel, followed by a pediment with an urn on top. Unfortunately, the upper half of the façade is heavily weathered. Unusually for Petra there is a large window above the central doorway. Between the four pilasters there are three niches, the central one still containing a heavily weathered bust. Inside is a large chamber with arched and square recesses in the walls. An inscription in the rear wall tells of its conversion into a church in 446/7 AD, while holes in the floor mark the placement of the chancery screen, altar and pulpit. The large central arched recess in the back wall and the ceiling of the chamber boast colourful swirling patterns in the limestone rock.

To the left of this, past a badly weathered façade with crow-step decoration, is the **Silk Tomb**, its façade also badly weathered and rather plain looking, but interesting for the colourful swirling patterns in the carved rock. These are amongst the best examples in Petra of the striking colours and patterns in the grain of the rock.

Continuing along the line, you come next to the **Corinthian Tomb**. The upper section of this monument, although heavily weathered, is unmistakably modelled on the Treasury. The lower section is unusual in that the three surviving doorways between the pilasters are each in a different style.

Next to it on the left is the **Palace Tomb**, amongst the largest of the monuments in Petra, its façade consisting of three tiers. The first tier has pilasters separating four large doorways which lead into individual chambers (unfortunately the two on the left side are heavily eroded). The second tier consists of another row of pilasters, while the third has largely collapsed or been eroded away. The façade is unusual in that parts of the upper tier had to be built-on as opposed to being carved. It is partly due to this that the upper section has suffered so badly. The origins of the Palace Tomb are not clear. It is believed to have been modelled on a Roman palace design (hence the name), perhaps even Nero's Golden House, although that would put its construction very late on. More likely it was the palace or tomb of a Nabatean king, perhaps Harith III. At the time of writing, the Palace Tomb was considered dangerous and had been fenced off pending restoration work.

A little further on, around the corner, you come to a stairway (see below). Just beyond this is the **Tomb of Sextius Florentinus**. A Latin inscription above the doorway identifies Sextius Florentinus as a Roman soldier who served in the early 2nd century AD, retiring in 127 AD from his position as Governor of Arabia. Most probably however the tomb is much older, having been acquired by him at a later date.

Petra

The stairway between the Palace Tomb and Tomb of Sextius Florentinus is the start of the route up to the Jebel Umm al-Amr High Place of Sacrifice. It is a steep 20-30 minute climb to the top. In places the stairway is newly-built or restored, elsewhere it is rock-cut, weathered and ancient. The remains to be found at the top are not as well-preserved or extensive as at the Jebel Madhbah High Place of Sacrifice. However, you can see traces of sacrificial areas cut into the flat rock of the summit, the heavy stonework of what was a dam built into a cleft, and the remains of various rock-cut water channels, caves and stairways. The views out over Petra are magnificent, particularly across to the Jebel Madhbah High Place of Sacrifice opposite, and down onto the Theatre. It is also possible to continue along to a point overlooking the Treasury, though you should not attempt to descend the gully from here down to the valley floor as it is extremely dangerous in places.

Jebel Umm al-Amr High Place of Sacrifice

Central City Ruins

Returning to the valley floor and following the course of the wadi-bed, the main path swings round to the left soon after the turning up to the Urn Tomb, bringing you to the central basin, where Petra's main urban centre was located. A colonnaded street runs east-west through the middle of the urban area, terminating in a monumental gateway which leads through to the *temenos* of the Qasr el-Bint, the only surviving temple in Petra which was constructed from free-standing stone blocks as opposed to being carved out of a rock-face. Along the south side of the colonnaded street is a stepped embankment where excavations have revealed market areas and the 'Great Temple', as well as further ruins higher up. To the north is the bed of Wadi Musa, on the far side of which is the Winged Lion Temple, and beyond this, the Petra Church and Ridge Church.

These ruins are perhaps not the most visually impressive in Petra, generally being in a far more advanced state of ruin than the rock-cut façades and consisting largely of the excavated foundations of buildings. However, from an archaeological point of view, the central city ruins are of great importance as an area of ongoing excavations which have revealed several different layers of activity, from the earliest Nabatean settlers through the entire Roman period to the mid-Byzantine period. As well as disproving the theory that the free-standing buildings at Petra were purely Roman in origin, ongoing research here has considerably advanced our understanding of the purpose of the various buildings.

Colonnaded Street, Nymphaeum and 'Upper Market'

The remains of the **Colonnaded Street** to be seen today are of Roman origin, dating either from the time of Trajan when Petra became part of the Roman province of Arabia, or else later, during the reign of Antoninus (138-161 AD) – a period of intense building works throughout the empire. However some experts have suggested that it was constructed earlier, perhaps during the reign of Rabbel II (70-106 AD) or Harith IV (9 BC-40 AD), while further excavations have revealed the existence of a much older, gravel-surfaced roadway of Nabatean construction lined with one- and two-storey buildings dating from the 3rd century BC. Much of the original limestone paving still remains, along with many of the pedestals of the columns which once lined the street.

Petra central city ruins

After I Browning
(adapted from Bachman)

Not to scale

1 Qasr el Bint
2 Altar
3 Temenos
4 Temenos Gate
5 Winged Lion Temple

6 Byzantine Tower
7 Nymphaeum
8 Shrine
9 Colonnaded Street
10 Upper Market

11 Middle Market
12 Lower Market
13 Propylaeum Steps
14 Great Temple
15 Small Temple

16 Roman House
17 Faroun Ruins
18 Pillar

A series of nine re-erected columns give some idea of what the street would have originally looked like, although you have to bear in mind that it once ran through a bustling urban area. On the right as you approach the Colonnaded Street from the Royal Tombs are the remains of a small **nymphaeum** consisting of a shrine and water fountain dedicated to the water spirits or Nymphs which played such an important role in both Nabatean and Roman mythology. A pistachio tree growing out of the ruins gives welcome shelter from the sun in summer.

Following the street westwards towards the Qasr el-Bint, you pass first a stairway on the left (originally graced by a monumental arch over it) leading up to a terrace generally referred to as the **'Upper Market'** or 'Upper Court' (of which there is little to see). Some of the **shops** on either side of this stairway have now been partially restored by ACOR; the one to the right of the stairway gives a good idea of their layout, though it was modified during the Byzantine era, perhaps after the earthquake of 363 AD. Between the 'Upper Market' and the Great Temple are two further terraces, largely unexcavated, known as the Middle and Lower Markets.

Just before the monumental gateway, a set of steps on the left leads up into what is termed the Great Temple. Covering more than 7,500 sq m, this vast structure was originally thought to be the town's *agora*. In 1921 the archaeologist W Bachmann suggested that it might be a temple, and work by the Brown University initially confirmed this theory. However, the discovery of a theatre-like structure in the 'temple' itself has forced archaeologists to admit that its exact nature remains something of a mystery. **Great Temple**

Clearly this was once one of the main architectural components of Petra. Centrally located, rising to a height of nearly 20 m and decorated with red and white stucco, it must have contrasted strikingly with the surrounding monuments. The complex comprised of a *propylaeum* (monumental entrance), a lower *temenos* (sacred area) and a monumental stairway leading up to the upper *temenos* where the 'temple' itself was located. The complex is believed to have originally been constructed in the late 1st century BC, during the reign of Malichus I (62-30 BC) and/or Obadas II (30-9 BC). Sometime during the late 1st or early 2nd century AD it was completely rebuilt and enlarged to its present form. Exhibiting a mixture of local Nabatean and Classical styles, it was lavishly decorated and included some unusual features such as capitals with carved elephant heads.

Excavation and restoration work is ongoing, but already the basic outline of this temple is clearly discernible. Though still fenced-in at the time of writing, you could still go inside and look around. Ascending the stairway from the colonnaded street (originally this would have been topped by a *propylaeum* or monumental entrance way), you find yourself in the **lower temenos** of the temple, parts of which are still paved with large hexagonal flagstones. On either side of the *temenos* were triple colonnades which ended in semi-circular *exedrae*. On the eastern (left-hand) side some of the columns of the triple colonnade have been re-erected, and the *exedra* partially reconstructed. Note the deep trench at the north end of this colonnade, revealing the depth of the foundations, and also part of the water storage and canalisation system which extends under the whole of the lower temenos.

Two stairways next to each of the *exedra* lead up to the forecourt of the **upper temenos**, from where a broad central stairway flanked by two narrower ones lead up to the portico of the 'temple' itself. Some of the huge columns of the portico have been partially re-erected, though perhaps more evocative are

Petra

those that still lie fallen in neat lines like dominoes, the victim presumably of the great earthquake of 363 AD.

It is the **'temple'** itself, standing in the centre of the upper temenos, which is the most unusual feature of the whole complex. Originally this was thought to follow the standard plan of a *cella*, or inner sanctuary, in which the 'holy of holies' (a statue of the temple god) would have been housed. However, the excavations carried out in 1998 revealed instead what appears to have been a small theatre (a *theatron* or *odeon*). Though badly damaged, five tiers of seating from the theatre's semi-circular *cavea* had survived, and the excavators believe that originally there may have been as many as 20 tiers, which would have accommodated somewhere between 550-630 people. Restoration and reconstruction of this unusual feature was in progress at the time of writing.

The presence of a theatre-like structure at the heart of what otherwise conforms exactly to the plan of a 'Great Temple' is intriguing. Martha Sharp Joukowsky, the archaeologist leading the excavations, does not believe that this was a temple which was later converted into a civic monument, on the grounds that such a transformation would have been seen as sacrilegious. Perhaps it was indeed a temple, though in this case it is unlike any previously discovered in the Middle East. Or maybe it served as a civic centre, perhaps representing the *bouleuterion*, where the city council (or *boule*) would meet. It may even have served a combined function, both as a temple and theatre, or as a council chamber and theatre. What is certain is that this monument confirms how much more there is still to be learnt about the cultural life of the Nabateans.

Monumental Gateway

The Monumental Gateway at the western end of the colonnaded street originally consisted of a triple-arch, although all that remains today are the four piers which once supported the arches. Excavations have revealed that the gateway was built in the 2nd century AD, after the colonnaded street had been completed. The paving of the street had to be dug up and was subsequently repaired and enlarged to form a small square. Approaching from the east, the piers are adorned with engaged half-columns set on half-pedestals, while on the west side are free-standing columns on pedestals in front of each pier. The gateway was also flanked by towers, but these are now completely in ruins. Originally it was believed that the gateway formed the western entrance to the town, but it has since been demonstrated that it was the entrance to a large *temenos* which preceded the Qasr al-Bint. The *temenos* would once have been partly surrounded by a colonnade, and along the south wall is a long double row of benches.

Qasr al-Bint Pharon

The Qasr al-Bint Pharon towers impressively at the far end of the open *temenos*, offset slightly to the left. Built to a huge scale with its basic structure still standing, it is possible to reconstruct in the imagination the four massive pillars at the top of the wide stairway which would have supported the entrance portico. Behind this is an enormous single doorway (still standing) to the inner temple. Inside, the dividing walls of a central altar-chamber (*adyton*) flanked by two side-chambers are still tied into the rear wall. In front of the entrance is the base of a large, square altar. The outer walls, particularly the east one which faces you as you approach from the monumental gateway, are well preserved, with two sections of crowning *entablature* still in place.

The name Qasr al-Bint Pharon means literally `Palace of the Pharaoh's Daughter', a reference to a local legend which relates how the princess who lived in the palace (the Pharaoh's daughter) vowed to marry the first man to successfully supply the palace with running water. According to the legend, eventually one man succeeded, with the help of `men, camels and God'. The story is slightly suspect in that the building was clearly a temple; according to one 4th century writer it was dedicated to Dusares (Dhu-Shara) and his virgin mother Al Uzza, a theory confirmed by Greek inscriptions and a fragment of an eye-idol discovered in the temple. On the other hand, such temples might also have served as royal palaces (a number of Nabatean rulers were after all deified). The temple was initially excavated and restored by the British School of Archaeology in Jerusalem, with the Jordanian Department of Antiquities continuing the work today. It dates from somewhere between 30 BC-40 AD.

Just beyond (west of) the Qasr al-Bint, and towering above it, is the mountain of Al Habees. At the northern edge a short stairway climbs up to a small **museum** housed in a tomb cut into the rock-face of the mountain. Inside is a small but interesting collection of pottery pieces, architectural fragments, sculptures and carved reliefs. Directly opposite the altar and entrance of the Qasr al-Bint there is a bridge giving access to the north side of the wadi, where the *Basin* restaurant is situated, and, within the same complex, a second, newer **museum**. This museum houses a beautiful and impressive collection of pottery, coins, terracotta figurines, bronze statuettes, jewellery, glassware, architectural fragments etc. There are excellent information panels giving detailed explanations of various aspects of the life and history of Petra. Also exhibited here are two interesting fragments of Nabatean mosaics dating from the 1st century AD which were recently discovered in the centre of Wadi Musa town.

Al Habees & its monuments

The mountain of **Al Habees** has two interesting monuments carved into the base of its eastern face. The most southerly of these is the so-called **Columbarium**, the Latin name given to a place where cremation urns are stored, usually in niches. The exterior of this simple rock-cut chamber, as well as the interior walls, are completely covered in small niches, giving rise to the name, although the niches appear to be far too small and impractically shaped to have ever held urns. Another theory is that it was used as a dovecote in Byzantine times. To the north of this is the **Unfinished Tomb** which is interesting for the insight it gives into the way in which the façades of Petra were carved, working from the top down.

Thus the upper half of this monument, including all the entablature and the capitals of the pillars, has been completed, while the lower half is bare rock except for a small doorway cut into it at ground level, probably at a much later date since its positioning interferes with one of the uncompleted columns. From the southern end of Al Habees, a new stairway cut into the rock leads up to the summit of the mountain. On top are the ruins of a **Crusader Fortress**. However it is the views which are most impressive, and useful as well, in that they help give an overview of the layout of the central city area.

The steep, rubble-strewn rise in the land to the south of the Qasr al-Bint has been described by Iain Browning as the `tip of an archaeological iceberg'. The slope is not a natural one, but rather the accumulated debris of centuries, which once excavated will no doubt reveal a great deal more about the central city area. A path leads from behind the Qasr al-Bint in a southeasterly direction to a lone standing column known as **Zibb Pharon** (the Pharaoh's Phallus). No convincing explanation as to its original function has been put forward as yet. An identical column lies fallen on the ground nearby, while to the east the ruins of a temple can be discerned. The columns do not appear however to have formed part of this temple complex.

Zibb Pharon & Az Zantur

Locally the column was clearly interpreted as a fertility symbol and, like so many of Petra's monuments, attributed to the Pharaohs. From the Zibb Pharon one path heads southwest, leading past Umm al-Biyara towards the

Snake Monument and Jebel Haroun beyond. A second path heads southeast towards the Wadi Farasa and the Jebel Madhbah High Place of Sacrifice. To the southeast of the Zibb Pharon, up on a small hillock, is an area of excavations known as **Az Zantur**. A sign by the excavations reads `Nabatean Chapel', although the site is in fact a mixture of Nabatean and Roman domestic housing. Only the lower courses of the walls remain and the site, which is still undergoing excavations, is of little interest to the non-specialist.

Temple of the Winged Lions
Crossing the wadi by the bridge directly opposite the Qasr al-Bint, if you turn right and then bear off to the right again up a slope, you reach the excavated remains of the **Temple of the Winged Lions** (also known as the Northern Temple or Temple of al-Uzza) up on a hillock. The site is fenced off since excavations are ongoing, and there is not that much for the untrained eye to see, although the intricately carved capitals decorated with floral patterns and winged lions (from which the temple gets its name) are impressive. First identified by Bachmann and others in 1921 as a gymnasium, detailed excavations carried out since 1974 by Dr Hammond of Utah University have revealed it to be an important temple. A road once crossed the wadi from the colonnaded street and led up to the temple, which consisted of a *temenos* surrounded by colonnades in the centre of which was a *cella*, also colonnaded (many of these have been re-erected).

The whole temple stood on crypt-like vaulted halls which acted as a podium. Around the edges of the temple were various dwellings and artisans' workshops. A statuette of Osiris dating from the 6th century BC was found on the site (probably stored there as a sacred relic), along with one of Isis in mourning, suggesting that the temple was dedicated to Osiris and Isis, who were identified locally with Dusares (Dhu-Shara) and Al Uzza. A fragment of inscription dated 26/27 AD (during the reign of Aretas IV) led some to fix this as the date of the temple's construction, though others date it to the late 1st century BC. Originally the temple was lavishly decorated with painted plaster, but after a fire in the early 2nd century AD partially destroyed it, it was clad in white and brown marble. It was finally completely destroyed by the earthquake of 363.

Petra Church
Continuing east from the Winged Lions Temple towards the Royal Tombs and then bearing off slightly to the left brings you to the rather unimaginatively named Petra Church. These remarkable remains were first discovered in 1990 by Dr Kenneth W Russell, and subsequent excavations here revealed a large triple-apsed basilica church measuring some 26 m by 15 m, with an atrium and baptistry. Impressive mosaics were found in both the side-aisles of the church, prompting the archaeologists to erect a protective structure over it. The site was only opened to the public in 1998.

The church is thought to date originally from the late 5th century AD. During the early 6th century AD it appears to have been enlarged, with most of the

Mosaic of the Personification of Spring (6th century AD), Petra Church

mosaics being dated stylistically to this period. Many of the architectural features appear to have been taken from ruined Nabatean and Roman buildings, and it is thought that the church may have been built over the ruins of an earlier Nabatean or Roman building. The discovery of thousands of glass *tesserae* scattered around the site has led archaeologists to believe that, as well as the floor mosaics, the upper parts of the walls, the semi-dome over

The Petra Papyri

In 1993 around 50 charred papyrus scrolls were discovered in a small room adjacent to the northeast corner of the Petra church. Although completely carbonized, the scrolls have been painstakingly unrolled and preserved at the American Centre of Oriental Research (ACOR) laboratory in Amman by an international team of experts. The scrolls, some of them up to 10 m in length, are of great importance in that they represent the largest collection of written material from antiquity ever found in Jordan. They date from late 5th to early 6th century AD and offer an invaluable insight into this period of Petra's history, which otherwise remains something of a blank. Those texts which have been translated so far consist of economic documents written in Greek. One is an inventory recording the property of a deceased man named Obodianus and relates the contracts and agreements which were made concerning loans, sales and inheritence of plots of land and houses. Another is the will of a man suffering from a terminal illness and relates the obligation of his heirs to care for his mother. Although they cannot be compared to the famous Dead Sea Scrolls in terms of their significance and state of preservation, the papyrus scrolls discovered at Petra promise to shed light on the social and economic life of Petra during this period and, hopefully, to give some insight into the fate of the Nabateans and their culture under early Byzantine rule.

the central apse and the arches over the capitals would also have been lavishly decorated with mosaics. The church appears to have suffered from a fire, followed later by an earthquake, perhaps that of 551 AD, after which it was abandoned. The discovery of such a large and lavishly decorated church here suggests that Petra continued to prosper well into the Byzantine era, and no doubt there are further monuments from this period awaiting discovery.

You enter first into the atrium, in the centre of which is a circular opening into a large water cistern. To the west of this (to your left as you enter), is the baptistry, one of the largest and best preserved in the Middle East. Inside is a font consisting of a cross-shaped basin sunk into a square platform. On the east side of the atrium are three entrances into the church itself. The mosaics paving the north and south side-aisles are beautifully preserved. The north aisle consists of three parallel rows of *roundels,* or medallions (84 in total), depicting various animals, birds and objects such as vases and water jars, as well as some human figures, all enclosed within a geometric border. The eastern end of the south aisle consists of six larger-sized *roundels* depicting animals enclosed within a border. The rest of the south aisle consists of three rows of geometric panels, the central one containing personifications of the four seasons, the ocean, earth and wisdom, while those flanking it on either side contain various birds, animals and fish. Traces of the original paving of the central nave can be seen, though most of it is a modern reconstruction.

Ridge Church

Continuing uphill from the Petra Church, up onto the ridge to the north, you arrive at the so-called 'Ridge Church'. Excavated between 1994-98 by ACOR, this church is much smaller and simpler than the Petra Church, perhaps reflecting the fact that it stood at the outer limits of the city centre. Only the foundations of the church remain, and there are no surviving mosaics. However, the panoramic views from up here are spectacular and well worth the climb. The Ridge Church dates from around the same period as the Petra Church, and appears to have been abandoned around the same time. A large cistern carved into the bedrock was discovered underneath the nave.

Petra

The Monastery (Ed Deir)

Alongside the Treasury, this is certainly amongst Petra's most impressive and best-preserved monuments. It takes around 45 minutes to one hour to get there, including side-trips, but the long steep climb involved is well worth the effort. The best time to arrive is in late afternoon when the sun falls directly on the Monastery façade, illuminating the rock to a rich golden yellow. Late afternoon is also when most of the climb is in shade, making the going that much easier in summer.

The path leads past the *Basin* restaurant on the right, soon giving way to rock-cut steps as it enters the Wadi ed-Deir. After a short distance there is a signpost indicating the **Lion Triclinium** down a narrow cleft to the left of the main path. Some scrambling over rocks is needed to reach this monument, so called because of the large, now severely weathered, lions carved into the rock on either side of the entrance. The entrance itself consists of an odd key-hole-shaped crack in the rock, a result of weathering on what was originally a separate doorway and window. Above this is a frieze with carved faces at either end and symbols in between, followed by a pediment.

Back on the main path, you pass first the entrance to Wadi Kharareeb on the right, before coming to a signposted path which branches off to the right up to **Qattar ed-Deir**. This is a strenuous 20-30 minute detour which can reasonably be skipped. The path leads you to a ledge sheltered by the overhanging cliff-face where there is a plain room and a number of niches and water tanks cut into the rock. The remains are not particularly impressive and the best thing about this detour are the spectacular natural formations and patterns to be seen in the sheer walls of the narrow gorge.

The main path continues to climb steeply through more spectacular rock formations and, shortly before reaching the summit, passes a steep-sided pinnacle on the left with a number of caves carved into the rock. Dubbed the **Hermitage**, there are various crosses carved into the walls of the cells, indicating that they were occupied during the Byzantine era, although nothing is known about their origin or precise function.

A short way further on is the **Monastery**, or **Ed Deir**. The climb may have seemed interminable and you might be thoroughly exhausted, but the spectacle which greets you is more than worth the time and effort spent slogging your way up there. This is the largest of Petra's monuments, towering to a height of over 40 m and measuring nearly 47 m in width. The doorway alone measures 8 m in height, dwarfing any figure framed within it into insignificance. It is generally agreed that this monument was a temple, although some experts have suggested that it was an unfinished royal tomb, pointing out

The Monastery
(Ed Deir)

that the niches do not appear to have held any statues. Its present name is derived from the Byzantine-era crosses found carved on the walls of the inner chamber. Given its enormous size, it must have played an important role in the religious life of the Nabateans. The temple façade has been carved deeply into a shoulder of the mountain to give a large courtyard area in front, presumably to accommodate a large congregation, and it seems likely that the climb up to it represented an important aspect of the rituals and ceremonies associated with the temple.

Stylistically, the Monastery mirrors closely the Khazneh and the Corinthian Tomb, differing only in that it has none of the detailed decoration found on the latter two. This simplicity of style serves to emphasize the grandeur and bold-ness of its scale. It is generally dated to around the middle of the 1st century AD, perhaps between 40-70 AD, making it in effect a culmination of the Helle-nistic styles first developed in the Khazneh and Corinthian Tomb. The inside consists of a large single chamber with a large niche in the rear wall. Steps lead up to the niche on either side, and above it is a segmented arch.

Opposite the Monastery there is a tea and cold drinks stall offering refresh-ments and shade from which to appreciate its grandeur. You can climb up onto the rock hillock behind for a better vantage point. It is also possible to climb up to the top of the monument itself, something obviously only for those with a head for heights, although the route up there is not in fact difficult. A set of rock-cut steps ascends from the rocky outcrop to the left of the façade as you face it, leading to an altar area half way up before continuing to a point where you can scramble round onto the dome of the urn. Continuing west past the Monastery brings you to a wide ledge with dramatic views out across the Wadi Arabah; the small white sanctuary of Nabi Haroun is also visible from here. A little further on there is a small cluster of caves, one of which is used by the *Basin* restuarant to serve meals to organized tours.

Turkmaniyeh Tomb

Across the bridge opposite the Qasr al-Bint, a wide, bare and exposed wadi ascends gently in a northeasterly direction with a good jeep track running along it. This is known variously as Wadi al-Turkmaniyeh or Wadi Abu Alleiqa, and leads up to the modern Bedouin village of Bdoul, on the road to Beida and El Barid. In the cliffs to the left as you ascend the wadi, there are various façades carved into the rock. After approximately 1 km (around 15 minutes walk), there is a temple façade on the left, close to the jeep track, known as the Turkmaniyeh Tomb. The lower half of this façade has been completely eroded away, most probably by flash floods. However, preserved between the two pilasters of the upper half is the longest Nabatean inscription to be found at Petra. The inscrip-tion is of great value in that it gives details of the additional features that origi-nally complemented the tomb façades. In this case there was a courtyard in front of the tomb, a colonnaded portico, gardens, a triclinium and water cisterns. All of these were presumably washed away by flash floods over the centuries, but it is worth remembering that most of the façades at Petra probably originally formed just one part of a far more extensive complex. The tomb is currently undergoing restoration as part of the Petra Stone Preservation Project.

Umm al-Biyara

The sheer rocky massif of Umm al-Biyara towers to a height of 1,178 m and dominates the whole Petra basin. Along the base of the cliffs of its eastern face there are numerous tomb façades carved into the rock displaying a wide vari-ety of styles. These can be reached by heading southwest from the Zibb Pharon (arriving at the Zibb Pharon from the Qasr al-Bint, take the right-hand fork in the path). The route to the summit of Umm al-Biyara is not obvious, as well as being difficult in places, and a guide is strongly recommended. If you enjoy strenuous climbs, it is well-worth the effort for the magnificent views from the top. The climb is best undertaken later in the day when the route is largely in shade. Allow at least 3-4 hours for the return trip and leave plenty of time to descend before darkness falls. After an initial scramble up a loose scree-slope, you join the original processional route, an unusually grandiose affair consisting of a smooth ramp chiselled deep into the rock to give smooth-sided vertical walls on either side. The ramp leads to a landing before doubling back to continue the ascent. Higher up it gives way to rock-cut stairs with precipitous drops on one side. The steps are now very badly worn and need to be negotiated with extreme care.

The large summit area is basically flat-topped, rising gently to its highest point in the northwest. Roughly in the centre are the excavated remains of an **Edomite settlement**. These excavations were carried out by the British archaeologist Crystal Bennett in the 1960s, an expedition of considerable logistical complexity which involved a team of archaeologists camping on the summit while all supplies were delivered by helicopter. The settlement has only been partially excavated, but has been dated with a fair degree of certainty to the 6-7th centuries BC. There are a total of eight large bell-shaped cisterns cut deep into the rock in a cluster near the northeast edge of the summit, and it is from these that the mountain gets its name (literally `Mother of Cisterns'). The cisterns are believed to be Edomite, suggesting that the Edomites developed rock-cutting techniques themselves, and perhaps passed them onto the Nabateans. Along the eastern edge of the summit, overlooking the Wadi Thugra and the central city ruins, are various unexcavated Nabatean remains, including at one point a set of steps which leads down to an artificial terrace at the very edge of the cliffs. The statue of a deity was found here and the spot was perhaps once the site of a temple.

Umm al-Biyara is associated in popular tradition with the biblical Sela (literally `rock'), from which the king of Judah, Amaziah, threw 10,000 Edomites to their death in revenge for raids they had carried out in southern Palestine (2 Kings 14: 7 and 2 Chronicles 25: 11-12). However the rule of Amaziah can be dated to 796-781 BC, at least 100 years before the Edomite settlement was established.

Wadi es-Siyagh

If you feel in danger of overdosing on monuments or wish to get away from the crowds, the Wadi es-Siyagh makes for a pleasant, undemanding walk and excellent picnic area, enjoyable mostly for the stunning natural beauty of the surrounding mountains and for the welcome contrast of lush green vegetation after so much bare rock. However, the tranquility of this wadi is sometimes shattered by the noise of a generator, one of several in the area which supply the *Basin* restaurant and Department of Antiquities offices with electricity. At the bridge leading from the Qasr al-Bint across to the *Basin* restaurant, follow the bed of the wadi around the base of Al Habees mountain and then bear right at the junction with the Wadi Kharroub (or Wadi Kharrubat Ibn Jurayma) to continue up the Wadi es-Siyagh. You come first to an ancient quarry, at the point where the wadi swings round to the left. Further on the wadi becomes increasingly green and wooded, being watered by the spring which emerges here, giving way eventually to a pleasant stream complete with rock-pools and even waterfalls when there are sufficient rains. This was one of Petra's main water sources and irrigation channels would once have carried the water to the central city area.

On the way back, you have the option of bearing right after the quarry instead of left. This takes you along the bed of the Wadi Kharroub and brings you out at a point to the south of the Qasr al-Bint, along the route to the Snake Monument.

Snake Monument

This is a longish walk, taking some 35-45 minutes to reach from the Qasr al-Bint. It is not however dangerous or particularly difficult to follow, despite the warning posted at the Zibb Pharon. Neither is it anything like as far as the local camel-touting Bedouins along the way insistently claim. Follow the path southeast from the Qasr al-Bint to the Zibb Pharon. Here the path forks; bear right to head southwest in the direction of Umm al-Biyara, descending to the Wadi Kharroub just before it forks. Cross the wadi and continue southwest along a good track which follows the right bank of the right fork. After a while the track crosses to the left bank and becomes just a path, climbing gently and steadily, before coming eventually to a steep rise of solid sandstone rock. To the right is a cluster of rock-cut chambers with a large Djinn Block above, while to the left is another large Djinn Block with a sign some way below it reading `Snake Monument'. The Snake Monument is in fact the square-based structure higher up and to the left, with what looks for all the world like a melting blob of ice-cream on top, rather than a snake. Over the crest of the rocky rise is an open expanse of higher ground with a small orchard and the seasonal *Al Nabat* tea/cold drinks stall opposite. If you continue a little further on, as you round the shoulder of cliffs to your right, the tiny white tomb of Nabi Haroun comes into view on the summit of Jebel Haroun.

Shrine of Nabi Haroun (Shrine of the Prophet Aaron)

The shrine of Nabi Haroun (the Prophet Aaron) is situated on the summit of Jebel Haroun, at 1,396 m the highest mountain in the area. By foot this is a long and strenuous full-day's excursion, although you can go by camel or donkey as far as the base of Jebel Haroun. A guide is strongly recommended since the final ascent is by no means clear. The route is the same as for the Snake Monument, though from the point where the shrine comes into view, it's still a deceptively long way off. The shrine is kept locked, and the key held by the Bedouins living close to the foot of the mountain. Bear in mind that this is a sacred place of pilgrimage for Jews, Christians and Muslims and as such casual tourists wandering up there simply for the view are not particularly welcome. Unless the shrine is of special significance to you, it's far from noteworthy, and while the views are spectacular, there are plenty of equally impressive ones which are much nearer and more easily accessible.

The shrine is revered as the place where the prophet Aaron is buried, with Jebel Haroun being identified with biblical Mount Hor. According to the Old Testament story:

"*At Mout Hor, near the border of Edom, the Lord said to Moses and Aaron, `Aaron will be gathered to his people. He will not enter the land I give to the Israelites, because both of you rebelled against my command at the waters of Meribah. Call Aaron and his son Eleazar and take them up Mount Hor. Remove Aaron's garments and put them on his son Eleazar, for Aaron will be gathered to his people; he will die there.' Moses did as the Lord commanded: they went up Mount Hor in the sight of the whole community. Moses removed Aaron's garments and put them on his son Eleazar. And Aaron died there on top of the mountain. Then Moses and Eleazar came down from the mountain, and when the whole community learned that Aaron had died, the entire house of Israel mourned him for thirty days.*" (Numbers 20: 23-29).

According to Muslim belief, this is also where Mohammed was first identified by Bahira, the guardian of the tomb, as a future Prophet. Mohammad, then aged 10, was en route to Damascus with his uncle Abu Talib when they climbed Jebel Haroun to make an offering. They were met by an excited monk who had seen Mohammed in a vision and been told that he would act as God's messenger and change the course of history. The monk who had the vision would have been one of the Greek Orthodox monks who cared for the shrine until the 13th century. At that time it was restored by the Mameluke Sultan Qalaun and then in 1459 the present shrine was built, as indicated by the inscription above the entrance.

Sabrah

This is at the least a half-day excursion, involving a good two-hour walk to get there from the central city ruins. If you feel like getting away from the crowds this is an excellent place to go. Sabrah was effectively a suburb of Petra, rather like Al Barid (see below). As such it contains many of the elements typical of Petra, including temple façades and a small theatre, but on a smaller scale. A distinctive feature are the plaster-coated columns which were painted a deep red, most probably a fashion which arrived from Rome.

Despite the impressive remains found here, it is far enough away from the main centre to deter the majority of tourists and so remains blissfully tranquil and atmospheric. A guide is recommended since the route is not always very clear, although there is no difficult scrambling or climbing involved. Essentially the route runs parallel to that leading to the Snake Monument, but follows the left-hand edge of the low hilly plain as you head southwest. From the Qasr al-Bint, walk up to the Zibb Pharon and then bear left at the fork. This takes you towards Zibb Attuf and one route up to the High Place of Sacrifice. Instead of ascending, bear off to the right, keeping the mountain to your left. There are numerous shepherds' paths traversing the low, hilly terrain making it easy to wander off-course, but if you can keep your general sense of direction you should not go too far wrong. It is also possible to return via the Snake Monument, although for this you really do need a guide.

Al Madras

On your way into Petra, just before you cross the dam and enter the Siq proper, there is a detour which can be made up to Al Madras. This was one of Petra's suburbs, and is particularly interesting for the inscription which was found in the area. The inscription confirms that the suburb was known to the Nabateans as Madras, making this the only part of Petra to bear its original name, and also identifies Dusares as the god of the area.

As the path approaching the dam swings round to the right, bear off to the left across the dry bed of the wadi and pick up a path through the trees on the other side. The path soon disappears onto solid sandstone rock, at which point you must look out for the small stone cairns which indicate the route. First you must cross a small gulley before passing through a landscape of bizarre dome-capped rock formations. At times a path worn into the rock, or else heavily weathered rock-cut steps, are vaguely disernable. Finally, a short steep climb brings you to an area of rock-cut chambers, stairs, niches, cisterns and water channels. If you explore further afield you will find more of these, as well as a small High Place of Sacrifice. The most impressive thing though is surely the view back across a forest of weathered sandstone domes (reminiscent of Cappadocia in Turkey).

Jebel Madhbah High Place of Sacrifice

The Nabateans had a fondness for high, exposed rock summits on which they would carry out ritual sacrifices. There are numerous examples of these ` High Places' all around Petra. The largest and most famous of these is on the summit of Jebel Madhbah. After passing the Treasury and before arriving at the Theatre, a signpost indicates the start of the rock-cut staircase which leads up there. At least 1½-2 hours are needed to go and come back by the same route, or longer if you wish to descend via a number of interesting monuments on the other side of the mountain (strongly recommended).

The ascent to the High Place takes around 30 minutes, following clearly marked (and in places recently restored) rock-cut stairs. Near the summit are various seasonal souvenir and tea/cold drinks stalls, followed soon after by two stone **Obelisks** up on a small plateau to your left, perhaps meant to mark the approach to the High Place. These have been created by chiselling away all of the surrounding summit, which must have been a monumental task. It has been suggested that they represent the two main Nabatean gods, Dushara (Dusares) and Al Uzza. If you climb up the slope opposite the obelisks (ie to your right when they first come into view), you pass the heavily ruined remains of a **Fortress**. This is generally believed to be of Crusader origin, although some suggest it might be Byzantine, Roman or even Nabatean in origin (according to the latter theory, it was built from the stone which was chiselled away to create the obelisks). Beyond the fortress ruins, rock-cut steps take you out eventually onto the flat, exposed summit of Jebel Madhbah, and the High Place itself. From here there are spectacular views in all directions, including southwest to Jebel Haroun, west to Umm al-Biyara and northeast to Jebel al-Khubtha.

The **High Place** consists of a large rectangular sunken courtyard with a small raised platform within it and, just to the west, a large rectangular altar platform. Three steps lead up to the altar platform, which has a square hole cut into it, perhaps to hold a representation of a deity. Just to the left (south) of the main altar platform there is a second, circular platform with a circular basin carved into it. There is a small drain in the basin, and a channel leading from it; this was perhaps used for ritual washing. The large sunken courtyard was most probably used as a congregational area for those witnessing the ritual sacrifices which were taking place. The small raised platform within it was perhaps used in the same way as the *shewbread* table on which bloodless offerings were laid in Israelite temples. The sunken courtyard is also equipped with drainage holes, although these most likely served simply to drain away rainwater.

The preceding explanation of the function of the different components of the High Place represents the current general consensus amongst experts. However the details of the ritual sacrifices, and of the circumstances in which they took place, remain entirely a matter of conjecture. The popularly-held belief is that human and animal sacrifices were made on a regular basis. The archaeologist A Starcky disputed this, suggesting that the Nabateans did not make human sacrifices at all, sticking entirely to animal sacrifices. However a Nabatean inscription found at Hegra relates how "*Abd Wadd, priest of Wadd, and his son Salim, and Zayd Wadd, have consecrated the young man Salim to be immolated to Dhu Gabat*". In addition, it is known that around this time human sacrifices used to be made on a regular basis to Al Uzza, involving the cutting of a boy's throat, as recounted by the pagan philosopher Porphyrius. However horrifying all this may appear to us today, it has to be remembered that the concept of sacrifice at that time had entirely positive connotations, signifying an affirmation of life and a renewal of the bonds between man and god.

Petra

The altar platform and sunken courtyard are striking for their excellent state of preservation, the lines and angles still clear and crisp, a fact all the more remarkable when you consider their exposed location. Based on the quality of the workmanship, it is generally assumed that these features were carved out in Nabatean times, although it seems likely that the area was used for ritual sacrifice by the Edomites also, and perhaps much earlier too. You can continue north along the ridge from the High Place and, if you scramble far enough, it is possible to get good views down onto the whole area of the central city ruins.

Returning to the gully that runs between the two obelisks to the south and the fortress ruins and High Place to the north, if you keep the obelisks to your left, you can pick up the path which leads down the western face of the mountain via the Wadi Farasa. At first the route is a little unclear, although small stone cairns mark the way and soon there is a clear path as well as rock-cut stairs in places. Following this route, you pass first the **Lion Fountain** on your left, consisting of a heavily weathered but clearly discernible lion carved into the rock. There are traces of a water channel above and it seems likely that a pipe fed water out of the lion's mouth to provide pilgrims with a drinking fountain. Immediately after this there is a section of steep steps, with traces of a water channel visible in the rock to your left.

You come next to the **Garden Triclinium** with a large **Cistern** next to it. The Triclinium opens onto a platform of rock, while the area in front of this was seen to resemble a garden plot, giving rise to the name. According to the sign it is a tomb, but the monument almost certainly served as a triclinium (a banqueting hall in honour of the dead). The design is simple, consisting of four columns, two of them free-standing, supporting a lintel. This forms a portico (the area in which the banquets were held), beyond which there is a small shrine. The cistern is lined and would have been used to store water which was channelled from the Braq springs 4 km to the south, right into the centre of Petra.

A little further along, on the left, is the **Roman Soldier Tomb**, and opposite a **Triclinium**. These two features once formed part of a single complex, with a central courtyard surrounded by a colonnaded portico joining the two. The Roman Soldier Tomb consists of four tall pilasters with a low-pitched pediment above. The central doorway has its own small pilasters (largely eroded away) supporting an entablature and pediment. In the upper level, between the four pilasters, are three niches each holding heavily weathered statues. It is from these statues that the tomb gets its name, with the central one, although headless, clearly being clad in Roman armour. Inside there are two large chambers, with the main one having a series of arched recesses in the walls, presumably to accommodate sarcophogi.

Although the Triclinium is distinctly unimpressive from the outside, the interior is particularly interesting since it is the only one in Petra with elaborately carved decoration. The side and rear walls have beautifully fluted half-columns carved into them, with niches in between, while the sandstone rock reveals beautiful swirling patterns and colours in its grain. Looking at the faces of the pillars which support the entrance from the inside you can get an idea of the original, crisply chiselled workmanship. Given the scale and splendour of the original complex, it was clearly designed for a figure of great standing. It has been suggested that the complex dates originally from some time in the 1st century AD, implying that the carved statues were added after the Roman annexation of Petra in 106 AD.

Shortly after, on the right, is the **Renaissance Tomb**, so called for its unique, elegantly executed façade. Two tall pilasters support a low-pitched pediment topped by an urn, very much in traditional Nabatean style, but the central doorway is framed by pilasters supporting a beautifully proportioned arch, a feature unique to this tomb, although quite closely reflected in the façade of the Sextius Florentinius Tomb.

Finally, the path takes you past the **Broken Pediment Tomb**. This tomb is situated up on a ledge facing north and is easily missed as you must turn and look back the way you came in order to see it. The façade is compact and simple, but interesting in that the device of a broken pediment is used in isolation, without a central *tholos* rising between the two ends of the pediment, as found in the Treasury and Monastery, and without the mass of other architectural detail which at times threaten to clutter up the classical Nabatean façades. In addition, this façade has good examples of the swirling patterns and colours typical of Petra's sandstone rock.

Continuing on, the wadi opens out and the path forks; bear right to keep following the line of the cliffs in a northerly direction. There are numerous small tomb façades carved into the cliff-side to your right, the best-preserved ones being higher up. Many of these display the distinctive Nabatean-style crow-step attic storey. If you keep following the line of the cliffs you end up back near the theatre. If you follow the track which branches off to the left you arrive in the vicinity of the Qasr al-Bint. Following the latter route takes you up onto the crest of a hillock and past a set of excavated ruins on the right just below the track, signposted `Nabatean Chapel' but better known as the Az Zantur site. From here you can cut straight across to the solitary standing column of Zibb Pharon, or else follow the wide loop of the track, before continuing down to the Qasr al-Bint and central city ruins area.

Essentials

Sleeping

The growth in the number of hotels in Wadi Musa has been dramatic over the last 5 years or so; there are now numerous establishments covering the full range from cheap budget places through to 5-star international hotels. There is currently a great deal of competition between them, and although it does get extremely busy during peak times (notably in Apr), making it necessary to book in advance, for the rest of the year supply far outstrips demand. The result is that there is a huge variation in prices according to the season and how busy it is. Off-season when it is quiet some excellent deals can be negotiated, with some hotels advertising discounts of up to 25% while others can easily be bargained down even further.

Phone code: 03
Note that all hotels have been categorized here according to their peak season rates

The majority include breakfast in the room price, and many also offer half board deals (breakfast and dinner); check exactly what is included. Check also whether tax and service (up to 23%) are included. Almost all the hotels in Petra show videos of *Indiana Jones and the Last Crusade*, which features the Treasury in its closing scenes, and also *Lawrence of Arabia*, which features the landscapes of nearby Wadi Rum. The hotels listed below have been grouped according to their location. Those down by the entrance gate have the obvious advantage of being within easy walking distance (maximum 5 mins) of the entrance to Petra. Those in Wadi Musa town, and on the road between Musa Spring and Wadi Musa, are less convenient in that you have to drive down to the entrance gate. On the other hand, most of these hotels offer free transportation to and from the entrance gate, though the lift down is sometimes more reliable than the lift back. The hotels along the road to Taybet village are all luxury affairs whose star attraction is the stunning views.

L *Mövenpick*, T2157111, F2157112, hotel.petra@moevenpick.ch Suitably luxurious rooms with all the mod cons. Full conference and banqueting facilities. *Al Iwan* and *Al*

Down by the entrance gate

Saraya restaurants, *Al Maqa'ad* bar, roof garden and library. Swimming pool, steam room, gym. Shopping arcade, *Hertz* car hire, *Cairo-Amman* bank, travel agents. This was the first *Mövenpick* hotel to open in Jordan, and is arguably Petra's most luxurious. Lavishly furnished and with an architecturally imposing central courtyard. Excellent service all round. **L Petra Forum** (part of *Inter-Continental* chain), T2156266, F2156977, petra@interconti.com Low-rise complex with mixture of chalet-style and standard rooms, nearly all with balcony and excellent views of Petra mountains. All rooms recently renovated to a high standard and tastefully furnished in traditional style with all the mod cons. Restaurants, bars, conference/banqueting facilities, swimming pool, tennis court, horse riding, children's playground. Also a tiny 'museum' featuring artefacts from ACOR's excavations of the Petra Church and Great Temple complex. Guests here can make use of the facilities at the nearby *Petra Forum Guesthouse*, and have meals at the *Basin* restaurant in Petra itself added to their hotel bill. **Camper-vans** can stay in the car park here and use toilet/shower facilities.

AL Petra Forum Gesthouse, T2156266, F2156977, petra@interconti.com Sister hotel of the *Petra Forum*, and also owned by the *Inter-Continental* chain. Situated right by the entrance to the site, this was the first hotel in Petra. Comfortable rooms with a/c, TV/dish, IDD, minibar and attached bath. Restaurant, *Cave* bar (see under Bars, below). Fantastic location and access to all the facilities at the *Petra Forum* hotel next door make this an excellent value choice.

A Edom, T2156995, F2156994, edom@go.com.jo Reasonably comfortable rooms with a/c, TV/dish, IDD, minibar, attached bath and balcony. Restaurant, bars, conference room. A large, modern monstrosity of a hotel. **A Petra Palace**, T2156723, F2156724, ppwnwm@go.com.jo Pleasant, comfortable rooms with a/c, TV/dish, phone, fridge and attached bath (best rooms are those on 1st floor with French windows opening onto a courtyard with a small swimming pool; also good are the rooms

Wadi Musa

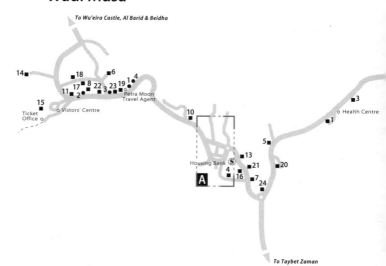

To Wu'eira Castle, Al Barid & Beidha

Petra Moon
Travel Agent

Ticket Office

Vistors' Centre

Housing Bank $

A

To Taybet Zaman

N

Related map
A Wadi Musa centre,
page 280

0 metres 200
0 yards 200

■ **Sleeping**	6 Candles	12 Musa Spring	17 Petra Inn
1 Acropolis	7 Cleopatra	13 Peace way	18 Petra Moon
2 Al Anbat I	8 Edom	14 Petra Forum	19 Petra Palace
3 Al Hidab	9 King's Way Inn	15 Petra Forum	20 Sela
4 Amra Palace	10 Moon Valley	Guesthouse	21 Shara Mountain
5 Araba	11 Mövenpick	16 Petra Gate	22 Silk Road

on 4th floor sharing large sun terrace). Large restaurant, nicely furnished bar. Well-run hotel, good value. **A** *Silk Road*, T2157222, F2157244. Reasonably comfortable rooms with a/c, TV/dish, phone and attached bath. OK but a bit overpriced. Restaurant. The complex below the hotel includes a shopping arcade, the *Rum Studio & Lab* (for Kodak film and machine processing), *International Traders* (agents for *American Express*), *Petra Turkish Bath* (see under Sports) and the *Al Mehbash* restaurant.

B *Candles*, T2157311, F2156954. Reasonably comfortable rooms with a/c, TV/dish, phone, minibar, attached bath and balcony. Restaurant, summer terraces (excellent views). Deals mostly with groups, but worth trying if they are quiet. **B** *Petra Moon*, T/F2156220. Rooms with heater, TV/dish, phone and attached bath. Restaurant. Popular with groups. Rather tacky decor, but good location.

D-E *Sunset*, T2156579, F2156950. Choice of rooms with TV, heater, phone and attached bath, or slightly cheaper without TV, or **E** category with shared bathroom. Also **F** category dorm beds (JD4 per bed) out of season. Rather spartan and unimaginative place, but friendly, reasonably clean and good value (this is the cheapest place down by the site entrance). *Sunrise* restaurant downstairs.

B *Amra Palace*, T2157070, F2157071, amrapalace@index.com.jo Comfortable though somewhat characterless rooms with a/c, heater, TV/dish, phone and attached bath. Restaurant, off-road parking and small garden out front. **B-C** *Al Anbat II*, T2157200, F2156888, alanbath@joinnet.com.jo Clean, pleasant rooms on 4 floors (some with great views) with fan, heater, phone, TV/dish and attached bath. Restaurant on top floor. Very flexible on prices.

Wadi Musa town

C *El Rashid*, T2156800, F2156801, rashid@joinnet.com.jo Comfortable though rather small rooms with heater, TV/dish, phone and attached bath. Also larger 'deluxe' rooms. *Al Hayek* restaurant. Modern hotel, clean but characterless. **C** *Elgee*, T2156701, F2157002. Clean, comfortable rooms (some with good views) with small fan, heater, TV, phone and attached bath. Restaurant, small bar. A bit characterless.

C *Peace Way*, T/F2156963, peaceway@index.com.jo Small but comfortable rooms with fan, heater, TV/dish, phone and attached bath. Arabic 'tent' restaurant and terrace upstairs. **C** *Rose City*, T2156440, F2156448. Clean but mediocre rooms with heater, TV, phone, fridge and attached bath. Restaurant. **C-D** *Treasury*, T2157274. Simple but clean rooms with heater and attached bath. Restaurant with nice views. Quiet residential location. Well run. Friendly management. **C-D** *Moon Valley*, T2156824, F 2157131. Nicely furnished, pleasant rooms (some with good views) with heater, phone and attached bath. Rooftop restaurant. Friendly management.

D *Shara Mountain*, T/F2157294. Small but clean rooms with heater and attached bath. Restaurant with pool table.

E *Cleopatra*, T/F2157090. Small but pleasant rooms with heater and attached bath. Sleep on roof for JD2. Meals served. Friendly, helpful staff.

Petra

To King's Highway (North)

Ain Musa (Moses Spring)

To Wadi Rum & Aqaba

2

12

9

F *Orient Gate*, T/F2157020. Choice of doubles with attached or shared bath (JD10/6). Also dormitory rooms with attached or shared bath (JD3.5/2 per bed), or sleep on the roof (JD2). Clean, decent sized rooms with heater and fan. Restaurant upstairs. Friendly place, working hard on its backpacker reputation and gaining in popularity. **F** *Petra Gate*, T/F2156908, petra-gate-hotel@hotmail.com Choice of double rooms with attached or shared bath (JD8/6). Also dormitory (bunk beds, a bit cramped but good value at JD2 per bed). Basic but clean. Free use of kitchen. Cosy, nicely furnished reception. Friendly manager. Good budget option.

Musa Spring & the road down to Wadi Musa town

L *Hayat Zaman* (under construction), situated down in the wadi to the north of the road between Musa Spring and Wadi Musa town. 5-star resort complex scheduled to open in 2001. **AL** *Kings' Way Inn*, T2156799, F2156796, resrv@kingsway-petra.com Comfortable, nicely furnished rooms with a/c, TV/dish, IDD and attached bath. Restaurant, bar, swimming pool. New lobby and more rooms under construction at the time of writing. Modern, suitably plush hotel, but a long way from the site.

B *Sela*, T2157170, F2157173. Comfortable rooms with a/c, TV/dish, IDD, minibar and attached bath. Restaurants and bar. Very plush and fancy modern hotel. Good value. **C** *Al Anbat I*, T2156265, F2157965. Comfortable rooms (some with great views) with heater, TV/dish, phone, fridge and attached bath. Also comfortable **F** category dormitory rooms (3-6 bed) with heater and attached bath, excellent value at JD4 per bed, or sleep on a mattress in the 'greenhouse' (a tin-roofed conservatory) for JD2. Restaurant. New wing of chalet rooms complete with 'Turkish bath' complex under construction. Private off-road parking area, popular with overland groups. **C** *Al Hidab*, T2156763, F2157496. Small but comfortable rooms with a/c, heater, TV, phone and attached bath. Restaurant and bar upstairs. Grand lobby, but otherwise rather characterless. **C** *Araba*, T/F2156107. Simple but clean rooms with heater and attached bath. Best rooms are at the rear, with balconies and excellent views (good value), others are nothing special. Restaurant.

D-E *Valley Stars*, T2156095, F2156914. Clean, simple rooms with small a/c units in summer, heater and attached bath. Sleep on roof for JD2. Meals served. A bit rundown, but very friendly and helpful manager. **E-F** *Musa Spring*, T2156310, F2156910. Doubles with heater, TV and attached or shared bath (JD14/8). Best rooms at the front, with proper windows; others are a bit cell-like. Also dormitory rooms with attached or shared bath (JD5.500/4), or sleep on the roof for JD2. Restaurant. One of the longest-established hotels in Petra. Very friendly and helpful manager. Popular with backpackers. **F** *Acropolis*, T2157352, F2157052. Fairly basic but reasonably clean doubles with phone, heater and attached or shared bath (JD10/8). Also dormitory rooms with attached bath (JD3 per bed) or sleep on the roof for JD2. Free use of kitchen.

Taybet road **L** *Grand View*, 4 km from Wadi Musa, T2156871, F2156984 (reservations in Amman via *Al Tawfiq* hotels, T06-4652415, F06-4652417,

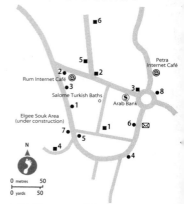

Wadi Musa centre

■ Sleeping	● Eating
1 Al Anbat II	1 Al Janoob
2 Elgee	2 Al Shami
3 El Rashid	3 Al Wardeh al-Shamieh
4 Orient Gate	4 Cleopatra
5 Rose City	5 Petra Nights
6 Treasury	6 Petra Pearl
	7 Treasury
	8 Wadi Petra Restaurant & Bar

nazzalco@nets.com.jo). Facilities include restaurant, bar, swimming pool, conference hall, shopping and travel agent. A truly palatial hotel with stunning views out over Petra mountains (especially at sunset). **L** *Petra Plaza*, 4 km from Wadi Musa, next door to the *Grand View*, T/F2156407 (reservations in Amman T06-4639197, F06-4642401). Facilities include restaurant, bar, swimming pool, fitness centre, banquet/conference hall and nightclub. Slightly less ostentatiously palatial than the *Grand View*, but every bit as luxurious and benefiting from the same stunning views. **L** *Petra Panorama*, 6 km from Wadi Musa, T2157390, F2157389, panorama@index.com.jo (reservations in Ammam T06-568704, F06-5684706). Opened in 1999. Some rooms with large terraces, all with views. Facilities include restaurant, bar, swimming pool and shops. **L** *Nabatean Castle*, 6 km from Wadi Musa, next door to *Petra Panorama*, T2157201, F2157209 (reservations in Amman T06-4610723, F06-4610724). Only some rooms with views. Facilities include restaurants, bars, indoor swimming pool, and tennis courts. Very grand lobby, but rather gloomy, and overall not as stylish/swish as the others. **L** *Taybet Zaman*, 10 km from Wadi Musa, below modern village of Taybet, T2150111, F2150101. A new development consisting of a traditional village of Ottoman-period houses lovingly restored and equipped with all the mod cons to give a luxury resort bursting with character; a welcome change from the usual luxury blandness. Facilities include restaurants, bars, swimming pool, Turkish bath, conference/banquet facilities, museum, traditional `souk' and bakery. Regular evening events and entertainments. Very elegantly and convincingly done, with stunning views out over Petra mountains. Worth a visit even if just to look (and for the drive), but very pricey (right at the top of the **L** category price range).

Eating

Practically all of Petra's numerous hotels have restaurants attached, or are at least able to provide meals. The inclusive breakfasts offered by many of the medium to cheaper range hotels are generally poor value and not very inspiring, consisting of bread, cheese, jam, butter and an egg. The buffet dinners in the cheaper hotels likewise tend to be rather basic, though in the mid-range hotels they can be reasonably good value.

The *Al Saraya* restaurant in the *Mövenpick* hotel offers buffet lunches and dinners for JD15.500 per head inclusive; not exactly cheap, but the quality is excellent and if you feel like indulging yourself this is the place to come. The food at the *Petra Forum* hotel also has an excellent reputation; the evening buffet here costs JD9 per head. Buffet lunches and dinners at the *Taybet Zaman* resort cost around JD12.500 per head.

In the parade of shops just up from the *Mövenpick* hotel, there is a branch of **Pizza Hut**, with the usual selection of pizzas etc. Next door, **Papazzi** offers a selection of pasta and pizza dishes for JD2.500-8.500, as well as Arabic dishes for JD3.500-4 each. Next door again is the **Red Cave**, with cave-style decor, which serves Arabic food for around JD7 per head and sometimes lays on buffet meals (JD6/4 for full/vegetarian). A little further up, below the *Silk Road* hotel, *Al Mehbash*, serves mainly Arabic food in comfortable surroundings for around JD10 per head. A little further up again is the **Rose City** restaurant, which does good buffet meals for around JD3. Next door, the **Sunrise** restaurant (below the *Sunset* hotel) serves buffet evening meals (Arabic cuisine) for JD3-6 depending on the season (low season, prices go down in an attempt to lure people in), or à la carte for around JD5 per head. Continuing up the hill, just past the *Petra Moon* travel agents, the **Middle East** is a clean, pleasant place serving the usual range of Arabic food at somewhat inflated prices (around JD7-10 per head). Next door is the **Tafili**, which does good Arabic food for around JD5 per head.

There are several restaurants **in Wadi Musa town** itself, most of them at the budget end of the range. However, Petra being something of a tourist trap, there are practically no genuinely budget places. Entering Wadi Musa and following the one-way system as it loops round to the south, the *Al Wardeh al-Shamieh* is an excellent local diner, simple but clean, with seating on two floors. They serve the usual range of fuul, hummus, falafel, chicken, meat grills etc, or you can get take-away falafel and shwarma sandwiches downstairs. Unfortunately, they have a dual pricing policy, with tourists paying 2-3 times what locals are charged, pushing the price of a meal up to around JD5, or JD2-3 for vegetarian. Round the corner on the main drag (one-way heading down towards Petra), the *Al Shami* is a basic but friendly Syrian-run place (perhaps the only genuine budget diner in town), which serves good shwarma and falafel sandwiches, as well as fuul, fatteh, hummus etc. You can eat well here for JD1-2. Continuing around the one-way system, the *Al Janoob* serves hummus, grills etc for around JD3 per head. The *Treasury* serves a selection of traditional Arabic dishes (including `hummas, foal and flafil'), as well as buffet lunches. Across the road, the **Petra Nights** has a nice rooftop terrace. Continuing round, the *Cleopatra* and the **Petra Pearl** both lay on buffet lunches and dinners; as with the *Sunrise*, prices vary according to the season, from around JD3-6 per head. Right on the main roundabout is the **Wadi Petra**, a large restaurant serving reasonable Arabic food for around JD3 per head, but more popular in the evenings as a cheap (and somewhat sleazy) bar.

Entertainment

Bars & nightlife   The *Cave Bar* at the *Petra Forum Guesthouse* is housed in a Nabatean cave. A small Amstel here costs JD2.500, or JD5 for a can of Guinness. They have a small 'library' of CDs, from which you can select the music you want to drink to. The poolside bar at the *Petra Forum* hotel next door has great views and is not quite so tacky. The bar in the *Petra Palace* hotel is comfortable and nicely furnished. A can of Guinness/Murphy's costs JD4.250/5 and a small Amstel JD2.500. The bar in the *Wadi Petra* restaurant is cheaper, though it is a srictly males-only kind of place.

Some of the larger hotels provide evening entertainment if they have groups staying and will generally allow non-guests to attend also; try at the *Petra Forum* or *Movenpick*. The *Taybet Zaman* resort, 11 km from Wadi Musa, also provides evening entertainment. There are also occasional traditional Bedouin-style evenings with food, dancing and singing laid on for groups at Al Barid (or Little Petra), 9 km from the Visitors' Centre.

Turkish baths   A very nice way to relax those aching limbs after a long day's sightseeing. There are currently three 'Turkish baths' enterprises in and around Wadi Musa, with more planned. *Salome Turkish Bath*, situated in the centre of Wadi Musa town, T2156926. Furnished and arranged inside in traditional style with marble baths and steam rooms and a central sitting area for taking tea and refreshments afterwards. Full works including scrub-down, massage and tea afterwards JD15. There are separate changing areas for men and women, though the steam rooms are mixed. Women can make a special reservation if they wish (minimum number around 7). *Petra Turkish Bath*, situated below the *Silk Road* hotel, T2157085. Recently opened. Similar arrangement to the *Salome Turkish Bath*. Full works including scrub-down, massage, tea etc JD15. *Hammam*, part of the *Taybet Zaman* resort complex, T2150111. As well as being far and away the nicest, surprisingly this is also the cheapest of the 'Turkish baths', costing JD12 for the full works. The steam room is mixed, but there are separate changing areas and massage rooms. The management insist that their male masseur is entirely trustworthy, but can arrange for a female masseuse on request.

Shopping

There is certainly no shortage of souvenir and handicraft shops and stalls, both inside and outside the site. The usual range of goods can be found, including the ubiquitous bottles filled with layers of coloured sand to create desert scenes and pictures, and an incredible number of different Petra-theme kitschy souvenirs. All the more expensive hotels have their own shops, which can be good for newspapers, magazines, books, maps and guides, as well as film, toiletries etc. A new development (scheduled to open sometime in 2001) is the *Elgee Souk* in the southern part of Wadi Musa town, a complex of restored Ottoman buildings which will house handicraft shops, cafés etc.

Film is fairly readily available (this must after all be one of the most photographed sites in the Middle East), either in the hotel shops or else from many of the souvenir shops; the *Rum Studio and Lab*, below the *Silk Road* hotel is probably the best place. It generally has fairly fresh stocks of *Kodak* film and also does processing. There is a reasonable selection of food shops in Wadi Musa and it is worth preparing a packed lunch for yourself for when you are inside the site.

Sports

Use of the swimming pool, steam room and gym at the *Mövenpick* hotel costs JD10 per day for non-guests. Use of the swimming pool only at *Taybet Zaman* costs JD10 per day. Use of the swimming pool at the *Petra Forum* hotel is cheaper at JD6 per day. The small but pleasant pool at the *Petra Palace* hotel is the best value at JD3 per day. **Swimming & fitness**

The *Petra Forum* hotel has its own **tennis courts** and also offers **horse riding**. Non-guests can make use of both these facilities if they book in advance. **Other**

Tour operators

Petra Moon, situated next door to the *Petra Palace* hotel, down near the entrance gate to Petra, T2156665, F2156666, www.petramoon.com Locally-based tour operator with an excellent reputation and considerable experience. Can arrange 'adventure tours', including horse/camel treks, hiking and camping, as well as 'eco-tours' and 'archaeological tours'. Able to cater for large or small groups, including tailor-made tours for couples or individuals. Also helps run 'Petra by Night' tours of the Petra ruins (currently every Mon and Thu evening, departing from the Visitors' Centre at 2030, JD12 per person, advance booking necessary). Two other local tour operators (also agents for the 'Petra by Night' tours) are *La Bedouina*, T2157099, and *Zaman*, T2157722.

Transport

Taxis are readily available outside the site, in Wadi Musa and at Musa Spring. A taxi from the entrance of the site to Musa Spring should in reality only cost JD1 (or 150 fils by service taxi), but in practice you will have to fight hard to get one for JD2. The Visitors' Centre tends to support an overall policy of higher fares for tourists and taxi drivers certainly don't disagree. The quoted fares from the Visitors' Centre to Al Barid/Beidha (wait and return) is JD10, to Showbak (wait and return) JD10, and to Taybet Zaman (one way) JD5. Taxis are more than happy to undertake long-distance runs to Wadi Rum, Aqaba etc, though again they charge inflated rates (eg Wadi Rum/Aqaba JD20/25). Many of the hotels further from the site entrance offer free transport back and forth. If you want to avoid the hassle of bargaining down a taxi each time, it is worth checking that your hotel does offer this service. **Local**

Petra

Car hire There is a branch of **Hertz** inside the *Mövenpick* hotel (contact the hotel or try their mobile; T079-649815). Note that if you want to hire a car from here, you must arrange it in advance; most easily done through their head office in Amman.

Long distance With the exception of the *JETT* coaches, which depart from the Visitors' Centre down by the entrance to Petra, all the other minibus services depart from the roundabout in the centre of Wadi Musa town. (The *JETT* ticket office is temporarily housed in the small, easily-missed *Jeff's Bookshop*, one of several tourist shops outside the Visitors' Centre.) Most hotels can arrange for the *JETT* coach – and the minibuses to Amman, Wadi Rum and Aqaba – to pick you up from your hotel if you let them know the day before. There is talk of a new bus station being established at Musa Spring, though a final decision has yet to be made. Note that the fares quoted below are tourist prices, being 2-3 times what locals are charged. The timings for all the services listed below are subject to frequent changes, so you are advised to check the situation the day before.

Amman: the *JETT* coach services to Amman currently only operate on Tue, Fri and Sun, departing at 1500 (JD5.500). They may increase this to a daily service (as it was in the past), but no one seems to know for sure. There are also regular minibuses to Amman; up to 5 between 0600-0800 (depending on demand), and usually a further one at 1100 (JD2.500). **Wadi Rum**: 1 minibus daily at 0600 (JD3). **Aqaba**: 4 minibus daily, departing between 0600-0800, and usually a 5th one at around 1500. **Ma'an**: regular minibuses every 30 mins or so until around 1600 (JD1.500; on this route you may only be charged the 'locals' rate of 500 fils). There are regular connections from Ma'an to Amman, Aqaba, Kerak and the turning off the Desert Highway for Wadi Rum. **Kerak**: occasional services (depending on demand) at 0600 (JD3), though the more more reliable option is to go via Ma'an. **Showbak**: usually at least 1 departure daily between 0600-0800, depending on demand.

Directory

Banks The branch of the ***Arab Bank*** inside the Visitors' Centre, by the entrance to the site, is open 0830-1430, Fri 0900-1100, closed Sat. It can change TCs (commission JD5 up to US$500, JD7 for US$500+) and cash (no fee). The branch of the ***Cairo-Amman Bank*** inside the *Mövenpick* hotel is open 0830-1500, closed Fri and Sat. It can change TCs (JD6.200 commission) and cash (no fee). It also deals with *Visa* cards and acts as an agent for *Western Union Money Transfer*. The main branch of the ***Arab Bank*** is in Wadi Musa itself (see map) and has a cash machine which accepts *Visa, Mastercard, Cirrus* and *+Plus* cards. There is also a branch of the ***Housing Bank*** in Wadi Musa with a cash machine which accepts *Visa, +Plus* and *Visa Electron* cards. Many of the larger hotels also change money, but at well below the bank rate. *American Express* are represented by *International Traders*, below the *Silk Road* hotel, T2157711. They can arrange replacements for lost or stolen TCs, but cannot cash them.

Communications **Internet** The cheapest place is currently the smoky ***Rum Internet Café***, on the main street in the cente of Wadi Musa town, T2157906. Internet access here costs JD2.500 per hr (minimum 30 mins). Nearby, the ***Petra Internet Café*** charges JD4 per hr, or JD3 after 2000. Though more expensive, it is nicely furnished with a real café attached. There is also an internet café attached to the *Middle East restaurant*, down towards the entrance gate to Petra, though this is the most expensive at JD5 per hr. Note that at the time of writing, there were hopes that a 'lease line' would be installed at Petra in the near future, which will result in internet access charges dropping significantly. **Post** The main post office is in Wadi Musa town, near the roundabout. There is also a branch inside the Visitors' Centre, and another one beside the *Mussa Spring* hotel at Musa Spring. All are open 0700-1400, 7 days. **Telephone** There are *Alo* and *JPP* cardphones at the Visitors' Centre, in the parade of hotels etc on the main road just outside, in Wadi Musa town, and outside the post office up at Musa Spring.

Medical services There are excellent medical facilities at Petra. Inside the site there are emergency facilities at the *Basin* restaurant and museum complex, including oxygen. Just outside the site, next to the *Petra*

Forum hotel, there is a *Polyclinic*, T2157161, with an English-speaking doctor on call 24 hrs. Just above the village of Wadi Musa there is a *Health Centre*, T2156025, with full facilities including X-rays, operating theatre, dentist, pharmacy and analysis lab. Ambulances are available from either the Polyclinic or the Health Centre, while a helicopter is available for serious injuries within the site. A new hospital is under construction along the road to Taybet.

Sites around Petra

There are a few other sites around Petra within easy driving distance which are worth visiting. If you arrive in Petra in the afternoon and do not wish to pay to enter just for the half-day, Al Barid (also known as Little Petra) is free to get in and gives a good taster of what is in store. The drive to Taybet Zaman meanwhile is particularly spectacular at sunset. The luxury hotels en route make excellent places to enjoy the view over a drink, while the restored Ottoman village-cum-luxury hotel at Taybet Zaman is also worth a visit and often lays on evening entertainments.

Approaching the Visitors' Centre and car park from Wadi Musa, take the signposted right turn by the *Mövenpick* hotel. This road climbs gently northwards, skirting the mountains which guard Petra to the west. After approximately 1 km you pass the now somewhat paltry ruins of **Wu'eira Crusader Castle** perched on a hilltop to your left. The castle dates from between 1108-1116 AD and was abandoned around the time that Salah ud-Din drove the Crusaders from the region. However, it is the surrounding landscape of bizarrely rounded and weathered rock formations which catch the eye rather than the ruins themselves.

Al Barid (Little Petra) & Beidha

After 3 km you pass through the modern Bedouin village of Bdoul (also known as Umm Sayhoun), constructed to house the Bedouin families who once lived amongst the ruins. At the north end of the village there is a checkpost and fork off to the left which marks the start of a road leading down to Petra's central city area. Continuing straight on, after a further 5 km, you reach a T-junction. Turn sharp left for Al Barid and Beida, continuing for 1 km until you reach the road-head. Turning right at the T-junction, there is a left turn immediately after which leads down to Wadi Arabah (this road soon deteriorates into a very rough track requiring 4WD), while continuing straight takes you in the direction of Showbak (at the time of writing, this road was being resurfaced).

From the road-head, where there are various souvenir and refreshments tents, the entrance to **Al Barid** is straight ahead. Al Barid was one of Petra's more prosperous suburbs. You pass first a remarkably well-preserved temple façade on your right before passing through a mini-Siq. Once through this, there is a second well-preserved façade higher up in the cliff-face on the left, with a set of rock-cut stairs climbing steeply up just before. Following the narrow wadi-bed you pass more rock-cut chambers (the majority badly weathered) as well as numerous rock-cut stairs leading to various small High Places of Sacrifice. Further on the cliffs close-in sharply to leave just a narrow cleft, accentuating the bizarre weathered rock formations on either side. A set of heavily worn steps climb up into the cleft and, if you can negotiate your way past the massive stone which blocks the way towards the top, you reach a ledge overlooking a larger wadi below. It is possible to scramble down into this wadi and explore further.

Facing the entrance to Al Barid, a rough track bears off to the left from the road-head leading to the excavated site of **Beidha**, a 10-15 minute walk.

Petra

Although to the untrained eye there is not a great deal to see here, in archaeological terms it is of major importance. The site was first discovered by the archaeologist D Kilbride in 1956, and although extensive work has been done on it over the years, the excavations are far from complete. The remains of the small settlement found here date back to the Pre-Pottery Neolithic period (7000-6500 BC) when man was making the transition from nomadic hunter-gathering to settled agriculture and animal husbandry. The majority of the tools found here are of flint and bone, while querns (stone mills for grinding grain) were found in abundance. A few crude clay items were also found, including a bowl and the figure of a horned ibex, perhaps representing the first experiments at manufacturing things from alternative materials. A total of six levels of settlement were excavated, each representing a distinct period and displaying a clear progression in the design of the buildings, from simple round dwellings to more complex rectangular structures. Kilbride also found evidence of a much earlier period of occupation, dating from 10,000-8000 BC, a time when the people in the region were still semi-nomadic hunter-gatherers.

The road to Taybet Zaman The drive to Taybet Zaman is truly spectacular and is worth undertaking one evening simply to experience the sun setting behind the mountains of Petra. If you are travelling by your own transport and heading down to Aqaba, you can continue along this road to join the Desert Highway further south. From Wadi Musa, head up towards Ain Musa and turn right at the roundabout opposite the *Valley Stars* hotel (you can also join the Taybet road directly from Wadi Musa, but it is easy to go wrong). The road heads south, following the east side of a deep valley, while off to the west, across the valley, are the mountains that guard Petra. Mindful of the potential of this stunningly beautiful 'scenic road' as a tourist attraction in its own right, the Petra Regional Council has had it widened and resurfaced, making it one of the best in the country. Thus today it is a somewhat indulgent 4-lane highway with optimistically vast parking areas at strategic viewpoints along the way.

Unfortunately, a road of such perfect quality is seen by many locals as an open invitation to race flat-out along it, with the result that there have already been several fatalities in the short time since it was completed. After 4 km you pass the *Grand View* and *Petra Plaza* hotels next-door to each other, followed by the *Petra Panorama* and *Nabatean Castle* hotels 2 km further on. Entering the modern village of Taybet (10 km from Wadi Musa, also written Taybeh or Tayyibeh), the road reverts abruptly to a narrow, pot-holed affair. A poorly signposted right turn in the village points the way down to the restored Ottoman village-resort of *Taybet Zaman* resort (see Essentials below).

Ain Musa (Musa Spring) The small cluster of buildings on the main road when you first arrive at the head of Wadi Musa are easily overlooked. However, on the right (facing down towards Petra) is a small domed whitewashed building. This marks the spot where the spring which still feeds Wadi Musa rises; according to local tradition (and hence the name) this is also the spot where Moses struck the rock and brought forth water.

Petra to Wadi Rum

There are two possibilities for the first part of the route from Petra to Wadi Rum. The first (and more scenic) option is to take the road just above Wadi Musa town leading to Taybet Zaman (see above). Continue straight past the turning for Taybet Zaman (10 km from Wadi Musa), and after a further 3 km or so, bear sharp right (following the road round to the left takes you to Eil, see below). Continue straight through the village of Rajifa (or 'Ar Rajif'), and then bear right again at the next junction you come to (13 km from the last junction; signposted for 'Ras an-Naqab' and 'Aqaba'). Just under 16 km further on you come to the Desert Highway. Turning right here to head south, it is another 42 km to the turning for Wadi Rum (left takes you to the exit for Ma'an, and north towards Amman).

The second option is to bear right at the junction by Musa Spring (coming from Petra/Wadi Musa town). After 13 km you come to the village of Basta, where there is a turning left to a small area of excavations in the village, the **Basta Neolithic Village** which, as the name suggests, is the remains of a Neolithic village, contemporary with the Beidha remains discovered near the Petran suburb of Al Barid (see above). Continuing straight along the main road, around 2 km further on you pass through the small village of **Eil**, passing a right turn signposted to 'Rajif' and 'Taibeh' (Taybet) and then second right turn signposted to Aqaba, Sadakah and Farthakh (both turnings join up with the first route via Taybet Zaman and Rajif). Continue straight on, forking right after 4 km to arrive after a further 8 km at a T-junction. Turn right here, passing through the small village of Muraygah, to join the Desert Highway heading south (8 km beyond the T-junction). Having joined the desert highway, you pass after 8 km the `Rajif Junction' and turning for Petra. Soon after, the road soon begins to descend steeply from its high plateau and then continues south through open desert, with a taste of the spectacular scenery typical of Wadi Rum stretching away to the east. The road passes the town of Quwayra off to the left, before arriving at the left turn for Wadi Rum (clearly signposted), opposite the village of Rashidiyeh.

Taking the turning, continue straight on this road, passing a turning to the village of Salhia. After 17 km you reach a fork and checkpost; continue straight for Wadi Rum, 11 km further on (bearing off to the left takes you to the Bedouin village of Disi).

Petra

Wadi Rum

10

Wadi Rum

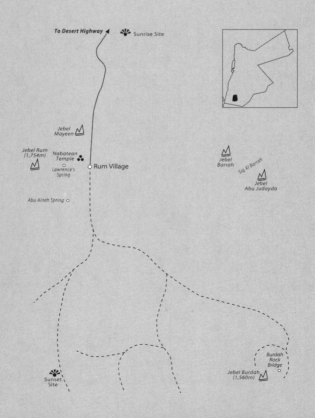

So many of the tour groups visiting Wadi Rum stay only for a few hours (often in the middle of the day when the sun bleaches much of the colour out of the scenery) before rushing off again, which largely defeats the purpose of coming here in the first place. In order to really appreciate it you need to spend at least one night in Wadi Rum, to witness the fantastic spectacle of the changing colours of light on rock and sand which come with dawn and sunset, and to absorb something of the atmosphere and tranquility of the desert. If possible, having savoured the sunset, spend a night out under the stars, away from the barking dogs and noise of Rum village. It is then that you really get a sense of `Rumm the magnificent...vast, echoing and godlike' which so captivated Lawrence.

While some of the romance of the place may now have been eroded by the building of a metalled road right into its heart, by the steady haphazard sprawl of Rum village, and the hordes of tourist coaches which descend each day, it still remains an awesome place. Huge pillars of sandstone rock rise abruptly and majestically from the sandy desert floor, their cliffs, sheer in places or else twisted and weathered into outlandish shapes, towering to heights of over 1,500 m.

Wadi Rum

TE Lawrence's Wadi Rum

"The crags were capped in nests of domes, less hotly red than the body of the hill; rather grey and shallow. They gave the finishing semblance of Byzantine architecture to this irrisistible place; this processional way greater than imagination. The Arab armies would have been lost in the length and breadth of it, and within the walls a squadron of aeroplanes could have wheeled in formation. Our little caravan grew self-conscious, and fell dead quiet, afraid and ashamed to flaunt its smallness in the presence of the stupendous hills.

Landscapes, in childhood's dream, were so vast and silent. We looked backward through our memory for the prototype up which all men had walked between such walls toward such an open square as that in front where this road seemed to end. Later, when we were often riding inland, my mind used to turn me from the direct road, to clear my senses by night in Rumm and by the ride down its dawn-lit valley towards the shining plains, or up its valley in the sunset towards that glowing square which my timid anticipation never let me reach. I would say, 'Shall I ride on this time, beyond the Khazail, and know it all?' But in truth I liked Rumm too much." (TE Lawrence, Seven Pillars of Wisdom).

A quote from TE Lawrence is of course obligatory when it comes to Wadi Rum. Lawrence is at his most effusive whenever he talks about the natural beauty of the desert, and becomes positively poetical when he turns to the subject of Wadi Rum. However, this area of outstanding natural beauty was made famous to the outside world not so much by his description of it in the Seven Pillars of Wisdom as by the fact that David Lean shot the desert scenes of his epic film 'Lawrence of Arabia' here.

Ins and outs

Getting there Public transport to and from Wadi Rum is pretty appalling. There are just 2 buses daily between Aqaba and Wadi Rum, and 1 bus daily between Petra and Wadi Rum (see under Transport in the Essentials section below for more details). There are no direct services between Amman and Wadi Rum. However, any of the buses running along the Desert Highway between Aqaba and Amman or Ma'an pass the turning for Wadi Rum, from where you can hitch the remaining 28 km to Wadi Rum itself. There is a bus shelter at the turning, and though you will probably have to pay for your lift, you are unlikely to have to wait more than 30 mins or so.

Entry fees There is an entrance fee of JD1 per person payable at the checkpost just before you reach the village. If you intend to drive your own 4WD around Wadi Rum, there is an extra charge of JD4 per vehicle. 40% of the money raised from entrance fees goes to the *Resthouse* (where you are entitled to a cup of tea), while 60% goes to local community projects. Note that when Wadi Rum is established as an RSCN National Park (see next page), a new visitors' centre will be built around 8 km before the existing *Resthouse*, with no private vehicles being allowed beyond this point. Entry fees will go up and there will be considerably tighter controls on 4WD, camel and horse 'safaris' within the National Park.

Tourist information The tourist information (T2018867) and tourist police (T2018215) are based in the *Resthouse*. They are mainly useful for organizing guides and transport for jeep or camel trips into Wadi Rum, and for contacting guides with experience of rock-climbing. The prices charged for jeep and camel trips to the most popular spots in Wadi Rum are fixed and are listed on the wall of the resthouse (see next page). A guide for walking or climbing will cost in the region of JD25-30 per day.

The RSCN Wadi Rum National Park

Although already officially listed as a 'Protected Area', in practice little has been done to protect Wadi Rum's unique natural environment. Each year the number of visitors increases significantly, with ever more jeeps taking tourists out into the desert. The uncontrolled movement of vehicles through the desert, along with the excessive burning of firewood (and to a certain extent overgrazing), is having a disastrous impact on the sparse vegetation cover of the area. Litter is becoming a serious problem at some of the the more popular sites, as is graffiti, while the growing popularity of rock climbing raises a whole new set of issues. The continued hunting of Wadi Rum's endangered Ibex population is also a major problem.

In recent years the government has approached the RSCN and asked it to put together a plan for protecting Wadi Rum's fragile ecosystems and managing tourism in the area on a more sustainable basis. This is the first time that the RSCN has worked in partnership with the government. The fact that there is already a well-established tourist industry in the area which is the major (and often the only) source of income for many Bedouin families means that any changes will have to be introduced slowly, with the cooperation of local people. At present there is considerable resistance to the RSCN plans. For a start, many Bedouin proudly identify themselves as hunters. They are also understandably suspicious of attempts to regulate the tourism which has become so important to their livelihoods.

The National Park will encompass an area of some 500 sq km, making it the largest in Jordan. At the time of writing, the RSCN was predicting that the Park would be up and running within three years, though there has already been a considerable amount of 'drift'; a reflection of the many conflicting interests which have to be accommodated. There is a small RSCN office in a building just beyond the Resthouse, on the same side of the road, or contact the RSCN in Amman (see page 115) for more details of recent developments at Wadi Rum.

The summer months from Jun through to early Sep are the hottest in Wadi Rum with daytime temperatures often reaching 40°C, making any strenuous activity such as walking or climbing particularly exhausting and essentially impractical. From late Sep onwards, temperatures begin to fall significantly with the days being warm and sunny, but not unbearable. This lasts all the way through to late May/early Jun, when temperatures again begin to rise. Even in summer, temperatures fall dramatically at night; if you are planning on camping out, make sure you have a good sleeping bag and warm clothing. Most of the rainfall comes between November and April, usually in the form of brief, heavy downpours. Jun through to Sep are generally completely dry. Thus the best time to visit Wadi Rum is really any time outside the summer months. Spring has the advantage of longer days, and this is also when the desert is at its greenest. However, climbers and walkers should bear in mind the very real risk of flash-floods in gullies and ravines. Bear this in mind also when choosing a campsite. Christmas and New Year are popular and it can get quite busy then.

Best time to visit

Wadi Rum

Flora and fauna

Although on the surface Wadi Rum may appear inhospitable and barren, the desert here is in fact a complex ecosystem rich in life. Those fortunate enough to spend a while here and see the dramatic transformation which a little rain brings, carpeting the desert floor in flowers and wild grasses, can attest to this. Even during the dry months, a short walk into the Wadi S'Bach near the resthouse reveals what a little water can do in this otherwise parched

Pre-historic and Nabatean Wadi Rum

There is evidence of man's presence here since earliest times in the form of numerous pre-historic and Nabatean drawings, inscriptions and constructions. Most of the drawings depict animals and hunting scenes or stylized human figures. Most of the inscriptions found in the region are of Thamudic origin (named after the ancient Arabian tribe of Thamud) and date from the 3rd century BC to 2nd century AD. Other inscriptions are in Greek or Minaean, the former reflecting the Greek influence on the region following Alexander the Great's conquest in 332 BC, while the latter were probably left by merchants from the southern Arabian state of Ma'in in Yemen, who controlled the incense trade before being supplanted by the Nabateans. Aramaic inscriptions, left by the Nabateans, can also be found, as well as much later

Kufic inscriptions left by early pilgrims en route to or from Mecca and Medina.

There is plenty of evidence that early man also worked to modify the environment to his advantage, most obviously by building dams, water channels and cisterns in order to collect and control the flow of water. Such remains, mostly of Nabatean origin, have been found scattered all over the region. Finally, although no great centre of civilisation existed here as at Petra, the remains have been found of what must have been a fairly substantial Nabatean temple close to the resthouse. A number of other Nabatean temple or sanctuary remains have also been found elsewhere in the region, suggesting that there was some form of permanent settlement here during the Nabatean period.

wilderness. Bushes such as tamarisk and artemesan form the bulk of the scrub vegetation. Near sources of spring water these are complemented by numerous other bushes and plants, including wild watermelon, as well as palm trees. Higher up, juniper trees can also be found, although these are becoming increasingly rare. The desert is also rich in herbs and medicinal plants, of which the local Bedouin have a detailed and extensive knowledge.

Unless you spend quite a bit of time in Wadi Rum and seek out the more isolated spots, you are unlikely to come across much in the way of wildlife. Ibex, jackals and the Arabian sand cat can still be seen roaming around remote high mountain areas (though in ever decreasing numbers), as well as the more common hyrax. Smaller mammals include gerbils, jirds and numerous other rodents. Reptiles are common and include gheckos, agama and fringe fingered lizards, as well as Palestinian vipers, sand snakes and the horned cerastes snake, the latter being much feared by the Bedouin. Other nasties include the camel spider, black widow and various scorpions, although the chances of coming face to face with any of these, let alone actually being bitten or stung by them, is very remote. Birds are numerous in the region; birds of prey include vultures, buzzards and eagles, while ravens, partridges, pidgeons, sparrows, finches, larks and warblers are all common.

Rock climbing and trekking

For most it is enough simply to be amidst the vast and spectacular desert scenery of Wadi Rum. But for anyone with the merest trace of a predilection for clambering around over rocks, the mountains of Wadi Rum present an irresistible temptation. In the early 1980s the Ministry of Tourism commissioned a British climber, Tony Howard, to expore the area and map the possibilities from a rock climber's point of view.

He has produced a book `*Treks and Climbs in Wadi Rum*', now in its third edition (1997), which gives detailed information on nearly 300 climbing

Camel and 4WD hire

The standard charges for jeep and camel trips are listed below to give some idea in advance of costs, but bear in mind that they will go up over time. Officially all arrangements should be made through the resthouse, although it is sometimes possible to negotiate a deal informally with the local Bedouins. Make sure that all the details have been understood and agreed before setting out (eg price, length of time, where you are going, arrangements if staying out overnight etc). The charges for 4WD hire are expensive, so it is well worth trying to get a group of half a dozen people together to share the cost.

Destination	KM	Camel	4WD
1 Nabatean Temple	1	JD2 (30 mins)	-
2 Lawrence Spring	6	JD7 (2 hrs)	JD7 (30 mins)
3 Khazali (via 2)	14	JD16 (4 hrs)	JD15 (1½ hrs)
4 Sunset Site (via 2 & 3)	22-26	JD40 (overnight)	JD18 (2½ hrs)
5 Burdah Rock Bridge (via 2 & 3)	40-45	JD40 (overnight)	JD32 (3 hrs)
6 Sand Dune	25	JD20 (5 hrs)	JD18 (2 hrs)
7 Full day safari	-	JD20 (full day)	JD45 (full day)

routes in the Wadi Rum region, as well as background information on the area. And so it is that visitors to Wadi Rum today can hardly fail to notice the persistent presence of brightly dressed, slightly odd-looking characters who disappear early each day with a restless glint in their eyes.

The sport is still very much in its youth in Jordan and you need to bring all your own equipment. There are a few local Bedouins who are now qualified to lead and guide western-style ascents. As Tony Howard points out, the local Bedouin have been scaling the various mountains in the region while on hunting expeditions for generations; all that was needed was to get to grips with all the new-fangled accessories which Westerners brought with them. Ask at the resthouse to be introduced to a competent guide. There is also a visitors' book at the resthouse with lots of useful comments and advice on routes from climbers. This is particularly useful for up-to-date information on recent changes to routes brought about by weathering and earthquakes.

If hanging precariously from vertiginous cliff faces is not your cup of tea, there are plenty of non-technical walks and scrambles which you can do. A booklet entitled *Walks and Scrambles in Wadi Rum*, published by Al Kutba (1993) and written by Tony Howard and Diana Taylor gives good, detailed descriptions of these, complete with useful sketch-maps. If you wish to explore the area in any detail, a copy of this booklet is highly recommended. A new book by the same team, *Jordan; Walks, Treks, Caves, Climbs and Canyons* (Cicerone Press, 1999), also includes a section on Wadi Rum which combines a selection of the walks and less strenuous climbs.

Wadi Rum

Tourist Code

Limit desertification; make no open fires and discourage others from doing so on your own behalf. Even dead wood plays a role in the desert's ecosystem. It is also the only source of fuel for many Bedouin families.

Remove litter, burn and bury paper (toilet paper should also be burned before burying with wastes).

Keep spring water clean.

Plants should be left to flourish in their natural environment.

Wildlife should not be disturbed.

Do not inscribe the rocks with names or graffiti.

When taking photos, respect privacy; ask permission and use restraint.

Giving anything to children encourages begging. A donation to a village project is a better way to help.

If necessary, show your driver or guide that you are concerned about the environment.

As a guest, show respect; showing that you value local traditions encourages local pride and reinforces local culture.

Respect for local etiquette earns you respect; when in the desert, loose lightweight clothes are preferable to revealing shorts, skimpy tops and tight fitting action wear, all which are considered offensive. Hand-holding between opposite sexes or kissing in public are likewise considered offensive in Muslim society.

Observe standard charges for food, accommodation, travel and souvenirs and remember that any bargains you strike may only be possible because of the low income of others. Please help local people gain a realistic view of life in Western countries.

Wadi Rum may change you, please do not change it.

(Adapted from the tourist code printed in Treks and Climbs in Wadi Rum, itself based on the Himalayan Tourist Code, published by Tourism Concern).

Sights

Around the Resthouse

There are a number of pleasant and interesting walks which can be undertaken in the immediate vicinity of the resthouse. These take in what `sights' there are here besides the natural landscape. There are also plenty of scrambles and climbs you can do in the vicinity of the resthouse. The narrow ridge which rises directly from the resthouse camping area up to the peak of Jebel al-Mayeen to the north is described as a `moderate scramble' in the Howard/Taylor book ("requiring a `head for heights' and some confidence on easy rock up to Grade 2. Safety rope sometimes advisable"). The first sections are the easiest and you can scramble up as far as you feel comfortable to get excellent views out across Wadi Rum before it starts to get more difficult. You can also descend into the Wadi S'Bach on the far (east) side of the ridge, where a spring waters palm trees and shrubs, and from there walk across to the Nabatean Temple and then up to Lawrence's Spring.

Nabatean Temple A short walk west from the resthouse towards the east face of Jebel Rum brings you to the remains of a Nabatean temple dating from around the 1st century AD. Head towards the large watertank visible close to the base of Jebel Rum; the ruins are to the left of this. Only the basic outline of the square courtyard remains, along with the lower courses of the walls and some sections of columns. Alongside the great monuments of Petra these remains are very meagre, though they are important in that they confirm the existence of some sort of permanent Nabatean settlement here.

Wadi Rum

Continuing southwest from the Nabatean Temple, you enter the Wadi Shelaali. A good path zigzags up to Lawrence's Spring. The main source of the spring is now enclosed within a stone and concrete structure, making it difficult to bathe here as Lawrence did, but you can lean inside and take a drink. Various ancient rock drawings and inscriptions are dotted around, along with more recent additions, and there are long sections of a rock-cut water channel of Nabatean origin which once led down to the temple.

Lawrence's Spring (Ain Shelaali)

Around 3 km to the south of Rum village is the spring and campsite of Abu Aineh. This can be reached easily by walking directly south from Rum village and then bearing off to the right to reach the sandy `cove' at the foot of the mountains. Alternatively, from Wadi Shelaali you can scramble up over a small pass to the west of Jebel Ahmar and then skirt along the base of the cliffs before scrambling up to a second small pass and over into a small valley which leads down to Abu Aineh. This is an easy scramble though the second pass is

Abu Aineh

Wadi Rum

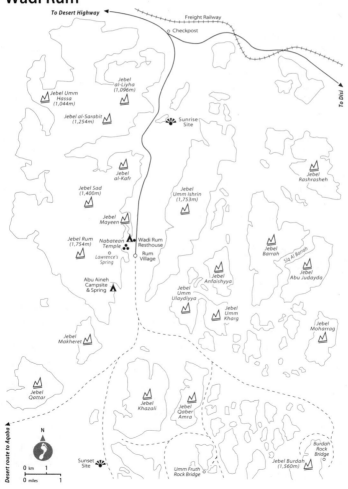

Burdah Rock Bridge

not that obvious and easily missed. There is usually a small Bedouin camp at Abu Aineh, close to the spring, where you may be offered tea. This makes for a wonderfully secluded spot in which to camp, away from the noise of Rum village, and is easily reached on foot.

In order to explore much beyond the areas mentioned above, you really need to hire a camel or 4WD (see page 295). Unless you have a specific plan or itinerary of your own, the Bedouin drivers will take you around a circuit of popular locations to match the amount of time and money you have to spend. These might take in the best spots from which to view the sunrise or sunset, or dramatic features such as the **Al Barrah Siq**. One of the most popular (and most photographed) spots is the **Burdah Rock Bridge**, a natural feature which has been weathered out of the rock over centuries.

The desert route to Aqaba It is possible to drive from Rum village all the way to Aqaba on desert tracks which take you south through the heart of Wadi Rum before bearing west through various wadis, either to meet up with the Desert Highway about 12 km north of Aqaba or to emerge on the Red Sea coast just north of the Saudi border. It is between 50-70 km to Aqaba, depending on the route taken. The route is not obvious in places and it is essential that you go with an experienced guide. You are advised to inform the resthouse before setting off.

Essentials

Sleeping and eating

Phone code: 03 There is no hotel as such at Wadi Rum, only the **G** *Wadi Rum Resthouse*, T2018897. This consists of a large restaurant and **camping** in the sandy yard behind. There are small 2-man tents available here, which cost JD3 per person (mattress and bedding included), as well as larger tents which sleep 8-12 people (same price), or you can pitch your own tent for JD1 per person. Alternatively, you can sleep on the roof of the resthouse for JD2 per person. Caravans and campervans are charged JD5 per vehicle. Toilet and shower facilities are provided and if you time it right you can even have hot water. The *Abou Aineh Camp,* approximately 3 km south of the Resthouse, makes for a quieter and more secluded spot, with its own spring and a small Bedouin camp, though there are no toilet or shower facilities here.

The *Resthouse* restaurant is the main venue for food. The buffet lunch or dinner costs JD6 per head, while breakfast is JD3. Alcohol is also served here. The large dining hall acts as a focal point and is the obvious place to meet people if you wish to get a group together to hire a vehicle for example. Longer-term visitors can negotiate use of the kitchen facilities at the *Resthouse*. A large Bedouin tent in the back yard is used for group meals and occasional evening entertainment. There are a couple of small restaurants which have been opened by local Bedouins a little further down the street from the *Resthouse*, on the opposite side.

Shopping

There are several small shops just beyond the resthouse. The **Peace Bazaar and Bookshop** has the best selection of books and maps, including the Tony Howard/Diana Taylor *Treks and Climbs in Wadi Rum* and *Walks and Scrambles in Wadi Rum*, as well as postcards and various souvenirs. In terms of food, you can usually find rice, lentils, biscuits, dried fruit and tins of tuna etc, though the availability of such items is far from guaranteed. If you want to stock up on food and supplies for a trip into Wadi Rum, you are strongly advised to buy everything you need beforehand in Aqaba.

Tour operators

The *Resthouse* can arrange tours in Wadi Rum (including overnight camping, food etc). Many of the tour operators in Aqaba also arrange all-inclusive jeep safaris to Wadi Rum.*The Desert Guides*, c/o *Alcazar* hotel, Aqaba, T03-2014131, F03-2014133, mobile T079-587472. This small tour operator specialises in horse trekking tours. Run by 2 European women, Emmanuelle Lançon and Susie Shinaco, between them they have an excellent selection of horses and considerable experience of organising horse trekking tours in Jordan. At the time of writing, they were planning to base themselves permanently at Wadi Rum. *Eco-Tourism Development Project*, situated on the Desert Highway, a little to the north of the Wadi Rum turning, T2042032. Run by the Noor al-Hussein Foundation, this project has its own fleet of new 4WD vehicles and organises its own 'safaris' around the Wadi Rum area. It's more expensive than hiring a vehicle in Rum village itself, but their vehicles are more comfortable, and a percentage of the proceeds go towards funding local projects.

Transport

Departures from Wadi Rum are somewhat erratic. Check the night before exactly when your bus is scheduled to leave. Be sure to be ready in plenty of time as the buses sometimes leave early if they are already full, but be prepared also to wait around for an hour or so. **Petra**: 1 bus daily, departing at 0800-0900, JD3. **Aqaba**: 1 bus daily departing at 0700-0800, and if there is sufficient demand, a second bus at around 1200. **Amman**: take a bus or hitch to the junction with Desert Highway, from where there is regular passing transport heading north. Likewise, if you miss the bus, hitch to the junction and pick up transport from there. The main transport hub is at **Ma'an**, just off the Desert Highway 75 km to the north, from where there are regular buses to Amman, Aqaba and Petra. If you are coming from Aqaba or Petra on a bus not going directly to Wadi Rum, ask to be dropped off at the turning off the Desert Highway, from where it is usually fairly easy to hitch into Wadi Rum itself.

Directory

Medical services There is a brand new *Medical Centre* in Rum village (T2032957) which is well equipped to deal with climbing accidents and most other emergencies. The nearest fully equipped hospital is at Aqaba. Make sure you have your own basic first-aid kit in case of minor accidents. In a major emergency, the Air Force will organize an airlift, but this may take some time and will certainly be expensive. **Communications** There are a couple of *Alo* cardphones outside the *Resthouse*, and a couple of *JPP* cardphones outside the *Peace Bazaar and Bookshop*. There is also a post box at the *Resthouse*, though mail posted in Aqaba or Amman will reach its destination considerably more quickly.

Wadi Rum

Wadi Rum to Aqaba

Heading south along the Desert Highway from the Wadi Rum turn-off, after 25 km you pass an interchange and left turn for the Saudi border and sea port to the south of Aqaba. Continue straight on, past a right turn (for Aqaba airport, the border crossing to Eilat, and the Dead Sea highway/Wadi Arabah Highway to Amman), to arrive in Aqaba, 42 km from the Wadi Rum turn-off. As you approach Aqaba, you are confronted first by a view in the distance of the sprawling mass of Eilat across the border in Israel. It is only further on that the much smaller town of Aqaba comes into view.

Aqaba

11

Aqaba

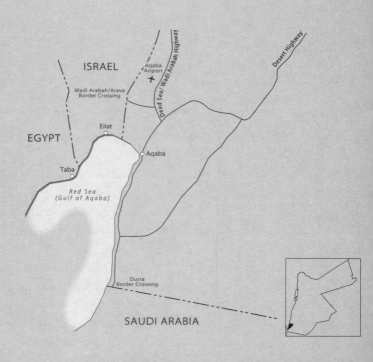

Situated at the northern tip of the Gulf of Aqaba, about 335 km south of Amman, Aqaba is Jordan's Red Sea resort, with 27 km of sandy beaches, splendid coral reefs and warm seas. Behind it are groves of palm trees and the impressive purple escarpment of the Jordanian Heights (especially attractive at sunset). As a sea and sun holiday destination, Aqaba is still somewhat overshadowed by Eilat, its larger and better known neighbour across the border in Israel, and by the resorts along Egypt's Sinai coast. However, in terms of sports and leisure facilities (though not entertainment) Aqaba is starting to catch up, with major developments such as the new Mövenpick hotel-resort providing a clear indication of the shape of things to come. In the meantime, Aqaba remains a relatively small town, friendly and relaxing, with a charm which its larger competitors have long since lost. At the same time, it offers excellent diving facilities for those who wish to explore the Red Sea's fascinating and colourful underwater world, as well as sailing, watersports, and the chance to simply sit on the beach and soak up the sun – even in the depths of winter – or sample a delicious selection of seafood. For those arriving here after travelling down through the rest of Jordan, it provides an ideal place to relax and unwind, while those arriving from Egypt or Israel can be sure of a warm welcome.

Ins and outs

Getting there Aqaba's airport has regular scheduled connections with Amman, as well as occasional charter flight connections with various places in Egypt. There are also regular sailings between Aqaba and Nuweiba in Sinai (Egypt). Many visitors also arrive from Eilat, just a stone's throw away across the Wadi Arabah/Arava border crossing with Israel. There are regular a/c coach services between Amman and Aqaba. Bus and minibus connections between Aqaba and Wadi Rum and Petra are less frequent, and if you are not on a tight budget it is worth considering chartering a private taxi. For further airport information see page 319.

Getting around The centre of Aqaba is small enough to explore on foot (to walk the length of the Corniche from the Fort to most northerly of the luxury hotels, the *Coral Beach*, takes around 30 mins), though there are plenty of private taxis cruising the streets if the heat is getting to you. To get to the various places along the coast to the south of Aqaba you need take catch a minibus from the traffic lights on the Corniche by the Fort, or hire a private taxi. To get to/from the airport, or the Wadi Arabah/Arava border crossing with Israel, a private taxi is the easiest option, although there are also occasional service taxis.

Orientation The main road from the north (you will also arrive by this road if coming from the airport or Israeli border crossing) leads directly into the centre of Aqaba and down to the Corniche. Along the northern section of the Corniche is a stretch of public beach, followed by a string of luxury hotels each with their own segments of private beach. Along the southern section of the Corniche are more public beaches, followed by the Fort and Museum. To the west of the southern section of the Corniche is the commercial heart of Aqaba, where the majority of the shops, markets, restaurants and budget hotels are located. The coast road south from Aqaba takes you past the passenger ferry terminal, Marine Aquarium, Club Murjan, southern public beaches, National Tourist Campsite and Royal Diving Centre, before arriving at the Saudi border (27 km from the centre of Aqaba).

Best time to visit Basically, Aqaba is at its best any time outside the summer months of Jun, Jul and Aug, when temperatures reach a sweltering 35-40°C. During spring (Mar-May) and autumn (September-November) temperatures average a very pleasant 24°C, while in winter (Dec-Feb) the average is around 16°C (in marked contrast to the rest of the country, where it can be bitterly cold during these months). Sea water temperatures in summer are 26°C and in winter a most pleasant 20°C. The period of the annual *Hajj* (which falls in Feb for the next few years) is perhaps best avoided; at this time Aqaba experiences a massive influx of Muslim pilgrims en route to and from Mecca. Many hotels are fully booked during this period (particularly in the mid-range and budget categories) and sailings to and from Sinai are disrupted.

Tourist information The tourist information office (T2013731, F2013363) is housed in the same building as the Aqaba Museum, adjacent to the fort. Open daily from around 0800-sunset. They can provide you with the Jordan Tourism Board's free Aqaba map/pamphlet, but otherwise they are of limited help. There is also a tourist information office at the Wadi Arabah/Arava border crossing with Israel.

History

The Old Testament gives details of King Solomon's sailing ships leaving Ezion-Geber (possibly present-day Aqaba) loaded with copper. Recent excavations at Tell Khuleifa (see below), between Aqaba and the Israeli border, produced a number of copper smelters. A major trade route from Damascus in

Syria via Petra through Sinai into Egypt utilizing this port was used by the Edomites and the Nabataeans. The Roman Tenth Legion was also stationed here. In the Early Arab period (638-1099 AD) the port established here, Aila/Ayla, was a major transit point for Muslim pilgrims performing the *Hajj* to Mecca. During the 12th century AD, the Crusaders made use of Aqaba's strategic position before Salah ud-Din took control of the area.

Aqaba fort was erected in the 16th century AD, with the town subsequently becoming part of the Ottoman Empire. During the World War I Arab revolt the fort was used by Prince Faisal and his troops as a base for attacks on the

Aqaba

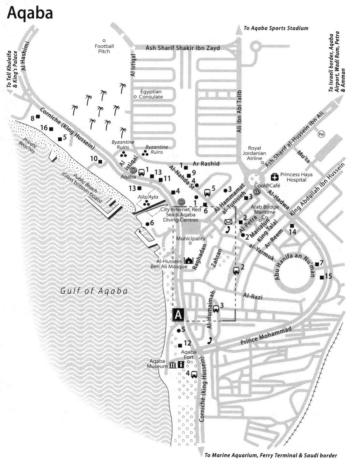

| 0 metres | 300 |
| 0 yards | 300 |

N

■ **Sleeping**
1 Al-Cazar
2 Al-Noman
3 Al-Zaitouna
4 Aqaba Gulf
5 Aquamarina Beach
6 Aquamarina City
7 Aquamarina Royal
8 Coral Beach
9 Jordan Suites & Harley's Place bar
10 Juhani Camp
11 Miramar
12 Moon Beach
13 Mövenpick

14 Oryx Suites
15 Petra International
16 Radisson SAS Aqaba

● **Eating**
1 Captain's & Chili House
2 China
3 Mankal Chicken Tikka
4 Pizza Hut
5 Qalat Jdoundna
6 Romero

🚌 **Transport**
1 Jett Bus Station
2 Minibus & Service taxi stand
3 Minibuses to Kerak
4 Minibuses to Saudi border
5 Trust International Bus Station

Related maps
A Aqaba centre,
page 314

Aqaba

Ottomans. The fate of Aqaba in the settlement after World War I was first decided by the British in the difficult post-war settlement with the French government. Lloyd George, the British prime minister, proposed in mid-1919 that British garrisons be withdrawn and replaced in the north and west by French troops and in the east by Arab troops. The Arab side were to have authority in Aqaba and Amman. Palestine (west of the Jordan River) remained under British occupation. Aqaba was important as an outlet to the sea but was also important since it had been captured from the Turks by the Saudi Arabian Huweitat tribe in 1916.

In 1922 when the Mandate Government was established, Aqaba town was allocated to Transjordan, though remaining garrisoned by the British. The line dividing Palestine from Transjordan was stated at being "all territory lying to the east of a line drawn from a point 2 miles west of the town of Aqaba on the Gulf of that name up the centre of the Wadi Araba..." At that stage there was little settlement at the head of the Gulf of Aqaba other than a small Arab town and a minor British military base.

Between 1922 and 1948 the town grew slowly. Its functions as a port were limited since the area was without shelter and thus open to winds and squalls. The coral reefs and islands at the entrance to the Gulf were also an impediment to ocean transport. Transjordan's occupation of Aqaba was contested by King Ibn Saud until a treaty of friendship and good neighbourliness was signed in 1933 between Transjordan and Saudi Arabia (though Jordanian occupation of Aqaba and Ma'an was not fully accepted until 1965). In 1965 King Hussein exchanged a significant area of the Jordanian desert (around 600 sq km) with the Saudis for a further 12 km of coastline, thus giving space to expand. In the new area, to the south towards the Saudi Arabian border, is Jordan's only commercial port, served by a freight railway track carrying phosphate from Al-Hesa.

Sights

Aqaba Fort Aqaba's small fort is credited to Khayer Bey al-'Ala'i who built it during the reign of the penultimate Mameluke Sultan, Al Ashraf Qansuh al-Ghawri (1501-1516 AD), though it was twice restored during the period of Ottoman rule (1587 and 1628). During World War I the Turkish garrison was shelled by the British navy, and following the withdrawal of the Ottoman forces, the Hashemite coat of arms was raised above the entrance, and is still in place today. It was subsequently used as a caravanserai for Egyptian pilgrims on their way to and from Mecca, before being restored in 1964.

The main entrance to the fort is flanked by semi-circular towers, each with a medallion containing Arabic inscriptions invoking the glory of Allah. The entrance leads through into a cross-vaulted room with a band of Arabic inscription around the walls singing the praises of the Mameluke Sultan Al Ashraf Qanush al-Ghawri ("Sultan of Islam and the Muslims...slayer of the unbelievers and polytheists... reviver of justice in the universe.." etc). From here an inner doorway with a *machicolation* above

Tell Khuleifa

0 metres 1
0 yards 10

Storehouse/Granary

First Fortification

Second Fortification

Guard Rooms

Entrance

leads through a second entrance chamber, this one with a domed ceiling, and into the main courtyard of the fort. At the time of writing, a large canopy and stage had been erected in the centre of the courtyard, used to host evening entertainments for tour groups. The upper level of rooms on the north side of the fort (above the entrance) have been extensively restored, allowing you to climb up and explore. Some of the rooms around the courtyard on ground level now house various souvenir/craft shops. Much of the western side of the fort is still in ruins – the result of the British bombardment during World War I. ■ *Open daily 0800-sunset. Entry Free.*

Aqaba Museum

The building to the rear (seaward side) of the fort served for a time as the residence of Sharif Hussein bin Ali, the great-grandfather of the late King Hussein and Sharif of Mecca. Today it is home to the Aqaba Museum, which contains a small and moderately interesting collection of artefacts. The first room is given over primarily to artefacts from the excavations at Ayla, including various pottery items and coins. The main exhibit consists of large limestone blocks recovered from the Egyptian Gate, inscribed with verses from the Qur'an in Kufic script. Interpretation boards provide a good explanation of the history of Ayla and a plan of the site. The second room has more artefacts from Ayla, including fragments of carved ivory, medallions etc. The third room contains artefacts and detailed explanations of the excavations carried out at Wadi Rum (mostly of the Nabatean temple there), as well as a variety of pottery pieces and architectural fragments from other sites around southern Jordan. ■ *Open daily 0800-sunset. Entry JD1.*

Ayla/Aila

Hemmed in by the Corniche, Royal Yacht Club and *Mövenpick* hotel, what appears to be an empty building lot opposite the *Miramar* and *Aqaba Gulf* hotels is in fact the remains of medieval Aqaba (known then as Ayla, or Aila). The excavations here are not exactly awe-inspiring, but the site is worth a quick look.

Founded soon after the Muslim Arab conquest of the region, sometime around 650 AD, Ayla quickly grew into an important port-town on the transit route for Muslim pilgrims travelling between Egypt, Syria and the holy cities of Mecca and Medina. The height of its prosperity came during the Abbasid period (750-950 AD), as a result of extensive trade links with Egypt, Yemen, Syria, Iraq and even China. Ayla went into decline during the Fatimid period (950-1100 AD), and was finally abandoned following its capture by the Crusaders in 1116 AD. The Ayyubid and Mameluke period town was subsequently established in the vicinity of the fort.

Ayla consisted of a rectangular settlement surrounded by walls with semi-circular towers at regular intervals and a gate in the centre of each wall. Two main streets, running between each of the gates divided the settlement into four quadrants. Today, the dry bed of a wadi runs through the site. On the northeast side, where you enter the site from the Corniche, was what has been dubbed the '**Syrian Gate**' (of which nothing survives). From here a main street ran past the remains of what has been identified as a **mosque** on the left, dating originally from the mid-7th century, but substanially rebuilt following an earthquake duing the Abbasid period. Further on, in the centre of the settlement, is the so-called **pavilion building**, which perhaps served as the governor's residence.

Excavations here have revealed two levels of occupation, the earlier dating from the Umayyad period and the later from the late Abbasid or early Fatimid period. Turning right here, an excavated stretch of street complete with the foundations of shops and houses leads to the `**Egyptian gate**', in the northwest wall. This gate is the oldest, dating from around 650-800 AD, though substantial modifications were made in the Abbasid and Fatimid periods. The '**Hejaz**

Aqaba

Gate', across the wadi to the southeast of the pavillion building, is today within the grounds of the Royal Yacht Club. Little remains to be seen of the **'Sea Gate'**, in the southwest wall facing the public beach. ■ *Unrestricted access. Entry free.*

Tell Khuleifa This site is difficult to get to, and really only for those with a specialist interest. First discovered in 1933 and largely excavated between 1938-40 by Nelson Glueck, the site of Tell Khuleifa has been tentatively identified with the biblical **Ezion-Geber** *"which is near Eloth on the shore of the Red Sea, in the land of Edom"* (I Kings 9: 26) where Solomon established his fleet. The site comprises a casement fortress that was later destroyed and replaced by some form of fortified settlement between the 8th and early 6th centuries BC. However a reappraisal of Glueck's work by Pratico, under the auspices of the American Center of Oriental Research (ACOR) has shed doubt upon this identification, suggesting that the *"site provides no clear archaeological evidence, either ceramic or architectural, for its identification with the Ezion-Geber of Israel's wilderness tradition* (Numbers 33: 35-36) *or even Solomon's reign in the 10th century BC* (I Kings 9: 26-28); *indeed the site provides only questionable evidence for the 9th century BC* (I Kings 22: 47-48)". As with Eilat, it is quite conceivable that remains that could have led to a positive identification have long since been built over during the construction of the modern town. It is also possible that any remains may have been completely washed away by the flash-floods that periodically inundated the site prior to the construction of water control measures. ■ *The site is located to the northwest of the town centre, in a military zone close to the border with Israel. Contact the Department of Antiquities (in the same building as the museum) if you are interested in visiting; they can arrange for the revelant permits from the Military Intelligence Department. There is no paved access to the site, so you will need a 4WD vehicle.*

Marine Aquarium The aquarium is part of Aqaba's Marine Science Station. If you've been to the Aquarium and Underwater Observatory in Eilat there's little point coming here, though at JD1 to enter, it's far cheaper and the staff are very helpful. The living displays are actually quite impressive (though no match for seeing them in their natural environment), but the various fish preserved in glass bottles are a bit sad. Hopefully, this is as close to a stone fish (*Synanceia verrucosa*), lion fish (*Pterois radiata*) or turkey fish (*Pterois volitans*) that you will ever come. There is an excellent book published by the Marine Science Station on sale here; *Fishes of the Gulf of Aqaba* (1997) by Maroof A Khalaf and Ahmad M Disi, with lots of colour plates (JD20); and also a booklet entitled *A guide to the sea shore of Jordan* by NC Hullings and M Wahbeh (JD2.500). ■ *Open daily 0800-1700. Entry JD1. Located 9 km south of the centre of Aqaba, T2015145, F2013674. Either catch a minibus from the traffic lights opposite the fort (500 fils), or take a private taxi (JD2-3).*

Around Aqaba

A popular full-day cruise destination from Aqaba is Pharaoh's Island, just off **Pharaoh's** the Sinai coast in Egyptian waters. There is a restaurant on the island and the **Island** remains of a Crusader castle, as well as great swimming and snorkelling in the surrounding waters.

Marine archaeologists excavating the sea bed between the island and the mainland discovered the remains of two ships dating to the Byzantine period (324-638 AD), whilst greater depths revealed artifacts from the 2nd century BC. Excavations on the island have led to the tentative identification of the site with Ezion-Geber (see above). The lagoon on the west side of the island is not natural, suggesting that prior to the construction of the breakwater, it was an open bay. The island was also used as an anchorage in later years, with fortified remains from the Hellenistic (332-37 BC) and Byzantine periods (324-638 AD). The Crusader fortress was built in 1116, during the reign of King Baldwin I of Jerusalem, and subsequently lost to Salah ud-Din in 1170. Though recovered by Reynald of Châtillon, it was lost again to the Mamelukes in the 13th century. ■ *Trips are arranged by the Aquamarina Beach hotel. They cost JD24 per person including lunch (minimum 10 people). The island is in Egyptian waters, so you must submit your passport the day before so that the relevant permit can be obtained. Departures are at around 1000, returning by 1630.*

Beaches

Aqaba's beaches, like those of neighbouring Eilat, feature `building site' type sand and are not particularly picturesque. Their real attraction lies below the water, where the large expanses of coral teeming with fish make snorkelling a fascinating experience. Within Aqaba itself there are two stretches of **public beach** with free access, one between the *Mövenpick* and *Aquamarina Beach* hotels, and the other between the Royal Yacht Club and the Fort. These are reasonably clean, though though they can get very busy. Western women should be prepared for the possibility of some unwanted attention (though these days this is more the exception than the rule). **Glass-bottom boats** can be hired at these beaches by those who want to view the coral without getting wet (JD5 per half-hour, bargain very hard). The luxury hotels (*Mövenpick*, *Aquamarina Beach*, *Radisson SAS* and *Coral Beach*) along the northern section of the Corniche each have their own private stretch of **private beach**, which you must pay to use (from JD2.500-JD6), though this also entitles you to use their swimming pools.

The beaches along the coast to the **south of Aqaba** are more attractive than those in the town itself. *Club Murjan*, 1 km to the south of the Marine Aquarium (see under Sailing and Watersports, below) was allowing people to use its stretch of beach for free at the time of writing, though an entrance fee may be introduced in the future. The *National Tourist Campsite*, just over 1 km further south again (see under Camping in Essentials), charges 500 fils per person per day to use its long stretch of beach. Unfortunately, it features a string of rather unattractive metal shade structures, and despite the attempts to raise environmental awareness, is still strewn with litter. On the other hand, the snorkelling around here is excellent.

About 2 km further south there is a turning signposted for the *Red Sea Marine Peace Park* (this in theory extends from the Marine Aquarium down to the Royal Diving Centre). Apart from a couple of ugly concrete structures, the beach here features much more tasteful palm-frond shades and is otherwise free from any development (for the time being at least; there are grandiose plans for major luxury resort complexes just inland all along the southern coast). Entry is free. The *Royal Diving Centre*, 3 km further south again (17 km from central Aqaba; see under Diving, below), charges a JD2 entrance fee. The beach here is spotlessly clean, and facilities include a salt-water swimming pool, showers and changing rooms, and a snack bar. Snorkelling equipment is readily available for hire at all the above beaches.

Diving

The Red Sea waters off Jordan's 27 km stretch of coastline between Aqaba and the Saudi border boast a wealth of coral reefs and other marine life (see also under Land and Environment in the Background chapter for more details), and offer a surprisingly rich and varied selection of diving opportunities to suit all levels of ability and experience. In 1985, a Lebanese ship, the *Cedar Pride*, was purposely sunk offshore just to the south of the National Tourist Campsite to provide a wreck dive. The fact that the majority of the dive sites are easily accessible from the shore makes them particularly suitable for beginners, and ideal for snorkelling. Many of the reefs are known by different names according to which dive centre you consult, while some are sub-divided differently. However, all the dive centres know the coastline in great detail and will take you to the best places to suit your ability and the prevailing weather conditions.

Diving is possible all year round in the Red Sea; even in winter, when air temperatures might be down to 10°C, sea temperatures remain above 20°C (although winds can make for choppy conditions, reducing visibility). Spring and autumn are the best seasons, if only because it is not unbearably hot on land.

Although there has been a certain amount of damage to the coral due to the careless handling of phosphates at the modern commercial port, Jordan's reefs and marine life are in much better shape than Israel's tiny, over-dived areas, and also many of Egypt's most popular sites. Sheer force of numbers is a major factor here, with a staggering 2 million dives or so occuring annually in Egypt, and over 700,000 in Israel, as compared with around 20,000 in Jordan. The establishment of the **Red Sea Marine Peace Park** along the coast between the Marine Science Station and the Royal Diving Centre promises to ensure that the diving industry is developed and managed sustainably in Jordan. However, pollution from the land is another important factor, and discharges from the extensive resort complexes planned for the coastline south of Aqaba represent a major threat to the reefs' ecosystems.

Courses & dive centres There are currently 5 diving centres in and around Aqaba, all of which offer a good level of service. All are registered with PADI (Professional Association of Diving Instructors) and offer PADI courses. Note that if you already have a PADI qualification, you must be able to produce your certificate and log book, or you will have to take a PADI Review course (you will also have to take this course if you have not dived for a long time). Absolute beginners can opt for a PADI 'Discover Scuba' package. These include a sea dive to a maximum depth of 6 m with a qualified instructor taking full charge. The first stage of PADI qualification is the Open Water course, which takes around 5 days (depending on weather conditions) and includes a minimum of 10 sea dives, followed by the Advanced Open Water course. In addition, there are various speciality courses you can do (deep diving, night diving, navigation, rescue diver, medic/first aid, etc), or you can train to become a Divemaster (which allows you to teach). The prices given below were correct at the time of writing, although some of the more obviously better deals may give way to higher prices at peak times. Discounts are available for bookings of multiple dives. Always check whether the price quoted for a PADI Open Water course includes certification and log book. Some dive centres charge for this separately.

Aqaba

Conserving the Coral Reefs

Divers are by definition very aware of the stunning beauty and diversity of coral reefs. They are also a major cause of their destruction. Coral is remarkably fragile and equally slow-growing. By touching, knocking, scraping and breaking the coral, divers can inadvertently cause significant damage. As well as physically impeding growth, this damage exposes the coral to attack by bacteria, in the same way as any other wound. However, divers can take simple and practical steps to minimise unnecessary damage;

Don't touch, kneel on or kick corals
They are delicate animals which are damaged when touched

Don't stir up the sand
Sand settling on coral inhibits its feeding and limits growth; in suspension it reduces the sunlight's penetration with the same effect.

Don't collect souvenirs
Many dive sites are heavily visited and could become rapidly depleted of their resources.

Don't feed the marine life
Feeding interferes with the reef's natural food chains. It can produce dependency and in some cases aggression in normally non-aggressive species.

Don't catch marine life
Fishing and spearfishing is prohibited in National Parks/Protected Areas.

Do control your buoyancy and body/equipment placement
Much damage is done unknowingly. Proper buoyancy control is crucial; practice away from reefs. Be aware of trailing guages and alternate air sources which can drag along the reef.

Do respect aquatic life
For the most part, the fish appear indifferent or mildly inquisitive towards divers. However excessive attention, or activities such as hitching lifts on dolphins or turtles can cause stress and interfere with mating behaviour.

Do collect any rubbish you see
Litter is a significant and blatantly unnecessary cause of damage to the reef.

Do inform divers if they are damaging the reef or acting irresponsibly
Many people act out of ignorance; speaking up helps raise environmental awareness.

Do report damage to the reef, injured marine life or other disturbances
As a diver, you are in a position to contribute towards the monitoring of reef ecosystems.

Aqaba International Dive Centre, Corniche (around side of large complex next door to *Aqaba Gulf* hotel), T/F2031213, diveaqaba@yahoo.com Shore dives only. JD18 per shore dive. PADI introductory/review course JD20. PADI Open Water diving course JD200. PADI Advanced Open Water diving course JD180. Prices include all equipment, transport etc. Run by Ahmad Qatawneh, who has been diving since 1964.

Aquamarina Diving Club, *Aquamarina Beach* hotel, T2016250, F2032630, www.aquamarina.com The only outfit to offer boat dives (but not shore dives). 2 dives daily at 0900 and 1400; get there 30 mins beforehand. JD17.400 per boat dive (including tank, weight belt and transportation), plus JD14.500 for all the other equipment you need (regulator, BCD etc). 'Discover Scuba' package JD48, including all equipment. PADI Open Water diving course JD248. Advanced Open Water Diving Course JD180. (Both the Open Water and Advanced Open Water courses include all equipment, but not the cost of your certificate and log book).

Red Sea Dive Centre, Corniche (around side of large complex next door to *Aqaba Gulf* hotel), T2022323, F2018969, rsdiving@go.com.jo Shore dives only. JD20 per shore dive. PADI 'Discover Scuba' package JD42. PADI Open Water diving course JD245. PADI Advanced Open Water diving course JD210. Above prices include all equipment, transport etc. Established in 1992 and run by Mohammad al-Momany. Also offers excellent value packages consisting of 10 dives plus 7 nights accommodation in comfortable appartments for JD210 per person; single supplement JD70 (equipment includes tank and weight belt only; regulator, BCD etc extra).

Royal Diving Centre, situated 17 km to the south of Aqaba, T2017035, F2017097, royaldiving@yahoo.com Arguably the best run of the dive centres, displaying a very high level of environmental awareness. Established in 1986 and currently run by the enthusiastic and helpful Ahmad al-Qatawneh (no relation to the manager of the *Aqaba International Diving Centre*). Spotlessly clean beach, salt-water swimming pool, shower/changing facilities and snack bar. Shore dives (boat dives can be arranged with advance notice). JD15 per shore dive. PADI 'Discover Scuba' package JD35. PADI Review dive JD30. PADI Open Water diving course JD220. PADI Advanced Open Water diving course JD160. Also BSAC (British Sub-Aqua Club) courses. Shuttle bus between Aqaba and diving centre free for divers (will pick-up from your hotel).

Sea Star Diving Centre, *Al-Cazar* hotel, corner of Ar-Rashid/Al-Nahda St, T2014131, F2014133. Dive centre facilities at *Al-Cazar* hotel, and also at *Club Murjan* (from where most the dives take place). Shore dives only. JD24 per shore dive. PADI 'Discover Scuba'/'Scuba Review' packages JD34. PADI Open Water diving course JD280. PADI Advanced Open Water diving course JD195. The UK agent for *Sea Star* is *Aquatours* (www.aquatours.com); good deals on inclusive accommodation and diving packages available if you book in advance through them.

Snorkelling If diving doesn't appeal, snorkelling is an excellent way to look in on the underwater world. In fact you can see almost everything you might expect to on a dive with a snorkel and mask. In the shallower water around the coral reefs there is a staggering variety of small fish which, together with the corals, are all the more brilliantly coloured for being nearer the surface and so better lit. In deeper water, the visibility is so good that you can see fish perfectly clearly at 10 m, alongside the divers with all their equipment. All the dive centres listed above hire out snorkelling equipment and are happy to take snorkellers along with them; as well as taking care of transportation, this gets you directly to the best snorkelling areas (which are invisible from the land). Snorkelling equipment is also available for hire or sale at most of the hotels and beaches, and numerous other places around Aqaba. Hire of snorkel, mask and fins costs anywhere between JD2-7 per day, and wetsuits around JD3 per day).

Sailing and watersports

In the centre of Aqaba, the *Aquamarina Beach* hotel offers waterskiing (JD4.350 for around 10 mins, or you can be towed around on an inflatable yellow 'banana' for JD2.180), jet skiing (JD1 per min), windsurfing (JD5 per hr) and Laser or Erplast sailing dinghies (JD5 per hr).

Club Murjan, situated 10 km south of Aqaba centre, T2018335. This new beach centre has excellent sailing and windsurfing facilities, with good equipment and qualified instructors. Topper and Topaz dinghies are available for rent (JD20 for 2 hrs, or JD30 for the day), as well as the faster Topaz Trez and Topper Sports 16 (both only for experienced sailors). Hobie-cats and the like are also on order. Windsurfers cost JD10-15 for 2 hrs, or JD25 for the day, and there are canoes available. Sailing and windsurfing courses lasting 3 or 5 days cost JD70/100. You can also hire mountain bikes here (JD5 per hour, or JD25 for the day) to explore various trails in the hills just inland. There is a restaurant and bar here, as well as a small fresh water swimming pool, and a good long stretch of beach with excellent snorkelling.

Essentials

Sleeping

There is quite a range of accommodation in Aqaba, though to really get the best deal some ruthless bargaining is necessary; this applies to the most expensive places as well as the budget hotels. In most cases you should at least be able to bargain the price down into the price classification below – possibly further. This is often true of the high as well as the low season. Price categories below are for the high season, before bargaining. Don't forget the government tax and service (23%) which is added to your bill in the more expensive hotels.

Exactly when the high season occurs varies for different categories of hotels. For the luxury and upper-range hotels and beach resorts, which get most of their business from organised group tours, it is late Mar-Jun and Sep-Dec (advanced booking is advisable during these periods). For the mid-lower range hotels, which tend to rely more on visiting Saudi families for business, it is from May-Jul. At the budget end of the market, the popular backpacker hotels are at their busiest during the spring and autumn months, though they are rarely completely full.

LL *Mövenpick*, Corniche, T2034020, F2039370, www.movenpick-aqaba.com Due to open some time in 2000. Massive resort complex (212 rooms) in two parts; one on the beach, the second on the other side of the Corniche and linked by a promenade/bridge over the road. Promises to be a super-luxurious extravaganza. Their stretch of beach, however, is tiny, although there is talk of them taking over the considerably larger beach-frontage of the now closed *Aqaba Beach* hotel; other reports suggest that the *Aqaba Beach* will be redeveloped by the Hilton group. **LL-L** *Radisson SAS Aqaba*, Corniche, T2012426, F2013426, www.radisson.com/aqabajo Choice of sea view or cheaper road-facing rooms, as well as a new wing with rooms overlooking 'garden' area. Restaurants, bar, conference and banqueting facilities, small swimming pool and short stretch of private beach. Recently renovated. Suitably luxurious (rooms in the main block very spacious), but otherwise unremarkable.

AL *Coral Beach*, Corniche, T2013521, F2013614. Recently refurbished to a high standard. All rooms with balcony and sea view. Restaurant, bar, small circular swimming pool, short stretch of private beach. A relatively small luxury hotel, without the facilities of others in the same price category in Aqaba, but ideal if you are after somewhere quieter and more manageable. German Honorary Consulate located here.

A *Aqaba Gulf*, Corniche, T2016636, F2018246. Functional rooms with a/c, TV/dish, fridge, phone and attached bath. Rather expensive for a hotel not right on the beach and with no balconies. Restaurant, swimming pool, tennis court, shops, *Petra Tours* travel agent. **A** *Aquamarina Beach* (aka *Aquamarina I*), Corniche, T2016250, F2032630, www.aquamarina.com Rather mediocre rooms (best ones have sea view) with a/c, TV/dish, phone, minibar, attached bath and balcony. Restaurant, bar, small swimming pool, sauna, games room. Very small stretch of private beach, plus a large jetty. *Aquamarina* diving centre and watersports (see above), tour operator, *Arab Bank* ATM outside main gate (*Visa, Mastercard, Cirrus, +Plus, Visa Electron*). Leisure facilities somewhat out-shine the hotel itself. **A** *Aquamarina City* (aka *Aquamarina II*), Al-Nahda St, T2015165, F2032633, www.aquamarina.com Comfortable, spacious rooms (those at rear have sea views) with a/c, TV/dish, IDD, minibar and attached bath. Restaurant, bar, night club, swimming pool, jacuzzi, sauna and massage/fitness centre. Guests have full use of all the facilities at the *Aquamarina Beach* hotel. **A** *Aquamarina Royal* (aka *Aquamarina III*), Abu Hanifa an-Nu'man St, T2032634, F2032639, www.aquamarina.com Comfortable, spacious rooms (some have excellent views out over Aqaba, Eilat and the sea) with a/c, TV/dish, IDD, minibar and attached bath. Restaurant on top floor, pleasant roof terrace (great views). Located away from the centre (and a long way from the beach) in a new residential area. Guests have full use of all the facilities at the *Aquamarina Beach* hotel (a shuttle bus operates between the two). **A** *Jordan Suites*, Al-Nahda St, T2030890, F2030893, sihs@firstnet.com.jo Comfortable, spacious suites with a/c, TV/dish, phone and attached bath. Separate bedroom and sitting room/kitchen area with sink, cooker and fridge. Also 2 family suites each with 2 bedrooms (1 double, 1 twin). Coffee shop, *Harley's Place* bar downstairs. **A** *Petra International*, Prince Mohammad St, T2016255, F2014270, petrah@go.com.jo Comfortable, spacious rooms with a/c, TV/dish, IDD, minibar and attached bath (some with balconies and great views). Restaurant, bar, roof terrace, tiny swimming pool, sauna and fitness centre. Very similar to *Aquamarina Royal*, both in terms of the level of facilities and location, but wider variety of rooms.

B *Al-Cazar* (or *Alcazar*), corner of Ar-Rashid/Al-Nahda St, T2014131, F2014133. Comfortable rooms arranged around open-air courtyard with a/c, fan, TV/dish, phone fridge attached bath and balony. Restaurant, bar, swimming pool, *Sea Star* diving centre, shuttle bus to *Club Murjan* (see under Sailing and Watersports, above), *Desert Guides* travel agent. **B** *Al-Shuala*, Raghadan St, T2015153, F2015160. A/c, TV/dish, phone, fridge, attached bath. Rooms at front with balcony and good sea views. Comfortable, but rather naff '70s decor. Restaurant, coffee shop, roof terrace. Aimed very much at the Arab market. **B** *Al Zatari*, King Talal St, T2022970, F2022974. Recently opened hotel, a/c, TV/dish, phone, fridge, attached bath. Comfortable, though slightly naff decor. Some rooms with balcony and good sea views. Restaurant. **B** *Crystal*, corner of Corniche/Al-Razi St, T2022001, F2022006. Reasonably comfortable rooms with a/c, TV/dish, IDD, minibar and attached bath. Restaurant, bar and disco. Modern, centrally located hotel. Fairly good value for money, though only some rooms have sea views, and none have balconies. **B** *Moon Beach*, Corniche, T2013316, F2016500. Brand new hotel on beach front adjacent to fort. Comfortable rooms (those at front have sea views) with a/c, TV/dish, IDD, fridge and attached bath. Restaurant, roof terrace. Very good value (currently at bottom end of **B** category), while prices hold. **B** *Nairoukh 2*, Corniche, T2012980, F2015749. Comfortable and spacious rooms with a/c, TV/dish, phone and attached bath. Most rooms with good sea views; also some smaller/cheaper rooms without sea views. Restaurant, coffee shop, conference and banqueting facilities. Well-run hotel. Friendly manager. **B** *Oryx Suites* (aka *Family Suites*), Prince Mohammad St, T2018788, F2018789. Comfortable and

Aqaba centre

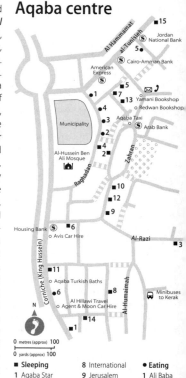

very spacious suites featuring separate bedroom, kitchen and dining room areas, a/c, TV/dish, IDD and attached bath. Also large 2-bedroom suites (double and twin), and some 4-bedroom, or you can join up standard suites. Excellent value (with discounts for longer stays), but a long way from the beach (comparatively). **B-C** *Al Zaitouna*, Al Hammamat al-Tunisieh St, T2019601, F2019605, zaitounahotel@yahoo.com Choice of old wing with larger rooms and balconies, or new wing with smaller but better furnished rooms. All rooms with a/c, TV/dish, phone, fridge and attached bath. Two restaurants. Centrally located, well run hotel. Helpful management. Good value. **B-C** *Miramar*, Corniche, T2014341, F2014339. Comfortable rooms with a/c, TV, phone, fridge, attached bath and balcony (rooms at front with sea views). Restaurant, bar, medium-sized swimming pool. Excellent value for money.

C *Aqaba Star*, Corniche, T2016480, F2018147. Passable rooms (though somewhat in need of refurbishment) with a/c TV/dish, fridge, attached bath and balcony (those at the front with sea views, but noisy due to the traffic on the Corniche below). Restaurant, coffee shop, good buffet breakfast included in room price. Helpful staff. **C** *Shweiki*, Al Hammamat al-Tunisieh St, T2022657, F2022659. Comfortable rooms with a/c, TV/dish, phone and attached bath. Rooms at front very spacious, with balcony; those at rear smaller, no balcony. Restaurant. Good value. **C-D** *Nairoukh*, off Raghadan St, T2019284, F2019285. A/c, TV, fridge and attached bath. Clean rooms, but small and without balconies. Restaurant. A little overpriced. Next door is **C-D** *Dweik*, T2012984, F2012985. A/c, TV/dish, phone, minibar and attached bath. Clean rooms, but rather naff decor. Restaurant.

D *Amira*, off Al Yarmouk St, T2018840, F2012559. Reasonable rooms with a/c, TV/dish, phone, attached bath and balcony. Restaurant. A little overpriced for what you get. **D** *International*, T/F2032486. Reasonably comfortable rooms with a/c, TV, phone and attached bath, but appallingly tacky decor. Restaurant, coffee shop. **D-E** *Al Nahr al-Khaled*, Al-Razi St, T2012456, F2012457. Choice of rooms with a/c, TV, fridge, attached bath and balcony, or simpler rooms with balcony, fan and shared bath only. Unassuming but clean, well run place. Simpler rooms in particular are good value. **D-E** *Al Noman*, Al Petra St, T2015142. Fairly basic rooms with a/c, TV, phone and attached bath. An unremarkable hotel and location, OK value if you bargain them down to around JD10 for a double, but otherwise not worth it. **D-E** *Red Sea*, off Raghadan St, T2012156, F2015789, redseahotel@firstnet.com.jo Pleasant rooms with fan, TV, phone, attached bath and balcony (some also with a/c), or much simpler rooms fan, attached bath and balcony only. Most rooms with sea views. Reasonably good value.

E *Al Khouli*, Zahran St, T/F2030152. Pleasant rooms with a/c, fan, TV/dish, phone, fridge, attached bath and balcony. Also smaller, quieter rooms, but without balconies. Friendly management. Good value. **E-F** *Jordan Flower*, Zahran St, T2014377, F2014378. Choice of doubles with attached or shared bath, all with fan, fridge and balcony (some with a/c). Also dormitories (3/4 bed, JD2.500 per bed) with fan and shared bath. Fairly clean. Popular with backpackers. **E-F** *Petra*, Zahran St, T2013746. Choice of doubles with attached or shared bath (some with balcony and/or a/c). Also dormitories with fan, balcony and shared bath (JD2.500 per bed), or sleep on covered roof area for JD2 (mattresses, toilet/shower facilities, great views). Popular with backpackers. **E-F** *Sagher*, off Corniche, T2016470. Reasonably clean rooms with fan (some rooms also have a/c), phone, fridge and attached bath. Fairly good value.

F *Jerusalem*, Zahran St, T2014815. Basic doubles with fan and shared bath for JD5 (better rooms with balcony; others are windowless boxes). Dormitory rooms with fan and shared bath JD1.500 per bed. A bit grotty, but equally cheap.

Camper vans and caravans are allowed to park up in the parking area adjacent to **Camping** Aqaba Fort free of charge, although there is no privacy here or toilet/shower facilities. Alternatively, there are 2 'official' camp sites.

Juhani Camp, located just off the Corniche, between the public beach and the luxury hotel private beaches (though without its own beach frontage). Some signs of renovations being carried out to the coffee shop here, but otherwise very basic. Shower and toilet facilities. JD1 per person to camp, or JD1.500 per person for campervans/caravans. *National Tourist Campsite*, situated 11 km to the south of Aqaba, occupying a long stretch of land between the road and the sea. The government-owned camping areas here are cheapest (JD1 per person for tents or campervans etc), but they are also furthest from the beach, have little shade and only very basic toilet/shower facilities. Closer to the beach are a number of privately run 'Bedouin camps' within palm-frond enclosures which act as wind-breaks and offer more privacy (JD2 per person). Some very simple palm-frond rooms were also under construction at the time of writing (modelled on the so-called 'camps' to be found at Dahab and elsewhere in Sinai), which will cost around JD5-10 per room when they are completed. A number of simple Bedouin tent/palm frond restaurants (good for fresh fish) and cafés are also being established. Entry to the beach area itself costs 500 fils (see under Beaches, above).

Eating

As well as the hotel restaurants, there's a good range of places to eat in Aqaba which offer more in the way of atmosphere and are worth checking out.

Expensive to mid-range *Al Far*, T2013740. Situated on the northern edge of the modern harbour (around 600 m to the south of the fort). Specialising in fish (from JD6), and with a selection of *mezze* dishes (though the menu is somewhat limited). Modern, mirror-glass building, rather spartan inside, but with a pleasant outdoor terrace. *Ali Baba*, corner of Al Hammamat al-Tunisieh and Raghadan St, T2013901. Huge menu, mostly Arabic but with some Continental dishes, and of course fish (from JD7 per dish). A popular place with a pleasant outdoor seating area which makes for a great place to watch the world go by. Alcohol served. *Captain's Restaurant*, Al-Nahda St (next door to the *Aquamarina City* hotel), T2016905. A small, pleasant restaurant styled as a boat, offering set-menu fish or mixed grill meals for JD9/7 respectively, or a selection of cheaper chicken or pasta dishes. *Hani Ali (Ata Ali)*, Raghadan St, T2015200. A similar set-up to the *Ali Baba* next door, though slightly cheaper, and with excellent ice creams and diet-busting sweets as an added speciality. *Mina House*, T2012699, F2013400. Housed in a pleasantly furnished wooden boat moored in the old fishing harbour (just to the south of the fort). Seating inside on two levels, or outside on the deck. Fish is the speciality here (all fish dishes JD7, except lobster for JD35), though they also serve chicken and meat, and a variety of *mezze* dishes. *Raman*, Corniche (just south of *Nairoukh II* hotel). Reasonable Arabic food for around JD5-7 per head. Pleasant seating indoors or out on the street. *Romero*, T2022404, F2012914. Situated in the Royal Yacht Club (off the large roundabout at the junction of Al Hammamat al-Tunisieh St with the Corniche). A classy restaurant (part of the *Romero* group) serving excellent Italian food. JD7 per head upwards (fish dishes JD8-12 each). Next door is a bar.

Cheap Al Shami, Raghadan St. One of a host of cheapish places along this street. Fairly good value Arabic cuisine (JD3-4 per head). Nice upstairs balcony with good views out over the Gulf of Aqaba. *Chili House*, Al-Nahda St (next door to the *Aquamarina City* hotel). Modern-style diner (eat in or take away) offering chili and spaghetti dishes, burgers, chips and sandwiches. Generous portions. Eat well for under JD3. *China*, Al-Petra St, T2014415. Offers good value Chinese dishes for JD2.500-JD5. *Mankal Chicken Tikka*, off Al-Nahda St (just up from the *Trust International* bus station), T2013633. Part of the chain. The chicken tikka (JD2 for two pieces) is good (large pieces, nicely spiced). Other options include chicken biriyani, shish tawouk and various *mezze* dishes. *Pakistan*, off Al

Hammamat al-Tunisieh St. Simple place serving excellent value budget Pakistani food. Eat well for JD2-3 per head. *Pizza Hut*, Al-Nahda St, T2016974. The usual range of pizzas (from just under JD2 to just under JD10), pasta, salads and starters. The special meal for two costs JD7.400. They will deliver to the main hotels in the immediate vicinity. *Qalat Jdoudna*, situated just off the Corniche, near the fort. From the Corniche, what you see is a juice bar facing the road; below it, around the back and facing the sea, is the *Qalat Jdoudna*, a newly opened diner offering shawarmas, grills, savoury pastries, sandwiches etc.

If you are after a quick snack, there are lots of shawarma places around the centre of **Snacks, juice** Aqaba; the *Altarboosh* on Raghadan St is worth a visit, if only to see the elaborate and **bars & cafés** entertaining flourishes of knife sharpening and serving theatrics. There are also a couple of good (if more subdued) shawarma places on Al-Nahda St opposite the *Aquamarina City* hotel. There are several good juice bars (also serving tea and coffee) along Al-Razi St, near the junction with Zahran St. An excellent traditional café, with shaded and peaceful seating outside, can be found on the pedestrian street across from the *Red Sea* hotel.

Entertainment

Nearly all the luxury and upper range hotels have their own bars. These can be some- **Bars &** what lacking in atmosphere, although many of them have 'happy hours' (for example **nightclubs** at the *After Eight* pub in the *Miramar* hotel from 1730, when a large Amstel costs JD2). The outdoor terrace of the *Ali Baba* restaurant is a nice spot for a drink, while the bar next door to the *Romero* restaurant in the Royal Yacht Club is very smart. *Harley's Place*, on Al-Nahda St (below the *Jordan Suites* hotel), is an American-style bar featuring big-screen TV/dish in the corner. A bit anodyne unless it's busy. Draught Amstel good value at JD2 per pint; cans of Guinness/Kilkenny overpriced at JD4.500. Also serves snacks (burgers, chips, Arabic *mezze* dishes etc). For budget drinks there are several liqueur stores around the town; a good one is *Joseph's*, opposite the *Red Sea* hotel (but note that drinking in public is frowned on, so be discreet).

There are `discos'/nightclubs at the luxury hotels, though they are pretty dire and utterly unable to compete with Eilat's nightlife.

Aqaba Turkish Bath, Corniche (next door to *Nairoukh II* hotel), T2031605. Open **Turkish baths** 0900-2100 in summer, 1000-2300 in winter. Friendly, well-run place, used to dealing with tourists. Women should book in advance (you need a group of at least four to make this viable). 'Turkish' (steam) bath, scrub, massage etc JD10.

Shopping

Redwan Library and *Yamany Library* both have a good selection of books and paper- **Books** backs, though the prices are hugely inflated. Jordanian and foreign newspapers are available (eg *The Observer* for JD3.500). Both have a good selection of snorkelling gear. Try also at the luxury hotels.

Handicraft/souvenir shops selling carpets, woven fabrics, jewellery, pottery etc can be **Handicrafts &** found all around the centre of Aqaba, particularly around Zahran St/Raghadan St, and **souvenirs** in all the luxury hotels. *Noor al-Hussein Craft Shop*, opposite the museum and tourist information office, T2013731, www.nhf.org.jo Open daily 0800-1900. Part of the Noor al-Hussein Foundation's network of shops, established with the aim of creating employment and income generating opportunities among poorer communities (and in particular for women) by promoting and providing outlets for Jordan's traditional crafts. Excellent range of hand-woven rugs, embroidered home furnishings, fabrics basketry, ceramics, glassware, jewellery, furniture etc. Not exactly cheap, but the merchandise is of a very high quality. A pleasure to look round (and no high pressure salesmanship), and worth visiting, if only to get an idea of what's available.

General Along Zahran St, in the commercial centre of Aqaba, there are numerous 'supermarkets' offering a wide range of groceries (including lots of imported luxury items), as well as an impressive array of fresh spices. Worth trying is the *Al Wafa Grocery*, next door to the entrance to the *Khouli* hotel, run by the ever friendly and helpful Fawzi, who loves to ply visitors with his own blend of 'romantica' coffee or cinnamon tea and lively conversation. As well as an excellent range of goodies, he offers a fax service and has internet access (T/F2013793, alwafa_sch@yahoo.com).

Sports

Swimming Aside from the sea of course, most of the luxury hotels have their own swimming pools which non-guests can use for a fee. Of those fronting onto the beach, the *Radisson SAS* and *Coral Beach* both charge JD6 (which includes access to the beach as well), while the *Aquamarina Beach* charges only JD2.500. The *Miramar* is even cheaper at JD2, though it has no beach access.

Tour operators

Petra Travel & Tourism, *Aqaba Gulf* hotel, Corniche, T2016636, F2018246, www.petratours.com Flight reconfirmations, hotel bookings, tours etc. Head office in Amman. *Bridge Travel*, Al Petra St, T2039222, F2035926, www.bridgetravel.com.jo Recently established, with offices in Syria and Lebanon also. Tailor-made tours, including diving, jeep 'safaris' etc. *Hillawi Desert Services*, Corniche (south of *Nairoukh II* hotel), T/F2013841. Specialises in jeep, camel, hiking and camping trips to Wadi Rum. *The Desert Guides*, *Al-Cazar* hotel, T, F2014133, mobile T079-587472. Offer a range of one-day (or longer) excursions to Wadi Rum, Petra, Dana, Dolphin Reef (Eilat), Pharaoh's Island (Sinai) etc. Horse-riding and camel trips a speciality (run by Emmanuel Lançon and Suzie Shinaco, who keep their own horses).

Transport

Local **To/from airport** There is no public transport to and from the airport, although many of the luxury hotels offer a free shuttle bus service. The standard fare for a private taxi from the town centre to the airport is JD5; coming from the airport, you may have to bargain hard.

To/from Wadi Arabah border crossing A private taxi between the town centre and the Wadi Arabah border crossing into Israel costs around JD4. Service taxis operate from the main bus/minibus station for JD1 per person, but only early in the morning. Coming from the border, it is usually much easier to find a service taxi. For more information on this border crossing into Israel, see page 317.

To/from ferry terminal A private taxi between the town centre and the ferry terminal costs around JD3. You can also catch a minibus from the Corniche (wait by the traffic lights opposite the fort), which runs past the entrance to the ferry terminal (8 km, 500 fils) en route to the Saudi border.

Car hire There are several car hire firms in Aqaba. On the whole they are more expensive than in Amman, though there is considerable room for bargaining. **Avis**, Corniche (near *Crystal* hotel), T2022883, mobile T079-656556. Small cars for JD45 per day (+13% tax). Discounts for longer periods; eg JD30 per day for 1 week, including tax and CDW. **Hertz**, Al-Nahda St (opposite *Aquamarina City* hotel, T2016206,

F2016125, hertz@go.com.jo Small cars from JD25 per day. Discounts of around 10% for 1 week, or 15% for 1 month. Minibuses or 4WD jeeps from JD75 per day. Helpful service. **Moon**, Corniche (south of *Nairoukh II* hotel, in same office as *Hillawi* tour operator), T2022232, F2019734. Small cars from JD35 per day. 4WD from JD45 per day. 8-seater minibuses from JD60 per day.

Taxis are readily available throughout Aqaba. The majority do not have meters and overcharging can be a problem, so always agree a price in advance. Short journeys within the town should not really cost more than 500 fils, though as a foreign tourist (and therefore infinitely rich) you may have to settle for JD1.

Air Aqaba airport is 10 km to the northwest of Aqaba, along the Dead Sea/Wadi **Long distance** Arabah Highway (see above for transport to and from the airport). Between them, *Royal Jordanian* and *Royal Wings* provide 2-3 flights daily between Aqaba and Amman. Note that some flights into Amman go to Queen Alia International Airport, while other go to Marka Airport (officially known as Amman Civil Airport). Flying time between Aqaba and Amman is 50 mins, with tickets costing JD30 one way. Bookings can be made through the *Royal Jordanian* office in Aqaba (see Directory, below). Schedules change frequently and cancellations are not uncommon.

Road The *JETT* coach station (T2015222) is on the Corniche, just west of the new *Mövenpick* hotel. A/c coaches to Amman depart 5 times daily (0700, 0900, 1100, 1400, 1600, approx 4 hrs, JD4). In Amman you will be dropped off at the *JETT* coach station on King Hussein St, about 1 km north of Abdali bus station. Tickets can be bought the day before (in any case you are advised to check timings, as these can change).

The *Trust International* coach station (T2032300) is on Al-Nahda St, opposite the *Aquamarina City* hotel. A/c coaches to Amman depart 4 times daily (0730, 1130, 1430, 1700, approx 4 hrs, JD4). In Amman you will be dropped off at the *Trust International* coach station, near 7th Circle. Tickets can be bought the day before and again you are advised to check timings.

The 'main' bus station is on King Talal St (see map). There's no real schedule as such, with services running on a `depart when full' basis. For **Wadi Musa/Petra** there are usually at least 2 minibuses daily, departing between 0800-1000, with a further 2 minibuses between 1200-1600 if there is sufficient demand (JD3). For **Wadi Rum** there is 1 minibus daily departing at around 0630-0700, with a further minibus at around 0900 if there is sufficient demand (JD1.500). There are frequent minibuses (approximately every 30 mins) to **Ma'an** (JD1) and **Quweira** (500 fils), which take you past the turning off the Desert Highway for Wadi Rum, from where you can hitch the remaining 28 km. From Ma'an there are frequent minibuses to Wadi Musa/Petra, and to Showbak, Kerak and Amman. There are coaches for **Amman's** Wahadat bus station, which depart approximately every hour (JD3, not as comfortable as the JETT or Trust International). Service taxis also operate to all the above destinations on a 'depart when full' basis. To charter a private taxi to Petra or Wadi Rum will cost around JD25/20 one-way respectively.

Irregular minibuses depart when full for **Kerak** from the yard on Al Humaimah St (see map). These go via the Dead Sea/Wadi Arabah Highway and cost JD1.500.

Sea The passenger ferry terminal is 8 km south of Aqaba (see above for getting to and from it). Regular **ferries** and faster **sea-cats** run from Aqaba to **Nuweiba** in the Sinai (Egypt). Several agencies sell tickets, though your best bet is to go direct to the *Arab Bridge Maritime Co* on Al Petra St, T2013235, F2013238. The office is open daily from 0830-1430 and 1730-1930, Fri 0830-1430. The `sea-cat' departs daily at 1200, takes 1 hr and costs US$28 (plus JD6 departure tax). The ferry service operates once or twice daily, depending on demand. If there is only one departure it leaves at 1500, if there are 2 they leave at 1200 and 1800. The journey takes around 3-4 hrs (though long delays are common). The fare is US$21 for foot passengers, US$20 for motorbikes, US$103 for cars and US$155 for caravans (plus JD6 departure tax). Bicycles go free. For both the 'sea cat' and the ferry you should arrive at the ferry terminal at least 1 hr beforehand, or 2 hrs if you are taking a vehicle. 'Sinai Permits' (see page 113) are available on the boat, but if you want a full Egyptian visa you should get it in advance from the consulate in Aqaba. Coming from Egypt, Jordanian visas are available on arrival.

Directory

Airline offices *Royal Jordanian* (including *Royal Wings*), Ash Sharif al-Hussein Ibn Ali St, T2014477, F2016555. Open daily 0800-1800, Fri 0800-1400.

Banks Changing money in Aqaba is easy. There are plenty of banks (most with ATMs) to be found in the centre of town (notably along Al Hammamat al-Tunisieh St). Most banks are open 0830-1230, 1530-1730, closed Fri. Licenced moneychangers, which generally do not close in the afternoon and stay open later, are to be found along Al Razi St, around the junction with Zahran St. The luxury hotels will also change money (cash or TCs), but at considerably lower rates. *Jordan National Bank*, Al Hammamat al-Tunisieh St. Charges 3% commission for changing TCs, with a minimum fee of JD3 (no charges on changing cash). Cash advances against *Mastercard*, but no ATM. *Cairo-Amman Bank*, Al Hammamat al-Tunisieh St. Charges JD6.200 commission for changing TCs (no charges on changing cash). Commission-free advances on *Visa* cards, and *Visa* ATM outside. Outside of normal banking hours you can go to their branch inside the same building as the *Arab Bridge Maritime Co*, on Al Petra St (open 0830-1430 and 1730-1930, Fri 0830-1430). Other good banks include the *Arab Bank*, Zahran St, with an ATM which accepts *Visa, Mastercard, Cirrus, +Plus* and *Visa Electron* (there is also an *Arab Bank* ATM at the gate of the *Aquamarina Beach* hotel) and the *Housing Bank*, Corniche (on corner of Al Razi St), with an ATM which accepts *Visa*. *American Express*, c/o *International Traders*, Al Hammamat al-Tunisieh St, T2013757, F2015316, aqaba.office@traders.com.jo Can arrange replacements for lost or stolen Amex TCs (or sell you further supplies), and offers a clients' mail service, but, being a travel agent, cannot cash TCs.

Communications Internet There is a growing number of internet cafés in Aqaba, and prices for internet access are falling steadily. Those along Al Hammamat al-Tunisieh St were still charging hugely inflated rates (up to JD7 per hr) at the time of writing. A few of the better/cheaper places are listed here, though this is a rapidly changing scene so you would do well to ask around for the current best deals. *Aqaba Internet Café,* Corniche (in same building as *JETT* office). Open 0900-2400. Internet access JD3 per hr; JD2 per hr after 1900. *City Internet Café*, Corniche (next door to *Aqaba Gulf* hotel, in same complex as *Red Sea* and *Aqaba International* dive centres). Open 0900-2400. Internet access JD3 per hr; JD2 per hr after 1800. *Cool@Café*, behind (south of) Princess Haya roundabout. Open 0900-2400. Internet access JD2 per hr. **Post** The Central Post Office is on Al Yarmouk St. Open 0800-1800, Fri 0800-1200. The poste restante service here is particularly chaotic; better to use the *American Express* clients' mail service (you don't need to be a customer). **Telephone** There are several *Alo* and *JPP* cardphones just outside the Central Post Office, with phonecards on sale at the nearby kiosks, and more cardphones dotted around the town. There are also several private telephone offices in the centre of town, though these are more expensive and only really of use for sending/receiving faxes.

Consulates Egyptian consulate, off Al-Istiqlal St (see map), T2016171. Open 0900-1500, closed Fri. Visa applications should be submitted between 0900-1200; if you get there early, it is usually possible to collect your passport the same day, just before the consulate closes at 1500. Tourist visas JD12/15 for single/multiple entry. Sinai Permits (see page 122) free.

Medical services *Princess Haya Hospital*, by roundabout at entrance to town, T2014111. Excellent facilities, including decompression chamber in case of diving accidents. There are several good pharmacies near the hospital, and a dispensary inside.

Useful phone numbers Tourist Police], T2019717. **Police**. T2012411. **Diving accidents**, T193.

Aqaba-Amman: two north-south routes

The King's Highway is undoubtably the most interesting route by which to travel between Amman and Aqaba, and is covered in detail in a separate chapter. However, there are two additional routes connecting these urban centres; the Desert Highway and the Dead Sea/Wadi Arabah Highway. Both are fast routes. In the case of the Desert Highway, this is really its only attraction, but the Dead Sea/Wadi Arabah Highway is also of interest in itself, taking you past a couple of important archaeological sites and through some stunning scenery as it follows the shores of the Dead Sea.

Dead Sea/Wadi Arabah Highway: Aqaba to Amman

Prior to the signing of the peace treaty with Israel, this route lay within a restricted military zone, and it is only in recent years that the various checkposts along the road have been done away with. It is a fast road, with very little traffic, although you have to watch out for the huge potash lorries which crawl along it, and the odd camel wandering across. It is a good idea to fill up with petrol before setting off, although there are now petrol stations at fairly regular intervals.

Following the main road leading northeast out of Aqaba, take the left turn signposted for 'Aqaba International Airport', just over 3 km from the town centre. Continue straight on past a left turn signposted for 'Eilat' (this road leads to the Wadi Arabah/Arava border crossing into Israel). Some 3 km further on (7 km from the turning off the Desert Highway) is **Aqaba Airport** to the left of the road, with a checkpost by the entrance. Continuing north, some 35 km further on, near the village of **Rahma**, there is a new petrol station and cafeteria. Another 37 km brings you to the small settlement of **Risha**, with a couple of very basic snack places and a police post. About 32 km beyond Risha there is another petrol station and small café. Another 20 km further on (136 km from Aqaba), there is a right turn signposted to Fidan and Qurayqira, from where you can reach the RSCN Feinan campsite in Wadi Feinan (part of the Dana Nature Reserve, see page 52).

Continuing north, around 39 km further on, there is a right turn for Tafila on the King' Highway. The next section takes you through the intensively farmed agricultural areas surrounding **Safi**, off to the east, before arriving at a right turn signposted for **Lot's Cave** and Safi itself, 19 km from the Tafila turning (for details of Lot's Cave, see page 235). After this, the fertile agricultural land gives way to a more industrial landscape of potash factories. Just under 4 km from the Lot's Cave turning there is a large 24 hour petrol station (the last one for around 160 km before you join the highway up to Amman). Just under 4 km further on again there is a major right turn leading up to Kerak, followed soon after by the small settlement of Mazraa, where there are a couple of very basic eateries. A little further north you get your first views of the Dead Sea stretching away to the west, with rocky mountains rising steeply up to the east, and the road snaking a path between them.

Some 25 km north the Kerak turning you come to a bridge across the **Wadi Mujib** where it emerges from its dramatic, sheer-sided gorge. This whole area to the east of the road is part of the RSCN Wadi Mujib Nature Reserve (see page 225). There is a small hut down by the wadi, close to the bridge, which acts as the RSCN reception centre. This is a popular picnic area, although you

Aqaba

must take an RSCN guide if you wish to explore the Wadi Mujib gorge upstream from the bridge (note also that there is a very real danger of flash floods in the gorge). Another 15 km or so brings you to the **Ain Zarqa Hot Springs**, to the right of the road. From here it is a further 23 km to the junction with the highway leading up to Amman, passing various hotel/resort complexes along the way. For details of the Dead Sea resorts, and the Ain Zarqa Hot Springs, see page 120.

Desert Highway: Amman to Aqaba

The Desert Highway is the fastest and most direct route linking Amman and Aqaba. It is also the most boring, taking you through a monotonous and unchanging desert landscape for most of the way. If you are driving, the volume of heavy lorry traffic along it can make it hard going at times. Nevertheless, if you are in a hurry, it is convenient.

Either take the route out of Amman as if to join the King's Highway and follow signs for the Desert Highway/airport/Aqaba. Or head south out of Downtown Amman along Prince Hassan St and keep going straight, past the exit for Azraq (8 km), the exit for Madaba (19 km) and the exit for the **Queen Alia International Airport** (35 km). After a further 30 km you pass a right turn signposted for `Dhaban'. This turning takes you past Umm ar-Rasas to Dhiban on the King's Highway. 27 km further on is Qatrana.

Qatrana   Situated 92 km from Amman, Qatrana is a popular halting place for transport along the Desert Highway, and is marked by various truck-stop diners lining the road. The best place however is the *Baalbaki Tourist Resort*, a few kilometres to the north of the main cluster of restaurants, T03-398080, F398156. This modern, well-run complex houses various shops, including an outlet of the *Noor al-Hussein Foundation* (for handicrafts), a good restaurant and accommodation (**B** category). Just over 2 km to the south of the main cluster of diners, there is a right turn leading into the centre of Qatrana, and 3 km beyond this there is a major right turn leading to Kerak.

Continuing south along the Desert Highway, you pass an exit signposted for Mazar and Mu'ata (126 km from Amman), which brings you out on the King's Highway just south of Mazar, passing close to the village of Dhat Ras. Next is an exit signposted 'Jurf al-Darawish Junction' (163 km from Amman), which brings you out on the King's Highway at Tafila. 23 km further on is an exit signposted for Petra, which joins the King's Highway just to the north of Showbak. Another 31 km or so brings you to an exit signposted for Ma'an, just to the east of the Desert Highway (this is the north exit for Ma'an; the south exit is 5 km further on; between the two there is an exit which leads northwest to join the King's Highway just to the north of Showbak, with a branch at Udruh to Petra).

Ma'an   Although there is nothing of special interest in Ma'an, it is a useful transport hub, with frequent minibuses and service taxis running from here to Amman and Aqaba, and fairly frequent minibuses to Wadi Musa (for Petra). There are also a couple of basic hotels and restaurants here if you get stuck or want to break your journey.

Sleeping and eating   Of the 3 hotels in Ma'an, the **E-F** *Krishan*, in the town centre (T2132043) is the cleanest, although the rooms (double JD10) do not have fans. The rooms at the front have balconies overlooking the main street. Downstairs is a restaurant. To the west of the town centre is the **E-F** *Shwaikh*, T2132428, which has reasonably clean rooms with fan, TV and smelly attached bath (JD10), or slightly cheaper ones with shared bathrooms. Just up the road is the **F** *Tabouk*, T2132452, offering tiny rooms with fan, TV and attached bath for JD4. The restaurant below the *Krishan* hotel serves reasonable food. There are several good restaurants along King Hussein St (to the south of the mosque) with chicken roasters and barbeque stands set out on the street, as well as lots of well-stocked fruit and vegetable shops.

Banks and transport Also on King Hussein St are branches of the *Arab Bank* and *Housing Bank*, both with ATMs. The bus station is tucked away in the residential area to the east of the southern section of King Hussein St. As well as regular services to Amman, Aqaba and Wadi Musa, there are reasonably frequent minibuses to Kerak and Showbak, and more erratic services to various other towns and villages in southern Jordan. There is no direct service to Wadi Rum; take an Aqaba-bound minibus as far as the turning off the Desert Highway, then hitch from there.

Continuing south along the Desert Highway, you pass two exits for Wadi Musa/Petra, the first around 10 km beyond the southern exit for Ma'an, and the second a little under 15 km further on. Both these exits take you to the road leading to Petra via Eil and Basta. Another 8 km to the south is the turning for Petra via Rajif and Taybet (see page 286 for details of the various routes between Petra and the Desert Highway). Soon after this turning, the road descends dramatically from its high plateau and continues south through open desert, with a taste of the spectacular scenery typical of Wadi Rum stretching away to the east. The turning for Wadi Rum itself is 42 km from the last turning to Petra, and from here it is another 42 km to Aqaba. For details of this last section of the Desert Highway between the Wadi Rum turning and Aqaba, see page 300.

Ma'an

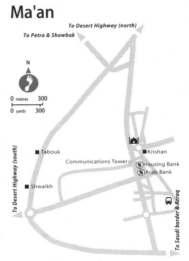

Aqaba

Background

12

Background

History

"As works of the imagination, the historian's work and the novelist's do not differ. Where they do differ is that the historian's picture is meant to be true." (RG Collingwood)

Although Jordan only came into existence as a nation-state during the 20th century, the land it occupies boasts a history dating right back to the earliest dawn of civilisation, and beyond, revealing traces of human activity stretching back as far as the Old Stone Age or Lower Paleolithic era (as much as one million years ago).

To describe Jordan as standing at the "crossroads of history and civilization" may sound like the clichéd hyperbole of tourist brochures, but geographically it has indeed acted as a causeway linking two of the great cradles of civilisation; Egypt and Mesopotamia. With the Mediterranean to the west and the vast deserts of Arabia to the east, this region has from time immemorial acted as a narrow corridor for movement between North Africa and Eurasia. Such was the importance of this route that when Moses led the Israelites along it, that it was already known as the King's Highway. Even today the modern road of this name follows an almost identical course.

Forming part of the so-called Fertile Crescent, Jordan's varied landscape and climate provided the ideal environment for settlement and agriculture to emerge as early as elsewhere in the region. However, it was never sufficiently productive to allow civilizations to prosper in their own right (with the exception perhaps of the Nabateans, who thrived by taxing the trade along the King's Highway). Instead, for most of its history, the land that comprises modern-day Jordan has acted as a battleground for the invading armies of more powerful neighbours, being periodically incorporated into their empires and, to a greater or lesser extent, influenced by their cultures. Small indigenous kingdoms did come and go, but they were generally fragmented and riven by infighting.

Jordan's modern history has been equally influenced by international events. Sharing borders with Israel, Syria, Iraq, Saudi Arabia and Egypt, it has been obliged to maintain a delicate and often highly pragmatic balancing act in order to ensure its own survival. The Arab-Israeli wars of 1947-9 and 1967 left Jordan with a massive population of Palestinian refugees, while the latter war saw the country shorn of the cherished Holy City of Jerusalem and the whole of the West Bank. Even before this traumatic dismemberment, many had dismissed Jordan as an unviable entity, too weak to stand up to its neighbours and lacking in the wealth and natural resources needed to survive economically. Yet today the country stands almost as a beacon of hope in the Middle East. Its economy, though by no means prosperous, has proved relatively stable. Socially and politically, against all the odds, it has acheived a remarkable level of cohesion, and even the seeds of a democratic process. Perhaps most importantly, however, in the context of a region dogged by deep-rooted conflicts and tensions, it has also earned itself international respect as the voice of restraint and moderation.

The Pre-Historic Era

The **Paleolithic** period stretches back to around 1,500,000 years ago in the Middle East. The oldest clear evidence of human activity in Jordan, found at the site of Ubeidiyeh in the northern Jordan valley, dates back to around 700,000 BC (during the Lower Paleolithic period). At this time the climate was

Hunter-gatherers

• •

👉 *Chronology of archaeological and historic periods*

Lower Paleolithic	*1,500,000 - 100,000 BC*
Middle Paleolithic	*100,000 - 40,000 BC*
Upper Paleolithic	*40,000 - 17,000 BC*
Epipaleolithic (Mesolithic)	*17,000 - 8500 BC*
Pre Pottery Neolithic	*8500 - 6000 BC*
Pottery Neolithic	*6000 - 4500 BC*
Early Bronze Age	*3300 - 2250 BC*
Middle Bronze Age	*2250 - 1550 BC*
Late Bronze Age	*1550 - 1200 BC*
Iron Age	*1200 - 539 BC*
Persian Period	*539 - 333 BC*
Hellenistic Period	*333 - 64 BC*
Roman/Nabatean Period	*64 BC - 395 AD*
Byzantine Period	*395 - 636 AD*
Early Islamic Period	
Arab Conquest	*632 - 661 AD*
Umayyad Period	*661 - 750 AD*
Abbasid Period	*750 - 969 AD*
Fatimid Period	*969 - 1171 AD*
Crusader Period	*1097 - 1291 AD*
Late Islamic Period	
Zengid and Ayyubid Periods	*1128 - 1260 AD*
Mameluke Period	*1260 - 1516 AD*
Ottoman Period	*1516 - 1918 AD*
Modern Period	*1918 AD - Present*

• •

much wetter. Large lakes occupied much of the region and vegetation was more extensive and abundant, supporing large mammals such as elephants and hippopatami. Neanderthal man was engaged in primitive forms of hunting and gathering, utilizing simple stone tools such as the Acheulien hand axe. The oasis around Azraq and the highlands around Kerak have revealed evidence of similar Neanderthal campsites dating from the Middle Paleolithic, scattered with the debris of hunted animals and stone tools.

During the **Epipaleolithic** or **Mesolithic** period (17,000-8500 BC) the region underwent major climatic and environmental changes. The end of the last Ice Age (which for Jordan had meant a wet temperate climate, or *pluvial* period), saw the lakes retreat and vegetation become sparser. The larger mammals were gradually replaced by smaller faster ones such as gazelles and wild goats. *Homo sapiens sapiens* first made their appearance around this time, developing more elaborate hunting skills to match the greater agility of their prey, as reflected in the appearance of more specialised stone tools (*microliths*) such as flint arrow-heads, spear-heads and knives. Simultaneously, the gathering of wild grains began to take on a greater importance, and the first semi-permanent settlements began to appear. The 'cultures' dating from this period are referred to as *Natufian*, after the first archaeological site of this kind to be discovered, at Wadi al-Natuf, a cave 27 km north of Jerusalem.

Early settlement All around the peripheries of the Middle East, the so-called Fertile Crescent (see next page) provided the ideal conditions for the development of settled agriculture. This occured towards the end of the Epipaleolithic (Mesolithic) period and during the early stages of the **Pre-Pottery Neolithic** period

Background

Jordan in history

The fact that Jordan only came into existence as a nation-state in 1946 poses certain problems when it comes to discussing the earlier history of this region. Historically, the area covered by present-day Jordan formed part of a much larger region generally referred to as 'Syria', though the actual definition of this term has shifted over the ages. The word itself was originally Greek, derived from the Semitic Suriyon, or perhaps the Babylonian Suri. Herodotus believed the term 'Syria' to be a corruption of 'Assyria', denoting the western parts of the loosely-defined Assyrian empire. By the Roman era, 'Syria' had come to mean "those regions of the Near East between Asia Minor and Egypt which belonged to the Roman empire" (indeed, the Roman conquest of 64 BC saw the creation of the Roman Provincia Syria, with Antioch as its capital). The Roman definition endured through the Byzantine era and, with the coming of the Muslim Arabs, though the terminology changed, the broad definition remained the same.

In Arabic, the region was referred to as Ash Sham or Bilad ash-Sham (literally 'The North' or 'The Country of the North'. From the point of view of the nomadic Arab tribes who conquered this region, it was indeed to the north of their heartlands in the depths of the Arabian desert; by the same token, they used the term al-Yaman (literally 'The South') to refer to southern Arabia, this term gaining currency in English as Yemen. In Europe, the term 'Syria' (or in French 'Syrie') continued to be used, and with the growing European influence in the region, became Arabised during the 19th century as 'Suriya'.

Thus a distinction needs to be made between 'geographical/historical Syria', which PK Hitti describes as "the lands between the Taurus and Sinai, the Mediterranean and the desert", and the modern nation-states of Jordan, Israel, Syria and Lebanon which today occupy this region.

Within geographical/historical Syria there were many other regional definitions, all of them vague and ill-defined. Modern-day Israel was, roughly speaking, Palestine, while in Europe the term 'Southern Syria' was largely interchangeable with 'Palestine', though it tended to include parts of what was otherwise referred to as 'Transjordan', the land across (to the east of) the Jordan river. During the period of British Mandate rule which followed the San Remo conference of 1920, the status (or indeed the extent) of 'Transjordan' was far from clear (see page 344). It was only in 1923 that the 'Emirate of Transjordan' was formally established, eventually gaining full independence as the 'Hashemite Kingdom of Jordan' in 1946.

(8500-6000 BC). In the Jordan Valley, wheat and barley appear to have been first cultivated around 10,000 years ago, while 8000 to 9000 years ago sheep and goats had been fully domesticated. Hunting and gathering still played an important role, while the domestication of sheep and goats still required at least a semi-nomadic lifestyle in order find suitable grazing. Gradually, however, small permanent settlements became more widely established.

During the **Pottery Neolithic** period (6000-4500 BC), baked clay (ceramic) wares make their appearance. This period witnessed a further marked reduction in levels of rainfall, and settlement tended to shift to riverside and coastal sites. Settlements such as Jericho (on the west bank of the Jordan river, in present-day Israel) were complemented by others at Beidha (near Petra), Ain Ghazal (near Amman), and in the northern Jordan Valley near its junction with the Yarmouk river. As well as practical pottery utensils, excavations at many of these sites have yielded intriguing clay figurines and skulls decorated with clay and cowrie shells, suggesting that some form of religious worship, or at least veneration of the dead, was practised.

The Desert and the Sown

*Viewing the Middle East as a whole, its single largest feature is the vast Arabian desert. This forms the core of the region, around which is a periphery of fertile land; the **Fertile Crescent**. This stretches in a broad arc from southern Jordan up through Lebanon and Syria following the eastern plateau of the Great Rift Valley, the Jordan River, Bekaa valley, the Lebanese and Syrian coastal plains and mountains and the Orontes river, right up to the Taurus mountains marking the border between Turkey and Syria, following them east and then bending southwards to follow the Euphrates and Tigris rivers right the way down though Iraq to the Arabian Gulf.*

In many ways, the ancient history of this region has been to a large extent shaped by the relationship between the central core of desert and the Fertile Crescent surrounding it. While the Fertile Crescent provided the best environment for the emergence of agriculture and permanent settlements, the desert itself was the source of successive waves of migrations. Nomadic tribes of the deserts gradually (and in some cases more abruptly and violently) moved into the fertile peripheries, displacing those that were already there and bringing with them their own new cultures and languages. In ancient times, the most important of these tribes included the Amorites, Aramaeans and indeed the Hebrews. All shared a common mother-tongue which developed into different languages, but still shared a basically Semitic root. More recently, the arrival of the Muslim Arabs and their conquest of the Middle East during the 7th century AD represents another such wave of migration from the desert interior into the fertile settled lands of the periphery.

The **Chalcolithic** period (4500-3300 BC) heralded the appearance of copper (first used in eastern Anatolia and central Iran). Village settlements based on agriculture spread throughout the whole of the region. Agriculture and animal husbandry both became more sophisticated. At sites such as Abu Hamid (to the north of Tell Deir Alla in the Jordan Valley), wheat and barley were complemented by pulses, olives and flax, while further south, dates and grapes were being cultivated. As well as sheep and goats, cattle and pigs were kept, and remains of dogs, donkeys, gazelle and foxes have also been found. Styles of pottery become more varied, while basalt was also being used for many utensils. Large complex wall paintings have also been discovered at sites such as Teleilat Ghassul near the Dead Sea. By now there was a thriving trade in obsidian with Anatolia.

The Ancient Era

The first cities and empires By the **Early Bronze Age** (3300-2250 BC), settled agricultural communities could be found across the Middle East. Gradually these grew in size and complexity, giving rise to the first city-states (urban centres supported by an agricultural hinterland). Initially, this process of urbanization took place at the opposite end of the Fertile Crescent, in southern Mesopotamia, where the **Sumerian** civilisation began to evolve from the 5th millenium BC. Here, an economy based on animal husbandry and large-scale irrigation of the river valleys between the Tigris and Euprates rivers produced substantial surpluses. This in turn allowed powerful city-states with specialized divisions of labour and complex social hierarchies and administrations to emerge. The most important of these was **Uruk** in southern Mesopotamia, the source of the 'Late Uruk' culture.

The most significant feature of the Sumerian civilisation was the development of a form of writing based on the cuneiform script. At the same time, from around 2900-2300 BC (a period in Syria generally referred to as the Early

Background

Syrian II period and in Egypt as the Early Dynastic period), the settlements at **Mari** (Tell Hariri) on the Euphrates and **Ebla** (Tell Mardikh) on the Central Plains to the south of Aleppo were also evolving into powerful city-states in their own right. Both developed their own systems of writing based on the cuneiform script of the Sumerians. In the Nile Delta meanwhile, a more or less identical process had led to the emergence of a unified **Egyptian** nation-state, the so-called Old Kingdom. On the Mediterranean coast, **Byblos** (Jbail) flourished as a result of its trading links with the pharaohs of the Old Kingdom, supplying them with timber from the cedar forests of Mount Lebanon which was used, amongst other things, in the construction of the pyramids.

The city-states which evolved in Jordan – at sites such as Bab adh-Dhraa in Wadi Araba, Zeiraqoun and Jawa – were smaller and less influencial, though they too clearly flourished, developing trade links as far afield as Egypt, Cyprus and Greece. All, however, were influenced by the upheavals of the **Middle Bronze Age** (2250-1550 BC). The traditional view holds that towards the end of the 3rd millenium BC, the region was overrun by the **Amorites**, a Semitic people who emerged from the deserts to the south and east, leading to the destruction of the city-states. Certainly, the archaeological record confirms the arrival and great influence of the Amorites around this time, but it now seems more likely that they found the city-states already in a state of decline, brought about by ecological pressures and social disintegration rather than invasion. By around 1900 BC, the city states of the region began once again to prosper, with those of the southern Levant coming under the influence of the Middle Kingdom pharaohs of Egypt.

During the 17th century BC the **Hyksos**, a people of mixed Semitic/Asiatic origin, swept through the Middle East, overthrowing the Middle Kingdom pharaohs and establishing their own dynasty in Egypt. The Hyksos brought with them innovations such as the composite bow and the horse and chariot (perhaps accounting for their success). Both in terms of the new military techniques they introduced, and the culture they brought with them (styles of pottery etc), they had a major influence on the region.

The **Late Bronze Age** (1550-1200 BC) saw further upheavals in the region. The expulsion of the Hyksos from Egypt by the first pharaoh of the 18th Dynasty (heralding the start of the 'New Kingdom') around 1550 BC was soon followed by a far greater **Egyptian** involvement in the region, particularly in the southern Levant and along the Mediterranean coast in centres such as Byblos and Ugarit.

Ancient superpower rivalries

The region which today comprises Jordan was to remain for the most part under Egyptian domination until the end of the Late Bronze Age, although the empires which emerged to the north certainly made their influence felt. First came the **Hittites**, a new peoples of Indo-European origin, who arrived from the northwest. These were complemented by the **Hurrians** and later the **Mittanites** who arrived from the northeast. The latter two blended into a federation known as the **Mittani** kingdom. For a time, the Egyptian, Hittite and Mittani empires formed a triangle of superpowers fighting for control of the region. Eventually the Mittani kingdom was absorbed into that of the Hittites, the struggle for supremacy becoming a straight battle between the Egyptians and Hittites. Byblos, along with Sidon and Tyre, allied themselves with Egypt, though their pleas for assistance in the face of the Hittite threat, as recorded in the famous Tell Amarna tablets discovered in Egypt, were largely ignored by the Egyptian pharaoh of the time. The armies of the two powers finally met head-on at Kadesh, though the outcome of the battle was inconclusive, with both sides claiming victory.

Despite these upheavals, it was during the Late Bronze Age that the first alphabets were developed, offering a massive improvement on the hugely complex cuneiform system first developed by the Sumerians, and the equally complex hieroglyphic system of the Egyptians. This momentous development occured initially at Ugarit during the 14th century BC, and later at Byblos towards the end of the 13th century BC, the latter being considered by many experts to represent the forerunner of our own alphabet.

It was also probably towards the very end of the Late Bronze Age that the famous **Exodus** took place, when Moses led the **Israelites** out of slavery in Egypt and back to the 'Promised Land', his successor Joshua leading the 12 tribes across the Jordan river into Palestine.

Iron Age
(1200-539 BC)

The start of the Iron Age saw two major migrations which coincided with fundamental changes in the region. The first was the violent invasion of the so-called **'Sea Peoples'**, about which remarkably little is known. As JD Muhly points out; "*While the Egyptian texts refer to massed invasions by land and by sea of various groups collectively known as the 'Peoples of the Sea', it has been notoriously difficult to find any trace of such people in the archaeological record. Only the **Phillistines**, who gave their name to what was thereafter known as Palestine subsequent to their settlement in the area as Egyptian garrison troops, can be identified in the archaeological context by their distinctive painted pottery.*" (JD Muhly in *Ebla to Damascus*). What is known however is that the arrival of these 'Sea Peoples' coincided with the collapse of the Hittite empire to the north and the decline of Egyptian influence in the southern Levant. More recently, scholars have begun to argue that, as in the case with the Amorites, this was perhaps as much due to ecological and social changes as it was to invasion.

In the wake of the 'Sea Peoples' came the **Aramaeans**, a semi-nomadic Semitic people who arrived from the deserts of Arabia and settled in central and northern Syria, blending with the small **Neo-Hittite** kingdoms which had arisen in the wake of the collapse of the Hittite empire, and establishing themselves also in Damascus.

To the south, the departure of the Egyptians had in effect left a power vacuum. This was filled by a series of small competing territorial states. The most important of these, running north to south roughly between Amman and Aqaba were the **Ammonite**, **Moabite** and **Edomite** kingdoms. These names appear to have been in use since the Late Bronze Age, but it was only now that they came to represent independent kingdoms.

To the west of the Jordan river, the **Israelites** were finally united under the leadership of King Saul (circa 1020-1004 BC) and then King David (1004-965 BC), the latter establishing Jerusalem as his capital around 997 BC. The balance of power between the Ammonites, Moabites, Edomites and Israelites continually ebbed and flowed. At first, King David and his successor King Solomon (965-928 BC) appear to have dominated the eastern states, forging a powerful empire in what is considered by many to be one of the 'golden ages' of Jewish history. After the death of Solomon, however, the Israelite kingdom became divided between Judah in the south and Israel in the north, and the kingdoms to the east began to reassert their independence.

Rabbath Ammon (modern-day Amman) flourished as the capital of the Ammonite kingdom, with archaeological evidence indicating that, in terms of its art at least, it was significantly more advanced than both Moab and Israel. King Mesha, the ruler of Moab from around 853-830 BC, recorded his military victories over the Israelites on the famous Mesha Stela (see page 223), thus providing for the first time an alternative literary source for this period other than the Old Testament. Edom, though remaining nominally under the

The biblical origins of the Ammonites, Moabites, Edomites and Israelites

In Genesis, the first book of the Old Testament, the story is related of how, after the destruction of Sodom and Gomorrah and the flight of Lot (see page 233), his two daughters slept with him, both producing sons who were to become the fathers of the Moabites and Ammonites respectively;

"Lot and his two daughters left Zoar and settled in the mountains, for he was afraid to stay in Zoar. He and his two daughters lived in a cave. One day the older daughter said to the younger, "Our father is old, and there is no man around here to lie with us, as is the custom all over the earth. Let's get our father to drink wine and then lie with him and preserve our family line through our father." ....So both of Lot's daughters became pregnant by their father. The older daughter had a son, and she named him Moab; he is the father of the Moabites of today. The younger daughter also had a son, and she named him Ben-Ammi; he is the father of the Ammonites today." (Genesis 19; 30-38).

It has to be remembered that the stories of the Old Testament were written from the point of view of the Israelites. Though related to the Israelites (Lot was a nephew of Abraham), the Ammonites and Moabites were more often than not at loggerheads with them. As B MacDonald points out; "This Israelite tale of the Ammonites and the Moabites was told partly to ridicule these racially related but rival nations, and partly to give folk etymologies for their names [In Hebrew Moab translates as "from my father", while Ben-Ammi translates as "the son of my people"]....no doubt the Ammonites and Moabites had their own derogatory stories about the Israelites." (B MacDonald, Ammon, Moab and Edom, 1994). Later in Genesis, the story is related of the origins of the Edomites and Israelites. Abraham's son Isaac had twins by his wife Rebekah;

"The Lord said to her, 'Two nations are in your womb, and two peoples from within you will be separated; one people will be stronger than the other, and the older will serve the younger.' When the time came for her to give birth, there were twin boys in her womb. The first to come out was red, and his whole body was like a hairy garment; so they named him Esau. After this, his brother came out, with his hand grasping Esau's heel; so he was named Jacob." (Genesis 25; 23-26).

'Esau' is translated as 'hairy'. He was also known as 'Edom' (literally 'Red'), and later in Genesis Esau is identified as the ancestor of the Edomites; "This is the account of Esau the father of the Edomites" (Genesis 36; 9). 'Jacob' is translated as 'he grasps the heel', and is interpreted as meaning 'he supplants' or 'he deceives'. The Old Testament goes on to recount how Jacob persuades Esau to give up his birthright (as the eldest son) and then tricks his father into giving him his blessing (Genesis 25 and 27). Later, Jacob changes his name to Israel, becoming the ancestor of the Israelites. To quote MacDonald again, as with the story of the Ammonites and Moabites, "Throughout Genesis, Esau, ie Edom, is continually portrayed in a poor light; to satisfy his immediate hunger, he sells his birthright (Genesis 25; 29-34); to his parents' grief he marries Hittite, ie foreign, women (Genesis 26; 34-35); and his future is one of subjugation to his brother Jacob, ie Israel (Genesis 27; 40)."

Thus the Bible suggests that the Ammonites, Moabites, Edomites and Israelites were all related. Though their biblical version of their origins cannot in any way be considered historical, it is widely accepted that all these tribes probably did form part of the great Aramaean migrations from the Arabian desert.

Background

---

control of Judah, clearly exercised considerable independence and also flourished, exploiting the rich mineral resources, particularly copper, to be found in the Wadi Arabah region. Indeed, it was the struggle for control over such mineral resources, and more importantly the lucrative trade along the King's

Highway, which fuelled the constant antagonism which existed between these kingdoms.

Along the Mediterranean coast, meanwhile, Phoenicia was experiencing its golden age, with the king of Tyre supplying Solomon with cedar for the building of the great Temple, and Phoenician ships voyaging throughout the Mediterranean and beyond, carrying out lucrative trade and establishing numerous colonies, most famously that of Carthage in North Africa.

From the 9th century BC a new empire, that of the **Assyrians**, arose in northern Mesopotamia and gradually extended its control southwards, making its presence felt in the southern Levant towards the end of the 8th century BC. Having captured Damascus ten years earlier, the Assyrian king Tiglath Pileser III invaded the kingdom of Israel in 722 BC, wreaking destruction on the land and driving its people into exile.

Statue of Yerah 'Azar, Ammonite King

Ammon, Moab and Edom by contrast seem to have fared better, paying tribute to the Assyrians in return for their autonomy, and benefitting from the relative stability which ensued.

In their turn, however, the Assyrians were overthrown by the **Neo-Babylonians** (or **Chaldeans**), who captured their capital Nineveh in 612 BC. Again, it was Israel which suffered most under the Neo-Babylonians. In 587 BC Nebuchadnezzar II attacked the kingdom of Judah, capturing Jerusalem, razing the Temple and sending the Jews into exile (the 'Babylonian Exile'). Though the Ammonite capital was also sacked, both Moab and Edom appear to have been largely unaffected.

Persian period (539-333 BC) Neo-Babylonian dominance of the region was short-lived, with the **Achaemenid Persians**, led by Cyrus the Great, capturing their capital Babylon in 539 BC, taking over control of their empire and extending it to include all of the Middle East, Egypt and Asia Minor. Persian rule was on the whole very well organised, with an excellent network of roads encouraging trade and communications within the empire. Cyrus allowed the Jews to return to their historical homeland and soon after the Temple at Jerusalem was rebuilt. When the Ammonites and Moabites attacked the newly re-established Jewish state, he even led a campaign to repulse them. Such adventures apart, the eastern kingdoms appear to have fared well under the Persians, with trade once again flourishing. Locally produced pottery, stone carvings and iron utensils were supplemented by imported goods from Babylon, while the palace architecture of the imperial rulers was adopted in many places, along with their script and seal motifs. On the Mediterranean coast, the cities of the Phoenicians, in particular Sidon, also flourished. The Sidonian fleet aided the Persians in their defeat of the Egyptians in 525 BC, and played a crucial role in their wars with the Greeks.

The Classical Era

Although the Persians were at first successful in their battles with the **Greeks**, ultimately it was the latter who triumphed, with Alexander the Great of Macedon defeating the forces of Darius III at the battle of Issus in 333 BC. When he died at Babylon in 323 BC, Alexander was only 33 years old and in the space of just 10 years had succeeded in creating an empire larger even than that of the Persians.

After his death, Alexander's empire was partitioned between his generals. Ptolemy I Soter gained control of Egypt and the southern Levant (including Damascus), founding what became known as the **Ptolemid** empire. Seleucus I Nicator meanwhile gained control of Mesopotamia, Asia Minor and northern Syria, establishing what became known as the **Seleucid** empire. Over the next century, the Seleucids extended their control southwards, driving the Ptolemids back into Egypt, though at the same time they lost Asia Minor to the Romans and Mesopotamia to the Parthians (who arose from the ashes of the Persian empire). Thus present-day Jordan came to be controlled by the Seleucids.

The Seleucids continued the process, begun under Alexander, of Hellenization. Cities such as Philadelphia (present-day Amman), Gerasa (Jerash), Pella and Gadara (Umm Qais), all flourished. Though the Greeks invariably claimed to have 'founded' such cities, most had already existed as small settlements. They did however lay out distinctive grid-patterns of streets and erected civic buildings and monuments, bringing with them Greek political and legal institutions, and indeed the Greek language. All the same, many of these cities were able to establish a high degree of autonomy within the empire, often amounting to near independence. The Seleucids, being relatively few in number, had no choice but to let them run their own affairs, albeit in a Hellenistic way. In the countryside, they made little or no impression.

By the 2nd century BC the Seleucid empire was beginning to crumble. The sacking of Jerusalem and desecration of the Temple there prompted the Maccabean revolt of 173 BC, which in turn led to the creation of the independent Jewish **Hasmonean** dynasty within Palestine. The Hasmoneans subsequently extended their power to the east of the Jordan river, capturing Jerash in 84 BC. At the same time, the **Nabateans**, who had already established themselves as a powerful, semi-independent trading state in Petra, began to push northwards. Under King Aretas III (84-56 BC), they briefly succeed in extending their empire to include Bosra (in southern Syria) and Damascus. Similarly, the Itureans, a local tribal dynasty from the Bekaa valley, began making raids on the coastal cities and inland centres. In the northern part of the empire, the Seleucids faced more serious threats from the Romans to the west, the Armenians to the north and the Parthians to the east

Hellenistic period (333-64 BC)

The final fall of the Seleucid empire came with the conquest of Antioch by the Roman general Pompey in 64 BC. The Romans created the province of Syria in their newly acquired territory and adopted Antioch as its capital. Initially, the Romans were much more concerned with their own internal power struggles, and at one stage the Parthians even succeeded in occupying much of Syria. Rome's bloody intrigues finally drew to an end with the abolition of the Roman Republic and the appointment of Octavian as the first Roman emperor in 29 BC.

Thus at first the Romans were only able to exercise loose political control, declaring the former city-states of the Seleucid empire 'free cities'. In the south, the Nabatean kingdom continued to exist as an independent entity, keeping Damascus until as late as 54 AD. After that it was pushed back into its former confines of Petra, though in 70 AD it pushed northwards again and

Roman period (64 BC-395 AD)

Background

briefly made Bosra the capital of its empire. Although Pompey had taken Jerusalem when he first conquered the region, a reduced Hasmonean kingdom was allowed to maintain its independence, a state of affairs which continued under the rule of the Herod the Great (37-4 BC) and his successors. By 44 AD however (following the death of Herod Agrippa I) it had been brought under direct Roman rule.

Octavian's rise to the position of emperor in 29 BC (after which he was known as Augustus Ceasar) heralded a gradual improvement in the overall state of affairs in the province of Syria. Though there were many areas over which they still had only nominal control, Roman rule brought with it peace and an orderly, efficient administration – the so called *Pax Romana* – which allowed the region to flourish economically. The loose federation known as the **Decapolis**, or 'Ten Cities' emerged, straddling the borders of present-day southern Syria and northern Jordan, with cities such as Jerash in particular benefitting from the north-south trade between Damascus and the Red Sea.

In Damascus, the former temple of Haddad was gradually expanded and converted into a temple dedicated to the Roman god Jupiter, and the principal *Via Recta* (the Straight Street of the Bible) was widened and colonnaded. Likewise, Baalbek began to rise to prominence as a major centre for the cult worship of Jupiter, work on its main temple nearing completion towards the end of Nero's reign (37-68 AD). In the Syrian desert Palmyra began to emerge as a major trading post on the direct route between Dura Europos and Emesa (Homs). Ironically, in the case of Palmyra, it was actually its position in the no-man's-land between Parthian and Roman power which helped it to flourish. Palestine, however, continued to cause problems, the Jews rising against Roman rule in 66 AD (the First Jewish Revolt). By 70 AD the revolt had been effectively crushed, with the Romans taking Jerusalem and destroying the Temple.

Throughout Jordan, it is the monuments of the Roman era which have survived, the ubiquitous building projects of the Romans having overlain those of the Greeks whom they replaced. Socially and culturally however, the region's Hellenistic influences continued to be felt long afterwards. Greek remained the official language, and the Romans relied heavily on pre-existing Hellenistic administrative structures.

In 106 AD, during the reign of Trajan, the empire was substantially reorganised. The Nabatean kingdom of Petra was incorporated into the empire and a new province of Arabia created alongside that of Syria, with Bosra as its capital. As a result of this, Palmyra entered its golden age, surpassing Petra in significance as a centre of trade. Jordan remained of major strategic significance, however, with Trajan overseeing the building of the **Via Nova Traiana**, so allowing Roman troops to move rapidly between Bosra and the Red Sea. Soon after, the Second Jewish Revolt (or Bar Kokhba Revolt) from 132-135 was even more brutally suppressed than the first. The marriage of Septimus Severus to the daughter of the High Priest of Homs, Julia Domna, in 187 heralded a 'Syrian' line of Roman emperors, ensuring a greater direct Syrian influence in the affairs of Imperial Rome.

During the rule of Caracalla (211-217) and his successor Elagabalus (217-222) however the empire began to descend into degeneracy. The reigns of Alexander Severus (222-235) and Philip the Arab (244-49) provided brief respites, but by that time Rome's empire in the Middle East was under serious threat. Since the late 2nd century, the advances of the Parthians to the east had become a major preoccupation. In the early part of the 3rd century the Parthians were replaced by the Sassanid Persians, who posed an even more pressing threat. In 256 Dura Europos, on the Euphrates in northern Syria, fell to the Sassanids. Four years later, the emperor Valerian was captured by the

Sassanids and disaster was only averted when the king of Palmyra, Odainat, defeated them the same year. This set the stage for the legendary Queen Zenobia to establish Palmyra as an independent kingdom until the emperor Aurelian captured it in 271.

Diocletian's rule (284-305) saw relative stability, but his death brought with it 20 years of civil wars between the newly created eastern and western administrations of the Roman empire. These only came to an end when Constantine managed to establish himself as sole emperor in 324, founding Constantinople as a second imperial capital in 330.

In 312 Constantine had himself converted to Christianity, which was already spreading throughout the empire, despite the attempts of Diocletian before him to suppress it. A year later, the Edict of Milan officially gave Christians the right to practice their religion, and by 380 Christianity had been adopted as the official religion of the Roman empire. Although the Byzantine period can be said to have effectively started earlier (according to some interpretations with the rise of Constantine to the position of sole emperor in 324), most historians date the Byzantine period from the official division of the Roman empire into East and West in 395, with the Eastern Roman Empire becoming known as the Byzantine empire. **Byzantine period (395-636 AD)**

Many of the former pagan temples of the Romans were converted into great churches during the Byzantine era, for example at Jerash and Petra. In addition, numerous Christian communities flourished, particularly in the so-called 'Dead City' region around Aleppo (and most famously at the pilgrimage site of St Simeon), but also throughout the rest of the empire. The Byzantine period in the Middle East spawned many fundamentally important innovations in religious architecture, the influence of which can still be seen today.

Under the reign of Theodosius II (408-50), the '100 Year Peace' was established with the Sassanids, and the region was able to prosper as it had done under the Romans. During the reign of Justinian (527-65), the Byzantine empire again came under repeated attacks from the Sassanids, who on several occasions made deep incursions into Byzantine territory. Nevertheless, Justinian's rule was also marked by a flowering of Byzantine culture and architecture. It was during Justinian's rule for example that Madaba flourished as a great centre of mosaic religious art.

In 602, under the leadership of Chosroes II, the Sassanids launched a massive invasion. By 614 they had reached right down into the southern part of the empire and captured Jerusalem. In addition, Antioch, Aleppo, Damascus and Jerash were all occupied. In 616 they simultaneously conquered most of Egypt and Asia Minor, laying siege even to Constantinople. In 622 the Byzantine emperor Heraclius led a counter-attack. His six year campaign against the Sassanids drove them from most of the empire, but his success was short-lived. The Byzantine empire was on its knees, and in no position to resist the onslaught of the new power emerging from the deserts of Arabia, that of the Muslim Arabs.

The Islamic Era

After the death in 632 of the founder of Islam, the Prophet Mohammad, the Arab tribes which he had welded together into such a formidable force set about conquering the fertile lands to the north and west. Led by the military commander Khalid ibn al-Walid, the Muslim Arab army captured Amman and Damascus in 635 and then withdrew to defeat forces of Byzantium at the Battle of Yarmouk in 636, effectively marking the end of Byzantine rule in the region. They again occupied Damascus the same year, and then proceeded to **Arab conquest (632-661 AD)**

Background

sweep through the lands of present-day Jordan, Syria and Lebanon, meeting little resistance from the local peoples. The new invaders at first made little impression. There were no forced conversions from Christianity to Islam, and the rulers they appointed were fair and just. By 656 the whole of Persia had also been conquered.

These conquests took place under the rule of Mohammad's first three successors, the caliphs Abu Bakr (632-34), Omar (634-44), and Uthman (644-56), who all maintained Medina as their capital. The fourth caliph, Ali (656-61), whose assumption of the title of caliph was opposed both by the kin of Uthman (who had been assassinated) and by others in Medina, moved the Arab Muslim capital to Kufa in southern Iraq. However the governor of Syria, Mu'awiya, was a close kinsman of Uthman, and he rose up in revolt. After Ali was murdered by disaffected members of his own camp, Mu'awiya assumed the title of caliph, thus founding the Umayyad dynasty.

The Umayyads (661-750 AD) Mu'awiya promptly made Damascus the seat of the caliphate and capital of the empire, heralding the start of one of the most glorious periods in the city's history, and that of the region as a whole. Jordan in particular benefitted, both from its proximity to the political heart of the empire, and from the annual passage of pilgrimage caravans through its territory en route between Damascus and the holy cities of Mecca and Medina. Under the Umayyads, the empire grew to its greatest extent and by the end of the 7th century it stretched from Spain in the west to the Indus river in the east.

Though their origins were nomadic, the Umayyads were quick to adopt many aspects of the civilisations which had previously existed in the lands they now ruled. As Albert Hourani comments; "Gradually, from being Arab chieftains, they formed a way of life patterned on that traditional among rulers of the Near East, receiving their guests or subjects in accordance with the ceremonial usages of Byzantine emperor or Iranian king." (Albert Hourani *A History of the Arab Peoples*). The synthesis of different influences – Graeco-Roman, Byzantine, Persian, Mesopotamian and indigenous – which occurred under the Umayyads is most graphically displayed in their architecture, and in particular their religious architecture. The famous Umayyad Mosque in Damascus, built during the reign of the sixth Umayyad caliph Khalid ibn al-Walid (705-15), is the most spectacular example of this. But the Umayyads were also responsible for many other monuments, including the hilltop palace in Amman and the so-called 'Desert Castles' to the east of Amman.

In retrospect, the Umayyads were seen as lax and corrupt by future Islamic dynasties. Certainly, they did not place a major emphasis on religion, concentrating instead on developing their empire economically and politically. But eventually they did indeed fall into degeneracy. The last truly great Umayyad caliph, Hisham (724-43) was followed in quick succession by a series of incompetent and debauched caliphs. The last of these, Marwan II, was overthrown following an uprising led by Abu al-Abbas, who went on to found the Abbasid dynasty. One grandson of Hisham did however manage to flee to Spain, maintaining the Umayyad lineage there for another 500 years.

The Abbasids (750-1258 AD) The Abbasids sought to bring Islamic rule back to the more rigorous and theocratic interpretations they felt it deserved. They transferred the seat of the caliphate to Iraq, first to Kufa and then Baghdad. In doing so, they abandoned the blending of eastern and western influences which characterised Umayyad rule and brought to the empire a distinctively Mesopotamian and Persian emphasis. Jordan, no longer close to the political heart of the empire, became a relatively insignificant backwater.

Initially, the Abbasids managed successfully to administer an empire which included the whole of the former Umayyad empire except Spain and Morocco. However, by the mid-9th century their power was beginning to fragment, with numerous local dynasties appearing. The **Tulunid** and **Ikhshidid** dynasties of Egypt in turn controlled Jordan and parts of southern Syria from 868 to 969. The latter were ousted by the **Fatimids**, who went on to make Cairo their capital in 973 and later extended their power into Syria. The Fatimids represented the Ismaili branch of Shi'ite Islam, and as such were a direct threat to the power of the Sunni Abbasids, having set up their own rival caliphate. In the north meanwhile, the **Hamdanid** and **Mirdasid** dynasties ruled in turn in Aleppo from 944-1070. Both however were only nominal rulers, being at one time or another subject to either the Fatimids to the south or the Byzantines to the north (the Byzantines were making the most of the chaos and trying to regain territory in their former empire).

While all this was happening, the **Seljuk Turks**, originally chiefs of the Oghuz tribes of Transoxania, had conquered Persia and established a kingdom there with Isphahan as their capital. Being Sunni Muslims, they came to the aid of the Abbasids, who were experiencing their own domestic problems in Baghdad. In return the Seljuk ruler forced the Abbasid caliph to recognise him as 'Sultan' (literally 'Sovereign') of the Universal State of Islam. Thus the Abbasids became in effect helpless puppets of the Seljuks. The Seljuks occupied Aleppo in 1070 and defeated the Byzantines at Manzikert in eastern Anatolia in 1071. By 1076 they had extended their control over most of Syria (including Damascus) and parts of Jordan, largely ousting the Fatimids, though they were never strong enough to completely expel them from Jordan. After 1095 two Seljuk rulers emerged in Syria with Aleppo and Damascus as their capitals. These rulers set up what was in effect their own rival dynasties, both only nominally subservient to the Seljuk sultan in Isphahan. Though the Abbasid caliphate continued to exist, nominally at least, until it was conclusively destroyed by the Mongols in 1258, in practice it faded into total insignificance.

During the first part of the 11th century, the Fatimid caliph Al Hakim had ordered the destruction of 30,000 churches in Egypt, Palestine, Jordan and Syria (including the Church of the Holy Sepulchre in Jerusalem). This, along with the pleas of the Byzantine emperor, who was becoming increasingly alarmed at the Seljuk threat, prompted Pope Urban II to call for a crusade to restore the Holy Lands to Christian control. **The First Crusade**

Thus the **First Crusade** set off from Europe, arriving in Syria in 1097. To their surprise, instead of a formidable enemy in the form of the Seljuk Turks, what they found was a region deeply divided and fragmented into numerous petty principalities. While the Crusaders were united by their religious mission of a 'Holy War', the Muslim peoples against whom they were marching were thoroughly embroiled in their own domestic conflicts. After a nine month siege they took Antioch, massacring many of its inhabitants, including its Greek Orthodox community. They then continued southwards along the Orontes river. Despite meeting little resistance, they were were by this time in a sorry state, riven by disease and famine. The shortage of food in particular was reaching crisis point, prompting the infamous massacre at Maarat al-Numan. Continuing south, they swung inland through the Homs Gap, briefly occupying the castle which was later to become Krak des Chevaliers. After unsuccessfully besieging Aqra (near Tripoli), they headed straight down the Mediterranean coast, turning inland again near Jaffa to arrive at Jerusalem. After just over a month, on 15 July 1099, the Holy City fell to the Crusaders, its inhabitants, like those of Antioch, being subjected to an indiscriminate massacre.

Three Crusader states were soon established under the rule of the principal leaders of the Crusade: the Kingdom of Jerusalem, which went to Godfrey of Bouillon; the Principality of Antioch, which had been left in the possession of Bohemond; and the County of Edessa (present-day Urfa in Turkey), which Baldwin, Godfrey's brother, had carved out for himself. After the fall of Jerusalem, Raymond St Gilles headed back north along the coast and laid siege to Tripoli. The siege cost him his life, but eventually Tripoli fell in 1109 and a fourth state, the County of Tripoli, was created. Meanwhile, other cities along the coast had fallen to the Crusaders and been incorporated into the Kingdom of Jerusalem or County of Tripoli. By the early 12th century the Crusaders controlled a narrow strip of land stretching along the whole of the eastern Mediterranean coast (and including also various inland sites in the coastal mountains), as well as the area around Edessa.

After capturing Jerusalem, the great majority of the soldiers of the First Crusade returned home. Though the Crusaders were to remain in the region for another 200 years or so, their numbers were always dangerously few. In the absence of manpower they resorted instead to building formidable castles which could be easily defended with the minimum of soldiers. Today, the best example of Crusader military architecture in Jordan is to be found at Kerak (see page 226).

The Crusaders quickly realised the importance of establishing some 'strategic depth' to their narrow strip of coastal territory. The highlands to the east of the Dead Sea and Jordan river were of particular significance in that whoever controlled them also controlled movement along the inland route between Syria and Egypt. Thus King Baldwin I (the successor to Godfey of Bouillon) crossed into present-day Jordan and established a castle at Showbak in 1115 (see page 242). This was followed by castles on Pharaoh's Island (in the Red Sea to the south of Aqaba), at Wu'eira (in the vicinity of Petra), Al Habees (inside Petra) and Tafila (on the King's Highway between Showbak and Kerak). The construction of Kerak castle came later, sometime around 1140, by which time the administrative district of **Oultre Jourdain** had been established (forming part of the Seigneury of Montreal, itself part of the Kingdom of Jerusalem).

The Zengids and Ayyubids (1128-1260 AD) A concerted response to the Crusaders came from the **Zengids**, nominally subservient to the Seljuks. The Zengid dynasty was founded by Zengi, who in 1124 had helped lead a Seljuk force in the relief of Aleppo from a Crusader siege. In 1128 he became the ruler of Aleppo. Under his rule, and that of his son Nur ud-Din (1146-74), Aleppo became a centre of resistance against the Crusaders.

In 1144 the County of Edessa fell to Nur ud-Din, prompting the **Second Crusade**. Their attempts to besiege Damascus failed and the whole expedition ended in something of a fiasco. By 1154 the Zengids had themselves gained control of Damascus, uniting the Muslim opposition to the Crusaders in Syria. In 1169 Nur ud-Din sent a huge force against the Fatimids in Egypt. Led by Salah ud-Din (better known to us as Saladin), the Zengid forces overthrew the Fatimids in 1171, restoring Sunni orthodoxy there and, nominally at least, the authority of the Abbasid caliph. Though the castle of Kerak came under siege no less than four times between 1169-74, it remained in Crusader hands. After Nur ud-Din's death, Salah ud-Din returned to Syria and by 1186 had succeeded in uniting all the Muslim lands from Cairo to Baghdad under the **Ayyubid** dynasty (named after his father Ayyub). In 1187, having defeated the Crusaders at the Battle of Hattin, he recaptured Jerusalem and also regained Acre, Sidon, Beirut and Byblos. The following year he conducted a whirlwind campaign which saw no less than 50 Crusader positions fall (including Kerak, Wu'eira and Showbak), although he avoided their most important and impregnable strongholds such as Krak des Chevaliers and Qalat Marqab (in present-day Syria), and Antioch (in present-day Turkey).

The fall of Jerusalem prompted the **Third Crusade**, which by 1191 had recaptured Acre. The King of England, Richard I (Richard the Lionheart) is perhaps the best-known figure of this Crusade, but despite twice coming to within sight of Jerusalem, he failed to take it. Instead, he signed a peace treaty in 1192 which guaranteed pilgrims free right of passage. After Salah ud-Din's death the following year, his successors failed to capitalise on the gains he had made and the Crusaders were able to recapture much of their former territory along the coast. The Ayyubid line continued until 1260, ruling from the twin capitals of Cairo and Damascus. It came to rely increasingly however on Turkish slaves to man its armies and administer its empire. These slaves grew in power, giving rise to what became known as the Mameluke dynasty (from *mamluk*, meaning 'owned').

The Ayyubid line in Damascus was brought to an abrupt end in 1260 by the invasion of the **Mongols**, who swept across Syria and the southern Levant leaving a trail of destruction in their wake. Already in Cairo the **Mamelukes** had risen to power in a coup in 1250, and they were able to decisively defeat the Mongols at the Battle of Ain Jalud in Palestine. One of the Mameluke generals at this battle was a man named Baibars, who subsequently made himself sultan and took over from the vanquished Ayyubids. Baibars (1260-77) proved himself to be a formidable adversary, unleashing the full force of his military genius on the Crusaders. By the end of his rule he had driven them from Antioch, Krak des Chevaliers and Safita. The offensive was continued by Qalaun (1280-90) who dislodged the Crusaders from Qalat Marqab, Lattakia and Tripoli, and by his successor Khalil who took Acre and Tartus in 1291. The Crusaders continued to cling to a tiny foothold on the coast, occupying the island of Arwad until 1302, but already they had been reduced to little more than an anachronism.

The Mamelukes (1260-1516)

The Mameluke genius was not however purely military. During the 14th century they also presided over a remarkable programme of building works, the legacy of which is still very much in evidence in Damascus (their second capital after Cairo), Aleppo and Tripoli. In Jordan, commercial and pilgrimage traffic moved freely along the King's Highway once again. Agriculture also flourished, with intensive irrigation schemes bringing large areas of the Jordan valley under cultivation. Sugar production became a major industry, both for the domestic market and for export. However, towards the end of the 14th century the Mamelukes were riven by internal power struggles which left their empire increasingly vulnerable to renewed attacks by the Mongols. The most devastating of these, led by Tamerlane, came in 1400, leaving a trail of destruction in its wake. Under the sultan Qait Bey (1468-95), the Mamelukes recovered somewhat, but they never achieved their former greatness, and in the first quarter of the 16th century they were overthrown by the Ottomans.

Painted jar from Mameluke period

The Ottoman Turks, who had already established themselves in Asia Minor during the middle of the 15th century and made Constantinople their capital, met little resistance when they swept into Syria, Jordan and Palestine in 1516, led by the sultan Selim I

The Ottomans (1516-1918)

(1512-20). Under his rule, the Ottomans extended their empire into Egypt, capturing the last Mameluke sultan, and even into Arabia, taking the Islamic holy cities of Mecca and Medina. His successor Suleiman the Magnificent (1520-66), further extended the empire to include Serbia, Hungary, Mesopotamia and all of North Africa except Morocco. Thus present-day Jordan formed just a tiny part of a vast empire.

The wider Middle Eastern region benefitted considerably from its incorporation into this new empire. An efficient administrative system was put in place, new trading links were established and ambitious building projects undertaken. It was during Suleiman's reign that the great Tekkiyeh as-Suleimaniyeh complex in Damascus was built. One of the first things Selim I had done on capturing Cairo was to proclaim himself caliph (since the final collapse of the Abbasid caliphate in 1258, the title had been held by a puppet of the Mamelukes). The Ottomans took great care also to ensure that the great pilgrimage route to Mecca, which they now controlled almost in its entirety, was managed properly. As a result, they soon succeeded in legitimising their assumption of the caliphate and establishing themselves as Protectors of the Faith. Damascus flourished in its role as the last great staging post on the *Hajj* to Mecca. Aleppo meanwhile was opened up to European traders by 'capitulation' treaties with the European powers and prospered even more vigorously, its souks and khans thronging with commercial activity. Jordan, however, appears to have fallen into relative decline. Though the Ottomans maintained the caravan and pilgrimage routes, other aspects of the social and economic infrastructure were clearly neglected. In many areas, intensive griculture gave way to semi-nomadic pastoralism, while towns and cities appear to have shrunk in size.

Inevitably for such a vast empire, Ottoman rule was rarely directly applied, with *Pashas* or local governors holding office in the major cities and exercising control over large administrative districts. As long as taxes were collected and paid on time, and peace maintained, the sultans in Constantinople were happy not to interfere. At times, the local governors, or even their subordinate tax collectors, were able tó carve out what amounted in effect to more or less fully independent kingdoms for themselves. The first Pasha of Damascus, Al Ghazali, declared his independence, though he was quickly ousted. In the mountains of Lebanon, the Emir Fakhr ud-Din II Maan ruled over a largely independent principality from 1590 to 1635, and the Emir Bashir Shihab II achieved a similar state of affairs in Lebanon from 1788 to 1840.

The 18th century saw a period of stagnation in the Ottoman empire, which was followed in the 19th century by a more serious revolt. The viceroy of Egypt, Mohammad Ali (1805-49) succeeded in establishing his own independent power base there, shaking off the authority of the Ottomans. His son, Ibrahim Pasha, carried the uprising into Jordan, Syria and Lebanon in 1831, ousting the Ottoman forces from the region and carrying out wide-ranging modernising reforms. At one stage it seemed that the Ottoman empire would collapse, but in 1840 the European powers chose to intervene on the side of the Ottomans, alarmed at this upset to the balance of power in the region and the threat that it posed to their interests.

The immediate result of greater European involvement was to open up the region to greater European influence. At the same time, at the heart of Ottoman political power in Constantinople, the Ottoman sultan was deposed in 1909 by the revolutionary movement known as the 'Young Turks', who established the Committee of Union and Progress (CUP). This brought with it an upsurge of Turkish nationalism which served to awaken amongst the Arab peoples a sense of their own Arab identity. Turkish nationalism was also behind the brutal genocide carried out against the Armenians during World War I.

The Modern Era

The modern political geography of the Middle East was largely shaped during the decade from 1914 to 1924. The onset of the First World War was of enormous significance to the region, which suddenly became a focus of international concern. The decision of the Ottoman Turks to ally themselves with the Central Powers (Germany and Austria-Hungary) placed them in direct opposition to the Allies. The harsh indifference of the Turks to local Arab populations, along with a breakdown of civic administration as the Turks focused their attentions on the war, brought widespread famine and epidemics. Arab feelings against the Turks increased, culminating in the Arab Revolt, with the Sharif of Mecca, Hussein Ibn Ali, the figurehead. **World War I & the Arab Revolt**

By the beginning of the 20th century, the emirate of Mecca (in the Hejaz peninsula of Arabia) was rather different to other political and administrative units found within the Ottoman empire. As Salibi observes "*it was neither a principality nor a province, but merely an office to which members of a particular line of Hijazi sharifs were regularly appointed*". More importantly, however, "*it represented a Muslim office of considerable antiquity, based in Islam's most holy city, and commanding general deference*". Crucially to the Arab world, "*it was the only Muslim institution which continued to be the preserve of an Arab dynasty long after political sovereignty in the world of Islam had passed into non-Arab hands*" (Kamal Salibi *The Modern History of Jordan*, 1993).

As the concept of Arab nationalism began to develop at the turn of the century, notably amongst the urban middle classes of Syria, it soon became clear that the only source of leadership to which they could turn was provided by the emirate of Mecca – an Arab dynasty of great Islamic standing that was directly descended from the Prophet. Among those who had recognised this fact were the British, who in 1882 had established themselves just across the Red Sea in Egypt. The contacts that the British had established early on with the various sharifian factions paid dividends when the Ottomans entered World War I on the side of the Central Powers.

When the CUP's puppet caliph Mohammad V declared the expected *jihad* against the Allies on behalf of the Islamic world, the impact on the Muslim populations in the Arab world and India was in fact negligible. The Ottoman-German advance into Aden did however mean that the Central Powers could threaten Allied shipping in the Red Sea and Suez Canal area (particularly now that the Germans had U-boats). Further, their armies could be resupplied and reinforced by way of the **Hejaz railway**, which ran through Jordan en route between Damascus and Medina. Thus, for the Allies (and British in particular) a revolt in the Hejaz and Syria against the Ottomans would not only disrupt the Central Powers resupply lines to Aden, it might actually cut off the whole of the Ottoman-German forces in southern Arabia. Henceforth efforts were made by the British staff at the Arab Bureau in Cairo to increase contacts with Sharif Hussein and his sons.

The subsequent call to armed revolt against the Ottoman empire that Sharif Hussein made in 1916 – the **Arab Revolt** - has been the subject of much reinterpretation over the years. How much the revolt was British-inspired and how much it was the result of an indigenous bid for Arab independence is a moot point. The fact that many of the desert tribesman appeared only to have joined for pay and the booty of conquest, and that many villages and towns remained at best neutral, at worst loyal to the Ottomans until their fate was decided, has left many questions surrounding the 'popular' nature of the revolt. Likewise, the revolt's actual military contribution to the war effort is often queried.

Background

Much of the controversy over the interpretation of the Arab Revolt centres on the role of **TE Lawrence** and the degree to which his account of it, most famously told in his book, *Seven Pillars of Wisdom*, is accurate or realistic. Sceptics argue that Lawrence vastly over-inflated and romanticized the significance of the revolt, and indeed his own role in it. Certainly, the Arab Revolt was of minor significance in the wider scheme of things. However it was important in that by harassing vital Turkish lines of communications, most notably the Hejaz railway line which Lawrence and his band spent so much time blowing up, it forced the Turks to tie up large bodies of troops defending strategically unimportant corners of the Arabian peninsula (Medina included), allowing the British to consolidate their military position in Palestine, Egypt and the Red Sea. Further, it should be made clear what Lawrence does and doesn't say in *Seven Pillars of Wisdom*. Though there are instances in the book where Lawrence appears to lie about his exploits (the 49 hour march across Sinai from Aqaba to Suez being one), he himself plays down both his own role and that of the Arab Revolt in the World War I. Indeed Lawrence describes the Arab Revolt as "a sideshow of a sideshow".

End of World War I & broken promises The triumphant entry of the Allies and the Arab nationalist forces into Damascus on 1 October 1918 signalled the final collapse of the Ottoman empire and defeat of the Central Powers. The end of the First World War saw Sharif Hussein's third son, **Feisal**, established in Damascus as the head of an Arab government that recognised the suzerainty of his father, the ruler of the Hejaz. Feisal however only controlled one of three Occupied Enemy Territory Administrations (this consisted of present-day Jordan, Syria and the inland areas of Lebanon, while the British controlled Palestine and the French the coastal areas as far north as present-day Turkey). Each of these OETAs was under the overall control of the British commander General Allenby who, while recognising Feisal's government, described it as 'purely provisional'.

Feisal attended the Paris Peace Conference of 1919 and secured the promise of an International Commission of Inquiry to look into the question of Syrian unity. The **King-Crane Commission**, as it became known, recommended that "*the unity of Syria be preserved, in accordance with the earnest petition of the great majority of the Syrian people*". However in response to increasing French pressure, Britain agreed in September 1919 to withdraw its troops from Syria and Lebanon. In January 1920 Feisal managed to negotiate an agreement with the French Premier Georges Clemenceau which allowed a temporary French military presence along the coast in return for French acknowledgement of Syrian unity and Feisal's rule over the interior. The end of Clemenceau's term in office saw the agreement repudiated and in response the General Syrian Congress proclaimed Feisal king of all Syria. A month later however, at the **San Remo Conference** in April 1920, Britain and France formally divided historic Syria between them, the French Mandate covering present-day Syria and Lebanon, while the British Mandate covered Palestine and Transjordan.

This put into effect the **Sykes-Picot Agreement** of 1916. Despite this secret wartime agreement to carve the region up between the British and French, the British had also entered into the so-called **'Hussein-McMahon Correspondence'** that had appeared (albeit vaguely) to commit Britain to assist the Arabs in attaining independence. In addition, in 1917, in a letter addressed to Lord Rothschild (and subsequently known as the **Balfour Declaration**), the British government appeared to commit itself to the establishment of a "*nation home for the Jewish people in Palestine*". Thus the Arabs were denied their own government, the region was divided along artificial lines, and the seeds of the bitter dispute over 'Palestine', still so fundamental to Middle Eastern politics today, were sown. It is interesting to note now how Israeli sources refer to the moral obligation of the Balfour Declaration whilst dismissing the other agreements as wartime expediency. Most Arab sources meanwhile focus on the perceived treachery of the British.

The San Remo Conference of 1920 saw Britain awarded the Mandate for Palestine and Iraq, whilst the French assumed the mandatory rights in Syria (and what was to become Lebanon). Despite having been proclaimed King of Syria by the General Syrian Congress that was convened in Damascus earlier that year, on 24 July 1920 Fesial (the leader of the Arab Revolt) was forced out of Damascus by the French.

Post World War I peace settlements

The status of the area known as **Transjordan** was rather muddy at this point. Ostensibly it was part of Britain's Palestine Mandate, administered from Jerusalem, though in reality the British recognized three separate governments in the area, with each having a special British adviser assigned from Jerusalem. The northern division was referred to as the Government of Ajlun, the central section became the Government of Salt, and the southern section was termed the Arab Government of Moab. The ad-hoc way in which these three governments operated is perhaps best summarized by the experiences of Major Alec Kirkbride, who was appointed to the post of adviser to the Arab Government of Moab. As he recounts in his book *A Crackle of Thorns*, upon arrival in Kerak it was soon made clear to him that the council of local clan chiefs were unable to agree on a leader, and so he was expected to rule! When **Abdullah**, second son of King Hussein of Hejaz, arrived at Ma'an on 11 November 1920 and declared his intention of redeeming the `Arab Kingdom of Syria', it was with something approaching relief that Kirkbride greeted him. As Kirkbride describes, "*So the National Government of Moab passed away quite painlessly, as did the other autonomous administrations in the north, and the Amir Abdullah set up a central administration in Amman*".

British policy in the Middle East at this point was largely being shaped by the newly appointed colonial secretary **Winston Churchill**, who had been charged with maintaining British influence in the region whilst at the same time reducing imperial costs. The result was the **Cairo Conference** of March 1921 that saw Feisal installed in Baghdad as King of Iraq (described at the time as "the best and cheapest solution"). Abdullah (who at the same General Syrian Congress of 1920 that proclaimed Feisal as King of Syria, had himself been proclaimed King of Iraq) was encouraged by the British to renounce any claims to the Iraqi throne since it was being prepared for his brother Feisal, though he was told that he could assume the rule of Transjordan on a temporary basis pending an Anglo-French agreement.

Emir Abdullah & the status of Transjordan

The following year the British presented their latest plans for their Palestine mandate to the League of Nations. Transjordan was to be excluded from the area of Britain's Palestine mandate, which was envisaged as some form of `national home for the Jews', and a new Anglo-Jordanian treaty was created to replace the former British Mandate over Transjordan. Thus on 15 May 1923, the **Emirate of Transjordan** was formally declared an independent constitutional state. Many of the provisions of the British Mandate still applied however with the new Emirate being prepared for full independence under the tutelage of the British high commissioner in Jerusalem. Abdullah was to rule as emir with the aid of a constitutional government and British advisers.

Jewish Zionists have never forgiven the British for removing Transjordan from the Mandate for Palestine, though many of the protestations use a highly selective view of history. For example, Benjamin Netanyahu claims that "*Britain*

Background

tore off Transjordan from the Jewish National Home ... With one stroke of the pen, it lopped off nearly 80% of the land promised the Jewish people". In actual fact, what form the `national home for the Jews' (as envisaged by the Balfour Declaration) would take was never made clear. Nevertheless, Netanyahu continues that the British action *"sanctioned the entry into Palestine of Abdullah, the Hashemite chieftain from Mecca, titled him emir, and created a new country called Transjordan (now Jordan), which to this day suffers from the artificiality of its birth".*

In fact the Zionists were not the only ones who were ill-disposed towards this turn of events. Abdullah is said to have been disappointed with his brother Feisal for going behind his back to secure the Iraqi throne, whilst King Hussein of the Hejaz was said to be extremely angry with both for having accepted what he saw as a British-made throne in Iraq and British terms for the rule of Transjordan.

Early years of the Emirate of Transjordan Under the terms of the 1923 agreement a small armed force, the Arab Legion, was established, commanded first by the British officer Captain Frederick Peake, and after 1939 more famously by Major John Bagot Glubb or `Glubb Pasha'. An annual subsidy of £150,000 provided the basis for the development of the Emirate in its early years. In 1928 a treaty was signed giving Transjordan a further degree of independence. A constitution for the new Emirate was written up and a Legislative Council established. Britain however still retained control over foreign affairs, the armed forces, communications and state finances. In 1934 the Emirate was allowed to appoint consular representatives in Arab countries and in 1939 the Legislative Council was converted into a regular Cabinet. The outbreak of World War II delayed any further moves towards independence.

On the international scene however Transjordan had begun to play its part, particularly with respect to the issue of Palestine. In 1937 the Peel Commission, sent by the British to report on the problem, presented a partition plan which envisaged *"an Arab state consisting of Transjordan and the Arab part of Palestine, and ... a Jewish state".* The Palestinians were represented by the Arab Executive Committee, under the control of Hajj Amin al-Husseini, Mufti of Jerusalem, who firmly rejected the recommendations of the Peel Commission. Abdullah on the other hand recognized the need for dialogue, certainly with the British and possibly with the Jews, and accepted the plan. He also advanced an alternative proposal to place the whole territory under his rule with a guarantee of autonomy for Jewish areas. In the eyes of many Palestinians (and other Arab states), Abdullah came to be seen as a political opportunist whose dedication to the Palestinian cause was suspect, and whose land dealings with the Jews were unacceptable.

Despite this damage to Abdullah's Arab political standing, Transjordan continued to participate in the ongoing negotiations. Abdullah participated in the Round Table Conference on Palestine held in London in 1939 (where the so-called 1939 White Paper was tabled, see below), again going against the current of public and political opinion by recommending its acceptance. Transjordan also took part in the preliminary discussions of 1943 and 1944 which subsequently led to the formation of the **Arab League** in 1945, of which it was a founding member – although it was to find itself once again isolated from the other members on the question of Palestine.

World War II & independence The spectre of war in Europe caused a massive about-face with regard to British policy in Palestine. The Balfour Declaration was soon recognized for what it really was; not a `moral obligation' but another piece of World War I wartime expediency. Thus it was swiftly dropped as the British sought to build bridges and mend fences with the Arab Middle East. The Zionists were naturally appalled by what they saw as this betrayal, yet unlike the Arabs, the Jewish strategists realized that they were playing a long-term game. In rejecting the new British offer of independence for a federal Palestinian state after a five-year transition period, with restrictions on Jewish immigration and land purchases during this period, the Arabs seemingly lost the initiative and the trust of the British policy makers. The British subsequently acted unilaterally, issuing the **1939 White Paper**, and though the Jews rejected it as totally unacceptable, the Palestinian Arabs (on Hajj Amin's instruction) denounced it also. In fact the only Arab leader who accepted it was Abdullah, who correctly surmised that it was probably the best deal of a bad lot.

Abdullah's Arab Legion served on the Allied side with distinction during the Second World War, though Alec Kirkbride (who was now serving as the British resident in Amman) recalls how he had to repeatedly reassure Abdullah that he had backed the right side (particularly when the French forces in neighbouring Syria and Lebanon joined Vichy France). At the conclusion of the war Abdullah was `rewarded' by the British for his loyalty, though his reward was not quite the prize he desired.

On 22 March 1946 the **Treaty of London** was signed between Abdullah and the British, which provided for independence for Transjordan (subject to some provisions, such as British military facilities on its territory in exchange for subsidizing the Arab Legion), and on 25 May 1946 the Transjordanian cabinet voted to change Abdullah's title from Emir to King (and the country's name from Transjordan to the **Hashemite Kingdom of Jordan**). This was a significant step, though still a far cry from the ambition that Abdullah had cherished ever since arriving in Ma'an in November 1920, namely to reclaim the Arab nation of Greater Syria.

Jordan's newly found independence was not graciously accepted by the rest of the world. Pressure from the Jewish lobby in the United States delayed recognition from that quarter (on the grounds that Transjordan was part of the land that had been earmarked as a `national home for the Jews'), whilst the Soviet Union went as far as blocking Jordan's admission to the UN (regarding Abdullah as the latest puppet of western imperialism).

Nevertheless, the status of Transjordan was not the main regional concern at this point; the future of Palestine continued to occupy the thoughts of the key policy makers. Having been condemned by the rest of the Arab world for backing the recommendations of the 1937 Peel Commission and the 1939 White Paper, King Abdullah joined the rest of the Arab League in condemning the call for partition in the 1946 Anglo-American Committee of Inquiry's report (even though it had been hinted at that the Arab parts of Palestine would go to Jordan). Abdullah also stood firm with the Arab League in rejecting the United Nations Special Committee on Palestine's partition recommendation in 1947, after Britain had unilaterally handed over the perceived poison chalice of Palestine to the UN.

The UN vote on the partition of Palestine was grudgingly accepted by the Zionists (on the grounds that it provided a starting point for future expansion), but was resoundingly rejected by the Arab world. However Jordan was perhaps the only Arab country that was really prepared for the inevitable consequence of this vote: war. The popular image of the war that greeted Israel's declaration of independence is one of the huge Arab world attempting to strangle the Jewish baby at birth. For example, Israeli prime minister Benjamin Netanyahu's view of events is as follows: "*Israel's ragtag forces were*

State of Israel & the 1947-49 war

Background

overwhelmingly out-numbered and out-gunned, possessing virtually no tanks, no artillery, and no planes. As the Arab armies invaded, Israel's life hung in the balance" (A Place Among the Nations, 1993). In fact, as Smith points out, "*the Israelis held a manpower advantage over the Arab armies, backed by much superior military training and commitment compared with that of the Arab troops ... there was no co-ordination of Arab military movements, as the participants were mutually suspicious of one another's territorial ambitions" (Palestine and the Arab-Israeli Conflict*, 1992). The only Arab army that was really a match for the Jewish forces in terms of training and equipment was Jordan's Arab Legion, which succeeded in gaining control of the West Bank, as well as the Old City and eastern districts of Jerusalem.

End of the 1947-49 war

The turning point of the war was the short armistice agreed in spring 1948. The Israelis took advantage of the break in hostilities to defy the UN arms embargo and purchase large quantities of weapons from Czechoslovakia and import arms stock-piled in Europe. The effect of the arms embargo on the Arabs was to prevent shipment of Western arms from Europe, and so the tide of the war was turned.

A series of armistices finally ended the war in 1949, with Jordan concluding its ceasefire agreement with Israel on 3 April 1949. The terms of the ceasefire agreement meant that Jordan (now formally recognized by the USA) stood in possession of East Jerusalem and the **West Bank**, representing a significant portion of the Arab state that had been envisaged in the UN partition plan. Spring 1950 saw new elections to the Jordanian parliament, with Palestinians being invited to both vote and stand for office. The result was a motion to `unite' the two banks of the Jordan River, and following a constitutional amendment, the `West Bank' became part of the Hashemite Kingdom of Jordan.

The implications of this action were enormous. The population of the `united' Jordan was now swollen to some 1.5 million, though less than a half of this figure were `native Transjordanians'. This population also included a significant number of Palestinian refugees, as many as 500,000 of whom were living in camps. A recurring Israeli criticism over the years has been the failure of the various Arab regimes to integrate these refugee populations (Israel itself absorbed some 500,000 or so Jews who were expelled from or forced to leave Arab countries). However the Arab League (and the Palestinians themselves) consciously chose not to offer (or accept) citizen status for fear of compromising Palestinian claims to their own homeland.

Jordan from 1951 to 1967

In July 1951 King Abdullah was assassinated while visiting the Al Aqsa Mosque in Jerusalem. He was succeeded by Talal, his eldest son. Talal however suffered from schizophrenia, which worsened after taking over as king. Within a year the situation was so bad that parliament voted that he should step down in favour of his son Hussein. During his brief reign King Talal presided over the writing of a new constitution making the government collectively responsible before parliament. This was ratified by the regency council which ruled in the interim between Talal stepping down and Hussein taking power.

On 2 May 1953, at the age of just 18, Hussein assumed the throne, a position which he held till his death in 1999. The early years of his reign were however turbulent ones, which saw numerous Prime Ministers come and go in quick succession. In 1954 Gamal Abdul Nasser came to power in the recently declared Republic of Egypt, and began to spread his doctrine of pan-Arab nationalism, which found a particularly sympathetic audience amongst the dispossessed Palestinians living in refugee camps in Jordan. Nasser's stance was also strongly anti-Western, and in particular anti-British. King Hussein at first tried to maintain a neutral stance, but in March 1956 he dismissed the British commander of the Arab Legion, `Glubb Pasha', in an attempt to quell rising unrest at home and demonstrate to neighbouring Arab states that he was no longer a puppet of the British.

Against the background of growing tension following Nasser's nationalization of the Suez Canal in July 1956 and the subsequent Israeli invasion of Sinai in October of that year (covertly encouraged by Britain and France, and then overtly supported by air-strikes and a military presence), a pro-Nasserist government was elected in Jordan in October 1956. The king and the government found themselves at loggerheads on a wide range of domestic and foreign policy issues, most notably over America's **Eisenhower Doctrine** of January 1957. This offered defence and economic aid to Middle Eastern states which felt threatened by Communism. King Hussein expressed a strong interest in the prospect of American economic aid, while at the same time his government was pressing for Jordan to officially recognize the Soviet Union and communist China. In April 1957 the pro-Nasserist government was forced by the King to resign. In the following weeks popular demonstrations spread throughout the country and there was an attempted coup. Finding himself in such a precarious position, King Hussein declared a state of emergency and imposed martial law.

Jordan's relations with Syria and Egypt had reached rock-bottom, and in June 1957 diplomatic ties with Egypt were severed. In February 1958 Egypt and Syria united to form the **United Arab Republic (UAR)**, marking the height of Nasser's power as a pan-Arab leader. Jordan meanwhile entered into a federal union with Iraq the same month, creating the **Arab Federation**. By July 1958 however a bloody Nasserist coup in Iraq resulted in the overthrow and massacre of the Hashemite royal family there. Jordan's federation with Iraq was over after just six months.

Most observers in the Arab world (and beyond for that matter) believed that King Hussein would soon go the same way as his Hashemite cousins in Iraq. King Hussein however still only 23 years old, was already an adept politician and born survivor. In 1960 he offered full Jordanian citizenship to all Palestinians within the country. Although this move was condemned by the UAR (with which Jordan had recently re-established relations), for many Palestinians it was a welcome move which resulted in a tangible improvement in their everyday lives.

Gradually Jordan managed to end its isolation in the Arab world. In 1961 Syria withdrew from the UAR, effectively bringing it to an end. In 1964 Nasser, whose position had been some what weakened (both by the collapse of the UAR and by his involvement in Yemen), invited his Arab neighbours, including Jordan, to attend a conference in Cairo. A plan was agreed to reduce the flow of water into Lake Tiberias (Sea of Galilee), in response to Israel's announcement that it was about to start drawing water from the Jordan River to irrigate the Negev desert. As a precaution against possible Israeli military action (the Israelis did in fact respond with air-strikes), the United Arab Command was created. This comprised of Lebanese, Syrian, Jordanian and Egyptian military forces under the command of the Egyptians. The conference also resulted in the formation of the **Palestinian Liberation Organization (PLO)**, dedicated to the liberation of Palestinian `occupied territory'; namely Israel. The headquarters of the PLO were to be in Amman.

The significance of the 1964 conference in Cairo for Jordan was that it placed it firmly in the camp of the other Arab states in their approach to Israel. To quote Salibi, King Hussein "*had apparently deemed it preferable for Jordan to join the*

Six Day War of 1967

Arab states in their frenzy and accept her share of the expected consequences, rather than remain in isolation, continually at the mercy of destabilizing forces from both without and within her frontiers" (Kamal Salibi, *The Modern History of Jordan*). *Fedayeen* (Palestinian guerrilla) attacks on Israeli territory increased dramatically in 1966, led both by the PLA (the armed branch of the PLO) and **Fateh**.

Fateh were a radical Palestinian group led by Muhammad Abdul-Rauful-Qudwa al-Husseini, better known as Yasir Arafat (or Abu Ammar), later to become the head of the PLO. The name Fateh, meaning `conquest', is an acronym in reverse of their full name, *Harakat al-Tahrir al-Watanial-Falastini*, or `Movement of Palestinian National Liberation'. Taken the right way round, the acronym Hataf means `demise' in Arabic; it was reportedly their initial sponsor King Feisal of Saudi Arabia who suggested reversing it. While the PLO were sponsored principally by Egypt, Fateh relied primarily on Syria for support.

The mounting tensions caused by the ever more daring raids of the *fedayeen*, coupled with incidents of open hostilities between Israel and its enemies (most notably the shooting down of six Syrian aircraft), were leading inexorably towards war. Syria had already entered into a mutual defence pact with Egypt, and Jordan now followed suit, resurrecting the lapsed 1964 United Arab Command. When Egypt expelled UN observers from Sinai, massed its troops along the border with Israel and closed the Straits of Tiran to Israeli shipping (thus blockading Israel's Gulf of Aqaba port of Eilat), in Israeli eyes the war had effectively begun.

Israel launched a pre-emptive strike against Egypt at 0745 on 5 June 1967, destroying most of the Egyptian air force within three hours. Syria and Jordan (and Iraq) meanwhile believing the reports of overwhelming victories for Egypt emanating from Cairo, launched their own attacks on Israel's western and northern flanks. By the end of the same day however the entire Jordanian air force had been wiped out, along with two-thirds of Syria's air force. A series of bitter infantry, artillery and tank battles ensued, but the outcome of the war had effectively already been determined by Israel's early attainment of complete air supremacy. Within six days Israel had defeated the combined might of the Arab armies, and by the time a UN-brokered ceasefire was imposed on 10 June, Israel controlled the whole of the Sinai peninsula, the Gaza Strip, the entire West Bank (including Jerusalem) and the Golan Heights.

Aftermath of the Six Day War For Jordan, the outcome of the Six Day War was particularly devastating. As well as losing all of the West Bank and the cherished Holy City of Jerusalem, more than 300,000 Palestinian refugees flooded across the Jordan River into a much-reduced Jordan, placing a further strain on an economy already in tatters from the war. In September 1967 the UN passed **Resolution 242**, calling for Israeli withdrawal from `occupied territories', and for all Middle Eastern countries `to live in peace within secure and recognized borders'. The resolution was backed by Jordan (indeed King Hussein helped draft it), but the PLO, Syria and Iraq refused to do so on the grounds that it implied recognition of Israel.

Jordan's long ceasefire line with Israel meanwhile became the focus for continued *fedayeen* attacks on Israel. The various Palestinian guerrilla groups in Jordan became steadily stronger, receiving substantial financial aid and armaments from the Gulf states. In Jordan, they also drew strength from the fact that more than half the population was Palestinian in any case. Many Palestinians felt betrayed by Jordan's refusal to allow the Palestinians in the West Bank to arm themselves and chose to blame Jordan for its loss. Such was their influence that they began to pose a threat to Jordanian sovereignty. Fateh became incorporated into the PLO, along with other radical Palestinian groups, and Yasir Arafat assumed the leadership of the PLO. Although he sought to improve relations with King Hussein, other more radical breakaway organizations, notably the PFLP (Popular Front for the Liberation of Palestine) and PDFLP (Popular Democratic ...), were by 1970 calling for the overthrow of the Jordanian monarchy. King Hussein had in 1969 met with President Nixon to discuss a possible peace agreement (the so-called Rogers Plan, based essentially on UN Resolution 242). To radical Palestinians this represented a betrayal of their cause.

The various Palestinian organizations in Jordan had practically become a `state within a state'. Jordanian national sentiment was turning against them and violent confrontations began to occur between the guerrilla groups and the Jordanian authorities. Things came to a head in September 1970. On 1 September there was an attempt on King Hussein's life. Between 6-12 September four international airliners were hijacked, three of them being taken to Jordan and blown up (after the passengers had been allowed off). On 15 September Palestinians took over the city of Irbid and declared a `people's government'. The next day Jordanian artillery started shelling the Wahadat and Husseini refugee camps on the outskirts of Amman, where the headquarters of the most militant Palestinian groups were based. According to PLO figures the death toll in the first 11 days of fighting was as high as 3,400.

Black September

Syria responded by sending 200 tanks into Jordan to help the Palestinians, but the Jordanian air force reacted quickly and they soon withdrew. The Jordanian offensive against the Palestinian guerrilla groups dragged on until July 1971 with various attempts by other Arab states to broker an agreement. Ultimately however these all failed and the PLO, along with all the other groups both within it and separate from it, were driven from the country. The PLO instead established itself in Lebanon, where much the same problems were to arise again.

In October 1973 Syria and Egypt launched another offensive against Israel. Timed to take place on Yom Kippur, the holiest day of the Jewish calendar, it became popularly known in Israel as the **Yom Kippur War**, and in Syria as the October War of Liberation. Jordan remained officially neutral, although it did send a token armoured brigade to help Syria.

Jordan from 1973 to 1991

Despite Jordan's actions against the PLO three years earlier, at the seventh Arab summit in 1974 (the so-called **Rabat Conference**) Jordan reluctantly backed a declaration recognizing the PLO as the "sole legitimate representative of the Arab people". In doing so, it implicitly relinquished its own claim to the West Bank. Since the PLO were refusing to talk to (or even recognize) Israel, it also effectively meant that there was no prospect of an agreement on the West Bank for the foreseeable future. From King Hussein's point of view it allowed him to reduce the influence of Palestinians in Jordan. Parliament was dissolved and reconvened, but this time without any Palestinian representatives from the West Bank, as had been the case before. Furthermore, it was decreed that no further parliamentary elections could be held until the issue of the West Bank had been settled.

In 1977 Anwar Sadat of Egypt visited Israel, leading to the **Camp David** accords of 1978 and a full Egyptian-Israeli peace treaty by 1979. The treaty was condemned by the rest of the Arab world as a sell-out in which Egypt had broken ranks with Arab solidarity against Israel. Egypt was expelled from the Arab League and Jordan, like most other Arab states, severed diplomatic links in protest. Meanwhile in 1978 King Hussein replaced parliament with a National Legislative Council, suspending elections indefinitely.

The outbreak of the **Iran-Iraq War** in 1980 turned attention away from the Israeli-Arab question. Jordan gave its backing to Iraq while Syria backed Iran. Over the period of eight years for which the war dragged on, this led to very tense relations between Jordan and Syria, at times bordering on hostilities.

In 1984, in the face of growing disaffection at home, King Hussein reconvened parliament and once again allowed West Bank Palestinians to be represented. This however was interpreted by the PLO as attempting to undermine its position as `sole representative' of the Palestinians. When King Hussein met with President Mubarak of Egypt in Washington and restored diplomatic relations with Egypt later that year, it was also suggested that Hussein was preparing to come to an agreement with Israel over the West Bank, with or without Palestinian backing. In 1985 King Hussein managed to get the PLO to sign the **Amman Accord**, which indirectly at least committed it to enter into negotiations with Israel on the basis of previous UN resolutions. The following year however with popular Palestinian opinion firmly against the agreement, Arafat was persuaded to renegade on the agreement and relations between Jordan and the PLO once again broke down. When the Palestinian popular uprising, which became known as the *Intifada* (literally `throwing off'), broke out in 1987 in the occupied territories, Jordan showed its support by giving it extensive coverage in the media.

There was however no improvement in relations with the PLO. The Palestinian question was a perennial problem for Jordan. According to some interpretations, the PLO's position as `sole representative' of the Palestinian people gave it a say in the fate of the Palestinians within Jordan itself. Indeed, the Israeli right winger Ariel Sharon had long presented Jordan as a possible alternative homeland for the Palestinians, popularizing the slogan 'Jordan is Palestine'. Anything King Hussein did for the West Bank Palestinians meanwhile was invariably interpreted as undermining the PLO's mandate. Only by fully relinquishing any claim to the West Bank could Jordan dissociate itself from the Palestinian question. This in turn would put the onus on the Palestinians in Jordan to decide for themselves whether or not to fully integrate into Jordanian society. Thus in July 1988, having once again dissolved parliament and put an end to West Bank representation in the legislature, King Hussein formally renounced Jordan's claim to the West Bank. Arafat in turn made the 'Algiers Declaration' in November of that year, declaring Palestinian 'statehood'. In an address to the UN General Assembly in December he renounced violence as a means of resolving interstate disputes and recognized the state of Israel.

In November 1989, after riots over increases in taxes and food prices, Jordanians were allowed to vote in the first general election since 1967, though these were still non-party elections. By 1992 however the ban on political parties had been lifted and martial law, also in force since 1967, revoked. In 1993 a one-person-one-vote system was put in place and the first multi-party elections for 34 years took place.

Gulf War　The Iraqi invasion of Kuwait in August 1990 and the subsequent multi-national `Desert Storm' operation of January 1991 presented a serious setback to Jordan's attempts to promote economic growth and stability. Overwhelming support amongst the Palestinian population for Saddam Hussein's actions prevented King Hussein from joining the anti-Iraqi coalition. As well as damaging relations with the US and its allies, Jordan once again found itself isolated from many of its Arab neighbours over the issue, including Syria. Jordan did however abide by the UN trade embargo on Iraq, at enormous cost to the economy.

In October 1991 Jordan participated in the Madrid conference on Arab-Israeli **Peace Process** peace, incorporating a Palestinian delegation into its own so as to circumvent the Israeli refusal to negotiate directly with the PLO. The talks themselves produced no major breakthroughs, but in September 1993, after secret negotiations in Oslo and much to everyone's surprise, Israel and the PLO signed a Declaration of Principles (DOP, more commonly referred to as the **Oslo Accords**) setting out the basis for a peace settlement.

On 25 July 1994 the signing of the **Washington Declaration** ended the theoretical state of war between Israel and Jordan. On 26 October of that year Jordan signed a formal peace treaty with Israel, the ceremony taking place in a tent straddling the border near the Wadi Arabah crossing.

The primary benefits of the peace treaty to Jordan have been economic. Tourism in particular has flourished, while cooperation on water issues and the economic development of the Jordan Valley and Dead Sea areas have started to yield positive results. Likewise, plans to integrate the Aqaba-Eilat region into a single district for tourism, industry, trade etc, and for cooperation on mutual ecological concerns, on research and development and professional training, are all promising. At the same time, Jordanian banks have started to open up in the Palestinian territories, the result of a separate agreement signed with the Palestinian National Authority in 1994.

The assassination of the Israeli Prime Minister Yitzhak Rabin in November **Assassination of** 1995 by a right-wing Jewish extremist came as a dramatic shock to the world. **Yitzhak Rabin** King Hussein made a moving address at his funeral, providing a poignant symbol of the new peace between the two countries and reinforcing the king's stature as a man dedicated to peace in the Middle East. However, the assassination effectively brought the Peace Process to a grinding halt. The elections which followed in May 1996 saw the right-wing Likud leader Benjamin Netanyahu narrowly beat the left-wing Labour leader Shimon Perez (the margin was just 50.5% against 49.5%). During his term in office, Netanyahu was widely seen as doing everything in his power to block any further progress in negotiations with the Palestinians, sowing a deep-seated sense of disillusionment amongst even the most optimistic of Jordanians as to the future prospects of the moribund Peace Process.

On 19 January 1999 King Hussein returned to Jordan after a six month absence **Royal intrigue &** during which he had been undergoing treatment for lymphatic cancer in the US. **the death of** Both the king and officials talked of a complete cure. King Hussein's brother, **King Hussein** Crown Prince Hassan, had filled the role of deputy for more than 30 years; during the king's absence he had effectively ruled the country and now seemed assured of the succession. However, speculation was also rife that the King intended to change his choice of heir from Hassan to one of his sons, with the 18 year old Hanza, the eldest of Queen Noor's sons, a favourite amongst pundits.

On the night of 26 January, exactly a week after his return, King Hussein was on his way back to the US. Few doubted that his cancer was active again. According to officials, the hour-long tour of Amman in a vintage Mercedes in driving rain which followed his arrival in Jordan had triggered an almost immediate relapse. In his wake he left a frenzy of confusion and speculation. That evening the king had dismissed his brother Hassan as crown prince in a letter accusing him of attempting to "fragmentise and politicise" the army, and of smearing Queen Noor and their children (according to some accounts, the text of the letter was published and broadcast on television even before Hassan had had time to read it). A hasty ceremony followed in the palace, in which Abdullah, his son by his English second wife Antoinette (Toni) Gardiner, was

Background

made crown prince. At the airport, an even more hurried ceremony saw him handed power as regent in the King's absence.

At the time, 'security forces' were quoted as arguing that King Hussein's decision to effectively disinherit his brother Hassan had originated in the events of the previous year when the king lapsed into a coma while undergoing chemotherapy in the US. "Hassan was going round telling everyone; 'He's dying, he's dying, he's not coming back', and started trying to sack some officers loyal to the king and put his own people in their places. He was preparing to take over." (Guardian, 27 January 1999).

On 5 February 1999, King Hussein once again flew back to Jordan from the US. This time he was on his deathbed. At 1143 on 7 February 1999, he died aged 63. Spanning some 46 years, King Hussein's rule had been the longest lasting, not only in the Middle East, but in the world. Present at King Hussein's funeral were more than 40 heads of state from around the world, including all the big names; Clinton, Yeltsin et al. Indeed, the roll-call surpassed even that for the funeral of Israeli Prime Minister Yitzhak Rabin following his assassination in 1995, both in terms of numbers and importance. In fact, the only leader of a neighbouring state unable to show his face personally was the Iraqi President Saddam Hussein, who sent his Vice President, Taha Mohieddin Ma'rouf instead. Bill and Saddam at the same funeral may have been an impossibility, but the event did witness President Assad of Syria trying hard not to rub shoulders with Israeli Prime Minister Benjamin Netanyahu and his entourage.

Recent developments in the region

Despite the international media hype of a potential power struggle in Jordan following King Hussein's death, the transition of power to his son Abdullah after 46 years of rule has been remarkably smooth. Having been sworn in as the new monarch of the Hashemite kingdom, King Abdullah II appointed his half-brother Hamza as crown prince. His brother, Prince Talal, advises on national security, while Talal's wife, Princess Ghida, directs the country's international press centre. Though the one-time Crown Prince Hassan has not assumed a public role, he has remained in the country, and the image presented publicly at least is very much one of family unity and a 'team effort'. For Abdullah himself, the new role as king of Jordan certainly came as an unexpected and sudden upheaval, but the country has experienced none of the unrest or instability that some predicted. In the wider region, however, there have been a number of momentous changes, all of which have fundamental implications for Jordan.

The May 1999 elections in Israel saw the virtual collapse of the Likud party (their share of parliamentary seats fell from 32 to just 19) and the subsequent resignation of Netanyahu as leader of the party. Such was the level of antagonism against Netanyahu that he even succeeded in alienating many of his own party colleagues, including Yitzhak Mordechai (Likud's Minister of Defence) and Yitzhak Shamir (a former Likud Prime Minister), both of whom voted against the party. In his place, the Labour leader Ehud Barak secured a convincing majority and went on to form a coalition government which brought many disparate groups under the Labour wing.

Many perceived the election result as a vote in favour of the Peace Process. However, early optimism that Barak would be able to reach a final agreement with the Palestinians, and even Syria, was soon replaced by a more realistic outlook. Negotiations between Israel and Syria initially looked promising, but by January 2000 they had been broken off. Syria adamantly refused to drop its demands for a complete Israeli withdrawal from the Golan Heights, while Israel insisted on retaining a narrow strip of land around the Sea of Galilee in order to protect its access to this vital water source. In March 2000, the US

President Bill Clinton and President Assad of Syria met in Geneva in an attempt to restart the talks, but without success.

Under intense pressure at home, Barak continued to press ahead regardless with his plans for a unilateral withdrawal from southern Lebanon. Though he had originally pledged that the withdrawal would be completed by July, events for once moved faster than predicted, and by the end of May the Israeli army had completely withdrawn from their infamous 'security' zone in southern Lebanon, ending 22 years of occupation.

Less than three weeks later, on 10 June 2000, the death of President Assad of Syria was announced. Assad, who had ruled over Syria with an iron fist for nearly 30 years, was considered to be one of the Middle East's most influencial and enigmatic leaders. So far at least, the transition of power to his son Bashar appears to be a smooth one. The young, western-educated Bashar is said to be keen to initiate a programme of reforms and modernisation very similar to that undertaken by King Abdullah II in Jordan. In terms of the Peace Process, however, Assad's death is widely seen as a major setback. Many argue that only Assad had the necessary stature and authority to broker a peace deal with Israel which would in effect represent a U-turn on more than half a century of uncompromising opposition to the very existence of the Jewish state. On the other hand, Bashar is a representative of the 'new order' in the Middle East, concerned more with developing his country economically and socially, rather than the old ideologies of confrontation. Whatever his aspirations, however, Bashar will have to move very slowly and cautiously if he is to keep the formidable military and secret police on his side.

More directly relevant to Jordan's future is the progress (or lack of it) on the Palestinian-Israeli track of the Peace Process. Yassar Arafat's pledge to declare an independent Palestinian state by 13 September 2000, supported by the PLO's Central Council, has placed renewed pressure on the negotiations. At the time of going to press, the talks between Ehud Barak and Yassar Arafat, brokered by Bill Clinton at Camp David, had broken up without an agreement. Evidently, thorny 'final status' issues such as the fate of Jerusalem and the return of Palestinian refugees proved too great an obstacle. While both leaders may be keen to reach an agreement, they are both equally vunerable to the hostile reactions of their respective constituencies, neither of which will take kindly to the inevitable compromises involved in any comprehensive settlement. Indeed, when Arafat returned to Gaza after the talks, he received a hero's welcome for refusing to compromise over the issue of Jerusalem. However, while the high-profile Camp David initiative failed, negotiations continue, spurred on by the fact that without an agreement, a return to violent confrontation seems almost inevitable.

Modern Jordan

Population

At around five million, Jordan's overall population is relatively small (Israel by comparison has a population of over six million, despite being only a third of its size). To a large extent, this reflects the fact that most of the country is semi-arid desert, supporting only minimal numbers of semi-nomadic Bedouin tribes. The majority of the population are to be found in the corridor of land running parallel to the Jordan River, Dead Sea and Wadi Arabah. In addition, the population is predominantly urban, with nearly 80% of Jordanians today living in the country's towns and cities.

Background

Basics

Population: 5,000,000 (August 2000 estimate)
Population growth rate: 3.05% (1999 estimate)
Life expectancy: 73 years (1999 estimate)
Total Fertility rate: 4.64 children born per woman (1999 estimate)
Language: Arabic (official), English also widely understood
Ethnic groups: Arab (98%), Circassian (1%), Armenian (1%)
Religion: Sunni Muslim (96%), Christian (4%)

GDP: US$15.5 bn (1998 estimate)
GDP real growth rate: 2.2% (1998 estimate)
GDP per capita: US$3,500 (1998 estimate)
Unemployment: 15% (official rate), 25-30% (estimated actual rate 1998)
Inflation: 4% (1998 estimate)
Balance of payments deficit: US$2.4 billion (1997 estimate)
External debt: US$7.5 bn (1998 estimate)
Defence spending: US$608.9 mn (1998 estimate, approx 7.8% of GDP)

Though the overall numbers may be small, with a growth rate in excess of 3%, Jordan's population is amongst the fastest growing in the world. In practical terms this means that the population will double in the next 20-25 years. For a country lacking in mineral resources such as oil, gas or coal, and deficient even in water resources, this puts an enormous pressure on both the economy and society. Such a high growth rate also means that the population is very young, with the under-15 age group accounting for 43% of the population. Although birth rates have dropped considerably in recent years, the large 'base' of younger people means that growth rates continue to be high. On the other hand, most indicators suggest that in the long term there will be a gradual reduction in the population growth rate.

Jordan's high overall rates of population growth have not been due to natural increase (births over deaths) alone, being complemented by periodic influxes of large numbers of Palestinian refugees over the years. The most dramatic movements of people were of course a direct result of the Arab-Israeli conflicts of 1948 and 1967, but the Gulf war of 1991 also saw more than 250,000 Jordanian migrant workers in Kuwait being forced to return home.

Society

Jordanian society is full of contrasts and anomolies. With more than 60% of the population made up of people of Palestinian descent, the region's troubled history has impacted on this small country to a far greater extent than any other in the region. Indeed, the plight of the Palestinians has in many ways been at the heart of Jordan's search for its national identity.

Education Jordan's record on education is generally good, though with such a youthful population, the pressures on this sector are enormous; around one-third of all Jordanians, in theory at least, are enrolled in an educational establishment of one sort or other. Free, compulsory primary and secondary education is provided to the age of 15, and an estimated 95% of school-age children are enrolled. The majority of primary and secondary schools in Jordan are government-run, though there is also a significant private sector, as well as UNRWA (United Nations Relief and Works Agency) schools catering specifically for Palestinian refugees. According to 1995 estimates, the overall literacy rate (the number of people over 15 who can read and write) was 86.6%, with a significant gap between males and females (males 93.4%, females 79.4%).

King Abdullah II and Queen Rania

Born in 1962 to the late King Hussein's second wife Muna Hussein (née Antoinette Gardiner), the 38 year-old Abdullah is amongst the youngest of a new generation of rulers in the Middle East (Bashar Assad, recently installed as President of Syria, is even younger at just 34). Like his father, Abdullah was educated at Sandhurst military college in Britain, studying also Arabic and politics at Oxford, as well as at Georgetown University in the United States.

Until his father unexpectedly named him as his successor to the throne, Abdullah was pursuing a successful but relatively low-profile career in the military. By 1998 he had been promoted to the head of Jordan's Special Forces, a position of considerable power, but still far from the blaze of media limelight which now follows him wherever he goes. Already, he has caught the public imagination by copying one of his father's favourite ploys and disguising himself for an incognito visit to a government hospital in order to see for himself what conditions there were really like. Such antics may help to make him popular with the Jordanian people, but he has also demonstrated a more serious purpose in instigating wide-ranging economic reforms at home, as well as various ground-breaking foreign

policy initiatives in the region. It is still very early days, and to a large extent his popularity at home and abroad is founded on the reputation of his father, but already he is showing signs of developing a stature for himself equal to that of the late King Hussein.

His wife, Queen Rania al-Yassin, though in Kuwait, is Palestinian (her family originally from Tulkarm in West Bank). She returned to Jordan in 1991, having been expelled from Kuwait following the Gulf War. Having met Abdullah in Amman, they married in 1993 and now have two children; a son, Hussein, born in 1994, and a daughter, Iman, born in 1996. Being an Arab Muslim, and also Palestinian, Queen Rania is seen as having an important role to play in promoting social cohesion in a country which is 60% Palestinian by descent. Strikingly beautiful and reputedly highly intelligent, she also looks set to become something of a champion of an international role model and champion of charitable causes. Hussein's third wife Queen Noor also filled this role with distinction, but being American by birth she was always seen as something of an outsider, and often criticised for an excessively fashion-driven and glitzy 'Westernised' lifestyle.

Although around three-quarters of the education budget goes on primary and secondary schooling, a major emphasis is also placed on higher education, in the form of both universities and community colleges. A particular focus has been on developing computing and information technology courses, the success of which can be seen in the enormous interest many young Jordanians have in computers and the internet. Women fare very well in Jordan's higher education system, accounting for 65.4% of cummunity college students and 42.2% of university students.

Health

Health care provision in Jordan is reasonably good as compared with other countries in the Middle East. This is reflected in the relatively high figures for life expectancy; in 1999 this was estimated at 73 years for the overall population (up from 68 years in 1994), 71 years for men, and 75 years for women. In 1995 there were 17.3 hospital beds per 10,000 people, a relatively high figure in the Middle East. There are some excellent private hospitals in the major towns and cities, complemented by good public sector facilities, particularly in poorer rural areas. The government places a major emphasis on primary care, for example providing a free programme of immunization which is estimated to have reached around 95% of children.

All change...

The enthronement of King Abdullah II of Jordan came less than a year after another young king, Mohammad VI of Morocco, succeeded his father. In Syria, meanwhile, the 34 year old Bashar has recently been sworn in as president following the death of Hafez al-Assad. These changes represent a sweeping away of the 'old order' of Middle Eastern leaders.

There are several still remaining, but it cannot be long before they too give way to a new generation. The 69 year old Yassar Arafat is looking increasingly frail, with a trembling lower lip and hands fuelling rumours of Parkinson's disease. In Egypt, President Hosni Mubarak is now 72. In Saudi Arabia, the 77 year old King Fahd is already seriously ill and barely able to walk since a stroke in 1995. Day-to-day affair of state are handled by his heir-apparent, Crown Prince Abdullah.

Exactly what the 'new order' of Middle Eastern leaders will bring to the region is impossible to predict, but most observers agree that it is likely to herald a more pragmatic approach to the Arab-Israeli problem, and a concerted drive towards modernisation and economic reform.

Free speech in Jordan

Jordan's record on human rights is not as good as its popular international image might suggest. In particular, the freedom of the press has consistently been compromised over the years. Journalists and editors are frequently arrested for supposed violations of the Penal Code and the provisions of the Press and Publications Law. Under Article 195 of the Penal Code, 'lèse majesté (literally 'offending the dignity of the king') is a criminal offence. Article 40 of the 1993 Press and Publications Law went further, imposing censorship over no less than ten very broadly defined topics, including the royal family, the armed forces and anything which could be construed as insulting to the heads of state of Arab, Islamic or 'friendly states'.

Over the years this censorship has been used to silence opposition to the Peace Process and discontent over the state of the economy. In August 1996, the doubling of the price of bread resulted in violent anti-government demonstrations in Kerak. Four journalists and an editor were arrested and charged with sedition for their coverage of the events. As a direct result of this coverage, in May 1997 the Press and Publications Law was amended by royal decree, expanding the definitions of the various topics liable to censorship. According to Human Rights Watch; "The broadly formulated language of the contents restrictions can be interpreted by the authorities to rule out the publication of virtually any critical news, information and analysis related to the conduct of public affairs by [the king], government ministers and ministries, and the internal security forces. In addition, news and other information related to foreign affairs is also affected by the ban on 'abusive remarks' about heads of state and material that 'sours' Jordan's bilateral relations. Similarly, news and commentary about religion, social relations and social affairs in Jordan could be sharply circumscribed by the broadly worded language which bans material deemed to be harmful to national unity, disparaging of religion, detrimental to the public interest, and promoting social 'disharmony' or 'perversion'."

The desire on the part of the authorities to prevent fanaticism and extremism gaining ground is perhaps understandable, but few would deny that these provisions are draconian and open to abuse. They have also produced some farcical situations. When the country experienced its worst snowstorms for decades in February 2000, the press were unable to give figures for the amount of snow that had fallen as the only government official allowed to release such figures was out of the country at the time!

One of the least savoury aspects of Jordanian society is the continuing curse of 'honour killings'. Under Article 340 of the Penal Code, a man who kills his wife or a close female relative "caught in adultery" or "an indecent [sexual] position" is exempted from the heavy jail term normally prescribed for murder, being liable to only to a considerably reduced sentence. This article is a reflection the deeply conservative nature of Jordanian society in relation to women, both in terms of Islam and tribal codes of conduct, although neither Islam nor tribal law actually sanctions such acts. In 1999, a total of 17 women died as a result of so-called 'honour killings'. In the majority of cases they were murdered by a brother on the basis of rumoured illicit sexual relations, although this may have amounted to no more than secret meetings.

This is an issue which deeply divides Jordanian society. In 1999, under direct instructions from King Abdullah II, the govermnent drafted a bill calling for the annulment of Article 340 in order to put an end to the 'mitigating excuse' for perpetrators of honour killings. In November 1999, this bill was rejected by the lower house, only to be accepted by the upper house the following month. After being returned to the lower house and again rejected, a joint session of both houses in February 2000 finally resulted in the bill being abandoned. However, with so many influencial figures in Jordanian society publicly opposed to Article 340, there is likely to be another attempt to annul this aspect of the Penal Code in the future.

Government and politics

The Hashemite Kingdom of Jordan is a constitutional monarchy. There is a National Assembly of two houses. The lower house (House of Representatives) is made up of 80 seats, with its members being elected by popular vote on the basis of proportional representation and serving for a term of four years. The upper house (Senate) consists of 40 members appointed by the king from designated categories of public figures, and also serving for a term of four years.

The king wields considerable powers as head of the armed forces, and through his ability to appoint the prime minister, the cabinet and the 40 members of the Senate. The king can only be thwarted in constitutional affairs by a two-thirds majority against him in both houses of the National Assembly. At the end of the day, however, his ability to dismiss prime ministers and reshuffle cabinets at will (both of which are measures to which King Hussein resorted to during his reign) effectively gives him ultimate power.

The king retains an interest in the Palestinian question despite severing all links with the West Bank in 1988. Jordan remains the holder of state documentation from the period of its rule on the West Bank between 1948 and 1967. King Hussein also regarded himself as the rightful guardian of Jerusalem and demanded a say in the future status of the city under the Peace Process, a position which King Abdullah II will no doubt maintain.

In the elections of 1997, no less than 75 seats in the House of Representatives went to moderate independents (including tribal representatives), the majority of whom support the monarchy. The next elections are scheduled for November 2001.

International relations

The late King Hussein, ever a pragmatist and moderate on foreign policy issues, was the architect of Jordan's peace treaty with **Israel**. Though a state of war with Israel only officially ended with the signing of the 1994 peace accords, as Lawrence Joffe points out, "Long before they signed peace with him ...,

Israelis regarded the king as a vital `stabilizing' influence in the region" and Jordan and Israel "had in fact maintained close ties on strategic issues since [the 1967 war]" (Lawrence Joffe, *Keesing's Guide to the Middle East Peace Process*). However, the repeated stalling of the Peace Process, and in particular Israel's policy of expanding settlements in the West Bank, has strained relations between the two countries. Essentially, until there is a comprehensive settlement between the Israelis and Palestinians, Jordan's options for fully developing its relations with Israel will remain severely restricted. Incidents such as the bungled Mossad assassination attempt in Amman on the Hamas activist Khaled Mesh'al in September 1997 (a bizarre James Bond-like parody in which undercover agents failed miserably to inject an `undetectable' poison into his ear and then `melt' into the Amman rush-hour) have done nothing to help matters.

Relations with **Syria**, never very friendly at the best of times, took a turn for the worse after Jordan's treaty with Israel, although diplomatic ties were never completely broken. In May 1999, King Abdullah II conducted a ground-breaking visit to Syria to meet personally with Assad. With Assad's son Bashar now installed as president, future prospects for a significant improvement in relations are very good. Abdullah and Bashar are said to be good friends, talking frequently on the phone and sharing a number of common interests.

Though relations with **Iraq** became somewhat strained for a time by the defection to Jordan of various senior aides to Saddam Hussein, fundamentally they continue to be good, reflecting the close economic ties between the two countries. The visit of the Jordanian foreign minister to **Saudi Arabia** in July 1995 was the first such high-level contact since the Gulf War and signalled a thawing in relations between the two, a trend which looks set to continue under King Abdullah II. Relations with **Egypt** have improved considerably now that both countries have peace treaties with Israel.

With regards to the **USA** and **Europe**, although Jordan's stance during the Gulf War was not well received, King Hussein continued to be recognized as a force for peace in the region. Since Abdullah came to the throne, there have been promises of substantial economic aid to help the country develop.

Economy

Jordan faced considerable difficulties in adjusting to the post-Gulf War situation. There was a loss of financial support from the oil-exporting states of the Arabian Peninsula in the form of subsidies as a front-line state and other goodwill benefits, a negative attitude towards supply of economic aid from the OECD states, a loss of remittance income from Palestinian migrant workers in the Arabian Peninsula states, and a loss of income from direct trade and transit trade with Iraq. Jordan relied on Iraq for most of its oil imports, which it was receiving free in repayment of debts incurred during the Iran-Iraq war. Iraq was also one of Jordan's principal export markets for agricultural and industrial products. The return of an estimated 250,000 Palestinian migrant workers had the short-term effect of nearly doubling unemployment to 30%. According to official figures, the unemployment rate in 1998 was 15%, though many economists argue that the actual rate is still 25-30%.

By 1993 external debt stood at US$7.9 bn and re-scheduling of debts was needed to prevent default. By 1999, the external debt had risen to US$11 bn, accounting for nearly 30% of the country's annual national budget. When he visited Britain in May 1999, Abdullah petitioned prime minister Tony Blair to support the cancellation of half of this debt.

The signing of peace accords with Israel in 1994 prompted a marked improvement in relations with the USA, which lifted restrictions on trade to Jordan through the port of Aqaba, and by 1995 had written off all of Jordan's substantial outstanding debts to the US. An international donors conference meanwhile promised US$200 mn in aid, and the IMF a further US$181 mn. At the time of King Hussein's funeral in February 1999, Clinton pledged to rush through a new US$300 mn aid package. In April 2000 Jordan and the European Union signed an accord which included a US$123 mn aid package and set 2010 as the date for a full dismantling of customs barriers and trade restrictions. In the same month, Jordan was accepted as a member of the World Trade Organisation (WTO).

Likewise, peace with Israel has started to yield tangible economic benefits, most notably in terms of tourism and trade. In 1998 Jordan exported goods totalling US$17 mn in value to Israel, representing an increase of more than three-fold on the 1996 figure of US$5 mn. This growth in exports to Israel is a direct result of an agreement signed in 1996 governing bilateral commerce between the two countries. Jordan's improved overall standing in the Arab world following the Gulf War also led to direct economic benefits. The Middle East and North Africa Conference hosted by Jordan, for example, contained plans for a US$25 bn regional investment package.

Since 1995, certain aspects of the economy have shown encouraging signs of improvements. Exports rose by 39% in that year (though from a very small base) and the IMF approved a loan of US$295 mn, pointing towards confidence in the future prospects of the economy. On the other hand, the Jordanian dinar remains weak and unemployment is still unacceptably high. Average per capita income in Jordan is barely one-fifteenth that of neighbouring Israel, and around 30% of the population are estimated to be below the poverty line. The economy continues to rely heavily on services, with this sector accounting for around 67% of GDP. Overall, the value of exports in most years are still less than half the value of imports.

Agriculture

Despite a powerful cultural attachment of part of the Jordanian population to arable farming and livestock herding, agriculture is not a major component of the economy. Only 4.5% of Jordan's land surface can be cultivated and just 7% of this is actually under irrigation at any one time. Agriculture accounts for only around 7% of the country's GNP and employs approximately 10% of the labour force. Scarcity of water is a major difficulty for the extension of farming. It is calculated that Jordan outstripped its renewable supplies of water available for agriculture in the mid-1980s. Major agricultural products include wheat, barley, citrus fruits, tomatoes, melons olives, sheep, goats and poultry.

Mineral resources

With obvious disappointment, and despite extensive searching, Jordan has failed to find the oil reserves with which its neighbours to the east and southeast are blessed. **Oil shale** (sometimes referred to as 'bituminous limestone' or 'bituminous marl') has been found in some quantity, though it is a somewhat poor consolation for the real thing. **Natural gas** deposits contribute towards the domestic energy budget, though on a global (or even regional) scale Jordan's reserves are deemed negligible.

The country's principal non-hydrocarbon mineral is **phosphates**, of which Jordan is one of the world's key suppliers. The Dead Sea region contains significant deposits of **potash**, though the eventual contribution to the Jordanian economy of other by-products (bromine, magnesium etc) is still uncertain. Other minerals mined in Jordan include small quantities of **copper**, **manganese**, **iron ore**, **glass sand**, **gypsum**, **kaolinite** and materials used in the construction industry such as **limestone**.

Background

Industry Manufacturing industry accounts for just under 15% of GDP, although outside phosphates and potash the manufacturing sector is small-scale. Some manufacturing is undertaken for the domestic market, both processing agricultural raw materials for dairy, jam and other food products and for light consumer goods such as clothing, tobacco, beverages etc.

Tourism Tourism is a major contributor to the Jordanian national income and an important employer throughout the country, with centres such as Aqaba and Wadi Musa (Petra) being largely reliant on this sector. Currently it is estimated that Jordan is earning around US$750 million annually from tourism, boosted by the Peace Process and the opening of the international entry point at Aqaba. In 1998, around 125,000 Israelis visited Jordan, accounting for just over 11% of foreign tourist arrivals in the country. A good deal of new investment in hotels is noticeable, particularly at Aqaba, Wadi Musa and Amman.

Culture

Religion

Islam The word Islam translates roughly as `submission to God'. The two central tenets of Islam are embodied in the creed "There is no god but Allah and Mohammad is his Prophet" ("*Lah Illaha illa 'llah Mohammad Rasulu'llah*"), which affirms the belief in the oneness of God and recognizes Mohammad as the divinely appointed messenger of God.

The *Qur'an* (generally referred to as the Koran in English) is Islam's holiest book. The word translates literally as `recitation' and unlike the Bible, the Qur'an is considered to be the *uncreated* (ie direct) word of God, as revealed to Mohammad through *Jibril* (the angel Gabriel). The text consists of 114 chapters, known as *suras*. Each sura is classified as Meccan or Medinan, according to whether it was revealed to Mohammad in Mecca or Medina. Most of the text is written in a kind of rhymed prose known as *saj*, and is considered by Muslims to be inimitable. Each chapter of the Qur'an begins with the words "*Bismillah al-Rahman al-Rahim*" ("In the name of Allah, the Merciful, the Compassionate"), an invocation which is also heard in numerous everyday situations.

In addition to the Qur'an, there is the *Hadith* body of literature, a record of the sayings and doings of Mohammad and his followers, which forms the basis of Islamic laws (*Shariat*), and precepts. Unlike the Qur'an, the Hadiths are recognized to have been written by men, and are therefore potentially flawed and open to interpretation. Thus they are commonly classified into four major categories according to their trustworthiness: *Sahih* (sound, true, authentic), *Hasan* (fair, good); *Da'if* (weak); and *Saqim* (infirm). The two most revered compilations of Hadiths are those by *al-Bukhari* and *Muslim*. It is in the interpretation of the Hadiths that most of the controversy surrounding certain Islamic laws and their application originates.

While Mohammad is recognized as the founder of the Islamic faith and the principle messenger of God, Muslims also regard him as having been the last in a long line of Prophets, starting with Adam and including both Moses and Jesus. They do not however accept Jesus as the son of God, but simply another of God's Prophets. Both Jews and Christians are considered *Ahl-e-Kitab* (`People of the Book'), the Torah and the Gospels being completed in Islamic belief by the Qur'an.

Nearly all Muslims accept six basic articles of the Islamic faith: belief in one God; in his angels; in his revealed books; in his Apostles; in the Resurrection

The Five Pillars of Islam

There are five practices or Akran, known as the Five Pillars of Islam, which are generally accepted as being obligatory to Muslims;

Shahada the profession of faith ("There is no god but Allah..."), which also forms the basis of the call to prayer made by the muezzin of the mosque.

Salat the ritual of prayers, carried out five times a day at prescribed times; in the early morning before the sun has risen above the horizon, in the early afternoon when the sun has passed its zenith, later when the sun is halfway towards setting, immediately after sunset and in the evening before retiring to bed. Prayers can be carried out anywhere, whether it be in a mosque or by the roadside, and involves facing towards the Ka'ba in Mecca and prostrating before God while reciting verses of the Qur'an.

Zakat the compulsory payment of alms. In early times this was collected by officials of the Islamic state, and was devoted to the relief of the poor, aid to travellers and other charitable purposes. In many Muslim communities, the fulfilment of this religious obligation is nowadays left to the conscience of the individual.

Sawm the 30 days of fasting during the month of Ramadam, the ninth month of the Muslim lunar calendar. It is observed as a fast from sunrise to sunset each day by all Muslims, although there are provisions for special circumstances.

Hajj the pilgrimage to Mecca. Every Muslim, circumstances permitting, is obliged to perform this pilgrimage at least once in his lifetime and having accomplished it, may assume the title of Hajji.

and Day of Judgement; and in his predestination of good and evil. Heaven is portrayed in Muslim belief as a Paradise filled with sensuous delights and pleasures. The idea of heaven as paradise predates Islam. Alexander the Great is believed to have used the term paradise to describe the walled Persian gardens that were found even before the birth of Christ. Hell on the other hand is portrayed as a place of eternal terror and torture, which is the certain fate of all who deny the unity of God.

Islam has no ordained priesthood or clergy. The authority of religious scholars, learned men, Imams, judges etc (referred to collectively as the *Ulema*), derives from their authority to interpret the scriptures, rather than from any defined status within the Islamic community. Many Muslims complain that their growing influence interferes with the direct, personal relationship between man and God which Mohammad originally espoused (and was indeed one of the reasons he was driven from Mecca, as it threatened the privileged position of the temple priests).

Sunnis & Shi'ites In the century following Mohammad's death, Islam divided into two major sects. Mohammad left no sons and therefore no obvious heir, and gave no instructions as to who should succeed him. There were two main contenders: **Abu Bakr**, the father of Mohammad's wife; and **Ali**, the husband of Mohammad's daughter Fatimah and his cousin. In the event Abu Bakr assumed the title of *caliph* (or vice-regent, from *Khalifat rasul-Allah*, `Successor to the Apostle of God'). He died two years later in 634 AD and was succeeded by **Umar** who was killed in 644. **Uthman**, a member of the powerful **Umayyad** family, was chosen to succeed him, but proved to be a weak leader and was murdered in 656.

At this point the aggrieved Ali managed to assume the title of caliph, thus ousting the Umayyads. However **Mu'awiya**, the governor of Syria and a member of the Umayyad family, soon rose up in revolt. The two sides met in battle at Siffin on the upper Euphrates, but both eventually agreed to arbitration by

Background

☞ Jihad; the sixth pillar?

Jihad, literally 'holy war' is considered by some Muslims to constitute the sixth pillar of Islam, although it has never been officially elevated to this status. The concept of jihad was the basis for the early expansion of Islam and was carried out very much in the literal sense of the word. A similar concept underpinned the Crusades of Europe's Christians. There are many contemporary examples of jihad, some of them rather controversial. The radical Shi'ite group Islamic Jihad saw itself, as their name suggests, as waging a holy war on the imperialist ambitions of America and Israel during the Lebanese civil war, and claimed responsibility for the bombing of the US embassy in Beirut in 1983. Hezbollah view their continuing fight against Israel in much the same light. Likewise Saddam Hussein, following his invasion of Kuwait, tried to rally support in the ensuing Gulf War by casting it as as a jihad against the evil designs of American infidels.

Many of the attitudes surrounding western perceptions of Islam are based on fears as to the wider implications of the concept. On the other hand, the word actually derives from an Arabic root meaning basically 'to strive', and many Muslims emphasise a less literal interpretation in terms of a personal spiritual striving against sin to attain greater closeness to God.

delegates from each side. However some members of Ali's camp resented this, seeing such a move as submitting the Will of God to human judgement. Eventually, Ali was murdered by one of his own supporters in 661 and Mu'awiya proclaimed himself caliph. Ali's eldest son **Hassan** set up a rival caliphate in Iraq, but was soon persuaded to abdicate. However the seeds of the schism in Islam had already been sown: between the Sunnis (those who accepted the legitimacy of the first three caliphs) and the Shi'ites (those who recognized only Ali as the first legitimate caliph). Later, when Mu'awiya died in 680, Ali's second son **Hussein** attempted to revolt against the Umayyads, but was defeated and killed in 681 at Karbala, providing the Shi'ites with their greatest martyr.

Followers of the **Sunni** sect, generally termed `Orthodox', account for over 80% of the population of Jordan. They base their *Sunna* (path, or practice) on the `Six Books' of traditions. They are organized into four orthodox schools or rites named after their founders, each having equal standing. The *Hanafi* is the most common, and the most moderate. The others are the *Shafii*, *Maliki* and *Hanbali*, the latter being the strictest. Many Muslims today prefer to avoid identification with a particular school, preferring to call themselves simply Sunni.

Followers of the **Shi'ite** (or Shia) sect account for only a small minority of the population of Jordan. Aside from the dispute over the succession of Mohammad, Sunnis and Shi'ites do not generally differ on fundamental issues since they draw from the same ultimate sources. However there are important differences of interpretation which partly derive from the practice of *ijtihad* ('the exercise of independent judgement') amongst Shi'ites, as opposed to *taqlid* (the following of ancient models) as adhered to by Sunnis. Thus Shi'ites divest far more power in their *Imams*, accepting their role as an intermediary between God and man and basing their law and practice on the teachings of the Imams.

The majority of Shi'ites are known as *Ithna asharis* or `Twelvers', since they recognize a succession of 12 Imams. They believe that the last Imam, who disappeared in 878 AD, is still alive and will reappear soon before the Day of Judgement as the *Mahdi* (one who is rightly guided), who will rule by divine right.

Ismailis The Ismailis are an offshoot of mainstream Shi'ite Islam. Following the death of the Sixth Shi'ite Imam Ja'far al-Sadiq in 765, there was a dispute as to the

Mohammad, the Holy Prophet of Islam

Mohammad, the founder of the Islamic faith, was born around 570 AD in the city of **Mecca** *in present day Saudi Arabia. His family were of noble descent, members of the house of* **Hashim***, belonging to the* **Abd Manaf** *clan and part of the* **Quraish** *tribal confederacy of Mecca. The Abd Manaf clan had a semi-priestly status, being responsible for certain functions during the annual pilgrimage to the Ka'ba in Mecca (the Ka'ba, the cube-shaped stone to which Muslims face when praying, predates Islam; Muslims believe that it was given to Adam when he was driven from Paradise and revere it as a sanctuary where closeness to God can be achieved; more scientific theories suggest that it is a meteorite).*

At the age of 40 Mohammad received his first revelations of the Qur'an and began preaching his message. He encountered stiff opposition from the

powerful Quraish leaders, the temple guardians and the rich traders, and was eventually forced to flee to **Medina***, known then as Yathrib (this event is known as the Hijra or flight and marks the beginning of the Islamic calendar). There he established himself and achieved a position of power, fighting three major battles with the Meccans before finally returning there in triumph two years before his death in 632 AD.*

In his lifetime he had become recognised as a prophet and founded the Islamic faith. Part of his success was in incorporating many aspects of the ancient Arabian religion, such as the pilgrimage to the Ka'ba, as well as aspects of Judaism and Christianity. But his success was not purely in religious terms. He was also an accomplished statesman who laid the foundations for what would later become a great Islamic empire.

rightful heir to the title of Imam, with his eldest son Ismail being passed over by the majority of Shi'ites in favour of his younger son Musa al-Kazim. The Ismailis however recognized Ismail as the rightful Imam. They are also known as *Sab'iya* or `Seveners' since, unlike the Twelver Shi'ites, they recognize only seven principal Imams after the death of the Prophet Mohammad. The philosophy of the Ismailis is a largely esoteric one, and a further name for them is the *Batiniyya* because of their emphasis on an esoteric (*batin*) interpretation of the Qur'an. Their theology is based on a cyclical theory of history centred around the number seven, which is considered to be of enormous significance. They are less restrictive in their customs and practice, allowing much greater freedom to women. Likewise, prayers are not linked to a specific formula. The mosque is replaced by a *jamat khana* which also serves as a community centre. Their spiritual head is the Agha Khan, who is considered a direct descendant of the Prophet Mohammad through his daughter Fatima.

Although first founded in the 8th century, they only really began to make their presence felt in North Africa from the beginning of the 10th century, going on to conquer Egypt in 969 and establish the powerful **Fatimid Dynasty** (named after the Prophet's daughter, Fatima) which flourished for the next two centuries, extending at the height of its power to include Egypt, Jordan, Syria, North Africa, Sicily, the Red Sea coast of Africa, Yemen and the Hejaz region of Arabia (including the holy cities of Mecca and Medina).

Under the Fatimids, however, the radical doctrines of the Ismailis (the source of their initial appeal) were gradually replaced by a more conservative outlook better suited to the responsibilities of such a powerful dynasty. This led to ideological conflicts which culminated in a major internal schism amongst the Ismailis. After the death of the eighth Fatimid caliph Al Mustansir in 1094, there was a dispute over his succession. The conservative elements within the court, led by the Commander of the Armies who had risen to a

Background

position of great personal power, installed Al Mustansir's younger and therefore more easily influenced son Al Mustali as caliph, dis-inheriting his older son Nizar, who was subsequently killed after attempting to revolt.

The followers of Al Mustali became known as *Mustalians* and the followers of Nizar as *Nizaris*. The Fatimid Dynasty, although it continued to rule in Egypt until 1171, was in terminal decline, finally being formally abolished by Salah-ud Din (Saladin) who restored Sunni orthodoxy and went on to establish the Ayyubid Dynasty. After the schism of 1094, the Mustalians (many of whom disowned the declining Fatimid Dynasty) established themselves on the outer peripheries of the Islamic world (notably in Yemen and India, where they are known today as *Boharis*). The Nizaris meanwhile began a period of intense political and doctrinal development in Persia, one outcome of which was the formation of the much feared **Assassins**, who established themselves in Syria from the beginning of the 12th century.

Though the Ismaili influence was important historically in terms of Fatimid rule, today they are a numerically insignificant minority in Jordan. Small numbers are still to be found in neighbouring Syria, but their main areas of settlement are in India and Pakistan, and to a lesser extent in Iran, Afghanistan, East Africa and Zanzibar.

Druze The Druze represent an offshoot of the Ismailis. Their religion developed in the 11th century AD, during the reign of the Cairo-based Fatimid caliph Al Hakim (996-1021). Al Hakim allowed himself to be declared a divine representation of God and substituted his own name for that of Allah in mosque services. This blasphemous act, together with heretical decrees such as banning people from fasting during Ramadan or undertaking the pilgrimage to Mecca, earned him the condemnation of mainstream Ismailis of the Fatimid court. Indeed his disappearance in 1021, taken by his followers as an act of divine *ghayba* (concealment) pending his eventual return, was probably the result of a discreet assassination.

In the meantime one of his closest disciples, Mohammad ibn Ismail al-Darazi, had left Egypt and began spreading the new faith in Syria (and particularly in the mountains of present-day Lebanon), where he found a more receptive audience amongst a people who had already been exposed to various heterodox interpretations of Islam. The term `Druze' is in fact an anglicized form of the Arabic word *durzi*, which was in turn derived from this missionary's name. As with the Alawis, very little is known about Druze beliefs or practices. Indeed, even the Druze themselves are divided between the *juhhal* (literally `ignorant') and the *uqqal* (literally `intelligent'), with only the latter being fully initiated into the doctrines of the faith. The Druze form an extremely tight-knit community, only ever marrying amongst themselves, and are said to have ceased accepting new members into their religion 20 years after the death of Al Hakim.

Historically, the Druze were concentrated in the Lebanon mountains, particularly the Chouf and Metn. However, following the 1860 massacre of as many as 10,000 Maronites at the hands of the Druze and the subsequent French intervention, many of them migrated to Syria, settling primarily in the Hauran. During the early 20th century small numbers moved across into present-day Jordan, where they can still be found in Jordan's own Hauran region in the north of the country, though they represent only a very small minority. In Lebanon they number around 170-200,000 and make up approximately 5% of the population, while in Syria they number around 430,000 but make up just 3% of the population. There are also around 80,000 Druze in modern-day Israel, concentrated in the Haifa and Golan regions.

Sufism is the mystical aspect of Islam, often described as the `science of the **Sufis** heart'. The word *Sufi* is most probably derived from the Arabic word *suf* meaning `wool', a reference to the woollen garments worn by the early Sufis. The Sufis do not represent a separate sect of Islam; rather they aspire to transcend sects, emphasizing the importance of personal spiritual development, to be found only through the Qur'an.

Nevertheless, various different Sufi orders did emerge, the most famous of them being the *Mawlawiyya* or **Whirling Dervishes**. This Sufi order originated in Turkey, inspired by the 13th century mystical poet Jalal ud-Din Rumi, and is best known for the whirling dance which forms part of their worship. The dance is performed to music and involves the chanting of the *dhikr*, a kind of litany in which the name of God is repeated over and over again. Historically the Sufis had considerable influence in the region, though the majority of the monuments they left behind are to be found in neighbouring Syria, particularly in Damascus. In the more up-market hotels of Amman you might be treated to arranged performance of Whirling Dervish dancing, while on the international scene a Damascus-based troupe of Whirling Dervishes have won widespread acclaim for their performances (though also attracting criticism for reducing what is supposed to be a spiritual act into a spectacle).

Christian theology has its roots in Judaism, with its belief in one God, the eter- **Christianity** nal Creator of the universe. Jesus, whom Christians believe was the Messiah or `Christ' (literally `Anointed One') and the son of God, was born in the village of Bethlehem, some 20 km south of Jerusalem. Very little is known about his early life except that he was brought up in a devout Jewish family. At the age of 30 he gathered a small group of followers and began to preach in the region between the Dead Sea and the Sea of Galilee. Two years later he was crucified in Jerusalem on the charge that his claim to be the son of God was blasphemous.

The New Testament of the Bible, which, together with the Old Testament, is the text to which Christians refer to as the ultimate scriptural authority, consists of four `Gospels' (literally `Good News'), and a series of letters by early Christians outlining the nature of Christian life.

Much of the early development of the Christian church took place within present-day Jordan. At first, Christians faced persecution within the Roman Empire, but gradually, as the faith spread, it became more widely accepted. In 313 AD the emperor Constantine issued the Edict of Milan, which formerly recognized the right of Christians to practice their faith, and in 380 AD the emperor Theodosius declared it the official religion of the Roman Empire.

Soon after, the Roman Empire was formally divided into East and West, with Constantinople (formerly Byzantium and today Istanbul) becoming the capital of the Eastern Roman Empire, better known as the Byzantine Empire. Under Byzantine rule, Christianity in the Middle East divided into numerous different churches. These different branches of the church arose out of somewhat obscure theological disputes over the nature of Christ, but also reflected the power struggles going on within the empire. Other regional centres of Christianity also developed their own theological doctrines and separate churches.

The orthodox **(Dyophysite)** view was that Christ was of two natures, divine and human, while the alternative view, that of the **Monophysites**, was that he was of one nature – purely divine. This latter interpretation was condemned as a heresy by the Council of Chalcedon in 451. The **Monothelite** doctrine, that Christ had two natures but one will, was seen as something of a compromise, and adopted by the Byzantine emperor Heraclius (610-641) as a means of providing a solution to the Dyophysite versus Monophysite schism which was threatening to tear the church apart. However in 680 AD the Sixth Ecumenical Council in turn condemned the Monothelite doctrine as heresy.

In the East, those who adhered to the orthodox (Dyophysite) view became known as **Melkites** (or Melchites), meaning literally `King's Men', in reference to the fact that they maintained their allegiance to the Byzantine emperor in Constantinople. The Byzantine emperors meanwhile regarded themselves as defenders of the **Orthodox** Church. Followers of the Monophysite, Monothelite and other `heterodox' (as opposed to orthodox) theologies meanwhile founded their own churches, including: the Antioch based **Syrian** or **Jacobite** church, named after Jacobus Bardaeus, a 6th century monk responsible for organizing the Monophysites of Syria into a church; the Egyptian **Coptic** church based at Alexandria; the **Armenian (Gregorian)** church; the **Nestorian (Chaldean)** church, founded by Nestorius of Cilicia in the 5th century; and the **Maronite** church which emerged in the 7th century.

To begin with, the Eastern Church of Constantinople and the Catholic (Latin) Church of Rome existed in broad, if at times uneasy, agreement, but over the centuries doctrinal differences intensified, culminating in the great schism of 1054, with the Eastern Church refusing to accept the supremacy of the Pope and recognizing instead the Patriarch of Constantinople as its head. Later, many of the independent churches in the East renounced the doctrines regarded as heretical by the Roman Catholic Church and acknowledged the supremacy of the Pope. They became known as **Uniate** Churches, but were allowed to retain their respective languages, rites and canon law in accordance with the terms of their union. At the same time, the independent churches continued to exist in parallel, with the exception of the Maronite church, which became fully united with the Roman Catholic Church. Thus today, there is in the Middle East the **Greek Orthodox** and **Greek Catholic** church, the **Syrian Orthodox** and **Syrian Catholic** church, and the **Armenian Orthodox** and **Armenian Catholic** church. In addition, the **Roman Catholic** church is itself represented. Later arrivals on the scene were the **Protestant** and **Anglican** churches, which began preaching in the Middle East during the 19th century.

In Jordan, the Greek Orthodox and Greek Catholic churches are the most important, although there are also small minorities of Armenian Catholics.

People

Arabs The vast majority of Jordanians (around 98% of the population) can be described as Arab, though the term is an extremely broad one, encompassing many different religious and ethnic groups. The Muslims, Christians, Bedouin and Palestinians of Jordan – each of them representing distinct communities – are all Arab. It is helpful, therefore, to look first at exactly what is meant by the term 'Arab', and how its meaning has evolved over time.

The earliest known use of the term 'Arab' comes from an inscription of the Assyrian king Shamaneser III, which refers to the *Arabi*. Thereafter it appears frequently, either as *Arabi* or *Arabu*, in Assyrian and Babylonian inscriptions. The term 'Arab' first appears in the Bible in Chronicles (2 Chronicles 17: 11), although it has been suggested that the 'mixed multitude' referred to in Exodus 12:38 as having accompanied the Israelites into the wilderness could equally be translated as 'Arabs' (in Hebrew, the word for each is *erev* and *arav* respectively, but in their written forms the vowels do not appear). More commonly, however, the Bible makes reference to the Ishmaelites. In Islamic and Hebrew tradition, the Arabs and the Hebrews are both descendants of the prophet Abraham, the Arabs through his son Ishmael and the Hebrews through his son Isaac. The birth of Isaac to Abraham's elderly wife Sarah meant that Ishmael (born to Abraham's concubine Hagar) was superseded as Abraham's natural heir, whose descendants would inherit the Promised Land. Ishmael instead went out into the desert (Genesis 21).

The traditional definition of an Arab, as reflected in the biblical interpretation, was a nomadic inhabitant of the deserts of northern and central Arabia. Indeed, the word 'Arab' is thought to have been derived from a Semitic root related to nomadism, perhaps the word *abhar* (literally 'to move' or 'to pass'), from which the word 'Hebrew' is also probably derived. On the other hand, settled agricultural communities were to be found in the Arabian peninsula even in biblical times, for example in the rain-fed uplands of present-day Yemen, which could also be termed 'Arab'. In addition, over the centuries many of the nomadic peoples traditionally recognized as Arabs themselves adopted a settled lifestyle based on agriculture and animal husbandry. Nevertheless, despite such anomolies, the broad definition of an Arab was to begin with fairly clear.

The definition of an Arab became more complicated with the arrival of Islam. As Peter Mansfield points out: "*The transformation achieved by the Holy Koran is unparalleled in the history of the world. When Mohammad began to recite his message the Arabs were despised and feared by their more civilized neighbours as licentious and violent nomads living on the edge of starvation, who worshipped idols, stones, trees and heaps of sand ... Yet before the Prophet's death 20 years later these scattered bands of idolatrous tribesmen had been welded into a single dynamic nation worshipping one all-powerful but compassionate deity. At the same time the sensible social laws of the Koran, skilfully adapted to the needs and conditions of Arabia, had raised the ethical standards of Arab society to an infinitely higher plane*" (Peter Mansfield, The Arabs). The Islamic faith as revealed by the Prophet Mohammad was clearly intended, initially at least, specifically for the nomadic tribes of the Arabian peninsula; ie the Arabs. The conquests of the 7th century, however, resulted in the creation of a vast Arab Empire based on the precepts of Islam. Thus, Arab and Muslim identities became very closely intertwined, though the two were never synonymous.

As Kamal Salibi points out: "*The Islamic conquests which were undertaken by the Arabs in the name of Islam were depicted as Arab conquests. This, viewed in one perspective, was true. The earlier Islamic conquests, though undertaken in the name of Islam, did result in the actualization of Arab political dominance in areas which had long been predominantly Arab in population - notably Syria and Iraq. It was highly arguable however whether or not the Islamic Empire of the Umayyad and Abbasid caliphs, which came to extend from the borders of Central Asia and the Indian Ocean to the Atlantic, was in fact an Arab Empire. Certainly the caliphate which stood at the head of this empire, though held by Arab Dynasties, was an Islamic rather than an Arab institution, representing an Islamic rather than Arab sovereignty. More important, the imperial civilization which reached its apogee under the Abbasid caliphs of Baghdad was an Islamic rather than Arab civilization, in which non-Arabs as well as Arabs participated. This civilization, in fact, had many of its leading centres outside the Arab world*" (Kamal Salibi, A House of Many Mansions). Later, the Arab nature of the Islamic Empire became even more tenuous, with the caliphate passing to the Turkish Ottomans. Kamal Salibi again: "*To the early Arab nationalists among the Muslims ... Arab nationalism essentially involved the reclamation of the Islamic caliphate, then held by the Turkish Ottomans, for a caliph of the Arab race.*"

Even more significantly, although Muslim and Arab identities came to be very closely identified with each other (at least by the Sunni Muslim majority in the region), there existed sizable minorities of Arab Christians (and indeed Jews), who had everything in common with their Muslim counterparts in terms of history, culture and language, but little in terms of religion. Ironically, the Christian Arabs were the first to articulate the concept of Arab nationalism, because they avoided the trap of confusing Arab and Muslim identities. To them: "*The Arab nation was amongst the greatest nations in history. It had a civilization prior to Islam, and a much more developed one after Islam. Christians had participated in the development of Arab civilization before and after Islam; and this civilization was not a purely religious one... but exhibited numerous traits which had no connection with religion whatsoever*" (Sati al-Husri, quoted in *A House of Many Mansions*, Kamal Salibi). To the minority Islamic sects of the region, the Shi'ites, Druze, Alawis etc, the idea that Arab history was inseparable from the history of the Sunni Islamic state was equally dubious, since it implied that they would always be relegated to a secondary position and excluded from power within it.

Thus the traditional definition of an Arab, as a nomadic inhabitant of the deserts of northern and central Arabia, was rendered inadequate by the 'arabization' of a far larger area, and much of what we today recognize as Arab culture and society has little in common with that of the nomadic desert tribes. Likewise, the tendency of mainstream Sunni Muslims to identify 'Arab' with 'Muslim' is flawed even within the Arab world, given the existence of non-Muslim Arab minorities, and completely untenable when you take into consideration the spread of Islam far beyond the bounds of the Arab world. Today, perhaps the nearest you can get to a definition of `Arab' is a native speaker of the Arabic language, though this remains a very loose definition, Arabic being the native tongue of around 120 million people across the Middle East and North Africa. As the language of Islam, it is also known to millions more Muslims outside the Arab world.

Bedouins   Native Jordanians are often characterized as 'Bedouin', but this is far from accurate since a greater proportion of the population are 'settled' Arabs who for centuries have relied on agriculture and in more recent times have formed part of Jordan's growing urban society.

The 40-50,000 persons of Bedouin extraction for the most part retain their semi-nomadic/pastoral lifestyle based on tribal traditions. They are earnestly wooed by the government and provide the bulk of recruits into the Jordanian armed forces. The late King Hussein in particular was seen as a patron and leader of this community. Despite the spread of educational and health facilities in tribal areas, the Bedouin look down on urban lifestyles. Most these days are transhumant herders of sheep and goats, moving with the help of mechanized transport from pasture to pasture through the seasons.

'Settled' Arabs   Many of the settled Arabs of the Jordan Valley, and other agricultural/urban areas, have more in common with their counterparts to the east of the Jordan River than with their Bedouin fellow-countrymen of the desert. Urban Jordanians have strong family traditions of their own, and no less of a sense of pride in history and civilization. There is a sizeable (and growing) social elite which is highly educated, talented and dedicated to the development of the country.

Palestinians   As much as 60% of the population is of Palestinian extraction, refugees of the bitter Arab-Israeli wars of 1947-9 and 1967, and more recently returnee migrant workers expelled as a result of the Gulf War. Palestinians have greatly enriched Jordanian political, economic and social life. Although a large proportion have become integrated and now carry Jordanian passports, there are still many who remain for the most part exiles in attitude and are regarded as a separate community by their hosts. Following the establishment of the

Palestine 'entity' in 1994, the question of the future of the Palestinians in Jordan has been opened up; at the simplest level, they will either have to admit full loyalty to Jordan or return to the new Palestine. However with the final status of the would-be Palestinian state still unsettled, the issue is far more complicated, both from the Palestinian and Jordanian point of view.

There is also a small community of Circassians – non-Arab Muslim refugees **Circassians** from the Russian Caucasus who came to Jordan in the 19th and 20th centuries. The majority are to be found in northern and eastern Jordan, concentrated in Amman, Jerash, Wadi Seer, Zarqa and Azraq.

The Arts

There is a long and illustrious tradition of literature and poetry in Arab culture. **Literature** The Qur'an is described by some as the greatest example of Arab literature, although to Muslims it is not really 'literature' at all, being the very words of God as revealed to the Prophet Mohammad. Historically, a great deal of the literature in Arab culture was religious in nature. At the same time, in the courts of the Islamic caliphs, poetic traditions of praise for the rulers developed, along with eulogies of nature and romantic love. Accounts of heroic deeds, the beauty of nature and the nature of human emotions were also themes central to the poetry of the nomadic Bedouin tribes of the desert. These poetic traditions were, however, entirely oral, passed down from generation to generation. Though many of these poetic traditions have been lost, some are still alive today, and a few have been committed to writing in the form of anthologies of folk tales in recent times.

In terms of contemporary literature, Jordan has tended to be somewhat eclipsed by Egyptian, Lebanese and Palestinian writers. In recent decades, however, an increasing number of specifically Jordanian writers have begun to make their mark both in the Middle East and internationally. Notable amongst modern writers in Jordan whose work has been translated into English are Abd al-Rahman Munif, Fadia Faqir, Ibrahim Nasrallah and Mu'nis Razzaz. A great many Palestinian authors and poets also have close connections with Jordan, having come to the country as refugees of the Arab-Israeli conflicts of 1949 and 1967, and in many cases settled there and adopted Jordanian citizenship.

As with literature, music in Muslim Arab culture was traditionally religious in **Music** nature. Indeed, a great deal of early poetry was meant to be sung. Likewise, the Qur'an is recited in a rhythmical, musical fashion, as is the call to prayer. At the same time, music was developed in the courts of the caliphs as a form of entertainment, an accompaniment to the more worldly poetry of adulation, particularly by the Umayyads. The frescoes decorating Umayyad Qasr Amra in the desert to the east of Amman depict many a scene of singing and dancing to the accompaniment of musical instruments. Amongst ordinary people, music played a central role in important social occasions such as weddings, as indeed it does today. A variety of traditional musical instruments can still be found in Jordan, including stringed instruments such as the *Oud* (a type of lute), as well as numerous different wind and percussion instruments.

Contemporary music in Jordan is very different. Practically none of it is indigenous, with the vast majority coming from that great power-house of Arabic music and culture, Egypt, and to a lesser extent from Palestinian and Lebanese culture. To most western ears, the music to be heard blaring from shops all over Downtown Amman (and practically any town centre in Jordan), takes some getting used to. Singers generally perform to the accompaniment of huge orchestras containing a mix of western and traditional instruments, with the overall effect somehow managing to evoke echoes of the 1930's alongside the distinctive wailing or crooning of Arabic lyrics.

Art Traditions of painting in Jordan go right back to the dawn of history in the form of rock art. Over the centuries, such traditions were developed in the form of decorative designs on pottery wares, with moulded figurines and sculpted pieces also making an appearance. By the Roman period, the decorative arts were already very advanced. During the Byzantine era, mosaics were an important medium for the artistic expression of religious themes, though the origins of mosaic art are actually to be found in Greek and Roman culture. Under Islam, depictions of the human form were considered blasphemous, leading to the destruction of much art at the hands of iconoclasts. Traditionally, Islamic art expressed itself in terms of geometric patterns, vegetal designs and, most importantly, calligraphy. There were of course exceptions to this, most notably during the Umayyad era, as shown so graphically in the beautiful frescoes of Qasr Amra.

Artistic expression in the Middle East during the Ottoman period was largely restricted to cultural centres such as Cairo, Beirut and Damascus, with the land of Jordan being something of a backwater. In the decades leading up to independence, the art scene in Jordan remained quiet. The wars and upheavals of the early decades of Jordan's history as an independent state restricted the development of the arts, though at the same time Palestinian artists living in Jordan increasingly made their mark and helped inspire Jordanian artists.

Today, Jordan has a thriving modern art scene, though it is restricted very much to Amman's urban elite. The founding of the Jordan National Gallery of Fine Arts in Amman in 1980 reflected the growing importance of artistic expression in Jordanian society. More recently, the founding in 1992 of the excellent Darat al-Funan (see page 78) under the auspices of the Abdul Hameed Shoman Foundation has helped establish Amman as an important centre for the arts in the Middle East. The vibrancy of Amman's art scene is reflected also in the numerous private galleries opening up all over the city.

Land and Environment

"Jordan itself is a beautiful country. It is wild, with limitless deserts where the bedouin roam, but the mountains of the north are clothed in green forests, and, where the Jordan river flows, it is fertile in summer and winter. Jordan has a strange, haunting beauty and a sense of timelessness. Dotted with the ruins of empires once great, it is the last resort of yesterday in the world of tomorrow. I love every inch of it. I love Amman, where I was born, and which I have seen grow from a township. I am still awed and excited each time I set eyes on the ancient city of Petra, approached by a defile so narrow that a dozen Nabateans could hold an army at bay. Above all I feel at home in the tribal black tents in the desert" (King Hussein bin-Talal, Uneasy Lies the Head: An Autobiography of HM King Hussein of Jordan, 1962).

Area and borders

The Hashemite Kingdom of Jordan today occupies an area of 92,140 sq km (making it roughly the same size as Portugal), having formally relinquished its claim to some 5,600 sq km of the West Bank in 1988. Jordan's odd geographical shape is due to its late emergence as a nation state and is based on designs created in the capitals of the major imperial powers. It represents compromises agreed in Versailles and London rather than local realities (though it is misleading to suggest that the country of Jordan was a European creation; only its borders).

Jordan's western border with Israel runs from the Gulf of Aqaba in the south to the confluence of the Jordan and Yarmouk rivers in the north. It passes through sea and lake or is aligned along river courses for much of its length and the hydrology of the Rift Valley has deeply affected this international border. Jordan's border with Syria is marked by the Yarmouk River in the northwest and runs through open desert in the northeast. Jordan has a short, straight stretch of desert border in the east with Iraq, but most of its vast, jagged, ruler-drawn eastern border is with Saudi Arabia. While Saudi Arabia originally disputed Jordan's rights to a frontage on to the Gulf of Aqaba, the Saudi kings were finally magnanimous, permitting Jordan to extend its area on the Gulf south from Aqaba against adjustments elsewhere. Jordan now has 17 km of coast, a useful access to the Gulf for commercial and tourist purposes.

Landscape

Jordan can be divided into three broad topographic regions; the Rift Valley to the west; the Trans-Jordan Plateau (upland mountain spine) in the centre; and the vast undulating desert lands to the east.

Described by PK Hitti as one of the "most singular features of the earth's surface", the Rift Valley forms part of the Great Syrian-African Rift Valley. This extends from Turkey in the north right the way down through Syria, Lebanon and Jordan, along the bed of the Gulf of Aqaba and Red Sea, and then through Eritrea, Ethiopia, Kenya, Tanzania, Malawi and Mozambique. Its geological origins are to be found some twenty to thirty million years ago when most of **Rift Valley**

Jordan: regional

Background

the southern Levant lay under the ocean, with only the granite peaks of Sinai protruding above sea-level. Early in the Miocene epoch, pressure on the earth's surface from both east and west forced the sea-bed upwards in two long, north-south running folds. These folds then became fissured, with the land to the east shearing and moving northwards several kilometres. At the same time, the land in the middle slumped downwards, pushing the emerging mountains on either side even higher up. Within Jordan itself, three distinct areas can be identified along the length of the Rift Valley; the Jordan Valley, Dead Sea and Wadi Arabah.

Jordan Valley Known in Arabic as the *Ghor*, or 'depression'), the Jordan Valley forms part of the border between Jordan and Israel (and the Palestinian controlled West Bank) as it runs north-south for around 100 km between Lake Tiberias (Sea of Galilee) and the Dead Sea. Averaging between 5-15 km in width, its most significant feature is that, like the Dead Sea, it is *below* sea level, starting at around 200 m below sea level at Lake Tiberias and descending to more than 400 m below sea level as it drains into the Dead Sea. Left to its own devices, the Jordan Valley would today consist predominantly of semi-arid desert steppe. However, this area has produced some of the earliest evidence of human activity in Jordan. The secret of course is water; wherever natural springs emerge the favourable climate and rich alluvial soils are able to support lush vegetation and the agricultural potential is excellent. This was the basis of pre-historic settlement at Pella, and the advent of modern irrigation projects have made this one of Jordan's most productive regions (for more on the agricultural development of the Jordan Valley, see under Economy).

The headwaters of the **Jordan river** are formed by three steams which all rise close to each other on the slopes of Mount Hermon. The upper section of the Jordan then flows through northern Israel before draining into Lake Tiberias. Around 10 km to the south of Lake Tiberias the **Yarmouk river** joins it from the east. With a catchment area of around 18,300 sq km (a quarter of which lies in Syria), the Jordan river represents the country's main surface water resource. The Yarmouk river, forming the western part of the border between Jordan and Syria (and also a small part of the border between Jordan and Israel), is its most important tributary, followed by the **Zarqa**. Despite its biblical fame and current importance as a surface water resource, the Jordan river is relatively small; "*a very tiny stream, rather a rivulet...compared with other rivers in the world*" (Stephan Libiszewski, *Water Disputes in the Jordan Basin Region and their Role in the Resolution of the Arab-Israeli Conflict*). Thus the total natural discharge of the Jordan river basin, including all its tributaries, is around 50 times less than the Rhine, 65 times less than the Nile, and 400 times less than the Mississippi (*ibid*).

Dead Sea The Dead Sea is arguably Jordan's most striking, and certainly its most unusual, topographical feature. In reality a huge inland lake, this vast expanse of lifeless, salt-laden water lies at some 412 m *below* sea level, making it the lowest point on the earth's surface. Its waters on the other hand have the highest salt content in the world (more than 20%, as compared with 5% for the world's oceans). Following the shearing and slumping which formed the Rift Valley, rainwater washed large quantities of limestone down from the mountains on either side, partially filling the rift and creating a large lake (the Lisan lake). Following the end of the last Ice Age (in Jordan a *pluvial* or rainy period), much of the lake's water evaporated to create what is now the Dead Sea.

The Dead Sea is fed by the Jordan River which drains into it from the north, and by the various wadis and springs which drain into it from the east and

The disappearing Dead Sea

For the last 10,000 years or so, the flow of water into the Dead Sea has been balanced by the high rates of evaporation from its surface, so maintaining a stable water level. However, the intensive exploitation of the Jordan river basin for irrigation purposes has upset this equilibrium, with dramatic consequences. During the early 1960s the surface of the Dead Sea was around 395 m below sea level, but by 1987 it had reached 407 m below sea level. According to current estimates, the Dead Sea is being lowered by as much as half a metre every year.

Originally, the Dead Sea was divided into two unequal sectors; a larger northern area with a maximum depth of up to 400 m, and a shallow, smaller southern basin. Between the two was a spit of land known as the Lisan Peninsula, with just a narrow channel of water - Lynch's Strait - joining them. In 1976, when the Dead Sea's level dropped to 401.5 m below sea level, Lynch's Straight dried out, leaving an ithsmus or interlaken separating its two halves. The shallower southern half quickly dried out entirely in the subsequent years, resulting in a massive 25% decrease in the surface area of the Dead Sea. Today, the evaporation ponds for the extraction of potash to be found in the southern sector rely on water pumped from the deeper northern sector.

This reduction in the Dead Sea's level and extent has been accompanied by an equally dramatic increase in salinity. Originally, the fresh water flowing in from the Jordan river tended to rest on the surface, resulting in a layer of less saline water with a dense column of saltier 'fossil' water below. With the reduced inflow, the surface layer of water has become progressively saltier, and therefore denser. Eventually, by the late 1970s, the surface layer reached the point where it was saltier and denser than the deeper water, with the result that the statified water column became inverted and the fossil water rose to the surface. Despite its name, the Dead Sea does support some life in the form of several species of bacteria and one species of algae. Found only in the surface layer of water, the more salt-sensitive algae have been for the most part killed off by the increased salinity, while the more salt-tolerant bacteria which fed on them have been reduced in number by the loss of their main food source. Occasionally, during particularly wet years, the original stratification of the water column has been restored and the algae have again flourished, but overall the delicate ecological balance which once existed appears to have disappeared for ever.

west. Being below sea level it has no outlet. Nor is its high salt content due to water from the Red Sea flowing into it; rather it is a product of the high evaporation rates which accompany the blistering heat, particularly during the summer, when as much as 25 mm are lost every 24 hours.

As well as common salt (sodium chloride), the waters of the Dead Sea are rich in magnesium chloride, calcium chloride and potassium chloride, the latter providing the raw material for the industrial production of potash, used in the manufacture of fertilizers, soaps and glass. These salts, together with a wide range of other trace elements, also give the water (and the mud below) significant theraputic properties, adding another aspect to the Dead Sea's tourist appeal.

Wadi Arabah

To the south of the Dead Sea the land climbs gently, reaching a maximum elevation of 192 m above sea level. Here a line of rocks and low hillocks, known in Arabic as the *charagi ar-rishi* (literally 'saddlebags of feathers'), forms the watershed between the Dead Sea and the Wadi Arabah. Thus the Wadi Arabah drains southwards into the Gulf of Aqaba, not north into the Dead Sea. Minimal rainfall and high evaporation rates mean that this watercourse is dry for most of the year, with wide swathes of desert and sand dunes occupying the broad, shallow valley on either side.

Trans-Jordan Plateau The Trans-Jordan Plateau or central upland spine comprises a series of low mountain ranges and plateaux (the Ajlun highlands and eastern plateau of the Great Rift Valley), extending north-south from the Syrian border to the Gulf of Aqaba. Sometimes referred to as the Jordanian Heights, this spine is broken by a series of broadly east-west valleys containing seasonal wadis that flow into the Jordan Valley and Dead Sea. Though the mountains and plateaux only reach altitudes of around 1,500 m above sea level, the sharp drop down into the Rift Valley has produced spectacular canyons such as Wadi Mujib and Wadi Hasa which cut across the route of the King's Highway. The Trans-Jordan Plateau also boasts substantial **aquifers** holding valuable reserves of ground water, though this finite resource is under growing pressure from increased demand from agriculture, industry and municipal usage.

Desert region An extension of the Arabian Desert, Jordan's desert region comprises more than three-quarters of the country's territory. For the most part this region is flint-strewn desert, though there are two broad divisions that can be identified. The north and northeast parts are actually a southward continuation of Syria's Hauran region, comprising lava and basalt landscapes formed by volcanic activity which took place around the same time as the Rift Valley was formed. To the south there are prominent outcrops of granite and sandstone, most spectacularly seen at Wadi Rum. Azraq Oasis, to the east of Amman, is a remnant of one of the many lakes which existed in this region during the last Pluvial period.

Red Sea Separating Arabia from northeastern Africa, the Red Sea represents a continuation of Jordan's Rift Valley system. At its northern end the Red Sea is split in two by the triangular mass of the Sinai peninsula. The western Gulf of Suez now connects with the Mediterranean via the Suez Canal, while the eastern Gulf of Aqaba reaches up to touch the southern tip of Jordan and Israel. The Gulf of Aqaba boasts a wealth of coral reefs supporting a rich diversity of exotic marine life.

This delicate ecosystem is particularly vunerable. The Gulf of Aqaba is very narrow, averaging just 20 km across, and only 180 km long. It is also semi-enclosed, with the result that any pollution or contamination remains concentrated within a small area. In addition, there is no steady inflow of fresh water (the Wadi Arabah is dry for most of the year), and rainfall amounts to just 25-30 millimetres annually. With a high concentration of industrial and tourism activities along its shores, the pressures on the Gulf of Aqaba's coral reefs and associated marine life are very great indeed. Municipal sewage from the numerous tourist resorts in neighbouring Egypt and Israel, industrial pollution from the loading of phosphates at Aqaba port, the threat of oil spills and unregulated diving are all taking their toll.

However, now that both Jordan and Egypt have signed peace treaties with Israel, there is considerable scope for multilateral cooperation on what after all is a natural resource which all three countries have a vested interest in preserving. Already there have been a number of initiatives at both the national and international level, though balancing environmental concerns with the demands of industry, commerce and tourism will always be problematic.

The importance of water in the Middle East

Water, the very basis of life, is scarce in the Middle East. As well as being of fundamental importance in terms of domestic consumption (for drinking, washing etc), water is also vital to industry and agriculture (this sector in fact consumes by far the largest share of Jordan's available water resources). Not only is the scant rainfall in the region highly unevenly distributed and seasonal in character, but most of it is lost to evaporation during the heat of the summer season. As a result, somewhere between 80-85% of Jordan can be termed arid. In Israel the figure is 60%, and in Syria 50-65%, with only Lebanon enjoying an abundance of water. Jordan, Israel and the Palestinian territories are all classified as being below the absolute scarcity level of 500 cubic metres of water per person annually. Jordan has the lowest level of domestic water consumption in the Arab world.

The Jordan-Yarmouk river basins represent the single most important source of water for both Jordan and Israel, acounting for more than a third of the national supply of each country. According to a US Geological Survey carried out in 1998, water usage in this area exceeds the estimated total renewable water supply by around 25%. The deficit is made up by tapping into non-renewable groundwater sources and underground aquifers (for example at Azraq, see page 135).

Moreover, with high levels of population growth, as well as the over-exploitation and pollution of existing water resources, the problem looks set to get ever worse. In this context, many commentators suggest that the next major confrontation in the Middle East will not be over land, but over the question of water (the so-called "Water Wars" scenario). Though it makes for a compelling argument, the reality is somewhat more complex.

In many ways, water has always been right at the heart of the Arab-Israeli conflict; hardly surprising when you consider its significance. In the aftermath of the Arab-Israeli war of 1948-9, Israel clashed repeatedly with Jordan and Syria over the question of water.

The role of water in the Arab-Israeli conflict

In 1955 the US helped to draw up the 'Johnston's Unified Plan' for the allocation of the waters of Jordan river and its tributaries. According to the plan, Israel was to receive a 40% share, while Jordan, Syria and Lebanon were to divide the remaining 60% between them. The plan was never officially accepted by the Arab parties, as it would have implied recogition of Israel. Instead, each country went ahead with their respective water diversion plans. Israel continued with its National Water Carrier project, consisting of an ambitious pipeline which would divert water from Eshed Kinrot on the northwest shore of Lake Tiberias and irrigate the country as far south as the Negev desert. Jordan meanwhile concentrated on developing its access to the waters of the Yarmouk river, which it shared with Syria.

Events began to come to a head in 1963 when, with the National Water Carrier pipeline nearing completion, Israel announced its intention to soon begin drawing water from Lake Tiberias. The impact of this was potentially devastating; were Israel it exceed its allocation under the Johnston Plan (which seemed likely given that the Arabs had rejected it), Jordan faced the prospect of the productive lands of the Jordan valley being turned to saline desert.

In response to this, in 1964 the Arab League launched plan to divert two of the major sources of the Jordan river. The Arab League plan would have cut the capacity of Israel's National Water Carrier by around one third and increased the salinity of Lake Tiberias, an equally devastating prospect for Israel's water supply system. Israel warned that it regarded such a project as a direct threat to its national security, and therefore as an act of war. It attacked the project several times between 1965-67 and, though only one aspect of growing Arab-Israeli tensions, many commentators have argued that these clashes contributed directly to the Six Day War.

During the Six Day War, Israel destroyed the works of a Jordanian dam on the Yarmouk which would have improved water diversion into Jordan's King Abdullah Canal. By occupying the Golan Heights, Israel also increased its

The ancient world of coral reefs

Coral reefs have existed on the planet for approximately 450 million years, with fossil evidence indicating that ancient reefs were every bit as complex as those of today. They are considered to be one of the two most productive natural ecosystems in the world, the other being the tropical rain forests. Both these systems are currently at risk as a result of excessive and negligent use.

Coral reefs are the largest natural structures in the world. They are the result of a remarkable relationship between coral animals, known as polyps, and microscopic algae (zooxanthellae) living in their tissues. The polyp, resembling a small sea anemone, is able to feed itself using stinging cells found on its tentacles which paralyse passing plankton. The plankton is digested but supplies only a small part of the nutritional requirements of the polyp. The remainder comes from the zooxanthellae which convert sunlight, carbon dioxide and their own wastes into oxygen and carbohydrates. These carbohydrates are also used by the polyp to make calcium carbonate in a process known as calcification. This material

forms the skeleton of the coral and eventually the framework of what we recognise today as coral reef. 137 species of coral are found on the reefs of the Gulf of Aqaba.

Coral reefs provide food and shelter for thousands of organisms which co-exist in complex inter-connected food chains. Different behavioural patterns permit many organisms to share the same area, yet all organisms share common objectives; to occupy space and protect that space, to feed and to reproduce. Organisms which are less successful in any of the above will, in time, disappear from the reef.

Coral reef ecosystems are in a constant state of change. Corals grow and provide the framework for extension of the reef. Simultaneously, the reefs are being broken down by animals living in or feeding on the structure (sponges, bivalves, urchins, fish). If corals are damaged then the complex equilibrium of the reef will be permanently altered. The result is loss of productivity and biodiversity, and in extreme circumstances the complete collapse of the entire ecosystem.

access to the Yarmouk, largely at Jordan's expense. In the ensuing decades, it consistently opposed any improvement of Jordan's intake system from the Yarmouk, and only recently has it lifted its veto on World Bank financing of a joint Jordanian-Syrian dam there. Likewise, the Israeli monopoly over the waters of the Upper Jordan has until very recently totally excluded Jordan from tapping this source. Such has been the level of tension between Jordan and Israel over the question of water, that the late King Hussein (not one to raise the spectre of conflict lightly) once publicly stated in an interview that water was the only issue which might precipitate a war with Israel (The Independent, 15 May 1990).

The role of water in the Peace Process The scarcity of water in the Middle East and the competing demands for it may seem on the surface to justify the "water wars" scenario so favoured by many commentators. However, in the case of Jordanian-Israeli relations at least, water issues have also proved to be a valuable tool in the Peace Process. Indeed, the settlement of bilateral water disputes is a centrepiece of the 1994 peace treaty between Jordan and Israel.

The progress made by Jordan and Israel on this issue reflects in part the fact that, since Jordan gave up its claim to the West Bank in 1988, there have been no major outstanding territorial disputes between the two countries, making negotiations on water far more straightforward. Even so, on the face of it, the water issue would appear appear to be a zero-sum game, with both parties competing for an excessive share of an insufficient resource. However, the treaty between Jordan and Israel is careful to make the redistribution of existing water resources only a minor component. A far greater emphasis is placed on cooperative 'win-win' projects which will actually increase the available water supply, as well creating a set of common interests and practical interdependencies which will hopefully help cement the peace between the two countries.

A major component of this cooperation involves the joint Jordanian-Israeli construction of a diversion/storage dam on the Yarmouk river at Adassiya, which will allow Jordan to fulfil its longstanding ambition of increasing the flow of water into the King Abdullah Canal. A similar joint water storage facility on the Lower Jordan river will catch the winter flood water which otherwise flows untapped into the Dead Sea, with the water going to Jordan. Along with the building of a treatment plant to purify saline spring water emerging around Lake Tiberias, this will increase Jordan's share of the waters of the Jordan river from virtually nothing to a minimum of 30 million cubic metres per year, while allowing Israel to maintain its present share. Finally, the two parties agreed to the forming of a Joint Water Committee which would "cooperate in finding sources for the supply to Jordan of an additional quantity of 50 million cubic metres per year of water of drinkable standard" (Annex II, Article 1.3). This last aspect of the treaty is certainly its most ambitious and uncertain, with potential projects including a costly "Peace Pipeline" bringing water in from outside the region (possibly from Turkey, Egypt or Lebanon), and a canal to carry water from the Red Sea or the Mediterranean into the Dead Sea – the so-called "Red-Dead" and "Med-Dead" projects (see below).

Although the water-related provisions of the 1994 treaty between Jordan and Israel represent one of the most promising examples of constructive long-term cooperation in the Peace Process, there are still major obstacles. At the time of the treaty, Jordan's Prime Minister and Chief Water Negotiator told the press that Jordan stood to gain at least 25% more water in the long term. According to Stephan Libiszewski, a more realistic figure is around 7% in the short term, and 15-20% in the long term. Although a pipeline transferring water from Lake Tiberias to Jordan (in exchange for water taken by Israel from the Yarmouk river) has been operational since 1995, none of the other major water storage/diversion projects have been completed as yet. The more ambitious long term projects, meanwhile, have barely made it to the drawing board, if that.

An added complication is that the existing treaty represents an agreement between Jordan and Israel only; Syria, Lebanon and the Palestinian territories, all of which have legitimate claims on the waters of the Jordan river basin, have yet to reach an agreement with Israel (or Jordan for that matter). From the Jordanian point of view, this is particularly worrying. Syria already extracts far more than its share of the waters of the Yarmouk as envisaged in the 1955 Johnston Plan, and according to some experts plans to further increase its share, which would have a direct impact on Jordan's supply from this source. Given the history of poor relations between Jordan and Syria, the prospect of a future dispute between the two over the Yarmouk river is highly possible. Without a comprehensive regional agreement on water sharing, the reality on the ground for Jordan is likely to fall far short of the ambitious projections of its treaty with Israel. In contrast, as long as Israel continues to occupy the Golan Heights and southern Lebanon, it is strategically well placed to protect its own share of the waters of the Jordan river basin.

The idea of a pipeline supplying water from outside the region was originally put forward by President Sadat of Egypt in 1979. The El Salaam (Peace) Canal he proposed would carry water from the Nile across the Sinai to Jerusalem

The "Peace Pipeline" concept

Background

(currently, a section of canal already exists linking the Nile and Sinai). Though technically feasible, such a project would be politically sensitive, requiring the cooperation of Sudan, Ethiopia and Uganda, all of which have rights to the waters of the Nile. It might also provoke protest from within Egypt, which itself suffers from regional water scarcity, even though the proposed canal would only draw the equivalent of 0.2% of Egypt's total annual water consumption. In 1993 President Moubarak suggested a variation extending only as far as the Egyptian-Gaza Strip/Israeli border town of Rafah, but as yet there has been no firm commitment to such a project.

Another, more ambitious project was proposed by the former president of Turkey, Turgat Özal, in 1987. He suggested taking water from Turkey's Seyhan and Ceyhan rivers, both of which currently flow untapped into the Mediterranean. He envisaged two pipelines, one carrying water south to Syria, Jordan, western Saudi Arabia and possibly Israel, and the other transporting it east to Kuwait, eastern Saudi Arabia, Oman and the United Arab Emirates. The cost of this project (estimated at some US$21 bn in 1990) has been the major sticking point, with some experts predicting that it would work out cheaper to desalinize sea water (a process itself considered prohibitively expensive on anything other than a very small scale). Moreover, such an approach would be unlikely to win favour with Syria, which is already engaged in an acrimonious dispute with Turkey over the waters of the Euphrates river, or with Israel, which tends to view self-sufficiency in water as being integral to its security.

The "Red-Dead" project Perhaps even more ambitious than any of the above options, and certainly more complex and uncertain, is the idea of a tunnel and/or canal linking the Red Sea with the Dead Sea. Initially, this was conceived as a way of generating hydro-electric power by exploiting the 400 m altitude difference between the two seas. Subsequently it was suggested that the power generated could be used to run desalization plants to supply water for domestic consumption and agriculture. Again, the economic viability of such a project is questionable. As well as an estimated price-tag of around US$3 bn, some experts have suggested that the water eventually produced would be so expensive as to make it only viable for luxury tourist complexes on the shores of the Dead Sea, or else for highly sophisticated intensive agriculture.

More worrying is the uncertainty surrounding the possible environmental impacts. Part of the rationale behind the project was that it would provide a means of reversing the steady fall in the level of the Dead Sea (see above). However, studies have suggested that replacing the inflow of freshwater from the Jordan river with salt water from the Red Sea could have a disasterous effect on the delicate ecological balance of the Dead Sea, with possible micro-climatic and even macro-climatic repercussions. A rapid increase in the volume of the Dead Sea (and therefore pressure on the sea bed) might also increase the likelihood of earthquakes or volcanic activity in this region of tectonic instability. Certainly, the rise in sea level would increase the salinity of nearby fresh water aquifers, as well as submerging a number of villages, roads and tourist resorts.

Towards sustainable water use Notwithstanding the best efforts of hydrologists and politicians, water scarcity will in all likelihood remain a fact of life for the vast majority in the Middle East for the forseeable future. Making the best possible use of what's already there is, therefore, a vital part of the equation. In Jordan, as in Israel, agriculture accounts for around 65-70% of water use, and it is here that the potential gains are the greatest. The open canals which account for more than a quarter of Jordan's irrigation system – principally in the Jordan valley – lose around 40% of their water through evaporation and leakage. At the farm level on the other hand, 86% of irrigation is already carried out using highly efficient drip or sprinkler systems. Across the border, Israel rightly claims to lead the world in terms of water-saving irrigation technologies and arid zone agriculture. Indeed, although agricultural output continues to rise steadily in Israel, the total amount of irrigation water used has been falling slowly since the mid-1980s. In terms of municipal and domestic use, there are also great efficiency savings to be made, as in industry. In the context of the Peace Process, the opportunities for sharing expertise in all these areas offer immediate benefits, as well as helping build constructive relations. In ecological terms also, the consequences of mismanagement and pollution of water resources demand a cooperative approach. In the lower Jordan river, for example, the combined effects of diverted saline water, industrial waste and irrigation run-off have made the water unsuitable even for agriculture. Cooperative measures to remedy the situation will bring this water back into use.

Climate

The Middle East region is subject to two major climate zones; **Mediterranean/European** and **continental/desert**. Together with Jordan's unique topographical features, most notably the Jordan Valley and the Dead Sea, these two climate zones determine its overall weather. At its simplest, the country experiences a cool/cold rainy season from mid-November through to early March, and a warm/hot dry season for the rest of the year.

For details of the best time to visit Jordan in terms of climate, see page 27

During the winter and early spring (mid-November to early March), the Mediterranean climate zone is dominant, with westerly winds blowing in from Europe. Much of the moisture carried by these winds is deposited as rain on the coastal mountains of Israel. This creates a 'rain shadow' effect further east, so that the valleys of the Great Rift system receive comparatively little rainfall. Some clouds do however make it inland, depositing significant amounts of rain on the mountains of the Ajlun highlands to the north of Amman, and lesser amounts on the mountains and plateaux to the east of the Dead Sea. Every now and again, exceptionally heavy thunderstorms are blown right across both mountain ranges and so reach the desert steppe. Usually coming in late winter or spring, the light rainfall which occurs in these circumstances causes the desert steppe to burst into life, with the valley floors becoming carpeted in a thin covering of grass and wild flowers. Thus there is a progressive decrease in rainfall as one goes from west to east, and a similar pattern as one goes from north to south. The higher altitudes of the Trans-Jordan Plateau make winter temperatures significantly cooler, while in the desert to the east it also gets very cold at night. In the south, however, the warming effect of Red Sea keeps winter temperatures above 15°C.

During the summer (late May to late September), the Mediterranean climate belt is pushed northwards and the region comes under the influence of the continental/desert climate of Africa. The overall climate during this period approaches the hot, arid conditions of the Sahara. The higher altitudes of the Trans-Jordan Plateau also moderate the summer heat, with the Ajlun highlands enjoying an essentially Alpine climate. In the desert steppe and the valleys of the Great Rift system, however, the summer months are ones of intense (though dry) heat with temperatures often reaching well over 40°C. Throughout Jordan rainfall is almost entirely absent during the summer.

Though spring and autumn are as a general rule the most pleasant in terms of climate (subject of course to local topography and what you are actually looking for), these seasons are also the time when hot winds occasionally blow in from the east or southeast. Known as the *khamsin*, meaning literally '50 days', in reference to the period for which they are supposed to last, these usually in fact only last for a few days at a time. They are however extremely uncomfortable, being accompanied by a significant rise in temperatures (by as much as 10°C) and a dramatic fall in humidity (to as little as 10%), in addition to which they also sometimes laden with fine sand from the desert.

Flora and fauna

The varied topography and contrasting climatic influences of this region combine to create a huge diversity of habitats. Added to this is the fact that the region stands at the junction of the European, Asian and African continents, with the result that just about every vegetation type from each of these is found within what is a comparatively small area. This diversity in theory also provides habitats for a large variety of wildlife, although in practice extensive over-hunting of most larger species of mammals has reduced their numbers to a bare minimum. On the other hand, the future for Jordan's flora and fauna looks more promising, with the Royal Society for the Protection of Nature (RSCN) working hard to reverse the destruction of the past. For more details of all Jordan's National Parks and Nature Reserves, see page 50.

Flora With its varied topography and climate, Jordan is home to around 2,225 species of flowering plants, with new species being discovered on a regular basis. The Ajlun highlands and the deep wadis which cut through the eastern plateau of the Rift Valley as they drain down to the Dead Sea have the richest vegetation. The Ajlun highlands consist of Mediterranean hill country dominated by forests of holly oak, Aleppo pine and pistachio. The Dana Nature Reserve is perhaps the best place to take in the enormous variety of vegetation to be found in Jordan, with almost every conceivable vegetation type represented at different levels as one descends from the high plateau down to the Dead Sea. In the Jordan Valley willow, oleander and tamarisk are found. Despite their harsh climate, the desert steppe regions also support a surprising variety of seasonal grasses, low shrubs, thorny bushes and trees. Throughout the country, spring heralds the blossoming of an almost unbelievable variety of wild flowers, some of them strikingly beautiful and very rare.

Fauna In the recent past Jordan was home to an equally rich variety of wildlife, although excessive hunting and the modification (or in some cases destruction) of their natural habitats has reduced many of these to near extinction. Where once onagers (wild ass), gazelle, oryx and ostriches roamed wild in the desert steppe to the east of Amman, these species now only survive in small numbers through the conservation efforts of the RSCN. The Shaumari Wildlife Reserve near Azraq is the focus for a captive breeding programme which is gradually reintroducing them into the wild. Similarly, the nearby Azraq wetlands once provided an important watering point for numerous species of migratory birds en route between Africa and Europe, as well as supporting indigenous wildlife such as buffalos, ducks, carp and catfish. Efforts to restore this important habitat are still in their early stages. The deep wadis draining into the Dead Sea (notably Wadi Dana and Wadi Mujib) are also the focus for conservation efforts to preserve species such as the Nubian ibex.

Overall, Jordan's record on conservation is far better than other Arab countries in the Middle East. Recent surveys have recorded no less than 77 different species of mammals, 92 species of reptiles and 420 species of birds (including seasonal visitors).

Footnotes

13

384

Footnotes

Useful words and phrases in Arabic

Learning just a few basic words and phrases of Arabic is not at all difficult and will make an enormous difference to your travelling experience. Being able to greet people and respond to greetings, point at something in the souks, ask 'how much?' and understand the reply, or recognise Arabic numbers on buses - such simple things are rewarding, enjoyable and of practical benefit. The greatest hurdle most people face is with pronounciation. Arabic employs sounds which simply do not occur in English, so your tongue and mouth literally have to learn to form new, unfamiliar sounds. It has been observed, perhaps a little unkindly, that the nearest most Westerners get to exercising the relevant muscles for intoning Arabic is when they vomit! With a little patience though you can soon pick up the correct pronounciation of most words (or at least good enough to make yourself understood). The following is just a very brief introduction. The Arabic transliterations are simplistic; at the end of the day there's no substitute to listening to and practicing with a native speaker. Once you are in the Middle East you will have plenty of opportunities to do this. Before you go, language books and tapes can get you started. *Colloquial Arabic (Levantine), published by Routledge, is a good package.*

Greetings and pleasantries

Hello (informal; 'hi')	*marhaba*
Hello ('welcome')	*ahlan wa sahlan* (or just *ahlan*)
Hello ('peace be upon you')	*asalaam alaikum*
Hello (response)	*wa alaikum as-salaam*
Goodbye	*ma'a salaama*
Good morning	*subah al-khair*
Good morning (response)	*subah an-noor*
Good evening	*musa al-khair*
Good evening (response)	*musa an-noor*
Good night	*tusba allah khair*
Good night (response)	*wa inta min ahalu*
How are you?	*kif halak/halik?* or *kifak/kifik (m/f)*
Fine, good, well	*qwayees*
Please	*min fadlak/fadlik (m/f)*
Thankyou	*shukran*
Thankyou very much	*shukran jazeelan*
Excuse me	*afwan*
Sorry	*aassif*
No problem	*mush mushkilay*
Congratulations!	*mabrouk!*
Thank God!	*hamdullilah!*

Small talk

What is your name?	*shoo ismak/ismik? (m/f)*
My name is...	*ismi...*
Where are you from?	*min wain inta/inti? (m/f)*
I am a tourist	*ana siyaha*

Useful expressions

If God wills it	*inshallah*
Yes	*naam/aiwa*
No	*laa*
Where is ...?	*wain...?*

How far?	*kam kilometre?*
Is there/do you have...?	*fi....?*
There is	*fi*
There is not, there's none	*ma fi*
How much?	*bikam/adesh?*
Expensive	*ghaali*
Cheap	*rakhees*
Good	*qwayees*
Bad	*mish mnih*
Enough, stop	*hallas*
Let's go	*yallah*
I understand	*ana afham*
I don't understand	*la afham*

Getting around

Airport	*al matar*
Bus station	*mahattat al bas/garagat*
Bus	*al bas/autobas*
Taxi	*taxi*
Service taxi	*servees*
Train station	*mahattat al qitar*
Car	*sayara*
Left	*yasaar*
Right	*shimal/yameen*
Straight ahead	*ala tuul*
Tourist office	*makhtab siyaha*
Map	*khareeta*
City centre/old city	*medina*
Hotel	*funduq*
Restaurant	*mataam/restauran*
Museum	*matthaaf*
Bank	*masraf/banque*
Chemist	*sayidiliya*

Documents

Passport office	*makhtab al jawazaat*
Passport	*jawas as safar*
Visa	*sima*
Permit	*tasrih*
Name	*ism*
Date of birth	*tarikha al mulid*
Place of birth	*makan al mulid*
Nationality	*jensiya*

Numbers

0	*sifr*
1	*wahad*
2	*itneen*
3	*talaata*
4	*arba'a*
5	*khamsa*
6	*sitta*
7	*sabba*
8	*tamanya*

9	*tissa*
10	*ashra*
11	*hidaash*
12	*itnash*
13	*talaatash*
14	*arbaatash*
15	*khamastash*
16	*sittash*
17	*sabbatash*
18	*tamantash*
19	*tissatash*
20	*ashreen*
21	*wahad wa ashreen*
22	*itneen wa ashreen*
30	*talaateen*
40	*arbaa'een*
50	*khamseen*
60	*sitteen*
70	*sabba'een*
80	*tamanteen*
90	*tissa'een*
100	*mia*
200	*miatein*
300	*talaata mia*
1,000	*alf*
2,000	*alfein*
3,000	*talaata alf*

Days and time

Sunday	*al ahad*
Monday	*al itneen*
Tuesday	*at talata*
Wednesday	*al arbaa*
Thursday	*al khamees*
Friday	*al juma*
Saturday	*as sabts*
Today	*al yoom*
Yesterday	*ams*
Tomorrow	*bukra*
Morning	*subah*
Afternoon	*ba'ad az-zohr*
Evening	*musa*
Day	*yoom*
Night	*lail*
Week	*usboo*
Year	*sana*
Now	*al-aan*
Before	*qabl*
After	*baad*

Glossary of architectural and general terms

A

Ablaq alternating courses of contrasting stone, typical of Mameluke and Ottoman architecture (Arabic)

acropolis fortified part of upper city, usually containing political, administrative, religious complex

adyton inner sancturay of the *cella* of a temple

agora open meeting place or market

architrave lowest division of an *entablature* or decorated moulding round arch, window etc

apodyterium changing rooms of a Roman baths

apse semicircular niche; in a Byzantine *basilica* this is always at the eastern end and contains the altar

atrium courtyard of a Roman house or forecourt of a Byzantine church

B

bab gate (Arabic)

barrel vault a vault in the shape of a half-cylinder

basilica a Roman building/Byzantine church of rectangular plan with a central *nave* flanked by two side-aisles and usually with an *apse* at one end.

bastion strongpoint or fortified tower in fortifcations

beit house (Arabic)

bimaristan hospital, medical school (Arabic)

bir well (Arabic)

birkat pool or reservoir

burj tower (Arabic)

C

caldarium hot room in Roman baths

capital crowning feature of a column or pier

caravanserai see *khan* (Arabic)

cardo maximus main street of a Roman city, usually running N-S and lined with colonnades

castrum fortified Roman camp

cavea semicircular seating in auditorium of Roman theatre

cella the inner sanctuary of a temple

chancel raised area around altar in a church

clerestory upper row of windows providing light to the nave of a church

crenellations battlements

cuneiform script consisting of wedge-shaped indentations, usually made into a clay tablet, first developed by the Sumerians

cupola dome

D

decumanus major E-W cross-street in Roman city, intersecting with the *cardo maximus*

deir monastery (Arabic)

donjon (or keep) main fortified tower and last refuge of a castle

diwan see *iwan*

E

entablature horizontal stone element connecting a series of columns, usually decorated with a cornice, frieze and architrave in in Greek/Roman architecture

exedra a recess in a wall or line of columns, usually semicircular and traditionally lined with benches

F

forum open meeting place or market

fosse ditch or trench outside fortifications

frieze central section of *entablature* in classical architecture, or more generally any carved relief

frigidarium cold room in Roman baths

G

glacis (or talus) smooth sloping surface forming defensive fortification wall

groin vault two intersecting *barrel vaults* forming ceiling over square chamber, also called a cross vault

H

hammam bath house (Arabic)

haremlek private/family quarters of an Ottoman house (Arabic)

hypogeum underground burial chamber

I

iconostasis screen decorated with icons separating the *nave* and *chancel* of a Byzantine or Orthodox rite church

iwan (or diwan/liwan) open reception area off courtyard with high arched opening (Arabic)

J

Jami' Masjid Friday congregational mosque (Arabic)

jebel hill, mountain (Arabic)

K

kalybe open-fronted shrine with niches for statuary

keep see *donjon*

khan hostel and warehouse for caravans and traders consisting of walled compound with accommodation, stables/storage arranged around a central courtyard (Arabic)

kufic early angular form of Arabic script (named after Kufa in southern Iraq)

L

lintel horizontal beam above doorway supporting surmounting masonry

liwan see *iwan*

loculus (plural *loculi*) shelf-like niche in wall of burial chamber for sarcophogus/corpse

M

madrassa Islamic religious school (Arabic)

Mar Saint (Arabic)

maristan see *bimaristan*

masjid mosque (Arabic)

medina old city (Arabic)

Footnotes

mihrab niche, usually semicircular and vaulted with a semi-dome, indicating direction of prayer (towards Mecca) (Arabic)

minaret tower of mosque (from Arabic)

minbar pulpit in mosque for preaching, situated to right of *mihrab*

muezzin man who recites the call to prayer (Arabic)

narthex entrance hall to *nave* of church

nave the central rectangular hall of basilica/church, usually lined with colonnades to separate it from the side-aisles

necropolis ancient burial ground

noria waterwheel (Arabic)

nymphaeum Roman monumental structure surrounding a fountain (dedicated to nymphs), usually with niches for statues

O

odeon small theatre or concert hall

orchestra paved semicircular area between stage and *cavea* of Roman theatre

P

pediment triangular, gabled end to a classical building

peristyle colonnaded corridor running around the edges of a courtyard

pier vertical roof support

pilaster engaged pier or column projecting slightly from wall

portico colonnaded porch over outer section of doorway

praetorium Roman governor's residence or barracks

propylaeum monumental entrance to a temple

Q

qadi Muslim judge (Arabic)

qalat castle, fortress (Arabic)

qibla marking direction of prayer, indicated in a mosque by the **mihrab** (Arabic)

qubba dome (Arabic)

R

revetment facing or retaining wall in fortification

ribat Muslim pigrim hostel or hospice

S

salemlek area of Ottoman house for receiving/entertaining guests

sanjak subdivision of an Ottoman *vilayet*

scaenae frons decorated stone façade behind the stage area of Roman theatre

seraya (or *serai*) palace (Arabic)

soffit the underside of a lintel

souk market (Arabic)

stele **(plural *stelae*)** narrow upright slab of stone, usually inscribed

T

talus see *glacis*

tariq road

tell artificial mound

temenos sacred walled temple enclosure surrounding *cella*

tepidarium warm room of a Roman baths

tessera **(plural *tesserae*)** small square pieces of stone used to form mosaic

tetrapylon arrangement of columns (usually four groups of four) marking major street intersections (eg between *cardo maximus* and *decumanus*) in Roman city

transept transverse section between nave and apse of church, giving a cruciform (cross) shape instead of basic rectangular shape
triclinium dining room of Roman house

V

via sacra sacred way used by pilgrims to approach shrine etc
vilayet Ottoman adminsistrative province
vomitorium (plural *vomitoria*) entrance/exit to theatre

W

wadi valley or watercourse with seasonal stream (Arabic)

Index

Y

Z

Map index

Shorts

Footnotes

Conversion tables

Weights and measures

Weight
1 kilogram = 2.205 pounds
1 pound = 0.454 kilograms

Length
1 metre = 1.094 yards
1 yard = 0.914 metres

1 kilometre = 0.621 miles
1 mile = 1.609 kilometres

Capacity
1 litre = 0.220 gallons
1 gallon = 4.546 litres
1 pint = 0.863 litres

Temperature

°C	°F	°C	°F
1	34	26	79
2	36	27	81
3	38	28	82
4	39	29	84
5	41	30	86
6	43	31	88
7	45	32	90
8	46	33	92
9	48	34	93
10	50	35	95
11	52	36	97
12	54	37	99
13	56	38	100
14	57	39	102
15	59	40	104
16	61	41	106
17	63	42	108
18	64	43	109
19	66	44	111
20	68	45	113
21	70	46	115
22	72	47	117
23	74	48	118
24	75	49	120
25	77	50	122

Footprint travel list

Footprint publish travel guides to over 120 countries worldwide. Each guide is packed with practical, concise and colourful information for everybody from first-time travellers to travel aficionados . The list is growing fast and current titles are noted below. For further information check out the website **www.footprintbooks.com**

Andalucía Handbook
Argentina Handbook
Bali & the Eastern Isles Hbk*
Bangkok & the Beaches Hbk*
Bolivia Handbook
Brazil Handbook
Cambodia Handbook
Caribbean Islands Handbook
Chile Handbook
Colombia Handbook
Cuba Handbook
Dominican Republic Handbook*
East Africa Handbook
Ecuador & Galápagos Handbook
Egypt Handbook Handbook
Goa Handbook
India Handbook
Indian Himalaya Handbook*
Indonesia Handbook
Ireland Handbook
Israel Handbook
Jordan Handbook*
Jordan, Syria & Lebanon Hbk
Laos Handbook
Libya Handbook*
Malaysia Handbook
Myanmar Handbook
Mexico Handbook
Mexico & Central America Hbk
Morocco Handbook
Namibia Handbook
Nepal Handbook
Pakistan Handbook

Peru Handbook
Rio de Janeiro Handbook*
Scotland Handbook
Singapore Handbook
South Africa Handbook
South American Handbook
South India Handbook*
Sri Lanka Handbook
Sumatra Handbook
Thailand Handbook
Tibet Handbook
Tunisia Handbook
Venezuela Handbook
Vietnam Handbook

* available autumn 2000

In the pipeline – Turkey, London, Kenya, Rajasthan, Scotland Highlands & Islands, Syria & Lebanon

Also available from Footprint
Traveller's Handbook
Traveller's Healthbook

Available at all good bookshops

Sales & distribution

Footprint Handbooks
6 Riverside Court
Lower Bristol Road
Bath BA2 3DZ England
T 01225 469141
F 01225 469461
E Mail info@
footprintbooks.com

Australia
Peribo Pty
58 Beaumont Road
Mt Kuring-Gai
NSW 2080
T 02 9457 0011
F 02 9457 0022

Austria
Freytag-Berndt Artaria
Kohlmarkt 9
A-1010 Wien
T 01 533 2094
F 01 533 8685

Belgium
Craenen BVBA
Mechelsesteenweg 633
B-3020 Herent
T 016 23 90 90
F 016 23 97 11

Canada
Ulysses Travel Publications
4176 rue Saint-Denis
Montréal
Québec H2W 2M5
T 514 843 9882
F 514 843 9448

Europe
Bill Bailey
16 Devon Square
Newton Abbott
Devon TQ12 2HR. UK
T 01626 331079
F 01626 331080

Denmark
Nordisk Korthandel
Studiestraede 26-30 B
DK-1455 Copenhagen K
T 3338 2638
F 3338 2648

Scanvik Books
Esplanaden 8B
DK-1263 Copenhagen K
T 33 12 77 66
F 33 91 28 82

Finland
Akateeminen Kirjakauppa
Keskuskatu 1
FIN-00100 Helsinki
T 09 12141
F 09 121 4441

Suomalainen Kirjakauppa
Koivuvaarankuja 2
01640 Vantaa 64
F 08 52 78 88

France
L'Astrolabe
46 rue de Provence
F-75009 Paris 9e
T 1 42 85 42 95
F 1 45 75 92 51

VILO Diffusion
25 rue Ginoux
F-75015 Paris
T 01 45 77 08 05
F 01 45 79 97 15

Germany
GeoCenter ILH
Schockenriedstrasse 44
D-70565 Stuttgart
T 0711 781 94610
F 0711 781 94654

Brettschneider
Fernreisebedarf
Feldkirchnerstrasse 2
D-85551 Heimstetten
T 089 990 20330
F 089 990 20331

Geobuch Gmbh
Rosental 6
D-80331 München
T 089 265030
F 089 263713

Gleumes
Hohenstaufenring 47-51
D-50674 Köln
T 0221 215650

Globetrotter Ausrustungen
Wiesendamm 1
D-22305 Hamburg
F 040 679 66183

Dr Götze
Bleichenbrücke 9
D-2000 Hamburg 1
T 040 3031 1009-0

Hugendubel Buchhandlung
Nymphenburgerstrasse 25
D-80335 München
T 089 238 9412
F 089 550 1853

Kiepert Buchhandlung
Hardenbergstrasse 4-5
D-10623 Berlin 12
T 030 311880

Greece
GC Eleftheroudakis
17 Panepistemiou
Athens 105 64
T 01 331 4180-83
F 01 323 9821

India
Roli Books
M-75 GK II Market
New Delhi 110048
T (011) 646 0886
F (011) 646 7185

Israel
Geographical Tours
8 Tverya Street
Tel Aviv 63144
T 03 528 4113
F 03 629 9905

Italy
Librimport
Via Biondelli 9
I-20141 Milano
T 02 8950 1422
F 02 8950 2811

Netherlands
Nilsson & Lamm bv
Postbus 195
Pampuslaan 212
N-1380 AD Weesp
T 0294 494949
F 0294 494455

Norway
Schibsteds Forlag A/S
Akersgata 32 - 5th Floor
Postboks 1178 Sentrum
N-0107 Oslo
T 22 86 30 00
F 22 42 54 92

Tanum
PO Box 1177 Sentrum
N-0107 Oslo 1
T 22 41 11 00
F 22 33 32 75

Olaf Norlis
Universitetsgt 24
N-1062 Oslo
T 22 00 43 00

Pakistan
Pak-American Commercial
Zaib-un Nisa Street
Saddar
PO Box 7359
Karachi
T 21 566 0418
F 21 568 3611

South Africa
Faradawn CC
PO Box 1903
Saxonwold 2132
T 011 885 1787
F 011 885 1829

South America
Humphrys Roberts
Associates
Caixa Postal 801-0
Ag. Jardim da Gloria
06700-970 Cotia SP
Brazil
T 011 492 4496
F 011 492 6896

Southeast Asia
APA Publications
38 Joo Koon Road
Singapore 628990
T 865 1600
F 861 6438

Spain
Altaïr
Balmes 69
08007 Barcelona
T 93 3233062
F 93 4512559

Bookworld España
Pje Las Palmeras 25
29670 San Pedro Alcántara
Málaga
T 95 278 6366
F 95 278 6452

Libros de Viaje
C/Serrano no 41
28001 Madrid
T 01 91 577 9899
F 01 91 577 5756

Sweden
Hedengrens Bokhandel
PO Box 5509
S-11485 Stockholm
T 8 6115132

Kart Centrum
Vasagatan 16
S-11120 Stockholm
T 8 111699

Lantmateriet Kartbutiken
Kungsgatan 74
S-11122 Stockholm
T 08 202 303
F 08 202 711

Switzerland
Artou
8 rue de Rive
CH-1204 Geneva
T 022 311 4544
F 022 781 3456

Office du Livre OLF SA
ZI 3, Corminboeuf
CH-1701 Fribourg
T 026 467 5111
F 026 467 5466
Schweizer Buchzentrum
Postfach
CH-4601 Olten
T 062 209 2525
F 062 209 2627

Travel Bookshop
Rindermarkt 20
Postfach 216
CH-8001 Zürich
T 01 252 3883
F 01 252 3832

USA
NTC/ Contemporary
4255 West Touhy Avenue
Lincolnwood
Illinois 60646-1975
T 847 679 5500
F 847 679 2494

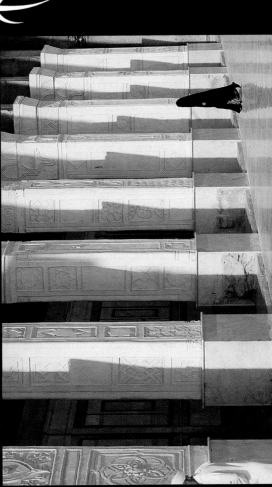

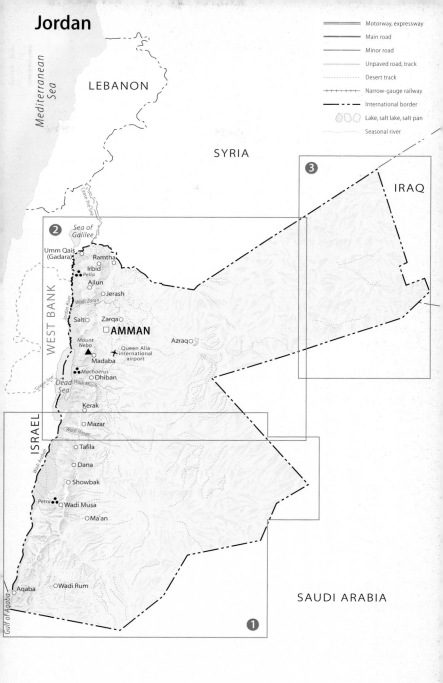

MA'AN

○ Al Jafr

A

B

6

SAUDI
ARABIA

C

MA'AN

SAUDI
ARABIA

N

0 km   10
0 miles   10

4

5

Map 2

SYRIA

ISRAEL

Lake Tiberias
(Sea of Galilee)

Golan Heights

Cease-fire line

A

Al Himma

Abila
(Quwayliba)

Umm Qais
(Gadara)

Beit Ras

Irbid

Ramtha

Ramtha/Deraa
border crossing

North
Shunah

Jabir/Nasib
border crossing

Prince Hussein
bridge
(Jordan River)
border crossing

Deir Abu
Said

Pella

Al Mashari

Zubia
Nature
Reserve

Al Hamra

IRBID

Qalat
ar-Rabaad

Ajlun

Mafraq

Umm
al-Jimal

Anjara

Jerash

Dibeen
National
Park

Tell Deir
Alla

Deir Alla

Wadi Zarqa

Mastaba

Qasr
al-Hallabat

Jordan River

Rummen Hill

Zai National
Park

Hammam
al-Sarakh

Prince
Mohammad
bridge

Muthallath
al-Misri

Salt

Zarqa

WEST
BANK

B

Al
Karama

Wadi
Seer

AMMAN

Iraq
al-Amir

Sahab

South
Shunah

Muwaqqar

Qasr Amra

King Hussein (Allenby)
bridge border crossing

Wadi
Kharrar

King
Abdullah
bridge

Suweimah

Tell Hisban

Hisban

Qasr
Mushatta

Queen Alia
International
Airport

Qasr Kharana

Mount
Nebo

Madaba

AMMAN

Ma'in

Hammamat
Ma'in

Machaerus

Mukawir

Lib

Mulagh

Dead Sea

Dhiban

Umm
ar-Rasas

Wadi Mujib
Nature Reserve

Lehun

Wadi Mujib

Green Line

Ariha

Qasr

King's Highway

Desert Highway

Sodom &
Gomorrah

Rabba

Qatrana

Qatrana
junction

Potash
City

Salt flats

Kerak

Map 1

Mutah

Mazar

AL KARAK

Deir Ain Abata
(Lot's Cave
Monastery)

Safi

Khirbet
Tannur

Dhat Ras

Hammamat
Afra

Hammamat
Borbita

Wadi Hasar

C

1

2

3

Map 3

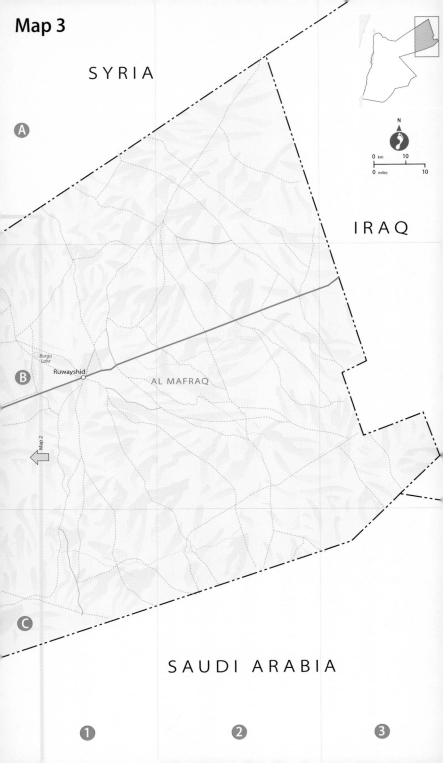

SYRIA

IRAQ

A

B

Burqu
Lake

Ruwayshid

AL MAFRAQ

Map 2

C

SAUDI ARABIA

N

0 km   10

0 miles   10

1   2   3

Will you help us?

We try as hard as we can to make each Footprint Handbook as up-to-date and accurate as possible but, of course, things always change. Many people write to us - with corrections, new information, or simply comments.

If you want to let us know about an experience or adventure - hair-raising or mundane, good or bad, exciting or boring or simply something rather special - we would be delighted to hear from you. Please give us as precise information as possible, quoting the edition number (you'll find it on the front cover) and page number of the Handbook you are using.

Your help will be greatly appreciated, especially by other travellers. In return we will send you details about our special guidebook offer.

email Footprint at:
jor1_online@footprintbooks.com

or write to:
Elizabeth Taylor
Footprint Handbooks
6 Riverside Court
Lower Bristol Road
Bath BA2 3DZ
UK

What the papers say

"*If the essence of real travel' is what you have been secretly yearning for all these years, then Footprint are the guides for you.*"
Under 26

"*Footprint Handbooks, the best of the best.*"
Le Monde, Paris

"*The guides for intelligent, independently-minded souls of any age or budget.*"
Indie Traveller

"*Intelligently written, amazingly accurate and bang up-to-date. Footprint have combined nearly 80 years experience with a stunning new format to bring us guidebooks that leave the competition standing.*"
John Pilkington, writer and broadcaster

Mail order
Available worldwide in bookshops and on-line. Footprint travel guides can also be ordered directly from us in Bath, via our website **www.footprintbooks.com** or from the address on the imprint page of this book.

Acknowledgements

This book could not have been written without the countless people along the way who helped in numerous different ways. It would be impossible to name them all, but a few who deserve particular mention include: Abdul Rahman Sabbagh at the Tourist Information Centre in Amman; Ignacio Arce at the Spanish Archaeological Mission in Amman; Qusay Ahmad, Ecotourism Manager, RSCN, Amman; Mohammad Yousef, Head of Research and Survey Section, RSCN, Amman; Khaled Haikal of the PR department of the Ministry of Tourism and Antiquities, Amman; Dr Mohammad Waheeb, director of excavations at Wadi Kharrar; Mohammad al-Balawneh; Archaeological Inspector, Deir Alla; Deeb Hussein, manager of the Pella Resthouse; Abdullah Qassem in Umm Qais; Ahmad al-Zouby, Educational Officer, Shaumari Nature Reserve; Majdi Salameh, Education Officer, Azraq Wetland Reserve; Kamal I Twal, manager of the Madaba Society Shop, Madaba; Abu Noor at Tell Hisban; Mahmoud Saoup, Assistant Director of Tourism, Kerak; Nidal Ali, tourist police officer at Hammamat Afra; Abd al-Razak Khwaldeh, Dana Nature Reserve; Ahmad al-Qatawneh, director of the Royal Diving Centre in Aqaba; Fawzi, manager of the Al Wafa minimarket in Aqaba; Samir Farouqa, of the Ministry of Tourism in Wadi Rum; Ali Farajat, Petra; Dr Zeidoun al-Muheisen and Engineer Mohammad al-Zoubi at the Petra Regional Planning Council, Petra; Lawrence Joffe, author of the Keesings Guide to the Middle East Peace Process (and a mine of useful information on all things Middle Eastern).

Thanks also to all those who bought the first edition of the Jordan, Syria & Lebanon Handbook, and in particular to those who wrote in or emailed us with their experiences, comments and suggestions.

Tim Sage deserves a special mention for producing such excellent line drawings for the book at such short notice. I would also like to thank all at Footprint Handbooks for their help and support. Finally, I would particularly like to thank Klair Allbuary for her seemingly limitless (?) patience throughout this project, for her help in proof-reading sections of the text so assiduously, and for generally being so wonderful.

Ivan Mannheim

Ivan Mannheim studied Geography at the School of Oriental and African Studies, University of London, finding time in-between to travel extensively in Asia and the Middle East. Ivan first became involved with Footprint Handbooks in 1991 when he contributed two chapters to the South Asian Handbook. After a brief office-bound spell working for a charity, he then went on to research and write the Pakistan Handbook with Dave Winter in 1995. The first edition of the Jordan, Syria & Lebanon Handbook, together with this new edition Jordan Handbook, have involved him in extensive travel throughout the Middle East, visiting each of the countries concerned several times in the course of his work. He lives in Dorset and, when not writing guidebooks, works as an apprentice organic vegetable grower. In his spare time he pursues his interests in sailing, walking and motorcycles.